TLS Cryptography In-Depth

Explore the intricacies of modern cryptography and the inner workings of TLS

Dr. Paul Duplys

Dr. Roland Schmitz

BIRMINGHAM—MUMBAI

TLS Cryptography In-Depth

Group Product Manager: Pavan Ramchandani
Publishing Product Manager: Neha Sharma
Senior Editor: Arun Nadar
Technical Editor: Arjun Varma
Copy Editor: Safis Editing
Project Coordinator: Ashwini Gowda
Proofreader: Safis Editing
Indexer: Pratik Shirodkar
Production Designer: Vijay Kamble
Marketing Coordinator: Marylou De Mello

First published: December 2023
Production reference: 203012024

Published by Packt Publishing Ltd.
Grosvenor House
11 St Paul's Square
Birmingham
B3 1RB, UK

ISBN 978-1-80461-195-1

www.packtpub.com

Contributors

About the authors

Dr. Paul Duplys is chief expert for cybersecurity at the department for technical strategies and enabling within the Mobility sector of Robert Bosch GmbH, a Tier-1 automotive supplier and manufacturer of industrial, residential, and consumer goods. Previous to this position, he spent over 12 years with Bosch Corporate Research, where he led the security and privacy research program and conducted applied research in various fields of information security. Paul's research interests include security automation, software security, security economics, software engineering, and AI. Paul holds a PhD degree in computer science from the the University of Tübingen, Germany.

Dr. Roland Schmitz has been a professor of internet security at the Stuttgart Media University (HdM) since 2001. Prior to joining HdM, from 1995 to 2001, he worked as a research engineer at Deutsche Telekom, with a focus on mobile security and digital signature standardization. At HdM, Roland teaches courses on internet security, system security, security engineering, digital rights management, theoretical computer science, discrete mathematics, and game physics. He has published numerous scientific papers in the fields of internet and multimedia security. Moreover, he has authored and co-authored several books. Roland holds a PhD degree in mathematics from Technical University Braunschweig, Germany.

Writing this book has been an amazing journey, and it is our great pleasure to thank the people who have accompanied and supported us during this time: our project coordinators at Packt Publishing, Ashwini Gowda and Arun Nadar, and our meticulous technical reviewers, Andreas Bartelt, Simon Greiner, and Christos Grecos.

About the reviewers

Andreas Bartelt holds a diploma in computer science (bioinformatics) and has specialized in cybersecurity topics for more than 20 years. He works at Robert Bosch GmbH as an expert in the field of cryptography and secures the deployment of cryptographic protocols such as TLS, IPsec, and SSH. Andreas is also a BSD enthusiast and has acquired extensive practical experience in securing POSIX-based operating systems (e.g., Linux) as well as their secure integration with hypervisors (e.g., Xen).

Dr. Christos Grecos (SM IEEE 2006, FSPIE 2023) is the chair and professor of the CS department at Arkansas State University. He was vice dean of PG research at NCI Ireland, chair of the CS department at Central Washington University (US), and dean of FCIT at Sohar University (Oman). He also has 13 years of experience in the UK as a professor, head of school, and associate dean for research. His research interests include image/video compression standards, processing and analysis, networking, and computer vision. He is on the editorial board of many international journals and has been invited to give talks at various international conferences. He has obtained significant funding for his research from several agencies, such as the UK EPSRC, UK TSB, the EU, and the Irish HEC.

Simon Greiner has been working as an automotive security expert for Robert Bosch GmbH, one of the largest automotive suppliers, for more than five years. He works in the lead engineering team for security and supports projects on different topics regarding security engineering, such as threat and risk analysis, security concepts, testing, and implementation security. He also supports pre-development projects on security topics, mainly in the context of autonomous driving. Before joining Robert Bosch GmbH, Simon obtained his PhD in computer science with a specialization in information security from the Karlsruhe Institute of Technology, Germany.

Table of Contents

Chapter 6: Transport Layer Security at a Glance   **107**

Part 2: Shaking Hands   **137**

Chapter 7: Public-Key Cryptography   **139**

Preface

Hello and welcome to *TLS Cryptography In-Depth*!

As you perhaps know, there are already many excellent books on cryptography out there, written by renowned experts in the field. So why did we write yet another?

First of all, we wanted to make cryptography easier to grasp by showing how the theory of cryptography is used in real-world cryptographic applications. It is impossible to provide a serious introduction to cryptography without delving deeply into abstract mathematical concepts, and this book is no exception. But oftentimes, these mathematical concepts are presented in a way that is difficult for a beginner to follow, and particularly to relate theory to practice, so it takes a lot of patience and energy until you get to the seemingly far-away applications. Finally, these applications are often presented quite briefly, almost like an afterthought.

Yet applications of cryptography profoundly affect our daily lives and are not remote at all. Perhaps most importantly, practically everybody who is surfing the web today uses web addresses starting with https, which stands for **Hypertext Transport Protocol Secure**, and the *Secure* part is realized by a cryptographic protocol called **Transport Layer Security**, or **TLS** for short. If you are using the Firefox browser, for example, and click on the padlock icon next to the URL you are visiting, a few clicks later, you will arrive at the technical details of the *Security* tab of the page info. Here, a typical entry could be as follows:

```
TLS_AES_128_GCM_SHA256, 128 bit keys, TLS 1.3
```

What do these abbreviations mean? Is this really a secure connection? Providing you with the knowledge necessary to answer these questions is one of the main goals of this book.

As we will see, much of present-day cryptography comes together in TLS. We therefore use TLS not just as an application but as a leitmotif of our book. That is, all cryptographic concepts are ultimately motivated by their appearance within the TLS protocol, and advanced cryptanalytic techniques such as linear and differential cryptanalysis are discussed only if they affect TLS protocol design.

TLS is a rather old protocol: its first version dates back to 1994 (under the name **Secure Sockets Layer**, or **SSL**). In 2018, TLS underwent a major revision: not only were many old, insecure cryptographic options deprecated but also protocol messages and their sequence were changed in the latest TLS version, 1.3. The underlying internet standard, IETF RFC 8446, however, is rather complex, densely written, and provides little in the way of motivation.

Therefore, our second reason for writing this book was to show how the design of TLS 1.3 is motivated by good cryptographic practices and earlier cryptographic attacks. Very often, we also dive deeply into TLS 1.3 specification and investigate the meaning of its various data structures. Therefore, you may also read this book as a detailed introduction to the TLS protocol and its nuts and bolts, or use it as a companion to IETF RFC 8446.

Who is this book for

In this book, we address two general audience groups:

- Students of mathematics, computer science, computer engineering, and related disciplines interested in modern cryptography and its deployment within TLS

- IT professionals such as cybersecurity specialists, security engineers, cryptographers, communication engineers, software developers, and administrators interested in the inner workings of TLS

We develop most concepts from scratch. However, some previous exposure to computer networking and fundamental mathematics will certainly help you.

What this book covers

The book starts with a general introduction to cryptography in *Part 1, Getting Started*. *Part 2, Shaking Hands*, and *Part 3, Off the Record*, are loosely organized around the most important subprotocols of TLS, the *handshake protocol* and the *record protocol*. Finally, *Part 4, Bleeding Hearts and Biting Poodles*, extensively covers known attacks on previous TLS versions at the handshake, record and implementation levels.

More specifically, this is what the individual chapters are about:

- *Chapter 1, The Role of Cryptography in the Connected World*, sets the scene by providing some answers to why there are so many insecure IT systems and how cryptography helps to mitigate our security problems.

- *Chapter 2, Secure Channel and the CIA Triad*, describes the general goals and objectives you can achieve with the help of cryptography and introduces cryptography's main protagonists, **Alice** and **Bob**, and their ubiquitous opponents, **Eve** and **Mallory**.

- *Chapter 3, A Secret to Share*, teaches you what a cryptographic key – a secret shared by Alice and Bob – really is, why it is needed to establish a secure channel, and how long it has to be for Alice and Bob to communicate securely.

- *Chapter 4, Encryption and Decryption*, explains how keys are used together with cryptographic algorithms to encrypt and decrypt secret messages, and describes the prerequisites for secure encryption and decryption.

- *Chapter 5, Entity Authentication*, covers **entity authentication**, an important security objective from the CIA triad that assures Alice of the identity of Bob.

- *Chapter 6, Transport Layer Security at a Glance*, concludes *Part 1, Getting Started*, by taking a first look at **Transport Layer Security (TLS)** and explores the role of the World Wide Web in the development of TLS.

- *Chapter 7, Public-Key Cryptography*, explains the mathematical techniques that enable secure key transport and key agreement over an insecure channel.

- *Chapter 8, Elliptic Curves,* introduces special mathematical objects that are widely used within TLS 1.3 because they allow the use of much shorter keys compared to traditional public-key cryptography schemes.

- *Chapter 9, Digital Signatures,* covers an important application of public-key cryptography which provides message integrity and authenticity and ensures another special security objective called **non-repudiation**.

- *Chapter 10, Digital Certificates and Certification Authorities,* shows how Bob can verify the authenticity of Alice's public key by relying on a **trusted third party**.

- *Chapter 11, Hash Functions and Message Authentication Codes,* explains hash functions and message authentication codes, the main cryptographic mechanisms to ensure the authenticity of messages.

- *Chapter 12, Secrets and Keys in TLS 1.3,* examines in detail the different types of secrets and keys Alice and Bob establish during the TLS 1.3 Handshake protocol.

- *Chapter 13, TLS Handshake Protocol Revisited,* zooms out of the cryptographic details and gives a high-level description of the TLS handshake using state machines for the TLS server and the TLS client.

- *Chapter 14, Block Ciphers and Their Modes of Operation,* discusses how the TLS Record protocol uses block ciphers and their modes of operation to protect application data transmitted between Alice and Bob.

- *Chapter 15, Authenticated Encryption,* introduces a special block cipher mode of operation that combines encryption and message authentication in a single algorithm.

- *Chapter 16, The Galois Counter Mode,* gives a detailed description of the authenticated encryption algorithm that all TLS 1.3 implementations must support.

- *Chapter 17, TLS Record Protocol Revisited,* zooms out of technical and mathematical details again and revisits the TLS Record protocol by showing how the cryptographic mechanisms covered so far fit together.

- *Chapter 18, TLS Cipher Suites*, covers the combinations of ciphers and cryptographic algorithms that any TLS 1.3 endpoint must support and implement.

- *Chapter 19, Attacks on Cryptography*, describes attacks on cryptographic schemes and cryptographic protocols from a conceptual perspective.

- *Chapter 20, Attacks on the TLS Handshake Protocol*, studies actual, real-world attacks on the Handshake protocol in earlier TLS versions. These attacks either try to get hold of the key established during the handshake or to impersonate one of the communicating parties.

- *Chapter 21, Attacks on the TLS Record Protocol*, explores attacks on TLS records that aim to extract the data transmitted in the encrypted records.

- *Chapter 22, Attacks on TLS Implementations*, covers attacks that exploit implementation bugs in software stacks implementing TLS.

To get the most out of this book

Simply be curious! Since we develop most concepts from scratch, you don't need any additional literature, information sources, or tools to follow the book. If you decide to delve deeper into cryptography than what is covered in the book, you will find numerous useful references in the bibliography.

For readers interested in hands-on experiments with TLS, we describe several simple experiments that you can replicate (and extend) on any computer with the *OpenSSL* toolkit installed on it. The code listings in the corresponding chapters contain complete instructions, so there is nothing extra to download.

If you are generally interested in modern cryptography, you may skip sections describing how the individual cryptographic primitives and mechanisms are used in TLS 1.3. However, we recommend you have at least a cursory look at *Part 4, Bleeding Hearts and Biting Poodles*, to get an idea of why getting cryptography right is hard.

If you are interested specifically in TLS 1.3, we recommend reading the book side by side with RFC 8446. Moreover, as you are likely familiar with basic cryptography, you may skip *Part 1, Getting Started.*

Conventions used

There are a number of text conventions used throughout this book.

`Code in text` indicates code words in text, database table names, folder names, filenames, file extensions, pathnames, dummy URLs, user input, and Twitter handles. Here is an example: "If the client provides parameters, for example, the set of specific cryptographic algorithms or a `key_share` value it wants to use for the TLS handshake, that are not supported by the server, the server replies with a `HelloRetryRequest` message."

A block of code is set as follows:

```
struct {
    uint16 length = Length;
    opaque label <7..255 > = "tls13" + Label;
    opaque context <0..255 > = Context;
} HkdfLabel;
```

Any command-line input or output is written as follows:

```
$ gh repo clone duplys/tls_lab
$ cd tls_lab/openssl_docker
$ docker build . -t openssl310
```

Get in touch

Feedback from our readers is always welcome.

General feedback: If you have questions about any aspect of this book, mention the book title in the subject of your message and email us at customercare@packtpub.com.

Errata: Although we have taken every care to ensure the accuracy of our content, mistakes do happen. If you have found a mistake in this book, we would be grateful if you would report this to us. Please visit `www.packt.com/support/errata` and fill in the form.

Piracy: If you come across any illegal copies of our works in any form on the Internet, we would be grateful if you would provide us with the location address or website name. Please contact us at copyright@packt.com with a link to the material.

If you are interested in becoming an author: If there is a topic that you have expertise in and you are interested in either writing or contributing to a book, please visit `authors.packtpub.com`.

Share Your Thoughts

Once you've read *TLS Cryptography In-Depth*, we'd love to hear your thoughts! Scan the QR code below to go straight to the Amazon review page for this book and share your feedback.

https://packt.link/r/1804611956

Your review is important to us and the tech community and will help us make sure we're delivering excellent quality content.

Download a free PDF copy of this book

Thanks for purchasing this book!

Do you like to read on the go but are unable to carry your print books everywhere? Is your eBook purchase not compatible with the device of your choice?

Don't worry, now with every Packt book you get a DRM-free PDF version of that book at no cost.

Read anywhere, any place, on any device. Search, copy, and paste code from your favorite technical books directly into your application.

The perks don't stop there, you can get exclusive access to discounts, newsletters, and great free content in your inbox daily

Follow these simple steps to get the benefits:

1. Scan the QR code or visit the link below

https://packt.link/free-ebook/9781804611951

2. Submit your proof of purchase

3. That's it! We'll send your free PDF and other benefits to your email directly

Part 1

Getting Started

In this part, we set the scene for the **Transport Layer Security (TLS)** protocol. After discussing the history of the internet and TLS, we introduce the three basic security services provided by TLS, namely, *confidentiality*, *integrity* and *authenticity*, and give a first, high-level overview of TLS.

More specifically, we look at the role of cryptography in the modern connected world and highlight the reasons why **Secure Sockets Layer (SSL)**, a predecessor of TLS, was invented in the early 1990s. Next, we explain why connectivity and complexity are the main drivers of cybersecurity and, in turn, cryptography in the modern connected world. We then introduce two cryptographic concepts: the *secure channel* and the *CIA triad*. We then show what cryptographic keys are, how the confidentiality of information transmitted between two parties can be protected using encryption and decryption, and how these parties can ensure that they are actually talking to each other rather than to an attacker. Finally, we give a high-level overview of the TLS protocol to illustrate how the theoretical concepts of cryptography are applied in TLS.

This part contains the following chapters:

- *Chapter 1, The Role of Cryptography in the Connected World*

- *Chapter 2, Secure Channel and the CIA Triad*

- *Chapter 3, A Secret to Share*

- *Chapter 4, Encryption and Decryption*

- *Chapter 5, Entity Authentication*

- *Chapter 6, Transport Layer Security at a Glance*

1

The Role of Cryptography in the Connected World

In this introductory chapter, we try to provide some answers to the following questions:

- Why are there so many insecure IT systems?

- How can cryptography help to mitigate our security problems?

Our core argument is that the simultaneous growth of connectivity and complexity of IT systems has led to an explosion of the attack surface, and that modern cryptography plays an important role in reducing that attack surface.

After a brief discussion of how the field of cryptography evolved from an exotic field appreciated by a select few to an absolutely critical skill for the design and operation of nearly every modern IT product, we will look at some recent real-world security incidents and attacks in order to illustrate our claim. This will allow you to understand why cryptography matters from a higher strategic perspective.

1.1 Evolution of cryptography

Over the past four decades or so, cryptography has evolved from an exotic field known to a select few into a fundamental skill for the design and operation of modern IT systems. Today, nearly every modern product, from the bank card in your pocket to the server farm running your favorite cloud services, requires some form of cryptography to protect it and its users against cyberattacks. Consequently, it has found its way into mainstream computer science and software engineering.

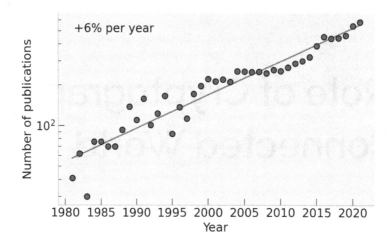

Figure 1.1: Number of publications at IACR conferences on cryptology over the years

Cryptography and its counterpart cryptanalysis were basically unknown outside of military and intelligence services until the mid 1970s. According to [172], *Cryptography is the practice and study of techniques for secure communication in the presence of adversaries*; it deals with the development and application of cryptographic mechanisms. Cryptanalysis is the study of cryptographic mechanisms' weaknesses, aimed at finding mathematical ways to render these mechanisms ineffective. Taken together, cryptography and cryptanalysis form what's called cryptology.

In 1967, David Kahn, an American historian, journalist, and writer, published a book titled *The Codebreakers – The Story of Secret Writing*, which is considered to be the first extensive treatment and a comprehensive report of the history of cryptography and military intelligence from ancient Egypt to modern times [93]. Kahn's book introduced cryptology to a broader audience. Its content was, however, necessarily restricted to *symmetric cryptography*. In symmetric cryptography, the sender and receiver of a message share a common secret key and use it for both encrypting and decrypting. The problem of how sender and receiver should exchange the secret in a secure way was considered out of scope.

This changed in 1976, when the seminal paper *New Directions in Cryptography* by Whitfield Diffie and Martin Hellman appeared in volume IT-22 of IEEE Transactions on Information Security [49]. In that publication, Diffie and Hellman described a novel method for securely agreeing on a secret key over a public channel based on the so-called *discrete logarithm problem*. Moreover, they suggested for the first time that the sender and receiver might use different keys for encrypting (the *public key*) and decrypting (the *private key*) and thereby invented the field of *asymmetric cryptography*.

Figure 1.2: From left to right: Ralph Merkle, Martin Hellman, Whitfield Diffie [69]

While there were scientific works on cryptography dating back to the early 1970s, the publication by Diffie and Hellman is the first publicly available paper in which the use of a private key and a corresponding public key is proposed. This paper is considered to be the start of cryptography in the public domain. In 2002, Diffie and Hellman suggested their algorithm should be called Diffie-Hellman-Merkle key exchange because of Ralph Merkle's significant contribution to the invention of asymmetric cryptography [185].

In 1977, the three MIT mathematicians Ron Rivest, Adi Shamir, and Len Adleman took up the suggestion by Diffie and Hellman and published the first asymmetric encryption algorithm, the RSA algorithm [151], which is based on yet another well-known mathematical problem, the factoring problem for large integers.

Figure 1.3: From left to right: Adi Shamir, Ron Rivest, Len Adleman [152]

The invention of asymmetric cryptography did not make symmetric cryptography obsolete. On the contrary, both fields have complementary strengths and weaknesses and can be efficiently combined in what is today called *hybrid cryptosystems*. The **Transport Layer Security (TLS)** protocol is a very good example of a hybrid cryptosystem.

Today, cryptography is a well-known (albeit mostly little understood in depth) topic in the IT community and an integral part of software development. As an example, as of July 2022, the OpenSSL library repository on GitHub contains over 31,500 commits by 686 contributors. Cryptography is also an integral part of numerous computer science and information security curricula, and numerous universities all over the world offer degrees in information security.

Why did this happen, and which factors led to this development and popularized cryptography within a comparably short period of time? To a large extent, this paradigm shift is a result of three—arguably still ongoing—developments in information technology that radically changed the role of cryptography in the modern connected world:

- The advent of the internet and the ever increasing need to transfer large amounts of data over untrusted channels, which also fostered the development of TLS

- The introduction of connectivity into nearly every new product, from toothbrushes to automobiles

- The ever increasing complexity of IT systems, specifically increasing hardware and software complexity

We will now discuss each of these factors in turn.

1.2   The advent of TLS and the internet

We'll now turn to the original theme of this book, TLS and the cryptographic tools it is made of. TLS is a protocol designed to protect data sent over the internet, so we'll start with a brief look into the early history of the internet.

Despite its origins as a research project financed by the **Defense Advanced Research Projects Agency (DARPA)**, the research agency of the Department of Defence of the United States, most of the main physical components of the internet, such as cables, routers, gateways, and so on, can be (and are) accessed by untrusted third parties. In the early days of the internet, this was not considered a problem, and very few (if any) security measures were introduced into TCP and IP, the internet's main protocol workhorses, and none of them involved cryptography. However, with more and more people using the internet, and the ever increasing available bandwidth, more and more services kept appearing on the internet, and it was quickly realized that to do real business over the internet, a certain amount of trust was needed that sensitive data such as credit card numbers or passwords did not fall into the wrong hands. Cryptography provides the answer to this problem, because it can guarantee **confidentiality** (i.e., no one can read the data in transit) and **authenticity** (i.e., you can verify that you are talking to the right party). TLS and its predecessor SSL are the protocols that implement cryptography on the internet in a secure, usable way.

Starting in 1995, SSL was shipped together with Netscape Navigator to clients. While server-side adoption of SSL was slow at first, by the end of 2021, according to the **Internet Security Research Group (ISRG)**, 83% of web pages loaded by Firefox globally used HTTPS, that is HTTP secured via TLS [87].

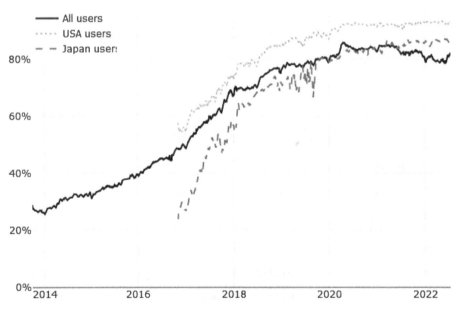

Figure 1.4: Percentage of web pages loaded by Firefox using HTTPS [88]

This is a huge success for TLS and the field of cryptography in general, but with it also comes a huge responsibility: we need to constantly monitor whether the algorithms, key lengths, modes of operations, and so on used within TLS are still secure. Moreover, we need to understand how secure algorithms work and how they can interact with each other in a secure way so that we can design secure alternatives if needed.

Maybe we should already stress at this early stage that TLS is not a remedy for all the problems mentioned here. TLS provides *channel-based security*, meaning that it can only protect data in transit between a client and a server. TLS is very successful in doing so, and how *in detail* TLS uses cryptography to achieve this goal is the main theme of this book. However, once the data leaves the secure channel, it is up to the endpoints (i.e., client and server) to protect it.

Moreover, cryptography by itself is useless in isolation. To have any practical effect, it has to be integrated into a much larger system. And to ensure that cryptography is effectively protecting that system, there must be no security holes left that would allow an attacker to circumvent its security.

There is a well-known saying among cybersecurity professionals that the security of a system is only as strong as its weakest link. Because there are so many ways to circumvent security – especially in complex systems – cryptography, or rather the cryptographic primitives a system uses, is rarely the weakest link in the chain.

There is, however, one important reason why cryptography is fundamental for the security of information systems, even if there are other security flaws and vulnerabilities. An attacker who is able to break cryptography cannot be detected because a cryptanalytic attack, that is, the breaking of a cryptographic protocol, mechanism or primitive, in most cases leaves no traces of the attack.

If the attacker's goal is to read the communication, they can simply passively listen to the communication, record the messages and decrypt them later. If the attacker's goal is to manipulate the target system, they can simply forge arbitrary messages and the system will never be able to distinguish these messages from benign ones sent by legitimate users.

While there are many other sources of insecurity (e.g., software bugs, hardware bugs, and social engineering), the first line of defense is arguably secure communication, which in itself requires a secure channel. And cryptography as a scientific discipline provides the building blocks, methods, protocols, and mechanisms needed to realise secure communication.

1.3   Increasing connectivity

Connectivity allows designers to add novel, unique features to their products and enables new business models with huge revenue potential that simply would not exist without it.

At the same time, connectivity makes it much harder to build secure systems. Similar to Ferguson and Schneier's argument on security implications of complexity, one can say that there are no connected systems that are secure. Why? Because connecting systems to large, open networks like the internet exposes them to remote attacks. Remote attacks – unlike attacks that require physical access – are much more compelling from the attacker's perspective because they *scale*.

1.3.1   Connectivity versus security – larger attack surface

While connectivity enables a multitude of desired features, it also exposes products to remote attacks carried out via the internet. Attacks that require physical access to the target device can only be executed by a limited number of attackers who actually have access to that device, for example, employees of a company in the case of devices in a corporate network. In addition, the need for physical access generally limits the attacker's window of opportunity.

Connectivity, in contrast, exposes electronic devices and IT systems to remote attacks, leading to a much higher number of potential attackers and threat actors. Moreover, remote attacks – unlike attacks that require physical access to the target – are much more compelling from the attacker's perspective because they scale.

Another aspect that makes remote attacks practical (and, to a certain extent, rather easy) is the fact that the initial targets are almost always the network-facing interfaces of the devices, which are implemented in software. As we have seen, complex software is almost guaranteed to contain numerous implementation bugs, a number of which can be typically exploited to attack the system. Thus, the trend of increasing software and system complexity inadvertently facilitates remote attacks.

1.3.2 Connectivity versus marginal attack cost

Remote attacks are easy to launch – and hard to defend against – because their marginal cost is essentially zero. After a newly discovered security vulnerability is initially translated into a reliably working exploit, the cost of replicating the attack an additional 10, 100, or 100,000 devices is essentially the same, namely close to zero.

This is because remote attacks are implemented purely in software, and reproducing software as well as accessing devices over public networks effectively costs close to nothing. So, while businesses need to operate large – and costly – internal security organizations to protect their infrastructure, services, and products against cybersecurity attacks, any script kiddie can try to launch a remote attack on a connected product, online service, or corporate infrastructure essentially for free.

1.3.3 Connectivity versus scaling attacks

To summarize, connectivity exposes devices and IT systems to remote attacks that target network-facing software (and, thus, directly benefit from the continuously increasing software complexity), are very cheap to launch, can be launched by a large number of threat actors, and have zero marginal cost.

In addition, there exists a market for zero-day exploits [190] that allows even script kiddies to launch highly sophisticated remote attacks that infest target systems with advanced malware able to open a remote shell and completely take over the infested device.

As a result, connectivity creates an attack surface that facilitates cybersecurity attacks that scale.

1.4   Increasing complexity

While it can be argued that the problem of increasing complexity is not directly mitigated by modern cryptography (in fact, many crypto-related products and standards suffer from this problem themselves), there is no doubt that increasing complexity is in fact a major cause of security problems. We included the complexity problem in our list of crucial factors for the development of cryptography, because cryptography *can help limit the damage* caused by attacks that were in turn caused by excessive complexity.

Following Moore's law [191], a prediction made by the co-founder of Fairchild Semiconductor and Intel Gordon Moore in 1965, the number of transistors in an integrated circuit, particularly in a microprocessor, kept doubling roughly every 2 years (see *Figure 1.5*).

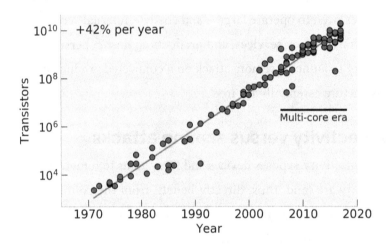

Figure 1.5: Increasing complexity of hardware: Transistors. Data is taken from https://github.com/barentsen/tech-progress-data

Semiconductor manufacturers were able to build ever bigger and ever more complex hardware with ever more features. This went so far that in the late 1990s, the Semiconductor Industry Association set off an alarm in the industry when it warned that productivity gains in **Integrated Circuit (IC)** manufacturing were growing faster than the capabilities of **Electronic Design Automation (EDA)** tools used for IC design. Entire companies in the EDA area were successfully built on this premise.

Continuously growing hardware resources paved the way for ever more complex software with ever more functionality. Operating systems became ever more powerful and feature-rich, the number of layers in software stacks kept increasing, and software libraries and frameworks used by programmers became ever more comprehensive. As predicted by a series of software evolution laws formulated by early-day computer scientists Manny Lehman and Les Belady, software exhibited continuing growth and increasing complexity [181] (see also *Figure 1.6*).

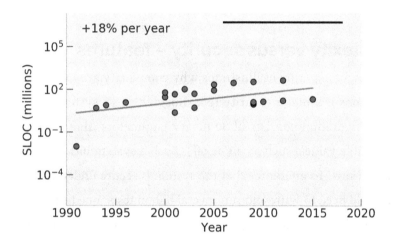

Figure 1.6: Increasing complexity of software: Source Lines of Code (SLOC) in operating systems. Data is taken from https://github.com/barentsen/tech-progress-data

Why should increasing complexity be a problem? According to leading cybersecurity experts Bruce Schneier and Niels Ferguson [65], *"Complexity is the worst enemy of security, and it almost always comes in the form of features or options"*.

While it might be argued whether complexity really is the *worst* enemy of security, it is certainly true that complex systems, whether realized in hardware or software, tend to be error-prone. Schneier and Ferguson even claim that *there are no complex systems that are secure*.

Complexity negatively affects security in several ways, including the following:

- Insufficient testability due to a combinatorial explosion given a large number of features

- Unanticipated—and unwanted—behavior that emerges from a complex interplay of individual features

- A high number of implementation bugs and, potentially, architectural flaws due to the sheer size of a system

1.4.1   Complexity versus security – features

The following thought experiment illustrates why complexity arising from the number of features or options is a major security risk. Imagine an IT system, say a small web server, whose configuration consists of 30 binary parameters (that is, each parameter has only two possible values, such as on or off). Such a system has more than a *billion* possible configurations. To guarantee that the system is secure under all configurations, its developers would need to write and run several billion tests: one test for each relevant type of attack (e.g., Denial-of-Service, cross-site scripting, and directory traversal) and each configuration. This is impossible in practice, especially because software changes over time, with new features being added and existing features being refactored. Moreover, real-world IT systems have significantly more than 30 binary parameters. As an example, the NGINX web server has nearly 800 directives for configuring how the NGINX worker processes handle connections.

1.4.2   Complexity versus security – emergent behavior

A related phenomenon that creates security risks in complex systems is the unanticipated *emergent behavior*. Complex systems tend to have properties that their parts do not have on their own, that is, properties or behaviors that emerge only when the parts interact [186]. Prime examples for security vulnerabilities arising from emergent behavior are **time-of-check-to-time-of-use** (**TOCTOU**) attacks exploiting concurrency failures, replay attacks on cryptographic protocols where an attacker reuses an out-of-date message, and side-channel attacks exploiting unintended interplay between micro-architectural features for speculative execution.

1.4.3   Complexity versus security – bugs

Currently available software engineering processes, methods, and tools do not guarantee error-free software. Various studies on software quality indicate that, on average, 1,000 lines of source code contain 30-80 bugs [174]. In rare cases, examples of extensively tested software were reported that contain 0.5-3 bugs per 1,000 lines of code [125].

However, even a rate of 0.5-3 bugs per 1,000 lines of code is far from sufficient for most practical software systems. As an example, the Linux kernel 5.11, released in 2021, has around 30 million lines of code, roughly 14% of which are considered the "core" part (arch, kernel, and mm directories). Consequently, even with extensive testing and validation, the Linux 5.11 core code alone would contain approximately 2,100-12,600 bugs.

And this is only the operating system core without any applications. As of July 2022, the popular Apache HTTP server consists of about 1.5 million lines of code. So, even assuming the low rate of 0.5-3 bugs per 1,000 lines of code, adding a web server to the core system would account for another 750-4,500 bugs.

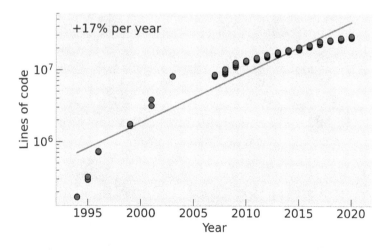

Figure 1.7: Increase of Linux kernel size over the years

What is even more concerning is the rate of bugs doesn't seem to improve significantly enough over time to cope with the increasing software size. The extensively tested software having 0.5-3 bugs per 1,000 lines of code mentioned above was reported by Myers in 1986 [125]. On the other hand, a study performed by Carnegie Mellon University's CyLab institute in 2004 identified 0.17 bugs per 1,000 lines of code in the Linux 2.6 kernel, a total of 985 bugs, of which 627 were in critical parts of the kernel. This amounts to slightly more than halving the bug rate at best – over almost 20 years.

Clearly, in that same period of time from 1986 to 2004 the size of typical software has more than doubled. As an example, Linux version 1.0, released in 1994, had about 170,000 lines of code. In comparison, Linux kernel 2.6, which was released in 2003, already had 8.1 million lines of code. This is approximately a 47-fold increase in size within less than a decade.

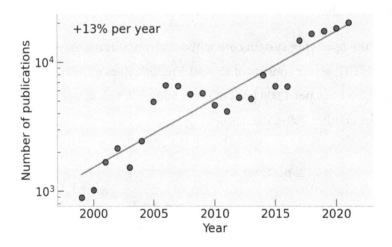

Figure 1.8: Reported security vulnerabilities per year

1.5 Example attacks

The combination of these two trends – increase in complexity and increase in connectivity – results in an attack surface explosion. The following examples shall serve to illustrate this point.

1.5.1 The Mirai botnet

In late 2016, the internet was hit by a series of massive **Distributed Denial-of-Service** (**DDoS**) attacks originating from the Mirai botnet, a large collection of infected devices (so-called *bots*) remote-controlled by attackers.

The early history of the Mirai botnet can be found in [9]: the first bootstrap scan on August 1 lasted about two hours and infected 834 devices. This initial population continued to scan for new members and within 20 hours, another 64,500 devices were added to the botnet. The infection campaign continued in September, when about 300,000 devices were infected, and reached its peak of 600,000 bots by the end of November. This corresponds to a rate of 2.2-3.4 infected devices per minute or 17.6-27.2 seconds to infect a single device.

Now contrast this with a side-channel or fault attack. Even if we assume that the actual attack – that is, the measurement and processing of the side-channel traces or the injection of a fault – can be carried out in *zero* time, an attacker would still need time to gain physical access to each target. Now suppose that, on average, the attacker needs one hour to physically access a target (actually, this is a very optimistic assumption from the attacker's perspective, given that the targets are distributed throughout the globe). In that case, attacking 200,000-300,000 devices would take approximately 22-33 *years* or 270 to 400 months (as opposed to 2 months in the case of Mirai).

Moreover, any remote attack starts at a network interface of the target system. So the first (and, oftentimes, the only) thing the attacker interacts with is software. But software is complex by nature.

1.5.2 Operation Aurora

In mid-December 2009, Google discovered a highly sophisticated, targeted attack on their corporate infrastructure that resulted in intellectual property theft [73]. During their investigation, Google discovered that at least 20 other large companies from a wide range of businesses had been targeted in a similar way [193].

This series of cyberattacks came to be known as Operation Aurora [193] and were attributed to APT groups based in China. The name was coined by McAfee Labs security researchers based on their discovery that the word *Aurora* could be found in a file on the attacker's machine that was later included in malicious binaries used in the attack as part of a file path. Typically, such a file path is inserted by the compiler into the binary to indicate where debug symbols and source code can be found on the developer's machine. McAfee Labs therefore hypothesized that Aurora could be the name of the operation used by the attackers [179].

According to McAfee, the main target of the attack was source code repositories at high-tech, security, and defense contractor companies. If these repositories were modified in a malicious way, the attack could be spread further to their client companies. Operation Aurora can therefore be considered the first major attack on software supply chains [193].

In response to Aurora, Google shut down its operations in China four months after the incident and migrated away from a purely *perimeter-based defense principle*. This means devices are not trusted by default anymore, even if they are located within a corporate LAN [198].

1.5.3 The Jeep hack

At the BlackHat 2015 conference, security researchers Charlie Miller and Chris Valasek demonstrated the first remote attack on an unaltered, factory passenger car [120]. In what later became known as the Jeep hack, the researchers demonstrated how the vehicle's infotainment system, Uconnect, which has both remote connectivity as well as the capability to communicate with other electronic control units within the vehicle, can be used for remote attacks.

Specifically, while systematically examining the vehicle's attack surface, the researchers discovered an open D-Bus over an IP port on Uconnect, which is essentially an inter-process communication and remote procedure call mechanism. The D-Bus service accessible via the open port allows anyone connected to the infotainment system to execute arbitrary code in an unauthenticated manner.

Miller and Valasek also discovered that the D-Bus port was bound to all network interfaces on the vulnerable Uconnect infotainment system and was therefore accessible remotely over the Sprint mobile network that Uconnect uses for telematics. By connecting to the Sprint network using a femtocell or simply a regular mobile phone, the researchers were able to send remote commands to the vehicle.

From that entry point, Miller and Valasek attacked a chip in the vehicle's infotainment system by re-writing its firmware to be able to send arbitrary commands over the vehicle's internal CAN communication network, effectively giving them the ability to completely take over the vehicle.

1.5.4 Commonalities

What do these examples have in common and how does it relate to cryptography? In a nutshell, these examples illustrate what happens in the absence of appropriate cryptography. In all three cases discussed, there was no mechanism in place to verify that the systems were talking to legitimate users and that the messages received were not manipulated while in transit.

In the Mirai example, anyone with knowledge of the IoT devices' IP addresses would have been able to access their login page. This information can be easily collected by scanning the public internet with tools such as nmap. So the designers' assumption that the users would change the default device password to a strong individual one was the only line of defense. What the security engineers should have done instead is to add a cryptographic mechanism to give access to the login procedure only to legitimate users, for example, users in possession of a digital certificate or a private key.

In the case of Operation Aurora, the perimeter defense doctrine used by the affected companies treated every device within the trusted perimeter (typically, within a corporate network) as trustworthy by default. On this premise, every device inside the perimeter had access to all resources and systems within that perimeter.

As a result, anyone able to walk inside a company building or trick an arbitrary employee into clicking on a malicious link and infect their computer with malware would have been able to access all systems within the perimeter.

As a response to Operation Aurora, Google and other companies replaced perimeter defense with a zero trust security model that establishes trust by evaluating it on a per-transaction basis instead of basing trust on the network location (the perimeter) [155]. At the core of the zero trust security model is the ability to securely authenticate users and resources in order to prevent unauthorized access to data and services. Secure authentication, in turn, is built upon cryptography.

Finally, in the Jeep hack example, the open D-Bus over IP port allowed anyone connected to the vehicle's infotainment system to execute arbitrary code in an unauthenticated manner. The possibility to access the vehicle remotely over the Sprint mobile network further increased the range of the attack. The system's designers apparently assumed that the Sprint mobile network is a secure perimeter. What they should have done instead is to add a cryptographic mechanism to ensure that only legitimate users could log in to the Uconnect system.

1.6 Summary

In this chapter, we have provided an overview of the recent history of cryptography, starting in the 1970s, and identified some global trends that explain why cryptography has become more and more important over the last few decades, to a point where it is practically around you every time you access the internet or use a connected device. In the next chapter, you will learn about the general goals and objectives you can achieve with the help of cryptography. In particular, you will get to know cryptography's main protagonists, Alice and Bob, and their ubiquitous opponents, Eve and Mallory.

2

Secure Channel and the CIA Triad

In this chapter, we discuss the fundamental objective of cryptography and computer security, namely enabling two parties to communicate securely over an insecure communication channel. As we will see shortly, this is not an easy task to accomplish because the communication needs to be secure against both passive and active attackers.

But how can we achieve security if the attacker is allowed to listen to the entire communication and even manipulate the messages sent over the channel? And what are the fundamental design principles that we must follow to build systems that can protect that communication?

To answer these questions, we will cover the most important cryptographic definitions, essential design principles, and central cryptographic goals. We will show how these goals can be achieved in principle, leaving the technical details for the chapters to follow. Finally, we will introduce the notion of a *secure channel*, which lies at the heart of TLS.

2.1 Technical requirements

This chapter introduces basic definitions, design principles, and goals and therefore requires no specific software or hardware.

2.2 Preliminaries

The fundamental objective of cryptography and computer security in general is to enable two persons, let's call them Alice and Bob, to communicate over an insecure channel so that an opponent, commonly called Eve, cannot understand or unnoticeably alter their messages [168]. Alice, Bob, and Eve can also be referred to as (communicating) *entities* or *parties* and may be people or machines. Alice and Bob are either a *sender* or *receiver*, that is, a legitimate transmitter or intended recipient, of the messages. Eve is an *adversary*, an entity that tries to compromise the information security between Alice and Bob.

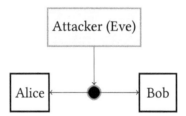

Figure 2.1: Legitimate communicating parties Alice and Bob transmit and receive information over an untrusted channel

Let's clarify terms by looking at some definitions:

- An **insecure** or **untrusted channel** is a channel an opponent, or **attacker**, can access. The capabilities of the attacker (that is, what the attacker can or cannot do on the channel) may vary and are part of the so-called **attacker model**.

- A **passive attacker** is an attacker who is only able to read information from an untrusted channel. In contrast, an **active attacker** is an attacker who can also insert their own information, or alter, replay, reorder, or delete the information on an untrusted channel.

Figure 2.2 illustrates the two fundamental attacker models in cryptography. Cryptographers use the attacker model to express the assumptions about the *power of the adversary*, that is, the actions the attacker is assumed to be able to take as well as their computational power.

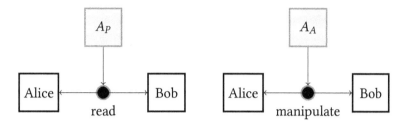

Figure 2.2: The two fundamental attacker models used in cryptography

The channel might be anything from a telephone line to a Wi-Fi network or satellite communication, and the information being sent from Alice to Bob can have an arbitrary structure – it might be numerical data, text, or simply some random blob. In computer science, blob, or binary large object, refers to a collection of binary data such as images, audio, or multimedia objects, or binary executables.

In numerous real-world applications, machine-to-machine or application-to-application communication needs to be secured. In this case, Alice could be equivalent to a web browser and Bob to a web server. Alternatively, Alice could be equivalent to an embedded device that is connected to the internet and Bob could be equivalent to a backend service the device is connected to.

Alice and Bob might even be the same person or entity, for instance, an electronic device. In this case, Alice is transmitting the information to her future self, that is, she wants to store the information securely.

Sometimes, Alice and Bob might engage in something called a *cryptographic protocol*, for example, to establish a key in a secure way, or in order to make sure they are really communicating with the correct entity. Here are precise definitions:

- A **cryptographic protocol** is a distributed algorithm defined by a sequence of steps that precisely specifies the actions required of two or more entities to achieve a specific cryptographic goal [117]. Transport Layer Security, one of the main topics of this book, is a cryptographic protocol for establishing a secure channel between Alice and Bob.

- In contrast, a **cryptographic mechanism** is a more general term referring to protocols, algorithms – specifying the steps followed by a single entity – and non-cryptographic techniques [117] such as trusted execution environments and role-based access control to achieve specific security objectives.

So, cryptographic mechanisms (and protocols among them) are tools with which Alice and Bob seek to achieve security objectives. But what precisely are these security objectives? There are several of them, and in the next three sections, we will explore the three most important ones.

2.3 Confidentiality

A fundamental need in secure communication is to ensure the privacy of the information transmitted between the communicating parties. In cryptography, this is referred to as *confidentiality* of data.

More precisely, *confidentiality is the ability to keep the content of information from all but those authorized to have it* [117]. Confidentiality therefore guarantees that no one except the sender and the intended receiver(s) of the information can read it.

In the classical scenario illustrated in *Figure 2.1*, these are two parties (Alice and Bob). In general, cryptographic mechanisms can be used to ensure confidentiality for any number of parties, for example, using the concept of group keys. In the simplest case, there is only one party involved, for example, a user encrypting their private data stored in the cloud or on a personal device such as a smartphone.

Figure 2.3 shows the classical scenario for confidentiality. The eavesdropper Eve has the capability r to read all messages sent between Alice and Bob over an insecure channel. Eve's goal is to recover the original plaintext from the messages transmitted over the channel (within a reasonable period of time).

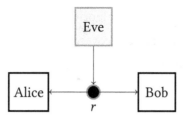

Figure 2.3: Alice and Bob must keep their communication confidential in the presence of Eve

There are many different ways to achieve confidentiality, such as physically protecting access to the media on which the private information is stored or exchanging private information in a way that both parties believe to be secure by design, such as in a private, face-to-face meeting. In contrast, cryptography focuses on mathematical algorithms – based on number-theoretic problems or the concept of pseudo-randomness – that *scramble* the message, before it is sent, in such a way that the private information becomes unintelligible for unauthorized parties.

An implicit assumption is that the communication channel between the legitimate parties is insecure, that is, that an eavesdropping adversary sees all *scrambled* messages and can store them for later processing. A cryptographic mechanism ensuring confidentiality must hold even if the messages observed by the eavesdropper are used in an offline attack.

If the goal of a cryptographic mechanism is to provide confidentiality, then a *passive* attacker is typically assumed. Recall from the last section that a passive attacker is supposed only to be able to read information from an unsecured channel [117]. While manipulating messages sent by Alice and Bob might interrupt the overall system – for example, lead to a denial-of-service attack if the legitimate parties are interpreting these messages to accomplish some kind of a computational or control task – this usually won't help the attacker to recover the original plaintext, so confidentiality will be preserved.

In cryptography, confidentiality is achieved using mathematical functions that transform the private information m, also referred to as *plaintext*, into a scrambled message $c = f_K(m)$, referred to as *ciphertext*. These functions are *bijective* meaning that for every such function f_K there is an inverse function, denoted by f_K^{-1}, which transforms the ciphertext back to the original plaintext. In other words, an algorithm mapping plaintext to ciphertext in such a way that the plaintext cannot be recovered does *not* provide confidentiality in a cryptographic sense. Note that bijectivity also implies that there are as many plaintexts as ciphertexts.

The infamous **Wired Equivalent Privacy (WEP)** hack illustrates what consequences a confidentiality breach can have in practice. WEP was a cryptographic algorithm that provided confidentiality for over-the-air transmissions in **Wireless Local Area Networks (WLANs)** defined in the IEEE 802.11 set of standards. Released in 1997 as part of the original 802.11 standard, WEP was recommended for all 802.11b- and 802.11g-compliant devices and included in most Wi-Fi routers by the late 1990s [52].

WEP was designed as a so-called *stream cipher* based on the RC4 algorithm as a key stream generator (see *Section 4.5.1* and *Section 4.5.2*, respectively). Because interference can cause bit errors and, consequently, packet loss in a wireless channel, the WEP key stream generation was restarted each time a frame of a message had been transmitted. This restart procedure relied on a so-called **Initialization Vector (IV)**, basically a 24-bit string. An attacker could therefore wait until an IV repeated after 2^{24} frames, which led to the repetition of the entire key stream. As is explained in *Section 4.3.2*, this is a serious security problem, especially if parts of the plaintext are already known, as is often the case with standardized network protocols.

In 2001, researchers published a complete cryptanalysis of WEP that recovered the secret key after eavesdropping on the wireless network [66]. Depending on the number of network packets available for inspection, the complete key could be recovered in as little as one minute [197].

2.4 Integrity

Integrity is the ability to **detect** data manipulation by unauthorized entities. By data manipulation, we mean unauthorized acts such as the insertion, deletion, or substitution of individual data chunks or entire messages. It is not required that manipulations as such are rendered impossible; given the multitude of possible communication channels, this would be an impossible task. Clearly, a passively eavesdropping attacker such as Eve does not have the capability to perform data manipulation. We, therefore, assume a more active attacker named *Mallory* who also has the capability to write on the communication channel (see *Figure 2.4*).

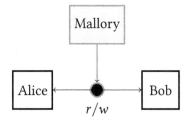

Figure 2.4: The malicious attacker Mallory has the capabilities r, w to read all messages sent between Alice and Bob and to write on the unsecured channel. Mallory's goal is to manipulate the messages in a way that is not noticed by Alice or Bob

At first glance, one might be tempted to think that a good encryption function should be able to provide both confidentiality and integrity when applied to plaintext. After all, if Mallory cannot see the plaintext and has to blindly manipulate the ciphertext c coming from Alice, this should be noticed by Bob, as decryption will fail to produce meaningful plaintext. While this is true in most cases, there are certain ways to encrypt where Mallory has a fairly good chance of getting away with her manipulations, for example, *stream ciphers* or the *Electronic Codebook Mode* (see *Chapter 4, Encryption and Decryption* and *Chapter 14, Block Ciphers and Their Mode of Operation*, respectively).

The real reason for keeping confidentiality and integrity separate from security services using different mechanisms goes deeper, however. There are many situations where integrity is needed but confidentiality is either not needed or even not wanted. A good example is provided by the header of an IP packet. Among other data fields, it contains the IP address of the recipient of the packet. While it is a good idea to provide integrity protection of the IP header (the IPSec protocol does just that), confidentiality would be counterproductive since intermediate gateways need to see the recipient's address to route the packet.

Attacks on the integrity of data can have severe consequences if they go unnoticed: important decisions might be based on wrong information, software systems might exhibit strange, inexplicable errors, and hardware-based systems could be physically damaged. A recent example of a data integrity attack is provided by the Stuxnet worm [106], allegedly composed in a joint effort by the NSA and the Israeli secret service Mossad to harm the Iranian nuclear program. Building upon a complex series of different attack vectors, Stuxnet finally managed to get access to the control software for centrifuges used to enrich uranium in Iranian nuclear facilities. By altering the control parameters, the centrifuges were made to run at a slightly higher speed than allowed and were rendered useless after a few months. Because of the long-term character of the attack, the real reason for the centrifuge failure was not detected for quite a long time.

Integrity can be achieved in a manner that is similar to detecting transmission errors in networking; basically, a cryptographic checksum h_K is computed over the data m that Alice wants to protect and appended to her message m. If Bob receives a message $(m, h_K(m))$, he can compute a checksum of his own over m. If this checksum does not equal $h_K(m)$, something has gone wrong: either there were transmission errors or someone has tampered with m.

Again, a secret parameter k has to go into the computation of the checksum. Otherwise, an intelligent attacker would be able to modify m to $\tilde{m}$ and alter the checksum so that it fits the modified $\tilde{m}$. Moreover, a checksum designed to detect transmission errors such as the **Cyclic Redundancy Check (CRC)** in networking will not be enough, as they can be easily forged even without knowing the secret k. Instead, one has to use secure hash functions, as discussed in *Chapter 11, Hash Functions and Message Authentication Codes*.

2.5 Authentication

Authentication is the ability to identify the source of the communication, both for the communicating parties and for the information itself. In other words, authentication refers to a cryptographic mechanism ensuring that the identity of communicating entities can be verified and that the source of a received message can be verified. Any two parties entering into a secure communication should authenticate each other and the data received with respect to their origin. This hints at the fact that there are actually two kinds of authentication: one to verify identities (*entity authentication*) and another to verify data origin (*message authentication*).

Authentication is one of the most important security goals in cryptography. After hash functions and digital signatures were discovered, authentication and confidentiality were classified as independent information security objectives [117]. Without authentication, however, there can be no genuine confidentiality because you can never be sure who you are talking to, even if the communication is in encrypted form. Today, confidentiality and authentication are often combined in *authenticated encryption schemes* (see *Chapter 15, Authenticated Encryption*).

It might even seem superfluous to differentiate between authentication and confidentiality. In practice, however, implementing one or the other can have fundamental implications on legal matters.

As an example, export control (legislation regulating the export of goods, software, and technology) restricts the export of items considered potentially harmful to the interest of the exporting country. Such items include arms, so-called dual-use goods with military potential, radioactive materials such as uranium, and cryptography.

In the case of cryptography, it is prohibited to export hardware or software that can be used for strong encryption to export controlled or sanctioned countries, entities, and persons. Strong encryption refers to encryption algorithms (see *Chapter 4, Encryption and Decryption*) deemed to be secure by national agencies and standardization bodies such as GCHQ or NIST. If the actual goal of a security system is to authenticate individual entities, such as a sensor in a car and an electronic control unit that uses the measurement data from that sensor, it might be more practical to use a cryptographic mechanism for authentication rather than encryption.

Another example where the separation of confidentiality and authentication makes sense is provided by two communicating parties located in different countries where one or both of the countries do not permit confidentiality in order to monitor all communications. While the legitimate parties are not allowed to use encryption, a mechanism for achieving confidentiality, they can still use a cryptographic algorithm to ensure the identity of each party as well as the origin of the information both parties receive.

2.5.1   Message authentication

Message authentication is the ability of the communicating party that receives a message to verify – through corroborative evidence – the identity of the party that originated the message [117]. This form of authentication is also referred to as **data origin authentication**.

Message authentication can be achieved by providing additional information together with the message. This information can be used by the receiving party to verify the identity of the party who sent the message – at least, this is true for asymmetric authentication protocols. In symmetric message authentication, we can only verify that a message was sent by someone in possession of the shared key (see also *Chapter 5, Entity Authentication*).

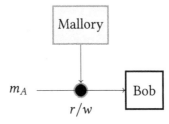

Figure 2.5: Message authentication allows Bob to verify that the message m_A he receives has indeed originated from Alice, despite malicious Mallory having the ability to read Alice's messages and write arbitrary messages to the unsecured channel

While message authentication ensures the origin of the message, it typically provides no guarantee of freshness. That is, with message authentication alone, it is not possible to say *when* the message was sent, only to verify its origin. As an example, imagine that Alice sends a message m_A to Bob today, but Mallory intercepts that message and deletes it from the unsecured channel. Mallory could then re-send m_A to Bob any time later, yet Bob would not be able to recognize that the message is delayed and is actually coming from Mallory rather than Alice.

The inability to determine whether a message is delayed or received out of order enables so-called *replay attack*, in which an authenticated message is sent a second time to the receiver, or *reflection attacks*, where an authenticated message is sent back to the sender. More details are given in *Chapter 19, Attacks on Cryptography*.

The lack of proper message authentication is the main cause for the notorious *false base station attacks*, which could originally be launched against 2G mobile networks and, because of the need for backward compatibility, also against 3G and 4G networks [143]. In these attacks, Mallory sets up a **False Base Station** (**FBS**), basically an antenna sending out a strong signal designed to lure mobile phones to connect to the FBS. The FBS then sends a standardized message to the phone to the effect that it does not support encryption. Therefore, the phone resorts to sending its speech data in plaintext to the FBS. If the phone is able to verify if the NullEncryption message is really coming from a legitimate network operator, the attack becomes infeasible.

Many other examples of attacks resulting from a lack of or faulty implementation of message authentication could be given. For example, email-based phishing attacks are only possible because email messages are not authenticated in most cases.

Message authentication is strongly related to integrity protection. After all, if Mallory modifies a message m_A coming from Alice to some $\tilde{m}_A$, thus breaking integrity, one might also argue that $\tilde{m}_A$ really is a new message coming from Mallory, but pretending to come from Alice. Therefore, one can say that message authenticity implies integrity.

2.5.2 Entity authentication

Entity authentication is the ability to assure one communicating party – using corroborative evidence – of both the identity of a second communicating party involved, and that the second party was actually active at the time the evidence was created or acquired [117]. This authentication type is also referred to as **identification**.

To achieve entity authentication, Alice and Bob typically engage in some kind of *authentication protocol*, which is a cryptographic protocol designed to achieve entity authentication.

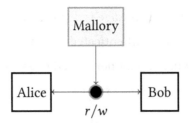

Figure 2.6: Entity authentication allows Bob to verify that the identity of the party he is communicating with is indeed Alice and that Alice is active during the identification. Malicious Mallory has the ability to read Alice's and Bob's messages and write arbitrary messages to the unsecured channel

In a typical example, Alice sends Bob a random, freshly generated challenge (for example, a random number) to which only Bob can respond correctly because Alice and Bob know a shared secret. After Bob has replied to Alice, he sends Alice a fresh, random challenge of his own and waits for the correct reply. If both replies from Alice and Bob are correct, the entity authentication is successful.

To prevent Mallory from compromising entity authentication by simply eavesdropping and replaying old messages, Alice and Bob need to verify each other's authenticity in real time, with non-repeating challenges. This is referred to as *timeliness* or *freshness*. Hence, both parties must be active in the communication.

This protocol is an instance of *mutual authentication* because Alice and Bob authenticate each other. If only Alice or only Bob needs to provide the correct answer to a random challenge, then this would be an example of *unilateral authentication*.

The hack of remote keyless entry systems deployed in VW Group vehicles built between 1995 and 2016 and the attack on the Hitag2 rolling code scheme, are prominent examples of attacks due to insufficient entity authentication [71].

A **Remote Keyless Entry (RKE)** system is used to lock and unlock a car without having to insert a physical key. To do this, RKE systems transmit data from the remote control embedded in the car key to the vehicle.

After a button is pressed, a radio transmitter in the car key generates a signal in a public radio frequency band (for example, the 315 MHz band in North America and the 433 MHz or 868 MHz band in Europe).

The first generation of RKEs was based on a constant secret code and is therefore an instance of *security by obscurity*, a very dangerous anti-pattern in system design where the security of a system depends solely on the secrecy of its design. When the constant code is leaked once, the security of all vehicles relying on such an RKE is instantaneously broken.

The second generation of RKE systems relies on so-called rolling codes. In rolling codes, a counter value is increased upon each button press. The counter value – together with some additional input – is used to compute the next valid rolling code message, which is encrypted in the car key and sent to the vehicle.

The vehicle decrypts the rolling code message and compares the result to the last stored counter value. The counter value is accepted and the car is locked or unlocked if the received value is larger than the stored one. If the received counter value is smaller than the stored one, the attempt to lock or unlock the car is rejected.

However, researchers [71] discovered that RKE systems designed by VW Group are based on a worldwide master key. Because the key is identical for all affected cars, it can be extracted by inspecting the firmware of a single vehicle (which is exactly what the researchers did). Knowing that key allows an attacker to lock and unlock a car after eavesdropping on a single rolling code message.

Hitag2 is another widely deployed RKE that is not specific to a single car manufacturer. The counter in the Hitag2 rolling code is not a step-wise increasing value as it is based on the output of a stream cipher (see *Chapter 4, Encryption and Decryption*). An attack reported in [71] requires Eve to eavesdrop on merely four to eight Hitag2 rolling codes and allows her to recover the cryptographic key in approximately one minute. With that, the attacker can create a clone of the original remote control.

These attacks work because the RKE systems lack a cryptographically secure entity authentication. When the car receives a rolling code, it has no means to verify that it is indeed communicating with the right car key and that the car key is active during the communication.

2.6   Secure channels and the CIA triad

So far, we have discussed three important cryptographic goals: confidentiality, integrity, and authentication. For the purposes of this book, the term *secure system* can be defined as a system that provides a combination of those three goals. Taken together, confidentiality, integrity, and authentication are oftentimes referred to as the *CIA triad*.

Some modern-day scholars and newer books on computer security use the term *availability* instead of *authentication* for the A in CIA. In this book, we deliberately stick to the classical definition. The main reason for this is that, strictly speaking, availability belongs to the realm of security engineering, not cryptography. While cybersecurity threats such as denial-of-service attacks are sometimes discussed in cryptography-related literature, a cryptographic protocol and mechanism by itself is in principle unable to guarantee availability. As a rather simple example, any cryptographic protocol assumes that Alice and Bob can send and receive messages. On the level of cryptographic protocol design, it simply makes no sense to define a protocol if you cannot assume that the information can flow from Alice to Bob and back.

With the definition of the term *secure* via the CIA triad, we can now restate the problem defined in the *Preliminaries* section earlier in this chapter more exactly as the problem of establishing a secure communication channel between Alice and Bob (or between a client device and a server) such that the data transferred is guaranteed to be confidential, authenticated, and unmodified (which is implied by the data being authentic).

A bit less formally, you can think of a secure channel as some kind of tunnel Alice and Bob can use to transfer their data. An attacker cannot see from the outside what is going on in the tunnel: they can neither see the plaintext data nor modify the encrypted data without being detected. Moreover, the tunnel endpoints are authenticated, so Alice can be sure she is really sending her data to Bob, and that any data she receives through the tunnel really comes from Bob.

2.7 Summary

In this chapter, we introduced the most important cryptographic definitions and described the main cryptographic goals, namely confidentiality, integrity, and authentication. We showed that combining these goals into the CIA triad allows Alice and Bob to establish a secure channel in the presence of both passive and active attackers.

In the next chapter, you will learn what a cryptographic key – a secret shared by Alice and Bob – is and why it is needed to establish a secure channel. In particular, you will learn why Alice and Bob should update keys frequently, and how long the key should be so Alice and Bob can communicate securely.

3

A Secret to Share

In the last chapter, we saw that in order to communicate securely over an insecure channel, Alice and Bob need a shared secret (or possibly more than one secret) that is only known to them. Once this is given, they can use cryptography to protect their communication against both passive attackers such as Eve and active attackers such as Mallory.

In cryptography, that shared secret is called a *key*, and we have seen that you can use a secret key K to establish a secure channel between Alice and Bob. But how do you actually generate a secure cryptographic key? How long should it be, and, perhaps most importantly, how can Alice and Bob agree on a key in a secure manner? In this chapter, we will try to provide a brief overview of these issues without becoming too engrossed in the mathematical details, which will be covered later.

In this chapter, we will cover the following topics:

- What is a key and what is a keyspace?

- What is the length of a key and how long should a key be?

- What is the difference between key transport and key agreement?

- What do the terms randomness and entropy mean and what roles do they play in cryptography?

3.1   Secret keys and Kerckhoffs's principle

Let's assume a plaintext m is mapped onto a ciphertext c. Earlier, we formalized this situation in the equation $c = f_K(m)$. You may have wondered why there is a parameter K. In cryptography, we distinguish between the encryption *algorithm f* and the *key K*. We can think of the algorithm as some kind of general template for how to perform encryption. The key is a (secret) parameter that transforms the general template into some specific instantiation that can be used to encrypt the plaintext. It is very important to distinguish between the two and not to treat f_K as a single entity, because the algorithm and the key have very different security requirements. This was realized first by the 19th-century cryptographer Auguste Kerckhoffs, who in 1883 formulated his famous principle that *a cryptosystem should be secure even if everything about the system, except the key, is known to the attacker* [189]. To understand the motivation behind this principle, think of some mechanical encryption devices as they were used by the military in the 19th century. These devices had to be manufactured somewhere, and many people got to see their specifications. Moreover, they could easily get lost in battle. So, it was not wise to assume that the mechanism, that is, the encryption algorithm, could be kept secret over a long period of time.

Kerckhoffs's principle was reformulated in the 20th century by information theory pioneer Claude Shannon succinctly as *the enemy knows the system* [161]. In that form, it is called **Shannon's maxim** [189].

Today, as encryption algorithms are implemented in software, we face the same situation: it is simply not possible to reliably hide the inner workings of an algorithm within the code implementing it. One recent example where the "security by obscurity" approach failed is provided by the CSS algorithm for scrambling the contents of DVDs [78]. The specification of the CSS algorithm was not public. In contrast, it was provided only to manufacturers of playing devices who were willing to sign an agreement with the content owners to the effect that the devices were refusing to create copies of the DVDs. However, the algorithm could be quickly reverse-engineered by analyzing a software-based DVD player.

Modern cryptographers even take Kerckhoffs' principle one step further by asserting that public algorithms are more secure than non-public algorithms because public algorithms can be scrutinized by an international community of experts.

3.2   Cryptographic keys

We saw in the last section that keys are extremely important because they are the only things that are supposed to be secret in a cryptosystem. But what exactly *is* a key?

A cryptographic key K comes from a large (but finite) set $\mathcal{K}$. This large set is called the *key space*. If we assume that K is some bit sequence of length N, then $\mathcal{K} = \{0, 1\}^N$ and the size of $\mathcal{K}$ is 2^N.

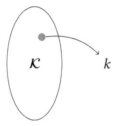

Figure 3.1: A cryptographic key k, the shared secret between Alice and Bob that ensures the security of their communication, is an element of a large (but finite) key space $\mathcal{K}$. If the length of the key is N bits, then the size of $\mathcal{K}$ is 2^N

Naturally, we only want Alice and Bob to know the key, so Eve should neither be able to guess K, nor should she be able to eavesdrop on K when it is exchanged or obtain K by other means. These other means can be anything from a malware attack on Alice or Bob to spying on the electromagnetic radiation emanating from their computer screens. However, these are attacks on the *endpoints* of the secure channel, and while being important and highly relevant, they are not the main focus of this book.

While passwords should never be used directly as cryptographic keys, they provide a very common example for a *shared secret* upon which a secure channel can be built. A password can be guessed by an attacker for two reasons:

- It can be inferred from some other information (for example, a simple generation rule)

- There are too few possibilities (that is, the password is too short)

You should easily recognize these potential problems from so-called password policies that oblige you not to choose a password that is contained in a dictionary and to choose a password that is sufficiently long. It is straightforward to reformulate these requirements for cryptographic keys in general. Adding the fact that the key needs to be agreed on in a secure manner, we get the following three basic requirements of cryptographic keys:

- The key is either exchanged or agreed upon between Alice and Bob in a secure way, that is, the CIA triad should be satisfied for the key exchange process

- The key should not contain any kind of information, or in other words, *the key should be generated in a completely random way*

- The keyspace $\mathcal{K}$ should be so large that is not possible to search through it within a reasonable time frame

The first requirement sounds rather strange as it seems we need to set up a secure channel first before we can exchange a key for setting up a secure channel. The second requirement is also rather tricky, as real randomness is quite hard to come by. The third requirement is the most straightforward, and we will deal with that one first.

3.2.1   One key for each task

In addition to the three basic requirements, it is a good practice in cryptography to have a unique key for each unique task. As an example, if Alice and Bob first authenticate each other (entity authentication) and then use message authentication to ensure their communication is not being manipulated by Mallory, they should use two different keys.

One key should be used only for entity authentication and the other key only for message authentication. Typically, the former key is a long-term, possibly **pre-shared key** (**PSK**), while the other is a more short-lived, so-called *session key* (see the next subsection).

While this might seem odd at first, having two distinct keys instead of one has a major advantage. If Mallory manages to compromise the key used for entity authentication, say, by mounting a side-channel attack on Alice's machine, the second key remains secure (at least for a certain period of time, namely until the next session key is negotiated). Mallory can now authenticate herself to Alice as Bob, but she still cannot send messages with the correct message authentication codes. Hence, the compromise of one key does not lead immediately to the total break of the entire security system.

In contrast, if a single key is used for all tasks, then regardless of the circumstances of how it is compromised, the entire security of that system is immediately broken. So, this best practice can be viewed as the cryptographic equivalent of not putting all your eggs in one basket.

3.2.2 Key change and session keys

Another good practice when dealing with cryptographic keys is to change them frequently. Regardless of what security measures they take, Alice and Bob can never rule out the possibility that their secret key becomes compromised.

There is always the chance that Mallory will find a new way to extract the key without breaking the underlying cryptography, for instance, by using a zero-day vulnerability to infest Alice's computer with malware. Alternatively, Eve might find a new, more effective cryptanalytic attack that breaks the protocol or mechanism used by Alice and Bob within a reasonable time frame.

By changing their secret key(s) frequently, Alice and Bob mitigate these risks. A frequently changing key limits the amount of information (for example, plaintext-ciphertext pairs or message authentication codes for given plaintexts) available to Eve for cryptanalysis.

More generally, frequently changing keys protects Alice and Bob against future algorithmic vulnerabilities or advances in cryptanalysis that would shorten a key's lifetime. As an example, if sufficiently large quantum computers with appropriate error correction (so that logical bits can be extracted from a large set of physical qubits in a stable way) ever become available, Eve could run Shor's algorithm for factorizing large numbers or finding discrete logarithms [163], [164] to break public-key algorithms such as RSA or ECC that are widely used today. However, Alice and Bob can at least mitigate this threat by changing the key faster than a quantum computer needs to execute Shor's algorithm.

Frequently changing keys also limits the exposure time of a key compromised by Mallory. If the extracted key is used only for a single communication session, Mallory cannot decrypt previous sessions and needs to repeat the extraction (and hope that her malware won't be detected by Alice's virus scanners, firewalls, and intrusion detection systems) to decrypt future sessions.

A cryptographic concept closely related to frequent key updates is the so-called *ephemeral* or *session* key. An ephemeral key is a key that is freshly generated for each new execution of a cryptographic protocol, for instance, for each new key agreement [63].

Ephemeral keys form the basis for *forward secrecy*, a security property of a cryptographic protocol that ensures that the compromise of long-term cryptographic secrets does not allow Eve to compromise previous sessions of the protocol. By generating a fresh key for every new session (and using the long-term secret for authentication only), a compromise of a single session key only affects data that is protected during that session by that particular key [187]. Moreover, even if a long-term secret is learned by Mallory, this will only affect *future* protocol sessions, because for them, entity authentication is compromised.

Intuitively, the term **forward secrecy** is somewhat misleading since it has the word "forward" in it, but actually describes a security property of past sessions. Basically, the idea behind forward secrecy is that the entire message traffic prior to the compromise of the long-term key(s) cannot be easily decrypted by the attacker. That is, the communication between Alice and Bob is locked securely in the past.

Here, *easily* means that the attacker cannot efficiently decrypt the communication unless she knows a polynomial-time algorithm for solving the underlying mathematical problem of the cryptographic protocol. For example, the **Discrete-Logarithm Problem (DLP)** underlies the **Diffie-Hellman (DH)** key agreement protocol. An attacker would therefore need a polynomial-time algorithm to solve that problem.

For a long time, problems such as DLP were believed to be computationally intractable, because for decades (DH, for instance, was introduced in 1976), no one was able to come up with an efficient method of solving them. That is essentially the reason why such problems form the basis of widely used algorithms in TLS. However, things have changed with the advent of quantum computers and Shor's algorithm [163]. Implemented on a quantum computer, Shor's algorithm can solve the DLP (and also the factoring problem used in the RSA cryptosystem) efficiently, that is, in polynomial time. Currently, quantum computers are not able to process the large numbers used in modern cryptography, but this might change over the next 10-15 years. Accordingly, DLP and the factoring problem are put by complexity researchers into a complexity class of their own called **bounded-error quantum polynomial-time (BQP)**, located somewhere between the complexity classes P (for *polynomial time*) and NP (for *non-deterministic polynomial time*) [123]. Of course, we will also need new, so-called *post-quantum* asymmetric algorithms for key exchange in due time, if only as insurance or fallback.

3.3 Key space

The security of an encryption algorithm is subtly related to the notion of key space. Simply put, a key space refers to encryption/decryption key pairs. The size of a key space determines how many of these pairs are available in a cryptographic algorithm (recall that in a symmetric algorithm, the encryption and decryption keys are the same, but in asymmetric cryptography they are different).

Clearly, the key space must be sufficiently large to prevent brute-force attacks (by means of an exhaustive search). But it would be very dangerous to assume an encryption algorithm is secure based on its key space size only.

A case in point: consider a simple type of cipher, the so-called *polyalphabetic substitution ciphers*, where the plaintext letters are substituted by ciphertext letters using multiple substitution alphabets. If the plaintext letters from the Roman alphabet are always substituted by a letter coming from the same alphabet, there are 26! possibilities for doing this (the number of possible permutations of the 26 letters). Consequently, a polyalphabetic substitution cipher that uses three distinct alphabets has a key space size of $(26!)^3$. This is approximately 7×10^{79} possible keys.

Assume someone comes up with an algorithm (a program) for a brute-force attack on a polyalphabetic substitution cipher where testing a single key hypothesis is computationally equivalent to a single floating-point operation. Then, searching half of the preceding key space would require 3.5×10^{79} operations (a typical assumption in cryptography is that an attacker doing an exhaustive key search will – on average – need to search half of the key space before they discover the right key).

As of June 2022, the TOP500 project, which ranks and details the 500 most powerful non-distributed computer systems in the world, lists Frontier as the currently fastest supercomputer in the world. Frontier, which was built by the Cray corporation for the US Department of Energy's Oak Ridge National Laboratory, performs 1.102×10^{18} floating-point operations per second.

Testing half of our key space on Frontier would take approximately 3.1×10^{61} seconds. This equals to roughly 0.86×10^{59} hours, or 0.35×10^{58} days, or 0.1×10^{56} years, that is, 10^{46} *billion* years. To set this into perspective, today's astronomers estimate the age of the universe (the time elapsed since the Big Bang) to be about 14 billion years.

Clearly, the key space size of a polyalphabetic substitution cipher is too big to break using brute force. Such ciphers, however, can be easily broken using statistical analysis techniques.

3.4 Key length

The key space $\mathcal{K}$ is large but finite. So, in principle, it is possible to search through it completely until the correct key K has been found. Such an attack is called a *brute-force* attack. Whether a brute-force attack is possible *within a reasonable time frame*, that is, within the time span the protected information is valuable for Eve, depends not only on the size of the key space but also on the speed of the latest computing technology and the resources Eve has at her disposal (this is part of the attacker model). This means key recommendations can (and do) vary over time.

For reasons of cost and usability, you should not always suppose the strongest possible attacker is after you. Thinking about the means an attacker realistically has at his or her disposal is part of the so-called *attacker model* in IT security. After that, you try to make your system secure against the specific type of attacker you have defined in your attacker model. When it comes to key length, however, it doesn't hurt to think of Eve as a representative of the NSA or some other government-sponsored security agency with basically unlimited financial resources.

For symmetric cryptographic mechanisms, the key length is the bit length of the secret key. For public-key algorithms (see *Chapter 7, Public-Key Cryptography*), key length refers to different things depending on the specific algorithm [63]:

- For RSA, it is the bit length of the RSA modulus n

- For algorithms based on the DLP in F_p^*, it is the bit length of p

- For algorithms based on the DLP in an elliptic curve over the finite field F_n, it is the bit length of n

Key length, together with a few other parameters, determines the security level of a cryptographic mechanism [63]. We say that a security level of n bits is achieved if any attack on that particular cryptographic mechanism needs 2^n (efficient) calculations, for example, 2^n encryptions with the AES block cipher [63].

Considering the computational capabilities of today's computers and taking into account the development of semiconductor technology for the foreseeable future (approximately five years), cryptographic mechanisms are currently required to achieve a security level of at least 112 bits; recommended key lengths for block ciphers and message authentication codes are 128 bits.

However, progress in semiconductor manufacturing and the introduction of fundamentally new cryptanalytic techniques, such as the application of a cryptographically relevant quantum computer, might require the adaptation of these recommendations in the medium term and a switch to 192 or even 256 bits.

Besides the key length, there are a few other parameters that affect the overall security of a cryptographic system [63]. For example, the digest length of a message authentication code is an important parameter for the security level. For block ciphers, their block width is an important security parameter.

3.5 Crypto-agility and information half-life

Because fundamental advances in cryptanalysis cannot be reliably predicted, especially for prolonged periods of time, it is desirable to design security systems in such a way that the transition to longer keys (or stronger cryptographic mechanisms) is possible and, ideally, easy to do. This concept is called *crypto-agility*. It is an important feature of a secure system: when, for example, NIST looked for a new standard block cipher algorithm (the **Advanced Encryption Standard**, or **AES**; see *Chapter 14, Block Ciphers and Their Modes of Operation*) in a competition held between 1997 and 2000, all candidate algorithms had to support varying key lengths of 128, 192, and 256 bits.

Conceptually, crypto-agility is to information security what software updates are to software engineering. A well-designed security system takes into account that at some future point in time, it *will* face some previously unknown attacks. Because the specific attacks are unknown at design time, the system must be specified and implemented in a way that makes it easy to change the key lengths or even replace the cryptographic mechanisms.

However, while crypto-agility allows efficient patching of a security system in case of (unexpected) cryptanalytic advances, it doesn't protect against *offline* attacks. This is especially critical if Alice and Bob need to keep their information confidential.

Eve can monitor the communication between Alice and Bob, store that data, and decrypt it later – maybe even some years later – when new cryptanalytic attacks or more powerful computing equipment become available. Thus, there remains a fundamental risk to the long-term protection of confidentiality [63].

The extent to which Alice's and Bob's data is susceptible to this risk depends on the *half-life* of their information, that is, the period of time within which their information is valuable for an attacker. As an example, say Alice operates a stock trading platform and transmits stock prices to Bob. Based on this information, Bob makes his trading decisions and sends them back to Alice to place his orders. In this case, the information that Alice and Bob exchange has a very short half-life: if Eve manages to decrypt that data a year later, she most likely won't gain anything (and there will be no harm to Bob).

If, on the other hand, Alice is a government agency sending classified information to Bob about who works on what project in that government's embassy, then it's an entirely different matter. If Eve can decrypt such information, it will likely have serious implications for Alice and Bob, even if Eve needs 10-20 years to succeed.

As a result, besides best practices such as frequent key updates, crypto-agility, and reduction of the transmission and storage of confidential data to the absolutely necessary extent, the key length of cryptographic algorithms should also be chosen by taking into account the half-life of the information these algorithms must protect.

A consequence of this is that the *practical* impact of cryptanalytic advances and progress in semiconductor technology heavily depends on the specific information to be protected. As an example, even if cryptographically relevant quantum computers will be built, numerous applications – at least initially – won't be affected.

3.6 Key establishment

To communicate securely, Alice and Bob need to share the secret key in advance. According to [117], Def. 1.63, "**key establishment** *is any process whereby a shared secret key becomes available to two or more parties for subsequent cryptographic use*".

In principle, Alice and Bob might meet in person in a cafe and establish a shared secret. However, apart from the logistic problems, this approach does not scale very well: in a group of n people, each possible pair needs to establish a key of its own. As there are $\frac{n(n-1)}{2}$ pairs, 100 people would need about 5,000 personal meetings. Obviously, an automated method of key establishment is in order.

Key establishment is a broad term in which we can further distinguish between *key agreement* and *key transport*. In a key agreement protocol, both parties involved have an influence on the final result, which is a shared key. The DH key exchange protocol mentioned in the first chapter is a prime example of a key agreement protocol. In a key transport protocol, on the other hand, one party (usually Alice) generates a key and sends it to Bob in a secure way.

3.6.1 Key transport

Key transport is a key establishment process in which one participant (Alice) selects the key, encrypts it, and distributes it to the other participant (Bob) [132]. Alice may generate the key herself or acquire it from some other source.

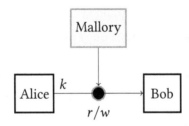

Figure 3.2: In key transport, one party (Alice) generates the secret key k and securely transmits it to another party (Bob). The transmission is done over an unsecured channel where an active attacker Mallory can read and manipulate data

Key transport can be performed using both public-key (or asymmetric) cryptography as well as with symmetric cryptography. If public-key cryptography is used, Alice encrypts the key to be transported using Bob's public key and sends this information to Bob. Bob then decrypts the data received with his private key.

NIST Special Publication 800-175B [14] provides an example of a public-key cryptography-based key transport. Bob, the receiving party, is required to have a public-private key pair that can be used for the key transport. The transport is accomplished in two steps:

1. Alice acquires an authentic copy of Bob's public key PK_{Bob}, generates a symmetric key k to be transported, encrypts k using Bob's public key, and sends the result $c = E_{PK_{Bob}}(k)$ to Bob.

2. Bob uses his private key to decrypt the ciphertext, thereby obtaining the key k (optionally, Bob confirms the key reception to Alice to ensure that they both now have the same key).

If Alice and Bob want to use symmetric cryptography instead, there must be a long-term secret K that they have already shared somehow. From K, both can derive a **Key-Encrypting Key (KEK)** on a regular basis. To transport a session key SK to Bob, Alice encrypts it with KEK and sends the result to Bob. Bob now uses KEK to decrypt and retrieve the session key.

3.6.2 Key agreement

From a security perspective, key transport has a fundamental downside compared to key agreement. If Alice generates the key and sends it to Bob (key transport), Bob can never be sure whether that key is sufficiently random.

This might seem quite paranoid at first (which is true for the cryptography mindset, but for a good reason), but Alice could unknowingly have a flaw in her random number generation or be tricked by Mallory, for example, to use an inadequate source of entropy.

Moreover, key transport typically relies on a long-term secret. If this secret gets lost, keys that were transported earlier also become known to Eve, meaning key transport does not provide forward secrecy. Thus, with key transport, Bob effectively needs to rely on Alice's security capabilities and security posture when obtaining the shared secret key.

In contrast, key agreement is a key establishment process where the resulting secret key depends on data contributed by both Alice and Bob. Because both Alice and Bob provide their random input, neither of them can compute the secret key independently without the contribution of the other party.

As a result – in contrast to key transport – Bob can be sure that the shared secret key established during the key agreement is secure even if Alice's input can be seen or guessed by the attacker.

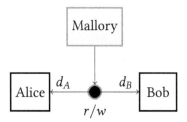

Figure 3.3: In key agreement, the secret key is generated from the information d_A provided by Alice and d_B provided by Bob. Neither Alice nor Bob can predetermine the value of the secret key k independently of each other. The information d_A and d_B is transmitted over an unsecured channel, so Mallory can read and manipulate that data

Let's take a look at an example of a key-agreement process where Alice uses a static key pair and Bob uses an ephemeral key pair [14]. The key agreement is carried out in four steps:

1. Bob acquires an authentic copy of Alice's static public key PK_{Alice}, for instance, from a so-called **Certification Authority (CA)**. In this key agreement example, PK_{Alice} is Alice's contribution to the key agreement.

2. Bob generates an ephemeral (i.e., short-lived) key pair and sends its public key part EPK_{Bob} to Alice, keeping the private key part to himself. The ephemeral public key EPK_{Bob} is Bob's contribution to the key agreement.

3. Alice and Bob use a mathematical operation involving their own private key and the other party's public key to generate a shared secret k.

4. Both parties derive from k one or more additional keys to protect their subsequent conversation.

Ideally, a process called *key confirmation* is performed at the end of the key agreement to ensure that both Alice and Bob have generated the same identical key. For example, both could compute a **Message Authentication Code** (**MAC**; see *Chapter 11, Hash Functions and Message Authentication Codes*) of the previously exchanged messages involving the shared secret and send the resulting MACs to each other. Key confirmation is an important part of the TLS handshake protocol (see *Chapter 6, Transport Layer Security at a Glance*).

3.7   Randomness and entropy

In cryptography, the security of most protocols and mechanisms depends on the generation of random sequences of bits or numbers. These sequences must have a sufficient length and be *random* in a very specific sense: we do not want an attacker to be able to guess part of or the whole sequence. To make this idea more precise, cryptographers use the concept of *entropy*.

You might be familiar with the notion of entropy from physics. There, entropy is a fundamental property of any complex system and, loosely speaking, describes the tendency of such systems to disorder. As an example, take a gas being injected into a container. At first, the gas particles will still be clustered closely together. But as time passes by, the gas particles will float around and distribute themselves randomly within that container. They do so because the latter configuration offers more possible states (i.e., locations and velocities) for the gas particles; in other words, the entropy of the latter configuration is higher. In that sense, entropy is inevitable in physics because it only increases over time.

3.7.1   Information-theoretic definition of entropy

Cryptography uses the entropy definition from information theory. The information theoretical concept of entropy is defined with the help of random variables.

Let X be a random variable that can take some values $x_1, x_2, \ldots, x_n$ with probability $P(X = x_i) = p_i$. Because the p_i are probabilities, we must have $0 \leq p_i \leq 1$ for each i and $\sum_{i=1}^{n} p_i = 1$.

Now we can define the *entropy* of X as

$$H(X) = - \sum_{i=1}^{n} p_i \log_2(p_i)$$

The entropy $H(X)$ can be seen as a mathematical measure of the average amount of information provided by an observation of X [117]. As an example, X could be the outcome of a six-sided die roll. Then, X would take its values from the finite set $1, 2, \ldots, 6$ with probability $P(X = x_{1\ldots6}) = 1/6$ and the sum of all possible outcomes $\sum_{i=1}^{6} p_i$ being 1. The entropy of X is

$$H(X) = - \sum_{i=1}^{6} \frac{1}{6} \log_2 \left(\frac{1}{6} \right) = -\frac{1}{6} \times 6 \times \log_2 \left(\frac{1}{6} \right) = \log_2(6) \approx 2.58$$

Alternatively, entropy can be viewed as the uncertainty about the outcome before X is observed. This uncertainty is highest if all n outcomes of X are equally likely. In this case, $H(X)$ takes on its maximum value $\log_2(n)$.

To illustrate, assume we have an unaltered six-sided die X_1 and a manipulated six-sided die X_2 that always gives a 3 or a 6 with equal probability. Clearly, the uncertainty of observing X_1 – the surprise about the outcome – is larger than that of X_2 because we know in advance that X_2 will give a 3 or a 6. Indeed,

$$H(X_2) = - \sum_{i=1}^{2} \frac{1}{2} \log_2 \left(\frac{1}{2} \right) = -\frac{1}{2} \times 2 \times \log_2 \left(\frac{1}{2} \right) = \log_2(2) = 1$$

As this example shows, entropy can also be used for approximating the average number of bits required to encode the elements of X. Since the entropy of X_1 is 2.58, we need 3 bits to encode them. In contrast, because $H(X_2) = 1$, a single bit is sufficient to encode the outcomes of X_2.

3.7.2 Entropy in cryptography

So, why is entropy so fundamental to cryptography? If the source used to generate secrets (or unique values used in cryptographic protocols) has a poor entropy, the number of values that can be possibly drawn from that source will be limited, and some values will be (much) more likely than others.

That, in turn, makes it much easier for Eve to mount a brute-force attack by exhaustively searching the key space because there are much fewer values to test and Eve can concentrate on the most common ones. This is exactly what happens in password-guessing attacks: Eve knows exactly which passwords are the most likely to be chosen by Alice and starts her attack with a list of the most common ones.

As another example, consider the key space of the AES-256 encryption algorithm. Its size is 2^{256}. If the AES-256 key was selected using a truly random source, Eve would have to try on average 2^{255} candidate keys before she comes to the correct key. If, on the other hand, Alice generates the key by first choosing a 32-bit random number and then turning it into a 256-bit key using some complicated but deterministic expansion algorithm E, then Eve needs to try only 2^{31} possible keys on average (obtained by running every possible 32-bit random number through E).

To prevent this, Alice and Bob must generate the keys or, in case of key agreement, the keying material, using sources that have enough entropy. In other words, they need to generate them randomly.

Therefore, cryptography employs random or pseudo-random number generators for generating keys. According to [117], "*a **Random Number Generator (RNG)** is a device or algorithm that outputs a sequence of statistically independent and unbiased binary digits*". We now turn to the difference between true randomness and pseudo-randomness.

3.7.3 True randomness and pseudo-randomness

Modern algorithms such as *Yarrow* [99] or *Fortuna* (see chapter 10 of [65]) generate secret keys for use in cryptographic algorithms and protocols by accumulating entropy from several **True Random Number Generators (TRNGs)** and combining it using hash functions (see *Chapter 11, Hash Functions and Message Authentication Codes*) and block ciphers (see *Chapter 14, Block Ciphers and Their Modes of Operation*).

A TRNG generates random numbers based on the randomness of a physical process such as thermal noise, the photoelectric effect, or other quantum phenomena. Such processes are unpredictable in principle and therefore offer high entropy. For cryptographic purposes, unpredictability is the most important feature of a TRNG. *Figure 3.4* illustrates the working principle of a TRNG.

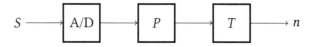

Figure 3.4: Basic architecture of a TRNG. A physical process S is used as a source of randomness. The fluctuations in S are converted into raw bits using an analog-to-digital (A/D) converter. The raw bits are post-processed to ensure sufficient entropy, for instance, by taking several raw bits and XORing them into a single bit. The resulting bit sequence is subjected to a built-in test T that ensures that the TRNG works as specified. If T passes successfully, the TRNG outputs a random number n

A good TRNG example is the well-known online service random.org, which offers true random numbers on the internet. These numbers are generated from atmospheric noise captured by a radio and post-processed to ensure high entropy. Atmospheric noise is caused by natural atmospheric processes, for example, lightning discharges in thunderstorms [183].

Another illustrative example is provided by the wall of *lava lamps* in the lobby of the San Francisco office of the cloud service provider *Cloudflare*. A video feed of this wall is used to generate additional entropy that is made available to the production system [45]. Because the flow of a lava lamp is highly unpredictable, the luminance values of the pixels in the video feed can serve as entropy sources.

Unfortunately, as these examples show, the generation of truly random bits is an inefficient (and expensive) procedure in most practical environments. Fortunately, pseudo-random number generators can be used to mitigate the problem.

A **Pseudo-Random Number Generator (PRNG)**, shown in *Figure 3.5*, is a deterministic algorithm that takes a comparably short sequence of truly random numbers or bits and outputs a much longer sequence of numbers or bits that *appears* to be random. Clearly, PRNG output is not really random. Ideally, however, an attacker cannot efficiently distinguish the output of a PRNG from a truly random sequence of the same length.

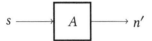

Figure 3.5: Basic architecture of a PRNG. The PRNG takes a comparably short seed s, i.e., a short sequence of truly random numbers or bits, and uses a deterministic algorithm A to produce a longer sequence of numbers n'

Apart from looking like a random sequence, for a **Cryptographically Secure Pseudorandom Number Generator (CSPRNG)**, unpredictability is the most important feature, just like for TRNGs. In this context, unpredictability means that even if part of the output sequence becomes known, Eve still cannot predict the next number in the sequence.

3.8 Summary

In this chapter, we have introduced the most important cryptographic notions and concepts revolving around keys, including entropy and randomness. We have seen that we should use different keys for different purposes and that they should be regularly updated. We also learned that the length of a key should depend on the half-life of the information the key is supposed to protect.

In the next chapter, we will see how keys are used together with cryptographic algorithms to encrypt and decrypt secret messages. We will even see an example of a truly unbreakable cipher.

4

Encryption and Decryption

In this chapter, we explain the concepts of encryption and decryption, describe the prerequisites needed for effective encryption and decryption, and illustrate these procedures using examples based on AES-256. On completion, you will be familiar with the cryptographic notions of encryption and decryption, and the core aspects that make modern encryption and decryption algorithms secure. Besides providing a precise definition of symmmetric cryptosystems, we will provide some more details on more advanced concepts we touched upon in the last chapter, such as the following:

- Information-theoretical security

- Computational security

- True randomness versus pseudorandomness

4.1 Preliminaries

In this chapter, we are going to talk about how to achieve confidentiality, the first of the three security goals in the CIA triad. For this, we need *encryption* (and also *decryption*) functions. In order to be able to describe these functions precisely and to put them into the right context, we need some mathematical jargon.

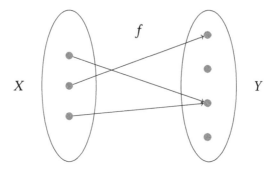

Figure 4.1: A function f can be seen as a table in which every element in set X is assigned to precisely one element in set Y

First of all, the term *function* has a precise mathematical meaning. A *function f* is a mapping from a set X (called the *domain of f*) to some other set Y (called f's co-domain) such that each element in X is mapped to precisely one element in Y, as illustrated in *Figure 4.1*. Symbolically, ones writes $f : X \rightarrow Y$.

If x is an element of the set X, formally written as $x \in X$, and the function f maps x to an element $y \in Y$, then y is said to be the *image* of x, and x is said to be a *preimage* of y. Formally, we write $y = f(x)$ in this situation.

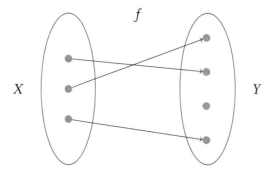

Figure 4.2: Function f is a one-to-one function if each element in its co-domain Y is the image of at most one element of its domain X. In other words, each element in Y has at most one preimage in X

A function $f : X \rightarrow Y$ is called *one-to-one* if each element in the co-domain Y is the image of at most one element in the domain X, as shown in *Figure 4.2*. If a function is one-to-one **and** the images of all elements in X, the function's domain, make up the entire set Y, then such a function is called a *bijection*. Note that the function shown in *Figure 4.2* is not bijective, because there is an element in Y without a preimage in X. A bijective function is illustrated in *Figure 4.3*. In this case, an *inverse function* $f^{-1} : Y \rightarrow X$ can be formed which basically reverses the action of f.

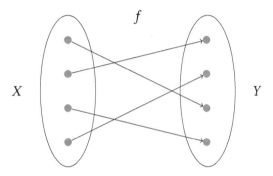

Figure 4.3: Function f is a bijection when it is one-to-one and the images of all elements in X, the function's domain, make up the entire set Y

The inverse function $f^{-1} : Y \rightarrow X$ maps each image $y = f(x) \in Y$ onto its preimage $x \in X$. This works because, for a bijective function, preimages always exist and are unique in X.

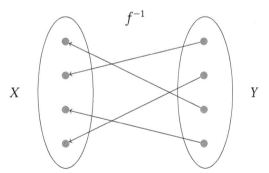

Figure 4.4: An inverse function of f, written as f^{-1}, reverses the action of f by mapping each element in Y to its preimage in X

In symmetric cryptography, we use certain functions f to *encrypt* things, and the inverse functions f^{-1} to *decrypt* things, that is, to reverse the encryption operation.

4.2 Symmetric cryptosystems

To recap from *Chapter 2, Secure Channel and the CIA Triad*, confidentiality is achieved using functions $f_K : \mathcal{M} \to C$ that transform the private information m, also referred to as *plaintext*, into a scrambled message $c = f_K(m)$, referred to as *ciphertext*. Here, f_K is an encryption function. It maps a plaintext m from some larger set $\mathcal{M}$, the *plaintext space*, to a ciphertext c which, in turn, is an element of some larger set C, the *cipher space*.

The functions f_K must be bijections, so that we can form the inverse functions, denoted by f_K^{-1}, which transform the ciphertexts back to the original plaintexts. The inverse functions are the decryption functions. The bijectivity of the f_K also means that $\mathcal{M}$ and C have the same number of elements.

In order to specify a complete *symmetric cryptosystem*, we need to define all of its ingredients:

- The plaintext space $\mathcal{M}$ and the cipher space C

- The keyspace $\mathcal{K}$

- The encryption function $f_K : \mathcal{M} \to C$

- The decryption function $f_K^{-1} : C \to \mathcal{M}$

Figure 4.5 illustrates the *encryption function* or encryption operation. The encryption function has two inputs: the plaintext message $m \in \mathcal{M}$ and the secret key $K \in \mathcal{K}$. They are mapped to the ciphertext $c \in C$. For convenience and better readability, it is common in cryptographic literature to use the notation e_K for the encryption function instead of the more formal f_K. Encryption functions are *the* fundamental tools of cryptography. In combination with additional cryptographic mechanisms, such as message authentication codes or digital signatures, encryption functions allow Alice and Bob to communicate securely over an unsecured channel. This holds both in the presence of passive as well as active attackers [168].

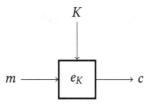

Figure 4.5: Working principle of encryption. The encryption function e_K produces the ciphertext $c \in C$ from the plaintext message $m \in \mathcal{M}$ and the secret key $K \in \mathcal{K}$

The *decryption function* or decryption operation, illustrated in *Figure 4.6*, is the reverse process. Here, the input is the ciphertext $c \in C$ and the secret key $k \in \mathcal{K}$. The input is mapped back to the original plaintext message $m \in \mathcal{M}$. Similar to encryption, decryption in cryptographic literature is often denoted as d_K instead of the more formal f_K^{-1}.

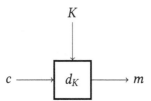

Figure 4.6: Working principle of decryption. The decryption function d_K takes as input the ciphertext $c \in C$ and the secret key $k \in \mathcal{K}$, and maps it back to the original plaintext message $m \in \mathcal{M}$

By taking together the encryption and decryption functions shown here, we can build a symmetric encryption scheme because the same key K is used to both encrypt and decrypt the messages. We will take a look at an example of encryption and decryption shortly.

Encryption functions are oftentimes used as building blocks for other, composite cryptographic mechanisms. These include key establishment schemes, message authentication codes to ensure the authenticity and integrity of messages, as well as protocols for entity authentication.

4.3   Information-theoretical security (perfect secrecy)

The historical roots of encryption are in military and diplomatic communications. The first encryption schemes were perhaps invented by the ancient Greeks and Romans. These encryption schemes have survived until today in the form of examples for easily breakable ciphers and can be found in virtually any textbook on cryptography.

Another famous historical example is provided by the Enigma encryption machine, which was used by the Axis powers in World War II. Due to its large key space, this sophisticated rotor-based machine was deemed unbreakable by its inventors. However, building on the work of Polish mathematicians and using (for the time) massive computing power, the Allies were able to prove them wrong [171]. Judging from these historical examples, one might get the impression that all encryption schemes can be broken. However, it is possible to devise *provably secure* encryption schemes.

An encryption scheme that is *provably secure* even against attackers with unlimited computational capabilities is called *perfectly secret* (not to be confused with perfect forward secrecy from *Chapter 3, A Secret to Share*) or *information-theoretically secure*. In a nutshell, this is achieved by constructing an encryption system that produces ciphertexts which provably – in the sense of mathematical proof – have not enough information for Eve to succeed regardless of her computational and cryptanalytic capabilities. In an example we shall see shortly, the ciphertext provably contains no information about the plaintext at all.

Let's make this a bit more formal.

*An encryption scheme is called **perfectly secret** if for any probability distribution over $\mathcal{M}$, every message $m \in \mathcal{M}$, and every ciphertext $c \in C$, it holds that:*

$$Pr[M = m | C = c] = Pr[M = m] \tag{4.1}$$

Here, $Pr[M = m]$ is the probability that the plaintext message is m and $Pr[M = m | C = c]$ is the so-called conditional probability that the plaintext message is m given that the corresponding ciphertext observed by Eve is c. This definition was introduced by Claude Shannon, the inventor of Information Theory, in [162].

What does the preceding mathematical definition say? Well, it tells us that Eve's chances of determining what the plaintext was given the ciphertext c (left-hand side of the definition) are the same if Eve is trying to guess the plaintext without any knowledge of the ciphertext (right-hand side of the definition). In other words, the ciphertext leaks no information whatsoever about the corresponding plaintext in addition to what Eve already knows about the plaintext. For example, Eve might already know that the plaintext is formed by a single bit. Then her guessing probability is $\frac{1}{2}$ and observing c will not improve her chances. Thus, regardless of computational resources at her disposal, the best Eve can do is to guess what the plaintext message was.

In the same report [162], Shannon also provided three criteria that have to be fulfilled so that a symmetric encryption scheme is perfect:

- The plaintext space $\mathcal{M}$ must be as large as the cipher space C and the keyspace $\mathcal{K}$

- For every possible $m \in \mathcal{M}$ and every possible $c \in C$ there should exist a key $k \in \mathcal{K}$ such that $c = e_k(m)$

- All keys should occur with equal probability

4.3.1 A first example

Let's construct an example of a perfectly secret encryption scheme based on these requirements. It will also help you get a grip on the ingredients of a symmetric cryptosystem given in the previous section.

We want to encrypt the roman letters a, b, g by mapping them onto their counterparts in the greek alphabet α, β, γ. Formally, this means that $\mathcal{M} = \{a, b, g\}$ and $C = \{\alpha, \beta, \gamma\}$. Because of requirement 1, we will also need three keys, so let's say $\mathcal{K} = \{1, 2, 3\}$. Now we need three encryption functions e_1, e_2, e_3, all having $\mathcal{M} = \{a, b, g\}$ as domain and $C = \{\alpha, \beta, \gamma\}$ as co-domain. We can find them by observing requirement 2.

We start by defining e_1 by its action on the elements of $\mathcal{M}$: $e_1(a) = \alpha, e_1(b) = \beta, e_1(g) = \gamma$. Note that each element of C appears on the right-hand side of exactly one equation. Had we defined $e_1(b)$ to be α instead, the resulting function would not have been bijective.

For e_2, we need to change something. We cannot simply repeat the definition for e_1, because in this case, we would not be able to satisfy requirement 2 (remember there are only three encryption functions overall). So let's switch to new plaintext-ciphertext pairs, by saying $e_2(a) = \beta, e_2(b) = \gamma, e_2(g) = \alpha$. Note again that e_2 is bijective.

Looking at the pairs we have defined so far, we see there are only three plaintext-ciphertext pairs left. They define the third encryption function: $e_3(a) = \gamma, e_3(b) = \alpha, e_3(g) = \beta$.

And we are done! The action of the decryption functions d_1, d_2, d_3 can be deduced by following the arrows in *Figure 4.7* from right to left. For a truly perfectly secret cryptosystem, we only need to take care that all three keys are chosen with equal probability, that is $1/3$ in this case.

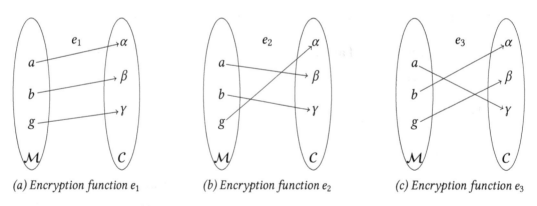

(a) Encryption function e_1 (b) Encryption function e_2 (c) Encryption function e_3

Figure 4.7: The three encryption functions constructed in our example

We can even check for ourselves that this cryptosystem is perfect. Let's assume that Eve observes the cipher $c = \gamma$ on the channel. From her knowledge of the plaintext space $\mathcal{M}$ alone, she has a probability of $1/3$ of guessing the correct plaintext.

Because of Kerckhoff's principle, however, we must also assume that Eve knows exactly how the encryption functions e_1, e_2, and e_3 work. By analyzing them, Eve can, for example, deduce that the following relation holds:

$$Pr[m = a|c = y] = Pr[k = 3].\qquad(4.2)$$

This is because only e_3 maps a onto y. But all keys occur with equal probability, so the probability that a is the plaintext after Eve has observed the ciphertext y is $1/3$, the same as her guessing probability.

4.3.2   The one-time pad

The prime example of a perfectly secret encryption scheme is the so-called *one-time pad*, also known as the Vernam cipher.

It was first described by Frank Miller in 1882 and re-invented by Gilbert Vernam in 1917, who also patented the cipher in 1919. The original version of the Vernam cipher had a cryptographical weakness because the bits on the key tape were reused after having been used once. The one-time use of the key tape was introduced later by Joseph Mauborgne who conjectured that cryptanalysis would be impossible if the key bits were completely random and never reused [192]. About 25 years later, Claude Shannon, was able to show mathematically that the one-time pad is indeed perfectly secret.

The one-time pad can be easily described in terms of the previous example. Here, $\mathcal{M} = C = \mathcal{K} = \{0, 1\}$. The encryption functions are e_0 and e_1, where $e_0(0) = 0, e_0(1) = 1$ and $e_1(0) = 1, e_1(1) = 0$. In this case, there is, however, a more compact way to describe the encryption process: We can write it as

$$c = m \oplus k\qquad(4.3)$$

where $\oplus$ denotes a bit-wise exclusive OR (XOR) operation. If you take two bits b_0, b_1 and apply the XOR operation onto them, $b_0 \oplus b_1$ will yield zero whenever both bits have the same value (that is, both are zero or both are one) and one whenever the bits have a different value.

So far, we have only considered encrypting single bits. If the plaintext m consists of l bits, we simply repeat the encryption process l times, *where each time the key bit k is chosen randomly*. If we slightly extend our notation for the key k to mean a random bitstring of length l, we may write again

$$c = m \oplus k \tag{4.4}$$

where m, c, and k are all bitstrings of length l.

Likewise, the decryption operation in the one-time pad scheme is performed by computing

$$m = c \oplus k \tag{4.5}$$

To re-iterate, the one-time pad is perfectly secret because, if Eve observes a ciphertext c, she is unable to get additional information about the corresponding plaintext m from c. This is because for every possible m we can find a corresponding key k such that $c = m \oplus k$.

In addition, every key occurs with the same probability, so no key has a higher probability than the others. As a result, every possible m is equally likely to have been encrypted and the ciphertext c reveals nothing about the plaintext.

As you might have guessed though, perfect secrecy – like most things in cryptography – is a trade-off. There is no free lunch, and a number of very inconvenient requirements for all practical purposes must be fulfilled for perfect secrecy to work.

First, the secret key must be as long as the message to be encrypted. This not only makes it more difficult to securely store the key, but also means that Alice and Bob must securely exchange the same amount of information that they are going to encrypt *beforehand*. But then – since they must exchange a secret key that is as long as the message – they can also exchange the message itself.

In other words, a perfectly secure scheme like the one-time pad effectively only allows encryption in the "time domain": if Bob manages to securely get an l-bit secret key to Alice today, she can use that key tomorrow to encrypt an l-bit message for Bob.

Second, to remain secure, every key can be used only once – that's why it is called the one-time pad. Using the same key k twice immediately leaks information because:

$$c_1 \oplus c_2 = (m_1 \oplus k) \oplus (m_2 \oplus k) = m_1 \oplus m_2 \tag{4.6}$$

This is a problem if certain parts or statistics about m_1 or m_2 are known. This knowledge can then immediately be transferred to the other message.

For these reasons, the one-time pad is very rarely used in practice. It remains important, however, to know that such a thing as a perfectly secure cipher actually exists. For other, not perfectly secure encryption schemes, it provides a benchmark to strive for.

4.4 Computational security

Compared to information-theoretical security, the concept of *computational* security is weaker in the sense that such cryptographic schemes can, in principle, be broken if Eve has enough time and sufficient computational resources.

However, the amount of computations needed to break a computationally secure scheme is so large that a break is absolutely infeasible in practice. As an example, if a scheme cannot be broken with a probability higher than 10^{-40} in 300 years using the fastest supercomputer available today (or in the near future), then that cryptographic scheme is sufficiently secure for all practical purposes.

On the positive side, computational security bypasses the limitations of perfect secrecy. As discussed in [97], perfect information-theoretical security suffers from the required key length: the secret key that Alice and Bob need to exchange before they can start communicating securely must have the same length as the overall length of *all* messages that will be ever encrypted with that key. Computational security overcomes this problem by weakening the notion of perfect secrecy in the following two aspects:

- We guarantee security only against attacks that Eve can execute in a practically relevant or feasible amount of time. In the context of cryptography, such (attack) algorithms are also called *efficient* and we will see shortly what that specifically means.

- Eve might succeed with some very small probability. In computationally secure encryption schemes, the ciphertext *does* carry a tiny bit of information about the plaintext so that, unlike with perfect secrecy, the probability of Eve succeeding is a bit higher than her guessing probability. However, this probability is still so tiny that Alice and Bob need not be concerned about it in practice.

We'll now analyze the situation that arises if Eve uses randomized algorithms to attack Alice and Bob. These algorithms are not always faster than their deterministic counterparts, but there is a certain probability that they are. This can improve Eve's overall success probability, so Alice and Bob should be aware of these algorithms.

4.4.1   Asymptotic approach and efficient computation

To account for future advances in computing technology, software or hardware optimized for a specific type of attack, and potential differences in the desired security level (e.g., average internet user versus government agency), modern cryptography uses a so-called *asymptotic* approach rooted in complexity theory [97].

The asymptotic approach treats the execution time of an attack as well as Eve's probability to succeed with that attack as *functions* of the so-called *security parameter n*, which is simply the key length in many cases. When Alice and Bob initialize the encryption scheme – for instance, when they exchange the secret key k – they choose a specific value for n (in practice, they choose a particular standardized variant of that encryption scheme with n having a pre-defined length, e.g., 128, 256, or 512 bits).

A *polynomial p* is a special kind of function that can be written in the form

$$p(n) = \sum_{i=0}^{N} a_i n^i \tag{4.7}$$

for some numbers a_i and input n.

An algorithm A is said to run in *polynomial time* if we can find a polynomial p, so that for any input x to A of length n, the computation of A terminates after **at most** $p(n)$ steps, which means we are always looking at bounds for the worst case.

Polynomials are used to classify the running time of an algorithm, because they grow with their input in a controllable way. In most cases (as in this section), we are only interested in the asymptotic behavior of the polynomial (that is, the growth for very large n. This behavior is governed by the largest power of n appearing in the polynomial (its *degree* N). If, for example, the running time of an algorithm can be described by a polynomial of degree 3, we say the algorithm is in $\mathcal{O}(n^3)$.

In complexity theory, the terms *efficient* and *polynomial running time* are often used synonymously for algorithms. Thus, in the context of computational security, efficient (attack) algorithms that Eve can execute in a practically feasible amount of time are probabilistic algorithms having a runtime that is *polynomial in n* [97].

In other words, for an efficient algorithm, there must be some constants a, c, so that the running time T increases like $a \cdot n^c$ with the security parameter n. Any attack algorithms that require a super-polynomial amount of time are ignored because they are not considered to be realistic threats.

A *probabilistic* or *randomized* algorithm is one that employs a degree of randomness as part of its logic or procedure [195]. Such algorithms effectively have the capability of making random decisions, which makes them *non-deterministic*.

The reason probabilistic algorithms are used in the context of computational security is that they can be faster than their deterministic counterparts. Even if this is not guaranteed, we can ignore them in our assessment of the security of an encryption scheme. Quicksort, a well-known algorithm for in-place sorting, is a good example of this phenomenon (which is not limited to cryptanalysis).

Quicksort is a divide-and-conquer algorithm that sorts an array by selecting a so-called pivot element from that array and partitioning the other elements into two sub-arrays depending on whether they are less than or greater than the pivot [194]. It can be mathematically shown that Quicksort is more likely to finish faster if it selects the pivot elements uniformly at random.

The fact that probabilistic algorithms could finish in fewer steps makes them more suitable for modeling the capabilities of an attacker as they allow to make a more conservative assumption from the defender's point of view. To be sure, any encryption scheme that is secure against a probabilistic polynomial time attack is also secure against its deterministic version [97].

4.4.2   Negligible probabilities

As discussed earlier in this chapter, computational security allows having encryption schemes that Eve might break with some very small probability. As long as this probability is negligible, such schemes are considered secure.

But how specifically small does a probability need to be to be considered *negligible*? In cryptography, this is precisely defined using negligible functions. A *negligible function* is a function that decreases faster toward zero with n than the reciprocal of any polynomial. More formally, a function f is negligible if for every polynomial p there exists an N such that for all integers $n > N$ it holds that:

$$f(n) < \frac{1}{p(n)} \tag{4.8}$$

As an example, both the functions 2^{-n} and $2^{-\sqrt{n}}$ are negligible (although they approach zero at different rates).

If Eve might break an encryption scheme E with the probability of $1/p(n)$ for some (positive) polynomial p, E is considered insecure. In contrast, if Eve can break that scheme with a probability that is asymptotically smaller than $1/p(n)$ for *every* polynomial p, then the scheme is consider secure because the probability of Eve's success is so tiny that it can be neglected.

Events that occur with a negligible probability (using the precise definition given earlier) are so unlikely to happen that they can be ignored in practice [97]. Thus, in the context of computational security, the breaking of an encryption scheme that happens with negligible probability can be ignored.

To summarize, in the realm of computational security, an encryption scheme is considered secure if, for every *probabilistic polynomial-time* attack, the probability of that attack being successful is negligible [97].

The preceding security definition is asymptotic because it employs the concept of negligible probability. Recall that negligible probability allows Eve to succeed for small values of the security parameter n. But when that value crosses some threshold N, the probability of Eve succeeding becomes so small we can neglect it.

4.5 Pseudorandomness

Computational security is built on the concept of *pseudorandomness*, the idea that bit strings (that is, ciphertexts) can look completely random even though they are not.

Pseudorandomness enables us to build (computationally) secure symmetric encryption schemes where a relatively short key, let's say 128 bits long, is used to securely encrypt multiple terabytes of plaintext messages.

In a nutshell – the precise mathematical details are, of course, much more complex – this works because a polynomial-time attacker cannot distinguish between a pseudorandom string and a truly random string. This means that, for the attacker, the ciphertext looks like it has been produced by a one-time pad, using the pseudorandom string as a key.

Pseudorandom strings can be created using a *pseudorandom generator*. This is a deterministic algorithm that takes a short, truly random string as input and expands it into a long pseudorandom string [97]. *Figure 4.8* shows a pseudorandom generator G takes as input a short, truly random string s and expands it into a much longer pseudorandom string t. In the computational security model, this allows us to construct secure encryption schemes that can encrypt a large number of messages using a single short key.

We have already come across pseudorandom generators in the earlier section on *True randomness and pseudorandomness* in *Chapter 3, A Secret to Share*, where we discussed their role in generating keys. Now we see that they can also be used to simulate a one-time pad.

Figure 4.8: A pseudorandom generator G

The short, truly random input of a pseudorandom generator is called a *seed*. The seed must be chosen uniformly at random to have sufficient entropy and must be kept secret. In addition, the seed must be large enough so that no polynomial-time attacker has enough time to test all possible seeds. Finally, an attacker should be practically unable to predict the next output bit of the pseudorandom generator (to put it more formally, an attacker using a polynomial-time algorithm should have a negligible advantage over pure guessing).

Figure 4.8 and the pseudorandom generator definition given earlier in this section tell us what its required behavior is but not how to achieve it. If we want to actually build a pseudorandom generator, we obviously need to find a mathematical function that Eve cannot invert. Otherwise, Eve could easily recover s by simply computing the inverse function G^{-1} for any given t.

Even though no mathematical proof of their existence has been found so far, there is a consensus in modern cryptography that pseudorandom generators exist because they can be constructed from so-called *one-way functions*.

*A function f from a set X to a set Y is called a **one-way** function if f(x) is easy to compute for all x ∈ X, but for essentially all elements y ∈ Y it is computationally infeasible to find any x ∈ X such that f(x) = y.* [117].

To make things even more complicated, there is also no mathematical proof for the existence of one-way functions. Proving this would be equivalent to solving the famous P versus NP problem, one of the six remaining most difficult mathematical problems selected by the Clay Mathematics Institute at the turn of the second millennium. However, mathematicians (and cryptographers) consider it very likely that one-way functions exist because there are several long-standing problems such as integer factorization that have no known algorithms that could solve them in polynomial time.

4.5.1 Stream ciphers

Using a pseudorandom generator, we can construct a symmetric cryptosystem, shown in *Figure 4.9*. By looking closely at the lower part of the figure, you'll recognize that this cryptosystem emulates the one-time pad encryption discussed earlier in this chapter. However, unlike the original one-time pad, this encryption scheme uses a *short* truly random string K (the key) instead of the much longer pad, which needs to have the same length as the message to be encrypted. This kind of cryptosystem is called a *stream cipher*. Here, the pseudorandom generator G is used to produce a random-looking stream of key bits, which is in turn used to encrypt plaintext m by XORing it with the pseudorandom pad k, just like in the one-time pad.

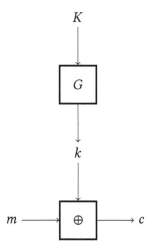

Figure 4.9: Computationally secure encryption scheme based on a pseudorandom generator

The XOR operation $\oplus$ in *Figure 4.9* – that is, the encryption operation itself – uses the pseudorandom string k obtained from the pseudorandom generator G. Because no polynomial-time algorithm can distinguish between a pseudorandom and a truly random string, this encryption scheme is computationally secure against eavesdropping attackers (so-called *ciphertext-only* attacks) [97]. Of course, for stream ciphers the same limitation applies as for the one-time pad: the key stream k must not repeat or be reused, otherwise, we run into the problems shown in *Equation 4.6*.

4.5.2   RC4

RC4 is a stream cipher that was very popular in the past because of its simplicity, speed, and apparent security. It also found heavy use within TLS until around 2013, when practical attacks on it were published [3]. As a consequence, use of RC4 within TLS was prohibited in 2015. The reason for discussing it here is to provide a relatively simple example of the inner working of a stream cipher. Later in this book, when discussing the modes of operation of block ciphers in *Chapter 14, Block Ciphers and Their Modes of Operation*, we will get to know more secure ways to construct stream ciphers.

The following description of RC4 is based on the account in [158]. RC4 consists of a state array S holding 256 bytes S_i, which are filled linearly at the beginning: $S_i = i, 0 \leq i \leq 255$. The initial seed, or key K consists of ℓ bytes K_j, where each key byte is written as a number between 0 and 255 and is used to address the entries of the state array. With the help of K, the state array is shuffled by selecting certain entries and swapping them:

for $0 \leq i \leq 255$ **do**

$\quad S_i \leftarrow i$

end for

$j \leftarrow 0$

for $0 \leq i \leq 255$ **do**

$\quad x \leftarrow i \pmod{\ell}$

$\quad j \leftarrow (j + S_i + K_x) \pmod{256}$

swap S_i and S_j

end for

After the initial shuffling phase, S is further shuffled and one byte S_t is selected to encrypt the first plaintext byte via bitwise XOR. After that, the shuffling and byte selecting go on until all N plaintext bytes P_n have been encrypted to cipher bytes C_n:

$i \leftarrow 0$

$j \leftarrow 0$

for $1 \leq n \leq N$ **do**

$\quad i \leftarrow (i + 1) \pmod{256}$

$\quad j \leftarrow (j + S_i) \pmod{256}$

swap S_i and S_j

$\quad t \leftarrow (S_i + S_j) \pmod{256}$

$\quad C_n \leftarrow P_n \oplus S_t$

end for

The effect of encrypting a file by RC4 can be nicely visualized by applying it on a grayscale image (see *Figure 4.10*). In a grayscale image, each pixel has a luminance value between 0 and 255 (i.e., it is a byte), therefore we can simply encrypt the luminance values pixelwise using the RC4 output.

Figure 4.10: Encrypting a grayscale image with RC4

Obviously, all visual structure has disappeared from the cipher image. But the cipher image also looks random at a statistical level (see *Figure 4.11* and *Figure 4.12*):

- While the distribution of luminance values in the plaintext image has a distinct shape, in the cipher image basically all luminance values occur with the same frequency, as they should in a random image. This results in the flat histogram on the right of *Figure 4.11*.

- In natural images, the luminance values of neighboring pixels are strongly correlated. The encryption process destroys this correlation, as *Figure 4.12* shows for the case of horizontally neighboring pixels. Similar figures could be produced for vertically or diagonally neighboring pixels.

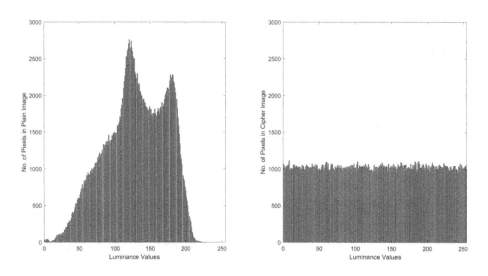

Figure 4.11: Frequency distribution of luminance values. Left: plaintext image; Right: cipher image

For *Figure 4.12*, the luminance values of 3,000 randomly selected pixels were compared to their horizontal neighbors. In a natural image, the luminance changes slowly and therefore the luminance values of neighboring pixels tend to be largely the same. In a cipher image, on the other hand, there should be no correlation left, and this is clearly shown on the right-hand side of the figure.

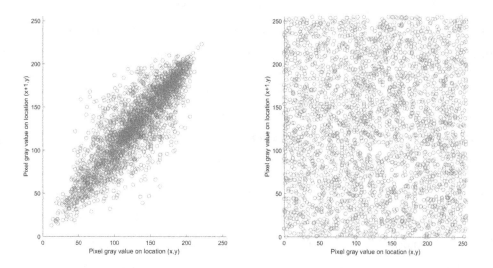

Figure 4.12: Correlation of 3,000 randomly selected, horizontally neighboring pixels. Left: plaintext image; Right: cipher image

We'll now discuss a new kind of attack, where Eve can feed plaintexts of her choice to an encryption server.

4.5.3 Pseudorandom functions and chosen-plaintext attacks

Being secure against passive eavesdropping is oftentimes not enough in practice. Encryption schemes must also be secure against so-called *chosen-plaintext attacks*. In a nutshell, a chosen-plaintext attack describes the situation where Eve can ask Alice or Bob to encrypt multiple messages of Eve's choice, and do so in an *adaptive* manner. That means Alice is made to encrypt specific plaintext messages based on the ciphertexts that resulted from the encryption before. Cryptographers refer to such a setting as an *oracle* (in our case, an encryption oracle).

The practical relevance of chosen-plaintext attacks is due to the fact that many modern systems interact with users who, in turn, determine what data is being processed or transmitted by these systems. For example, web servers send and receive information based on external requests by users accessing these web servers. In a real-life attack, malicious JavaScript loaded from Mallory's server can induce Eve's browser to repeatedly resume a previous TLS session with Bob's server, thereby sending encrypted session cookies to Bob.

When trying to defend encryption schemes against chosen-plaintext attacks, we are using so-called *pseudorandom functions*. According to the Encyclopedia of Cryptography and Security [95], "*A **pseudorandom function** is a deterministic function of a key and an input that is indistinguishable from a truly random function of the input*".

This means we are looking at a function F that has two input parameters: K (the key) and a second input x (the data variable). At first sight, this looks a lot like the encryption functions from *Section 4.2*. But here, we are not interested in the confidentiality of x, but in the output $F_K(x)$, which should look random for any random choice of K and any input x, that is: the function F_K should not be distinguishable from some truly random function g having the same domain and co-domain as F_K.

It can be mathematically shown that pseudorandom functions exist if and only if pseudorandom generators exist. As a result, pseudorandom functions are built using the same hard mathematical problems that pseudorandom generators are based on.

Equipped with a pseudorandom function, we can now build an encryption scheme shown in *Figure 4.13* that is computationally secure against chosen-plaintext attacks. The pseudorandom function F takes a key K and, for *every* new message m, a fresh value r as inputs, and outputs a pseudorandom string k, the equivalent of the pad in the original one-time pad scheme. It is important that the $r-$ values do not repeat, that is, they should be so called *nonces* (numbers used once). In principle, nonces can be generated using simple counters, but other constructions are also possible. Finally, the plaintext message m is encrypted using the XOR operation with k to obtain the ciphertext c. Because the nonces are not allowed to repeat, the string k (essentially, the pad) is independent from the pads used in previous encryptions.

Because a fresh value of r is used for every new message m, the encryption scheme in *Figure 4.13* is *probabilistic*: encrypting the same message m twice will result in two

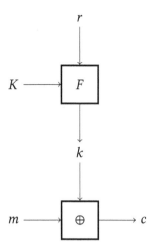

Figure 4.13: Encryption scheme secure against chosen-plaintext attacks

completely different ciphertexts (as long as r is not reused). Therefore, it is not possible for an attacker to predict what the next ciphertext will look like.

4.6 Summary

In this chapter, we covered a lot of ground. With the goal of confidentiality in mind, we have formally defined symmetric cryptosystems and have seen that perfectly secure cryptosystems do exist. Inspired by the prime example of a perfectly secure cipher, the one-time pad, we looked for less expensive ways to achieve a desired level of security. This led us to weaken the concepts of perfect security and true randomness and to look at computational security and pseudorandomness instead. These concepts will be important tools in what's to follow.

In the next chapter, we will look at another important security objective from the CIA triad, namely authentication.

5

Entity Authentication

In *Chapter 2, Secure Channel and the CIA Triad*, we saw that Alice and Bob need the CIA triad – the combination of the cryptographic goals confidentiality, integrity, and authentication – to establish a secure communication channel in the presence of both passive and active attackers. We defined what authentication is, gave several examples illustrating what happens when authentication goes wrong, and briefly discussed the two types of authentication used in cryptography, namely message authentication and entity authentication.

In this chapter, we are going to cover authentication – in particular entity authentication – in much more detail. Particularly, we will discuss the following:

- Why entity authentication is absolutely necessary to establish a secure channel

- The mathematical properties of cryptographically secure authentication

- Why password-based authentication is rather weak

- Several types of cryptographic protocols for strong authentication

Integrity and confidentiality, the other two properties of the CIA triad, will be covered in detail in *Chapter 11, Hash Functions and Message Authentication Codes*, and *Chapter 14, Block Ciphers and Their Modes of Operation*, respectively.

5.1 The identity concept

Let's recall from *Chapter 2, Secure Channel and the CIA Triad* that *entity authentication* is the ability to assure one communicating party – using fresh supporting evidence – of the identity of a second communicating party and to ensure that the second party was actually active when the supporting evidence was generated [117].

But what do we actually mean by the term *identity*? According to the Merriam-Webster online dictionary, identity is *the distinguishing character or personality of an individual* as well as *the condition of being the same with something described or asserted*. In cryptography, identity typically refers to a unique property of a communicating party. This actually can mean a lot of things; it might be the name that can be found in your passport, or the pseudonym you have chosen for yourself when posting on `www.dogforums.com`. As communicating parties very often involve computers, it might also be the name of a server. In the TLS context, it is most often the **Fully Qualified Domain Name (FQDN)**. So, the term **identity** can have many different meanings that change from context to context.

Identity plays an important role in cryptography and, in particular, in secure communication. In addition to keeping a message sent by Bob to Alice confidential, Alice needs assurance that this message is indeed from Bob. The following example illustrates why identity verification is important for security.

Imagine that Alice and Bob are two generals besieging Eve's stronghold. Although Eve is too weak to break the siege, Alice and Bob must act in a coordinated manner if they want to succeed. That is, in order to capture Eve's stronghold, Alice and Bob must attack simultaneously.

To communicate with each other, Alice and Bob use messengers (after all, the internet will not be invented for the next 500 years or so). The messengers are trustworthy but Alice and Bob do not know each other's messengers in advance.

To deliver their message, a messenger has to cross a valley controlled by Eve's army and, therefore, can be captured. If this happens, the genuine messenger is replaced by Eve's messenger, who delivers a message of Eve's choice to Alice or Bob. This way, Eve can easily defeat Alice and Bob by faking a message. Namely, if Alice sends Bob a message that they both shall attack at a certain time, and Eve captures the messenger, she can simply replace Alice's original message with a fake one saying that Alice will attack at a different time. If, instead, Alice's message tells Bob not to attack yet, Eve can present Bob with a message to attack right away. In both cases, Alice and Bob lose.

This example illustrates that in certain situations, the confidentiality and integrity of the information alone are not sufficient. Alice and Bob need to be sure that the message they are receiving actually originates from the other legitimate party. This means Alice and Bob are in need of the security objective **message authentication**.

Let's come back into the present and imagine that Alice and Bob are engaged in some kind of real-time interaction, such as a phone call. But something about Bob's voice seems strange to Alice. It might just be some atmospheric noise, or could it be that Bob's phone has been stolen? In this case, Alice wants to verify the identity of the party she is currently interacting with, in other words, she needs **entity authentication** or, synonymously, **identification**. For example, she might ask Bob a question that only Bob could answer, such as "Where did we first meet?" and, based on the answer, decide whether she is really talking to Bob.

Note that in both examples, neither message authentication nor entity authentication directly leads to a secure channel between Alice and Bob. This is because after the authenticity of Alice's message and the identity of Bob are verified, an attacker might still take over the channel, for example, by pushing Bob away from his phone. In order to get a secure channel, Alice and Bob need to establish a key between them by way of an

authenticated key exchange. However, entity authentication forms an important part of authenticated key establishment – after all, you need to be sure *with whom* you are going to share a secret key.

5.1.1 Basic principles of identification protocols

The simple exchange of a question and an answer between Alice and Bob described previously can be seen as a rudimentary *identification protocol*. We touched on this subject in *Section 2.5, Authentication* in *Chapter 2, Secure Channel and the CIA Triad*, and will now provide some more details.

But before diving into the details, we first need to introduce some basic definitions used in the context of identity and identity verification in cryptography.

In cryptography, the communicating party who assures themselves of the identity of the other communicating party is called the *verifier*. The communicating party claiming a specific identity is called the *claimant*. The claimant performs some calculations that only they can perform (we'll see later how that works) and the verifier validates that these calculations are correct and that the identity declared by the claimant is their actual identity. This prevents the threat of *impersonation*, the act of assuming someone else's identity.

Recall from the *Section 2.5, Authentication* in *Chapter 2, Secure Channel and the CIA Triad* that a *cryptographic protocol* is a distributed algorithm specifying the action required of two or more entities to achieve a specific security objective [117]. Because in entity authentication, we are interested in verifying who we are interacting with, a cryptographic protocol is a suitable framework for this task.

Figure 5.1 shows the working principle of a typical cryptographic protocol for identity verification. The verifier requests the claimant to send her a message, let's call it m, which demonstrates that the claimant is in possession of some secret that only the genuine party can know by design. In response, the claimant computes and sends message m to the verifier. Upon receiving m, the verifier checks the correctness of the message and accepts the claimant's identity if the check is successful. Such cryptographic protocols are referred to as *identification protocols* or *entity authentication protocols.* When analyzing the security of such protocols, we need to bear in mind that in most cases the channel that is used to exchange the protocol messages is insecure. In particular, this means that even after the identity check, an attacker might still take over the channel. This problem can only be resolved by combining entity authentication with authenticated key establishment, which we will discuss in the next section.

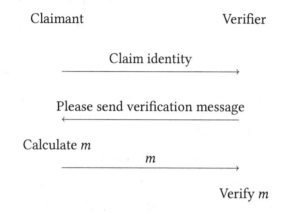

Figure 5.1: *Working principle of entity authentication protocols*

Figure 5.1 shows a situation where only the claimant authenticates against the verifier. This is called a *uni-lateral authentication.* Oftentimes, the verifier and claimant switch roles after the claimant has authenticated so that the other party also authenticates. This process is called *mutual authentication.*

5.1.2   Basic factors for identification

In information security, there are three basic ways for a legitimate party, say Alice, to prove their identity:

- *Something Alice knows.* Identity is proven based on some unique knowledge that no one except Alice is supposed to have. Examples of this type of identity proof include passwords, personal identification numbers, and secret cryptographic keys.

- *Something Alice has.* Identity is proven based on the possession of a unique item that, by design, only Alice can have. Examples of this type of identity proof include passports, magnetic-striped cards, hardware keys (such as FIDO), chip cards contained in badges, or handheld password or PIN generators (for example, the ones found in chipTAN schemes).

- *Something Alice is.* Identity is proven based on an intrinsic or inherent feature that is unique to Alice. Examples include human fingerprints, human DNA, and biometrics such as handwriting, voice, retinal patterns, or hand geometries, and typing timings on a keyboard. In this case, a so-called *feature vector* is extracted from the actually measured data, which is supposed to be robust (that is, it basically looks the same) against changes in lighting conditions, distance from the sensor, and so on. This feature vector is then matched against corresponding entries in a database.

Often, these factors are combined in what is called *multi-factor authentication.* For example, to withdraw money from an ATM, you need your credit card (something you have), but you also need your PIN (something you know). The basic idea behind multi-factor authentication is very simple: in order to break such a scheme, an attacker would have to attack several channels instead of one, which significantly raises the effort and lowers the success probability of the attack.

5.2   Authorization and authenticated key establishment

In computer security, the main purpose of entity authentication is to control access to an asset or a resource, say a money withdrawal from an ATM, a file on the disk, or an administrative interface of a web application. This is because access rights – what a user is allowed to do and what not – are typically tied to the user's identity. The property of computing resources being available only to authorized entities is called *authorization* [173]– another important security objective that relies heavily on entity authentication.

Entity authentication is also necessary to establish a secure channel. If Alice wants to securely communicate with Bob, she not only needs to protect the messages transmitted between her and Bob over an insecure communication channel but also ensure that she is indeed talking to Bob. As illustrated in *Figure 5.2*, if Eve can impersonate Bob, all security would be lost even if the messages themselves can neither be decrypted nor manipulated. For this reason, entity authentication is typically an integral part of key establishment protocols.

While key exchange without entity authentication (so-called *anonymous key exchange*) is possible in principle, it has the huge drawback that you cannot be sure about who you have exchanged the key with. On the other hand, you can certainly do entity authentication without key exchange (the authentication process at the ATM is an example of this), but there is a certain danger that the connection is *hijacked* after the authentication, meaning an attacker replaces Alice without Bob noticing. Both attacks can be avoided if Alice and Bob agree on a shared (and authenticated) key as part of the authentication protocol.

A protocol that provides *key authentication* is called *authenticated key establishment*. Key authentication guarantees that only specifically identified parties get hold of the secret key established during a key exchange. In other words, if Alice and Bob perform an *authenticated* key establishment, Alice is assured that no one except Bob can learn that secret key. This implies that Bob needs to authenticate himself to Alice. If Bob also needs assurance that only Alice can gain access to the secret key, this can be done by performing an authenticated key exchange with *mutual* authentication.

Related to key authentication, *key confirmation* is the assurance that the other communicating party is in possession of a particular secret key. As an example, if Alice and Bob have previously established a secret key k, then, later on, Bob can perform key confirmation to reassure himself that Alice is still in possession of k.

To perform key confirmation, Bob would typically send Alice a message containing (mathematical) evidence that Bob is indeed in possession of key k. There are several ways that Bob can demonstrate this. As an example, Bob can either compute a one-way hash of k, use k in a keyed hash function, or encrypt known plaintext using k.

Alternatively, Bob can use a so-called *zero-knowledge proof.* Zero-knowledge proofs can be used to demonstrate the possession of a key without leaking any additional information about its value.

By combining key authentication and key confirmation, Alice and Bob achieve *explicit key authentication.* With explicit key authentication in place, Alice can verify that Bob actually possesses key k (and vice versa).

5.3   Message authentication versus entity authentication

What happens if message authentication or entity authentication fails? We can answer this question by looking at *Figure 5.2* again. There are two ways in which Eve can manipulate messages sent from Bob to Alice. Eve's first option, illustrated on the left-hand side in *Figure 5.2*, is to break the message authentication of the communication between Alice and Bob by suppressing the original messages, changing them, or replacing them with messages of her own. Eve's other option, shown on the right-hand side in *Figure 5.2*, is simply to replace Bob in the communication and receive Alice's messages instead of Bob, or send Alice any message of Eve's choice, thereby breaking entity authentication.

The difference between entity authentication and message authentication is further illustrated by the notorious email-based phishing attacks you are all familiar with. In this case, an attacker sends you an email allegedly coming from your bank, telling you there is a problem with your online banking account and that you have to log in within the next 24 hours, otherwise your account will be canceled. Helpfully, there is also a link provided in the email for you to log in. If you click on that link, the attacker has achieved their first goal: you believe the email really comes from your bank, which is a violation of message authentication.

Clicking on the link will bring you to some web server controlled by the attacker. It certainly claims to be the banking server, it may even look like the banking server, but it isn't the banking server. If you fail to notice this, entity authentication is broken, and you provide your login credentials to some fake server. Luckily, TLS provides us with the means to verify whether we are really connected to our banking server or not.

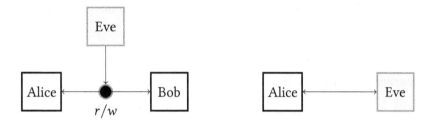

Figure 5.2: Eve can succeed either by attacking the communication channel or by impersonating Bob

Another fundamental difference between message authentication and entity authentication is the fact that message authentication does not guarantee timeliness. Using message authentication, Alice can be assured that Bob is indeed the source of a message m she received and that the message was not altered during transmission. However, Alice has no way to tell whether Bob sent the message m a minute or a year ago.

Entity authentication, on the other hand, involves validating the claimant's identity in real time through dedicated communication between the claimant and the verifier [117]. If Alice and Bob execute an entity authentication protocol before exchanging messages, Alice knows that Bob is actually online and, as a result, that the messages she receives from Bob are fresh. This, in turn, protects Alice against so-called replay attacks, where Eve replays Bob's messages that she recorded in the past.

5.4 Password-based authentication

Password-based authentication is arguably the most common way used to authenticate humans to electronic devices. An average internet user has about 70 to 80 passwords to identify themself to websites they visit and services they use [130].

Most existing password schemes use *time-invariant* passwords. The user initially chooses a string of characters, typically short enough so they can memorize it. From this point in time onward, that password is associated with the user ID, for instance, the username or the email address entered during registration.

The password is a secret shared between the user and the electronic system. Hence, from a cryptographic perspective, password-based authentication is a symmetric mechanism (it is based on a common secret) that provides unilateral authentication. The authentication is unilateral because the user authenticates themself to the system, but the system – an electronic device or a web service – does not authenticate itself to the user. Note, however, that in most instances of password-based authentication, a secure channel is created between user and server via TLS before the user sends their password, and this includes server authentication.

To access the electronic system, the user enters their user ID and password. The user ID is the claimed identity, and the password is the evidence to prove that claim. The system looks up the given user ID and checks whether the password provided by the user matches the password stored (in whichever form) on the system. The fact that the user knows the password – which is established by the user revealing the password to the system – is accepted by the system as proof of the user's identity. As a result, the system grants the user access to certain system resources, such as a computer account or web service.

In its most basic form, password-based authentication therefore takes the form depicted in *Figure 5.3*. The claimant sends their identity to the verifying system, along with a matching password. The system then checks whether the provided password indeed belongs to the claimed identity. Based on the result of this check, the system grants certain rights to the claimant. For example, after a successful login at amazon.com, you get the right to inspect your previous orders. This is called *authorization* and can be seen as an advanced kind of security service built on top of entity authentication.

Note, however, that there are important questions left open in this scheme: how do we protect the password on its way from the user to system? How is the password stored at the system's site in a secure way? We will return to these questions shortly, but first, a bit of history.

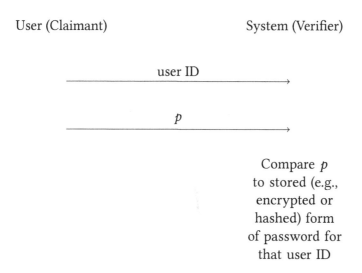

Figure 5.3: Working principle of password-based authentication

5.4.1 Brief history of password-based authentication

Password-based authentication was introduced in the early 1960s when the first time-sharing systems, such as the famous **Compatible Time-Sharing System (CTSS)** and, later on, Multics, were developed at the Massachusetts Institute of Technology.

A key problem the designers of these systems faced is that they – unlike earlier mainframe computers – were used by multiple people, each having their own private files. To protect access to these files, an authentication mechanism had to be added, and passwords were chosen for their simplicity and low usage of computing resources [116].

From these early time-sharing systems, passwords found their way into operating systems such as Unix, BSD, and Xenix as well as their many derivatives, such as SunOS, AIX, FreeBSD, Solaris, and Linux. Eventually, password-based authentication established itself as the main authentication method in IT systems.

Although passwords have many well-known, serious security problems (see the *Disadvantages of password-based authentication* section later in this chapter), they remain the dominant authentication mechanism on the internet and, in general, in IT systems [81] since they are easy to implement and have relatively good usability.

The diversity of technical systems and the usability of authentication, especially for non-technically-savvy users, are prime examples of the many barriers preventing the move beyond alphanumeric passwords [81].

IT systems that require user authentication are very heterogeneous, ranging from embedded smart home appliances to personal computers, tablets, and smartphones to web services and social media sites. To date, no other alternative authentication solution covers all these systems and services.

Moreover, passwords are conceptually simple and therefore usable even for people without a significant technical background. Stronger authentication mechanisms, such as two-factor authentication or the use of dedicated hardware keys, require much higher technical proficiency and put additional effort on the user.

5.4.2   Storing passwords

As early as 1977, the *Multics Security Evaluation* report by US Airforce's Electronic Systems Division [54] identified the login password file of any operating system as an attractive target because the information contained in this file enables undetected impersonation attacks and, as a result, a long-term exploitation of the system.

This attack vector was deemed especially critical if exposed to attackers who are not always authorized users of the system. For such attackers, obtaining a legitimate user's password provides an entry into the system that would not exist otherwise. The report [54] also considered the possibility of passwords appearing in memory dumps and concluded that password files must be protected.

In the early 1970s, Needham [202] was the first to note this security weakness and therefore proposed to store encrypted passwords together with the user ID. Needham's proposal included the use of a one-way function as there was no need to decrypt the passwords since the password supplied by the user must only be encrypted and compared to the ciphertext of the password stored for that user on the system.

The rationale for this approach was that even if an attacker could get hold of the file with encrypted passwords and their user IDs, it would be impossible for her to compute the plaintext passwords from the ciphertexts.

In *Chapter 4, Encryption and Decryption*, we briefly introduced the concept of one-way functions. These functions are also referred to as *hash functions*, and we are going to cover them in detail in *Chapter 11, Hash Functions and Message Authentication Codes*. For now, it is sufficient to recall that these functions are easy to compute but computationally infeasible to revert. Roughly speaking, this means that given some input x and a hash function f, it is easy to compute the hash value $y = f(x)$, but it is impossible to efficiently obtain the original input x given the hash value y.

Modern operating systems such as Linux use hash functions to store the hash values of passwords rather than the passwords themselves. The rationale is that even if an attacker gets hold of a hashed password, they cannot use it to log in as the victim because the password system requires the plaintext password. Moreover, because a hash function is a one-way function, the attacker should not be capable of obtaining the original password from its hash value.

However, it turns out that this is still not sufficient to protect passwords against practical attacks. While it is impossible to invert a hash function, Eve can employ a method known as *dictionary attack*. She can simply compute hash values for all words (or word combinations) in a dictionary – which can also be a list of compromised or common passwords – and compare them to the stolen hash value of a password.

However, simply computing the hash values of all possible words of a given length formed of 64 characters (a-z, A-Z, 0-9) and storing the hash values along with the words would result in huge files that are difficult to handle. But in a so-called *rainbow table* [134], only the results of repeatedly hashing the most common passwords are stored in so-called *hash chains* (actually, it is enough to store only the starting value s and end value e for each chain, as the intermediate values can be easily re-computed if needed).

We will discuss the details of an attack based on rainbow tables a bit later in *Section 19.7* of *Chapter 19, Attacks on Cryptography*. But basically, the attack works like this.

Suppose Eve has found the value $y = hash(x)$ in a stolen database and wants to find a matching *preimage x*. She creates a hash chain of her own starting with y and checks whether one of the resulting hash values coincides with one of the end values e stored in the rainbow table. This means that there is a high probability that $y = hash(x)$ is contained in the hash chain belonging to e.

Suppose that the hash chain ending with e starts with s. Eve then re-computes the hash chain, starting with s until she reaches the value y. The preceding value x in the chain has y as its hash value and will therefore be accepted as the password, even though it may not be the same as the original password.

This technique is known as a *time-memory tradeoff*. In this case, we are saving storage space by sacrificing some computation time that is needed to re-create the hash chains. In any case, it seems that by using rainbow tables, Eve would be able to break short or simple passwords that can be found in dictionaries.

There is, however, a relatively simple remedy against pre-computed hash tables: password systems used in practice employ a so-called *salt*, a random string that is freshly generated for each new password. The salt is hashed together with the password and stored in cleartext, together with the resulting hash value and the corresponding user ID. Salting does not make dictionary attacks impossible, but it makes them much harder because for every password, the attacker has to go through the hashing effort anew and cannot rely on pre-computed tables.

The Linux operating system stores the hashed passwords along with their salts and the user IDs in the /etc/shadow file. There are various algorithm options for the hash algorithm. The hash algorithm used is indicated numerically after the user ID (see *Figure 5.4*).

In *Figure 5.4*, the alice entry 6 means that the SHA-512 algorithm was used for hashing. The value elkQzDDD is the salt. The 512-bit hash value follows thereafter.

Figure 5.4: The etc/shadow *file in Ubuntu Linux*

Meanwhile, there are also other schemes, such as PBKDF2 [96], which were originally invented to derive a symmetric key from a password, but which may also be used to verify a password in a secure way.

5.4.3 Disadvantages of password-based authentication

In the previous section, we learned of several disadvantages of password-based authentication related to password storage. It turns out that passwords have even more drawbacks related to usability, time invariance, and human psychology.

From a usability perspective, the user must be able to correctly enter the password and, thus, successfully authenticate themselves on the system with high probability. This is, of course, easy to achieve if the user chooses a short and easy-to-remember password such as iloveyou or 1234.

However, as the **Have I Been Pwned (HIBP)** online service [83] will tell you, `iloveyou` has appeared 2,330,348 times in past data breaches and is therefore an utterly insecure password; it is certainly in every password dictionary, and its hash value is in every rainbow table you can download from the internet.

Choosing a strong password, such as `0(a<*ZS>jBUvNLym?oIp8d!PN4`, increases security but also makes it much more likely for the user to mistype while entering their password. This – as well as the time needed to enter a complicated character string – turns password-based authentication using strong passwords into a hassle for the user.

Moreover, strong passwords are not only error-prone and time-consuming to enter, but also difficult for humans to memorize. As a result, users either choose a short but insecure password or a complicated, secure one that they write down, preferably in an easily accessible place such as on a sticky note. This way, passwords get exposed to potential attackers in physical proximity, for example, in a co-working space.

Users also tend to choose passwords based on everyday words or popular phrases that they can easily remember. Many passwords therefore have low entropy and can be easily cracked using dictionary attacks, which we discussed earlier in this chapter [7].

Passwords can also be stolen using social engineering attacks, phishing emails, malware, key loggers, and man-in-the-middle attacks. According to recent statistics from the cybersecurity industry [142], nearly 98% of cybersecurity attacks rely on social engineering, the most popular method being to deliver phishing emails.

On a more fundamental level, many of the security weaknesses of passwords result from them being *time-invariant*. If Eve can trick Alice into disclosing her password – whether by using a social engineering attack, by eavesdropping on Alice while she enters it, or by cracking a leaked password file – there is nothing Alice can do to restore her security. Eventually, Alice might, of course, try and change her password. But even this might fail because Eve already has changed the password to something Alice does not know. In the instance of time when a password is compromised, its time-invariant nature immediately allows Eve repeated unauthorized access to Alice's account [81].

Taken together, these drawbacks make passwords a form of *weak authentication*. The good news is that instead of relying on passwords, we can use cryptographic protocols for entity authentication that avoid most of these drawbacks and, as a result, offer *strong authentication*.

5.5 Challenge-response protocols

The working principle of cryptographic challenge-response protocols is illustrated in *Figure 5.5*. Claimant Bob proves his identity to verifier Alice by demonstrating that he knows a secret that, by design, is known only to Bob (and, potentially, Alice). However, unlike with basic password-based authentication, as shown in *Figure 5.3*, Bob does *not* reveal the secret on the communication channel.

Instead, Bob responds to a time-variant challenge. Computing the correct response requires both Bob's secret and the challenge. The challenge, for example, a number, is chosen by verifier Alice randomly and secretly at the beginning of the protocol.

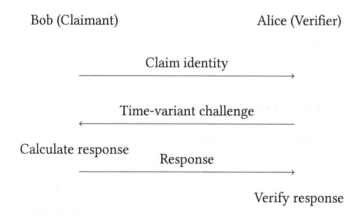

Figure 5.5: Working principle of entity authentication protocols

Why are challenge-response protocols more secure than passwords, and how do they overcome the drawbacks of password-based authentication we discussed previously?

First, the claimant never discloses the secret. Unlike with passwords, the secret used in a challenge-response protocol never leaves the claimant's machine (or whatever form of storage the claimant uses to store their secret). What is transmitted from the claimant to the verifier is a response generated using the claimant's secret.

Because the claimant's secret is typically a cryptographic key that has sufficient entropy, and the response is obtained by encrypting (or decrypting) the challenge with that key, or by computing a key-dependent hash value of the challenge, recovering the claimant's secret from the response would require the attacker to break the encryption or hashing algorithm. Luckily, this is practically infeasible for modern encryption algorithms such as AES.

Second, a challenge-response protocol always employs a time-*variant* challenge generated by the verifier. Most importantly, this means that the challenges will not repeat. A repeating or constant challenge would mean that the response also stays the same, and an active attacker, Mallory, could impersonate Bob simply by replaying a previously eavesdropped response. A time-variant challenge, on the other hand, means the response has a new value for each protocol run. As a result, even if Eve manages to read all communication between Alice and Bob, the response from one execution of a challenge-response protocol does not provide her with any information she could use to impersonate the claimant Bob in future protocol executions.

5.5.1 Ensuring freshness

In challenge-response protocols, the *freshness* of messages describes the property of being recent in the sense of originating subsequent to the beginning of the protocol run [117]. Time-variant parameters provide uniqueness and timeliness guarantees and prevent replay and interleaving attacks [117]. Non-repeating challenges can be generated very simply by using pseudorandom numbers (but be careful: if n-bit numbers are generated, they will start to repeat after roughly $2^{n/2}$ numbers; see also *Section 11.4.1, Collision resistance* in *Chapter 11, Hash Functions and Message Authentication Codes*), monotonically increasing counters, or even timestamps (if Alice and Bob are synchronized in time). Such non-repeating numbers are also called *nonces*, an abbreviation of *number used once*.

While random numbers do not have any prerequisites to ensure timeliness, counters require both claimant and verifier to store the state, and timestamps require them to have distributed clocks.

The verifier must control the time-variant parameter to guarantee timeliness or uniqueness. The verifier may control the parameter explicitly, for instance, by choosing the random number, or implicitly, for instance, using a common logical clock time.

If the challenges come from a pseudo-random generator, additionally, there is no way for an attacker to anticipate the value of the challenge for the next protocol execution.

In challenge-response protocols, Alice (the verifier) sends a nonce to Bob. Bob, in turn, responds with a message whose construction requires the knowledge of the random number (and, for instance, a secret shared by Alice and Bob). If Bob's response is valid, it is deemed to be *fresh* [117] because that random number links Alice's challenge to Bob's response.

Counters or sequence numbers serve as unique identifiers of a message. Like random numbers, counters prevent message replay. If counters are used, Alice and Bob accept a message only if the counter value has not been previously used. The simplest counter scheme is to start at zero (or one) and increment the counter value with each successive message. A less restrictive policy would accept any counter values as long as they are increasing, thereby tolerating messages lost due to benign communication errors.

Timestamps are more versatile compared to random numbers and counters. In addition to ensuring timeliness, timestamps can be used to implement time-limited access and detect forced delays [117].

If timestamps are used in a challenge-response protocol, the party sending the message reads their local timestamp and binds it to the message using a cryptographically secure technique. The receiving party gets the current time from their local clock and subtracts from it the received timestamp. The message is accepted if the timestamp difference is within an acceptable window.

To use timestamps securely, both the claimant and verifier need clocks that are loosely synchronized and protected against manipulation. In addition, they must synchronize their local clocks to account for the clock drift. Moreover, the maximum clock skew must be compatible with the chosen acceptance window [117].

5.5.2   Challenge-response using symmetric keys

In challenge-response protocols using symmetric keys, the claimant and the verifier share a (typically high-entropy) secret K. An obvious approach to entity authentication is to send a nonce as a challenge $RAND$ to the claimant and to expect the encrypted challenge as a response: $RES = E_K(RAND)$ (see *Figure 5.6*). Of course, the challenge numbers need to be fresh, as explained in *Section 5.5.1*.

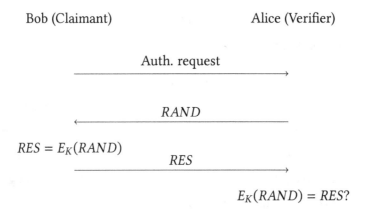

Figure 5.6: Authentication based on symmetric encryption

As an example of a real-life authentication protocol based on symmetric keys, we take a look at the **4th generation (4G)** mobile phone standard LTE [67]. In the LTE **Authentication and Key Agreement (AKA)** protocol, the home network and the user share a 128-bit symmetric key Ki. At the user's site, the key is stored in a protected hardware location called the **Universal Integrated Circuit Card (UICC)**. On this chip card, the same cryptographic algorithms are implemented as are used by the home network.

One of the basic problems in mobile phone communication is to allow *roaming* for the user, that is, using the service of a network different from the user's home network. The goal of the LTE AKA protocol is mutual authentication between UICC and the home network and key agreement between UICC and the serving network *without* disclosing Ki to the serving network.

The basic process is shown (in simplified form) in *Figure 5.7*:

1. The UICC sends the **International Mobile Subscriber Identity (IMSI)** to the **Serving Network (SN)**.

2. The SN transfers the IMSI to the user's **Home Network (HN)**.

3. The HN generates a random challenge $RAND$. Based on the shared key Ki, it also computes the expected response $XRES$, an authentication token $AUTN$, and a local session key K_{ASME} by using a set of different encryption algorithms and key derivation functions. Ultimately, these functions are based on the AES algorithm.

4. The HN bundles these parameters into a so-called *authentication vector* and sends it to the serving network. The serving network stores $XRES$ and K_{ASME} and sends the challenge $RAND$ along with $AUTN$ to the UICC.

5. The UICC verifies the correctness of the $AUTN$ token and thereby authenticates the HN. If this is successful, it computes the response RES and sends it to the serving network. Based on Ki and $RAND$, it also computes K_{ASME}.

6. The SN checks whether RES equals $XRES$. After successful authentication, both the UICC and the SN start to use K_{ASME} to protect the current call data on the air interface.

Note that the SN never gets to see the shared secret Ki. It only acts as an intermediary in the authentication process, with the one exception of verifying that $XRES = RES$. It needs to know K_{ASME}, however, because it handles the actual communication with the mobile. Although the SN does not directly authenticate in this protocol, false base station attacks, as described in the *Message authentication* section in *Chapter 2, Secure Channel and the CIA Triad*, become impossible, as an attacker posing as a legitimate SN would not be able to obtain an authentication vector from the HN.

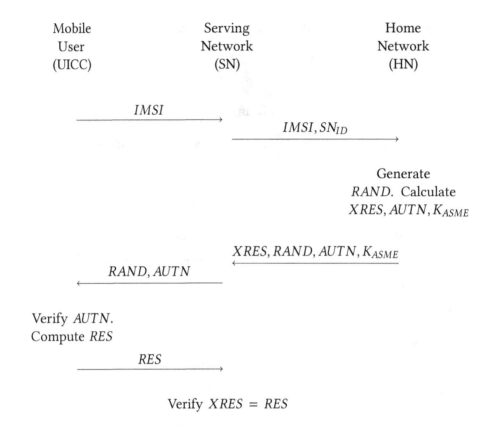

Figure 5.7: AKA protocol in LTE, the 4G mobile phone standard

The session key K_{ASME} is used to derive confidentiality and integrity keys for the ongoing call. LTE also offers partial anonymity by creating temporary user identities, but for bootstrapping the AKA protocol, the IMSI has to be sent in cleartext at least once. In 5G networks, the user ID is always encrypted with the public key of the home network [157].

5.5.3 Challenge-response using (keyed) one-way functions

The second option in a symmetric challenge-response protocol is to use *one-way* or *hash functions* to compute the responses. The shared secret K is hashed together with the random challenge *RAND* (see *Figure 5.8*). How this is done will be discussed in detail in *Chapter 11, Hash Functions and Message Authentication Codes.*

Because of the one-way property of the hash function, observing the challenge and corresponding response does not enable Eve to compute K (or parts of it). Again, the challenges must be fresh to prevent replay attacks.

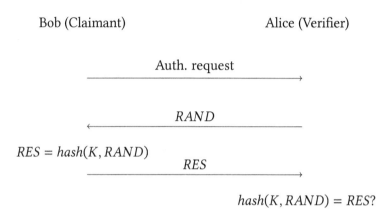

Figure 5.8: Authentication based on keyed hash functions

As before, let's take a look at a real-world example. When trying to access a password-protected resource via HTTP, the server might ask you to authenticate via *HTTP digest authentication*. In this protocol, the response consists of a hash value over the URL of the requested resource, the random challenge, and the password PW. The details can be found in *Figure 5.9* (see also [68]).

While this approach seems very straightforward, it has a certain weakness. Although pre-computed hash tables do not work because of the changing random challenges, eavesdropping on a challenge-response pair still provides Eve with verifiable text when launching a dictionary attack.

For each guessed password, Eve can compute the corresponding response and compare it to the observed response. If the claimant uses a common password, Eve might be able to guess it correctly within an acceptable time frame. For this reason, the use of the HTTP digest authentication protocol is recommended over secure channels only.

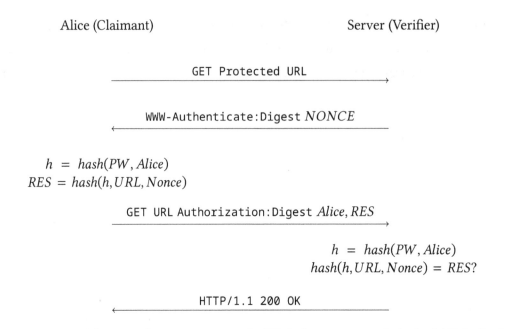

Alice (Claimant)   Server (Verifier)

GET Protected URL

WWW-Authenticate:Digest $NONCE$

$h = hash(PW, Alice)$
$RES = hash(h, URL, Nonce)$

GET URL Authorization:Digest $Alice, RES$

$h = hash(PW, Alice)$
$hash(h, URL, Nonce) = RES?$

HTTP/1.1 200 OK

Figure 5.9: HTTP digest authentication. Instead of PW, the response includes hash(PW, Alice), so that the server does not need to store PW in cleartext

5.5.4   Challenge-response using public-key cryptography

Challenge-response protocols can also be constructed using public-key cryptography. We will cover this subject in detail in *Chapter 7, Public-Key Cryptography*. For now, it suffices to say that unlike with symmetric crypto-systems, every party has a unique pair of keys, a public key that is, well, public, and a private key that the party keeps secret.

Everyone who wants to send Alice an encrypted message can use her public key to perform the encryption, but only Alice can decrypt that ciphertext using her private key. In the opposite direction, Alice can sign a message using her private key and anyone who has access to her public key can verify that it was indeed Alice who signed that message.

In the context of challenge-response protocols, the claimant has to demonstrate his knowledge of the private key. Thus, if Bob wants to prove his entity to Alice, he can decrypt a challenge Alice encrypted using his private key.

However, care must be taken not to turn the claimant into a decryption oracle! Eve could pretend to be Alice while Bob tries to authenticate himself and send Bob some previously captured messages that were encrypted with Bob's public key. Bob would assume this is a random challenge from Alice and would unknowingly decrypt messages for Eve.

To prevent this, the verifier Alice must prove to Bob that she knows the challenge. This is accomplished by prepending to the challenge a so-called *witness*, a value demonstrating that Alice knows the challenge without actually disclosing it.

As an example, Alice could compute the hash of the challenge and send it to Bob together with the encrypted challenge itself. Bob would decrypt the challenge with his private key, apply the hash function to the decrypted challenge, and compare the calculated hash to the received hash value. If these values do not match, Bob immediately terminates the protocol.

5.6 Summary

In this chapter, we covered entity authentication, a cornerstone of secure communication. We discussed what identity is and how identification protocols fundamentally work. We also covered basic factors for identification and discussed the connection between authorization and authenticated key exchange. We also worked out the differences between message authentication and entity authentication.

We covered password-based authentication, including challenges related to storing passwords as well as the fundamental shortcomings of password-based authentication. We then discussed how cryptographically secure challenge-response protocols avoid these drawbacks and introduced challenge-response protocols based on symmetric keys, hash functions and their key-dependent counterparts (also known as **message authentication codes** (MACs)), and public-key encryption.

In the next chapter, we will take a first glance at Transport Layer Security, the means to provide secure communication over an insecure network.

6

Transport Layer Security at a Glance

Before we dive into **Transport Layer Security** (**TLS**) cryptography in the next two parts of the book, we provide a high-level overview of the TLS protocol in this chapter. We will look at the role of the World Wide Web for TLS development, why SSL, the predecessor of TLS, was needed and how it was deployed in early web browsers, and how SSL eventually became TLS. Specifically, we will discuss the following:

- How the birth of the **World Wide Web (WWW)** led to the need for a protocol for secure communication on the internet

- The early history of SSL and TLS

- Basic TLS terminology

- How the CIA triad is realized in TLS and where TLS is located within the internet protocol stack

- An overview of the latest TLS version, 1.3

- Contrast TLS version 1.3 with its predecessor, version 1.2, and work out the major differences between these versions

- How the TLS 1.3 handshake protocol establishes the secret key between Alice and Bob

Upon finishing this chapter, you will have a good understanding of the TLS protocol, its historical background, and how TLS became what it is today.

This chapter covers *Section 1, Introduction*, and *Section 2, Protocol Overview*, of RFC 8446. However, we do not cover *Section 3, Presentation Language*, because it is only needed if you want to implement RFC 8446 [147], not understand the underlying cryptography.

Importantly, don't worry if you encounter TLS aspects you don't quite understand or technical details that don't quite add up when reading this chapter for the first time. Our purpose in this chapter is to give you a 10,000-feet view of TLS. If you want to connect all the dots in the big picture, you should come back to this chapter after reading *Part 2, Shaking Hands* and *Part 3, Off the Record* of the book where all the cryptographic primitives and mechanisms used in TLS are covered in depth.

6.1   Birth of the World Wide Web

Conseil Européen pour la Recherche Nucléaire, the European Organization for Nuclear Research, better known by its acronym **CERN**, is a European research organization operating the world's largest particle physics laboratory as well as the Large Hadron Collider, the world's largest high-energy particle collider [184]. CERN, which is located in Geneva, Switzerland, also hosts a large computing facility for storing and analyzing data collected in experiments.

In 1989, while working as an independent contractor at CERN, the British computer scientist Tim Berners-Lee invented the WWW [44]. Berners-Lee wrote a project proposal describing how information about accelerators and experiments at CERN can be managed using a distributed hypertext system [20].

Information Management: A Proposal

Tim Berners-Lee, CERN

March 1989, May 1990

This proposal concerns the management of general information about accelerators and experiments at CERN. It discusses the problems of loss of information about complex evolving systems and derives a solution based on a distributed hypertext system.

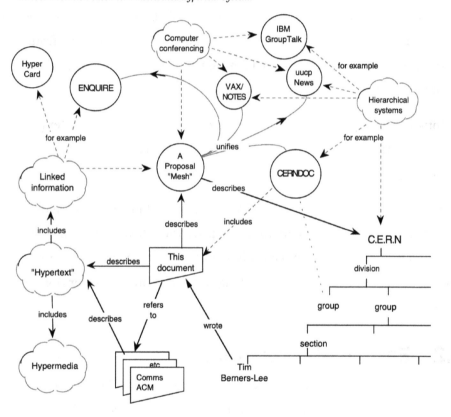

Figure 6.1: Project proposed at CERN by Tim Berners-Lee that led to the creation of the WWW

The report described what CERN needed from such a system and how it could be used to create and share information among CERN researchers.

From the beginning, the WWW was designed for easy access to information, with the early web pages containing links to information useful for scientists working at CERN. To achieve this, a way to link and access heterogeneous information as a web of nodes that the user can browse at will was needed. Berners-Lee, together with his CERN colleague Robert Cailliau, created a new protocol called **HyperText Transfer Protocol (HTTP)** to standardize communication between servers and clients [40].

To consume, add, and edit information in the WWW, Berners-Lee introduced a *browser*, a program that provided access to hypertext documents [21]. It had many features of today's web browsers and, in addition, offered functionality to modify WWW pages directly within the browser [44].

The original browser created by Berners-Lee ran on the NeXT computer platform, which only a few users could afford at that time. To overcome this limitation, a line-mode browser was developed at CERN that could run on any system [44].

In 1991, Berners-Lee released the WWW software, including the line-mode browser, the web server software, and a library for developers. The software was announced on internet newsgroups in August 1991 and quickly spread around the world. In December 1991, the first web server went online in the US, at the **Stanford Linear Accelerator Center (SLAC)** in California [44].

6.2 Early web browsers

At this point in time, two types of browsers were available to the early users of the WWW. The original browser developed by Berners-Lee had more sophisticated features but could only run on NeXT machines. The line-mode browser, on the other hand, could run on any platform but had fewer features and limited usability. After Berners-Lee's call to action for developers to join, individuals across the world started writing browsers, in particular for the X Window System[44].

In 1993, the **National Center for Supercomputing Applications (NCSA)** at the University of Illinois released the first version of its web browser called Mosaic, which was developed by Marc Andreessen and his colleagues [40]. Mosaic ran on the X Window System and provided web users a user-friendly graphical interface with the same sort of *point-and-click* graphical manipulations they were used to on their personal computers (see *Figure 6.2*). Shortly afterward, NCSA released Mosaic versions for PC and Macintosh.

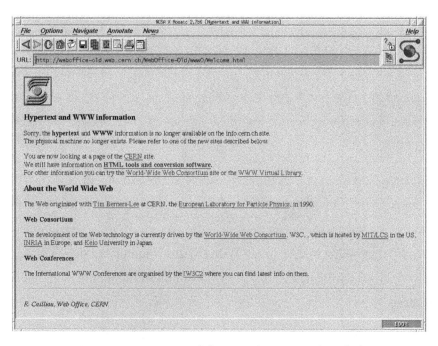

Figure 6.2: Mosaic web browser (source: Wikipedia)

In April 1994, Andreessen co-founded Netscape Communications Corporation. Their Netscape Navigator, a commercial product based on Mosaic, became the dominant web browser after it was released in December 1994 [40].

The availability of user-friendly web browsers on popular operating systems led to the rapid growth of the WWW. By the end of 1994, the web had 10,000 web servers, 2,000 of which were commercial, and a stunning 10 million users [44]. Individuals, institutions, and companies started extending web technology to realize new applications and address new needs. E-commerce and security turned out to be the most important features to be added soon.

6.3   From SSL to TLS

One of the first e-commerce applications was Book Stacks Unlimited, an online bookstore created by Charles M. Stack in 1992. The store began as a dial-up bulletin board, moved to the internet in 1994 in the books.com domain, and was eventually bought by Barnes & Noble [121].

In April 1995, John Wainwright, a computer scientist known for his pioneering work on object-oriented programming languages, ordered the first book ever sold by an online bookstore named after the South American river Amazon. It was Douglas Hofstadter's *Fluid Concepts And Creative Analogies: Computer Models Of The Fundamental Mechanisms Of Thought* [70].

More e-commerce sites and services quickly followed. The prominent eBay marketplace opened its doors in 1995. In 1996, IndiaMART started offering its services over the web. Netflix launched its subscription video-on-demand service in 1997. The PayPal online payment system went online in 1998 [196]. With the growing number of e-commerce sites and services on the newly created web, the security of online shopping quickly became a serious concern.

To address these security needs, in 1994 Netscape Communications started designing a new protocol they named **Secure Sockets Layer (SSL)** for establishing a secure channel between a web server and a web browser. SSLv1, the first version of the SSL protocol, had essentially no means to ensure the integrity of messages being transmitted, though.

The very first SSLv1 draft had no integrity protection at all. In subsequent revisions of that draft, a **Cyclic Redundancy Check (CRC)** was added. This, however, didn't solve the message integrity problem because CRC was originally designed as an error-detection code to detect *accidental* bit flips in communication messages. Unlike cryptographic hash functions, CRCs are invertible, and it is easy to find CRC collisions where two different messages lead to the same CRC value, allowing the attacker to undetectably change messages. As a result of these security flaws, Netscape never released the specification or implementation of SSLv1.

SSLv2, the second version of the SSL protocol, was publicly released in November 1994 and integrated into Netscape Navigator 1.1 in March 1995. In SSLv2, the CRC was replaced by MD5, a cryptographic hash function that was eventually broken in 2004 and is no longer secure.

However, soon after its release, a number of further security weaknesses were discovered in SSLv2. Among other things, the same cryptographic key was used for both encryption and message authentication. In addition, SSLv2 turned out to be vulnerable to length extension attacks and didn't protect the initial handshake or the explicit message close, making it vulnerable to man-in-the-middle attacks. Finally, SSLv2 was designed to support a single service and a fixed domain certificate, making it unusable with the popular feature of virtual hosting in web servers.

Learning from the previous security flaws, Netscape decided to re-design SSL from scratch and released SSLv3 in late 1995. SSLv3 fixed previous security problems and added a number of new features, including the use of the Diffie-Hellman key agreement protocol and the application of the Digital Signature Standard. In 2011, the specification of SSLv3 was published in the historical IETF document RFC 6101.

In May 1996, the **Internet Engineering Task Force (IETF)** formed a working group to standardize an SSL-like protocol. The standardization process took around three years and the **Transport Layer Security (TLS)** standard 1.0 was published as RFC 2246 in January 1999. While TLS 1.0 in principle closely resembled SSLv3, changes made to key expansion and message authentication turned it into a protocol without backward compatibility with SSLv3.

Almost seven years later, in April 2006, IETF published RFC 4346 defining the successor TLS version 1.1. Among the most important changes compared to TLS 1.0 was the added protection against cipher-block chaining attacks.

In 2008, IETF published RFC 5246 and with it a new version TLS 1.2. The most notable change was the addition of so-called authenticated encryption using the **Galois/Counter Mode (GCM)** and the **Counter with Cipher Block Chaining Mode (CCMP)** of the

Advanced Encryption Standard (**AES**) cipher (see *Chapter 14, Block Ciphers and Their Modes of Operation*).

After a number of practical attacks on TLS 1.2, work began on TLS 1.3 in August 2013. During this period, security researchers kept publishing attacks on TLS 1.2. Eventually, IESG approved the 28th revision of TLS 1.3 as a Proposed Standard. In August 2018, five years into its development, TLS 1.3 was published as RFC 8446. A compact overview of SSL and TLS history can be found at `https://www.feistyduck.com/ssl-tls-and-pki-history/`.

In March 2021, IETF published RFC 8996, which formally deprecates the previous TLS versions, 1.0 and 1.1. IETF gives several technical reasons for deprecating these TLS versions. First, they require the use of older cryptographic algorithms that are no longer considered secure. Second, they don't support state-of-the-art cryptographic mechanisms, most notably authenticated encryption with associated data. Third, the key establishment integrity and the authentication of peers depend on SHA-1, a hash function that was shown to have certain weaknesses by security researchers from CWI Amsterdam and Google in 2017. Although these weaknesses are not yet exploited in practical attacks, there was concern that this might happen in the future. Finally, the need to support four different TLS protocol versions would increase the misconfiguration likelihood.

6.4   TLS overview

The main task of the TLS protocol is to create a secure communication channel between two parties: server Alice and client Bob. The only thing that RFC 8446 assumes is a reliable, in-order data stream on the underlying transport layer. The two most widely used transport layer protocols are the **Transport Control Protocol** (**TCP**) and the **User Datagram Protocol** (**UDP**).

Thus, TCP lends itself to being a transport layer for TLS. In contrast, TLS doesn't work with protocols such as UDP that provide no guarantees regarding message delivery or the sequence of the messages. There is, however, a closely related alternative to TLS called **Datagram Transport Layer Security** (**DTLS**), which works on top of UDP and offers similar security guarantees to TLS [149].

6.4.1   TLS terminology

RFC 8446 uses the following terms to specify TLS. A **client** is an endpoint that initiates a TLS connection. A **server** is an endpoint that receives the request from the client to establish a TLS connection. A **handshake** is the initial negotiation between the client and the server for establishing the parameters, including the secret keys, for their TLS connection. A **sender** is the endpoint transmitting the data over an established TLS connection. In the TLS context, this data is referred to as a **TLS record**. A **receiver** is an endpoint receiving the TLS records.

6.4.2   CIA triad in TLS

As we would expect, TLS provides confidentiality, integrity, and authentication. Once a secure channel is established at the beginning of the TLS protocol, data transmitted over this channel can only be decrypted by the endpoints. This is also the reason why you will often encounter the term *end-to-end security* in the context of TLS.

Note that by itself, TLS doesn't hide the length of the transmitted data. This kind of information leakage where Eve learns metadata about the transmitted messages can compromise security. It represents an instance of traffic analysis attacks where the patterns of the communication – who communicates with whom, when, for how long, and so forth – are used to deduce secret information.

As an example, imagine a scenario where Bob can download three files of sufficiently different sizes, say 5 MB, 100 MB, and 500 MB, from a web server run by Alice. To determine which file Bob actually downloaded, Eve doesn't have to break the encryption algorithm; she can deduce this by simply looking at the amount of data transmitted from Alice to Bob.

To avoid this weakness, TLS endpoints can apply an operation called *padding*. Padding simply appends dummy bytes to TLS messages to hide the length of their actual payload data and, as a result, increases protection against traffic analysis.

Because TLS was created for the web, it was designed with the client-server model in mind. Here, the primary risk is that an attacker impersonates a server such as an online shop or a bank. Therefore, the server side is always authenticated, but client-side authentication is optional (and very rarely used on the internet).

TLS 1.3 offers two types of authentication. Alice and Bob can use symmetric cryptography with a **Pre-Shared Key (PSK)** or asymmetric cryptography, in particular algorithms such as RSA, **Elliptic Curve Digital Signature Algorithm (ECDSA)**, or **Edwards-Curve Digital Signature Algorithm (EdDSA)**, which we will learn more about in the upcoming chapters.

Finally, to complete the CIA triad, the TLS protocol has mechanisms to ensure that the data sent over a TLS-secured channel cannot be modified by an attacker without detecting the modification.

TLS ensures confidentiality, integrity, and authentication even in the presence of an active attacker, Mallory. A list of these attacks, including examples, is given in RFC 3552, which, among other things, describes the so-called *Internet Threat Model* used by most IETF standards.

The TLS protocol is application-independent. In other words, higher-level protocols can be built on top of TLS. However, TLS does not specify how to add security on higher layers using TLS. As an example, the TLS standard does not specify how authentication certificates exchanged during the initial TLS phase should be interpreted by the application or a higher-layer protocol. These details are left to the designers of applications and protocols running on top of TLS.

Moreover, TLS V1.3 is not directly compatible with previous TLS versions. However, it should still be possible that a TLS V1.3 client can connect to a TLS V1.2 server and vice versa. As a result, TLS defines a mechanism for the endpoints to negotiate a common version of TLS (if there is one that is supported by both endpoints).

6.4.3 TLS within the internet protocol stack

TLS is located between the application layer and the transport layer in the internet protocol stack (a simplified version of the OSI protocol stack; see *Figure 6.3*).

HTTP	SMTP	···
TLS		
TCP		
IP		

Figure 6.3: TLS within the internet protocol stack

Because of this position, TLS provides security services (confidentiality, integrity, and authentication) to the application layer, whereas the original transport layer is unaffected (and unprotected) by TLS. TLS can therefore be seen as a secure version of the transport layer, in the sense that it adds security services to the services already offered by TCP, such as session management. In most cases, the application layer protocol is HTTP, but other protocols, such as SMTP, can be (and are) protected by TLS as well.

For correct verification of **Message Authentication Codes (MACs)** within TLS, it is crucial that no network packets are lost on the lower layers and that the receiver is able to reconstruct their correct order. While the connection-oriented TCP has the ability to detect packet loss and to re-order packets, the faster, but less reliable, UDP does not have this ability. Therefore TLS only works on top of TCP.

6.5 TLS version 1.2

While we are largely focusing on TLS version 1.3 in this book, it is also instructive to take a look at version 1.2. Firstly, there are still many TLS servers that do not support version 1.3. Secondly, and more importantly, TLS version 1.2 and TLS version 1.3 share the same basic architecture. In particular, the basic steps in the so-called *handshake protocol* are the same but can be better explained in the context of TLS version 1.2, which is a bit less dense than the TLS version 1.3 handshake.

6.5.1   Subprotocols in TLS version 1.2

TLS version 1.2 consists of several subprotocols. Their location within the internet protocol stack and their relation to each other are shown in *Figure 6.4*.

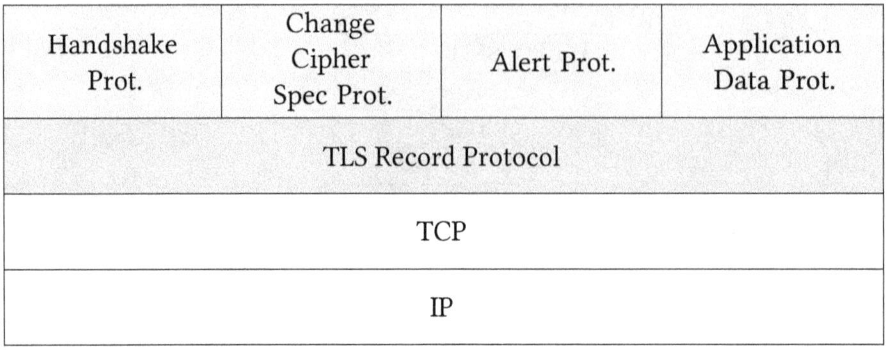

Handshake Prot.	Change Cipher Spec Prot.	Alert Prot.	Application Data Prot.
TLS Record Protocol			
TCP			
IP			

Figure 6.4: TLS subprotocols

- **Handshake protocol**: This protocol is invoked when the client and server meet for the first time or if they want to resume an earlier session. In the former case, they need to agree on a set of algorithms that protect the channel between them, agree on a shared secret, and authenticate each other. All this is organized by the handshake protocol. How it is done in detail is the main content of *Part 2, Shaking Hands* of this book.

- **Alert protocol**: If something goes wrong during the handshake protocol or record protocol, the alert protocol provides a pre-defined error code that indicates what exactly the problem was. For example, code 20 stands for bad_record_mac, a record with an incorrect MAC, and code 43 stands for unsupported_certificate.

- **Change cipher spec protocol**: This protocol consists of a single message with a pre-defined value that serves to signal a change in the ciphering strategy. It is usually displayed within the context of the handshake protocol, but it was defined as a separate protocol so that the message is not accidentally broken up into two records by the record protocol. Note that there is no change cipher spec protocol in TLS version 1.3 anymore, except when needed for backward compatibility.

- **Application data**: This protocol is basically a container for the application layer protocol being secured by TLS (e.g., HTTP).

- **Record protocol**: This subprotocol takes data from the higher-layer subprotocols (for example, Application data or the handshake protocol) and re-organizes them into chunks called *records*. These chunks are encrypted and integrity-protected by the record protocol and transferred to the lower layer protocol. How this is done in detail is described in *Part 3, Off the Record* of this book.

6.5.2 A typical TLS 1.2 connection

The following figure shows the interplay of the TLS subprotocols in a typical TLS connection until TLS 1.2. The TLS 1.3 handshake is much more compact by eliminating one entire roundtrip from the earlier version.

Note that the record protocol does not appear in *Figure 6.5*. This is because the record protocol is underlying all of the messages shown there. The first messages (until the first ChangeCipherSpec) are transferred in cleartext, and messages after that are encrypted.

Now, let's take a more detailed look at the messages in *Figure 6.5*.

Algorithm negotiation

In the very first message in *Figure 6.5*, ClientHello, the client proposes to the server a list of supported sets of algorithms for key establishment, digital signatures, encryption, and message authentication. These sets of algorithms are called *cipher suites*.

The ClientHello message also contains the protocol version, a random number, and optionally a session ID in case of session resumption (see *Section 6.5.3*). The server answers with its own ServerHello message, which contains a specific cipher suite chosen from the list, a SessionID, and a random number of its own. This concludes the algorithm negotiation phase. Note that all messages so far have been exchanged over an insecure channel.

While unauthorized changes in the cipher suites by an attacker can be detected afterward by way of the Finished message (see *Section 6.5.3*), so-called *version rollback attacks*, where

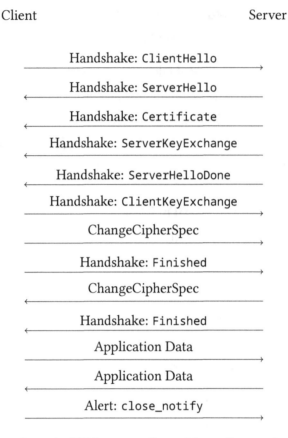

Figure 6.5: Overview of a typical TLS message flow without client authentication (up to version 1.2, adapted from [146])

the client and server are forced to use lower protocol versions than they actually support, are possible (see *Chapter 20, Attacks on the TLS Handshake Protocol*).

Key establishment

The key establishment phase starts with a Certificate message, which provides a copy of the server's public key to the client. The ServerKeyExchange message can take different forms, depending on the specific key exchange protocol algorithm chosen by the server (it might even be omitted altogether, but that is a very unusual choice nowadays). Without delving into the cryptographic details, the ServerKeyExchange message is typically a kind of Diffie-Hellman public key that has been dynamically generated for this session and that has been signed by the server in order to provide authenticity. The signature can be validated by the client using the public key from the previous `Certificate` message.

After the client has sent its own `ClientKeyExchange` message, algorithms and a shared secret are negotiated between the client and server, and the key establishment phase is concluded. The initial shared secret is called the **PreMasterSecret (PMS)**. Both parties now derive further encryption and message authentication keys from the PreMasterSecret by using so-called **Key Derivation Functions (KDFs)**.

Server authentication

After having agreed on a cipher suite and a shared key, bulk encryption can start. This is triggered by the `ChangeCipherSpec` protocol message. The next message, `Finished`, is the first encrypted handshake message and it is a very important one because it contains a key-dependent hash value of all previous handshake messages. This allows the server to verify whether the previous handshake messages, especially the `ClientHello` and `ServerHello` messages, have been tampered with. Without this retrospective integrity protection, an attacker would be able to downgrade the cipher suites negotiated at the beginning of the handshake. Moreover, the `Finished` message enables the server to check whether both parties have successfully derived the same keys. After the server has sent its own `Finished` message, the client can do the same. Moreover, by proving knowledge of the correct key for the `Finished` message, the server also proves that it knows the private key corresponding to the ephemeral key sent in the `ServerKeyExchange` message. Therefore, the server *authenticates* by way of a public-key-based challenge-response protocol as described in *Section 5.5.4, Challenge-resonse using public-key cryptography.*

Client authentication

Client authentication within the TLS handshake (as opposed to client authentication via some higher-layer protocol) must be explicitly requested by the server by means of the `CertificateRequest` message sent after `ServerKeyExchange` (not shown in *Figure 6.5*).

In response, the client will send its certificate and, if necessary, a chain of higher-order certificates (see *Chapter 10, Digital Certificates and Certificate Authorities*, for details) within the `ClientCertificate` message, which is followed by `ClientKeyExchange`. In order to finalize client authentication, another `CertificateVerify` message is needed, in which the client digitally signs the transcript of all previous handshake messages (see *Chapter 9, Digital Signatures*, for more information on digital signatures).

Note that client authentication is rarely requested by the server, lest the client is burdened by certificate management.

After the authentication phase, application data is protected: first, it is tunneled into the Application data subprotocol, which is in turn encrypted by the record protocol.

6.5.3   Session resumption

Establishing the value of the `PreMasterSecret` is computationally the most expensive part of the handshake because it involves public-key cryptography. TLS therefore includes a session resumption mechanism, where a client and server can reuse an already established session, including the cipher suite and the `MasterSecret` derived from `PreMasterSecret`. The client initiates the process by including the session ID of the previous session in its `ClientHello` message. If the server agrees to the resumption, it includes the same `SessionID` in its `ClientHello` message. There is no need to negotiate algorithms or keys. *Figure 6.6* shows the reduced handshake in this case. Note that reusing `MasterSecret` does *not* mean that the keys used for protecting the application data in a connection are the same as before. That's because these keys are derived from `MasterSecret` using the random numbers that are included in the `ClientHello` and `ServerHello` messages. These numbers are different for each connection, even when a session is resumed.

6.6   TLS version 1.3

In the years since its inception, TLS and its predecessor, SSL, have suffered a lot of attacks, both at the protocol level and the algorithm level (we will be discussing a few of them in *Part 4, Bleeding Hearts and Biting Poodles*). Step by step, these attacks have been mitigated in new TLS versions and extensions up to version 1.2. However, due to the need for backward compatibility and the resulting possibility for version rollback attacks, each new TLS

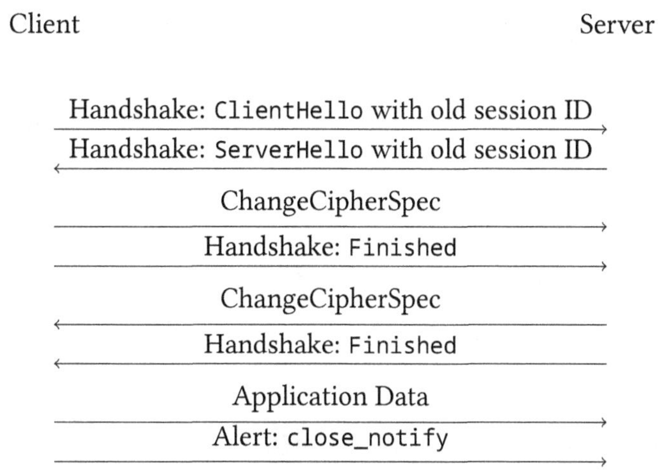

Client   Server

Handshake: `ClientHello` with old session ID →
← Handshake: `ServerHello` with old session ID

ChangeCipherSpec →
Handshake: `Finished` →

← ChangeCipherSpec
← Handshake: `Finished`

Application Data →
Alert: `close_notify` →

Figure 6.6: Overview of TLS session resumption (up to V1.2, adapted from [146])

version inherited the weaknesses of its predecessors. For example, the cumulative number of cipher suites in all TLS versions up to version 1.2 is 319, including a large number of outdated and insecure algorithms.

Therefore, in 2018, it was time for a larger clean-up: unsafe or unused options were removed in version 1.3, and version downgrade attempts are signaled to the client by the last eight bytes of `Server_Random`. Moreover, SSL version 3.0 has been generally deprecated.

While the basic subprotocol structure with a handshake protocol and a record protocol was retained in TLS version 1.3, some major changes were made within the handshake protocol. We will now take a detailed look at this new handshake and discuss the changes in comparison to version 1.2 in *Section 6.7, Major differences between TLS 1.3 and TLS 1.2*.

6.6.1 Handshake protocol

As in the earlier versions, the TLS handshake protocol allows Alice and Bob to agree on shared secret keys and corresponding symmetric cipher algorithms for establishing a secure channel. It supports three types of key exchange:

- Establishment of shared secret keys using the Diffie-Hellman key agreement protocol over finite fields, referred to as DHE in the TLS protocol specification, or elliptic curves, referred to as ECDHE. The last letter E in the acronyms stands for *ephemeral*, meaning that the public-key parameters are dynamically generated for each new session. TLS version 1.3 does not support the use of static, that is, long-term, public keys for key exchange.

- Use of a pre-shared symmetric key (PSK) that was previously distributed out of band, that is, not over the communication channel, that is to be protected using TLS, or established in a previous TLS session between Alice and Bob.

- Use of a pre-shared secret key in combination with DHE or ECDHE. In this case, the PSK is used to authenticate the DHE or ECDHE public keys.

The TLS handshake is performed when the client and the server communicate for the first time. In the remainder of this book, Alice will play the role of the server and Bob will play the role of the client. We also follow the notation of TLS messages and extensions used in RFC 8446 to make it easier for the reader to consult RFC 8446 for details alongside this book.

Using the handshake protocol, the client Bob and the server Alice agree upon the protocol version and the specific cryptographic algorithms to be used, perform a unilateral (the server proves its identity to the client) or mutual (both the server and the client prove their identity to each other) authentication, and exchange shared secret keys.

After a successful execution of the handshake, Alice and Bob can transmit data over a secure channel that guarantees confidentiality, integrity, and authenticity. If the handshake fails, Alive and Bob terminate their connection.

The TLS 1.3 handshake protocol consists of three phases. In the key exchange phase, Alice and Bob establish the shared keys and agree upon the cryptographic algorithms and primitives they are going to use for their TLS session. Bob, the client, sends the `ClientHello` message containing a random nonce, the versions of the TLS protocol that Bob supports, a list of symmetric ciphers and KDFs that Bob is able to compute, and either Diffie-Hellman key shares, PSK labels, or both. Optionally, Bob can send further information using additional TLS extensions, but we will not go into the details here.

Next, in the server parameters phase, additional handshake settings such as whether client authentication is performed are agreed upon. Alice, the server, processes Bob's ClientHello message to identify suitable cryptographic settings for the TLS session and responds with the corresponding ServerHello message.

The TLS 1.3 handshake protocol consists of three phases.

1. In the *key exchange phase*, Alice and Bob establish the shared keys and agree upon the cryptographic algorithms and primitives they are going to use for their TLS session. Bob, the client, sends the ClientHello message containing a random nonce, the versions of the TLS protocol that Bob supports, a list of symmetric ciphers and KDFs that Bob is able to compute, and either Diffie-Hellman key shares, PSK labels, or both. Optionally, Bob can send further information using additional TLS extensions, but we will not go into the details here.

2. Next, in the *server parameters phase*, additional handshake settings such as whether client authentication is performed are agreed upon. Alice, the server, processes Bob's ClientHello message to identify suitable cryptographic settings for the TLS session and responds with the corresponding ServerHello message.

   The ClientHello and ServerHello messages contain information to establish a shared secret, the *handshake secret.* If DHE or ECDHE key agreement is used, the ServerHello message includes the key_share TLS extension with Alice's secret Diffie-Hellman share. Moreover, Alice's share must be from the same group as one of the shares presented by Bob.

   If, on the other hand, key establishment based on PSKs is used, ServerHello contains the pre_shared_key extension to indicate which of the keys already shared by Alice and Bob shall be used. Alternatively, PSK and DHE or ECDHE can be used together. In this case, ServerHello contains both TLS extensions.

   At this point, the handshake secret is already known to Alice and she can derive a number of related keys from it. For example, Alice can protect all following handshake messages she sends to Bob using the so-called server_handshake_traffic_secret, and `client_application_traffic_secret_N` protects application data sent from Bob to Alice. This nicely illustrates the best practice we described in *Chapter 3, A Secret to Share* stating that every cryptographic key should be used for one task only.

Next, Alice sends Bob two messages containing the server parameters. The first message, `EncryptedExtensions`, contains responses to `ClientHello` extensions wich are unrelated to cryptographic settings. The second message, `CertificateRequest`, contains parameters for the client certificate – if Alice and Bob want to perform certificate-based client authentication (the message is otherwise omitted).

3. Finally, in the *authentication phase*, the server Alice and, optionally, the client Bob authenticate themselves, confirm the established shared key, and verify the integrity of the handshake. To achieve this, Alice and Bob exchange authentication messages.

   The `Certificate` message contains the endpoint's certificate and certificate-related TLS extensions for that certificate. If certificate-based authentication is not used, the server omits this message. Likewise, if the server does not send a `CertificateRequest` message, the `Certificate` message is omitted by the client.

   The `CertificateVerify` message contains a digital signature of the entire handshake protocol execution. The signature is computed using the private key that matches the public key in the `Certificate` message. This illustrates a cryptographic best practice to explicitly ensure that both communicating parties Alice and Bob sent and received identical data, thereby adding yet another protection layer against man-in-the-middle attacks.

   At the end of the TLS handshake, the server sends the `Finished` message containing a MAC over the entire handshake. This confirms the newly established secret key and binds the endpoint's identity to it.

   The client replies with its own authentication messages and the `Finished` message. After the `Finished` message from the client – and assuming the signature and MAC checks were successful – Alice and Bob derive the keys needed to protect the application data.

Figure 6.7 shows the complete default TLS 1.3 handshake as specified in RFC 8446. The asterisk (*) denotes optional TLS messages or extensions that are transmitted or omitted based on previous messages or chosen cryptographic parameters. Curly braces {} denote messages secured using shared secret keys derived from [sender]_handshake_traffic_secret. Finally, square brackets ([]) denote messages secured using shared secret keys derived from the secret called [sender]_application_traffic_secret_N.

Figure 6.7: Full TLS 1.3 handshake

6.6.2   Error handling in the TLS 1.3 handshake

In applied cryptography – similar to most other engineering areas that require some form of dependability – it is generally a good practice to plan for failure. The TLS standard specifies how to deal with failures during the initial handshake.

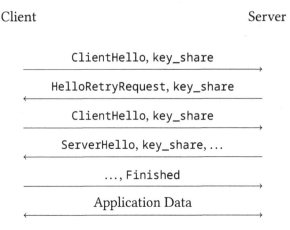

Figure 6.8: Message flow in TLS handshake with mismatched cryptographic parameters

In TLS, the so-called key_share *extension* contains the endpoint's cryptographic parameters, such as the elliptic curves and finite fields, that the endpoint supports for calculations performed during the TLS handshake.

If the client provides parameters, for example, the set of specific cryptographic algorithms or a key_share extension it wants to use for the TLS handshake, that are not supported by the server, the server replies with a HelloRetryRequest message. As shown in *Figure 6.8*, this message tells the client to restart the handshake with suitable cryptographic parameters.

If the client and the server cannot agree on cryptographic parameters that they both support, the server terminates the handshake and sends a corresponding message to the client.

For security reasons, the handshake transcript includes the initial ClientHello, HelloRetryRequest message exchange. The transcript is *not* reset with a new ClientHello message so that the cryptographic parameter re-negotiated is visible in the logs.

6.6.3 Session resumption and PSKs

As mentioned earlier in this chapter, in addition to an ad hoc key establishment using the handshake protocol, TLS also supports the use of pre-shared secret keys.

Note that the RFC 8446 document refers to a shared secret key as a **pre-shared key**. To a certain extent, this makes sense in order to differentiate between a secret key that was freshly established during the most recent handshake and a secret key established previous to the current execution of the TLS protocol. Fundamentally, however, any shared secret key must be established in advance. The terms *pre-shared secret key* and *shared secret key* are therefore equivalent in connection with session resumption, even if this blurs the distinction between previously shared long-term secrets and short-term (ephemeral) keys that have been established in a previous TLS session.

The long-term keys can be shared out of band, that is, not over the communication channel that is to be protected using TLS. As an example, Alice and Bob could meet in private to exchange the keys, pretty much how **Pretty Good Privacy (PGP)** keys are vouched for at PGP signing parties.

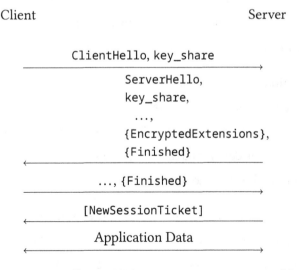

Figure 6.9: Message flow in TLS session resumption: initial handshake

Alternatively, the secret keys could have been established in a previous TLS session. In this case, TLS allows the establishment of a new TLS connection using these keys. This is called *session resumption* (see also *Section 6.5.3, Session resumption*, where it was discussed in the context of TLS version 1.2).

After a successful handshake – that is, after authenticating the server or both, the server and the client – the server sends the client the identity of a unique symmetric key derived during a previous handshake. In response, the client can use the identity of that shared key in future TLS handshakes if it wants to use that key again.

When the server accepts that shared key, the new TLS connection is cryptographically linked to the original TLS connection. In other words, the key established during the original handshake is used to shorten the process instead of executing a full TLS handshake.

TLS allows us to use PSKs in conjunction with a cryptographic key agreement protocol such as Diffie-Hellmann to ensure forward secrecy for session resumption. Alternatively, the pre-shared secret keys can be used as is. In this case, however, forward secrecy is not achieved. By now, you should know why this is so: if a PSK is used without an accompanying public-key-based key agreement protocol, losing it will compromise *all* sessions that used that key, including earlier sessions. If, on the other hand, the PSK is only used to provide authenticity to public keys, only future sessions are compromised, because in future sessions Eve might impersonate Alice or Bob.

Figure 6.9 shows the initial TLS handshake where the shared secret key is established. *Figure 6.10* shows the subsequent TLS handshake that uses the previously established key instead of performing a full key agreement. When a server authenticates itself using a PSK, neither `Certificate` nor `CertificateVerify` messages are sent. Rather, the server transmits a message telling the client to use the PSK.

In general, when pre-shared keys are used with TLS, they must have sufficient entropy (see *Chapter 3, A Secret to Share*). If Eve observes the handshake between Alice and Bob where a PSK is used, she can perform a brute-force attack on that key.

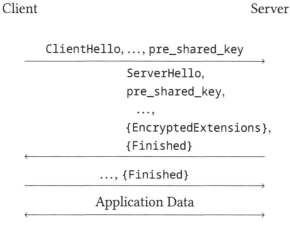

Client   Server

ClientHello, ..., pre_shared_key

ServerHello,
pre_shared_key,
...,
{EncryptedExtensions},
{Finished}

..., {Finished}

Application Data

Figure 6.10: Message flow in TLS session resumption: subsequent handshake

6.6.4 Zero round-trip time mode

If two TLS endpoints share a secret key, TLS 1.3 allows them to communicate over a secure channel right from the start. This is referred to as **0-RTT**, a **zero round-trip time** mode added in TLS 1.3 to save one round trip for the application data during the initial handshake, albeit with a decreased level of security. In other words, 0-RTT is a feature that allows TLS 1.3 to reduce the protocol latency by allowing client Bob to send data to server Alice in the first round-trip, without waiting for the Alice's response.

Figure 6.11 illustrates the 0-RTT mode. The client uses the shared key to authenticate the server and to establish a secure channel for the early data. The early data is simply added to the standard 1-RTT handshake. The remaining handshake is the same as the 1-RTT handshake with session resumption.

However, 0-RTT data is less protected. First, forward secrecy does not hold for this data because it is encrypted using keys derived from the PSK rather than fresh, randomly generated key shares.

Second, 0-RTT data is not protected against replay attacks. Regular TLS data is protected against this type of attack by the server's random variable. 0-RTT data, in contrast, does

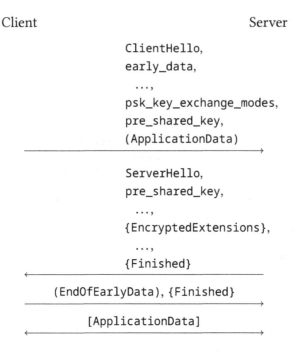

Client   Server

```
                        ClientHello,
                        early_data,
                            ...,
                        psk_key_exchange_modes,
                        pre_shared_key,
                        (ApplicationData)
```

```
                        ServerHello,
                        pre_shared_key,
                            ...,
                        {EncryptedExtensions},
                            ...,
                        {Finished}
```

```
            (EndOfEarlyData), {Finished}
```

```
                    [ApplicationData]
```

Figure 6.11: Message flow in a 0-RTT handshake introduced in TLS 1.3

not depend on the ServerHello message and therefore lacks fresh randomness from the server.

6.7 Major differences between TLS versions 1.3 and 1.2

While the focus of this book is to gain an in-depth understanding of the cryptography used in TLS 1.3, it is instructive to look at the changes TLS designers made between version 1.2 and version 1.3.

Insecure or unused cryptographic algorithms such as RSA, RC4, and SHA-1 and insecure modes of operation such as the **Cipher Block Chaining** (CBC) mode were either removed completely or, as in the case of SHA-1, only retained as legacy algorithms to ensure the verifiability of older certificates.

Further cryptographic improvements include the removal of compression, the **Digital Signature Algorithm (DSA)** (see *Chapter 9, Digital Signatures*), and client-generated ephemeral Diffie-Hellman groups.

A famous phrase in cryptography is that attacks only get better over time. Consequently, cryptographic algorithms and primitives do become insecure eventually and need to be exchanged. As a result, there are only five remaining cipher suites in TLS 1.3:

- TLS_AES_128_GCM_SHA25

- TLS_AES_256_GCM_SHA384

- TLS_CHACHA20_POLY1305_SHA256

- TLS_AES_128_CCM_SHA256

- TLS_AES_128_CCM_8_SHA256

Maybe you have noticed that public-key-based algorithms for key agreement are missing in these cipher suites. For comparison, look at this fairly common TLS 1.2 cipher suite:

- TLS_ECDHE_RSA_WITH_AES_128_GCM_SHA256

Here, key agreement is based on ECDHE, and the public keys are authenticated by means of RSA. The fact that these identifiers are missing in TLS 1.3 cipher suites does not mean there are no options in this area anymore. In the *refsubsec:TLSV13Handshake handshake protocol* section, we have seen there is still the choice between using PSKs, Diffie-Hellman based on finite fields, or ECDHE. However, these options are not negotiated by means of the cipher suites anymore, but by the form of the key shares offered by the client and server during handshake.

The remaining symmetric encryption algorithms in the cipher suites all support **Authenticated Encryption with Associated Data (AEAD)**, a modern and particularly secure encryption mode that combines confidentiality, data integrity, and message authentication in a single cryptographic scheme. We cover AEAD in more depth in *Chapter 15, Authenticated Encryption*. This is yet another example of an established cryptographic scheme such as the CBC mode of operation for block ciphers eventually becoming legacy and being replaced by newer, more secure alternatives.

Static Diffie-Hellman and RSA-based protocols for key transport were removed. As a result, every key exchange mechanism based on public-key cryptography guarantees forward secrecy in TLS 1.3. Forward secrecy is a highly desirable feature for any cryptographic protocol because it ensures post-compromise security. Even if Eve manages to break one TLS session, she needs to invest the same amount of computational work to break any *previous* session. This is also true if Eve manages to get hold of Alice's private key. Even with respect to *future* sessions, knowledge of a private key does not bring her any advantage, if she remains a purely passive attacker. As an active attacker, however, she will be able to impersonate Alice and thereby break any future sessions.

In addition, all handshake messages after `ServerHello` are encrypted in TLS 1.3. This is another example of further increasing the protocol's security by offering as small an attack surface to Eve as possible, especially considering that in the future Eve might discover attacks that are not known today.

KDFs used in TLS 1.3 have been redesigned to allow easier security analysis by cryptographers. This nicely illustrates how simplicity facilitates security. If a cryptographic protocol, mechanism, or primitive is simpler, it can be easier understood. As a result, it is more likely that any security flaws will be spotted by cryptographers. The corollary of this is that complex cryptographic mechanisms must be trusted less.

Finally, changes to the handshake state machine and the introduction of a single new PSK exchange made the protocol simpler. Improvements were also made to reduce the number of round trips during the handshake phase during the initial TLS session.

6.8 Summary

In this chapter, we looked into the motivation behind TLS, how it evolved to address the security needs of the WWW, and how it works from a 10,000-feet perspective.

In the course of this high-altitude overview, we introduced the TLS subprotocols, especially the handshake protocol and the record protocol, and looked into TLS 1.3 and 1.2 handshakes in somewhat more detail. Finally, we saw several examples of cryptographic good practices introduced in TLS 1.3. However, the ultimate reasons for some of the design choices in TLS 1.3 will only become clear once we look at some of the earlier attacks on TLS in *Part 4, Bleeding Hearts and Biting Poodles*.

This chapter also finishes the *Getting Started* part of this book. In the next part, *Shaking Hands*, we will cover the TLS handshake protocol and its underlying cryptographic building blocks in detail, and explain how and why they work to allow Alice and Bob to securely communicate with each other.

Part 2

Shaking Hands

In this part, we describe the purpose, properties, building blocks, design rationale, and inner workings of the TLS Handshake protocol.

More specifically, in this part, we aim to cover the *Handshake Protocol* chapter of the TLS specification provided in RFC 8446. We do so by discussing the appropriate cryptographic building blocks and their properties, and explaining TLS design decisions and the rationales behind them so that the technical background information needed to understand TLS 1.3 appears just before the relevant parts of the RFC 8446. On completion, you will have a detailed understanding of how the TLS Handshake protocol works and, on a more fundamental level, how secure key establishment must be done in practice.

This part contains the following chapters:

- *Chapter 7, Public-Key Cryptography*

- *Chapter 8, Elliptic Curves*

- *Chapter 9, Digital Signatures*

- *Chapter 10, Digital Certificates and Certification Authorities*

- *Chapter 11, Hash Functions and Message Authentication Codes*

- *Chapter 12, Secrets and Keys in TLS 1.3*

- *Chapter 13, TLS Handshake Protocol Revisited*

7

Public-Key Cryptography

So far, we have learned that secret keys are absolutely necessary to establish a secure communication channel. We have seen how one can use them to achieve different security objectives, and that you should use a different cryptographic key for each objective.

In this chapter, we will explain how key transport and key agreement over an insecure channel can be made to work in a secure manner. The solution to this problem is called public-key cryptography, in which there are two kinds of keys: *private keys*, which are to be kept secret, as usual, and are only known to a single entity, and *public keys*, which are – you guessed it – public.

In addition to explaining the fundamentals of public-key cryptography, we will also cover RFC 8446 Section 7 *Cryptographic Computations*, in particular subsection 7.4 *(EC)DHE Shared Secret Calculation*.

Summing up, in this chapter we will introduce you to the following topics:

- The mathematical structures in which public-key cryptography takes place: groups and fields

- Discrete logarithms and the Diffie-Hellman key exchange protocol

- The RSA algorithm

- Public-key cryptography within TLS and hybrid cryptosystems in general

There will be a lot of math to explain in this chapter, and we have tried to be as gentle as possible in this respect. Without the math, however, you would not be able to understand what is really going on. If you are already familiar with the basic mathematical structures, you may quickly skip over *Section 7.2, Groups* and *Section 7.6, Finite fields*.

7.1 Preliminaries

Recall our earlier definition of a symmetric cryptosystem from *Chapter 4, Encryption and Decryption*. A symmetric cryptosystem has the following ingredients:

- The plaintext space $\mathcal{M}$ and the cipher space C

- The keyspace $\mathcal{K}$

- The encryption function $f_K : \mathcal{M} \to C$

- The decryption function $f_K^{-1} : C \to \mathcal{M}$

Instead of f_K, in *Chapter 4, Encryption and Decryption*, we also wrote e_K (for encryption), and d_K (for decryption) instead of f_K^{-1}. In an *asymmetric cryptosystem*, the sender and receiver use different keys for encrypting and decrypting, respectively. The sender uses the receiver's *public key, PK*, for encrypting, and the receiver uses their *private key, SK*, for decrypting. This means the decrypting function d is not exactly the inverse function of e because it takes a different key as a parameter. In the present chapter, we are specifically interested in an *asymmetric encryption system*, which is defined by the following ingredients:

- The plaintext space $\mathcal{M}$ and the cipher space C

- The keyspace $\mathcal{K}$ is a set of key pairs $\{(PK_1, SK_1), \dots (PK_n, SK_n)\}$

- The encryption functions $e_{PK} : \mathcal{M} \to C$

- The decryption functions $d_{SK} : C \to \mathcal{M}$, so that

$$d_{SK}(e_{PK}(m)) = m$$

for all $m \in M$ and all key pairs

The security of public-key cryptography relies on the computational hardness of certain number-theoretical problems. This is also referred to as *intractability*. Recall from *Chapter 3, A Secret to Share*, that some mathematical problems are believed to be computationally intractable because for decades – or, in some cases, even centuries – no one managed to come up with an efficient algorithm for solving them. Efficient in this context refers to algorithms that run in polynomial time, at least for a non-negligible portion of all possible inputs.

To put it differently, we consider a mathematical problem to be easy (or tractable) if there is an algorithm that solves a non-negligible subset of all instances of that problem in polynomial time. On the other hand, a mathematical problem is hard if no efficient (that is, polynomial time) algorithms for solving it are known.

But how can we use such problems in public-key cryptography? The basic idea, as first formulated in [49], is to use so-called *trapdoor* or *one-way* functions. These are invertible mathematical functions that are easy to compute but computationally hard to invert. The easy part can be used for encrypting. The way to design a public-key cryptosystem is now to find a special piece of information, the *private key*, which makes the computation of the inverse function easy for the owner of the private key.

In what follows, we will explain the two most common mathematical problems used for public-key cryptography: the discrete logarithm and the factorization problem. The corresponding public-key-cryptosystems are the Diffie-Hellman key exchange protocol, the ElGamal cryptosystem, and the RSA cryptosystem.

7.2   Groups

Groups are the most basic mathematical structure in which public-key cryptography can take place. So, let's plunge right into the math and explain the properties of a so-called *abelian group*.

Let M be a nonempty set, and let $\star$ be an *operation* on M, which means $\star$ is a function $M \times M \rightarrow M$, which maps pairs of elements of M to elements of M. The pair $(M, \star)$ is called an *abelian group* G if the following properties hold:

- (G1) $\star$ is an *associative operation* that means for all cases of a, b, and $c \in M$, we have

$$a \star (b \star c) = (a \star b) \star c.$$

- (G2) In M exists a *neutral element* e with the property that for all cases of $a \in M$,

$$a \star e = e \star a = a.$$

- (G3) For all cases of $a \in M$ exists an *inverse element* $a^{-1} \in M$ with the property $a^{-1} \star a = a \star a^{-1} = e$.

- (G4) $\star$ is a *commutative operation*, which means for all cases of $a, b \in M$, we have

$$a \star b = b \star a.$$

The number of elements of M is called the *order* of the group G. Note that property (G4) is not strictly necessary for the pair of $(M, \star)$ to be a group. However, we will need this commutativity property later so that Diffie and Hellman can do their magical key exchange.

7.2.1 Examples of groups

Natural examples of abelian groups that immediately spring to mind are the following:

- The integer numbers $\mathbb{Z}$ with + as a commutative operation, 0 as a neutral element, and $(-a)$ acting as an inverse element for $a \in \mathbb{Z}$

- The rational numbers $\mathbb{Q}^* = \mathbb{Q} \setminus \{0\}$ with $\cdot$ as a commutative operation, 1 as a neutral element, and $a^{-1} = 1/a$ as inverse elements

If you need an example of a non-abelian group, take M as the set of invertible matrices with real entries and n rows and n columns, with $\cdot$ (matrix multiplication) as the operation. The fancy name for this group is $GL_n(\mathbb{R})$, or *general linear group*. Here, we can take the (n, n) identity matrix I as a neutral element and inverse matrices as inverse elements. But as you probably know, matrix multiplication is associative but not commutative.

However, we are not restricted to infinite sets to get an abelian group. Groups with a finite number of elements are called *finite groups*. An important example of a finite group is $M = \{0, 1\}$, with $\oplus$ as an operation. Recall from *Chapter 4, Encryption and Decryption*, that $\oplus$ is defined as the exclusive OR operation, so we have $0 \oplus 0 = 0, 0 \oplus 1 = 1, 1 \oplus 0 = 1$, and $1 \oplus 1 = 0$. From this, we can see immediately that 0 is the neutral element, 0 is inverse to 0, 1 is inverse to 1, and $\oplus$ is commutative. The associativity of $\oplus$ can also easily be checked. We can go even smaller and take $M = \{1\}$ and $\cdot$ as an operation. Naturally, this group is too small to be interesting.

However, these two small examples can be generalized to larger, but still finite, sets. Let $M = \{0, 1, \dots, n-1\}$ and $\star$ = addition modulo n, which means for $a, b \in M$ we set $a \star b = (a+b)$ mod n. This corresponds to our earlier example with $n = 2$. In a more general case, the neutral element is still 0, but the inverse element of a is given by $(-a) = n - a$, and it can be easily checked that addition modulo n is associative and commutative.

Can we again remove 0 from M and get an abelian group with the operation $\star$ = multiplication modulo n? Not always. If we take $n = 10$, for example, we won't be able to find an inverse element to $a = 2$. Moreover, $2 \star 5 = (2 \cdot 5) \mod 10 = 0$, which is not an element of M, so $\cdot$

is not even an operation on M. This happens for all elements a that are divisors of n, so the solution is to make n a prime number: $n = p$. The resulting group, consisting of the set $M = \{1, 2, ..., p - 1\}$ and the operation $\star$ being multiplication modulo p, is called $\mathbb{F}_p^*$. The reason for this symbolism will become apparent later when we discuss finite fields. As an example, the following table shows the multiplication table for $\mathbb{F}_5^*$:

$\cdot$ mod 5	1	2	3	4
1	1	2	3	4
2	2	4	1	3
3	3	1	4	2
4	4	3	2	1

Table 7.1: Multiplication table for $\mathbb{F}_5^*$

Using the $\star$ - operation within a group, we can formulate the discrete logarithm problem, which lies at the heart of the Diffie-Hellman protocol.

7.2.2   The discrete logarithm problem

If g is an element of a group $\mathbb{G}$ with operation $\star$, we can define *powers* of g by writing

$$g^x = \underbrace{g \star g \star \cdots \star g}_{x \text{ times}},$$

where g^0 is defined to be the neutral element e.

The group $\mathbb{F}_p^*$ has a special property: it is *cyclic*, which means we can always find some number $g \in \{1, 2, ..., p - 1\}$ so that all other elements in $\mathbb{F}_p^*$ can be written as powers of g. For example, take $p = 7$ and $g = 3$. Then $3^1 = 3, 3^2 = 2, 3^3 = 6, 3^4 = 4, 3^5 = 5, 3^6 = 1$.

The number g is called a *generator* or *primitive element* of the cyclic group $\mathbb{G}$. One can show that $g^n = e$, when n is the order of G. In $\mathbb{F}_p^*$, the primality of p guarantees there is always a generator $g \in \mathbb{F}_p^*$ (actually, there are quite a lot of them), and we have $g^{p-1} \mod p = 1$.

With these preliminaries, we are ready to formulate the **discrete logarithm problem**:

- **Given:** A group $G = (M, \star)$, $A \in M$, $g \in M$

- **Sought:** A positive integer number x so that $A = g^x$

  x is called the *discrete logarithm* of A to base g

For example, in $\mathbb{F}_{11}^*$, $x = 4$ is the discrete logarithm of $A = 5$ to base $g = 2$, because 2^4 mod $11 = 5$. Note that if g is a generator, the discrete logarithm problem always has a solution (that is, for all $A \in M$). Therefore, the discrete logarithm problem is often formulated with the assumption that G is a cyclic group and g is a generator of G, but this is not strictly necessary.

In some groups (including $\mathbb{F}_p^*$), the discrete logarithm problem is a hard problem. How hard it is exactly depends on the nature of the group operation $\star$. Consider, for example, the group $G = (\{0, 1, \ldots, n - 1\}$ with addition modulo n as the group operation. Then the discrete logarithm problem of finding a value for x so that $g^x = A$ reduces to $g \cdot x = A$. So, all we have to do is to find the multiplicative inverse of g modulo n (which can be done by using the extended Euclidean algorithm – see *Section 7.7, The RSA algorithm*, in this chapter for details) and multiply it by A to get $x = g^{-1} \cdot A$.

The fastest generic algorithms (that is, algorithms that do not use special properties of the group operation) for finding the discrete logarithm in a group of prime order p are the baby-step giant-step algorithm and Pollard's rho algorithm (see *Section 8.4, Security of elliptic curves* for details). These algorithms have a running time in $O(\sqrt{p})$, which is exponential in the bit length of p.

Another algorithm, the Pohlig-Hellman algorithm, is able to reduce the discrete logarithm problem in cyclic groups of composite order $n = p_1^{e_1} p_2^{e_2} \ldots p_s^{e_s}$ to s distinct problems in subgroups of prime order p_i. This is actually quite important, because the group order of $\mathbb{F}_p^*$ is $p - 1$, which is never prime! So, it is not sufficient just to choose a large prime p; we also have to take care that $p - 1$ does not have many small prime factors. For example, some prime numbers p are of the form $p = 2q + 1$, with q being another prime. In this case, the prime factors of $p - 1$ are 2 and q, and Pohlig-Hellman reduces the difficulty of the discrete logarithm problem by a factor of 2 only. For this reason, prime numbers of the form $p = 2q + 1$ are called *safe primes*.

Unfortunately, $\mathbb{F}_p^*$ is *not* a generic group. There are even faster algorithms for finding discrete logarithms, for example, the index-calculus method, which works especially well in $\mathbb{F}_p^*$ and has a sub-exponential running time in the bit length of p. However, if the bit length of p is larger than 2,048 bits, then the discrete logarithm problem in $\mathbb{F}_p^*$ is still considered to be hard.

The discrete logarithm problem can be seen as the inverse problem of computing powers of g, which only involves repeated applications of the group operation $\star$. So, as long as we are working in a group where the discrete logarithm problem is hard, we have a first example of a trapdoor function. In the next section, we will see how this can be used to exchange a secret key over an insecure channel.

7.3   The Diffie-Hellman key-exchange protocol

Alice and Bob communicate over an insecure channel. They can establish a shared secret K using the following protocol steps [49]:

1. Alice and Bob publicly agree on a cyclic group G and a corresponding generator g. Very often, this step is performed out of band long before the actual key agreement. For example, G and g might be specified in a public document.

2. Alice chooses a natural number α, where $1 < \alpha < N$, where N is the order of G. α is *Alice's private key* SK_{Alice}. She must not disclose this number to any other party.

3. Bob does the same as Alice: he independently chooses a number $1 < \beta < N$ as his private key SK_{Bob}.

4. Alice computes $A = g^{\alpha}$ in G and sends A to Bob. The number A (together with G and g) can be seen as *Alice's public key*: $PK_{Alice} = (g, G, A)$.

5. Bob computes $B = g^{\beta}$ in G and sends B to Alice. The number B (together with G and g) can be seen as *Bob's public key*: $PK_{Bob} = (g, G, B)$.

6. Alice computes $K_A = B^\alpha$. Bob computes $K_B = A^\beta$. However, both compute the same value K, because

$$K_A = B^\alpha = (g^\beta)^\alpha = g^{\beta\alpha} = g^{\alpha\beta} = (g^\alpha)^\beta = K_B$$

These protocol steps are also visualized in *Figure 7.1.* Can you see the trapdoor mechanism? The public parameters A and B can be computed easily enough via the power function in G, but in order to compute K, it seems an eavesdropping attacker would have to invert the power function and solve a discrete logarithm problem, which is supposed to be hard. Their private key, however, gives Alice and Bob a way to circumvent the need to compute discrete logarithms. Instead, they can keep on computing powers of group elements to arrive at the shared secret K. By using a **Key Derivation Function (KDF)**, as discussed in the previous chapter, actual cryptographic keys can then be derived from K.

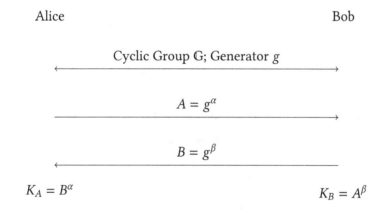

Figure 7.1: *Diffie-Hellman key exchange over a generic cyclic group* G

We will shortly discuss the security of this protocol, but let's turn to the original formulation of the protocol in the original paper [49] first. Here, the protocol is not described for a generic group G, but for the specific group $\mathbb{F}_p^*$. *Figure 7.2* shows what it looks like in this special case. Here, specifying a prime number p is sufficient to fix the group $\mathbb{F}_p^*$, and the powers of g in G become $g^x \mod p$ in this specific setting.

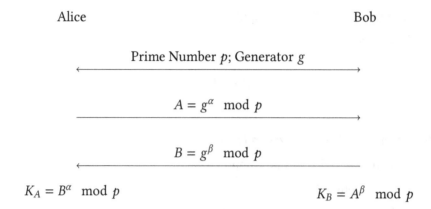

Alice   Bob

$$\text{Prime Number } p; \text{ Generator } g$$

$$A = g^{\alpha} \mod p$$

$$B = g^{\beta} \mod p$$

$$K_A = B^{\alpha} \mod p \qquad\qquad\qquad K_B = A^{\beta} \mod p$$

Figure 7.2: Diffie-Hellman key exchange over $\mathbb{F}_p^*$

For example, let's assume Alice and Bob use the prime $p = 11$ and the generator $g = 2$ as public parameters (you might check for yourself that $g = 2$ is indeed a generator). Alice's private key is $\alpha = 3$, so she computes $A = 2^3 \mod 11 = 8$ and sends A to Bob. Bob's private key is $\beta = 4$, so he computes $B = 2^4 \mod 11 = 5$ and sends B to Alice. Alice can now compute her version of the shared secret as $K_A = B^{\alpha} \mod p = 5^3 \mod 11 = 4$, while Bob computes $K_B = A^{\beta} \mod p = 8^4 \mod 11 = 4$.

7.4 Security of Diffie-Hellman key exchange

The security of the Diffie-Hellman protocol relies on the following three assumptions:

- The discrete logarithm problem is hard in the chosen group $\mathbb{G}$

- The Diffie-Hellman problem is hard in the chosen group $\mathbb{G}$

- The public keys of Alice and Bob are authentic

We will discuss each of these assumptions in turn.

7.4.1 Discrete logarithm problem

If Eve is passively eavesdropping on the protocol exchange shown in *Figure 7.1*, she sees the generator g and the public key values A and B coming from Alice and Bob, respectively. This means if Eve could efficiently solve the discrete logarithm problem in group $\mathbb{G}$, she could recover both private keys α and β. Armed with this knowledge, she could also compute the shared secret of Alice and Bob.

As discussed previously, we must ensure that the discrete logarithm problem is hard in G, so that an attacker cannot derive the private keys or the shared secret. For $\mathbb{F}_p^*$ this means that p must be a large prime (that is, $p \geq 2^{2048}$) and $p-1$ must not have many small divisors. Ideally, p is a safe prime.

While there is no formal mathematical proof for the discrete logarithm problem's intractability, mathematicians have strong reason to believe this is the case. Because of its role in cryptography, the discrete logarithm problem has attracted many researchers and has been extensively studied for the past 50 years. Yet, no one has so far been able to come up with an algorithm for solving this problem in polynomial time – at least not on conventional computers.

7.4.2 The Diffie-Hellman problem

There is another way Eve could attack a Diffie-Hellman key exchange. From observing $A = g^\alpha$ and $B = g^\beta$, she might somehow figure out the shared secret $K = g^{\alpha\beta}$. For this, she would need to solve the *generalized Diffie-Hellman problem*, which is defined like this:

Generic Diffie-Hellman problem

- **Given:** A finite cyclic group G, a generator g of G, and group elements $A = g^\alpha$ and $B = g^\beta$

- **Sought:** $K = g^{\alpha\beta}$

If we are working specifically in the familiar group $\mathbb{F}_p^* = \{1, 2, \ldots, p-1\}$, where p is a prime number, the Diffie-Hellman problem looks like this:

Specific Diffie-Hellman problem

- **Given:** A prime p, a generator g, and elements $A = g^\alpha \pmod{p}$ and $B = g^\beta \pmod{p}$

- **Sought:** $K = g^{\alpha\beta} \pmod{p}$

The Diffie-Hellman problem closely resembles the discrete logarithm problem, yet their exact relationship is not entirely clear. However, we can say this much: if it were possible to efficiently compute the discrete logarithms in G, then we could use this procedure to determine α from g^α (mod p) and subsequently compute $B^\alpha = g^{\alpha\beta}$. Therefore, if the discrete logarithm problem is not hard, then the Diffie-Hellman problem isn't hard either. By using a logical operation called *contraposition*, we can deduce that if the Diffie-Hellman problem is hard, then the discrete logarithm problem must be hard as well. Moreover, nobody has yet found a faster way to solve the Diffie-Hellman problem than by solving the discrete logarithm problem. For the time being, the hardness of the two problems is considered equivalent.

In addition to Diffie-Hellman key agreement, computational hardness of the Diffie-Hellman problem is also fundamental for the security of the ElGamal asymmetric encryption scheme. We will cover the ElGamal scheme in more detail later on in this chapter.

7.4.3   Authenticity of public keys

If Alice and Bob do not ensure that their public keys are authentic or do not verify their respective identities, they can suffer from a so-called **man-in-the-middle** attack, or **MITM** attack for short. In this attack, Mallory poses as Bob toward Alice and as Alice toward Bob, and provides her own public key to Alice and Bob. As a result, Alice and Bob will share a secret with Mallory, but not with each other. *Figure 7.3* illustrates the attack.

One way to defend against this kind of attack is to use certificates (see *Chapter 10, Digital Certificates and Certification Authorities*) to obtain authentic copies of public keys and to enhance the pure key-exchange protocol with additional mechanisms that can provide entity authentication (see *Section 7.9, Authenticated key exchange*).

Another option that can also be relevant in the TLS context is using pre-shared (symmetric) keys to authenticate the public keys of Bob and Alice. Similarly, the public keys themselves can be shared out of band prior to the actual key exchange protocol.

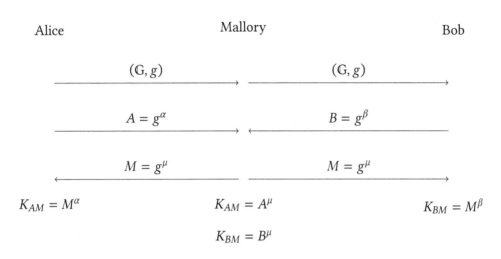

Figure 7.3: MITM attack on a Diffie-Hellman key exchange

7.5 The ElGamal encryption scheme

Without a doubt, you will have noticed that the Diffie-Hellman key exchange protocol is not yet a fully blown public-key scheme. While it accomplishes the task of sharing a secret over an insecure channel, which was the main motivation in thinking about public-key cryptosystems, it would still be nice to have actual encryption and decryption operations based on the discrete logarithm problem in the sense of *Section 7.1*.

Here, the ElGamal cryptosystem comes into play as an extension of the Diffie-Hellman key exchange protocol. The basic idea is very simple. Remember that in Diffie-Hellman key exchange, the triple $PK_{Alice} = (g, G, A)$ can be seen as Alice's public key. Assume Alice has published it on her web server. Bob wants to send Alice a message, so he retrieves (g, G, A). The key observation is now that as soon as Bob chooses a private key $SK_{Bob} = \beta$, he *already knows* the shared secret K_{AB} from the key exchange, so he might as well use it to encrypt his message m. Therefore, Bob sends the pair $(B = g^\beta, c = e_{K_{AB}}(m))$ to Alice, who can decrypt m by computing the shared secret $K_{AB} = B^\alpha$.

It only remains to specify the encryption function e. This relies on the observation that given a finite group G with group operation $\star$ and an arbitrary element $m \in G$, multiplying m by a random element $x \in G$ gives another random element $c \in G$. Because the distribution of c is independent from that of m, c carries no information about m. Thus, to encrypt a message $m \in G$ for Alice, Bob simply computes $c = m \star x$ and sends c and his public key $PK_{Bob} = B = g^{\beta}$ to Alice. To decrypt c, Alice first computes $x = B^{\alpha}$ and after that $x^{-1} \in G$. This can be done by the Extended Euclidean Algorithm (also see *Section 7.7*), which has a running time of $O(\log(x))$ and recovers Bob's original message via $c \star x^{-1} = m$.

This encryption scheme even gives us perfect security if x is completely random, and Alice and Bob share it in advance. However, if we use a pseudo-random x instead of a random element, and define the pseudo-random x to be the shared secret from the Diffie-Hellman key exchange, the security of the algorithm is preserved because the pseudo-random x will look random for eavesdropper Eve.

Summing up, the ElGamal cryptosystem consists of the following steps:

- **Plaintext Space and Ciphertext Space**: The plaintext space $\mathcal{M}$ and the ciphertext space $\mathcal{C}$ are given by the elements of a cyclic group G.

- **Key Pair Generation**: Alice chooses a cyclic group $(G, \star)$, a generator g, and an integer number α between 1 and the order of G. She computes $A = g^{\alpha}$ and publishes $PK_{Alice} = (G, g, A)$ as her public key, while she keeps $SK_{Alice} = \alpha$ secret.

- **Encryption**: Bob retrieves $PK_{Alice} = (G, g, A)$ and chooses some number β between 1 and the order of G and a message $m \in G$. He computes $B = g^{\beta}$ and $x = A^{\beta}$. Then he encrypts m by multiplication: $c = m \star x$. He then sends the pair (B, c) to Alice.

- **Decryption**: Alice computes $x = B^{\alpha}$, using her private key. She then finds $y = x^{-1} \in G$ and retrieves m via $c \star y = (m \star x) \star x^{-1} = m \star e = m$.

Figure 7.4 illustrates the ElGamal cryptosystem. It is easy to see that the security of ElGamal relies on the same three assumptions as the Diffie-Hellman key exchange protocol, namely computational hardness of the discrete-logarithm and Diffie-Hellman problems and authenticity of the public key.

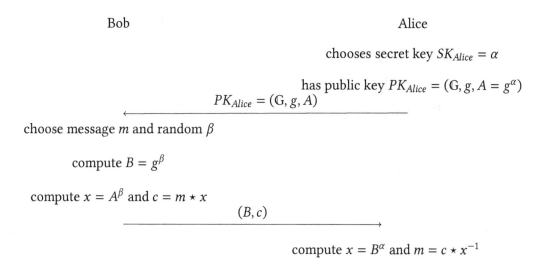

Bob   Alice

chooses secret key $SK_{Alice} = \alpha$

has public key $PK_{Alice} = (G, g, A = g^{\alpha})$

$PK_{Alice} = (G, g, A)$

choose message m and random β

compute $B = g^{\beta}$

compute $x = A^{\beta}$ and $c = m \star x$

(B, c)

compute $x = B^{\alpha}$ and $m = c \star x^{-1}$

Figure 7.4: The ElGamal cryptosystem in a generic cyclic group G

7.6 Finite fields

Fields are mathematical structures in which the basic arithmetic rules that we are used to hold true: in a field, we can add and multiply things together, and we can also reverse these operations, if we like. If we choose to combine addition and multiplication in a single expression, the so-called *distributive law* holds, which tells us we can factor common factors out of a sum. We are introducing finite fields here because they provide the stage for another important public-key cryptosystem, the RSA algorithm, which we will cover in *Section 7.7, The RSA algorithm*. Moreover, we can build other interesting cyclic groups out of finite fields, namely *elliptic curves*, which will be the subject of *Chapter 8, Elliptic Curves*.

To begin with, here are the formal requirements for a set M being a field:

- (F1) There is an operation $+$ on M so that $(M, +)$ forms an abelian group with neutral element 0

- (F2) There is an operation $\cdot$ on M so that $(M \setminus \{0\}, \cdot)$ forms an abelian group with neutral element 1

- (F3) For all $a, b, c \in M$, we have $a \cdot (b + c) = a \cdot b + a \cdot c$ (*Distributive Law*)

The most common examples of fields are the real numbers $\mathbb{R}$ and the rational numbers $\mathbb{Q}$. However, these sets have infinitely many elements, and in order to be usable in a computer, we need fields with a finite number of elements. This crucial number is also called the *order* of the field.

7.6.1 Fields of order p

In the last section, we already established that for a prime number p, the set $M = \{0, 1, \ldots, p-1\}$ forms an abelian group with respect to addition modulo p and $M \setminus \{0\} = \{1, \ldots, p-1\}$ forms an abelian group with respect to multiplication modulo p. Moreover, the distributive law holds for addition and multiplication modulo p. Thus $(M = \{0, 1, \ldots, p-1\}, +, \cdot)$ forms a field with p elements. This field is called $\mathbb{F}_p$. The group $\mathbb{F}_p^* = (\{1, \ldots, p-1\}, \cdot)$ is called the *multiplicative group* of $\mathbb{F}_p$. It can be shown that the multiplicative groups of finite fields are always cyclic.

7.6.2 Fields of order p^k

Are there any other finite fields than $\mathbb{F}_p$? It seems that the requirements that the order of the field must be a prime number is unavoidable, but it is actually possible to construct fields of order p^k, if we leave the known terrain of numbers and turn to other, more abstract objects as field elements. For example, one might arrange the elements of $\mathbb{F}_p$ in vector-like fashion, but it is difficult to find a multiplication operation that maps vector pairs on vectors and is invertible.

The way ahead is to look at polynomials of degree $\leq k - 1$ with coefficients $a_i \in \mathbb{F}_p$:

$$p(X) = \sum_{i=0}^{k-1} a_i X^i$$

Here, we have no intention of plugging in any values for the variable X. Instead, we are using these polynomials as mathematical objects of their own.

Let's define $\mathbb{F}_k[X]$ to be the set of all polynomials of degree $\leq k - 1$ with coefficients in $\mathbb{F}_p$:

$$\mathbb{F}_k[X] = \{\sum_{i=0}^{k-1} a_i X^i | a_i \in \mathbb{F}_p\}$$

First, we note that $\mathbb{F}_k[X]$ has p^k elements, because for each of the k coefficients there are p possibilities. For example, if we take $p = 2$ and $k = 2$, then $\mathbb{F}_2[X]$ has the following four elements:

$$p_0(X) = 0, p_1(X) = 1, p_2(X) = X, p_3(X) = X + 1$$

By using the $+$ operation from the underlying field $\mathbb{F}_p$, we can easily define a $+$ operation on $\mathbb{F}_k[X]$:

$$p(X) + q(X) = \sum_{i=0}^{k-1} a_i X^i + \sum_{i=0}^{k-1} b_i X^i = \sum_{i=0}^{k-1}(a_i + b_i)X^i \in \mathbb{F}_k[X],$$

so that $(\mathbb{F}_k[X], +)$ forms an abelian group with the 0 - polynomial as neutral element.

But if we try to do same thing with the $\cdot$ operation, we run into trouble, because the product of two polynomial of degree $\leq k - 1$ can have a degree $\geq k$. Analogously to $\mathbb{F}_p$, we need to do the multiplication modulo some polynomial M of degree k. This means, we first carry out the ordinary polynomial multiplication and divide the result by M, with some remainder polynomial $r \in \mathbb{F}_k[X]$. This remainder polynomial we define to be the product of p and q in $\mathbb{F}_k[X]$.

For example, let's consider $\mathbb{F}_2[X]$ again and let $M = X^2 + 1$. Then,

$$p_2(X) \cdot p_3(X) = (X \cdot (X + 1)) \mod M = (X^2 + X) \mod (X^2 + 1)$$

We can compute $(X^2 + X) : (X^2 + 1)$ using long division in $\mathbb{F}_2[X]$ and get the remainder $r = X + 1 = p_3(X)$. So we see that $p_2(X) \cdot p_3(X) = p_3(X)$.

So we have found a · operation for $\mathbb{F}_k[X]$. One can show that · is associative and $p(X) = 1$ is a neutral element, if we take 1 to be the multiplicatively neutral element in $\mathbb{F}_p$. However, we are not home free yet, because we will not always be able to find multiplicative inverses for the elements of $\mathbb{F}_k^*[X] = \mathbb{F}_k[X] \setminus \{0\}$.

Take, for example, $p_3 = X + 1$ in $\mathbb{F}_2[X]$. If we look for an inverse element with respect to multiplication modulo $M = X^2 + 1$, we get the following results (if you want to check them for yourself, bear in mind that $-1 = 1$ in $\mathbb{F}_2[X]$) :

$$p_1(X) \cdot p_3(X) = p_3(X), p_2(X) \cdot p_3(X) = p_3(X), p_3(X) \cdot p_3(X) = 0.$$

Analogously to the arithmetic in $\mathbb{F}_p$, in order to construct multiplicative inverses, we need to do the arithmetic modulo some prime element. That is, the result of every operation is taken modulo that prime element. Here, the prime elements are the *irreducible polynomials*, that is, polynomials that cannot be written as a product of two polynomials of degree one.

For example, our previous polynomial $M = X^2 + 1$ is not irreducible, because in $\mathbb{F}_2$, we have

$$X^2 + 1 = (X + 1) \cdot (X + 1)$$

On the other hand, $M = X^2 + X + 1$ cannot be written as a product of two polynomials of a smaller degree in $\mathbb{F}_2$. To see this, assume that

$$X^2 + X + 1 = (a_0 + a_1 X) \cdot (b_0 + b_1 X) = a_0 b_0 + (a_1 b_0 + a_0 b_1)X + a_1 b_1 X^2$$

By comparing coefficients, we see that $a_1 b_1 = 1$, which means $a_1 = b_1 = 1$. Analogously, we get $a_0 = b_0 = 1$. But in $\mathbb{F}_2$, this means $a_1 b_0 + a_0 b_1 = 0$, which is a contradiction. Hence $X^2 + X + 1$ is irreducible over $\mathbb{F}_2$.

Using $M = X^2 + X + 1$, we can now set up a multiplication table for the three elements of $\mathbb{F}_2^*[X]$ mod M as shown in *Table 7.2*.

· mod M	1	X	$X + 1$
1	1	X	$X + 1$
X	X	$X + 1$	1
$X + 1$	$X + 1$	1	X

Table 7.2: Multiplication table for $\mathbb{F}_2^*[X] \mod (X^2 + X + 1)$

Most importantly, there is a 1 in every row of the table, meaning that every element has a multiplicative inverse. So $\mathbb{F}_2^*[X]$ forms a group with respect to multiplication modulo M, and we have succeeded in constructing a field with $2^2 = 4$ elements (we must not forget to include the zero polynomial in the field). In general, it can be shown that for any prime p and degree k there are always irreducible polynomials M of degree k over $\mathbb{F}_p$. This means that, given a prime number p and a positive integer k, we can always construct fields of order p^k. There are at least three different notations for finite fields:

- If the irreducible polynomial M that is used to construct the field is given, it is denoted as $\mathbb{F}_p[X]/M$

- Alternatively, we can write $\mathbb{F}_{p^k}$ without stating the polynomial

- Finally, you often see $GF(p^k)$, where GF stands for *Galois Field*, after the French mathematician Evariste Galois (1811-1832).

7.7 The RSA algorithm

The RSA algorithm is named after its inventors, Ron Rivest, Adi Shamir, and Len Adleman (see *Chapter 1, The Role of Cryptography in a Connected World*, for a photo). Its trapdoor mechanism is based on the assumption that *factoring*, that is, finding the prime factors of a large integer n, is hard, while the inverse problem, namely multiplying prime factors to get n, is easy. While this trapdoor is certainly much easier to understand than the discrete-logarithm problem, understanding how exactly it can be used to realize a public-key cryptosystem requires a bit of math (again). We start by defining an odd-looking function.

7.7.1   Euler's totient function

No doubt you are familiar with prime numbers. To recap, p is a prime number if it has no divisors other than 1 and p. For two integer numbers a and b, we can always find a *greatest common divisor c*, or $c = gcd(a, b)$ for short. c is the greatest integer that divides both a and b. For example, 3 is the greatest common divisor of 42 and 15, so we can write $3 = gcd(42, 15)$. We can systematically find greatest common divisors with *Euclid's algorithm*. Here is how it works for $a = 42$ and $b = 15$:

$$42 = 2 \cdot 15 + 12, 15 = 1 \cdot 12 + 3, 12 = 4 \cdot 3 + 0$$

We start with an integer division of a by b with remainder r. In the next steps, the numbers change roles and the remainders become the new divisors, while the divisors become the new dividends. The algorithm stops if a remainder 0 is reached, which always happens at some point. The GCD is the remainder r occuring in the previous step – in this case, 3. Let's look at another example, $a = 35$ and $b = 9$:

$$35 = 3 \cdot 9 + 8, 9 = 1 \cdot 8 + 1, 8 = 8 \cdot 1 + 0$$

Here, we get $gcd(35, 9) = 1$, which means 35 and 9 do not share any common factors except 1. Such numbers are called *coprime*.

Euler's totient function is a function $\varphi : \mathbb{N} \to \mathbb{N}$ that counts for any input n how many numbers $x < n$ are coprime to n, which means how many $x < n$ there are with $gcd(x, n) = 1$. For example, there are 5 numbers smaller than 12 that are coprime to 12, namely 1, 3, 5, 7, and 11. So $\varphi(12) = 5$.

In general, in order to find $\phi(n)$ for some given n, we need the *prime factorization* of n, which means its unique decomposition into powers of prime numbers:

$$n = p_1^{e_1} \cdot p_2^{e_2} \cdot \dots \cdot p_k^{e_k}$$

Finding the prime factors of a given integer number n is called the *factorization problem*. In the easiest case, $n = p$ is a prime number itself. As a prime number, p does not have any divisors. So all numbers $< p$ are coprime to p, which means

$$\varphi(p) = p - 1,$$

if p is a prime. The next (and for us most important) case is when n is a product of two primes p and p: $n = p \cdot q$. Now there are $q - 1$ multiples of p that are *not* coprime to n, and $p - 1$ multiples of q that are not coprime to n. So the overall number of coprime numbers $< n$ is:

$$\varphi(n) = (n - 1) - (q - 1) - (p - 1) = n - p - q + 1 = (p - 1) \cdot (q - 1).$$

We are now ready to state the most important tool in the formulation of the RSA algorithm.

Euler's theorem

Let m be coprime to n. Then
$$m^{\varphi(n)} \mod n = 1.$$

For example, $\varphi(35) = 6 \cdot 4 = 24$, so according to Euler, $2^{24} \mod 35 = 1$. Indeed, $2^{24} = 16,777,216 = 479,349 \times 35 + 1$.

7.7.2   Key pair generation

Alice generates her RSA key pair with the following steps:

1. Generate two large primes p and q of about equal size. Compute their product $n = p \cdot q$ and $\varphi(n) = (p - 1) \cdot (q - 1)$. n is called the *public modulus*.

2. Choose a number $e > 1$ that is coprime to $\varphi(n)$. e is called the *encryption exponent*.

3. Compute a number d with $(e \cdot d) \mod \varphi(n) = 1$, which means: find the multiplicative inverse of e modulo $\varphi(n)$.

4. Publish the pair

$$PK_{Alice} = (e, n)$$

as a public key. Keep the number

$$SK_{Alice} = d$$

secret, along with p, q, and $\varphi(n)$.

There are a few things in this recipe we need to discuss before we move on to an example:

- How does Alice generate prime numbers of suitable length? She first generates a random number of the required length and then tests it for primality. The mathematical basis for these tests is an easy consequence of Euler's theorem:

Fermat's little theorem

Let p be a prime number. Then, for all $a < p$,

$$a^{p-1} \mod p = 1.$$

To test whether the number p is prime, we can check if a randomly chosen a satisfies Fermat's little theorem. This is called the *Fermat primality test* [109]. If $a^{p-1} \mod p \neq 1$, we can be sure that p is not prime. However, if $a^{p-1} \mod p = 1$, we cannot be sure that p is prime, as Fermat's little theorem is only a necessary condition for primality. Luckily, there is a refinement of the Fermat test called the *Miller-Rabin test*. It can be shown that if the Miller-Rabin test is successfully repeated t times with different numbers $a < p$, the probability of p being a prime is at least $1 - 2^{-t}$ (see [177], Theorem 3.18).

- Is there any danger of two people independently generating the same prime numbers? You probably know the ancient theorem by Euclid that states that there are infinitely many prime numbers. OK, but what if they are very thinly spread out in the large number regions that interest us?

We can deal with this issue by stating another important theorem from the late 19th century:

Prime number theorem

Let $\pi(N)$ be the number of prime numbers that are smaller than N. Then

$$\pi(N) \sim \frac{N}{\ln(N)}.$$

The $\sim$ symbol means that as N grows toward infinity, the two functions $\pi(N)$ and $\frac{N}{\ln(N)}$ grow in a similar way, or, to put it more technically,

$$\lim_{N \to \infty} \frac{\pi(N)}{\frac{N}{\ln(N)}} = 1$$

We can use the prime number theorem to roughly estimate the number of primes with a given size, for example, 1,024 bits. That's the number of primes between $N_1 = 2^{1024}$ and $N_2 = 2^{1023}$, which is

$$\pi(N_1) - \pi(N_2) \approx \frac{2^{1024}}{1,024} - \frac{2^{1023}}{1,023} \approx \frac{2^{1023}}{1,024} = 2^{1013}$$

- How can Alice find a number d so that $ed \mod \varphi(n) = 1$? For this, she can use an extension of Euclid's algorithm. Remember Euclid's algorithm computes the greatest common divisor of two input numbers a and b. Alice now applies Euclid's algorithm to e and $(p-1)(q-1)$, with the obvious result 1, because she has chosen e to be coprime to $\varphi(n)$. She then goes backward through Euclid's algorithm with the aim of finding a linear combination of e and $\varphi(n)$ that equals 1:

$$x \cdot e + y \cdot \varphi(n) = 1,$$

with x and y being integer numbers.

How this backtracking works exactly can be understood best when looking at the key pair generation example that follows. We can rewrite the linear combination in the form

$$x \cdot e = 1 + (-y) \cdot \varphi(n),$$

and this shows us that we have found a number x with $(xe) \mod \varphi(n) = 1$. Therefore, the number x is the secret key d Alice is looking for. If x happens to be negative, we can make it a positive number by adding $\varphi(n)$, which is the same as adding 0 modulo $\varphi(n)$.

Now let's look at a toy **Example for RSA key generation**:

- Alice chooses $p = 7$ and $q = 11$ as prime numbers. Then $n = 7 \cdot 11 = 77$ and $\varphi(n) = 6 \cdot 10 = 60$.

- As encryption exponent, Alice chooses $e = 17$.

- Alice now needs to compute a number d so that $17d \mod 60 = 1$. She applies Euclid's algorithm to 60 and 17 until she reaches 1 as the remainder:

$$60 = 3 \cdot 17 + 9$$

$$17 = 1 \cdot 9 + 8$$

$$9 = 1 \cdot 8 + 1$$

Now she solves these equations for the last remainder 1, starting with the last equation and successively replacing the other two remainders with their representation from the other equations:

$$1 = 9 - 1 \cdot 8 = 9 - 1 \cdot (17 - 1 \cdot 9) = 2 \cdot 9 - 17 = 2 \cdot (60 - 3 \cdot 17) - 17 = 2 \cdot 60 - 7 \cdot 17$$

The factor of 17 in this linear combination is -7, which is the same as 53 mod 60. Indeed, we have

$$17 \times 53 = 901 = (15 \times 60) + 1$$

So Alice sets $d = 53$ as her secret key.

- Alice publishes $PK_{Alice} = (17, 77)$ and keeps $SK_{Alice} = 53$ secret.

Alice has chosen $e = 17$ as her encryption exponent because the binary representation of 17 has few bits that are equal to 1. This makes it easier for Bob to encrypt messages for her, as we will see in the next subsection.

7.7.3 The encryption function

In order to send an encrypted message to Alice, Bob needs to obtain an authentic copy of Alice's public key $PK_{Alice} = (e, n)$. He then needs to encode his message m so that it fits into the plaintext space $\mathcal{M} = \{1, \dots, n - 1\}$. The ciphertext space C is the same as $\mathcal{M}$. The encryption function $e_{PK} : \mathcal{M} \rightarrow C$ works like this:

$$c = e_{PK}(m) = m^e \mod n$$

Encryption example

Let's assume Bob wants to send the message $m = 2$ to Alice. He retrieves Alice's public key $PK_{Alice} = (17, 77)$ from the key pair generation example and computes

$$c = 2^{17} \mod 77 = 18.$$

In general, Bob needs to compute powers of m for very large exponents e. There is an efficient algorithm for computing powers modulo n called *Square and Multiply*. It is based on the binary representation of e. Let the encryption exponent e consist of b bits:

$$e = \sum_{i=0}^{b} e_i 2^i \text{ with } e_i \in \{0, 1\}$$

Then we have

$$m^e \quad \mathrm{mod}\ n = m^{\sum_{i=0}^{b} e_i 2^i} \quad \mathrm{mod}\ n = \prod_{i=0}^{b} (m^{2^i e_i}) \quad \mathrm{mod}\ n$$

The powers m^{2^i} can be computed by repeated squaring of m, because

$$m^{2^{i+1}} = m^{2^i} \cdot m^{2^i} = (m^{2^i})^2$$

In order to get m^e, the squares m^{2^i} need to be multiplied, but only those where $e_i = 1$. Thus, fewer 1-bits in the binary representation of e mean less computational effort for Bob. Let's check the value given above for $c = 2^{17} \mod 77$ by re-computing it using the Square and Multiply algorithm (all values are given modulo 77):

- **Square**:

$$2^0 = 1, 2^1 = 2, 2^2 = 4, 2^4 = 4^2 = 16, 2^8 = 16^2 = 25, 2^{16} = 25^2 = 9$$

- **Multiply**:

$$c = 2^{17} = 2^{16} \times 2^1 = 9 \times 2 = 18$$

7.7.4   The decryption function

So Alice gets $c = m^e \mod n$ from Bob. How can she recover the plaintext? The decryption function $d_{SK} : C \to \mathcal{M}$ works like this:

$$m = d_{SK}(c) = c^d \quad \mathrm{mod}\ n,$$

where d is Alice's secret key. Why does this work? We have

$$c^d \quad \mathrm{mod}\ n = (m^e)^d \quad \mathrm{mod}\ n = m^{ed} \quad \mathrm{mod}\ n.$$

Remember that d was computed by Alice in such a way that $ed \mod \varphi(n) = 1$. Equivalently, we know that there is some integer k so that

$$ed = k \cdot \varphi(n) + 1$$

Using this expression as exponent, we get the following because of Euler's theorem:

$$c^d \mod n = m^{k \cdot \varphi(n)+1} \mod n = ((m^{\varphi(n)})^k \cdot m) \mod n = (1 \cdot m) \mod n = m$$

Note that in order to compute $c^d \mod n$, Alice can use the Square and Multiply algorithm described above. However, she has to use her private key d as exponent. In contrast to the encryption exponent e, she cannot control the number of ones in the binary representation of d. Therefore, decryption operations or generally operations that involve the private key are computationally more expensive than public key operations in RSA.

Let's continue our earlier example with Alice decrypting the cipher c:

Decryption example:

Alice gets $c = 18$ from Bob. Using her private key $SK_{Alice} = 53$, she computes

$$m = 18^{53} \mod 77 = 2$$

7.8 Security of the RSA algorithm

The security of the RSA algorithm relies on the following three assumptions:

- The factoring problem is hard for the given public modulus n

- The RSA problem is hard

- The public keys of Alice and Bob are authentic

We will discuss each of these assumptions in turn.

7.8.1   The factoring problem

If an attacker manages to compute the two prime factors p and q of the public modulus n, they can repeat the steps taken by Alice when she computed her key pair. In particular, an attacker could compute Alice's secret key and compromise the whole system. Therefore, the security of the RSA cryptosystem is crucially based on the intractability of the *integer factorization problem*, which is in general defined as follows:

Given a positive integer n, find its prime factors p_1 to p_k such that

$$n = p_1^{e_1} \times p_2^{e_2} \times \ldots \times p_k^{e_k},$$

where p_i are pairwise distinct primes.

The fastest algorithm to factorize *semiprimes*, which are numbers of the form $n = p \cdot q$ with p and q primes of approximately equal size, currently known is called the *Number Field Sieve* ([82], section 3.7.3). It has a subexponential (but not polynomial) running time in the bitlength of n.

Using the Number Field Sieve, the largest semiprime yet factored was RSA-240, a 795-bit number with 240 decimal digits, in February 2020 [38]. Therefore, public moduli with 1,024 bits, which were quite common in the past, cannot be considered secure anymore and should no longer be used. The American standardization authority NIST has compiled the following table of key lengths of comparable security strength for symmetric block ciphers (see *Chapter 14, Block Ciphers and Their Modes of Operation*) and asymmetric algorithms [126].

Note that a security strength of 80 bits is no longer considered adequate. We will amend *Table 7.3* in the next chapter with the corresponding numbers for Diffie-Hellman over elliptic curves.

Security strength (bits)	Block cipher	Length of RSA modulus n	Length of prime p in DH over $\mathbb{F}_p^*$
≤ 80	2-Key 3DES	1024	1024
112	3-Key 3DES	2048	2048
128	AES-128	3072	3072
192	AES-192	7680	7680
256	AES-256	15360	15360

Table 7.3: Equivalent key lengths of symmetric and asymmmetric algorithms

7.8.2 The RSA problem

The RSA problem concerns the security of the RSA encryption function. If Eve knows the public key of Alice, $PK_{Alice} = (e, n)$, and observes the cipher $c = m^e \mod n$, we ask whether Eve can find m without knowing the secret key $SK_{Alice} = d$.

More formally, the **RSA problem** is defined as follows:

- **Given:** A positive integer $n = p \cdot q$ that is a product of two distinct odd primes p and q, a positive integer e such that $gcd(e, (p-1)(q-1)) = 1$, and an integer $c < n$

- **Sought:** An integer $m < n$ such that $m^e = c \pmod{n}$

This problem can be summarized as the problem of finding e–th roots modulo n. In general, if Eve manages to factorize n, she can compute the secret key d and compute m via $m = c^d \mod n$. This is currently considered to be the fastest way to solve the RSA problem in general cases, so the difficulty of the RSA problem is closely tied to the integer factorization problem.

Therefore, the relation of the RSA problem to the factorization problem parallels the relation of the Diffie-Hellman problem to discrete logarithm problems.

There are, however, some special cases of the RSA problem that might go wrong. If the encryption exponent e chosen is very small, it might happen that $m^e \mod n = m^e$, that is, there is no wrap-around n and the RSA problem reduces to take an ordinary e–th root. In a similar vein, problems can arise if the same message m is enciphered with the public keys of r receivers, where each receiver uses the same e, but different moduli n_i. If Eve observes the r ciphers

$$c_1 = m^e \mod n_1, c_2 = m^e \mod n_2, \ldots, c_r = m^e \mod n_r,$$

she can compute a number c with

$$c = m^e \mod (n_1 n_2 \cdots n_r)$$

using the **Chinese Remainder Theorem (CRT)** (see e.g. [82], Theorem 2.25). Again, if there is no wraparound, m can be found by taking the ordinary e-th root of c. This is called the *Small Exponent Attack* on RSA. In practice, this issue is prevented by randomly padding each message before encryption.

7.8.3 · Authenticity of public keys

Another way for Mallory to attack the RSA cryptoystem is to tamper with Alice's public key. More specifically, Mallory might replace Alice's public key $PK_{Alice} = (e_A, n_A)$ with her own public key $PK_M = (e_M, n_M)$. If Bob does not notice the exchange, he will encrypt his message in a way that Mallory can decrypt. Therefore it is vital for the security of the RSA cryptosystem (and all other public-key cryptosystems) that the public keys are *authentic*, which means in this case that the binding between an entity and its public key can be verified by other parties. One way to achieve authenticity for public keys is *digital certificates*, which are the subject of *Chapter 10, Digital Certificates and Certification Authorities*.

7.9   Authenticated key agreement

The Diffie-Hellman protocol is a key agreement protocol because it establishes a shared secret between the communicating parties, but it is **not** an *authenticated key agreement* protocol. This is illustrated by the MITM attack on Diffie-Hellman we discussed earlier. The MITM attack is possible because Alice and Bob cannot verify each other's identity.

In 1992, cryptographers Whitfield Diffie, Paul van Oorschot, and Michael J Wiener published a paper describing *two-party mutual authentication protocols providing authenticated key agreement, focusing on those using asymmetric techniques* [50]. In addition to theoretical fundamentals, they also introduced the now well-known **Station-to-Station (STS)** protocol, illustrating authenticated key agreement in a simple, elegant manner.

Authenticated key agreement is a cryptographic protocol that allows Alice and Bob to verify each other's identities and establish a shared secret key in a single protocol run. To put it differently, the goal of an authenticated key agreement protocol is to establish a shared secret key between two communicating parties whose identities have been verified.

We are specifically interested in authenticated key agreement protocols based on public-key cryptography for reasons we elaborate on later in this section. For such protocols, it is typically assumed that the underlying cryptographic primitives such as an encryption algorithm or a hash function are secure.

In addition, the protocol must be secure against active attacker Mallory who is allowed to see all messages sent by Alice and Bob and can delete, manipulate, inject, and redirect messages. Mallory can also reuse message from previous protocol runs and initiate communication with arbitrary parties. In other words, an authenticated key agreement protocol must withstand both passive and active attacks.

Note that a denial of service attack in itself is not considered to break the security of an authenticated key agreement protocol. If Mallory manipulates or injects messages in the communication between Alice and Bob, and the protocol terminates as a result of Alice having seen different messages from those seen by Bob, the protocol is considered to be secure.

Moreover, Mallory's interference with the communication where she simply intercepts messages from Alice and Bob and then passes them along without manipulating them is not considered an attack.

A good cryptographic practice is to use protocols that are simple, work with a small number of messages, require a small number of fields in each message, and perform a minimum number of cryptographic computations. The reason for this is the observation, backed by numerous scientific publications and security incidents in the wild, that it is extremely easy to make mistakes when designing cryptographic protocols.

In authenticated key agreement protocols, it is highly desirable to combine authentication and key agreement to improve the protocols' security. If Alice and Bob use a protocol where authentication and key agreement are independent, Mallory can wait until the authentication is successfully completed and then impersonate Bob or Alice during the key agreement phase.

In contrast, when a protocol combines authentication and key agreement, Alice is assured that the secret key she has agreed upon is actually shared with Bob, not Mallory. The same guarantees apply for Bob.

In general, there are several more desirable properties for an authenticated key agreement protocol:

- *Perfect forward secrecy* ensures that the compromise of long-term secrets does not affect the security of the keys Alice and Bob have established in previous protocol runs

- *Direct authentication* – the validation of Alice's and Bob's identities directly during the protocol, not at the end of the protocol – prevents Mallory from misusing Alice or Bob as a mere signing service who unknowingly signs messages of Mallory's choice

- *Avoiding the use of timestamps* relaxes the implementation requirements for both Alice and Bob because there is no need for them to operate local clocks that must be periodically and securely synchronized with a trustworthy time source

In the cryptographic literature, direct authentication is sometimes referred to as *explicit* key authentication. It combines the assurance that only the identified, legitimate parties Alice and Bob are able to exchange the shared secret key – a property that is also called *(implicit) key authentication* – with the assurance that Alice and Bob are actually in possession of that particular secret key, a property called *key confirmation*.

7.9.1 The Station-to-Station (STS) protocol

A simple example that nicely illustrates fundamental design principles of an authenticated key agreement protocol is the **Station-to-Station (STS)** protocol [136]. The protocol is a combination of Diffie-Hellman key agreement and the exchange of digital signatures for authentication, a concept we will explain in a minute.

Figure 7.5 shows the basic STS protocol. Recall that $e_K(i)$ denotes the encryption of input i under the shared secret key K using a symmetric encryption algorithm e. A *hash function* is a function that maps an input of arbitrary length onto an input of fixed length, denoted here by $h(i)$ where i is the input. The input can consist of multiple parts $i_0, i_1, \ldots i_j$ that are concatenated to a single bit vector $i_0|i_1| \ldots |i_j$. Note that in order to be useful in cryptography, hash functions need to fulfill some additional properties, which we will discuss at length in *Chapter 11, Hash Functions and Message Authentication Codes.*

Finally, $sig_A(i)$ denotes a *digital signature* for input i generated with Alice's private key and $sig_B(i)$ denotes a digital signature generated with Bob's private key.

Digital signatures are a new concept we will have much more to say about in *Chapter 9, Digital Signatures.* For now, it is sufficient to know that a digital signature is generated using the communicating party's *private* key, which is, by design, only known to that party, and can be verified using that party's *public* key, which is known to all communicating parties.

As a result, only Alice can compute $sig_A(i)$ and only Bob can compute $sig_B(i)$. But they both can verify each other's signatures (for the input i, given that the input is known to the verifying party).

Note how the authenticity of Alice's and Bob's public keys plays a crucial role in the protocol's security: if Mallory can trick Alice into believing that a public key PK_M generated

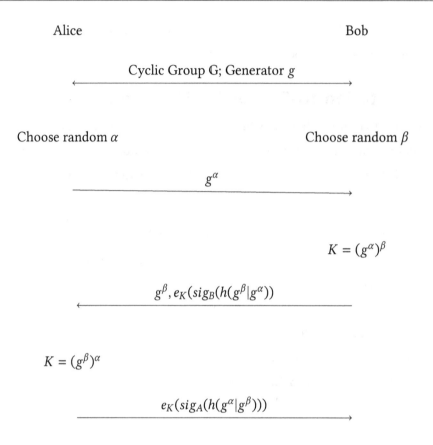

Figure 7.5: Basic STS protocol

by Mallory belongs to Bob, she can easily impersonate Bob by presenting Alice with a fake digital signature $sig_M(i)$ instead of the genuine $sig_B(i)$.

The basic STS protocol in *Figure 7.5* starts with Alice choosing a random number α and transmitting the exponential g^α to Bob. Bob, in turn, chooses a random β and computes $K = (g^\alpha)^\beta$. He then sends Alice the exponential g^β and signature of concatenated exponentials $g^\beta|g^\alpha$ encrypted with a symmetric key encryption algorithm under key K.

Upon receiving Bob's message, Alice computes $K = (g^\beta)^\alpha$. She then decrypts Bob's encrypted signature $e_K(sig_B(h(g^\beta|g^\alpha)))$ using key K she just computed and verifies the signature $sig_B(h(g^\beta|g^\alpha))$ using Bob's public key.

If the signature verification is successful, Alice generates her own signature $sig_A(h(g^\alpha|g^\beta))$, encrypts it using the shared secret key K, and sends the result to Bob. Analogous to Alice, Bob decrypts the received encrypted signature and verifies it using Alice's public key. If this verification is successful, the protocol is finished and Alice and Bob share an authenticated secret key K.

In *Figure 7.5*, you should easily spot that the security of the STS protocol relies on the inability of Eve to determine the random exponent α from g^α or β from g^β. As a result, the security of the STS protocol relies on the intractibility of the discrete logarithm problem.

In terms of cryptographic assurances, after Bob responds with his message, he has established a shared secret key with the other communicating party. However, Bob cannot know whether the other party is indeed Alice or an imposter – Mallory or Eve.

Luckily, Bob can rely on some trusted source in obtaining Alice's public key. Bob is therefore able to verify a digital signature generated by Alice. In her response, $e_K(sig_A(h(g^\alpha|g^\beta)))$, Alice signs the exponentials g^α and g^β, which are unique for this protocol run, with – and this is very important from the cryptographic perspective – the exponential g^β generated by Bob. In this way, Alice's signature $sig_A(h(g^\alpha|g^\beta))$ is tied to that specific protocol run.

Moreover, by sending Bob $e_K(sig_A(h(g^\alpha|g^\beta)))$, her signature encrypted with the shared secret key K, Alice implicitly proves to Bob that she is the communicating party who generated the random exponent α. As a result, Bob is able to verify that the party he communicated with is indeed Alice.

In a similar manner, Alice can verify that she indeed communicated with Bob while exchanging the keying material g^α, g^β based on Bob's response $g^\beta, e_K(sig_B(h(g^\beta|g^\alpha)))$. Just like with Alice, Bob's response ties his signature to the exponents and allows Alice to verify that it was Bob with whom she established the shared secret key K.

Note how STS has the desired authenticated key agreement properties discussed earlier in this section. First, STS uses fresh random challenges α, β rather than timestamps.

Second, Bob's and Alice's authentication is direct because they use the shared secret key K to encrypt their signatures.

Third, STS offers perfect forward secrecy – the only long-term secret keys are Alice's and Bob's private keys, which they use to sign the hash of the exponentials g^α and g^β. If Alice's or Bob's private key (or both) are somehow compromised, the security of the previous STS protocol runs is not affected provided the exponents α and β are random and are not reused between protocol runs. Then, the Diffie-Hellman problem prevents Eve (and Mallory) from determining these exponents from g^α and g^β, respectively.

In addition, the use of digital signatures implies that Alice and Bob do not need to contact a trusted third party, Trent, for every run of the STS protocol. In other words, once Alice and Bob have their own certificates as well as the certificate of Trent (stored in a secure memory that cannot be manipulated by Mallory), they can perform an authenticated key agreement using the STS protocol completely offline, without the need for any connectivity or additional infrastructure.

The Handshake subprotocol of TLS is currently perhaps the most widely deployed Authenticated Key Agreement (AKA) protocol.

7.10   Public-key cryptography in TLS 1.3

Equipped with the mathematical background on public-key cryptography, we can now explore how it is applied in TLS 1.3.

In the previous chapter, we learned that client Bob and server Alice exchange messages during the TLS handshake phase to establish all parameters necessary for deriving the TLS secrets and, subsequently, the TLS keys.

Technically, these cryptographic parameters are transmitted in the `key_share` extension of the `ClientHello`, `ServerHello` and, if needed, `HelloRetryRequest` messages.

7.10.1   Client key shares and server key shares

In a ClientHello message, the key_share extension – more precisely, its extension_data field – contains a value called KeyShareClientHello defined as follows:

```
struct {
    KeyShareEntry client_shares<0..2^16-1>;
} KeyShareClientHello;
```

The client_shares variable is a list of key shares offered by client Bob to server Alice in the initial ClientHello message. Generally, the client_shares list is ordered according to Bob's preference and starts with his most preferred key share. But Bob may also send Alice an empty client_shares list, letting her choose the group for the key share.

The basic data block size in the TLS 1.3 specification given in RFC 8446 is one byte. A *vector* is a one-dimensional array of data elements of the same type whose length may be fixed or variable. Notably, the length of a vector in the TLS 1.3 specification is always given as the number of bytes. This can be confusing at first since most programming languages, as well as programming literature, declare the length of an array or vector as the number of its elements.

The angle brackets <...> denote vectors of variable length. The numbers in the angle brackets specify the range of legal lengths using the <floor...ceiling> notation. When variable-length vectors are encoded, their actual length is prepended to the vector's contents. This length indication itself consumes as many bytes as are required to hold the vector's maximum legal length.

The elements of the client_shares list – that is, the TLS key shares – are of type KeyShareEntry shown in *Listing 1*. Each key share is composed of two variables. The group variable contains the name of the key share's specific group defined in the TLS specification. The key_exchange variable contains the actual cryptographic key share for either the finite field-based Diffie-Hellman (that is, Diffie-Hellman over the group $\mathbb{F}_p^*$) or for the elliptic curve Diffie-Hellman key agreement protocol. We will discuss elliptic curves in detail in the next chapter. For now, it suffices to know that points of an elliptic curve form an abelian group, so we can perform the general Diffie-Hellman key exchange protocol shown in *Figure 7.1*.

```
struct {
    NamedGroup group;
    opaque key_exchange<1..2^16-1>;
} KeyShareEntry;
```

Listing 1: TLS key shares

In a ServerHello message, the key_share extension contains a value called KeyShareServerHello shown in *Listing 2*. Note that in contrast to client Bob's KeyShareClientHello, server Alice's server_share is a single key share entry value. This is because Alice chooses one key share from the list offered by Bob.

```
struct {
    KeyShareEntry server_share;
} KeyShareServerHello;
```

Listing 2: Data in the key share extension of a ServerHello *message*

For the TLS handshake to work, server_share must be in the same group as one of the key shares offered by client Bob. Server Alice is not allowed to respond with a key share for any group that was not contained in Bob's supported_groups list he transmitted in his ClientHello message.

7.10.2   Supported groups

When client Bob starts a TLS handshake with server Alice and wishes to use the ECDHE or DHE key agreement protocol, he transmits the supported_groups extension listing the named groups that Bob supports. The groups are listed in the order of most to least preferred.

The extension_data field of supported_groups contains the value NamedGroupList as defined in *Listing 3*. The **Elliptic Curve Groups (ECDHE)** are the names of elliptic curves supported by the TLS 1.3 standard. These elliptic curves are defined in FIPS 186-4 and RFC 7748.

```
enum {
    /* Elliptic Curve Groups (ECDHE) */
    secp256r1(0x0017), secp384r1(0x0018), secp521r1(0x0019),
    x25519(0x001D), x448(0x001E),

    /* Finite Field Groups (DHE) */
    ffdhe2048(0x0100), ffdhe3072(0x0101), ffdhe4096(0x0102),
    ffdhe6144(0x0103), ffdhe8192(0x0104),

    /* Reserved Code Points */
    ffdhe_private_use(0x01FC..0x01FF),
    ecdhe_private_use(0xFE00..0xFEFF),
    (0xFFFF)
} NamedGroup;

struct {
    NamedGroup named_group_list<2..2^16-1>;
} NamedGroupList;
```

Listing 3: Named finite fields and elliptic curves supported in TLS 1.3

Similarly, **Finite Field Groups Diffie-Hellman (DHE)** contains the list of finite fields that client Bob and server Alice can use in Diffie-Hellman key agreement as an alternative to elliptic curve groups in the TLS 1.3 handshake. These fields are defined in RFC7919. Finally, the Reserved Code Points is a placeholder for private use as defined in RFC8126.

If Alice and Bob use the **Diffie-Hellman Ephemeral (DHE)** key agreement, client Bob sends server Alice a list of finite field groups that Bob supports. Alice picks one specific group out of that list. Her choice determines the finite field generator g and modulus p.

For the finite field-based Diffie-Hellman key agreement to be secure, Alice and Bob must choose secure cryptographic parameters. As an example, it has been shown [117] that the use of small private exponents with a random prime modulus p renders the computation of the discrete logarithm easy. For this reason, having a definition of suitable finite field groups is crucial.

All primes in the finite field groups used in TLS 1.3 are so-called *safe* primes. As discussed in *Section 7.2, Groups* a safe prime p has the form $p = 2q + 1$ where q is also a prime.

In practice, private Diffie-Hellman exponents are usually chosen independently and uniformly at random from $\{0, ..., p - 2\}$. When p is a safe prime, the most probable Diffie-Hellman key is only 6 times more likely than the least probable and the key's entropy is only 2 bits less than the maximum $lg(p - 1)$ [117].

With e denoting the base of the natural logarithm and $\lfloor ... \rfloor$ denoting the floor operation, the finite field groups defined in RFC 7919 and used in TLS 1.3 are derived for a given bit length b by finding the smallest positive integer x that creates a safe prime p of the form:

$$p = 2^b - 2^{b-64} + \lfloor 2^{b-130}e \rfloor + x * 2^{64} - 1$$

As an example, the 2,048-bit finite field group `ffdhe2048` is calculated as follows. The modulus equals to:

$$p = 2^{2048} - 2^{1984} + \lfloor 2^{1918} * e \rfloor + 560316 * 2^{64} - 1$$

The modulus' p hexadecimal representation is:

```
FFFFFFFF FFFFFFFF ADF85458 A2BB4A9A AFDC5620 273D3CF1
D8B9C583 CE2D3695 A9E13641 146433FB CC939DCE 249B3EF9
7D2FE363 630C75D8 F681B202 AEC4617A D3DF1ED5 D5FD6561
2433F51F 5F066ED0 85636555 3DED1AF3 B557135E 7F57C935
984F0C70 E0E68B77 E2A689DA F3EFE872 1DF158A1 36ADE735
```

```
30ACCA4F 483A797A BC0AB182 B324FB61 D108A94B B2C8E3FB
B96ADAB7 60D7F468 1D4F42A3 DE394DF4 AE56EDE7 6372BB19
0B07A7C8 EE0A6D70 9E02FCE1 CDF7E2EC C03404CD 28342F61
9172FE9C E98583FF 8E4F1232 EEF28183 C3FE3B1B 4C6FAD73
3BB5FCBC 2EC22005 C58EF183 7D1683B2 C6F34A26 C1B2EFFA
886B4238 61285C97 FFFFFFFF FFFFFFFF
```

The generator g equals 2, and the group has the size $q = (p - 1)/2$. The hexadecimal representation of q is:

```
7FFFFFFF FFFFFFFF D6FC2A2C 515DA54D 57EE2B10 139E9E78
EC5CE2C1 E7169B4A D4F09B20 8A3219FD E649CEE7 124D9F7C
BE97F1B1 B1863AEC 7B40D901 576230BD 69EF8F6A EAFEB2B0
9219FA8F AF833768 42B1B2AA 9EF68D79 DAAB89AF 3FABE49A
CC278638 707345BB F15344ED 79F7F439 0EF8AC50 9B56F39A
98566527 A41D3CBD 5E0558C1 59927DB0 E88454A5 D96471FD
DCB56D5B B06BFA34 0EA7A151 EF1CA6FA 572B76F3 B1B95D8C
8583D3E4 770536B8 4F017E70 E6FBF176 601A0266 941A17B0
C8B97F4E 74C2C1FF C7278919 777940C1 E1FF1D8D A637D6B9
9DDAFE5E 17611002 E2C778C1 BE8B41D9 6379A513 60D977FD
4435A11C 30942E4B FFFFFFFF FFFFFFFF
```

The `ffdhe2048` finite field group has an estimated security strength (based on the strength of symmetric key cryptographic primitives) of about 100 bits.

Keeping in mind the mathematical fundamentals of public-key cryptography we discussed earlier in this chapter, you might have spotted a small inconsistency in the TLS 1.3 specification language. The specification talks about elliptic curve groups and finite field groups. But we, of course, know that any field is automatically a group and that all elliptic curves are groups by definition.

In TLS 1.3, server Alice can send the `supported_groups` extension to client Bob. However, Bob is not allowed to act upon any data in `supported_groups` before he successfully completes the handshake with Alice. Bob may only use this information to adjust the list of named groups in his `key_share` extension in subsequent TLS sessions with Alice.

If server Alice has a group she prefers to those sent by client Bob in his key_share extension but is still willing to accept Bob's ClientHello message, she sends a supported_groups extension to communicate to Bob her preferences. Moreover, that extension lists all groups that Alice supports, even if some of them are currently unsupported by client Bob.

7.10.3   Finite Field Diffie-Hellman in TLS

When finite field groups are used, server Alice and client Bob execute the conventional Diffie-Hellman key agreement protocol as described in *Figure 7.2*. The secret Alice and Bob agree upon is converted into a byte string by encoding it in big-endian form and left-padding it with zeros up to the size of the prime. This converted byte string forms the Handshake Secret S_H, which is subsequently used as the shared Diffie-Hellman ephemeral secret in the TLS key schedule to further derive the client_handshake_traffic_secret (CHTS), the server_handshake_traffic_secret (SHTS), the derived_handshake_secret (dHS), and finally the master_secret (MS) (see *Section 12.3, KDFs in TLS*).

7.11   Hybrid cryptosystems

From the previous sections, you might have got the (correct) impression that using a public-key cryptosystem is rather costly in terms of computation time. For example, according to [177], p. 121 key generation in the RSA cryptosystem has an effort in $O(\ell^4 \log(\ell))$, where ℓ is the bitlength of the public modulus n, and encryption or decryption of an n-bit plaintext block takes $O(n^3)$ bit operations. Such an effort is unacceptable for the encryption of large amounts of data.

Therefore, most cryptographic systems used in practice today are *hybrid cryptosystems*. Hybrid cryptosystems combine the advantage of public-key cryptography of being able to bootstrap a secure communication channel to a previously unknown communicating party with the speed and efficiency of symmetric-key encryption, decryption, and hashing operations [188].

7.11.1 High-level description of hybrid cryptosystems

Figure 7.6 illustrates the basic architecture and the fundamental working principle of hybrid cryptosystems. A hybrid cryptosystem is composed of two separate cryptographic systems:

- A public-key cryptosystem *PKS* used as a secure means for the communicating parties Alice and Bob to establish a shared secret

- A symmetric-key cryptosystem *SKS* used to secure the actual (bulk) data by transforming it using a desired cryptographic operation.

A hybrid cryptosystem works by Alice and Bob first establishing a shared secret key k using a public-key cryptosystem *PKS* and mathematically verifiable credentials.

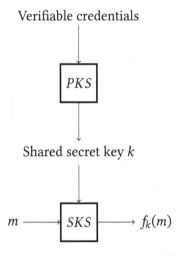

Figure 7.6: Working principle of a hybrid cryptosystem

We will have much more to say about how the verifiable credentials work in detail in *Chapter 10, Digital Certificates and Certification Authorities.* For now, it is sufficient to know that these credentials are constructed in such way that Alice can verify Bob's identity and Bob can verify Alice's identity. Or, more precisely, Alice can verify that the other communicating party claiming to be Bob is indeed Bob, and vice versa.

Most importantly, Alice and Bob can verify each other's identity even if they have never met before. This works by having a third party that both Alice and Bob trust – let's call him

Trent – vouch for Bob's and Alice's identities in advance. This act of vouching is encoded in the credentials so that Alice and Bob can perform the identity verification of the other party *without* the need to communicate with Trent.

Conceptually, the ability of communicating parties that never met before to verify each other's identities without the online, real-time support of a trusted third party solves the key distribution problem. In other words, public-key cryptography relieves Alice and Bob from having to share a common secret in advance.

In the second step, having established a shared secret key k, Alice and Bob use a symmetric-key cryptosystem SKS to compute a desired cryptographic function $f_k(m)$ on the bulk payload data m they want to secure.

Compared to public-key cryptographic schemes, symmetric-key schemes are orders of magnitude faster and much easier to implement because, unlike public cryptography, they do not require arbitrary-precision arithmetic where calculations are performed on huge numbers having hundreds of digits and limited only by the amount of working memory available in the computer.

As a result, cryptographic computations on large bulk data, for example, an audio or video stream of several gigabytes, can be done very efficiently and at high speed using a symmetric-key cryptosystem SKS.

7.11.2   Hybrid encryption

A hybrid encryption scheme is a specific type of hybrid cryptosystem that allows Alice and Bob to securely encrypt data they want to exchange over an insecure communication channel. *Figure 7.7* shows the architecture of a hybrid encryption scheme. It strongly resembles that of the hybrid cryptosystem and is composed of two parts:

- A public-key cryptosystem PKS used as a means to establish a shared secret key

- A symmetric-key encryption E used as a **Data Encapsulation Method (DEM)** to securely encrypt the actual (bulk) data using the newly established secret key [105].

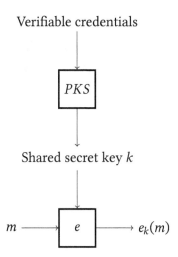

Figure 7.7: Architecture and working principle of hybrid encryption

Like with a general hybrid cryptosystem, shown in *Figure 7.6*, Alice and Bob first use the public-key cryptosystem to establish a shared secret key k. In the second step, they use a symmetric-key encryption e to encrypt plaintexts m under the key k.

A hybrid encryption system has the following cryptographic properties [105]:

- It ensures *secrecy* because Alice and Bob mutually verified their identities during the key agreement phase and therefore are the only communicating entities who know the shared secret key k. Alice and Bob can than use a symmetric key encryption e – for instance, the **Advanced Encryption Standard (AES)**, which we will discuss in detail in *Chapter 14, Block Ciphers and Their Modes of Operation* – that is secure against polynomial time adversaries. Consequently, Eve is not able to extract any information about m from the ciphertext $e_k(m)$, except its length.

- It allows *ubiquitous application* because Alice and Bob can verify each other's identity based on the credentials they present during the key agreement phase. As a consequence, Alice and Bob can securely establish a shared secret key even if they have never met each other before.

- The symmetric-key encryption e itself can be performed in ways that ensure *randomization* of the resulting ciphertexts. Randomization means that two identical plaintext messages m will yield two completely different ciphertexts. As a result, Eve has no way to determine whether a given plaintext corresponds to a specific ciphertext even if Eve knew one or more plaintexts that Alice or Bob encrypted.

Now let's take a look at a specific example of a hybrid encryption scheme.

7.11.3 Example – Hybrid Public Key Encryption

Hybrid Public Key Encryption (HPKE) is a hybrid encryption scheme defined in RFC 9180 [15]. It provides public-key encryption of plaintexts for the recipient public key and supports entity authentication.

HPKE is composed of a public-key cryptosystem, a KDF used for key derivation, and an encryption algorithm that offers **Authenticated Encryption with Associated Data (AEAD)**. We will cover AEAD in detail in *Chapter 15, Authenticated Encryption.*

Classical hybrid encryption, illustrated in *Figure 7.7*, uses public-key cryptography to transport or agree on a symmetric key. In contrast, if Bob wants to send Alice an encrypted message using HPKE, he generates a symmetric key k, encapsulates it with Alice's public key, and sends the encapsulated k alongside one or more ciphertexts of arbitrary size encrypted under k.

In its base mode, HPKE encrypts the payload data Bob wants to send to Alice to a public key [100] as shown in *Figure 7.8*. The base mode is the most commonly used HPKE mode.

Bob generates a shared secret key k and encrypts the plaintext message m that he wants to send Alice under key k. Bob then encrypts the key k using Alice's public key $PubK_A$ and sends this encapsulated key alongside the resulting ciphertext c to Alice.

Upon receiving the encrypted data c and the encapsulated shared secret key, Alice uses her private key $PrivK_A$ to recover the symmetric key k. To do this, she decrypts the encapsulated key $\tilde{k}$ to $k = d_{PrivK_A}(\tilde{k})$. She then uses k to decrypt the plaintext message m.

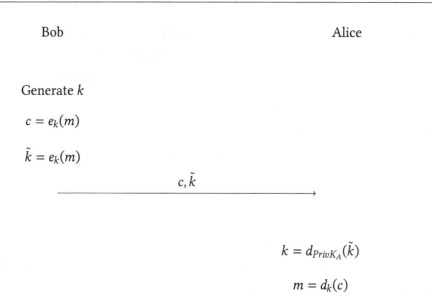

Bob   Alice

Generate k

$c = e_k(m)$

$\tilde{k} = e_k(m)$

$$c, \tilde{k}$$

$$k = d_{PrivK_A}(\tilde{k})$$

$$m = d_k(c)$$

Figure 7.8: Base mode of HPKE hybrid encryption scheme

We conclude this section with a general discussion of the use of hybrid cryptosystems today.

7.11.4   Hybrid cryptosystems in modern cryptography

Most popular cryptographic systems in use today are hybrid cryptosystems. TLS is a prime example of a hybrid cryptosystem – it uses public-key cryptography (more specifically, **Diffie-Hellman on Elliptic Curves (ECDH)**) to agree on a shared secret key required to establish a secure communication channel between Alice and Bob and then, as we will learn in *Part 2, Off the Record*, employs symmetric key cryptography to encrypt the bulk data.

Another example is the well-known **Secure Shell (SSH)** protocol, which was introduced in 1996 [203]. SSH uses public-key cryptography (for instance, the Diffie-Hellman key agreement protocol) for the symmetric key exchange and a DEM based on symmetric-key cryptography for bulk data encryption. Just like TLS, SSH acts on top of the transport layer.

The OpenPGP and PKCS #7 file formats, as well as protocols such as SMIME, are further examples of hybrid cryptosystems. As yet another example, a hybrid cryptosystem called ECIES is used to store the secret keys in the secure enclave of iOS devices [10].

7.12   Summary

In this chapter, we introduced the mathematical foundations of public-key cryptosystems and looked in detail at the two most important examples, the Diffie-Hellman key exchange protocol and the RSA cryptosystem. We also investigated how exactly public-key cryptography is used within TLS.

By now, you should be aware of a very substantial difference between Diffie-Hellman and RSA: while RSA has to work with integers, the Diffie-Hellman protocol works in principle with **any abelian group** G. The difficulty of the discrete logarithm problem, which lies at the core of the Diffie-Hellman protocol, varies from group to group. If we can find a group where it is especially difficult, the corresponding key lengths could be shorter in that group. This fact is what makes *elliptic curves* so attractive in modern cryptography. They are the topic of our next chapter.

8

Elliptic Curves

In the previous chapter, we got some first insights into how public-key cryptography can solve the key distribution problem even if Alice and Bob have never met before. More specifically, we learned how public-key cryptosystems can be built on two well-known problems from number theory: the discrete logarithm problem and the integer factorization problem.

Even after studying these problems for centuries – integer factorization, for example, was first investigated by the ancient Greeks – there are no known polynomial-time algorithms for these problems - at least not on conventional, non-quantum computers. For the time being, we therefore consider them to be computationally secure.

Nevertheless, to be secure in practice, cryptosystems based on the computational hardness of integer factorization or the discrete logarithm problem must operate on huge numbers. As an example, to achieve a security level equivalent to a 128-bit block cipher, the RSA cryptosystem must operate on integers whose binary representation has about 3,000 bits!

This poses a serious problem, especially for embedded systems and battery-powered devices such as smartphones where either the amount of computing resources or the amount of energy – or both – are limited.

Luckily, in 1985, two American mathematicians, Victor Miller and Neil Koblitz, proposed using so-called *elliptic curves* as a more efficient drop-in replacement for integers and finite fields over primes.

In this chapter, we will look at elliptic curves in detail. Specifically, we will do the following:

- Explain what elliptic curves are

- Discuss their mathematical properties

- Explain how to choose secure elliptic curves suitable for cryptographic purposes

- Discuss the elliptic curves used in TLS 1.3

- Show how they are used in the TLS protocol

Upon finishing this chapter, you will have a good understanding of what elliptic curves are, what properties they have that make them very useful for public-key cryptography, and how they are used in cryptographic algorithms, in particular those employed by TLS.

This chapter covers elliptic curve cryptography aspects defined in RFC 8446 in Sections 4 *Extensions* and 7 *Cryptographic Computations*, in particular Elliptic Curve Diffie-Hellman.

8.1   What are elliptic curves?

Historically, elliptic curves are rooted in so-called *Diophantine equations*, named after ancient Greek mathematician Diophantus of Alexandria. Diophantine equations are polynomial equations in two or more unknowns for which only integer solutions are of interest.

In the 19th century, these studies became more formalized and were extended to so called *algebraic curves*, which are the set of zeros of a polynomial of two variables in a plane.

Circles, as defined as the zeros of

$$x^2 + y^2 - R^2$$

and ellipses, defined as the zeros of

$$\frac{x^2}{a^2} + \frac{y^2}{b^2} - 1$$

are the most common examples of algebraic curves. However, elliptic curves are *not* ellipses. They arose from the study of so-called *elliptic integrals*, by which the arc length of ellipses is computed, and were intensively studied by pure mathematicians in the 19th and early 20th century. They are characterized by their amazing property of possessing a way to *add* curve points, so that the result is another point on the curve.

In 1985, Victor Miller and Neil Koblitz independently proposed using elliptic curves in public-key cryptography. According to [102], these were the reasons:

- Greater flexibility, because there are many elliptic curves to choose from

- The absence of subexponential algorithms for finding discrete logarithms on suitably chosen curves

Our goal in this section is to define mathematically what we really mean by the term *elliptic curve* and to discuss some of their properties.

8.1.1 Reduced Weierstrass form

Our story starts with the set of zeros of a general cubic polynomial in two variables – x, y:

$$ax^3 + bx^2y + cxy^2 + dy^3 + ex^2 + fxy + gy^2 + hx + iy + j = 0$$

This is an example of an *algebraic curve*.

Obviously, we must be able to add and multiply the x, y and the coefficients together, therefore we require them to come from a field $\mathbb{F}$, as defined in *Chapter 7, Public-Key Cryptography*. Through a series of coordinate transformations and after suitable re-naming of coefficients, we arrive at a much simpler equation, which is the defining equation for elliptic curves.

An *elliptic curve E* over a field $\mathbb{F}$ is the set of points (x, y), where x, y and the coefficients a_i are in $\mathbb{F}$, satisfying the equation

$$y^2 + a_1 x y + a_3 y = x^3 + a_2 x^2 + a_4 x + a_6, \text{ with } a_i \in \mathbb{F},$$

along with some special point O *at infinity.*

This is called the *Weierstrass form* of E. We will explain a bit later what this ominous point O really is, but let's start by looking at the defining equation. In the 19th century, mathematicians studied elliptic curves mostly over $\mathbb{R}$ or $\mathbb{C}$, and real numbers are the best field to visualize an elliptic curve, as in *Figure 8.1*.

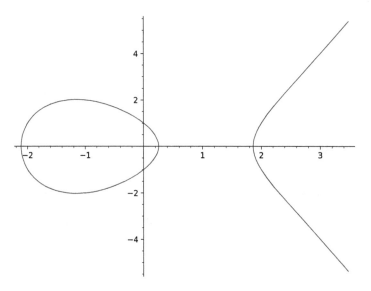

Figure 8.1: Elliptic Curve $y^2 = x^3 - 4x + 1$ over real numbers

Note the symmetry of the curve with respect to the x axis. This is because of the y^2 on the left-hand side of the curve equation. We can make sure all elliptic curves have this symmetry by making another coordinate transformation. If we use

$$y_{new} = y + \frac{a_1 x + a_3}{2}$$

instead of y, we can get rid of the xy term on the left-hand side. A similar change, $x_{new} = x + a_2/3$, frees us from the x^2 term on the right-hand side. After cleaning up and renaming the constants, we arrive at the *reduced Weierstrass form* of the elliptic curve,

$$y^2 = x^3 + ax + b.$$

However, this only works if we are allowed to divide by 2 and by 3, i.e. if $2 \neq 0$ and $3 \neq 0$ in $\mathbb{F}$. The fancy term for this requirement is *the field characteristic should be larger than 3*. If we work in a field $\mathbb{F}_p$, where $p > 3$, this is not a problem. But computers are especially efficient when dealing with bitstrings. Bitstrings live in the fields $\mathbb{F}_{2^k}$, which do have characteristic 2. In this case, there are two possibilities for the reduced form:

- The *nonsupersingular case*

$$y^2 + xy = x^3 + a_2 x^2 + a_6,$$

- The *supersingular case*

$$y^2 + a_3 y = x^3 + a_4 x + a_6.$$

For example, the curve $y^2 + y = x^3$ over $\mathbb{F}$ is supersingular. As it turns out, supersingular curves are not as secure as nonsupersingular curves (see *Section 8.4.2, Algorithms for solving special cases of ECDLP*). Luckily, the vast majority of elliptic curves are nonsupersingular [102].

8.1.2 Smoothness

Before we can start defining a group operation on the points of an elliptic curve, we need to add one requirement: The curve needs to be *smooth*. By this, we mean that the curve has well-defined tangent slopes everywhere. Take a look at curve E defined by $y^2 = x^3 - 3x + 2$ over real numbers (see *Figure 8.2*).

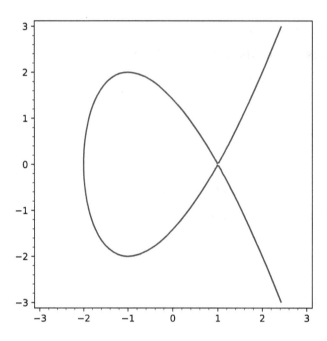

Figure 8.2: The singular curve $y^2 = x^3 - 3x + 2$ over real numbers

The point $(1, 0)$ of the curve does not have a unique tangent slope. Such points are called *singular points.* If we try to find a tangent slope by differentiating both sides of the defining equation with respect to x, we get $2yy' = 3x^2 - 3$, or $y' = \frac{3x^2-3}{2y}$. The behavior of this fraction is undefined if we plug in the singular point $(1, 0)$, meaning it takes two different limit values whether we approach $x = 1$ from the left or from the right. This comes from the fact that the right-hand side of the curve equation has a double zero at $x = 1$ (which means the derivative has a zero at $x = 1$ as well).

More generally, if the right-hand side of a curve E in reduced Weierstrass form is given by the cubic polynomial

$$x^3 + ax + b,$$

it can be shown that this polynomial has a double zero somewhere if and only if $16(4a^3 + 27b^2) = 0$. The factor 16 seems to be superficial, but it does matter if the characteristic of $\mathbb{F}$ is 2, because it is always zero in this case. We will not pursue this issue here, but refer you to [82], section 5.7 instead.

We therefore define an elliptic curve E in reduced Weierstrass form $y^2 = x^3 + ax + b$ over a field $\mathbb{F}$ of characteristic char($\mathbb{F}$) > 3 to be *smooth* or *nonsingular*, if the *discriminant*

$$\Delta = 4a^3 + 27b^2 \neq 0.$$

This ensures that the curve has well-defined tangents everywhere.

8.1.3 Projective coordinates

In order to get to grips with the mysterious point at infinity O, we need to extend the set of points that satisfy $y^2 = x^3 + ax + b$. We can do so by introducing yet another set of coordinates. Let $\mathbb{F}$ be a field. We look at triples (X, Y, Z), where X, Y, Z are from $\mathbb{F}$ and are not all zero at the same time. This looks like some three-dimensional space $\mathbb{F}^3$ without the origin, but we are only interested in lines through the origin, not at the single points, so we consider all points in $\mathbb{F}^3 \setminus \{0, 0, 0\}$ to be equivalent, if they lie on the same line through the origin. More precisely, we say that the triple (X_1, Y_1, Z_1) is equivalent to (X_2, Y_2, Z_2) if there is some factor $\lambda \in \mathbb{F}$ so that

$$(X_1, Y_1, Z_1) = (\lambda X_2, \lambda Y_2, \lambda Z_2)$$

The set of all equivalent triples (X, Y, Z) is called an *equivalence class*. Each equivalence class is called a *projective point*, and all projective points taken together form the *projective plane*.

The points of the ordinary or *affine* plane $\mathbb{F}^2$ can be mapped onto points of the projective plane: the affine point (x, y) corresponds to the projective point $(x, y, 1)$. Similarly, for $Z \neq 0$, the projective point (X, Y, Z) is equivalent to $(X/Z, Y/Z, 1)$, which can be identified with the affine point $(X/Z, Y/Z)$. This means, for $Z \neq 0$, there is a one-to-one correspondence between points of the affine plane and points of the projective plane. The projective points with $Z = 0$, however, do not have an equivalent in the affine plane. They can be thought of as adding a kind of horizon to the affine plane, that is infinitely far away.

What happens if we use projective coordinates $(X/Z, Y/Z)$ instead of the ordinary (x, y) in our equation for E? We get

$$\frac{Y^2}{Z^2} = \frac{X^3}{Z^3} + a\frac{X}{Z} + b.$$

Multiplying both sides by Z^3 to get rid of the denominators gives us

$$ZY^2 = X^3 + aXZ^2 + bZ^3.$$

Note that in this polynomial equation, all terms have the same overall degree 3. Polynomials of this form are called *homogeneous*. This homogeneous polynomial represents the projective version of the elliptic curve. It is satisfied by a projective point (X, Y, Z) with $Z \neq 0$ if and only if the corresponding affine point $(x, y) = (X/Z, Y/Z)$ satisfies $y^2 = x^3 + ax + b$. But what about the projective points with $Z = 0$? Plugging $Z = 0$ into the projective equation, we get

$$0 = X^3,$$

so X must be zero as well. But there is no restriction on Y apart from being non-zero, so we can choose $Y = 1$ and get another projective point $O = (0, 1, 0)$ as the solution of the projective equation. This point does not have an equivalent in the affine plane, but it can be visualized as lying on the infinitely far away end of the y axis.

Apart from providing a formal justification for having an additional point O at infinity on our elliptic curve, the use of projective coordinates is also more efficient when doing calculations on elliptic curves. We will return to this issue shortly when discussing the addition law for points on an elliptic curve.

8.2 Elliptic curves as abelian groups

Two points P and Q on a smooth elliptic curve E in reduced Weierstrass form can be added to give another point $R = P + Q$ on E. The addition process can be best understood by describing it as a geometrical recipe over the real numbers first.

8.2.1 Geometrical viewpoint

To find the sum of two points P and Q on E, we draw a line through P and Q first. One can show that this line must have exactly one additional intersection point with E. We find this point and form the mirror image of it with respect to the x axis by reversing the sign of its y coordinate. The result is the sum $P + Q$. This process is visualized in *Figure 8.3*.

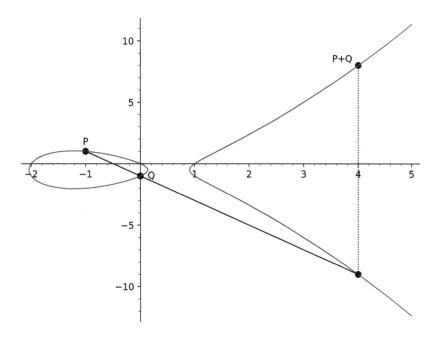

Figure 8.3: Elliptic curve point addition

Now let's look at some special cases:

- If $P = Q$, we form the tangent line t to E at P, find its intersection point with E and reverse the sign of its y coordinate. The result is the point $P + P = 2P$ (see *Figure 8.4*).

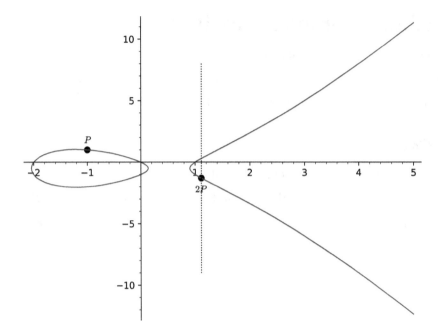

Figure 8.4: Point doubling on an elliptic curve

- If $Q = O$, we *define* $P + O$ to be P. This means that O serves as a neutral element for the point addition.

- If $P = (c, d)$ and $Q = (c, -d)$ have the same x coordinate c, the line $x = c$ joining them is vertical. It intersects E at the point at infinity O. This can be seen by writing $x = c$ in projective coordinates $x = X/Z$: we have $X/Z = c$. Multiplying by Z gives us the projective version of the connecting line:

$$X = cZ.$$

Clearly, the point $O = (0, 1, 0)$ lies on this projective line. But we have already established that O also lies on the curve, so O must be the point of intersection.

Replacing Y by $-Y$ in projective coordinates does not give a new point, so O is the final result of adding P and Q: $(c, d) + (c, -d) = O$. But this means that for a point

$P = (c, d)$ on E,

$$-P = (c, -d)$$

(see *Figure 8.5*).

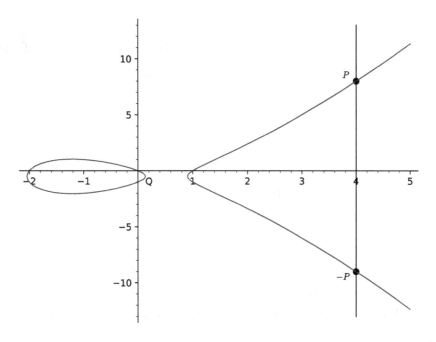

Figure 8.5: $P + (-P) = O$

Summing up, we have defined an operation + that maps a pair of points P and Q on E to their sum $P + Q$, which is also on E. The operation has O as a neutral element, and for a point $P = (c, d) \in E$, we can find its negative $-P = (c, -d) \in E$. It is also quite obvious that + is a commutative operation, because the order of P and Q does not affect the line joining them, so the end result of the adding process wil be the same. The only thing that remains to be checked before we can declare the pair $(E, +)$ to be an abelian group is the associativity law for +, that is, we need to prove that

$$P + (Q + R) = (P + Q) + R$$

for any points P, Q, R on E. This turns out to be a bit tricky, but it can be proved by using tools from projective geometry (see [102], p. 120, for example).

Summing up, we have proved that *a smooth elliptic curve E together with the point O at infinity forms an abelian group with respect to point addition as defined above.*

More generally, the zeros of a set of polynomials is called an *abelian variety*, if a group law can be defined on them. Abelian varieties can be seen as the generalization of elliptic curves, but as yet they have not found any applications in cryptography.

8.2.2 Explicit formulae

The geometrical viewpoint is nice to get an intuitive picture of point addition, but in order to actually implement things on a computer we need to have explicit formulae telling it what to do. Moreover, the geometrical picture is not valid anymore if we work in a finite field. Still, we can use the well-known tools from calculus and analytic geometry over real numbers to get explicit expressions for secants, tangents, intersection points, and so on, and finally, for the sum of points and point doubling on an elliptic curve. With a few small modifications, these formulae then carry over to finite fields. This is what you get for real, affine coordinates.

Let $P = (x_1, y_1)$ and $Q = (x_2, y_2)$ be points on a smooth elliptic curve in reduced Weierstrass form: $E : y^2 = x^3 + ax + b$. Let's add and double these points:

- **Point Addition:** Let $R = P + Q$. The coordinates (x_3, y_3) of R are given by:

$$x_3 = \left(\frac{y_2 - y_1}{x_2 - x_1} \right)^2 - x_1 - x_2$$

$$y_3 = -y_1 + \left(\frac{y_2 - y_1}{x_2 - x_1} \right) \cdot (x_1 - x_3).$$

- **Point Doubling:** Let $R = P + P = 2P$. The coordinates (x_3, y_3) of R are given by:

$$x_3 = \left(\frac{3x_1^2 + a}{2y_1} \right)^2 - 2x_1$$

$$y_3 = -y_1 + \left(\frac{3x_1^2 + a}{2y_1} \right) \cdot (x_1 - x_3).$$

Take, for example, the curve $E : y^2 = x^3 - 4x + 1$ and the points $P = (0, 1), Q = (3, 4)$. Then $\frac{y_2 - y_1}{x_2 - x_1} = 1$ and

$$x_3 = 1^2 - 0 - 3 = -2, y_3 = -1 + 1 \cdot (0 - -(2)) = 1.$$

So $R = P + Q = (-2, 1)$. Similarly, we get $2P = P + P = (4, 7)$.

The computationally most expensive part of the formulae above are the divisions, especially when carried out in a finite field $\mathbb{F}_p$, where division by x really means *multiplication by* x^{-1} mod p. We can save a lot of this effort, if we translate our formulae into projective coordinates, that is, by replacing $P = (x_1, y_1)$ and $Q = (x_2, y_2)$ with their projective counterparts $(X_1/Z_1, Y_1/Z_1, 1)$ and $(X_2/Z_2, Y_2/Z_2, 1)$. After a lot of algebra and a final multiplication to get rid of all denominators, the final result is (see [141]):

- **Point Addition** We set $U = X_1 Z_2 - X_2 Z_1$, $T = Y_1 Z_2 - Y_2 Z_1$ and $W = T^2 Z_1 Z_2 - U^2(X_1 Z_2 + X_2 Z_1)$. With these abbreviations, we get

$$X_3 = UW$$

$$Y_3 = T(X_1 Z_2 U^2 - W) - Y_1 Z_2 U^3$$

$$Z_3 = U^3 Z_1 Z_2$$

- **Point Doubling** We set $T = 3X_1^2 + aZ_1^2$. With this abbreviation, we get

$$X_2 = 2Y_1 Z_1 (T^2 - 4X_1 Y_1^2 Z_1)$$

$$Y_2 = T(8X_1Y_1^2Z_1 - T^2)$$

$$Z_2 = 8Y_1^3Z_1^3$$

Basically, we are trading a lot of multiplications and additions against the divisions in the affine case. The transfer back to affine coordinates is done by a single division, namely dividing all coordinates by the Z-coordinate value.

8.3 Elliptic curves over finite fields

Now let's see what elliptic curves over finite fields look like. As we established in the last chapter, there are only two kinds of finite fields: $\mathbb{F}_p = \{0, 1, 2, \dots, p - 1\}$, where p is a prime number, and $\mathbb{F}_p[X]/M$, where p is a prime number and M is an irreducible polynomial of degree n with coeffcients $a_i \in \mathbb{F}_p$. The essential difference between the two is that $\mathbb{F}_p$ has p elements, whereas $\mathbb{F}_p[X]/M$ has p^n elements. For this reason, $\mathbb{F}_p[X]/M$ is often called $\mathbb{F}_{p^n}$ without explicitly stating the polynomial M.

8.3.1 Elliptic curves over $\mathbb{F}_p$

We focus on the case $p > 3$, so that $char(\mathbb{F}_p) > 3$. Then it is always possible to generate the reduced Weierstrass form of the curve, and we can use the following definition.

Elliptic curve over $\mathbb{F}_p$

Let $p > 3$ be a prime number. An *elliptic curve* over $\mathbb{F}_p$ is the set of points (x, y) satisfying

$$y^2 = x^3 + ax + b \quad \mathrm{mod} \ p,$$

where $x, y, a, b \in \mathbb{F}_p$ and $\Delta = 4a^3 + 27b^2 \neq 0 \ \mathrm{mod} \ p$, together with some point O.

Note that here we have already included the smoothness condition in the very definition of an elliptic curve. What do these discrete elliptic curves look like? *Figure 8.6* provides an example, where $a = 5, b = 5$, and $p = 17$.

This discrete set of points does not bear much resemblance to the smooth curves we have drawn over $\mathbb{R}$ in the last section. Still, the explicit formulae for point addition and point

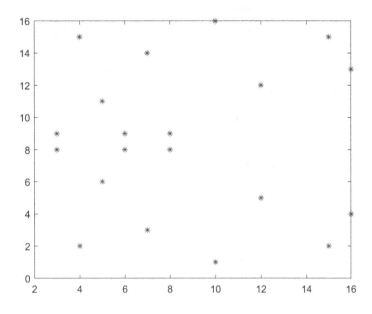

Figure 8.6: The curve $E : y^2 = x^3 + 5x + 5 \mod 17$

doubling given in the last section magically carry over to $\mathbb{F}_p$. We only need to observe that all calculations are being done modulo p, and that division really means multiplication with an inverse modulo p. So all elliptic curves over $\mathbb{F}_p$ defined in this way form an abelian group.

Recall from *Chapter 7, Public-Key Cryptography* that the number of elements of a group G is called its *order*. So what is the order of an elliptic curve E over $\mathbb{F}_p$? By manually counting the points in *Figure 8.6* (and not forgetting point O) we see that this special curve has 21 points. Unfortunately, there is no explicit formula giving us the number of points of an elliptic curve E in terms of a, b, and p, but we can try to estimate the number. An easy way to get an upper limit on the number of points is to assume that if we plug each possible x value from $\{0, 1, \ldots, p-1\}$ into the right-hand side of the curve equation, we get a perfect square modulo p every time. So each possible x value would provide two possible y values $y_{1,2} = \pm\sqrt{x^3 + ax + b}$, which gives us an upper limit of $2p + 1$ points (again, don't forget the point O).

Using much more advanced mathematical tools, we can get a much better estimate. **Hasse's theorem** (see [102], Chapter 6, Corollary 1.2) tells us that the number N of points of an elliptic curve E over $\mathbb{F}_p$ lies between $p + 1 - 2\sqrt{p}$ and $p + 1 + 2\sqrt{p}$.

So the number of points on E over $\mathbb{F}_p$ is quite close to p. This fact will become important a bit later, when we discuss the discrete logarithm problem on E.

8.3.2 Elliptic curves over $\mathbb{F}_{2^k}$

Although not strictly necessary in the context of TLS, for the sake of completeness, we'll also briefly discuss here how elliptic curves over $\mathbb{F}_{2^k}$ can be made a group. Readers who are not interested in these curves may safely skip this section.

Now, the characteristic of $\mathbb{F}$ is 2, so that our curve equations look different than before. Here, we focus on the non-supersingular case

$$y^2 + xy = x^3 + a_2 x^2 + a_6.$$

For these equations it can be shown that $\Delta = -a_6$, so for a smooth curve we add the requirement $a_6 \neq 0$.

What do these curves look like? As an example, we take the field $\mathbb{F}_{2^3}$, with $M(X) = X^3 + X + 1$ as generating an irreducible polynomial. The element $g(X) = X$ (or $g = (010)$ for short) generates the cyclic group $\mathbb{F}_{2^3}^*$, as $g^1 = (010)$, $g^2 = (100)$, $g^3 = (011)$, $g^4 = (110)$, $g^5 = (111)$, $g^6 = (101)$, $g^7 = (001)$. Therefore we can label the elements of $\mathbb{F}_{2^3}$ as the powers of g, plus the zero element $0 = (000)$.

Our example curve is given by

$$E : y^2 + xy = x^3 + g^2 x^2 + g^6$$

As $g^6 \neq 0$, it is smooth.

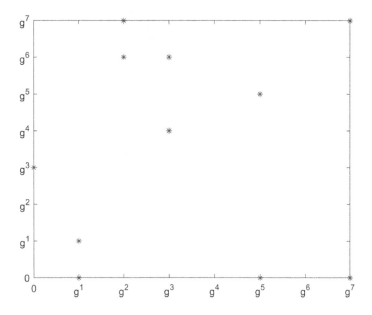

Figure 8.7: The curve $E : y^2 + xy = x^3 + g^2 x^2 + g^6$ over $\mathbb{F}_{2^3}$

Let's look for some points on E. For example, if we plug $x = g^3$ into the equation, we get

$$y^2 + g^3 y = g^9 + g^2 g^6 + g^6$$

as the condition for y. But $g^2 g^6 = g^8 = g^1$, and $g^9 = g^2$. As $g^1 + g^2 + g^6 = (010) + (100) + (101) = (011) = g^3$, the condition for y becomes

$$y^2 + g^3 y = g^3.$$

A little trial and error shows that $y = g^6$ provides a solution. Indeed,

$$(g^6)^2 + g^3 g^6 = g^{12} + g^9 = g^5 + g^2 = (111) + (100) = (011) = g^3.$$

So $P = (g^3, g^6)$ is a point on E, and $Q = (g^3, g^4)$ is another point on E with the same x coordinate. The set of all points on E (minus the point O at infinity) is shown in *Figure 8.7*.

Again, we can ask how many points there are on an elliptic curve over $\mathbb{F}_{2^k}$, and in this case the following version of Hasse's Theorem for $\mathbb{F}_{2^k}$ applies:

The number N of points of an elliptic curve E over $\mathbb{F}_{2^k}$ lies between $2^k + 1 - 2\sqrt{2^k}$ and $2^k + 1 + 2\sqrt{2^k}$.

Now let's turn to the arithmetic in elliptic curves over $\mathbb{F}_{2^k}$. The general intuition is the same as before, but the explicit addition and point doubling formulae change a little in this case because the reduced Weierstrass form looks different now.

Let $P = (x_1, y_1)$ and $Q = (x_2, y_2)$ be points on a smooth elliptic curve over $\mathbb{F}_{2^k}$ in reduced Weierstrass form: $E : y^2 + xy = x^3 + a_2x^2 + a_6$. Now, let's add and double these points:

- **Point Addition** Let $R = P + Q$ and let $s = \frac{y_1 - y_2}{x_1 - x_2}$. Then, the coordinates (x_3, y_3) of R are given by:

$$x_3 = s^2 + s + x_1 + x_2 + a_2$$

$$y_3 = s(x_1 + x_3) + x_3 + y_1.$$

  If $x_1 == x_2$, we set $R = P + Q = O$.

- **Point Doubling** Let $R = P + P = 2P$, where $P \neq (0, 0)$. Let $s = x_1 + y_1/x_1$. Then, the coordinates (x_3, y_3) of R are given by

$$x_3 = s^2 + s + a_2$$

$$y_3 = x_1^2 + (s + 1)x_3$$

  If $x_1 = 0$, we set $P + P = O$.

If $P = (\alpha, \beta)$ is a point on E, how can we find $-P$? According to the point addition formula, $-P$ must have the same x coordinate as P. However, we cannot set $-P = (\alpha, -\beta)$ as for the other fields, because in $\mathbb{F}_{2^k}$, we have $-\beta = \beta$, which would mean $-P = P$. But we can find $-P = (\alpha, \gamma)$ by looking at the defining equation.

If $P = (\alpha, \beta)$ is a point on E, then $y = \beta$ is a solution of

$$y^2 - \alpha y - \alpha^3 - a_2 \alpha^2 - a_6 = 0.$$

This means the left-hand side can also be written as

$$(y - \beta)(y - \gamma) = y^2 - (\beta + \gamma)y + \beta\gamma,$$

where y is the unknown y coordinate of $-P$. Equating coefficients, we see that $\beta + \gamma = \alpha$, or $\gamma = \alpha - \beta$, which is the same as $\gamma = \alpha + \beta$ in $\mathbb{F}_{2^k}$.

So for $P = (\alpha, \beta) \in E$, we have

$$-P = (\alpha, \alpha + \beta).$$

Again, we can conclude that elliptic curves over $\mathbb{F}_{2^k}$ in the form

$$y^2 + xy = x^3 + a_2 x^2 + a_6,$$

where $a_i \in \mathbb{F}_{2^k}, a_6 \neq 0$ form an abelian group with respect to point addition as defined above.

8.3.3 Discrete logarithms and Diffie-Hellman key exchange protocol

In *Section 7.2, Groups*, we defined the discrete logarithm problem for generic groups $\mathbb{G}$. We repeat the definition here for convenience:

- **Given:** A group $\mathbb{G} = (M, \star)$, $A \in M, g \in M$

- **Sought:** A positive integer number n so that $A = g^n$.

  n is called the *discrete logarithm* of A to base g.

The purpose of this section is to specialize this generic formulation to elliptic curve groups and to formulate the Diffie-Hellman key exchange protocol for elliptic curves.

Remember that in the earlier definition, g^n is an abbreviation for $g \star g \star \cdots \star g$, where the group operation $\star$ is applied n times. In an elliptic curve E, the group elements are points $P \in E$, and the group operation is an addition, traditionally written by a $+$ - sign. This means that $g^n = g \star g \star \cdots \star g$ becomes $P + P + \cdots + P = nP$.

Now we can re-formulate the **discrete logarithm problem for elliptic curves (ECDLP)**:

- **Given:** An elliptic curve E over $\mathbb{F}_p$, where $p > 3$, or over $\mathbb{F}_{2^k}$. A point $G \in E$ and a point P in the cyclic subgroup generated by G.

- **Sought:** A positive integer number n so that $P = nG$.

  n is called the *discrete logarithm* of P to base G.

We have added the requirement that P should be in the cyclic subgroup generated by G so that the ECDLP always has a solution.

Now, it is very easy to specialize the earlier generic formulation of the Diffie-Hellman key exchange protocol (see *Figure 7.1*) to elliptic curves:

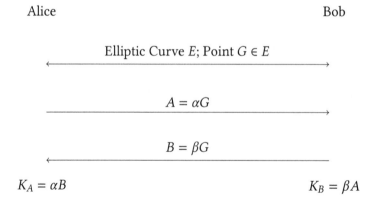

Alice   Bob

Elliptic Curve E; Point $G \in E$

$A = \alpha G$

$B = \beta G$

$K_A = \alpha B$ $K_B = \beta A$

Figure 8.8: Diffie-Hellman key exchange protocol over an elliptic curve E

As in the generic formulation, we should note that the first step of the protocol in *Figure 8.8*, namely publicly agreeing on a curve E and a point G on E, can be performed *a-priori*, which means at some time in the past, for example, by putting curve and point into a public standard.

The (random) numbers α and β are Alice's and Bob's secret keys, respectively, and should never be disclosed. They compute the same shared secret, because

$$K_A = \alpha B = \alpha(\beta G) = \beta(\alpha G) = \beta A = K_B$$

Diffie-Hellman key exchange example:

Take the elliptic curve

$$E : y^2 = x^3 + x + 1$$

over $\mathbb{F}_{97}$ and the public point $G = (76, 82)$ on E. Alice's secret key is the number $\alpha = 87$. She computes the public point $A = 87 \cdot G = (54, 31)$ and sends it to Bob. Bob's secret key is $\beta = 13$. He computes the public point $B = 13 \cdot G = (34, 32)$ and sends it to Alice.

Both then proceed to compute the shared secret point K on E:

- Alice computes $K_A = 87 \cdot (34, 32) = (45, 31)$

- Bob computes $K_B = 13 \cdot (54, 31) = (45, 31)$

They can now use the x coordinate of K as their shared secret.

Double-and-add algorithm:

Going through the previous example, maybe you have wondered how, for example, Bob computes $B = 13 \cdot G$ on E. One simple way would be just to add G to itself 13 times, but there is a better way to compute a product nP on E.

Just like in *Chapter 7, Public-Key Cryptography*, when we discussed the square-and-multiply algorithm for computing powers, we start by looking at the binary representation of the integer factor n:

$$n = \sum_{i=0}^{b} n_i 2^i \text{ with } n_i \in \{0, 1\}$$

Now we have

$$n \cdot P = \sum_{i=0}^{b} n_i (2^i \cdot P) = \sum_{i : n_i = 1} (2^i \cdot P)$$

The points $2^i \cdot P = 2 \cdot (2^{i-1} \cdot P)$ can be computed by repeated doubling of P. After that, the points $2^i \cdot P$, where $n_i = 1$, are added. Therefore this algorithm is called *double-and-add*. In contrast to the naive repeated adding approach, which has a running time in $\mathcal{O}(n)$, the double-and-add algorithm has running time in $\mathcal{O}(\log_2(n))$, which is a massive improvement.

If an attacker, Eve, tries to break the key agreement based on **elliptic curve Diffie-Hellman (ECDH)** or some other cryptographic mechanism that uses an elliptic curve, she will learn the curve's domain parameters, the base point G, and two points A, B on the curve, which are the product of G and some random, secret integers α and β, respectively.

Eve's goal is to determine a secret integer α from the product αG she can observe. Whether she can do this efficiently – that is, in a polynomial time – or not, depends on the computational hardness of the ECDLP in the cyclic subgroup $\mathbb{G}$ of E generated by the base point G.

While it is easy to solve ECDLP for cyclic groups with a small number of elements, it turns out that the best algorithms we know to solve it for large values require $\mathcal{O}(\sqrt{n})$ steps where n is the order of group $\mathbb{G}$, that is, the number of elements in that group.

As a result, if Alice and Bob want their cryptographic algorithm to have a security level of, say, 128 bits, they can simply choose a secure curve where the order of group $\mathbb{G}$ generated by a base point G is $n \geq 2^{256}$. This is because $\sqrt{2^{256}} = (2^{256})^{\frac{1}{2}} = 2^{128}$.

In the next section, we will discuss how secure curves can be chosen.

8.4   Security of elliptic curves

The security of cryptographic mechanisms based on elliptic curves relies on the following assumptions:

- The elliptic curve discrete logarithm problem is computationally hard for the chosen elliptic curve

- The chosen elliptic curve has no mathematical backdoors

- Alice's and Bob's public keys are authentic

- In the case of ECDH, the Diffie-Hellman problem is computationally hard in the cyclic group G generated by the base point G on the elliptic curve

In *Chapter 7, Public-Key Cryptography*, we already discussed – both for Diffie-Hellman key exchange as well as the RSA algorithm – why it is important for Alice's and Bob's public keys to be authentic. We also explained why the Diffie-Hellman problem must be computationally hard for the key agreement to be secure.

In this chapter, we will discuss how to fulfill the first two assumptions. We'll start by looking at the available algorithms for determining discrete logarithms over elliptic curves.

8.4.1 Generic algorithms for finding discrete logarithms

The naive algorithm for solving ECDLP computes $2G, 3G, 4G, ...$ all the way up to n, the order of the cyclic group G and compares the elements of this list to the term kG. Obviously, the algorithm requires $O(n)$ steps.

A much faster approach to solving ECDLP involves so-called *collision algorithms* that leverage the *birthday paradoxon*. This is a phenomenon known from probability theory that refers to the fact that it is easier to find collisions than specific elements in a set. As a result, these algorithms reduce the number of required steps from $O(n)$ to $O(\sqrt{n})$ [166].

To give you an idea how collision algorithms work, we will now describe two such algorithms, the *Babystep-Giantstep algorithm* and *Pollard's Rho algorithm*. We have deliberately left out the more subtle mathematical details. If you want to completely understand the mathematics behind these algorithms, [166] is a good source of information.

Shanks' babystep-giantstep algorithm

Let G be a base point on an elliptic curve E and G be a cyclic group of order n generated by G. Further, let P be an element of G. That is, $P = kG$. The babystep-giantstep algorithm proposed by the American mathematician Daniel Shanks finds the unique integer k and, thus, solves ECDLP as follows:

1. Compute $N = \lceil \sqrt{n} \rceil$, the smallest integer that is greater than or equal to $\sqrt{n}$.

2. Compute the *babysteps* as the list of elements

$$G, \ 2G, \ 3G, \ ..., \ NG$$

3. Express k as $k = i + jN$ and compute the *giantsteps* as the list of elements

$$kG - NG, \ kG - 2NG, \ ..., \ kG - (N - 1)NG$$

4. Look for a collision between the babysteps and the giantsteps by iterating through $0 \leq i, j < N$. If $iG = kG - jNG$ for some specific values of i and j, then the unique integer k is equal to $i + jN$.

The collision between iG (from the babystep list) and $kG - jNG$ (from the giantstep list) allows you to determine k and, thus, solve ECDLP. This is because, if we substitute k by the expression $i + jN$ from step 3, it holds for the giantstep $kG - jNG$ that:

$$kG - jNG = G(k - jN) = G(i + jN - jN) = iG$$

Thus, the algorithm returns the desired integer k as $i + jN$ using the values of i, j for which the collision happens. Because the algorithm needs to compute $\sqrt{n}$ babysteps and giantsteps, it is easy to see that it requires $\mathcal{O}(\sqrt{n})$ steps.

Pollard's ρ algorithm

This algorithm for solving the discrete logarithm problem was proposed in 1978 by the British mathematician John Pollard. With a slight modification, it can also be used to solve ECDLP.

As with the previous algorithm, let G be a base point on an elliptic curve E and $\mathbb{G}$ be a cyclic group of order n generated by G. Further, let $P = kG$ with some unknown k.

Pollard's ρ algorithm finds k and, therefore, solves ECDLP as follows:

1. Split the group G into three sets of roughly the same size and select a random mapping $f : G \rightarrow G$. If the mapping $f : G \rightarrow G$ is sufficiently random, one can prove that a collision should be expected after $\sqrt{\pi n/2}$ elements where n is the order of group G (see, for instance, [166] for detailed mathematical proof).

2. Using step 1, find numbers a, b, c, and d such that:

$$aP + bG = cP + dG$$

3. Once these numbers – that is, the collision – are found, rewrite the preceding equation as:

$$aP - cP = dG - bG$$

which is equivalent to:

$$(a - c)P = (d - b)G$$

and, since $P = kG$, can be rewritten as:

$$((a - c)k)G = (d - b)G$$

4. Based on the preceding equation, observe that $(a - c)k = (d - b)$ (mod n). Therefore, $k = (d - b)(a - c)^{-1}$.

Like Shanks' algorithm, Pollard's ρ algorithm requires $O(\sqrt{n})$ steps. Both algorithms are *generic* in the sense that they can be applied to the discrete logarithm problem in any group, that is, they do not use any special properties of elliptic curves. Here lies the real advantage of working with elliptic curves compared to other, less abstract groups such as $\mathbb{F}_p^*$. Apart from some special cases, *there are no known shortcuts for computing discrete logarithms in elliptic curves.* We'll now look at these special cases.

8.4.2   Algorithms for solving special cases of ECDLP

Because of their mathematical properties, some elliptic curves allow you to take shortcuts when solving ECDLP. In 1991, mathematicians Alfred Menezes, Scott Vanstone, and Tatsuaki Okamoto published an algorithm that reduces ECDLP to a DLP in the multiplicative group of a finite field.

They showed that for supersingular elliptic curves, the reduction takes probabilistic polynomial time. This, in turn, can undermine the security of an elliptic curve because subexponential algorithms are known for solving DLP in finite fields.

The **Menezes-Vanstone-Okamoto (MOV)** algorithm uses a so-called *bilinear map e* to map two points on an elliptic curve E defined over a field $\mathbb{F}_q$ to an element in the finite field $\mathbb{F}_{q^d}$ where d is the *embedding degree* specific to the elliptic curve E.

Let G be a base point on an elliptic curve E and G be a cyclic group of order n generated by G. Further, let Q be another point on curve E that has order n and is linearly independent to G, in other words, there is no such m that $Q = mG$.

Finally, let $P = kG$ with some unknown, unique integer k that we must find to solve ECDLP. The MOV algorithm solves ECDLP as follows:

1. Compute the bilinear maps $e(G, Q)$ and $e(kG, Q)$.

2. Observe that – because e is bilinear – the following equation holds:

$$e(kG, Q) = e(G, Q)^k$$

3. Based on the observation in step 2, set $u = e(G, Q)$ and $v = e(kG, Q)$. It holds that:

$$v = e(G, Q)^k = u^k$$

4. Solve the DLP in the finite field $\mathbb{F}_q^d$ by finding the unique integer k given u^k and u.

As a result, the MOV algorithm reduces solving ECDLP on the elliptic curve E to solving DLP in the finite field $\mathbb{F}_{q^d}$. Whether this has an impact on the security of an elliptic curve or not depends on the specific choice of the curve.

For most randomly chosen elliptic curves, the MOV algorithm reduces ECDLP on these curves to a much harder DLP in the corresponding finite field [166] because the embedding degree d is very large.

However, some curves can be mapped to finite fields with a small embedding degree where solving DLP is computationally feasible. As an example, let E be a supersingular elliptic curve defined over the finite field $\mathbb{F}_p$ where $p \geq 5$ is a prime.

Now suppose we choose as the base point a point G of order n that divides the total number of points on E. In that case – we omit the exact mathematical explanation here – n has an embedding degree 2 in $\mathbb{F}_p$. As a result, ECDLP on a supersingular elliptic curve over $\mathbb{F}_p$ can be reduced to solving DLP in $\mathbb{F}_{p^2}$ for which subexponential algorithms are known [166]. This is also the reason why, in general, supersingular curves are not be used in elliptic curve cryptography.

Another special case are so-called *anomalous* elliptic curves. An anomalous elliptic curve E is a curve defined over a finite field $\mathbb{F}_p$ where $p \geq 3$ and the number of points in E is equal to p. For such curves, the following algorithm can be used to solve ECDLP:

1. Let P, G be points in anomalous elliptic curve E defined over a finite field $\mathbb{F}_p$, and $P = kG$ with the unknown unique integer k.

2. Choose a second elliptic curve E' defined over the field of p-adic numbers $\mathbb{Q}_p$ whose reduction modulo p is the original curve E.

3. Lift points P, G to points P', G' in E' (again, we omit the mathematical details of how this is done or why it works).

4. Compute $pa = \log_E(pP')$ and $pb = \log_E(pG')$.

5. Finally, compute $k = a^{-1}b \pmod{p}$.

Because of these efficient algorithms to solve the ECDLP, anomalous and supersingular elliptic curves are mostly ruled out for cryptographic purposes. So, which properties does a *secure* elliptic curve need to have?

8.4.3   Secure elliptic curves – the mathematical perspective

From the preceding discussion, it should be clear that not every elliptic curve is suitable for cryptography. An elliptic curve used for cryptographic purposes must be *cryptographically strong*, which is just another way of saying that the ECDLP instance for this curve must be computationally hard.

In their *Technical Guideline 03111: Elliptic Curve Cryptography* [42], the German Federal Office for Information Security define the following four criteria an elliptic curve must fulfill for the ECDLP to be computationally hard:

- The order n of the base point G is a sufficiently large prime number (as of today, it must be at least 224 bits)

- The order n must be different from prime p used to define the finite field $\mathbb{F}_p$ to avoid the elliptic curve being anomalous

- The specific ECDLP instance must not be reducible to the DLP in a multiplicative group $\mathbb{F}_{p^r}$ for a small integer r (in other words, it must hold that $p \neq 1 \pmod{n}$ for all $1 \leq r \leq 10^4$)

- The class number of the principal order belonging to the endomorphism ring of the curve should be at least 200

As we will see later in this chapter, all elliptic curves supported by the TLS 1.3 standard meet the above criteria and so – from the mathematical point of view – can be considered to be cryptographically strong. This means the prime numbers involved and therefore the key lengths required for elliptic curves can be chosen much smaller than for RSA or Diffie-Hellman over $\mathbb{F}_p^*$ (see [126]):

Security Strength in Bits	Block Cipher	Length of RSA Modulus n	Length of prime p in DH over $\mathbb{F}_p^*$	Order of public base point G in ECDH
≤ 80	2-Key 3DES	1024	1024	160-223
112	3-Key 3DES	2048	2048	224-255
128	AES-128	3072	3072	256-383
192	AES-192	7680	7680	384-511
256	AES-256	15360	15360	≥ 512

Table 8.1: Equivalent key lengths of symmetric and asymmmetric algorithms

8.4.4 A potential backdoor in Dual_EC_DRBG

Dual_EC_DRBG is a pseudorandom number generator based on elliptic curve cryptography. From 2006 to 2014, it was among the algorithms officially recommended by NIST in their *Special Publication 800-90A Random Number Generation Using Deterministic Random Bit Generators*. In 2014, NIST withdraw the algorithm based on substantial suspicion in the cryptographic community that the algorithm contained a cryptographic backdoor inserted by NSA, the authors of the algorithm.

Even before its official publication, numerous renowned cryptographers voiced concerns about Dual_EC_DRBG's security because the algorithm's design lends itself to a backdoor insertion. More importantly, the absence of a backdoor could only be verified by the algorithm's designers.

Figure 8.9 shows a generic architecture of a pseudorandom number generator. Initially, the internal, secret state s is seeded using a truly random seed s_0, for example, the sequence of the computer mouse coordinates, the time between the keyboard taps or the hard disk latency. From there on, state s is used as input into a cryptographically secure hash function $h()$ to produce pseudorandom numbers r.

The hash function h is deterministic. Given a constant (or repeating) state s, it would therefore produce identical output r. To avoid this, function $g(s)$ – for example, a second hash function – is used to update state s. If the value of s was s_0 in the current iteration, the value for the next iteration would be $g(s_0)$.

Obviously, if Eve knew the value of s, she could predict every future r because she could compute every subsequent state $g(s)$ and, knowing that state, every subsequent output $r = h(g(s))$. Fortunately, because h is a cryptographically secure hash function, it is computationally infeasible for Eve to reverse it. Hence, Eve cannot reconstruct s from r.

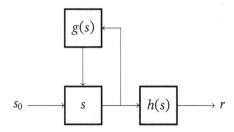

Figure 8.9: Basic architecture of a pseudorandom number generator

Figure 8.10 shows the architecture of the Dual_EC_DRBG pseudorandom number generator.

Analogous to the generic architecture in *Figure 8.9*, a truly random seed s_0 is initially used to seed the internal, secret state s. Next, the algorithm multiplies an elliptic curve point P by s to obtain an intermediate value r. Finally, to produce a pseudorandom number, Dual_EC_DRBG multiplies a second elliptic curve point Q by r and outputs the x coordinate of the resulting point rQ, the 16 most significant bits being discarded [165].

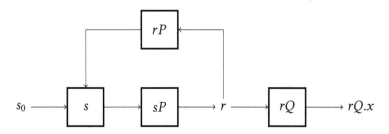

Figure 8.10: Architecture of the Dual_EC_DRBG pseudorandom number generator

To break Dual_EC_DRBG, Eve must compute r given rQ (we can neglect the fact that she does not know the 16 most significant bits of rQ because 16 bits can be easily brute-forced). Computing r from rQ is equivalent to solving ECDLP, and we learned earlier in this chapter that solving ECDLP for cryptographically secure elliptic curves is computationally hard.

As a result, operation rQ can be in principle viewed as a one-way function, making it impossible for Eve to determine Dual_EC_DRBG's secret internal state s from its output rQ. However, this only holds if the points P and Q were chosen randomly.

For the Dual_EC_DRBG specification in NIST's Special Publication 800-90A, no explanation was given how its designers at NSA generated P and Q. As an example, based on what is publicly known, no NUMS numbers were used. Without such assurance, there is a risk of the following cryptographic backdoor. Assume that P and Q were chosen such that:

$$P = eQ$$

for some secret number e known only to Dual_EC_DRBG designers. If this is the case and Eve, being one of the algorithm's designers, knows that secret e, then she can compute:

$$e(rQ)$$

Because $e(rQ)$ is associative, Eve can express it as $r(eQ)$. Because $P = eQ$, Eve can compute:

$$r(eQ) = rP = s,$$

thereby obtaining the secret internal state s. With the knowledge of s, Eve can calculate every subsequent pseudorandom number rQ and every subsequent internal state s.

While there is no definitive proof that Dual_EC_DRBG contains the above backdoor, the classified NSA files leaked by Edward Snowden in 2013 revealed the existence of a clandestine NSA operation codenamed BULLRUN whose aim was to break the encryption of online communication by inserting vulnerabilities into encryption systems and IT equipment. Based on Snowden's leaked files, the New York Times reported that the NSA deliberately became the sole editor of the Dual_EC_DRBG standard and concluded that the standard indeed contained a backdoor.

8.4.5   Secure elliptic curves: security engineering perspective

As illustrated by the Dual_EC_DRBG example, the mathematical perspective on the security of elliptic curves is not sufficient. As cryptographers Dan Bernstein and Tanja Lange explain in their SafeCurves initiative [22], preventing backdoors in cryptographic mechanisms based on elliptic curves requires *rigidity*.

Rigidity refers to a curve generation process where the number of curves that can be generated is limited or, to put it in the words of Bernstein and Lange, where the *ECC security story is as simple as possible*.

With rigidity, Eve can only succeed if some curve in that limited set is vulnerable to a secret attack known only to Eve. In contrast, without rigidity, Eve can simply generate curves until she finds one that is vulnerable to her secret attack.

A fully rigid curve generation process must be therefore completely explainable. An example given in [22] is a curve generation process where the following applies:

- Only prime numbers larger than 2^{224} are used for security reasons

- The smallest prime larger than 2^{224} is chosen for efficiency reasons

- Only curves of the shape $y^2 = x^3 - 3x + b$ are considered for efficiency reasons

- The smallest positive integer b is used that meets the security criteria

Similarly, rigidity must also be used when selecting elliptic curve-based parameters for cryptographic algorithms like points P and Q used in Dual_EC_DRBG. Only then is it possible for parties other than the algorithm designers to arrive at a reasonable degree of confidence that the algorithm has no backdoors. We'll now take a look at the specific curves defined in TLS 1.3.

8.5 Elliptic curves in TLS 1.3

Elliptic curves provide one option within the TLS handshake protocol for server Alice and client Bob to agree on a shared secret. First of all, Alice and Bob have to negotiate whether they want to use elliptic curves at all, and which curve they are going to use.

The `supported_groups` extension that client Bob sends to server Alice in his `ClientHello` message to negotiate the cryptographic parameters contains a list of groups that Bob wants to use to establish the secret key with Alice via ECDH. The list is ordered according to Bob's preference in descending order.

Technically, the `supported_groups` extension has a field called `extension_data`. This field contains a value of the type `NamedGroupList`, defined as shown in *Listing 4*.

```
struct {
    NamedGroup named_group_list<2..2^16-1>;
} NamedGroupList;
```

Listing 4: `NamedGroupList` *in* `supported_groups` *extension*

Each entry in `NamedGroupList` is a named group supported in the TLS 1.3 standard. When elliptic curve cryptography is used, these named groups refer to specific elliptic curves that Alice and Bob can use to establish their secret shared key via ECDH when using TLS 1.3. The valid choices for a `NamedGroup` – including the supported elliptic curves – are defined as shown in *Listing 5*.

The values `secp256r1(0x0017)`, `secp384r1(0x0018)`, `secp521r1(0x0019)`, `x25519(0x001D)`, and `x448(0x001E)` indicate the named elliptic curves supported by the TLS 1.3 standard. These curves are defined either in the **Federal Information Processing Standards (FIPS)** publication *FIPS 186-4 Digital Signature Standard (DSS)* [128] or in **Internet Research Task Force (IRTF)** *RFC 7748 Elliptic Curves for Security* [86].

The value range `ecdhe_private_use(0xFE00..0xFEFF)` is reserved for private use as defined in RFC 8126. RFC 8126 outlines the guidelines for writing an IANA considerations

```
enum {
    /* Elliptic Curve Groups (ECDHE) */
    obsolete_RESERVED(0x0001..0x0016),
    secp256r1(0x0017), secp384r1(0x0018), secp521r1(0x0019),
    obsolete_RESERVED(0x001A..0x001C),
    x25519(0x001D), x448(0x001E),

    /* Finite Field Groups (DHE) */

    ffdhe2048(0x0100), ffdhe3072(0x0101), ffdhe4096(0x0102),
    ffdhe6144(0x0103), ffdhe8192(0x0104),

    /* Reserved Code Points */
    ffdhe_private_use(0x01FC..0x01FF),
    ecdhe_private_use(0xFE00..0xFEFF),
    obsolete_RESERVED(0xFF01..0xFF02),
    (0xFFFF)
} NamedGroup;
```

Listing 5: Named finite fields and elliptic curves supported in TLS 1.3

section in RFCs. These guidelines ensure that parameter values used for the protocol's extensibility have no conflicting uses.

For all IETF protocols, the role of a central record keeper that coordinates the allocation of these values and, by doing this, ensures interoperability, is filled by the **Internet Assigned Numbers Authority (IANA)**.

Any parameters or values declared as for *private use* according to RFC 8126 are for *private or local use only, with the type and purpose defined by the local site* and IANA makes no attempt to *prevent multiple sites from using the same value in different ways*. Thus, TLS 1.3 theoretically even allows Alice and Bob to choose their own elliptic curves (which is not advisable from a cryptographic point of view unless Alice and Bob know exactly what they are doing).

The obsolete_RESERVED value ranges seen in *Listing 5* exist for legacy reasons. These values refer to groups used in previous TLS versions. However, these groups – mostly specific elliptic curves from previous TLS versions – have various practical or theoretical weaknesses, or have been used very little in the past. As a result, the TLS 1.3 standard considers these curves obsolete. As a result, if Alice and Bob want to use TLS version 1.3, they are not permitted to use the insecure obsolete_RESERVED curves.

8.5.1   Curve secp256r1

Digital Signature Standard FIPS-186 [128] specifies 15 elliptic curves that the **National Institute of Standards and Technology (NIST)** recommends for use by the US federal government. All 15 curves were generated using a method described in the IEEE 1363-2000 and the ANS X9.62 standards.

Curve secp256r1 is one of the elliptic curves defined in FIPS-186. In the standard, it is referred to as curve P-256. The curve is defined over a prime field $\mathbb{F}_p$ with the prime $p = 2^{256} - 2^{224} + 2^{192} + 2^{96} - 1$, hence the name P-256.

Curve P-256 is defined by the equation:

$$y^2 = x^3 - 3x + b$$

The coefficient -3 (mod p) in the term $-3x$ was chosen for reasons of computational efficiency. The coefficient b is generated based on the output of a cryptographic hash function, making P-256 a *pseudo-random* curve. In FIPS-186, the hash function used is the – in the meantime outdated and insecure – SHA-1 algorithm.

More precisely, coefficient b is computed in two steps:

1. Taking a 160-bit input seed specified for curve P-256 and computing SHA-1 output c for this seed value.

2. Then computing b such that $b^2 c = -27$ (mod p).

As an example, the SHA-1 input seed for curve P-256 in hexadecimal notation is:

```
c49d3608 86e70493 6a6678e1 139d26b7 819f7e90
```

P-256's security strength is equivalent to that of a 128-bit block cipher. In other words, with the currently known cryptanalytic techniques, Eve would need to perform 2^{127} guesses on average to break a cryptosystem whose security is based on curve P-256. However, this only applies as long as Eve has no access to a large enough quantum computer.

8.5.2   Curve secp384r1

Curve `secp384r1` is another elliptic curve over the prime field defined in FIPS-186 where it is referred to as curve P-384. It is defined over the prime field $\mathbb{F}_p$ with $p = 2^{384} - 2^{128} - 2^{96} + 2^{32} - 1$.

Like P-256, the elliptic curve P-256 has the form:

$$y^2 = x^3 - 3x + b$$

with the SHA-1 seed value for generating coefficient b defined as:

```
a335926a a319a27a 1d00896a 6773a482 7acdac73
```

Curve P-384 has the security strength of 192 bits against attacks using classical computers.

8.5.3   Curve secp521r1

The third NIST curve included in the TLS 1.3 standard is curve `secp521r1`. It is also defined in FIPS-186 where it is referred to as curve P-521. P-521 is defined over the prime field $\mathbb{F}_p$ with $p = 2^{521} - 1$.

Like P-256 and P-384, the curve P-521 is defined by the equation:

$$y^2 = x^3 - 3x + b$$

with the SHA-1 seed value for coefficient b being:

```
d09e8800 291cb853 96cc6717 393284aa a0da64ba
```

The security strength of curve P-521 is 256 bits. As with all elliptic curves, this only holds as long as Eve uses classical computers. If a large enough quantum computer is ever built and Eve can use it to attack the elliptic curve-based key establishment phase between Alice and Bob, she will be able to determine their secret key in polynomial time.

From the security perspective, there is a potential downside all three NIST curves – P-256, P-384, and P-521 – have in common. Specifically, it has to do with these curves being pseudo-random.

Previously in this chapter, we saw that the security of elliptic curve cryptography – for instance, the security of the key establishment between Alice and Bob when they use the ECDH protocol – depends on the computational hardness of ECDLP.

We also discussed that not all elliptic curves are suitable for cryptography as there are curves for which ECDLP can be solved in practice even using today's classical computers. As a result, such curves are not suitable for cryptographic applications.

When parameters defining an elliptic curve, for instance, its coefficients, are given without a concise explanation of how one has arrived at these specific values, there is a risk of a *cryptanalytic backdoor.* Specifically, Eve might have found a new attack known only to her and propose to standardize one or more curves that are vulnerable to this attack [22].

NIST curves P-256, P-384, and P-521 are generated using SHA-1 seeds that cannot be explained. As a result, some cryptographers voiced concerns that these curves might be deliberately chosen to have a mathematical weakness only known to the **National Security Agency (NSA)**, which helped NIST to specify them.

NIST has claimed that the use of SHA-1 to compute coefficient b ensures the curves were not predetermined because of the following:

- It can be verified that b is derived from the specific seed

- Given the properties of cryptographic hash functions, it is computationally infeasible to find an input seed that yields the desired hash value

However, Bernstein and Lange pointed out [22] that having enough computing resources, an attacker could simply generate curves for a large number of random parameters until they find a weak curve.

8.5.4   Curve 25519

Curve 25519 is defined in RFC 7748, where it is referred to as curve25519. It was proposed in 2005 by the American-German cryptographer Dan Bernstein [24] and attracted interest from the wider cryptographic community after the discovery of a potential backdoor in the **Dual Elliptic Curve Deterministic Random Bit Generator (Dual_EC_DRBG)** algorithm based on the then-popular standardized elliptic curve P-256.

curve25519 is an elliptic curve over a prime field $\mathbb{F}_p$ where p is equal to $2^{255} - 19$, hence the name of the curve. It is a so-called *Montgomery curve* defined by the equation:

$$y^2 = x^3 + 486662x^2 + x$$

Montgomery curves are simply a special form of elliptic curves defined by equations of the form $By^2 = x^3 + Ax^2 + x$ where $B \neq 0$ and $A \neq \pm2$.

curve25519 offers a security level of approximately 128 bits. In other words, the curve25519 security level is roughly equivalent to that of a 128-bit block cipher. Importantly, curve25519 is generated in a deterministic way to meet a number of required (security) properties. Why is this important? As discussed earlier in this chapter, if the generation process of a specific elliptic curve can be fully explained, Alice and Bob are assured that the curve was not generated to be weak.

Otherwise, Eve could join a standardization effort and propose standardizing an elliptic curve vulnerable to some secret attack that only Eve knows about. As a result, as long as that attack remains unknown to the public, Eve would be able to completely break the security of the communication channel between Alice and Bob completely unnoticed, that is, without having to tamper with the communication traffic.

curve25519 properties allow you to implement constant-time computation and a scalar multiplication that, by design, will never produce exceptions. The constant execution time is ensured by the design of curve25519 where the same sequence of computations is done for all secret key values.

As a result, Alice and Bob can use X25519 (the key agreement scheme based on curve25519) implementations that are resistant to various types of so-called *side channel analysis*, an implementation-level attack exploiting the statistical link between the intermediate values processed by a cryptographic algorithm and physical quantities such as instantaneous power consumption, execution time, or cache-based timing patterns, just to name a few.

In addition, cryptographic computations based on curve25519 are fast on a wide range of instruction set architectures. Thanks to careful design choices, cryptographic operations on curve25519 can be performed about twice as fast compared to other elliptic curves with a similar security level.

8.5.5 Curve 448

Curve 448 is also defined in RFC 7748 where it is referred to as curve448. It was proposed in 2015 by the American computer scientist and cryptographer Mike Hamburg [79] for inclusion in TLS, in order to equip the TLS standard with a cryptographically strong curve alongside curve25519.

curve448 is named after the prime $2^{448} - 2^{224} - 1$ used for the prime field $\mathbb{F}_p$ over which the curve is defined. curve448 is a Montgomery curve defined by the equation:

$$y^2 = x^3 + 156326x^2 + x$$

and offers a security level of roughly 224 bits. RFC 7748 describes this security level as a trade-off between computational performance and more conservative assumptions about the capabilities of future attackers.

In particular, the much lower security level of 128 bits offered by elliptic curves such as curve25519 is sufficient to ensure security against classical computers. The introduction of *cryptographically relevant* quantum computers, on the other hand, would break even curve448. However, designers of security systems might prefer a higher security level to accommodate future advances in cryptanalysis of elliptic curves, especially in applications without strict performance requirements.

The term *cryptographically relevant* quantum computer refers to a quantum computer capable of breaking public-key cryptography used in practice, that is, public-key cryptography with practically relevant security level. This, in turn, requires the quantum computer to have a sufficient number of logical qubits – in the order of several thousands – that can be made to preserve their coherence for several days to weeks using quantum error correction.

As of January 2023, the largest commercial quantum computer is IBM's Osprey with 433 physical qubits [138]. However, its predecessor, IBM's Eagle quantum processor, released in 2021, had 127 qubits [13] and IBM has a 1,121-qubit quantum processor Condor on their roadmap for 2023 [107]. Although one has to differentiate between physical and logical qubits (the latter being harder to realize), one has to state that if the number of qubits continues to grow like this, quantum computers might indeed pose a problem for public-key cryptography in the future.

Like X25519, X448 is designed to be resistant against popular types of side channel attacks, especially against *timing attacks* that try to exploit small differences in the execution time of a cryptographic algorithm based on the internal values it processes. To eliminate this information leakage, computations on curve448 defined in RFC 7748 are designed to have constant execution time regardless of the actual internal values being processed.

8.5.6 Elliptic curve Diffie-Hellman in TLS 1.3

If Alice and Bob use the ECDH key agreement with elliptic curves secp256r1, secp384r1, or secp521r1, they follow the ECKAS-DH1 scheme defined in the IEEE 1363-2000 standard illustrated in *Figure 8.11*.

When using the ECKAS-DH1 scheme, Alice and Bob first agree on the secret value derivation primitive. IEEE 1363-2000 standards defines two possible choices: **Elliptic Curve Secret Value Derivation Primitive, Diffie-Hellman version (ECSVDP-DH)** and **Elliptic Curve Secret Value Derivation Primitive, Diffie-Hellman version with cofactor multiplication (ECSVDP-DHC)**.

Given a point G on an elliptic curve, ECSVDP-DH computes the shared secret value as follows:

1. Take the secret random number α of one communicating party, say Alice, and the public key share βG of the other communicating party, say Bob, and compute an elliptic curve point $P = \alpha(\beta G)$.

2. Terminate the protocol if P equals O, the point at infinity.

3. Otherwise, output the x coordinate of P as the shared secret value.

In contrast, ECSVDP-DHC computes the shared secret value using the following steps:

1. If Alice and Bob want the calculations to be compatible with ECSVDP-DH, compute an integer $t = h^{-1}\alpha \pmod{n}$. Otherwise, set t to one communicating party's, say Alice's, secret random number α. Here, n is the order of the group $\mathbb{G}$ generated by the base point g, and h is the so-called *cofactor* of the elliptic curve, that is, the number of subgroups holding the points of the elliptic curve.

2. Using the other communicating party's, say Bob's, public key share βG, compute an elliptic curve point $P = ht(\beta G)$.

3. Terminate the protocol if P equals O, the point at infinity.

4. Otherwise, output the x coordinate of P as the shared secret value.

Next, Alice and Bob agree on the key derivation function. IEEE 1363-2000 specifies two possible choices: SHA-1 (which is no longer secure) and RIPEMD-160. With these two parameters set, Alice and Bob exchange their public key shares αG and βG, and use the selected secret value derivation primitive to compute the shared secret key.

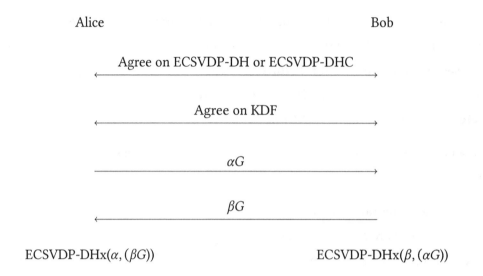

Figure 8.11: ECKAS-DH1 key agreement scheme defined in the IEEE 1363-2000 standard

If Alice and Bob use the elliptic curves 25519 or 448, they compute αG and βG, respectively, and exchange these values in the KeyShareEntry.key_exchange structure. Here, G is the standard public base point on the elliptic curve chosen by them.

Next, Alice computes the shared secret value as $\alpha(\beta G)$ and Bob computes it as $\beta(\alpha G)$. The resulting value is used raw, without post-processing. However, Alice and Bob must verify that the computed Diffie-Hellman shared secret is not an all-zero value. If it is an all-zero value, they must immediately terminate the TLS session.

8.5.7   ECDH parameters in TLS 1.3

Both server Alice and client Bob encode their ECDH parameters in the KeyShare structure, in the key_exchange opaque field of a KeyShareEntry. When elliptic curves secp256r1, secp384r1, or secp521r1 are used, the key_exchange field stores the serialized value of the UncompressedPointRepresentation structure shown in *Listing 6*.

The variables X and Y in *Listing 6* are a binary representation of x coordinate and y coordinate in network byte order. The size of the variables X and Y is determined by the parameters of the elliptic curve that Alice and Bob agreed upon.

```
struct {
    uint8 legacy_form = 4;
    opaque X[coordinate_length];

    opaque Y[coordinate_length];
} UncompressedPointRepresentation;
```

Listing 6: Uncompressed elliptic curve point representation in TLS 1.3

As an example, if the curve used is secp256r1, then both X and Y use 32 octets – if necessary, left-padded by zeros. In the case of the secp384r1 curve, X and Y have the size of 48 octets each and 66 octets each for the secp512r1 curve.

If Alice and Bob use one of the curves secp256r1, secp384r1, or secp521r1, they must validate each other's public values. That is, Alice needs to verify that Bob's public value βG is a valid point on the elliptic curve, and Bob must do the same for Alice's public value αG. This includes the verification of the following for the public value:

- It is not the identity element $\mathbb{O}$ (that is, not the point at infinity)

- It has the expected representation for its coordinates x and y in the underlying finite field

- It is a point on the correct elliptic curve

- It has the correct order

Altogether, the verification criteria ensure that the public values αG and βG are in the correct elliptic-curve subgroup and are not identity elements.

In contrast to previous TLS versions, TLS 1.3 does not allow you to negotiate the point format. This is a good example of how simplicity favors security: if only a single format is accepted, the risk of implementation bugs in the parser code is significantly reduced.

8.5.8   Example: ECDH with curve x25519

RFC 7748 [86] specifies how Alice and Bob must perform ECDH using curve 25519. The protocol is illustrated in *Figure 8.12* and we will follow the notation in RFC 7748 in case you want to look into that standard for more detailed information.

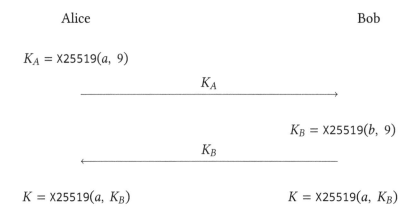

Figure 8.12: ECDHE with curve 25519 as specified in RFC 7748

First, Alice generates a random 32-byte private key, a. She then uses the X25519() function for scalar multiplication on the Montgomery form of the x25519 curve and computes:

$$K_A = \text{X25519}(a,\ 9)$$

where 9 is the u-coordinate of the base point. It is encoded as a byte with value 9, followed by 31 zero bytes.

The u-coordinate is simply part of the pair (u, v) representing the coordinates on a Montgomery curve. Every u-coordinate is an element of the underlying finite field $\mathbb{F}_{2^{255}-19}$.

The X25519 function takes a scalar and a u-coordinate as input and outputs the u-coordinate of the result of scalar multiplication. Thus, the inputs and the output of X25519 are 32-byte strings. Their encoding is specified in RFC 7748.

Alice then transmits K_A to Bob. Analogous to Alice, Bob also generates his private 32-byte key b, computes:

$$K_B = \text{X25519}(b, \ 9),$$

and sends K_B to Alice. Using these values, Alice computes:

$$K = \text{X25519}(a, \ K_B)$$

and Bob computes:

$$K = \text{X25519}(a, \ K_A)$$

In the last step, it is advisable for Alice and Bob to verify that K is not an all-zero value and immediately terminate the protocol if this is the case. Otherwise, if K is not an all-zero value, Alice and Bob now share a secret because it holds that:

$$\text{X25519}(a, \ \text{X25519}(b, \ 9)) = \text{X25519}(b, \ \text{X25519}(a, \ 9)) = K.$$

8.6 Summary

In this chapter we learned about how to use elliptic curves in cryptography and especially within TLS. Elliptic curves are a special kind of mathematical structure that allows for a commutative group operation. It turns out that the discrete logarithm problem in these groups is harder than in other, more common groups such as $\mathbb{F}_p^*$. Moreover, they offer great flexibility via their curve parameters. We have seen how to perform Diffie-Hellman key exchange using these curves, and how secure curves are chosen to be used within the TLS handshake protocol.

In the next chapter, another application of asymmetric cryptography is introduced, namely *digital signatures*. Digital signatures are important tools for providing integrity protection and authenticity, but they can also serve yet another security service, namely *non-repudiation*. In this respect, they are very similar to physical, handwritten signatures.

9

Digital Signatures

In previous chapters, we learned about public-key cryptography and, in particular, public-key cryptography based on elliptic curves. In this chapter, we will take a detailed look at *digital signatures*, a very important cryptographic mechanism based on public-key cryptography.

We are going to see how sender Alice can generate digital signatures for arbitrary messages and how receiver Bob can verify these signatures, thereby verifying that the messages were not manipulated and were actually sent by Alice.

More precisely, in this chapter, we will cover the following topics:

- RSA-based signatures

- Signatures based on discrete logarithms

- The Digital Signature Algorithm

- The Elliptic Curve Digital Signature Algorithm

- The digital signature algorithms used in TLS 1.3

9.1   General considerations

Assume Alice has generated herself a key pair (PK_{Alice}, SK_{Alice}) within some asymmetric cryptosystem. If Alice uses her private key SK_{Alice} to compute some output $s = sig_{Alice}(x)$ based on an input x, this is an operation that can, at least in principle, only be performed by Alice because she is the only one to know SK_{Alice}. This is fundamentally different from the situation when symmetric cryptosystems are used because here, at least two parties know the key K and can perform the same operations.

The fact that only Alice can compute s for some given input x motivates us to interpret sig_{Alice} as a *digital signature*. However, for this to work in practice, some important points need to be clarified:

- There must be some way to *verify* that Alice has produced the signature and that the signed document has not been changed since it has been signed. As this should be possible for any party, the verification step should not involve any secret information, but must be based on the public key PK_{Alice}.

- It must not be possible for an attacker to deduce SK_{Alice} from the signature value s, or to compute s by some other means without knowing SK_{Alice}.

- As with physical, handwritten signatures, the length of the digital signature should be independent from the length of a signed document m. This can be achieved by applying SK_{Alice} on a fixed-length hash value $x = H(m)$ instead of m itself.

- As we have seen in *Chapter 7, Public-Key Cryptography*, operations involving the private key are costly. This is another reason for working with (cryptographic) hash values, which will be shorter than the original documents in most cases.

The use of cryptographic hash functions in connection with digital signatures typically requires at least one important security property of the hash function H, namely *collision resistance*. This means that it must be hard for attacker Eve to find two different inputs x_1, x_2 with the same hash value $H(x_1) = H(x_2)$.

If Eve cannot construct arbitrary collisions, she is also unable to construct a specific collision where she is given some message m, and has to find another input message $\tilde{m}$ so that $H(\tilde{m}) = H(m)$. This weaker form of collision resistance is also called *second preimage resistance* and is of special importance for digital signatures: if Eve manages to find a second preimage $\tilde{m}$, we have

$$sig_{Alice}(\tilde{m}) = sig_{Alice}(m)$$

and Eve could replace m with $\tilde{m}$.

We will discuss collision resistance in greater detail in *Chapter 11, Hash Functions and Message Authentication Codes*. For now, we will simply assume that H is a *secure cryptographic hash function*, which means H is a hash function that has this property.

Based on this assumption, digital signatures can be used as tools for message authentication and entity authentication (see *Chapter 15, Authenticated Encryption*). But because no one but Alice can have produced the signature s over m, Alice cannot repudiate afterward having signed m, or having sent a message involving the signature. This property constitutes a new security objective called *non-repudiation*. Digital signatures are the only cryptographic mechanism by which non-repudiation can be achieved.

In the next two sections, we will see how, in principle, digital signatures can be realized based on the asymmetric cryptosystems we learned about in the previous two chapters. As they are based on the same mathematical problems (factorization problem or discrete logarithm problem), digital signatures basically inherit the same security properties as the corresponding asymmetric cryptosystems. Note however that in order to fully specify a real-world digital signature scheme, many more details need to be fixed, such as how to encode and pad the message, how to generate and use nonces, and so on. You can find some of these nuts and bolts later in this chapter in *Section 9.4, Digital signatures in TLS*.

9.2 RSA-based signatures

An RSA-based signature is generated by applying the private key part of the RSA key pair to the hash value of the message m to be signed. To recap from *Chapter 7, Public-Key*

Cryptography, Alice's RSA key pair has the public key part $PK_{Alice} = (e, n)$, where n is the product of two large primes p and q, and e is some number that is coprime to $\varphi(n) = (p - 1)(q - 1)$. Alice's private key, on the other hand, takes the form $SK_{Alice} = d$, where $d = e^{-1} \mod \varphi(n)$.

To encrypt some message m for Alice, Bob must encode m so that it is a number between 1 and $n - 1$. The cipher is then given by

$$c = m^e \mod n.$$

Alice can decrypt it using her private key d via

$$m = c^d \mod n.$$

In order to **sign** m, we can simply switch the order of the two operations, and use the private key d for encryption, except that we do not encrypt m itself, but its hash value $H(m)$. To be specific,

$$sig_{Alice}(m) = s = H(m)^d \mod n.$$

Alice sends m along with the signature $s = sig_{Alice}(m)$ to Bob.

In order to **verify** the signature, Bob first obtains an authentic copy of Alice's public key $PK_{Alice} = (e, n)$. He then hashes m and checks whether the resulting value matches

$$sig_{Alice}(m)^e \mod n = H(m)^{de} \mod n = H(m).$$

The last equation holds for the same reason that RSA decryption works: because of Euler's theorem (see *Chapter 7, Public-Key Cryptography*), we have $H(m)^{de} \mod n = H(m)$.

To give a concrete example, we let Alice use the same RSA key pair she generated in our example in *Section 7.7.2, Key pair generation* in *Chapter 7, Public-Key Cryptography*:

$$PK_{Alice} = (e, n) = (17, 77) \text{ and } SK_{Alice} = d = 53$$

We assume further that the message m to be signed has hash value $H(m) = 5$. Then

$$sig_{Alice}(m) = 5^{53} \mod 77 = 59.$$

Alice sends the pair $(m, 59)$ to Bob. Using $PK_{Alice} = (17, 77)$, Bob can verify the signature by first applying the hash function H on m. Assuming m has not been changed during transit, he will get $H(m) = 5$ as the result. Now Bob applies Alice's public key to the signature value:

$$sig_{Alice}(m)^d \mod n = 59^{17} \mod 77 = 5,$$

which matches $H(m)$. So, Bob is satisfied that Alice has signed the message m and that m has not been changed since.

9.3 Digital signatures based on discrete logarithms

Other than for RSA signatures, we cannot create a signature based on discrete logarithms simply by encrypting the message m with a private key. This is because in the Diffie-Hellman protocol, we only agree on a shared secret between Alice and Bob. In the ElGamal scheme, Alice uses this shared secret, but not her private key for encryption. Moreover, Alice needs Bob's public key to compute the shared secret. A digital signature scheme should work without knowing any other public keys than the signer's, however.

The solution is to compute a number that depends on the private key α and to add this number to the hash value of the message to be signed. This number is masked with another secret parameter k so that the private key cannot be computed from the signature. The basic scheme can be found in the paper by ElGamal [62] from 1985. However, today, ElGamal signatures are not widely used because in 1990, Schnorr [160] found an improvement in the basic ElGamal scheme that is more efficient and uses shorter signatures. A closely related algorithm is known as the **Digital Signature Algorithm** (**DSA**) and was adopted in 1991 by the **National Institute of Standards and Technology** (**NIST**) as the **Digital Signature Standard** (**DSS**) for the United States.

Note that in the latest version of the DSS [135], the DSA over a finite field is no longer approved for signature generation, and only the **Elliptic Curve DSA (ECDSA)** shall be used. Nevertheless, we discuss the DSA over finite fields in the next subsection because it still needs to be implemented in order to verify earlier signatures generated by DSA. Moreover, we think that the ECDSA is easier to understand if the DSA is discussed first.

9.3.1   Digital Signature Algorithm (DSA)

To set up the scheme, Alice and Bob agree on the following parameters [102]:

- A prime q of N bits, where N must not be larger than the bitlength of the hash function H (see *Chapter 11, Hash Functions and Message Authentication Codes*) used for signing.

- A second, larger prime p so that q is a large divisor of $p - 1$.

- A generator g of the cyclic subgroup of $\mathbb{F}_p^*$ of order q. In order to do so, Alice and Bob choose a random $g_0 \in \mathbb{F}_p^*$ and check if

$$g_0^{(p-1)/q} = 1 \quad \mod p.$$

If this is *not* the case, $g = g_0^{(p-1)/q} \mod p$ is a generator.

To generate her signing key, Alice performs the following steps:

1. She takes a random α, where $0 < \alpha < q$ as her secret signing key SK_{Alice}.

2. Her public key is $PK_{Alice} = A = g^\alpha \mod p$.

To sign a message m, Alice takes the following steps:

1. She applies a hash function H to m. The result $H(m)$ should be in the range $0 < H(m) < q$.

2. She picks a random integer k, where $0 < k < q$, computes $g^k \mod p$, and sets

$$r = (g^k \mod p) \mod q.$$

3. Finally, Alice finds an integer s such that

$$sk = H(m) + \alpha r \mod q,$$

or equivalently,

$$s = k^{-1}(H(m) + \alpha r) \mod q.$$

Her signature is the pair $sig_{Alice}(m) = (r, s)$. She sends $(m, sig_{Alice}(m)) = (m, (r, s))$ to Bob.

To verify Alice's signature, Bob first obtains an authentic copy of Alice's public key $PK_{Alice} = A$. He then proceeds as follows:

1. He applies the hash function to m and gets the number $H(m)$.

2. He then computes $u_1 = s^{-1}H(m) \mod q$ and $u_2 = s^{-1}r \mod q$.

3. He then computes $g^{u_1} A^{u_2} \mod p$. If the result agrees with r modulo q, the signature is verified.

The scheme works because

$$g^{u_1} A^{u_2} \mod p = g^{s^{-1}H(m)} g^{\alpha s^{-1} r} \mod p = g^{s^{-1}(H(m)+\alpha r)} \mod p = g^k \mod p$$

Moreover,

$$r = (g^k \mod p) \mod q,$$

because this was how Alice had defined the number r when she signed m.

It is important that the integer k in the signing step is chosen individually for each message m to be signed. Otherwise, if k is the same for two messages m_1, m_2, the first part r of the signature is the same. Moreover, we have

$$s_1 k = H(m_1) + xr \mod q,$$

$$s_2 k = H(m_2) + xr \mod q.$$

Eve can solve this system of equations for k:

$$k = (s_1 - s_2)^{-1} \cdot (H(m_1) - H(m_2)) \quad \mathrm{mod}\ q$$

Now Eve can forge Alice's signature over some message m_{Eve}.

Indeed, $sig_{Alice}(m_{Eve}) = (r, s_{Eve})$, where

$$r = g^k \quad \mathrm{mod}\ p, \text{ and } s_{Eve} = k^{-1} \cdot (H(m_{Eve}) - H(m_1)) + s_1 \quad \mathrm{mod}\ q$$

Example: To set up the scheme, Alice and Bob agree on the prime numbers $q = 11$ and $p = 23$. Then $2^{p-1/q} = 2^2 = 4 \neq 1 \mod 23$, so they can use $g = 4$ as the generator.

Now, Alice chooses $\alpha = 3$ as her signing key SK_{Alice}. Consequently, her public key is $PK_{Alice} = A = 4^3 \mod 23 = 18$. In order to sign her message m, she applies the hash function on it and gets $H(m) = 5$ as the result. She now picks $k = 7$ randomly and computes the number

$$r = (g^k \mod p) \mod q = (4^7 \mod 23) \mod 11 = 8 \mod 11 = 8$$

Now, she needs to find $7^{-1} \mod 11$. Because $7 \cdot 8 = 56 = 1 \mod 11$, she gets $7^{-1} = 8$ and can compute the second part of the signature:

$$s = k^{-1} \cdot (H(m) + \alpha r) \mod q = 8 \cdot (5 + 3 \cdot 8) \mod 11 = 1$$

Alice sends $(m, (r = 8, s = 1))$ to Bob.

In order to verify the signature, Bob hashes m and gets $H(m) = 5$, if the message was not modified during transit. He also needs to compute $s^{-1} \mod q$. But $s = 1$, so $s^{-1} = 1$ as well. He can now compute $u_1 = s^{-1} H(m) \mod q = 5 \mod 11 = 5$ and $u_2 = s^{-1} r \mod q = 8 \mod 11 = 8$.

Bob now computes

$$g^{u_1} A^{u_2} \mod p = (4^5 \cdot 18^8) \mod 23 =$$
$$((1024 \mod 23) \cdot (11019960576 \mod 23)) \mod 23 = (12 \cdot 16) \mod 23 = 8.$$

This number needs to agree with $r = 8$ (modulo q). But $q = 11$, so Bob gets $8 \mod 11 = 8 = r$, and the signature is verified.

9.3.2 Elliptic Curve Digital Signature Algorithm (ECDSA)

When transferring the DSA algorithm to an elliptic curve E, we just switch the group from $\mathbb{F}_p^*$ to E, so the basic steps will stay the same. We just have to ensure that we switch the objects correctly:

- In DSA, $p - 1$ signifies the group order of $\mathbb{G} = \mathbb{F}_p^*$ and q signifies the order of the cyclic subgroup generated by $g \in \mathbb{G}$. In ECDSA, the group order of E is N, where N is the number of points on E, and n is the order of the cyclic subgroup generated by the multiples of $G \in E$. N can be estimated by using Hasse's theorem (see *Chapter 8, Elliptic Curves*), and n is automatically a divisor of N, because it is the order of a subgroup of E.

- Numbers, if they signify how often a group operation is applied, remain being numbers in the ECDSA. On the other hand, a number A, when seen as an element of $\mathbb{F}_p^*$, becomes a point P on E. In particular, this means that Alice's private key α is still a number in ECDSA, whereas her public key PK_{Alice} becomes a point on E.

- The group operation is written additively in E, so powers g^x become products xG on E, and products $x \cdot y$ become sums $P + Q$ on E.

Bearing this in mind, formulating the ECDSA is not very difficult:

To set up the scheme, Alice and Bob agree on:

- An elliptic curve E of order N over some finite field $\mathbb{F}$

- A point $G \in E$, which generates a large cyclic subgroup of order n

To generate her signing key, Alice performs the following steps:

1. She takes a random α, where $0 < \alpha < n$, as her secret signing key SK_{Alice}.

2. Her public key PK_{Alice} is the point $A = \alpha \cdot G \in E$.

To sign a message m, Alice takes the following steps:

1. She applies a hash function H to m. The result $H(m)$ should be in the range $0 < H(m) < n$.

2. She picks a random integer k, where $0 < k < n$, computes the point $P = k \cdot G = (x_P, y_P)$ on E, and sets

$$r = x_P \mod n.$$

3. Finally, Alice finds an integer s such that

$$sk = H(m) + \alpha r \mod n,$$

or equivalently,

$$s = k^{-1}(H(m) + \alpha r) \mod n.$$

Her signature is the pair $sig_{Alice}(m) = (r, s)$. She sends $(m, sig_{Alice}(m)) = (m, (r, s))$ to Bob.

To verify Alice's signature, Bob first obtains an authentic copy of Alice's public key $PK_{Alice} = A$. He then proceeds as follows:

1. He applies the hash function to m and gets the number $H(m)$.

2. He computes the numbers $u_1 = s^{-1}H(m) \mod n$ and $u_2 = s^{-1}r \mod n$.

3. He computes the point $V = u_1G + u_2A = (x_V, y_V)$ on E. If $x_V \mod n = r$, the signature is verified.

Of course, for ECDSA the same cautionary remark applies as for DSA: the random integer k must be generated individually for each message m to be signed.

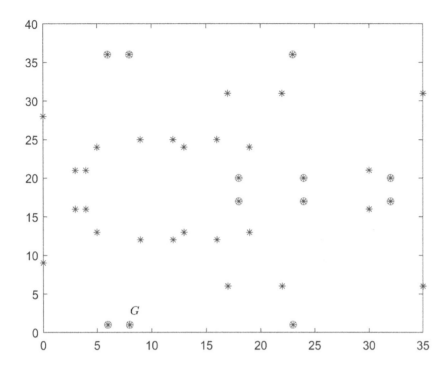

Figure 9.1: The curve $E \; : \; y^2 = x^3 + 7$ over $\mathbb{F}_{37}$. The points of the subgroup generated by $G = (8, 1)$ are drawn with an additional o symbol

Example: Let Alice and Bob use the curve $E \; : \; y^2 = x^3 + 7$ over $\mathbb{F}_{37}$ and the public point $G = (8, 1)$ on E. Then the order of E is $N = 39$, and the order of the subgroup generated by G is $n = 13$. *Figure 9.1* shows this curve, with the points of the subgroup generated by G highlighted.

In order to generate her key pair, Alice chooses $\alpha = 9$ as her private key and computes the point $A = \alpha G = 9 \cdot (8, 1) = (23, 1)$ as her public key.

Now, assume Alice wants to sign a message m with the hash value $H(m) = 4$. To do this, she chooses $k = 7$ and computes $P = k \cdot G = 7 \cdot (8, 1) = (18, 20)$. Therefore, $r = 18$ mod $13 = 5$. In order to compute s, we need the modular inverse of $k = 7$ modulo 13.

Because $2 \cdot 7 = 14 = 1 \mod 13$, we get $k^{-1} = 2$. Now

$$s = k^{-1}(H(m) + \alpha r) \mod n = 2(4 + 5 \cdot 9)) \mod 13 = 98 \mod 13 = 7.$$

So, Alice sends

$$sig_{Alice}(m) = (r, s) = (5, 7)$$

to Bob, along with m.

To verify Alice's signature, Bob first obtains an authentic copy of Alice's public key $PK_{Alice} = A = (23, 1)$. He then computes the hash value over m. If m was not changed during transmission, he will get $H(m) = 4$. Next, Bob computes the numbers

$$u_1 = (s^{-1}H(m)) \mod n = (2 \cdot 4) \mod 13 = 8,$$

$$u_2 = (s^{-1}r) \mod n = (2 \cdot 5) \mod 13 = 10$$

Now, he can compute the point V on E:

$$V = u_1 G + u_2 A = 8 \cdot (8, 1) + 10 \cdot (23, 1) = (32, 20) + (8, 36) = (18, 20)$$

Finally, because $x_V \mod n = 18 \mod 13 = 5 = r$, the signature is verified.

9.4 Digital signatures in TLS 1.3

To agree upon the signature algorithms they want to use during their TLS session, Alice and Bob use two TLS 1.3 extensions. The algorithms for verifying digital signatures in certificates – a topic we will cover in detail in *Chapter 10, Digital Certificates and Certification Authorities* – are transmitted in the `signature_algorithms_cert` extension. The algorithms for digital signatures in `CertificateVerify` messages are transmitted in the `signature_algorithms` extension.

Oftentimes, the set of digital signature algorithms that server Alice implements is different from the one that client Bob implements. The purpose of the `signature_algorithms_cert` extension is to allow Alice and Bob to communicate the algorithms they support and, as a result, determine which algorithms they can use for their TLS session.

If Alice and Bob omit the `signature_algorithms_cert` extension, then the signature algorithms specified in the `signature_algorithms` extension are also used for calculating and verifying digital signatures in certificates.

When client Bob wants server Alice to authenticate herself using a certificate, Bob must send Alice the `signature_algorithms` extension with his choice of signature algorithms. If, on the other hand, server Alice uses certificates to authenticate herself, and client Bob does not send the `signature_algorithms` extension, then Alice immediately terminates the TLS handshake and sends the `missing_extension` extension alert to client Bob.

The `signature_algorithms_cert` and `signature_algorithms` extensions both have a field called `extension_data`. This field carries a data structure called `SignatureSchemeList`, which contains a list of digital signature algorithms that client Bob can use. Listing 7 shows the `SignatureSchemeList` data structure.

```
struct {
    SignatureScheme supported_signature_algorithms<2..2^16-2>;
} SignatureSchemeList;
```

Listing 7: Data structure holding the digital signature algorithms Bob can use.

Each entry in `SignatureSchemeList` is a value of an enumeration type `SignatureScheme`, shown in *Listing 8*. A `SignatureScheme` value refers to a specific digital signature algorithm that client Bob is willing to accept. The algorithms in `SignatureSchemeList` are listed in descending order of Bob's preference.

```
enum {
    /* RSASSA-PKCS1-v1_5 algorithms */
    rsa_pkcs1_sha256(0x0401),
    rsa_pkcs1_sha384(0x0501),
    rsa_pkcs1_sha512(0x0601),

    /* ECDSA algorithms */
    ecdsa_secp256r1_sha256(0x0403),
    ecdsa_secp384r1_sha384(0x0503),
    ecdsa_secp521r1_sha512(0x0603),

    /* RSASSA-PSS algorithms with public key OID rsaEncryption */
    rsa_pss_rsae_sha256(0x0804),
    rsa_pss_rsae_sha384(0x0805),
    rsa_pss_rsae_sha512(0x0806),

    /* EdDSA algorithms */
    ed25519(0x0807),
    ed448(0x0808),

    /* Legacy algorithms */
    rsa_pkcs1_sha1(0x0201),

    -- snip --

} SignatureScheme;
```

Listing 8: Digital signature algorithms supported in TLS 1.3

We'll now turn to the RSA-based signature algorithms in TLS, before we look at the ECDSA-based algorithms.

9.4.1   RSASSA-PKCS1-v1_5 algorithms

The RSASSA PKCS1 version 1.5 algorithms rsa_pkcs1_sha256, rsa_pkcs1_sha384, and rsa_pkcs1_sha512 are defined in *RFC 8017 PKCS #1: RSA Cryptography Specifications*

Version 2.2. The hash functions – SHA-256, SHA-384 and SHA-512 – are definded in FIPS 180-4 Secure Hash Standard [129].

RFC 8017 specifies public-key cryptography algorithms – including so-called *signature schemes with appendix* – based on RSA, the public-key cryptosystem we learned about earlier, in *Chapter 7, Public-Key Cryptography*.

The RFC 8017 digital signature algorithms consists of a routine to generate a signature and a routine to verify a signature. The signature generation routine computes a message signature using the signer's private RSA key, and the signature verification routine verifies a given signature for a given message using the signer's public RSA key.

If Bob wants to verify a signed message *m* he received from Alice, he must have the message *m* itself. This is why the digital signature algorithms specified in RFC 8017 – in contrast to schemes with message recovery – are referred to as signature schemes with appendix.

The signature algorithms in RFC 8017 combine signature verification and signature generation routines with a signature encoding method. To sign a message she wants to send to Bob, Alice does the following:

- Encodes the message

- Converts the encoded message into an integer representation

- Computes the digital signature of the integer representation

To verify the signature for the message received from Alice, Bob first recovers the message integer representation from the signature. He then converts the integer representation into an encoded message. Finally, Bob performs the verification operation on that encoded message and on the original message he received from Alice. If the result is the same, he accepts the message to be genuine.

RSASSA-PKCS1-v1_5 algorithms combine two functions – **RSA Signature Primitive, version 1 (RSASP1)** and **RSA Verification Primitive, version 1 (RSAVP1)** – with an encoding method called EMSA-PKCS1-v1_5.

If the private RSA key has the form (n, d) where n is the public modulus and d is the secret exponent, and m is the integer between 0 and $n - 1$ representing a message Alice wants to sign, she computes the RSASP1 function as:

$$s = m^d \pmod n$$

where s is an integer representative of the signature $(0 < s < n - 1)$.

Similarly, if (n, e) is Alice's public RSA key, s is the integer representation of the signature, Bob computes the RSAVP1 function as:

$$m = s^e \pmod n$$

where m is the integer representation of the message Bob has received from Alice.

The RSASP1 function operates on an integer representation of a message. This representation is obtained by applying the EMSA-PKCS1-v1_5 encoding method. This deterministic encoding method takes three inputs:

- The hash function h to be used

- The message M to be encoded

- The desired length l of the encoded message

It returns an l-byte-encoded message m. A message encoded using EMSA-PKCS1-v1_5 is guaranteed to be large and to look somewhat random. This, in turn, prevents attacks on the signature where multiplicative relationships between different message representations are computed by factoring these representations into a set of small values.

These attacks illustrate why the input to the RSA signature generation function must be constructed in a secure manner and why the EMSA-PKCS1-v1_5 encoding uses a cryptographically secure hash function.

More precisely, the EMSA-PKCS1-v1_5 encoding is computed as follows:

1. Compute $H = h(M)$.

2. Encode the ID of the hash function h and the hash value into an ASN.1 value of type `DigestInfo` T with **Distinguished Encoding Rules (DER)**.

3. Generate an $l - l_T - 3$-byte string P of `0xff` values where l_T is the length of the DER encoding of T.

4. Concatenate P, DER encoding T, and additional padding into the string

$$m = \texttt{0x0001} \parallel P \parallel \texttt{0x00} \parallel T.$$

5. Output m.

With the EMSA-PKCS1-v1_5 encoding function and the RSASP1 function in place, Alice can generate the digital signature S for a plaintext message M. She does this as follows:

1. Compute the EMSA-PKCS1-v1_5 encoding for the input message M:

$$m' = \texttt{EMSA-PKCS1-V1\_5-ENCODE}(M, k)$$

where k is the size RSA modulus n in bytes.

2. Compute the integer representation for the encoded message m' as

$$m = \texttt{OS2IP}(m')$$

where `OS2IP` is an octet-string-to-integer data conversion primitive that takes a byte string and converts it into a non-negative integer.

3. Compute the RSASP1 function using the integer representation m and Alice's private key (n, d) as inputs to obtain the signature as integer representation s:

$$s = \texttt{RSASP1}((n, d), m)$$

4. Convert the integer representation s into a byte string S as

$$S = \text{I2OSP}(s, l)$$

where I2OSP is a data conversion primitive that takes a non-negative integer and outputs a byte string of length l.

5. Output signature S.

To verify Alice's digital signature for the message he received, Bob needs three inputs:

- Alice's public RSA key (n, e)

- The byte string M representing Alice's message whose signature Bob wants to verify

- The signature S itself

With these inputs, Bob performs the signature verification using the following steps:

1. Check that the signature length is l bytes, reject the signature otherwise.

2. Convert signature S into its integer representation:

$$s = \text{OS2IP}(S)$$

3. Compute the RSAVP1 function using Alice's public key (n, e) and the signature's integer representation s:

$$m = \text{RSAVP1}((n, e), s)$$

4. Convert the message integer representation m obtained in the previous step into the encoded message m':

$$m' = \text{I2OSP}(m, l)$$

5. Compute the EMSA-PKCS1-v1_5 encoding for the received message M to produce a second encoded message m'':

$$m'' = \texttt{EMSA-PKCS1-V1\_5-ENCODE}(M, l)$$

6. If $m' = m''$, the digital signature is valid. Otherwise, the signature is invalid.

In *Chapter 7, Public-Key Cryptography*, we learned that the security of the RSA algorithm relies on the computational hardness of the factoring problem and the RSA problem. Moreover, the public key of the signing party – Alice in the preceding examples – must be authentic. Because the fastest known factoring algorithms have subexponential (but not polynomial!) running times (on conventional computers), cryptographers consider computing the e-th roots modulo n for large enough n to be computationally infeasible. With this assumption and the assumption that the hash function used in EMSA-PKCS1-V1_5 encoding is cryptographically secure, EMSA-PKCS1-V1_5 generates secure digital signatures.

In other words, without knowing Alice's private RSA key, Eve cannot forge a signature in polynomial time. In addition, because the EMSA-PKCS1-V1_5 encoding includes the use of a cryptographically secure hash function, Eve must find collisions for that specific hash function if she wants to find a message that produces the same signature as some previous message signed by Alice. By definition, this is also computationally infeasible for a cryptographically secure hash function.

9.4.2 RSASSA-PSS algorithms

The TLS 1.3 `SignatureScheme` data structure defines two types of RSASSA-PSS algorithms: algorithms with public key OID rsaEncryption and algorithms with public key OID RSASSA-PSS.

An **Object Identifier (OID)** is a unique number standardized by the **International Telecommunication Union (ITU)** and ISO/IEC to globally and unambiguously identify an object, attribute, or concept.

The OID rsaEncryption identifies a specific representation of the RSA public and private keys [94]. The public key is represented by the RSA modulus n and the RSA public exponent e. The private key is represented by a set of values that includes the RSA modulus n, the RSA public exponent e, the RSA private exponent d, the secret primes p and q, the exponents d (mod $p - 1$) and d (mod $q - 1$), and the coefficient q^{-1} (mod p).

OID RSASSA-PSS identifies the RSASSA-PSS encryption scheme. `AlgorithmIdentifier` field associated with OID RSASSA-PSS specifies the hash function, the mask generation algorithm, and the length of the salt. Supported hash functions are SHA-256, SHA-384, and SHA-512, where the number indicates the length of the hash value in bits. The digest used in the mask generation function corresponds to the hash function used for signing, while the length of the salt is equal to the length of the hash value.

RSASSA-PSS algorithms combine the RSASP1 and RSAVP1 functions with an encoding method called EMSA-PSS, and the mask generation function 1 defined in RFC 8017.

The EMSA-PSS encoding is configured by selecting a hash function, a mask generation scheme, and the length of a salt. A message M is encoded using EMSA-PSS as follows:

1. Compute the hash value $H = h(M)$.

2. Generate a random salt s.

3. Concatenate the previously computed values to:

$$M' = \texttt{0x00 00 00 00 00 00 00 00}\|H\|s$$

4. With the result from the previous step, compute the hash value $H' = h(M')$.

5. Generate a `0x00`-byte string P of a suitable length defined in RFC 8017, and compute $D = P\|\texttt{0x01}\|s$.

6. Compute the mask $\mu = \mathrm{MGF}(H', l)$, where MGF is the chosen mask generation function and l is the number of bytes determined by the values computed in the previous steps.

7. Compute the masked value D_m as $D_m = D \oplus \mu$. Here, the operator $\oplus$ denotes exclusive OR.

8. Output $M' = D_m \| H' \| 0xbc$.

To generate the signature for message M with her private RSA key (n, d), Alice performs the following steps:

1. Compute the EMSA-PSS encoding of the plaintext message M:

$$M' = \text{EMSA-PSS-ENCODE}(M, l - 1)$$

with l being the length of the RSA modulus n.

2. Convert the encoded message M' to its integer representation as

$$m = \text{OS2IP}(M')$$

3. Compute the integer representation of the signature:

$$s = \text{RSASP1}((n, d), m)$$

4. Convert s to a byte string of length k as:

$$S = \text{I2OSP}(s, k)$$

5. Output the signature S.

After receiving the message M and the accompanying signature S from Alice, Bob uses Alice's public key (n, e) to verify the signature as follows:

1. Convert signature S into its integer representation as:

$$s = \text{OS2IP}(S)$$

2. Compute the integer representation of message M using the RSAVP1 function and Alice's public RSA key (n, e):

$$m = \text{RSAVP1}((n, e), s)$$

3. Convert m into the encoded message M':

$$M' = \text{I2OSP}(m, l')$$

where l' is the byte length $n - 1$.

4. Compute the EMSA-PSS verification function on message M and the encoded message M' to determine whether they are equal:

$$\text{EMSA-PSS-VERIFY}(M, M', n - 2)$$

In contrast to other RSA-based signature schemes defined in RFC 8017, RSASSA-PSS is probabilistic rather than deterministic because it incorporates a randomly generated salt. The salt increases the security of the signature scheme by enabling a more conservative security proof than deterministic alternatives.

9.4.3   ECDSA algorithms

The ECDSA algorithms `ecdsa_secp256r1_sha256`, `ecdsa_secp384r1_sha384` as well as `ecdsa_secp521r1_sha512` are defined in the **American National Standards Institute (ANSI)** X9.62 standard [6]. The corresponding elliptic curves are defined in the ANSI X9.62 and FIPS 186-4 [128] standards, and the hash functions are defined in the FIPS 180-4 standard [129].

We already learned how ECDSA works in principle earlier in this chapter. The ECDSA algorithm instances supported in TLS 1.3 are merely variations based on specific elliptic curves, `secp256r1`, `secp384r1`, and `secp521r1`, and the specific hash functions, SHA-256, SHA-384, and SHA-512, respectively.

The ECDSA digital signature scheme was originally proposed by the Canadian mathematician and cryptographer Scott Vanstone in 1992 in response to NIST's initial DSS proposal.

In 1998, ECDSA was accepted as **International Standards Organization (ISO)** standard 14888-3. One year later, it was accepted as ANSI standard X9.62. Finally, in the year 2000, ECDSA was accepted as **Institute of Electrical and Electronics Engineers (IEEE)** standard 1363-2000 and FIPS standard 186-2 [91].

The ANSI X9.62 standard contains instructions for generating the elliptic curve to be used with ECDSA *verifiably* at random. This is crucial for the trustworthiness of any cryptographic algorithm based on elliptic curves. Without this property, Eve could undermine the algorithm's security by joining the standardization process and proposing a weak elliptic curve for which she knows a secret attack.

To ensure an elliptic curve was generated at random, X9.62 describes a procedure where the domain parameters of the curve are outputs of a cryptographic hash function, namely SHA-1. The input to the hash function serves as proof that the elliptic curve was indeed generated at random.

Another argument that has been put forward for generating curves verifiably at random concerns future cryptanalytic advances in elliptic curves. If, so the argument goes, there are rare classes of weak elliptic curves that will be discovered by cryptanalysts in the future, the likelihood that such a curve would be generated at random is very low.

Today, the SHA-1 hash function is no longer secure. However, even replacing it with a cryptographically secure alternative, such as SHA-512, does not provide any serious security guarantees in the age of cloud computing where computing resources are available in abundance, at least if one is willing to pay the corresponding bill. With enough computational power at hand, Eve could simply hash random inputs and generate elliptic curves using the hash function's output as domain parameters until she finds a weak curve.

Consequently, the fact that Alice and Bob can verify the domain parameters of an elliptic curve to be the output of a cryptographic hash function applied to some input does not, in itself, guarantee that the curve is secure. In addition, the choice of the input must be *rigid*: the argument for choosing that specific input must be as simple as possible [22].

Unfortunately, renowned cryptographers are skeptical about the security of the ECDSA algorithms ecdsa_secp256r1_sha256, ecdsa_secp384r1_sha384, and ecdsa_secp521r1_sha512 included in the TLS 1.3 standard because the NIST curves secp256r1, secp384r1, and secp521r1 were not generated in a rigid process.

Dan Bernstein refers to these NIST curves as *manipulatable* [22] because their generation process uses a large unexplained input and, as a result, Eve has a large number of possible curves to choose from.

To illustrate this, Bernstein provides a hypothetical example where the procedure for generating a curve takes the equation $y^2 = x^3 - 3x + h(s)$, with s being a large random seed and h being a cryptographic hash function. Regardless of how strong h is, Eve can run the generation process for a large number of values for s and check each resulting curve $y^2 = x^3 - 3x + h(s)$ for vulnerability to the secret attack known to Eve. Given today's computing resources, this would work even if only one curve in a billion is susceptible to Eve's secret attack [22].

9.4.4 EdDSA algorithms

The ed25519 and ed448 algorithms are instantiations of the **Edwards-Curve Digital Signature Algorithm (EdDSA)** with the elliptic curves edwards25519 and edwards448, respectively. The algorithms are defined in *RFC 8032 Edwards-Curve Digital Signature Algorithm (EdDSA)*.

The ed25519 algorithm offers roughly 128-bit security. This is in line with the security level recommended by common cryptographic guidelines. As an example, Germany's Federal Office for Information Security Technical Guideline *Cryptographic Mechanisms: Recommendations and Key Lengths* [64] specifies key lengths for information that requires long-term protection. Such information is defined as *"information whose confidentiality is intended to be maintained significantly longer than the period of time for which the Technical*

Guideline makes predictions about the suitability of cryptographic mechanisms, that means well beyond 2028". The Technical Guideline recommends a security level of at least 120 bits.

The `ed448` algorithm offers approximately 224-bit security level. While `ed25519` offers sufficient security – unless cryptographically relevant quantum computers are invented – the `ed448` algorithm is provided for designers looking for ways to hedge the risk of significant cryptanalytic developments in elliptic curve cryptography.

EdDSA is a variant of Schnorr's signature algorithm with Edwards curves. More precisely, the EdDSA algorithm is defined by 11 parameters, which we list here for completeness:

- An odd prime p defining the finite field $\mathbb{F}_p$ over which the elliptic curve used by the EdDSA algorithm is defined.

- An integer $2^{b-1} > p$ defining the size of EdDSA public keys and EdDSA signatures. The public keys are exactly b bits long, and the signatures are $2b$ bits long. Typically, b is a multiple of eight so that both the public keys and the signatures have an integral number of bytes.

- A $(b-1)$-bit encoding for elements of the finite field $\mathbb{F}_p$.

- A cryptographic hash function h that generates a $2b$-bit hash H.

- An integer c, the base-2 logarithm of the so-called *cofactor* equal to either two or three. The secret EdDSA scalars are multiples of 2^c.

- An integer n where $c \leq n < b$. Secret EdDSA scalars have the size of $n + 1$ bits with the most significant bit always set to 1 and the least significant bit always set to 0.

- A non-square element d from the finite field $\mathbb{F}_p$, typically chosen as the nearest value to 0 that produces an acceptable elliptic curve.

- A second non-square element a from the finite field $\mathbb{F}_p$. To achieve good computational performance, the values typically chosen for a are either -1 (if $p \mod 4 = 1$) or 1 (if $p \mod 4 = 3$).

- An element B from the set $E = \{(x, y) | x, y \in \mathbb{F}_p \text{ and } a \cdot x^2 + y^2 = 1 + d \cdot x^2 \cdot y^2\}$.

- An odd prime l such that the scalar multiple lB equals 0 and $2^c l = \#E$ where $\#E$ is the number of points on the elliptic curve.

- A so-called *prehash* function PH. The EdDSA variant *PureEdDSA* uses the identity function as the prehash function, that is, $PH(M) = M$ for a message M. Another EdDSA variant called *HashEdDSA* uses a cryptographic hash function to prehash the input message, for example, $PH(M) = SHA - 512(M)$. Note that PureEdDSA is the variant used in TLS 1.3. For collision resistance, it does *not* rely on the collision resistance of the underlying hash function.

The points on the elliptic curve form a group under addition, that is:

$$(x_3, y_3) = (x_1, y_1) + (x_2, y_2)$$

The neutral element for this group is (0,1). The explicit formulas for computing the points x_3 and y_3 are

$$x_3 = \frac{x_1 \cdot y_2 + x_2 \cdot y_1}{1 + d \cdot x_1 \cdot x_2 \cdot y_1 \cdot y_2}$$

and

$$y_3 = \frac{y_1 \cdot y_2 - a \cdot x_1 \cdot x_2}{1 - d \cdot x_1 \cdot x_2 \cdot y_1 \cdot y_2}$$

Unlike with many other elliptic curves, these formulas have the advantage of being complete. That means they are valid for all points on the elliptic curve, without exceptions. Specifically, the denominators in these formulas are non-zero for all input points.

Now, if Alice wants to generate an EdDSA signature for message M, she first needs a key pair consisting of a private EdDSA key and a public EdDSA key. To obtain the EdDSA private key, Alice simply generates a random b-bit string k.

To obtain the EdDSA public key, Alice first uses the cryptographic hash function h to compute $H = h(k)$, the hash of her private key. She then computes:

$$s = 2^n + \sum_{c}^{n-1} 2^i \cdot H_i$$

In binary representation, s is simply a bit string of length n where the n-th bit is set to 1, the bits from the $n - 1$-th to c-th bit are set to the corresponding bit values of Alice's private key hash H, and the last 2 or 3 bits – depending on which value is chosen for c – are set to 0.

Using s, Alice computes the scalar multiple of B, the point on the elliptic curve we chose as the generator of the group (or subgroup) we want to work with:

$$A = sB$$

Finally, Alice computes $ENC(A)$ where ENC is a specific encoding defined in RFC 8032. The resulting $ENC(A)$ is Alice's public EdDSA key.

To generate an EdDSA digital signature for message M under her private key k, Alice needs to compute the PureEdDSA signature of the prehashed message $PH(M)$. Recall that PureEdDSA is simply an EdDSA where the prehash function PH is the identity function, that is, $PH(M) = M$.

To compute the PureEdDSA signature, Alice first computes two intermediate values R and S as follows:

1. Compute the hash $r = h(H_b \| ... \| H_{2b-1} \| M)$ using the bitwise concatenation of the previously computed hash H and Alice's message M.

2. Compute R as the scalar multiple $R = rB$.

3. Using the previously computed value s, compute S as:

$$S = (r + h(ENC(R) \, \| \, ENC(A) \, \| \, PH(M)) \cdot s) \pmod{L}$$

4. Output $ENC(R) \parallel ENC(S)$ as the PureEdDSA signature of M.

To verify the PureEdDSA signature for Alice's message M, Bob has to perform the following steps:

1. Parse the PureEdDSA signature $ENC(R) \parallel ENC(S)$ to obtain the values R and S.

2. Compute $H = h(ENC(R) \parallel ENC(A) \parallel M)$.

3. Verify that:

$$(2^c \cdot S) \cdot B = 2^c \cdot R + (2^c \cdot h) \cdot A$$

   holds in E.

4. Reject the signature if parsing fails or the above equation does not hold. Otherwise, accept $ENC(R) \parallel ENC(S)$ as a valid PureEdDSA signature of M.

EdDSA has several advantages compared to other digital signature schemes. First, it can be efficiently computed on various computer architectures and does not require a unique random number for each signature. This is especially advantageous for embedded systems where the available computing resources are always limited, and microcontrollers typically have no hardware-based random number generator.

Second, EdDSA uses small public keys and produces compact digital signatures. For the ed25519 algorithm, the public key is only 32 bytes and the digital signature is only 64 bytes. For the ed448 algorithm, the public key has 57 bytes and the digital signature has 114 bytes.

For comparison, the size of a signature generated with an RSASSA-PKCS1 v1.5 algorithm is l bytes, where l is the byte length of the RSA modulus n. Thus, if Alice uses RSA with, say, a 4,096-bit modulus, the size of the signature would be 512 bytes. And Alice *should* use RSA with a 4,096-bit modulus because achieving 128-bit security requires the modulus to be at least 3,200 bits, while the standard RSA settings used in practice are 1,024, 2,048, and 4,096 bits.

Third, the formulas used in EdDSA are complete in the sense that they are valid for *all* points on the curve. Consequently, there is no need to perform computationally expensive point validation for untrusted public values.

Finally, the PureEdDSA variant ensures collision resistance by construction. As a result, a potential collision of the hash function used in EdDSA does not break the signature scheme.

9.4.5 Legacy algorithms

The legacy algorithms define cryptographic algorithms as being deprecated because of known cryptographic weaknesses, specifically the SHA-1 hash function when used in either RSASSA-PKCS1 v1.5 or ECDSA.

The algorithms contained in this section of the TLS 1.3 `SignatureScheme` data structure concern only signatures appearing in digital certificates. In TLS 1.3, they are not allowed in `CertificateVerify` messages.

9.5 Summary

In this chapter, we learned how public key cryptography can be used to generate digital signatures, an extremely important cryptographic mechanism providing message authenticity and non-repudiation. We covered both RSA-based signatures and signatures based on discrete logarithms. Finally, we looked into digital signature algorithms used in TLS 1.3 in more detail.

In the next chapter, we will learn how *digital certificates* and *certification authorities* are used to ensure the authenticity of Alice's public key that Bob uses to securely communicate with Alice and verify her signatures. Without authenticity, attacker Eve could trick Bob into believing that her public key is that of Alice. As a result, Eve would be able to read any message Bob encrypts for Alice using the fake public key and generate a valid digital signature for any message apparently sent by Alice.

10

Digital Certificates and Certification Authorities

In the previous two chapters, we discussed the nuts and bolts of public key cryptography and digital signatures. In the current chapter, we delve into the details of the infrastructure needed to verify the authenticity of public keys. We will see that digital signatures play an important part in this: digital certificates are digitally signed documents, where a trusted third party warrants that a public key belongs to a certain entity, whereas certificate authorities are the entities responsible for issuing certificates. More precisely, we will look at so-called X.509 certificates including the following:

- Data fields

- Enrollment

- Revocation

- Trust model

After describing the format of a digital certificate and the processes needed to issue and verify a certificate in general, we turn to RFC 8446 and describe the usage of certificates and certificate authorities within TLS. Here, you will learn the following:

- What TLS extensions look like and how certificate requests are transmitted from Alice to Bob

- How Alice and Bob agree on the signature algorithm

- Which TLS handshake protocol messages are used to transmit the certificates

10.1   What is a digital certificate?

Remember from *Chapter 7, Public-Key Cryptography*, that public keys, more precisely their numerical representation **and** their relation to a certain entity, must be *authentic*. Otherwise, an attacker, Eve, might exchange her own public key with Alice's and could read Alice's messages. Digital signatures, on the other hand, create the same need for authentic public keys: If Eve manages to exchange PK_{Alice} with her own public key, she can sign with her own private key but claim that the signature was created by Alice, with potentially catastrophic consequences for Alice.

Yet, so far, we have not discussed how we can achieve authenticity for public keys in the best possible way. Luckily, digital signatures, as discussed in the last chapter, provide us with a way to ensure authenticity. What we need is a digitally signed statement that binds together a public key with a corresponding entity. These statements are so important that they have a name of their own:

*A digitally signed document stating that a certain public key belongs to a certain entity is called a **digital certificate**.*

Note that because of the non-repudiability of the digital signature, the signing party bears a certain responsibility that the information contained in the certificate is correct. Very often, the signing parties of a certificate are companies or governmental organizations. In this case, the signer of a certificate is called a **Certification Authority** or **CA** for short.

10.2 X.509 certificates

Because digital certificates are exchanged and automatically interpreted by various entities and systems, there must be a standard prescribing the format and data fields of a digital certificate. The oldest and most important digital certificate standard is called X.509, with v3 being its newest version.

In X.509, digital certificates are *always* issued by a CA. X.509 is an offspring of X.500, an early attempt by the OSI at a global directory structure, in which every entity has a globally unique **Distinguished Name (DN)**. A distinguished name, in turn, is a collection of **Relative Distinguished Names (RDNs)**. This naming scheme was also adopted for X.509 certificates. For example, according to his X.509 certificate, one of the authors of this book has the distinguished name C = DE, O = Hochschule der Medien, CN = Roland Schmitz, where C stands for *Country*, DE stands for Germany, O stands for *Organization*, and CN stands for *Common Name*. The CN should be unique within the organization so that, globally, the DN forms a unique identifier. Interestingly, the first version of X.509 did not include the option to use an e-mail address as the CN. This had to be added in later versions.

The DN of the certificate owner is one of the minimum eight data fields in an X.509 certificate. We will now discuss these in turn.

10.2.1 Minimum data fields

According to X.509v1, a digital certificate has to contain at least the following eight data fields:

- **Version number**: This is the version number of the X.509 standard in use. Current certificates should always have the version number 3.

- **Serial number**: The serial number of the certificate. It must be unique within all certificates issued by the CA.

- **OID of signature algorithm**: **OID** stands for **Object Identifier**, a globally unique identifier of an object standardized by the **International Telecommunication**

Union (ITU) and the **International Organization for Standardization (ISO)**. Here, the OID of the algorithm used for signing the certificate is provided.

- **Issuer name**: The DN of the issuing CA.

- **Subject name**: The DN of the certificate owner.

- **Subject public key info**: This includes the OID of the public key algorithm and the public key of the owner itself.

- **Validity period**: The validity period of the certificate is specified by a Not Before / Not After pair of dates.

- **Signature value**: The signature value of the CA's signature over the certificate.

Figure 10.1 shows some of these minimum data fields for the certificate of the web server www.amazon.com within Google Chrome's certificate viewer.

It soon turned out that the minimum data fields defined in X.509v1 were not enough in practice. For example, there is no way to specify the purpose of the public key contained in the certificate or to link the certificate to a *certificate policy*, a document that allows a relying party to assess the level of trust to put in the certificate.

10.2.2   X.509v3 extension fields

In X.509v3, a syntax for defining arbitrary certificate extensions was specified. Moreover, there is a list of extensions that are now a fixed part of the standard. Note that most of these extensions are optional parts of an X.509 certificate. However, each extension is marked as *Critical* or *Not Critical*. If the relying party detects a critical extension it does not support, the certificate must be classified as Not Valid. Here is a list of some of the most often used extensions:

- **Certificate Authority Key ID** *(Not Critical)*: An identifier of the CA's public key in case it has several public keys in use. It is recommended to use the hash value of the public key as an identifier.

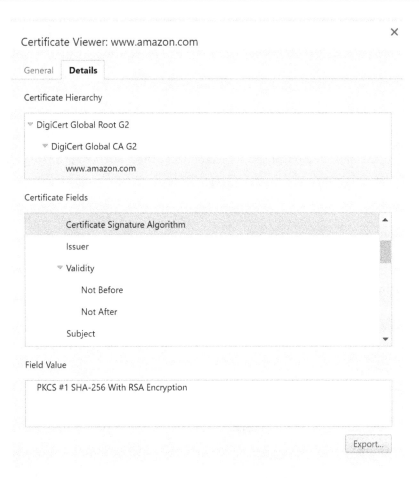

Figure 10.1: X.509v3 certificate of www.amazon.com *as shown by Google Chrome's certificate viewer*

- **Certificate Subject Key ID** *(Not Critical)*: An identifier of the certificate owner's public key in case more than one public key is available. It is recommended to use the hash value of the public key as an identifier.

- **Certificate Subject Alternative Name** *(Not Critical)*: This extension can be used to associate alternative, non-X,500-based names to the certificate owner.

- **Issuer Alternative Name** *(Not Critical)*: This extension can be used to associate alternative, non-X.500-based names to the certificate issuer.

- **Certificate Key Usage** (May be *Critical* or *Not Critical*): The Key Usage extension defines the purpose of the key contained in the certificate. Examples for possible purposes of TLS server certificates are `digitalSignature`, `keyEncipherment`, or `keyAgreement`.

- **Extended Key Usage**: (May be *Critical* or *Not Critical*): If this extension is marked as *Critical*, the indicated purposes, for example, `Server Authentication` replace the purposes given in the **Certificate Key Usage Extension**. Otherwise, the purposes given in this extension extend and explain the purposes in the Certificate Key Usage Extension.

- **CRL Distribution Points** *(Not Critical)*: This extension defines how **Certificate Revocation Lists (CRLs)** can be obtained.

- **Authority Information Access (AIA)** *(Not Critical)*: Information on services offered by the issuer of the certificate, especially about **Online Certificate Status Protocol (OCSP)** servers.

- **Certificate Policies**: (May be *Critical* or *Not Critical*): The Certificate Policies extension describes one or more certificate policies. Each policy contains an OID and further optional qualifiers. Moreover, the extension may include a URI to the issuer's **Certificate Practice Statement (CPS)**. In contrast to a certificate policy, a CPS does not apply to a single certificate, but describes the technical and organizational measures a CA takes for secure operation. It is therefore well suited to assess the level of trust to put into a CA.

- **Basic Constraints** *(Critical)*: This extension specifies whether the presented certificate is a CA certificate or a so-called *End Entity Certificate*, that is, a certificate belonging to a person or a system, which cannot be used to sign other certificates. If the certificate is a CA certificate, the maximum path length for certificate chains can be constrained by means of this extension.

Note that the above *Critical/Not Critical* classification might differ from the guidelines of the Certification Authority Browser Forum (CA/Browser Forum), a consortium of certification authorities, web browser vendors, and companies providing PKI-based applications. The CA/Browser Forum guidelines govern the issuing and management of X.509v3 certificates, including those used for TLS [43].

Figure 10.2 shows some of the extension fields for the certificate of the `www.amazon.com` web server.

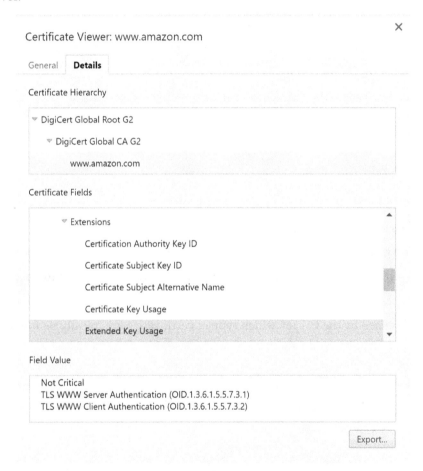

Figure 10.2: X.509v3 certificate extensions of `www.amazon.com` *as shown by Google Chrome's certificate viewer*

Looking at these extensions, you can find a few terms and concepts we have not yet discussed. Let's start with the question of how Alice can actually obtain an X.509 certificate from a CA.

10.2.3   Enrollment

The process by which Alice obtains a certificate from a CA is called *enrollment*. There are various options for doing this, but in the most common scenario, Alice first computes a key pair (PK_{Alice}, SK_{Alice}). She then generates a **Certificate Signing Request** (**CSR**) and sends it to the CA. The CSR is signed by Alice and contains the following data:

- Alice's DN

- Public key info (public key algorithm and public key)

- Intended key usage (the CA does not have to adhere to this usage)

- Signature algorithm OID

- Signature value

Upon receipt of the CSR, the CA first verifies the signature by using the public key contained in the CSR, thus making sure the CSR is a valid request. The CA then has to make sure that the information given within Alice's DN is correct. For example, Alice could be requested to appear in person at the CA's so-called **Registration Authority** (**RA**) and to authenticate by means of a passport. However, other, less costly (and less secure) options are available. Which option is used by the CA for which type of certificate can typically be found in the certificate policy.

After the CA has successfully verified Alice's identity, the certificate is generated and sent to Alice. Since the certificate contains no secret information, it can be made publicly available by the CA.

10.2.4   Certificate revocation lists

We have seen that each certificate comes with its own validity period, after which a certificate will automatically become invalid. But sometimes it becomes necessary to invalidate a certificate, although the validity period has not expired yet. This process is called *certificate revocation*.

The most dramatic reason for certificate revocation could be a private key compromise at Alice's site. This means an attacker can sign in Alice's name and the only way to stop this impersonation attack is to invalidate the certificate, so that signatures using this key can no longer be verified. In most cases, however, the reasons for certificate revocation are more mundane, for example, the DN of the certificate owner could have changed, for example, because of marriage or change of affiliation.

In practice, Alice and her CA will agree on a revocation password, which Alice can provide via an offline channel, for example, telephone, to the CA. The CA will then add the serial number of the certificate to a **Certificate Revocation List** (**CRL**), a signed list of revoked certificates along with the reasons for revocation (see *Figure 10.3*).

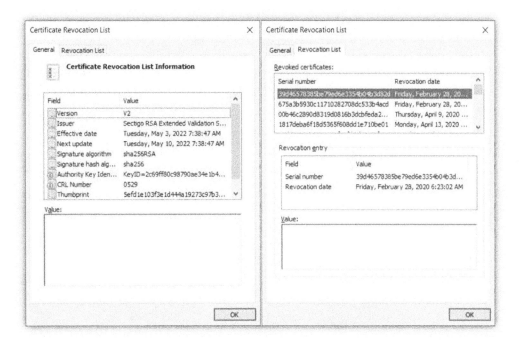

Figure 10.3: A certificate revocation list

There are, however, a few drawbacks associated with using CRLs. They include each and every certificate that has ever been revoked during the operation of the CA, so they can be rather long and contain a lot of irrelevant information. Moreover, they are typically updated once a week, so it could be seven days until a revoked certificate appears on it. Finally, if the private key of a CA gets lost, all certificates issued by this CA are supposed to be put on the CRL. However, it is not clear how this should work with a compromised CA. For this reason, browser manufacturers such as Google or the Mozilla Foundation are moving away from CRLs.

10.2.5   Online Certificate Status Protocol (OCSP)

An alternative to CRLs is to use an **Online Certificate Status Protocol (OCSP)** [110] server, as indicated in the **Authority Information Access** certificate extension. Compared to CRLs, OCSP provides a more timely revocation information. An OCSP client can transmit a status request for a specific digital certificate to an OCSP responder. By default, the client should not process the certificate until it receives a response from the OCSP responder (however, this is not always the case, as discussed shortly).

OCSP is a simple protocol where the relying party (the OCSP client) wishing to check the status of a certificate sends a request containing the serial number of the certificate to the OSP server (or *responder*). The OCSP server responds with a signed message containing the requested certificate status, the time the response was generated, and the signature algorithm OID. More specifically, an OCSP request that client Bob can send to server Alice is composed of the following:

- A protocol version

- A service request

- A target certificate identifier

- Potential extensions that the OCSP responder might process

An OCSP response that server Alice sends to client Bob is composed of the following:

- A version of the response syntax

- An identifier of the OCSP responder

- The timestamp when the response was generated

- The responses for each of the certificates in the preceding OCSP request

- Any optional extensions

- The digital signature algorithm identifier

- The digital signature computed over the hash of the OCSP response

Each response for an individual certificate is composed of the following:

- The target certificate identifier

- The certificate status value

- The time interval in which the response is valid

- Any optional extension

The OCSP specification defines three possible values for the status of a digital certificate:

good: Indicates that the certificate with the requested certificate serial number has not been revoked within its validity interval. The OCSP responder can use the optional extensions to send the OCSP client additional information such as the issuance and validity of the certificate. This might be necessary because the state *good* does not imply that the requested certificate was ever issued or that the point in time when the OCSP response is generated is within the time interval where the certificate is valid.

revoked: Indicates that the certificate with the requested certificate serial number has been revoked. The certificate can be revoked either temporarily or permanently.

unknown: Indicates that the OCSP responder has no knowledge of the requested certificate serial number. This is typically the case when the OCSP request contains a certificate issuer that is not known and not served by the OCSP responder.

As already mentioned, the OCSP response messages are digitally signed in order to provide message authenticity. The private key used to sign these messages must belong to one of the following entities:

- The certification authority that issued the certificate pointed to in the OCSP request.

- A trusted OCSP responder whose public key is trusted by the OCSP requester.

- An OCSP responder designated by the certification authority. Such an OCSP responder has a special certificate that was issued by the certification authority. This certificate indicates that the OCSP responder is allowed to issue OCSP responses on behalf of that CA.

TLS 1.3 supports the use of OCSP during the handshake, in that the TLS client Bob has the option to ask the TLS server Alice to send him status information about Alice's certificate during their TLS handshake. Server Alice then transmits her OCSP response in an extension in the `CertificateEntry` that contains the corresponding certificate. More precisely, the `status_request` extension contains the `CertificateStatus` data structure, which client Bob must interpret according to the OCSP response specification in RFC 6960.

Server Alice may also request client Bob to send her an OCSP response with Bob's certificate. She does it by sending an empty `status_request` extension in her `CertificateRequest` message. If, in turn, client Bob sends server Alice an OCSP response, the `status_request` extension in his TLS message contains the `CertificateStatus` data structure.

While OCSP enables the relying party to check the status of a certificate in real time, it has some issues of its own. More importantly, if no OCSP response is received, the browser has to decide whether to accept the certificate or not. Very often, the default behaviour in this case is to accept the certificate (so-called **Soft Fail**). However, a malware affecting the browser might also actively suppress OCSP responses and provoke the Soft Fail.

These problems may be resolved within TLS (version 1.2 or later) by using the *OCSP Stapling* TLS extension (see section 8 of [59]: TLS clients have the option to include an extension of type `status_request` in their (extended) `client_hello` message. The TLS server responds by sending (or *stapling*) a `CertificateStatus` message immediately after its `Certificate` message. Basically, the `CertificateStatus` message is a signed OCSP response from an OCSP server the client trusts. In order to get those, the certificate owner themself asks at regular intervals for OCSP responses from the OCSP servers.

If the OCSP response provided by the server is not satisfactory for the client, the client must abort the connection with a `bad_certificate_status_response` alert. Thus, the Soft Fail problem is resolved. Moreover, the burden of getting the OCSP responses is transferred from the relying parties to the certificate owners, and the web servers visited by the clients are no longer revealed to the OCSP provider.

10.2.6   X.509 trust model

Generally speaking, there are three steps in verifying a certificate:

- Verify that the certificate has not been revoked

- Verify that the certificate is valid (for instance, verify the certificate's extensions and its validity period)

- Verify the signature of the CA over the certificate

As discussed earlier, the first step consists of either consulting a CRL or an OCSP server. But to verify the signature over a certificate (or a CRL or an OCSP response), we need an authentic copy of the CA's public key – in other words, we need another certificate, in which the original CA is the subject. In X.509, these CA certificates are issued by a *higher-order* CA, which in turn has a certificate from an even higher-order CA, so that a hierarchical tree structure emerges with a *Root CA* at the top, which certifies itself (see *Figure 10.4*).

The `Path Length Constraint` within the **Basic Constraints** extension field limits the number of CA certificates that may follow a CA certificate down the tree until the EE certificate under consideration is reached. For CA_0 in *Figure 10.4*, for example, the path length constraint could be set to 0, whereas for CA_1, the path length constraint should be at least 1, lest verification of the end entity certificates for C, D, and E fails.

In practice, a CA is rarely certified by another, independent CA. Rather, there are instances within the same company that act as root CAs for their own intermediate CA instances. From a security perspective, this is equivalent to a CA self-signing its own public key. This means that, in most cases, the relying parties cannot transfer the question of whether to

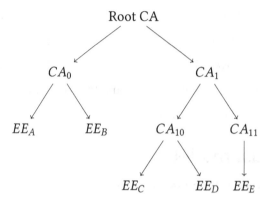

Figure 10.4: X.509 hierarchical trust model. An arrow from X to Y means that X certifies Y.
EE stands for End Entity

trust a particular CA to some independent higher-order instance, but must base their trust decisions entirely on the publicly available information about a CA, for example, the CPS. Although modern browsers contain lists of trusted CAs, it is not entirely clear how these lists come about, and they should be no substitute for making your own decisions.

10.3   Main components of a public-key infrastructure

A **Public-Key Infrastructure (PKI)** is a system that is able to issue, distribute, and validate certificates. While a CA is an important part of a PKI, the two terms are not the same. In order to limit the potential damage in case of a compromise, it is customary that the various operational tasks of a PKI are taken over by logically separate functional entities within the PKI, which have their own private keys. One of these is the CA. We will now take a closer look at all these entities:

- **Certification Authority (CA)**: Within a PKI, the CA is responsible for creating, signing, and issuing the certificates. Moreover, all certificates issued by the CA should be archived in a secure manner.

  When looking at *Figure 10.4*, it quickly becomes clear that a CA is a single point of failure within a PKI. It is therefore mandatory to run the CA within a specially secured environment with strictly enforced access control rules. Nevertheless, there have been incidents in the past where CAs have been compromised by an attacker, and we will discuss one such incident in the next section.

- **Registration Authority (RA)**: The RA is the instance Alice sends her certificate signing request in the course of the enrollment. The RA checks the data provided by Alice in the CSR. Depending on the security level of the requested certificate, this check can happen online or offline (for example, by Alice having to appear in person at the RA and present her passport). If the check is successful, the data is forwarded to the CA, which generates a corresponding certificate.

- **Directory Server (DIR)**: The directory server stores the certificates issued by the CA and makes them publicly available over a searchable directory.

- **Validation Authority (VA)**: The VA is responsible for issuing CRLs and/or running the OCSP server. As such, they form another critical component of the PKI and should be secured accordingly.

- **Time Stamping Server (TSS)**: A TSS signs documents along with the current time and date. Therefore, it can be used to prove that a document existed at a certain time. If Alice, for example, loses her private key and revokes her certificate, it is important to know which of the documents Alice has signed previously already existed *before* she revoked her certificate. Otherwise, Alice could claim that basically all documents she has ever signed were actually not signed by herself but by an attacker who stole her private key.

Another application is the so-called **Signed Certificate Timestamps (SCTs)**. By way of an SCT, the CA records the exact time a certificate was issued. SCTs can be delivered to a relying party either by directly embedding them into the certificate's extension (see *Figure 10.5*), by sending them in a TLS extension during the TLS handshake or as part of a response to an OCSP stapling request [51].

Embedded SCTs

Log ID	EE:CD:D0:64:D5:DB:1A:CE:C5:5C:B7:9D:B4:CD:13:A2:32:87:46:7C:BC:EC:DE:C3:51...
Signature Algorithm	SHA-256 ECDSA
Version	1
Timestamp	Tue, 17 Jan 2023 22:53:24 GMT
Log ID	73:D9:9E:89:1B:4C:96:78:A0:20:7D:47:9D:E6:B2:C6:1C:D0:51:5E:71:19:2A:8C:6B:8...
Signature Algorithm	SHA-256 ECDSA
Version	1
Timestamp	Tue, 17 Jan 2023 22:53:24 GMT
Log ID	48:B0:E3:6B:DA:A6:47:34:0F:E5:6A:02:FA:9D:30:EB:1C:52:01:CB:56:DD:2C:81:D9:B...
Signature Algorithm	SHA-256 ECDSA
Version	1
Timestamp	Tue, 17 Jan 2023 22:53:24 GMT

Figure 10.5: SCTs embedded in a certificate

10.4   Rogue CAs

If a CA is compromised, it will issue certificates for web servers with a fake identity, and impersonation attacks are the consequence, breaking entity authentication within TLS. The most serious incident of this kind goes by the name of *Operation Black Tulip*: In July 2011, an attacker took control of the Dutch CA *DigiNotar* (for more details, see *Section 19.5.2* in *Chapter 19, Attacks on Cryptography*) and issued fraudulent certificates for *.google.com and other important domains [199].

The main target of the attack seemed to be 300,000 Iranian Gmail users, who lost their credentials for various Google services, including Google Mail and Google Docs due to the attack. The real source of the attack was never disclosed. Initially, many signs pointed toward the Iranian government, but later on, the well-known security researcher Bruce Schneier also blamed the NSA [41].

How should we deal with a rogue CA, especially the certificates issued by it? Of course, a CA compromise is a valid reason for certificate revocation, but we can neither trust a

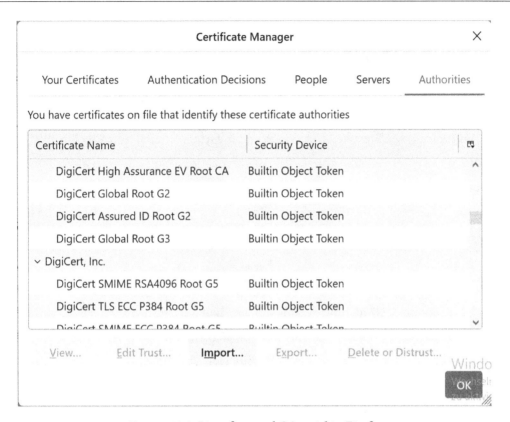

Figure 10.6: List of trusted CAs within Firefox

CRL nor an OCSP response signed by a rogue CA. Moreover, in most cases, we cannot rely on some independent, higher-order CA to revoke the certificate of the rogue CA. There is, however, a list of trusted CAs within modern browsers (see *Figure 10.6*), and indeed, trust in the DigiNotar CA was withdrawn by all major browsers by September 2011.

This example shows that the major browser manufacturers do have the potential to act like some global root CA. In 2015, Mozilla introduced *OneCRL*, where CA certificate revocation information is gathered centrally, then pushed out to client browsers on an almost daily basis. For this, all available CRLs are crawled, and revoked CA certificates as well as revoked high-profile end entity certificates, which may have a large impact on Firefox users, are included. Moreover, following a security incident such as Black Tulip, CA certificates may be entered manually into OneCRL [60]. Google's Chrome browser uses a similar mechanism known as *CRLSets*. The basic idea behind both OneCRL and CRLSets is to concentrate on CA certificates to reduce the size of the lists and to rely on OCSP stapling for end entity certificates.

Another promising innovative initiative from browser manufacturers is called *CRLite* [108]. CRLite aims to include *all* revoked certificates and is currently being tested by Mozilla [89]. In CRLite, the browsers locally store certificate revocation information in a compressed form that needs only a few megabytes of storage. The browser downloads daily updates, taking up storage space in the order of kilobytes. Most importantly, these lists can be held locally, so that no privacy issues arise from checking the status of a certificate.

10.5   Digital certificates in TLS

Now we will take a look at how certificates are handled within the TLS handshake protocol. We start by discussing TLS extensions, which provide a way to transport data in request-response type message exchanges within TLS. The rest of the section is broadly organized according to the TLS extensions dealing with digital certificates and certification authorities.

10.5.1   TLS extensions

Some TLS messages include the tag-value data structure shown in *Listing 9* and referred to as an *extension*. The extension_type field specifies the type of the extension, and the extension_data field stores the corresponding data.

```
struct {
    ExtensionType extension_type;
    opaque extension_data<0..2^16-1>;
} Extension;
```

Listing 9: Data structure of a TLS extension

Typically, TLS extensions are used in a request-response message exchange: client Bob sends an extension request in his ClientHello message, and server Alice replies with an extension response in her `ServerHello`, `EncryptedExtensions`, `HelloRetryRequest`, or `Certificate` message.

If server Alice sends an extension request in her `CertificateRequest` message, client Bob may respond with a `Certificate` message.

10.5.2   Encrypted extensions

In TLS 1.3 handshake, server Alice sends the `EncryptedExtensions` message immediately after her `ServerHello` message. At this point, Alice and Bob have agreed on a secret and have subsequently derived a shared key. The `EncryptedExtensions` message is the first encrypted message in the TLS handshake. The data structure is shown in *Listing 10*.

```
struct {
    Extension extensions<0..2^16-1>;
} EncryptedExtensions;
```

Listing 10: TLS encrypted extension data structure

10.5.3   Certificate request

If server Alice authenticates herself to client Bob using a certificate, she may request Bob to present his certificate too. This request must be sent directly after `EncryptedExtensions` and the corresponding message has the structure shown in *Listing 11*.

```
struct {
    opaque certificate_request_context<0..2^8-1>;
    Extension extensions<2..2^16-1>;
} CertificateRequest;
```

Listing 11: Server Alice's certificate request

The preceding is a good illustration of how optional interaction between communicating parties can be added to a cryptographic protocol to further improve security, if this is desired by Alice and Bob. Requiring client Bob to also prove his identity, in this case using a digital certificate, results in a *mutual* authentication where both client Bob as well as server Alice can verify each other's identity and so know whom they are communicating with.

10.5.4   Signature algorithms in TLS certificates

In *Chapter 9, Digital Signatures*, we learned that TLS 1.3 has two extensions for client Bob to specify which signature algorithms shall be used in the TLS session with server Alice:

- The `signature_algorithms` extension specifies algorithms to be used for signatures in `CertificateVerify` messages

- The `signature_algorithms_cert` extension, if used, specifies algorithms to be used for signatures in certificates

The `signature_algorithms` extension was introduced in TLS version 1.2 so that the client can indicate to the server which signature algorithms and hash algorithms can be used in digital signatures of that particular TLS session.

The `signature_algorithms_cert` extension was added in TLS version 1.3 so that TLS endpoints that support different sets of algorithms for certificates and in the TLS itself can clearly communicate their capabilities. RFC 8446 specifies that TLS 1.2 implementations should also process this extension.

In these extensions, the `extension_data` field contains a list of `SignatureScheme` values in a descending order of client Bob's preference. Each such value is a single signature algorithm that Bob is willing to verify.

Bob may use `signature_algorithms_cert` extension to tell Alice which certificate-specific signature algorithms he wants to use to validate X.509 certificates. Otherwise, if the `signature_algorithms_cert` is omitted, algorithms specified in `signature_algorithms` are also used for calculating and verifying digital signatures in certificates.

As a result, using the `signature_algorithms_cert` extension, TLS clients that support different sets of algorithms for certificates and in the TLS itself can signal this to a TLS server in an unambiguous way.

If client Bob wants server Alice to authenticate herself using a certificate, he must send at least the `signature_algorithms` extension (optionally, Bob may also send Alice the `signature_algorithms_cert` extension).

If server Alice can only authenticate herself using a certificate but client Bob sends no `signature_algorithms` extension, then Alice immediately aborts the TLS handshake and sends a `missing_extension` alert.

10.5.5 Certificates and TLS authentication messages

Recall that at the end of the TLS 1.3 handshake, client Bob and server Alice exchange *authentication messages* shown in **bold** in *Figure 10.7*. The same set of messages is used whenever client Bob and server Alice perform certificate-based authentication (authentication based on a pre-shared key happens as a side effect of the key exchange).

The set of authentication messages is composed of the `Certificate`, `CertificateVerify`, and `Finished` messages, as shown in *Listing 12*. These messages are protected using keys derived from `client_handshake_traffic_secret` and `server_handshake_traffic_secret`. Upon receiving server Alice's authentication messages, client Bob responds with his authentication messages.

The `Certificate` message contains either Alice's or Bob's certificate and any per-certificate extensions. This message is omitted by server Alice if certificate-based authentication is not used in that TLS session and by client Bob if Alice did not send the `CertificateRequest` message (which would indicate that Alice wants Bob to authenticate himself using his digital certificate).

The `CertificateVerify` message carries the digital signature over the entire TLS handshake. The signature is generated using the private key that corresponds to the public key in the respective `Certificate` message. As an example, the signature in Alice's `CertificateVerify` message is generated using Alice's private key. Alice's corresponding public key is contained in the certificate that Alice sends to Bob in her `Certificate` message. If certificate-based authentication is not used, this message is omitted.

```
enum {
    X509(0),
    OpenPGP_RESERVED(1),
    RawPublicKey(2),
    (255)
} CertificateType;

struct {
    select (certificate_type) {
        case RawPublicKey:
            /* From RFC 7250 ASN.1_subjectPublicKeyInfo */
            opaque ASN1_subjectPublicKeyInfo<1..2^24-1>;
        case X509:
            opaque cert_data<1..2^24-1>;
    };

    Extension extensions<0..2^16-1>;
} CertificateEntry;

struct {
    opaque certificate_request_context<0..2^8-1>;
    CertificateEntry certificate_list<0..2^24-1>;
} Certificate;

struct {
    SignatureScheme algorithm;
    opaque signature<0..2^16-1>;
} CertificateVerify;

struct {

    opaque verify_data[Hash.length];
} Finished;
```

Listing 12: Authentication messages in TLS handshake

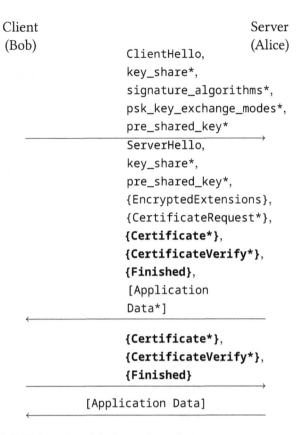

Figure 10.7: Full TLS 1.3 handshake with authentication messsages shown in **bold**

The Finished message contains a so-called **Message Authentication Code (MAC)** over the entire TLS handshake. We will cover message authentication codes in detail in the next chapter on *Hash Functions and Message Authentication Codes*. For now, it suffices to know that they can be used as cryptographically secure checksums.

With this, Alice and Bob use the Finished message to verify that all handshake messages sent by Bob were not manipulated en route and were indeed received by Alice, and vice versa. As a result, the Finished message provides key confirmation, binds the identities of Alice and Bob to the exchanged secret keys, and, if the pre-shared key mode is used, authenticates the TLS handshake.

More generally, the `Finished` message illustrates a best practice in the design of cryptographic protocols where at the end of the protocol, the communicating parties verify that they had the same view of their interaction, for example, that no other messages were received except those that were actually sent and that no messages were lost.

10.5.6   The `Certificate` message

The `Certificate` message contains the endpoint's – server Alice's or client Bob's – certificate chain.

Server Alice sends the `Certificate` message to client Bob whenever the key exchange Alice and Bob agreed upon uses certificate-based authentication. This is the case for all TLS 1.3 key exchange methods except TLS handshake based on a pre-shared key.

Client Bob sends a `Certificate` message if and only if server Alice has requested him to authenticate himself using the `CertificateRequest` message. If Alice requested Bob authenticate himself using a certificate, but Bob has no suitable certificate at hand, he sends a `Certificate` message containing no certificates. More precisely, Bob sends a `Certificate` message with the `certificate_list` field having a length of zero. The structure of the `Certificate` message is shown in *Listing 13*.

If the `Certificate` message is received in response to a `CertificateRequest` message, the `certificate_request_context` variable stores an identifier for the certificate request. When server Alice requests client Bob authenticate himself using a certificate, Alice can supply an additional context, which client Bob would return to bind his certificate to Alice's request. If client Bob does not authenticate himself using a certificate (which is the most common case on the internet), `certificate_request_context` has a length of zero.

The `certificate_list` field contains a chain of `CertificateEntry` data structures. Each `CertificateEntry` stores a single digital certificate together with its corresponding set of extensions.

```
enum {
    X509(0),
    RawPublicKey(2),
    (255)
} CertificateType;

struct {
    select (certificate_type) {
        case RawPublicKey:
            /* From RFC 7250 ASN.1_subjectPublicKeyInfo */
            opaque ASN1_subjectPublicKeyInfo<1..2^24-1>;
        case X509:
            opaque cert_data<1..2^24-1>;
        };
    Extension extensions<0..2^16-1>;


} CertificateEntry;

struct {
    opaque certificate_request_context<0..2^8-1>;
    CertificateEntry certificate_list<0..2^24-1>;
} Certificate;
```

Listing 13: Structure of the Certificate *message*

The extensions field consists of certain extension values for a CertificateEntry, including OCSP status for server certificates and the SignedCertificateTimestamp extensions. The extensions in the Certificate message from server Alice must match those found in client Bob's ClientHello message. Similarly, extensions in the Certificate message from client Bob have to match those in server Alice's CertificateRequest message.

Server Alice's certificate_list must never be empty. In contrast, client Bob may send an empty certificate_list if he has no appropriate certificate to respond to server Alice's authentication request with.

10.5.7   The `CertificateVerify` message

The `CertificateVerify` message provides explicit proof that the sender—either client Bob or server Alice—indeed has the private key corresponding to its certificate. Moreover, the `CertificateVerify` message allows you to verify the integrity of the TLS handshake up to this point. *Listing 14* shows the structure of the `CertificateVerify` message:

```
struct {
    SignatureScheme algorithm;
    opaque signature<0..2^16-1>;
} CertificateVerify;
```

Listing 14: Structure of the `CertificateVerify` *message*

The `algorithm` field in *Listing 14* holds the signature algorithm used to generate the signature. The content covered by the signature includes the TLS handshake context and the certificate.

The signature is computed over a concatenation of the following data:

- A string consisting of 64 bytes having a value of 32

- The `TLS 1.3, server CertificateVerify` string for server Alice's signature and the `TLS 1.3, client CertificateVerify` string for client Bob's signature

- A single byte having value 0 that acts as a separator

- The content to be signed

The context string secures TLS against cross-protocol attacks by providing a way to differentiate between the signatures generated in different contexts.

Server Alice sends the `CertificateVerify` message when she authenticates herself to client Bob using a certificate. Client Bob sends `CertificateVerify` whenever he authenticates himself using a certificate. If sent, the `CertificateVerify` message is transmitted immediately after the `Certificate` message and immediately before the `Finished` message.

For example, if the transcript hash consists of 32 bytes having the value 01, the content covered by the signature in server Alice's CertificateVerify message reads like this:

```
202020202020202020202020202020202020202020202020202020202020
202020202020202020202020202020202020202020202020202020202020
544c5320312e332c20736572766572204365727469666963617465566572966
79
00
010101010101010101010101010101010101010101010101010101010101
```

The sender of the CertificateVerify message computes the signature by taking the following data as input:

- The data covered by the signature

- The private key corresponding to the public key in the sender's certificate transmitted in the previous TLS message

When server Alice sends the CertificateVerify message, the digital signature algorithm Alice uses must be one of the algorithms that client Bob specified in his signature_algorithms extension.

When client Bob sends the CertificateVerify message, the digital signature algorithm must be among those specified in the supported_signature_algorithms field of the signature_algorithms extension in the CertificateRequest message.

The above illustrates how TLS addresses potential compatibility issues in a heterogeneous environment where different clients must communicate with different servers, with the endpoints likely supporting different digital signature algorithms.

The receiver of the CertificateVerify message verifies the digital signature. The verification process takes the following data as input:

- The data covered by the signature

- The public key in the certificate from the corresponding Certificate message

- The digital signature in the received `CertificateVerify` message

If the verification is not successful, the receiver terminates the TLS handshake and sends a `decrypt_alert` alert to the other communicating party.

10.5.8   Server certificate selection

When server Alice sends her certificate to client Bob, the certificate must have the following properties:

- The certificate must be an X.509v3 certificate (unless Alice and Bob negotiate a different certificate type).

- The public key of the server must be compatible with the selected authentication algorithm from client Bob's `signature_algorithms` extension. Possible signature algorithms are RSA, ECDSA, or EdDSA.

- The **Certificate Key Usage** field (discussed earlier in this chapter, in the *X.509V3 Extension Fields* section), must include the `digitalSignature` value. The signature algorithm must match the signature scheme specified in Bob's `signature_algorithms` and `signature_algorithms_cert` extensions.

- The `server_name` and `certificate_authorities` extensions are used to select the certificate.

All certificates sent by server Alice must be signed by the digital signature algorithm specified by client Bob. Self-signed certificates are not validated and, therefore, can be signed with any digital signature algorithm.

If server Alice is not able to provide a certificate chain where all certificates are signed using the signature algorithms specified by client Bob, she continues the TLS handshake by sending Bob a certificate chain of her choice that might use signature algorithms not supported by client Bob.

If Bob is not able to construct a valid certificate chain using the certificates provided by Alice and decides to abort the TLS handshake, he sends a corresponding certificate-related alert. The default alert is `unsupported_certificate`.

10.5.9   Client certificate selection

When client Bob sends his certificate to server Alice, Bob's certificate must have the following properties:

- The certificate must be an X.509v3 certificate (unless Alice and Bob negotiate a different certificate type).

- If the `certificate_authorities` extension was present in the `CertificateRequest` message, at least one of the certificates in Bob's certificate chain should be issued by one of the specified certification authorities.

- The certificate must be signed using one of the digital signature algorithms specified in the `signature_algorithms` extension of the `CertificateRequest` message.

- If the `CertificateRequest` message from server Alice has a non-empty `oid_filters` extension, the client certificate must contain all extension OIDs recognized by client Bob. This extension is covered in detail in the next subsection, *OID filters*.

This concludes the list of requirements on client certificates in TLS. These requirements become relevant only if server Alice sends a `CertificateRequest` message to client Bob.

10.5.10   OID filters

Using the `oid_filters` extension, server Alice can send client Bob a set of pairs (Object Identifier (OID), value) that Bob's digital certificate should match. If Alice decides to do so, she sends the `oid_filters` extension in her `CertificateRequest` message.

The structure of the `oid_filters` extension is shown in *Listing 15*. The `filters` variable holds a list of certificate extension OIDs with their corresponding values as defined in RFC 5280 *Internet X.509 Public Key Infrastructure Certificate and Certificate Revocation List (CRL) Profile*.

```
struct {
    opaque certificate_extension_oid<1..2^8-1>;
    opaque certificate_extension_values<0..2^16-1>;
} OIDFilter;

struct {
    OIDFilter filters<0..2^16-1>;
} OIDFilterExtension;
```

Listing 15: Structure of the `oid_filters` *extension*

If server Alice sends client Bob a non-empty `oid_filters` extension, the certificate included in Bob's response must contain all specified extension OIDs that Bob recognizes.

All specified values must be present in server Bob's certificate for every extension OID that Bob is able to recognize. According to the TLS 1.3 specification, Bob must ignore any unrecognized certificate extension OID.

If client Bob ignores some of the required certificate extension OIDs and, as a result, the certificate that Bob presents to server Alice does not satisfy her request, Alice may either continue with the TLS handshake without appropriate certificate-based client authentication or terminate the TLS handshake and transmit the `unsupported_certificate` alert.

10.5.11   Receiving a Certificate message

TLS endpoints have to follow certain rules when validating digital certificates. If client Bob receives an empty `Certificate` message from server Alice, Bob must immediately terminate the TLS handshake and send the `decode_error` alert.

If, on the other hand, client Bob sends an empty `Certificate` message to server Alice, Alice is free to decide whether she continues the TLS handshake without proper authentication of client Bob—or, more precisely, a party claiming to be Bob—or terminates the TLS handshake and sends the `certificate_required` alert.

Moreover, if the certificate chain received from client Bob is flawed—as an example, if it is not signed by a certification authority that Alice knows and trusts—Alice may continue or terminate the TLS handshake as she prefers.

If Alice or Bob receives a certificate that they would need to validate using any signature algorithm that uses the insecure MD5 hash function, they must immediately terminate the TLS handshake and send the `bad_certificate` alert. The TLS 1.3 specification recommends Alice and Bob do the same if they receive a certificate that must be verified using a SHA-1 based signature algorithm.

Instead, the TLS 1.3 specification recommends all TLS endpoints transition to signature algorithms that use SHA-256 or stronger hash functions. In addition, TLS 1.3 allows a digital certificate that contains a key for one signature algorithm to be signed with a different signature algorithm.

10.5.12 The `certificate_authorities` extension

Finally, we turn to certificate authorities within TLS. TLS in itself places hardly any requirement on CAs, except that they should be able to issue X.509 certificates. However, Alice and Bob can use the `certificate_authorities` extension to specify which certification authorities they support and which should be used by the receiving TLS party to select the appropriate certificates.

Client Bob sends the `certificate_authorities` extension in his `ClientHello` message. Server Alice sends the `certificate_authorities` extension in her `CertificateRequest` message. `certificate_authorities` contains the `CertificateAuthoritiesExtension` data structure, as shown in *Listing 16*.

In `CertificateAuthoritiesExtension`, field `authorities` holds a list of the distinguished names of suitable CAs. The CA names are represented in the DER-encoded format. The `authorities` variable also contains the name of the trust anchor or the subordinate CA. As a result, server Alice and client Bob can use the `certificate_authorities` extension to specify the known trust anchors as well as the preferred authorization space.

```
opaque DistinguishedName<1..2^16-1>;

struct {
    DistinguishedName authorities<3..2^16-1>;
} CertificateAuthoritiesExtension;
```

Listing 16: `CertificateAuthoritiesExtension` *data structure*

10.6 Summary

In this chapter, we have discussed digital certificates as a means to provide authenticity for public keys, and the bodies that issue certificates, **Certification Authorities** (**CAs**). In particular, we looked at the minimum set of data that needs to be presented within a certificate, and the optional parts of a certificate.

Regarding CAs, we discussed their tasks and the processes for obtaining and validating certificates. We have also seen how CAs fit into the larger structure needed to manage public keys, the **Public-Key Infrastructure** (**PKI**).

After these more general considerations, we looked in detail at how digital certificates are handled within the TLS 1.3 handshake protocol.

The next chapter will be more technical again, as it discusses hash functions and message authentication codes. Apart from digital signatures (which also use hash functions), they are the main cryptographic mechanisms for providing authenticity to handshake messages.

11

Hash Functions and Message Authentication Codes

In previous chapters, we touched upon message authentication and its importance for applied cryptography. We also used the terms *cryptographic hash function* and *message authentication code* (based on symmetric key cryptography), which are the underlying cryptographic mechanisms to realize message authentication. However, we did not give a formal definition of these terms and did not discuss their mathematical properties.

In this chapter, we take a deep dive into hash functions and message authentication codes. After explaining why message authenticity and integrity are crucial for security, we will cover one-way functions, mathematical properties of hash functions, as well as their underlying building blocks, such as the Merkle-Damgard construction.

Moreover, we will discuss how message authentication codes work and learn about a popular algorithm called HMAC. Finally, we will take a look at where hash functions and message authentication codes are used in TLS 1.3.

If you read RFC 8446, the IETF standard specifying TLS 1.3, you will notice that hash functions are sprinkled across almost the entire document. We combine this information in a single place to give a better overview. In particular, we cover the following aspects of the RFC 8446 standard:

- The hash function in the ClientHello message

- Hash functions in TLS 1.3 signature schemes

- Hash functions in the authentication messages of the TLS 1.3 handshake protocol

- The handshake protocol transcript hash

- Hash functions in TLS key derivation

Upon completion of the chapter, you will have a comprehensive understanding of hash functions and message authentication codes as well as their application in TLS 1.3. In terms of skills acquired, you will have gained the following:

- An understanding of the need for authenticity and integrity and why it cannot be achieved using encryption only

- Familiarity with one-way functions, a pre-requisite for hash functions, and their mathematical properties

- Knowledge of the formal definition of hash functions, their properties, such as collision resistance, and the primitives used to construct hash functions

- An understanding of message authentication codes and how they can be constructed from hash functions

- An overview of where and which hash functions and message authentication codes are used in TLS 1.3

11.1 The need for authenticity and integrity

Imagine Alice being a control computer in a train control system and Bob being a board computer installed within a train. For a more realistic scenario, let's assume the train control system is a positive train control. This means that the train is only allowed to move if it receives an explicit *move* message from the train control. Otherwise, the train does not move.

Further, assume that there are two different move messages that onboard computer Bob can receive from control computer Alice:

- Message m_s instructing the train to move slowly, for example, before entering a train station

- Message m_f instructing the train to move fast

In addition, to secure the train control against cyberattacks, the communication channel between Alice and Bob is protected using a cryptographic mechanism that provides confidentiality only. That is, Alice and Bob share a secret key k and can compute an encryption function e_k to make their communication unintelligible to the attacker, Mallory. However, they have no means to detect manipulation of the encrypted messages. The setup is illustrated in *Figure 11.1*.

Now, while Mallory cannot read the clear text communication between Alice and Bob, she can record and manipulate the encrypted messages. So, when Alice sends Bob the message $e_k(m_f)$, Mallory simply changes it to the message $e_k(m_s)$. Upon receiving the manipulated message, Bob decrypts it and obtains m_s. Because m_s is a legitimate message in the train control system, the onboard computer Bob accepts it and makes the train go slower than it is supposed to go, resulting in a delay at the next train station.

In cryptographic terms, the above attack works because Bob cannot verify the integrity of the message he received. After decrypting the message, Bob can determine whether it is in principle a valid train control message, but he has no way to check if it was manipulated en route.

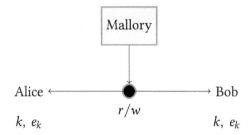

Figure 11.1: Example setting ensuring confidentiality, but not integrity and authenticity

Next, imagine a scenario where the train is halted for safety reasons, say, waiting for another train coming from the opposite direction to pass. Since our example is a positive train control, no messages are sent by the control computer Alice to the onboard computer Bob and, as a result, the train remains halted. What happens if Mallory sends the message $e_k(m_s)$ to Bob?

Upon receiving $e_k(m_s)$, Bob decrypts it and obtains the clear text message m_s telling the train to move slowly. Again, m_s is a valid message in the train control system and so is processed by onboard computer Bob. The train is set in motion and, as a result, causes an accident if there is no human operator in the loop to react in a timely way.

From the cryptographic perspective, the above attack is possible because Bob cannot verify the authenticity of the received message $e_k(m_s)$. While he can check that the plain text message m_s is a valid message, Bob cannot determine whether it was actually sent by Alice or by someone else. In other words, Bob is not able to verify the *origin* of the message. Moreover, there is no way for Bob to verify the *freshness* of the message, which opens up further attack possibilities for Mallory (this was already discussed earlier, in *Section 2.5, Authentication* in *Chapter 2, Secure Channel and the CIA Triad*).

11.2 What cryptographic guarantees does encryption provide?

On a more fundamental level, the attacks described in the above examples work because Alice and Bob, as illustrated in *Figure 11.1*, can only use encryption e_k.

Intuitively, it might seem as if encryption protects Alice's and Bob's messages against manipulation by Mallory because the ciphertext hides the plaintext message and Mallory cannot know how to manipulate the encrypted message in a meaningful way. But this is completely wrong! Encryption provides *no* guarantees for message integrity or authenticity.

We can convince ourselves that this is indeed the case by taking a closer look at the one-time pad encryption scheme from *Chapter 4, Encryption and Decryption.*

Recall that the one-time pad encrypts a message m under the key k as:

$$c = m \oplus k$$

where $\oplus$ denotes a bit-wise exclusive OR (XOR) operation. If you take two bits b_0, b_1 and apply the XOR operation to them, $b_0 \oplus b_1$ will yield zero whenever both bits have the same value (that is, both are zero or both are one) and one whenever the bits have a different value.

To decrypt a message encrypted under the one-time pad scheme, the receiver computes:

$$m = c \oplus k$$

In the case a one-time pad is used, it is very easy for Mallory to manipulate the ciphertext c because every bit flip in the ciphertext leads to the same bit being flipped in the decrypted message.

In other words, if Mallory has a ciphertext c that encrypts Bob's message m, she can easily generate a manipulated ciphertext c' that encrypts the same message as m, but with one or more bits of Mallory's choice flipped.

Thus, even a perfectly secret – that is, information-theoretically secure – encryption scheme does *not* provide message integrity. The same is true for stream ciphers because, as we have seen in *Chapter 4, Encryption and Decryption*, their encryption operation is identical to encryption using the one-time pad: the plaintext is simply XORed with the key stream.

Intuitively, one might think that block ciphers – a class of much stronger encryption algorithms we will learn about in *Chapter 14, Block Ciphers and Their Modes of Operation* – are resilient against the above manipulations and would offer some degree of integrity. After all, modern block ciphers are pseudorandom permutations where a one-bit change in the plaintext results in the change of roughly half of the bits in the ciphertext.

As a result, if Mallory changes only a single bit in ciphertext c to obtain a manipulated ciphertext c', the decryption result $p' = d_k(c')$ will be totally different from the genuine decryption result $p = d_k(c)$. It turns out, however, that even this property does *not* help with message integrity and authenticity!

As an example, if a block cipher is used in the so-called **electronic codebook (ECB)** mode (more on this in *Chapter 14, Block Ciphers and their Modes of Operation*) and Mallory flips a bit in the i-th block of the ciphertext, only the i-th block of the plaintext will change when Bob decrypts the manipulated ciphertext.

Alternatively, Mallory can manipulate the order of blocks in the original ciphertext c to obtain a manipulated ciphertext c'. When Bob decrypts c', he will obtain a manipulated plaintext p' where the individual blocks are identical to those of the genuine plaintext p, but their order is manipulated (their order is the same as in c').

If only encryption is used, Bob is not able to detect these manipulations. Moreover, this is independent of the type of symmetric key encryption algorithm used by Bob. We can therefore conclude that encryption alone provides only confidentiality, but *not* message integrity or authenticity.

11.3   One-way functions

In *Chapter 4, Encryption and Decryption*, we learned that the notion of computational security is built on the concept of pseudorandomness, the idea that bit strings can look completely random even though they are not. In fact, pseudorandom generators, functions, and permutations form the basis of modern symmetric key cryptography. As being one-way is also one of the defining properties of a cryptographic hash function, we chose to include a more formal discussion of this property in this section, even though it is fundamental for the whole of cryptography.

This is because mathematicians have proved that pseudorandom generators, functions, and permutations can be constructed from *one-way functions*.

As a result, the existence of one-way functions is equivalent to the existence of any non-trivial symmetric-key cryptography [97]. This means, if we can find functions that we can prove to be one-way, we can use them to construct symmetric-key cryptographic schemes, for example, symmetric-key encryption algorithms or keyed hash functions, that are provably computationally secure.

The good news is that there is a number of functions mathematicians have studied for decades that exhibit one-way properties. We will cover some of the most prominent examples of such candidate one-way functions in a minute.

The bad news is that the currently known candidate one-way functions are much less efficient than constructions actually used in practice, say a modern block cipher. Bridging this gap between theory and practice is one of the most important open research problems in modern cryptography as it allows you to build *provably-secure* pseudorandom generators, functions, and permutations.

11.3.1 Mathematical properties

A function $f : X \rightarrow Y$ is called a **one-way** function if $f(x)$ is easy to compute for all $x \in X$, but for essentially all elements $y \in Y$ it is computationally infeasible to find any $x \in X$ such that $f(x) = y$ [117]. Such an x is called a **preimage** of y.

Here, *easy to compute* simply means that for any given $x \in X$, Alice and Bob can compute $f(x)$ in polynomial time.

The requirement that it is computationally infeasible for Eve to find any $x \in X$ such that $f(x) = y$ means that a one-way function must be hard to invert. Since modern cryptography is about specifying cryptographic algorithms that are secure against a probabilistic polynomial-time attacker – to put it more precisely, that can be broken by a probabilistic polynomial-time attacker with only negligible probability – a function f is considered hard to invert if no probabilistic polynomial-time algorithm is capable of finding a preimage $x \in X$ for any given element $y \in Y$, except with negligible probability.

The definition of what it means for a function to be hard to invert might seem complicated at first. But it actually only excludes two extremes:

- It is always possible to *guess* a preimage x. Since we can choose the size of the *range* of f, that is, the set $\{y = f(x) \in Y | x \in X\}$, when designing a cryptographic algorithm, we can make the likelihood of a successful guess arbitrarily small, but never zero. As a result, we need to account for the fact that Eve could find a preimage y for a randomly chosen x with negligible probability.

- It is always possible to find a preimage of y by brute-force searching the domain of $f(x)$, that is, by simply trying all values of x until one produces the correct y. Such a brute-force search requires exponential time. As a result, we exclude this extreme by requiring f to be computationally infeasible to invert only for probabilistic polynomial-time algorithms.

Summing up, a function $y = f(x)$ is said to be *one-way*, if it is hard to invert for *all* values of y. If there is a probabilistic polynomial-time algorithm that can invert f for some values of y with a non-negligible probability—even if this probability is very small—then f is *not* a one-way function.

Because the brute-force search runs in exponential time and always succeeds, the existence of one-way functions is an assumption about computational complexity and computational hardness [97]. In other words, it is an assumption about the existence of mathematical problems that can be solved in principle, but cannot be solved efficiently.

11.3.2   Candidate one-way functions

With the current knowledge in complexity theory, mathematicians do not know how to unconditionally prove the existence of one-way functions. As a result, their existence can only be assumed. There are, however, good reasons to make this assumption: there exists a number of very natural computational problems that were the subject of intense mathematical research for decades, sometimes even centuries, yet no one was able to come up with a polynomial-time algorithm that can solve these problems.

According to the fundamental theorem of arithmetic, every positive integer can be expressed as a product of prime numbers, the numbers being referred to as *prime factors* of the original number [74]. One of the best known computational problems that is believed to be a one-way function is *prime factorization*: given a large integer, find its prime factors.

The first table of prime factors of integers was created by the Greek mathematician Eratosthenes more than 2,500 years ago. The last factor table for numbers up to 10,017,000 was published by the American mathematician Derrick Norman Lehmer in 1909 [178].

Trial division was first described in 1202 by Leonardo of Pisa, also known as Fibonacci, in his manuscript on arithmetic *Liber Abaci*. French mathematician Pierre de Fermat proposed a method based on a difference of squares, today known as Fermat's factorization method, in the 17th century. A similar integer factorization method was described by the 14th century Indian mathematician Narayana Pandita. The 18th century Swiss mathematician Leonhard Euler proposed a method for factoring integers by writing them as a sum of two square numbers in two different ways.

Starting from the 1970s, a number of so-called *algebraic-group factorization algorithms* were introduced that work in an algebraic group. As an example, the British mathematician John Pollard introduced two new factoring algorithms called the $p - 1$ algorithm and the rho algorithm in 1974 and 1975, respectively. The Canadian mathematician Hugh Williams proposed the Williams' $p + 1$ algorithm in 1982.

In 1985, the Dutch mathematician Hendrik Lenstra published the elliptic curve method, currently the best known integer factorization method among the algorithms whose complexity depends on the size of the factor rather than the size of the number to be factored [204].

Moreover, a number of so-called general-purpose integer factorization methods whose running time depends on the size of the number to be factored have been proposed over time. Examples of such algorithms are the Quadratic Sieve introduced in 1981 by the American mathematician Carl Pomerance, which was the most effective general-purpose algorithm in the 1980s and early 1990s, and the General Number Field Sieve method, the fastest currently known algorithm for factoring large integers [39].

Yet, except for the quantum computer algorithm proposed in 1994 by the American mathematician Peter Shor, none of the above algorithms can factor integers in polynomial time. As a result, mathematicians assume that prime factorization is indeed a one-way function, at least for classical computers. Shor's algorithm, on the other hand, requires a sufficiently large quantum computer with advanced error correction capabilities to keep the qubits stable during the entire computation, a technical challenge for which no solutions are known as of today.

Another example of a function believed to be one-way is a family of permutations based on the discrete logarithm problem. Recall that the discrete logarithm problem involves determining the integer exponent x given a number of the form g^x where g is a generator of a cyclic group. The problem is believed to be computationally intractable, that is, no algorithms are known that can solve this problem in polynomial time.

The conjectured one-way family of permutations consists of the following:

- An algorithm to generate an n-bit prime p and an element $g \in \{2, \dots, p-1\}$

- An algorithm to generate a random integer x in the range $\{1, \dots, p-1\}$

- The function $f_{p,g}(x) = g^x \pmod{p}$

Function $f_{p,g}(x)$ is easy to compute, for example, using the square-and-multiply algorithm. Inverting $f_{p,g}(x)$, on the other hand, is believed to be computationally hard because inverting modular exponentiation is equivalent to solving the *discrete logarithm problem* for which no polynomial-time algorithms are known to date, as discussed in *Chapter 7, Public-Key Cryptography*.

11.4 Hash functions

A **hash function** is some function *hash* that maps an arbitrarily long input string onto an output string of fixed length n. More formally, we have $hash : \{0,1\}^* \rightarrow \{0,1\}^n$.

A simplistic example of a hash function would be a function that always outputs the last n bits of an arbitrary input string m. Or, if $n = 1$, one could use the bitwise XOR of all input bits as the hash value.

However, these simple hash functions do not possess any of the properties required from a cryptographically secure hash function. We will now first discuss these properties, and afterward look at how secure hash functions are actually constructed.

11.4.1 Collision resistance

Cryptographic hash functions are hard to construct because they have to fulfill stringent requirements, which are motivated by their use within **Message Authentication Codes** (**MACs**) (see *Section 11.5, Message Authentication Codes*) and Digital Signatures (see *Chapter 9, Digital Signatures*).

Recall, for example, that in the RSA cryptosystem, Alice computes a digital signature over some message m as

$$sig_{Alice}(m) = (hash(m))^d \mod n,$$

where d is Alice's private key and n is the public module. Alice then sends the pair $(m, sig_{Alice}(m))$ to Bob.

If Eve observes this pair, she can compute $hash(m)$ using Alice's public key $PK_{Alice} = (e, n)$ via

$$hash(m) = (sig_{Alice}(m))^e \mod n$$

Eve now knows $hash(m)$ and the corresponding preimage m. If she manages to find another message $\tilde{m}$ with the same hash value (a so-called *second preimage*), m and $\tilde{m}$ will have the same signature. Effectively, Eve has signed $\tilde{m}$ in Alice's name without knowing her private key. This is the most severe kind of attack on a cryptographic hash function.

Therefore, given m and $hash(m)$, it must be computationally hard for Eve to find a second preimage $\tilde{m}$ such that $hash(m) = hash(\tilde{m})$. This property of a cryptographic hash function is called *second preimage resistance* or *weak collision resistance*.

Note that when trying out different input messages for the hash function, collisions must occur at some point, because *hash* can map longer messages onto shorter messages. In particular, if the given hash value $hash(m)$ is n bits long, a second preimage $\tilde{m}$ should be found after $O(2^n)$ trials. Therefore a second preimage attack is considered successful only if it has a significantly smaller complexity than $O(2^n)$.

A weaker form of attack occurs if Eve manages to find **any** collision, that is, any two messages m_1, m_2 with

$$hash(m_1) = hash(m_2)$$

without reference to some given hash value. If it is computationally hard for Eve to construct any collisions, the *hash* is called *strongly collision resistant*.

Again, when trying out many different candidate messages, collisions will naturally occur at some point, this time after about $2^{n/2}$ trials. This smaller number is a consequence of a phenomenon commonly known as **Birthday Paradox**, which we will discuss in detail in *Section 19.7, Attacks on hash functions* in *Chapter 19, Attacks on Cryptography*.

Consequently, an attack on strong collision resistance is considered successful only if it has a significantly smaller complexity than $O(2^{n/2})$. This also shows that in general, that is, assuming there are no cryptographic weaknesses, hash functions with longer hash values can be considered to be more secure than hash functions with shorter hash values.

Note that strong collision resistance of a hash function implies weak collision resistance. Hash functions that are both strongly and weakly collision resistant are called **collision resistant hash functions (CRHF)**.

11.4.2   One-way property

In *Chapter 5, Entity Authentication*, we showed how passwords can be stored in a secure way on a server using hash functions. More specifically, each password is hashed together with some random value (the **salt**) and the hash value is stored together with the corresponding user ID. This system can only be secure if it is computationally difficult to *invert* the hash function, that is, to find a matching input for a known output. The same requirement emerges if the hash function is used in a key-dependent way in order to form a MAC (see *Section 11.5, Message authentication codes*).

In order to put this requirement in a more precise way, we only need to apply our earlier definition of a one-way function from *Section 11.3, One-way functions*, to hash functions:

*A hash function hash is said to be **one-way** or **preimage resistant**, if it is computationally infeasible to find an input m for a given output y so that y = hash(m).*

As is the case for second preimages, preimages for a given n-bit output will occur automatically after $O(2^n)$ trial inputs. Hash functions that are preimage resistant and second preimage resistant are called **one-way hash functions (OWHF)**.

11.4.3   Merkle-Damgard construction

Our previous discussion of requirements on a secure hash function shows that in order to achieve collision resistance, it is important that all input bits have an influence on the hash value. Otherwise, it would be very easy to construct collisions by varying the input bits that do not influence the outcome.

How can we accommodate this requirement when dealing with inputs m of indeterminate length? We divide m into pieces (or *blocks*) of a fixed size, then you deal with the blocks one after the other. In one construction option, the block is *compressed*, that is mapped onto a smaller bit string, which is then processed together with the next block.

The *Merkle-Damgard scheme* has been the main construction principle for cryptographic hash functions in the past. Most importantly, the MD5 (128-bit hash), SHA-1 (160-bit hash), and SHA-2 (256-bit hash) hash functions are built according to this scheme. Later in this chapter, in *Section 11.7, Hash functions in TLS*, we will look at the SHA-family of hash functions in detail, as these functions play an important role within TLS.

For now, we'll concentrate on the details of the Merkle-Damgard scheme. In order to compute the hash value of an input message m of arbitrary length, we proceed according to the following steps:

- Separate message m into k blocks of length r, using padding if necessary. In the SHA-1 hash function, input messages are *always* padded by a 1 followed by the necessary number of 0-bits. The block length of SHA-1 is $r = 512$.

- Concatenate the first block m_1 with an initialization vector IV of length n.

- Apply a *compression function comp* : $\{0, 1\}^{n+r} \rightarrow \{0, 1\}^n$ on the result, to get

$$h_1 = comp(m_1 \parallel IV) \in \{0, 1\}^n.$$

- Process the remaining blocks by computing

$$h_i = comp(m_i \parallel h_{i-1}) \text{ for } 1 \leq i \leq k.$$

  Note that each h_i has length n.

- Set

$$hash(m) = h_k.$$

Note that finding a collision in *comp* implies a collision in *hash*. More precisely, if we can find two different bit strings y_1, y_2 of length r so that $comp(x\|y_1) = comp(x\|y_2)$ for some given n–bit string x, then we can construct two different messages $m, \tilde{m}$ with the same hash value:

$$m = m_1 \parallel m_2 \parallel \ldots \parallel m_j = y_1 \parallel \ldots \parallel m_k$$

$$\tilde{m} = m_1 \parallel m_2 \parallel \ldots \parallel \tilde{m}_j = y_2 \parallel \ldots \parallel m_k$$

The article [8] lists a number of generic attacks on hash functions based on the Merkle-Damgard scheme. Although in most cases these attacks are far from being practical, they are still reason for concern about the general security of the scheme.

11.4.4 Sponge construction

Sponge construction is used in the formulation of the SHA-3 standard hash algorithm *Keccak* [26]. It works by first *absorbing* the input message into some state vector $\vec{S}$ (the sponge). After one block has been absorbed, the state vector is permuted to achieve a good mixing of the input bits. After all input blocks have been processed, the n bits of the hash value are *squeezed* out of the sponge.

The detailed construction is as follows:

1. Separate message m into k blocks of length r.

2. Form the first state vector $\vec{S}_0 = 0^b$, that is, a string consisting of b 0's, where $b = 25 \times 2^l$, and $b > r$.

3. **Absorb:** For each message block, modify state vector $\vec{S}_{i-1}$ by message block m_i and permute the result via some bijective *round function* $f : \{0, 1\}^b \rightarrow 0, 1^b$:

$$\vec{S}_i = f(\vec{S}_{i-1} \oplus (m_i \| 0^{b-r})), 1 \leq i \leq k.$$

The final result is a b-bit vector $\vec{S}_k$, into which the message blocks have been *absorbed*.

4. **Squeeze:** We are now squeezing n bit out of the state vector $\vec{S}_k$.

If $n < r$, we simply take the first n bit of $\vec{S}_k$:

$$h(m) = \text{trunc}(\vec{S}_k, n).$$

Otherwise, we form the following string of length $(12 + 2l + 1) \times r$ by repeatedly applying the round function f on $\vec{S}_k$:

$$H = \text{trunc}(\vec{S}_k, r) \, \| \, \text{trunc}(f(\vec{S}_k), r) \, \| \, \dots \, \| \, \text{trunc}(f^{(12+2l)}(\vec{S}_k), r)$$

Afterward, we pick the first n bits again:

$$h(m) = \text{trunc}(H, n).$$

We will now see how hash functions are used to form **Message Authentication Codes (MACs)**.

11.5   Message authentication codes

If Alice wants to securely transmit a message m to Bob, she must use a so-called **Message Authentication Code (MAC)** to prevent Eve from tampering with that message. More precisely, a MAC prevents Mallory from doing the following:

- Modifying m without Bob noticing it

- Presenting Bob a message m' generated by Mallory, $m' \neq m$, without Bob noticing that m' was *not* sent by Alice

Therefore, a MAC helps us to achieve the two security objectives *integrity protection* and *message authentication* (see *Chapter 2, Secure Channel and the CIA Triad* and *Chapter 5, Entity Authentication*). Note that a MAC cannot prevent the tampering itself, nor can it prevent message replay. The active attacker Mallory can always manipulate the genuine message m, or present Bob with the message m' and pretend that it was sent by Alice. A MAC only gives Bob the ability to *detect* that something went wrong during the transmission of the message he received. Bob cannot reconstruct the genuine message m from a MAC. In fact, he cannot even determine whether the wrong MAC results from an attack by Mallory or from an innocuous bit flip caused by a transmission error. Later in this chapter, we will see that this property has fundamental implications on the use of MACs in safety-critical systems.

If Alice and Bob want to secure their messages with MACs, they need to share a secret k in advance. Once the shared secret is established, Alice and Bob can use MACs as illustrated in *Figure 11.2*. The sender Alice computes the MAC t as a function of her message m and the secret key k she shares with Bob. She then appends t to message m—denoted by $m\|t$—and sends the result to Bob. Upon receiving the data, Bob uses the message m, the MAC t, and the shared secret k to verify that t is a valid MAC on message m.

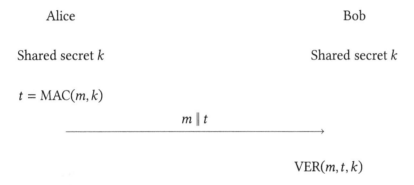

Figure 11.2: Working principle of MACs

So how are MACs actually computed?

11.5.1 How to compute a MAC

Basically, there are two options to form a MAC. The **first option** closely follows the approach we adopted to compute digital signatures in *Chapter 9, Digital Signatures*. Back then, we hashed the message m first and encrypted the hash value with the signer's private key:

$$sig_{Alice}(m) = E_{PK_{Alice}}(hash(m))$$

Analogously, using their shared secret k, Alice and Bob could compute

$$MAC_k(m) = t = E_k(hash(m))$$

as MAC. Here, encryption is done via some symmetric encryption function, for example, a block cipher (see *Chapter 14, Block Ciphers and Their Modes of Operation*). Note that if Alice sends $m\|t$ to Bob and Eve manages to find another message $\tilde{m}$ so that $hash(m) = hash(\tilde{m})$, then Eve can replace m with $\tilde{m}$ without being noticed. This motivates the *collision resistance* requirement on hash functions described in *Section 11.4, Hash functions*.

However, even if we are using a collision-resistant hash function, in a symmetric setting where Alice and Bob both use the same key k, one might ask whether it is really necessary to agree on and deploy two different kinds of algorithms for computing a MAC. Moreover, hash functions are built for speed and generally have a much better performance than block ciphers.

The **second option** for computing a MAC therefore only uses hash functions as building blocks. Here, the secret k is used to modify the message m in a certain way and the hash function is applied to the result:

$$MAC_k(m) = t = hash(m, k).$$

This option is called a *key-dependent hash value*. In which way k should influence the message m, depends on how the hash function is constructed. In any case, if Eve is able to reconstruct the input data from the output value $hash(m, k)$, she might be able to get part of or even the complete secret key k. This motivates the *one-way property* requirement on hash functions described in *Section 11.4, Hash functions*. A well-proven way to construct a key-dependent hash called **HMAC** is defined in [103].

11.5.2 HMAC construction

The HMAC construction is a generic template for constructing a MAC via a key-dependent hash function. In this construction, the underlying hash function *hash* is treated as a black box that can be easily replaced by some other hash function if necessary. This construction also makes it easy to use existing implementations of hash functions. It is used within TLS as part of the key derivation function HKDF (see *Section 12.3, Key derivation functions in TLS* within *Chapter 12, Key Exchange*).

When looking at the way hash functions are built, using either the Merkle-Damgard or the Sponge Construction, it quickly becomes clear that input bits from the first message blocks are well diffused over the final output hash value. Input bits in the last message blocks, on the other hand, are only processed at the very end and the compression or the round function, respectively, is only applied a few times on these bits. It is therefore a good idea to always *append* the message to the key in key-dependent hash functions. The simple construction

$$MAC_k(m) = hash(k\|m)$$

however, suffers from so-called *Hash Length Extension Attacks*, if the hash function is constructed according to the Merkle-Damgard scheme. Here, an attacker knowing a valid pair $(m, MAC_k(m))$ can append another message m_A to the original message m and compute the corresponding MAC without knowing the secret key k. This is because

$$MAC_k(m\|m_A) = hash(k\|m\|m_A) = comp(MAC(k, m)\|m_A),$$

where *comp* is the compression function used for building the hash function.

In the HMAC construction, the input message m is therefore appended *twice* to the keying material, but the second time in a hashed form that cannot be forged by an attacker. More specifically, for an input message m and a symmetric key k, we have

$$HMAC_k(m) = hash(k' \oplus opad\|hash(k' \oplus ipad\|m)),$$

where:

- *hash* : $\{0,1\}^* \rightarrow \{0,1\}^n$ is some collision-resistant OWHF, which processes its input in blocks of size r.

- k is the symmetric key. It is recommended that the key size should be $\geq n$. If k has more than r bits, one should use $hash(k)$ instead of k.

- k' is the key padded with zeros so that the result has r bits.

- *opad* and *ipad* are fixed bitstrings of length r: *opad* = 01011100 repeated $r/8$ times, and *ipad* = 00110110 repeated $r/8$ times. Both *opad* and *ipad*, when added via $\oplus$, flip half of the key bits.

In this construction, the hash length extension attack will not work, because in order to forge $MAC_k(m\|m_A)$, an attacker would need to construct $hash(k' \oplus ipad\|m\|m_A)$. This is impossible, however, as the attacker does not know $hash(k' \oplus ipad\|m)$.

More generally, the HMAC construction does not rely on the collision-resistance of the underlying hash function, because a collision in the hash function does not imply the construction of a colliding HMAC.

11.6   MAC versus CRC

Can we construct a MAC without a cryptographic hash function and without a secret key? Let's take a look at the *Cyclic Redundancy Check* (CRC), which is popular error-detecting code used in communication systems to detect accidental errors in messages sent over a noisy or unreliable communication channel.

The working principle of error-detecting code is for the sender to encode their plaintext message in a redundant way. The redundancy, in turn, allows the receiver to detect a certain number of errors – that is, accidental bit flips – in the message they receive. The theory of channel coding, pioneered in the 1940s by the American mathematician Richard Hamming, aims to find code that has minimal overhead (that is, the least redundancy) but, at the same time, has a large number of valid code words and can correct or detect many errors.

CRC is so-called *cyclic code*, that is, a block code where a circular shift of every code word yields another valid code word. The use of cyclic code for error detection in communication systems was first proposed by the American mathematician and computer scientist Wesley Peterson in 1961.

Cyclic code encodes the plaintext message by attaching to it a fixed-length check value based on the remainder of a polynomial division of the message's content. The receiving party repeats that calculation and checks whether the received check value is equal to the computed check value.

The algebraic properties of cyclic code make it suitable for efficient error detection and correction. Cyclic code is simple to implement and well suited to detect so-called *burst errors*. Burst errors are contiguous sequences of erroneous bits in communication messages and are common in many real-world communication channels.

CRC code is defined using a *generator polynomial* $g(x)$ with binary coefficients 0 and 1. The plaintext message, encoded as another polynomial $m(x)$, is divided by the generator polynomial. The CRC is then computed by discarding the resulting quotient polynomial and taking the remainder polynomial $r(x)$ as CRC, which is subsequently appended to the plaintext as a checksum. The whole arithmetic is done within the finite field $\mathbb{F}_2$, therefore the coefficients of the remainder polynomial are also 0 and 1.

As an example, we can compute an 8-bit CRC using the generator polynomial $g(x) = x^2 + x + 1$. To encode a message, we encode it as a polynomial, divide it by the generator polynomial $x^2 + x + 1$, and take the remainder of this division as the CRC check value to be appended to the plaintext message.

So, to encode a two-byte message 0x0102, Bob would interpret it as the polynomial $m(x) = x^8 + x$, divide it by $x^2 + x + 1$ using polynomial division, and get a remainder polynomial $r(x) = 1$. In hexadecimal notation, the remainder has the value 0x01. He would then append the remainder value as the CRC check value and transmit the message 0x010201 to Alice.

Upon receiving the message, Alice would perform the same computation and check whether the received CRC value 0x01 is equal to the computed CRC value. Let's assume there was an error during transmission – an accidental bit flip – so that Alice received the message 0x010101. In that case, the CRC value computed by Alice would be 0x02 and Alice would detect the transmission error.

At first glance, this looks very similar to a MAC and, especially in systems that already support CRCs, it might be tempting to use CRC as a replacement for a MAC. Don't! Recall that MACs are built on top of cryptographic hash functions, and cryptographic hash functions are collision-resistant. CRCs, on the other hand, are *not* collision resistant.

As an example, *Listing 17* shows the Python code for computing CRC-8. This CRC uses generator polynomial $x^2 + x + 1$ and outputs an 8-bit CRC value.

```python
def crc8(data, n, poly, crc=0):
    g = 1 << n | poly  # Generator polynomial
    for d in data:
        crc ^= d << (n - 8)
        for _ in range(8):
            crc <<= 1
            if crc & (1 << n):
                crc ^= g

    return crc
```

Listing 17: Python code for computing CRC-8 using generator polynomial $x^2 + x + 1$

Now, if you compute CRC-8 checksum values for different 2-byte messages using the code shown in *Listing 18*, you can quickly verify yourself that messages 0x020B, 0x030C, 0x0419, and many others have the same CRC value of 0x1B.

```
for i in range(0,256):
    for j in range(0, 256):

        if crc8([i,j], 8, 0x07) == 0x1b:
            print(f"Message {hex(i)}, {hex(j)} has CRC 0x1b")
```

Listing 18: Python code to compute CRC-8 for different 2-byte messages

Consequently, if Alice and Bob were to use CRCs to protect their message integrity against malicious attacker Mallory rather than accidental transmission errors, it would be very easy for Mallory to find messages that have an identical CRC check value. That, in turn, would allow Mallory to exchange a message that Bob sent to Alice without her noticing it (and vice versa). And that is exactly the reason why a MAC needs to be collision-resistant. Moreover, and maybe even more importantly, even if Mallory cannot be bothered to find collisions for the CRC value already in place, he can simply compute the matching CRC value for a message of his choice and replace both the message and the CRC. This is possible because there is no secret information going into the CRC. To summarize, a CRC will only protect you against accidental, random transmission errors, but not against an intelligent attacker.

11.7 Hash functions in TLS 1.3

We'll now take a look at how hash functions are negotiated within the TLS handshake and how they are subsequently used in the handshake.

11.7.1 Hash functions in ClientHello

Recall that Alice and Rob use the TLS handshake protocol to negotiate the security parameters for their connection. They do it using TLS handshake messages shown in *Listing 19*. Once assembled by the TLS endpoint – that is, server Alice or client Bob – these messages are passed to the TLS record layer where they are embedded into one or more TLSPlaintext or TLSCiphertext data structures. The data structures are then transmitted according to the current state of the TLS connection.

```
enum {
    client_hello(1),
    server_hello(2),
    new_session_ticket(4),
    end_of_early_data(5),
    encrypted_extensions(8),
    certificate(11),
    certificate_request(13),
    certificate_verify(15),
    finished(20),
    key_update(24),
    message_hash(254),
    (255)
} HandshakeType;
```

Listing 19: TLS 1.3 handshake messages

One of the most important TLS handshake messages is ClientHello since this message starts a TLS session between client Bob and server Alice. The structure of the ClientHello message is shown in *Listing 20*. The cipher_suites field in ClientHello carries a list of symmetric key algorithms supported by client Bob, specifically the encryption algorithm protecting the TLS record layer and the hash function used with the HMAC-based key derivation function HKDF.

```
struct {
    ProtocolVersion legacy_version = 0x0303;      /* TLS v1.2 */
    Random random;
    opaque legacy_session_id<0..32>;
    CipherSuite cipher_suites<2..2^16-2>;
    opaque legacy_compression_methods<1..2^8-1>;
    Extension extensions<8..2^16-1>;
} ClientHello;
```

Listing 20: TLS 1.3 ClientHello message

11.7.2   Hash Functions in TLS 1.3 signature schemes

Recall that server Alice and client Bob also agree upon the signature scheme they will use during the TLS handshake. The `SignatureScheme` field indicates the signature algorithm with the corresponding hash function. The following code shows digital signature schemes supported in TLS 1.3:

```
enum {
    /* RSASSA-PKCS1-v1_5 algorithms */
    rsa_pkcs1_sha256(0x0401),
    rsa_pkcs1_sha384(0x0501),
    rsa_pkcs1_sha512(0x0601),

    /* ECDSA algorithms */
    ecdsa_secp256r1_sha256(0x0403),
    ecdsa_secp384r1_sha384(0x0503),
    ecdsa_secp521r1_sha512(0x0603),

    /* RSASSA-PSS algorithms with public key OID rsaEncryption */
    rsa_pss_rsae_sha256(0x0804),
    rsa_pss_rsae_sha384(0x0805),
    rsa_pss_rsae_sha512(0x0806),

    /* EdDSA algorithms */
    ed25519(0x0807),
    ed448(0x0808),

    /* RSASSA-PSS algorithms with public key OID RSASSA-PSS */
    rsa_pss_pss_sha256(0x0809),
    rsa_pss_pss_sha384(0x080a),
    rsa_pss_pss_sha512(0x080b),

    -- snip --

} SignatureScheme;
```

We'll now discuss the SHA family of hash functions in detail.

SHA-1

SHA-1 is a hash algorithm that was in use from 1995 as part of the FIPS standard 180-1, but has been deprecated by NIST, BSI, and other agencies due to severe security issues with regard to its collision resistance. In 2005, a team of Chinese researchers published the first cryptanalytic attacks against the SHA-1 algorithm. These theoretical attacks allowed the researchers to find collisions with much less work than with a brute-force attack. Following further improvements in these attacks, NIST deprecated SHA-1 in 2011 and disallowed using it for digital signatures in 2013.

In 2017, a team of researchers from the CWI Institute in Amsterdam and Google published *Shattered*, the first practical attack on SHA-1, by crafting two different PDF files having an identical SHA-1 signature. You can test the attack yourself at `https://shattered.io/`.

Finally, in 2020, two French researchers published the first practical chosen-prefix collision attack against SHA-1. Using the attack, Mallory can build colliding messages with two arbitrary prefixes. This is much more threatening for cryptographic protocols, and the researchers have demonstrated their work by mounting a PGP/GnuPG impersonation attack. Moreover, the cost of computing such chosen-prefix collisions has been significantly reduced over time and is now considered to be within the reach of attackers with computing resources similar to those of academic researchers [64].

While SHA-1 must not be used as a secure cryptographic hash function, it may still be used in other cryptographic applications [64]. As an example, based on what is known today, SHA-1 can be used for HMAC because the HMAC construction does not require collision resistance. Nevertheless, authorities recommend replacing SHA-1 with a hash function from the SHA-2 or SHA-3 family as an additional security measure [64].

SHA-256, SHA-384, and SHA-512 hash functions

SHA-256, SHA-384, and SHA-512 are hash algorithms from the Secure Hash Algorithm-2 (SHA-2) family. The algorithms are defined in *FIPS 180-4, Secure Hash Standard (SHS)* [129], the standard specifying NIST-approved hash algorithms for generating message digests, and are based on the Merkle-Damgard construction.

The suffix of the SHA-2 algorithms denotes the length of the message digest in bits [140]. As an example, the message digest of SHA-256 has a length of 256 bits. *Table 11.1* summarizes the message size, block size, and digest size of all SHA-2 hash family algorithms.

Algorithm.	Message size (bits)	Block size (bits)	Digest size (bits)
SHA-1	$< 2^{64}$	512	160
SHA-224	$< 2^{64}$	512	224
SHA-256	$< 2^{64}$	512	256
SHA-384	$< 2^{128}$	1024	384
SHA-512	$< 2^{128}$	1024	512
SHA-512/224	$< 2^{128}$	1024	224
SHA-512/256	$< 2^{128}$	1024	256

Table 11.1: Basic properties of SHA-2 hash family algorithms

All SHA-2 hash algorithms use a set of similar basic functions, only with different lengths of input and output. Every SHA-2 algorithm uses the following functions where x, y, and z are either 32-bit or 64-bit values, $\oplus$ denotes exclusive-OR, and $\wedge$ denotes bitwise AND:

- $Ch(x, y, z) = (x \wedge y) \oplus (\neg x \wedge z)$

- $Maj(x, y, z) = (x \wedge y) \oplus (x \wedge z) \oplus (y \wedge z)$

SHA-256 functions

In addition to the preceding functions, SHA-256 uses four logical functions. Each function is applied to a 32-bit value x and outputs a 32-bit result:

$$\sum_{0}^{256}(x) = ROTR^2(x) \oplus ROTR^{13}(x) \oplus ROTR^{22}(x)$$

$$\sum_{1}^{256}(x) = ROTR^6(x) \oplus ROTR^{11}(x) \oplus ROTR^{25}(x)$$

$$\sigma_0^{256}(x) = ROTR^7(x) \oplus ROTR^{18}(x) \oplus SHR^3(x)$$

$$\sigma_1^{256}(x) = ROTR^{17}(x) \oplus ROTR^{19}(x) \oplus SHR^{10}(x)$$

In the preceding functions, $ROTR^n(x)$ denotes a circular right-shift operation applied to a w-bit word x, using an integer $0 \leq n < w$, defined as $(x \gg n) \vee (x \ll w - n)$, and $SHR^n(x)$ denotes a right-shift operation applied to a w-bit word x, using an integer $0 \leq n < w$, defined as $x \gg n$.

SHA-512 functions

Similar to SHA-256, SHA-384 and SHA-512 also use four logical functions. However, the functions are applied to a 64-bit value x and output a 64-bit result:

$$\sum_{0}^{512}(x) = ROTR^{28}(x) \oplus ROTR^{34}(x) \oplus ROTR^{39}(x)$$

$$\sum_{1}^{512}(x) = ROTR^{14}(x) \oplus ROTR^{18}(x) \oplus ROTR^{41}(x)$$

$$\sigma_0^{512}(x) = ROTR^1(x) \oplus ROTR^8(x) \oplus SHR^7(x)$$

$$\sigma_1^{512}(x) = ROTR^{19}(x) \oplus ROTR^{61}(x) \oplus SHR^6(x)$$

SHA-256 constants

SHA-256 uses 64 32-bit constants $K_0^{256}, K_1^{256}, \ldots, K_{63}^{256}$ that are the first 32 bits of the fractional parts of cube roots of the first 64 prime numbers.

SHA-384 and SHA-512 constants

SHA-384 and SHA-512 use 80 64-bit constants $K_0^{512}, K_1^{512}, \ldots, K_{79}^{512}$ that are the first 64 bits of the fractional parts of cube roots of the first 80 prime numbers.

Preprocessing the message

All hash functions in the SHA-2 family preprocess the message before performing the actual computation. The preprocessing consists of three steps:

1. Padding the plaintext message to obtain a padded message that is a multiple of 512 bits for SHA-256 and a multiple of 1,024 bits for SHA-384 and SHA-512.

2. Parsing the message into blocks.

3. Setting the initial hash value $H^{(0)}$.

For SHA-256, the padded message is parsed into N 512-bit blocks $M^1, M^2, \ldots, M^N$. Because every 512-bit input block can be divided into 16 32-bit words, the input block i can be expressed as $M_0^i, M_1^i, \ldots, M_{1}^i 5$ where every M_j^i has the length of 32 bits.

Similarly, for SHA-384 and SHA-512, the padded message is parsed into N 1,024-bit blocks $M^1, M^2, \ldots M^N$. Because a 1024-bit input block can be divided into 16 64-bit words, the input block i can be expressed as $M_0^i, M_1^i, \ldots, M_{1}^i 5$ where every M_j^i has the length of 64 bits.

Setting the initial hash value

Before the actual hash computation can begin, the initial hash value H^0 must be set based on the specific hash algorithm used. For SHA-256, $H^{(0)}$ is composed of the following 8 32-bit words – denoted $H_0^{(0)}$ to $H_7^{(0)}$ – which are the first 32 bits of the fractional parts of the square roots of the first 8 prime numbers:

$$H_0^{(0)} = \text{6a09e667}$$
$$H_1^{(0)} = \text{bb67ae85}$$
$$H_2^{(0)} = \text{3c6ef372}$$
$$H_3^{(0)} = \text{a54ff53a}$$
$$H_4^{(0)} = \text{510e527f}$$
$$H_5^{(0)} = \text{9b05688c}$$
$$H_6^{(0)} = \text{1f83d9ab}$$
$$H_7^{(0)} = \text{5be0cd19}$$

For SHA-384, $H^{(0)}$ is composed of eight 64-bit words denoted $H_0^{(0)}$ to $H_7^{(0)}$, the words being the first 64 bits of the fractional parts of the square roots of the ninth through sixteenth prime numbers:

$$H_0^{(0)} = \text{cbbb9d5dc1059ed8}$$

$$H_1^{(0)} = \text{629a292a367cd507}$$

$$H_2^{(0)} = \text{9159015a3070dd17}$$

$$H_3^{(0)} = \text{152fecd8f70e5939}$$

$$H_4^{(0)} = \text{67332667ffc00b31}$$

$$H_5^{(0)} = \text{8eb44a8768581511}$$

$$H_6^{(0)} = \text{db0c2e0d64f98fa7}$$

$$H_7^{(0)} = \text{47b5481dbefa4fa4}$$

For SHA-512, $H^{(0)}$ is composed of the 8 64-bit words – denoted $H_0^{(0)}$ to $H_7^{(0)}$ – which are the first 64 bits of the fractional parts of the square roots of the first 8 prime numbers:

$$H_0^{(0)} = \text{6a09e667f3bcc908}$$

$$H_1^{(0)} = \text{bb67ae8584caa73b}$$

$$H_2^{(0)} = \text{3c6ef372fe94f82b}$$

$$H_3^{(0)} = \text{a54ff53a5f1d36f1}$$

$$H_4^{(0)} = \text{510e527fade682d1}$$

$$H_5^{(0)} = \text{9b05688c2b3e6c1f}$$

$$H_6^{(0)} = \text{1f83d9abfb41bd6b}$$

$$H_7^{(0)} = \text{5be0cd19137e2179}$$

The way the constants for the initial hash value $H^{(0)}$ were chosen for the SHA-2 family hash algorithms – namely, by taking the first 16 prime numbers, computing a square root of these numbers, and taking the first 32 or 64 bits of the fractional part of these square roots – is yet another example of nothing-up-my-sleeve numbers.

Because prime numbers are the atoms of number theory and the square root is a simple, well-known operation, it is very unlikely that these constants were chosen for any specific reason.

The choice of the constants is natural and their values are limited because only the first 16 prime numbers are used. As a result, it is very unlikely that someone could design a cryptographic hash function containing a backdoor based on these constants.

Message digest computation

Recall that for SHA-256, the message is first padded to have a length that is a multiple of 512. To compute the SHA-256 message digest, the message is parsed into N 512-bit blocks $M^{(1)}, M^{(2)}, \dots M^{(N)}$ is processed as shown in *Algorithm 1*.

The term $M_t^{(i)}$ denotes specific 32 bits of the 512-bit block $M^{(i)}$. As an example, $M_0^{(i)}$ denotes the first 32 bits of block $M^{(i)}$, $M_1^{(i)}$ denotes the next 32 bits of block $M^{(i)}$, and so on, up to $M_{15}^{(i)}$. Moreover, the SHA-256 algorithm uses a so-called *message schedule* consisting of 64 32-bit words W_0 to W_63, 8 32-bit working variables a to h, and 2 temporary variables T_1, T_2. The algorithm outputs a 256-bit hash value composed of 8 32-bit words.

Computation of the SHA-512 message digest, shown in *Algorithm 2*, is identical to that of SHA-256, except that the message schedule consists of 80 64-bit words W_0 to W_{79} and the algorithm uses 8 64-bit working variables a to h and outputs a 512-bit message digest composed of 8 64-bit words.

Moreover, the term $M_t^{(i)}$ now denotes specific 64 bits of the 1,024-bit block $M^{(i)}$. That is, $M_0^{(i)}$ denotes the first 64 bits of block $M^{(i)}$, $M_1^{(i)}$ denotes the next 64 bits of block $M^{(i)}$, and so on, up to $M_{15}^{(i)}$.

Finally, the SHA-384 hash algorithm is computed exactly like SHA-512, except the following:

- The initial hash value $H^{(0)}$ for SHA-384 is used

- The final hash value $H^{(N)}$ is truncated to $H_0^{(N)} \| H_1^{(N)} \| H_2^{(N)} \| H_3^{(N)} \| H_4^{(N)} \| H_5^{(N)}$ to produce a 384-bit message digest

---

Algorithm 1 Computation of the SHA-256 message digest.

Require: Padded message M parsed into N 512-bit blocks $M^{(1)}$ to $M^{(N)}$
Ensure: 256-bit message digest $H_0^{(N)} \| H_1^{(N)} \| H_2^{(N)} \| H_3^{(N)} \| H_4^{(N)} \| H_5^{(N)} \| H_6^{(N)} \| H_7^{(N)}$

for $i = 1 \ldots N$ **do**

$$W_t \leftarrow \begin{cases} M_t^{(i)} & \text{for } 0 \leq t \leq 15, \\ \sigma_1^{256}(W_{t-2}) + W_{t-7} + \sigma_0^{256}(W_{t-15}) + W_{t-16} & \text{for } 16 \leq t \leq 63 \end{cases}$$

$$a \leftarrow H_0^{(i-1)}, \quad b \leftarrow H_1^{(i-1)}, \quad c \leftarrow H_2^{(i-1)}, \quad d \leftarrow H_3^{(i-1)}$$
$$e \leftarrow H_4^{(i-1)}, \quad f \leftarrow H_5^{(i-1)}, \quad g \leftarrow H_6^{(i-1)}, \quad h \leftarrow H_7^{(i-1)}$$

  for $t = 0 \ldots 63$ **do**
  $$T_1 \leftarrow h + \Sigma_1^{256}(e) + Ch(e, f, g) + K_t^{256} + W_t$$
  $$T_2 \leftarrow \Sigma_1^{256}(a) + Maj(a, b, c)$$
  $$h \leftarrow g, \quad g \leftarrow f, \quad f \leftarrow e, \quad e \leftarrow d + T_1$$
  $$d \leftarrow c, \quad c \leftarrow b, \quad b \leftarrow a, \quad a \leftarrow T_1 + T_2$$
  end for

$$H_0^{(i)} \leftarrow a + H_0^{(i-1)}, \quad H_1^{(i)} \leftarrow b + H_1^{(i-1)}, \quad H_2^{(i)} \leftarrow c + H_2^{(i-1)}, \quad H_3^{(i)} \leftarrow d + H_3^{(i-1)}$$
$$H_4^{(i)} \leftarrow e + H_4^{(i-1)}, \quad H_5^{(i)} \leftarrow f + H_5^{(i-1)}, \quad H_6^{(i)} \leftarrow g + H_6^{(i-1)}, \quad H_7^{(i)} \leftarrow h + H_7^{(i-1)}$$
end for

return $H_0^{(N)} \| H_1^{(N)} \| H_2^{(N)} \| H_3^{(N)} \| H_4^{(N)} \| H_5^{(N)} \| H_6^{(N)} \| H_7^{(N)}$

Algorithm 2 Computation of the SHA-512 message digest

Require: Padded message M parsed into N 1024-bit blocks $M^{(1)}$ to $M^{(N)}$

Ensure: 512-bit message digest $H_0^{(N)} \| H_1^{(N)} \| H_2^{(N)} \| H_3^{(N)} \| H_4^{(N)} \| H_5^{(N)} \| H_6^{(N)} \| H_7^{(N)}$

for $i = 1 \dots N$ **do**

$$W_t \leftarrow \begin{cases} M_t^{(i)} & \text{for } 0 \leq t \leq 15, \\ \sigma_1^{512}(W_{t-2}) + W_{t-7} + \sigma_0^{512}(W_{t-15}) + W_{t-16} & \text{for } 16 \leq t \leq 63 \end{cases}$$

$a \leftarrow H_0^{(i-1)}, \quad b \leftarrow H_1^{(i-1)}, \quad c \leftarrow H_2^{(i-1)}, \quad d \leftarrow H_3^{(i-1)}$

$e \leftarrow H_4^{(i-1)}, \quad f \leftarrow H_5^{(i-1)}, \quad g \leftarrow H_6^{(i-1)}, \quad h \leftarrow H_7^{(i-1)}$

for $t = 0 \dots 63$ **do**

$\quad T_1 \leftarrow h + \Sigma_1^{512}(e) + Ch(e, f, g) + K_t^{512} + W_t$

$\quad T_2 \leftarrow \Sigma_0^{512}(a) + Maj(a, b, c)$

$\quad h \leftarrow g, \quad g \leftarrow f, \quad f \leftarrow e, \quad e \leftarrow d + T_1$

$\quad d \leftarrow c, \quad c \leftarrow b, \quad b \leftarrow a, \quad a \leftarrow T_1 + T_2$

end for

$H_0^{(i)} \leftarrow a + H_0^{(i-1)}, \quad H_1^{(i)} \leftarrow b + H_1^{(i-1)}, \quad H_2^{(i)} \leftarrow c + H_2^{(i-1)}, \quad H_3^{(i)} \leftarrow d + H_3^{(i-1)}$

$H_4^{(i)} \leftarrow e + H_4^{(i-1)}, \quad H_5^{(i)} \leftarrow f + H_5^{(i-1)}, \quad H_6^{(i)} \leftarrow g + H_6^{(i-1)}, \quad H_7^{(i)} \leftarrow h + H_7^{(i-1)}$

end for

return $H_0^{(N)} \| H_1^{(N)} \| H_2^{(N)} \| H_3^{(N)} \| H_4^{(N)} \| H_5^{(N)} \| H_6^{(N)} \| H_7^{(N)}$

11.7.3 Hash functions in authentication-related messages

In the previous chapters, we discussed that TLS uses the following messages uniformly, that is, as a common set, for authentication, key confirmation, and handshake integrity:

- Certificate

- CertificateVerify

- Finished

Server Alice and client Bob always send these three messages as the last messages of the TLS handshake.

Recall that server Alice and client Bob compute their TLS authentication messages all uniformly by taking the following inputs:

- Their digital certificate and their private key to be used for signing

- The so-called *Handshake Context* that contains all handshake messages to be included in the transcript hash

- The BaseKey used to compute a MAC key

Based on the preceding inputs, the authentication messages contain the following data:

- The Certificate to be used for authentication, including any supporting certificates in the certificate chain

- The CertificateVerify signature over the value of
  Transcript-Hash(Handshake Context, Certificate)

- The MAC Finished, computed using the MAC key derived from from BaseKey, over the value of

  Transcript-Hash(Handshake Context, Certificate, CertificateVerify)

The CertificateVerify message

Recall that Alice and Bob use the CertificateVerify message to explicitly prove that they indeed possess the private key corresponding to the public key in their certificate. In addition, CertificateVerify is used to ensure the TLS handshake's integrity up to this point. The structure of CertificateVerify is shown in *Listing 21*.

The signature field contains the digital signature, and the algorithm field contains the signature algorithm that was used to generate the signature. Hash output of the Transcript-Hash(Handshake Context, Certificate) function is the data covered by the digital signature.

```
struct {
    SignatureScheme algorithm;


    opaque signature<0..2^16-1>;
} CertificateVerify;
```

Listing 21: TLS 1.3 CertificateVerify message

The Finished message

Recall that Finished is the last handshake message in the authentication block, and that this message provides authentication of the TLS handshake and authentication of the keys computed by server Alice and client Bob. The structure of the message is shown in *Listing 22*.

```
struct {
    opaque verify_data[Hash.length];
} Finished;
```

Listing 22: Structure of Finished message in TLS 1.3

To generate a correct Finished message, Alice and Bob use a secret key derived from the BaseKey using the HKDF-Expand-Label function:

```
finished_key = HKDF-Expand-Label(BaseKey, "finished", "",
Hash.length)
```

Both Alice and Bob must verify the correctness of the Finished message they receive and immediately terminate the TLS session if Finished is corrupted. The verify_data field is computed as follows:

```
verify_data = HMAC(finished_key, Transcript-Hash)
```

The Transcript-Hash is a hash value computed over Handshake Context, Certificate, and CertificateVerify. The values for Certificate and CertificateVerify are included in verify_data computation only if they were present in the TLS handshake, that is, if either server Alice or client Bob have used digital certificates to prove their identity. Now we are going to explain how Transcript-Hash is computed in detail.

11.7.4   Transcript hash

Alice and Bob use transcript hash – the hash value of the transcript of TLS handshake messages – for many cryptographic computations in TLS. The value of the transcript hash is computed by first concatenating the handshake messages and then applying a hash function to this concatenated value:

$$\text{Transcript-Hash}(m_1, m_2, \ldots, m_n) = h(m_1 \| m_2 \| \ldots \| m_n)$$

where $m_1, m_2, \ldots, m_n$ are the TLS handshake messages and h is a hash function.

More precisely, the following handshake messages – but only those that were actually sent – are used in the following order as input for the transcript hash:

1. ClientHello

2. HelloRetryRequest

3. ClientHello

4. ServerHello

5. EncryptedExtensions

6. Alice's CertificateRequest

7. Alice's Certificate

8. Alice's CertificateVerify

9. Alice's Finished

10. `EndOfEarlyData`

11. Bob's `Certificate`

12. Bob's `CertificateVerify`

13. Bob's `Finished`

What, in general, is the use of a transcript of a cryptographic protocol? After a protocol run is finished, the transcript allows Alice and Bob to explicitly verify that they both saw the same messages being exchanged. This, in turn, creates an additional hurdle for Mallory to mount a man-in-the-middle attack by sending Alice a message m_i and Bob a different message m_i'.

11.7.5 Hash functions in TLS key derivation

Recall that in order to derive TLS session keys, Alice and Bob use HKDF defined in RFC 5869 (specifically, its `HKDF-Extract` and `HKDF-Expand` functions) as well as the following two functions:

```
HKDF-Expand-Label(Secret, Label, Context, Length) =
HKDF-Expand(Secret, HkdfLabel, Length)
```

and

```
Derive-Secret(Secret, Label, Messages) = HKDF-Expand-Label(Secret,
Label, Transcript-Hash(Messages), Hash.length)
```

The hash function used in `Transcript-Hash`, `HKDF-Extract`, and `HKDF-Expand` is the hash algorithm defined in the TLS cipher suite. `Hash.length` is the output length of that algorithm in bytes. Finally, `Messages` means the concatenation of the TLS handshake messages transmitted by Alice and Bob during that specific handshake session. The `HkdfLabel` is a data structure shown in *Listing 23*.

```
struct {
    uint16 length = Length;
    opaque label<7..255> = "tls13 " + Label;
    opaque context<0..255> = Context;
} HkdfLabel;
```

Listing 23: The HkdfLabel data structure

11.8 Summary

In this chapter, we learned how hash functions and message authentication code work, what mathematical properties they have, and how to construct them. Moreover, we covered several popular mechanisms, such as HMAC and the SHA-256, SHA-384, and SHA-512 algorithms from the SHA-2 hash algorithm family. Last but not least, we looked into the application of hash functions and message authentication code in the TLS 1.3 handshake protocol.

This chapter introduced the last building block required to understand how the TLS handshake protocol works in detail. Congratulations: you now know what Alice and Bob actually do to establish a TLS session!

In the next chapter, we will wrap up TLS 1.3 handshake. To do this, we will zoom out of the cryptographic details and give a higher-level description of TLS handshake using state machines for the TLS server and TLS client, which are specified in RFC 8446. Moreover, we will show how you can use s_client, a TLS client program from the popular OpenSSL toolkit, to conduct your own experiments with TLS.

12

Secrets and Keys in TLS 1.3

In *Chapter 7, Public-Key Cryptography*, and *Chapter 8, Elliptic Curves*, we discussed how Alice and Bob can establish a key K in principle, using key transport or key agreement mechanisms based on public-key cryptography. In the present chapter, we will see how these mechanisms are implemented within the TLS 1.3 handshake. We will see what the messages look like that server Alice and client Bob exchange, how the shared master secret is established, and how further, context-specific secrets and keys are derived in the scope of TLS 1.3's key derivation schedule.

To this end, we will describe the TLS key establishment process, the key derivation functions used in TLS 1.3, and the generation and updating of the shared secret keys. In addition, we will take a detailed look at *key exchange messages* defined in Section 4.1 of RFC 8446 [147], the official IETF specification of TLS V1.3. In particular, we will cover the following aspects:

- Cryptographic negotiation

- The ClientHello The message

- The ServerHello message

- The `HelloRetryRequest` message

On completion of the chapter, you will have a thorough understanding of the various secrets and keys within TLS 1.3 and their relationship and the options for secure cryptographic key establishment in TLS.

In terms of skills, you will gain the following:

- Knowledge of the different secrets and keys within the TLS protocol and how they depend on each other

- Familiarity with the **Key Derivation Functions** (**KDFs**) used within TLS

- An understanding of how key exchange options are negotiated within TLS

In order to achieve these skills, we have to dive rather deep into the TLS 1.3 specification, which might seem a bit tedious to those who are mainly interested in the mathematical principles of key establishment. If you belong to this group, you may safely skip this chapter and proceed directly to the next one.

12.1   Key establishment in TLS 1.3

Using the TLS handshake protocol, Alice and Bob negotiate the cryptographic algorithms and key sizes. They also exchange the key shares that are required to establish the master secret. Further context-specific shared secrets and keys are then derived from this master secret according to TLS 1.3's key derivation schedule. The secure communication channel is based on a subset of these derived secret keys.

The basic principle of TLS key establishment is shown in *Figure 12.1*. First, Alice and Bob negotiate cryptographic algorithms, key sizes, and exchange key shares. In the second step, Alice and Bob derive a number of context-specific TLS secrets, and in particular, a shared master secret. Each secret depends on the keying material as well as the label and the context used as inputs to generate that secret.

Finally, in the third step, Alice and Bob use the TLS secrets to derive a number of keys according to TLS 1.3's key derivation schedule. Because the derived TLS secrets are context-specific, no further labels or additional information is needed to derive the TLS keys. However, due to context-specific secrets as input for the key derivation, the secret TLS keys are also context-specific:

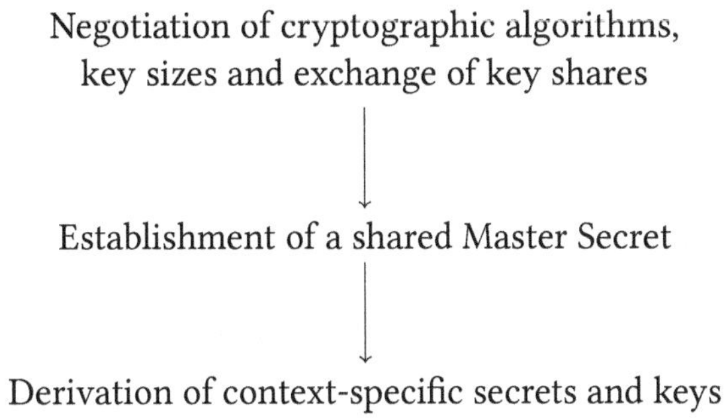

Negotiation of cryptographic algorithms,
key sizes and exchange of key shares

↓

Establishment of a shared Master Secret

↓

Derivation of context-specific secrets and keys

Figure 12.1: A high-level view of key establishment in TLS 1.3

We will cover each of the three steps shown in *Figure 12.1* in detail. As we have seen, the first step, exchange of key shares and establishment of a shared master secret over an insecure channel, can only be accomplished using a good deal of math, which is explained in *Chapter 7, Public-Key Cryptography*. In the present chapter, we will focus on TLS 1.3's key derivation schedule, that is, the process of deriving further, context-specific secrets and keys from an initial secret.

12.2   TLS secrets

We saw in *Chapter 3, A Secret to Share*, that a good cryptographic system has multiple keys so that every key is used for a single purpose only. TLS is no exception, and in this chapter, we are going to discuss in detail what cryptographic keys client Bob and server Alice need to establish a secure TLS channel.

However, before discussing the cryptographic *keys*, we first need to understand what TLS *secrets* are and how they are derived. TLS uses a three-step approach for generation of cryptographic keys, in which the keys are generated from the secrets:

1. Alice and Bob first establish a shared master secret.

2. They derive context-specific secrets from the master secret.

3. Finally, they derive context-specific keys from these derived secrets.

Note that there is no conceptual (or cryptographic) reason to differentiate between secrets and keys. But because the TLS 1.3 specification uses this terminology and we want to provide a trustworthy guide to this specification, we felt the need to do the same differentiation here.

Table 12.1 gives an overview of secrets used in the TLS protocol and briefly explains their purpose. Don't worry if the sheer number of TLS secrets looks overwhelming at first.

To help you, we compiled a series of graphics illustrating how the specific TLS secrets and TLS keys are interconnected. You will find the graphics at the end of the next section, *Key derivation functions in TLS*. In the remainder of this section, we are going to look into every TLS secret in more detail.

12.2.1   Early secret

TLS 1.3 offers the option for Alice and Bob to use a pre-shared secret key *PSK*. This is a key Alice and Bob have previously agreed on independent of TLS. If Alice and Bob use a *PSK* for their TLS handshake, they derive the **early secret** from *PSK* and use it as **input keying material (IKM)** to generate `binder_key`, `client_early_traffic_secret`, and `early_exporter_master_secret`, which will be explained later in this chapter.

12.2.2   Binder key

The binder key is used to establish a binding between Alice's and Bob's pre-shared secret key and their current TLS handshake as well as between the current TLS handshake and the previous TLS handshake where that PSK was generated. In other words, Bob uses the binder to prove to Alice that he indeed knows the PSK associated with the identity known to Alice.

Alice uses the PSK binder to verify that Bob actually knows the correct PSK before actually executing a PSK-based TLS handshake. If the verification fails or Bob does not present the binder to Alice, she immediately aborts the TLS handshake. This ensures that Alice does not execute a PSK-based handshake without verifying that Bob actually knows the PSK.

Secret	Purpose
Early secret	Used to generate key material if Bob and Alice use a **pre-shared key (PSK)** for their TLS handshake.
Binder	Establishes a binding between the PSK and current TLS handshake.
Early traffic secret	Used by Bob to encrypt early handshake traffic if the PSK is used for the TLS handshake.
Exporter secrets	Secrets that can be used outside of the TLS protocol to derive additional secret keys for higher-layer protocols or applications running on top of TLS.
Derived secrets	Intermediate secrets used as salt arguments for deriving TLS secrets.
Handshake secret	This secret is the result of the handshake. It is either derived from the early secret in case a *PSK* is in place or from a Diffie-Hellman key exchange between Alice and Bob. It is used as input to generate the following two TLS secrets: Bob's handshake traffic secret and Alice's handshake traffic secret.
Handshake traffic secrets	Used to generate TLS handshake traffic keys, one for Bob and one for Alice.
Master secret	Used as input to generate the following two TLS secrets: Bob's application traffic secret and Alice's application traffic secret.
Application traffic secrets	Used to generate TLS application traffic keys. Like with handshake traffic keys, one key is for Bob and one is for Alice.
Resumption master secret	Used for session resumption.

Table 12.1: Overview of secrets used in TLS (see also [53])

By binding a previous TLS session where the binder key was generated to the current TLS handshake, this mechanism also allows Alice to implicitly verify that Bob did not suffer a man-in-the-middle attack. If Mallory managed to perform a successful man-in-the-middle attack, Alice and Bob would have a different PSK and this would prevent a subsequent TLS session resumption.

12.2.3   Bob's client early traffic secret.

If a PSK is used for the TLS handshake, `client_early_traffic_secret` can be used to generate a key that allows Bob to encrypt early application data in the first `ClientHello` message of the TLS handshake. This key is only used by Bob.

12.2.4   Exporter secrets

Exporter secrets are secrets used to derive additional secret keys for use outside of the TLS protocol. Some higher-level protocols use TLS to establish a shared secret key and afterward use TLS keying material for other protocol-specific purposes. This, in turn, requires exporting keying material to higher-layer protocols or applications as well as agreeing on the context in which that keying material will be used.

For example, the DTLS-SRTP protocol first uses **Datagram-TLS (DTLS)** to exchange secret keys and selects the **Secure Real-Time Transport** Protocol **(SRTP)** protection suite. Subsequently, it uses DTLS `master_secret` to derive SRTP keys.

To enable this, TLS offers a mechanism called Key Material Exporter, details of which are defined in RFC 5705 [145]. The exported values are referred to as **Exported Keying Material (EKM)**. In TLS, `early_exporter_master_secret` and `exporter_master_secret` are examples of EKM generated at different stages of the TLS handshake.

TLS exporters have the following cryptographic properties:

- They allow Bob and Alice to export the same EKM value

- For attacker Eve who does not know the `master_secret`, EKM is indistinguishable from a random number

- Bob and Alice can export multiple EKM values from a single TLS connection

- Even if Eve learns one EKM value, she learns nothing about other EKM values or the `master_secret`

12.2.5   Derived secrets

These are intermediate secrets that are used as salt arguments for the HKDF-Extract function (which we will shortly discuss in detail). The HKDF-Extract function, in turn, generates the Handshake Secret and the Master Secret.

12.2.6   Handshake secret

This secret is the final result of the handshake. It is either derived from the Early Secret if a PSK is in place or from the secret Alice and Bob have exchanged during a Diffie-Hellman. The Handshake Secret is used to derive the `client_handshake_traffic_secret` for Bob and the `server_handshake_traffic_secret` for Alice.

12.2.7   Handshake traffic secrets

Bob subsequently uses the `client_handshake_traffic_secret` secret and Alice uses the `server_handshake_traffic_secret` secret to generate secret keys for their handshake traffic encryption.

12.2.8   Master secret

The Master Secret is used to derive the `client_application_traffic_secret0` for Bob and the `server_application_traffic_secret0` for Alice. These secrets can be updated later during a TLS session, hence their index 0.

12.2.9   Application traffic secrets

The `client_application_traffic_secret0` is used by Bob and the `server_application_traffic_secret0` is used by Alice to generate corresponding secret keys for encryption of the application data. These keys allow Alice and Bob to establish a secure channel for the bulk application data. TLS also has an optional mechanism to update these secrets and, in turn, these keys during a TLS session.

12.2.10   Resumption master secret

This secret is used to derive the pre-shared secret key for TLS session resumption. After a successful handshake, Alice can send Bob the identity of a PSK derived during that handshake. Bob can then use this PSK identity in subsequent TLS handshakes with Alice in order to signal his desire to use the associated PSK.

We now turn to the question of how the secrets are derived from the exchanged keying material.

12.3   KDFs in TLS

TLS uses four different functions to derive secrets: HKDF-Extract, HKDF-Expand, HKDF-Expand-Label, and Derive-Secret. All these functions are based on the **Hashed Message Authentication Code (HMAC)**-based **Extract-and-Expand Key Derivation Function (HKDF)** defined in RFC 5869 [104].

We will have much more to say on hash functions, message authentication codes, and key derivation function in *Chapter 11, Hash Functions and Message Authentication Codes.* For now, it is sufficient to treat HKDF as an abstract function, as shown in *Figure 12.2*. It takes keying material as input and returns one or more secret keys as output:

Figure 12.2: High-level view of the HKDF function

HKDF follows an *extract-then-expand* approach consisting of two logical stages. The rationale for this two-step approach is explained nicely in the introduction of [104]: *"In many applications, the input keying material is not necessarily distributed uniformly, and the attacker may have some partial knowledge about it (for example, a Diffie-Hellman value computed by a key exchange protocol) or even partial control of it (as in some entropy-gathering applications). Thus, the goal of the extract-stage is to concentrate the possibly dispersed entropy of the input keying material into a short, but cryptographically strong, pseudorandom key. In some applications, the input may already be a good pseudorandom key; in these cases, the extract-stage is not necessary, and the "expand" part can be used alone. The second stage expands the pseudorandom key to the desired length; the number and lengths of the output keys depend on the specific cryptographic algorithms for which the keys are needed."*

Now, let's take a look at the extract-and-expand-functions in HKDFs.

12.3.1 HKDF-Extract

HKDF-Extract, or H_E for short, implements the first stage of the HKDF, which takes the keying material as input and extracts a fixed-length pseudorandom key K from it. In particular, it is involved in the derivation of the handshake secret S_H and the master secret S_M (see *Figure 12.9* and *Figure 12.11*, respectively).

HKDF-Extract is illustrated in *Figure 12.3*. It takes two inputs: a salt and an **input keying material (IKM)**. The salt is a non-secret random value. If no salt is provided, HKDF-Extract takes a string of zeros of the length equal to that of the hash function output. HKDF-Extract outputs a **pseudorandom key (PRK)**. The PRK is calculated as PRK = HMAC-Hash(salt, IKM). Since HKDF-Extract is based on the HMAC construction, which is in turn a construction template that can use different hash functions [103], HKDF-Extract can also use different cryptographic hash functions.

A new TLS secret is derived using HKDF-Extract with the current TLS secret state as salt and the PSK – established out of band or derived from the `resumption_master_secret` instance of a previous TLS session – or the DHE or ECDHE based shared secret that Alice and Bob have established during the current TLS handshake as IKM.

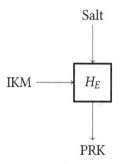

Figure 12.3: HKDF-Extract function used for TLS key derivation

12.3.2 HKDF-Expand

The second stage of the HKDF function expands a PRK to a pseudorandom bit string of the desired length, which can then be used to derive secret keys. HKDF-Expand is illustrated in *Figure 12.4*.

HKDF-Expand takes three inputs: a pseudorandom key PRK (which must have at least the length of the output of the hash function used), an optional context and application-specific information *info*, and the desired length in bytes of the output keying material L.

The output of HKDF-Expand is an L-byte long **Output Keying Material (OKM)**. The OKM is calculated by first calculating the following N values, where N is the result of the ceiling function applied to $(L/HashLen)$:

$$T(0) = \text{empty string(zero length)}$$

$$T(1) = \text{HMAC-Hash}(\text{PRK}, T(0)|info|0x01)$$

$$T(2) = \text{HMAC-Hash}(\text{PRK}, T(1)|info|0x02)$$

$$\cdots$$

$$T(N) = \text{HMAC-Hash}(\text{PRK}, T(N-1)|info|N)$$

where | denotes the bit-wise concatenation. The HMAC construction for key-dependent hash values is explained in *Section 11.5, Message authentication codes.* After that, the OKM is built by taking the first L octets of $T = T(1)|T(2)|...|T(N)$.

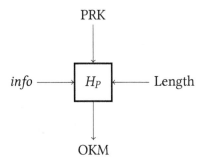

Figure 12.4: The HKDF-Expand function H_P

After each invocation of the HKDF-Extract function, the HKDF-Expand function is invoked one or more times.

12.3.3 HKDF-Expand-Label

HKDF-Expand-Label (or H_{EL} for short) is a pseudorandom function as shown in *Figure 12.5.* Recall this means that it can be efficiently computed for any given input, but it cannot be efficiently distinguished from a uniformly random function [37].

HKDF-Expand-Label takes a secret, the desired length of the output L, and an HKDF-Label as input, and expands them to OKM.

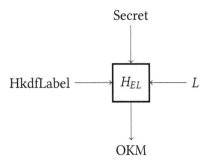

Figure 12.5: The HKDF-Expand-Label function H_{EL}

The `HkdfLabel` data structure is defined as in *Listing 24.* It essentially consists of a label and a context. All labels used in TLS 1.3 are strings. The context might have zero length.

```
struct {
    uint16 length = Length;
    opaque label<7..255> = "tls13 " + Label;
    opaque context<0..255> = Context;
} HkdfLabel;
```

Listing 24: HkdfLabel data structure

HKDF-Expand-Label illustrates a cryptographic good practice where keying material and, in turn, keys are derived for a specific purpose using a label and a context as inputs to the KDF.

12.3.4 Derive-Secret

Finally, the TLS 1.3 Derive-Secret function *DS* is defined as shown in *Figure 12.6.* It takes a secret, a label, and TLS messages as input, and outputs one of the TLS secrets listed in *Table 12.1.* In the subsequent step, these secrets will be used to derive the TLS keys.

As a result, multiple calls to Derive-Secret can be used to derive keying material for different secret keys even with the same secret as input as long as different messages are used to compute the transcript hash.

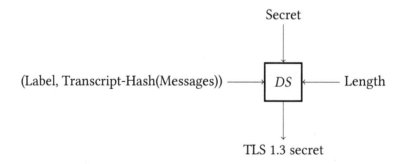

Figure 12.6: The Derive-Secret function DS

Derive-Secret implements a clever way to bind the keying material to previous messages exchanged during a specific execution of a cryptographic protocol. This is desirable from a cryptography perspective because it causes Alice and Bob to derive completely different secret keys and, as a result, leads to a failure of the cryptographic protocol since Alice cannot understand what Bob encrypted or authenticated, and vice versa.

This approach implements an implicit protection against man-in-the-middle attacks. Even if Mallory manages to intercept and manipulate messages exchanged by Alice and Bob, she cannot trick them into deriving an identical secret key because Alice's message transcript will be different from Bob's message transcript.

As illustrated in *Figure 12.7*, Alice and Bob start by deriving the Early Secret S_E and an intermediate secret S_0 (which will be used for further computations). Eventually, Alice and Bob will establish a secure TLS channel by deriving the shared cryptographic keys from these secrets.

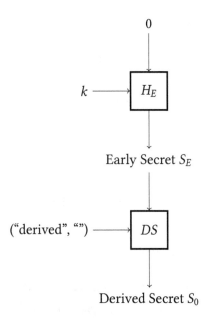

Figure 12.7: *Derivation of the TLS early secret and first derived secret* S_0

If a specific TLS secret is not available, a zero value – a string of 0-valued bytes – is taken as input. As an example, if the pre-shared key PSK is not used, the early secret will be computed as follows:

```
Early_Secret = HKDF-Extract(0, 0)
```

Next, Alice and Bob compute the binder key k_{bind}, `client_early_traffic_secret` and `early_exporter_master_secret` as shown in *Figure 12.8*. The binder key may be used to establish subsequent TLS sessions, and the early traffic secret and the exporter Master Secret are used to calculate the corresponding keys.

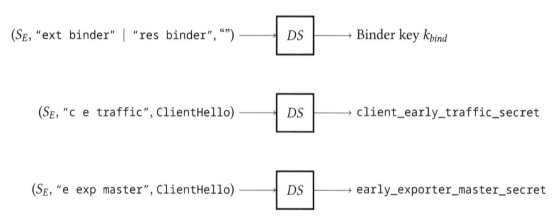

Figure 12.8: Derivation of TLS binder key, client early traffic secret and early exporter master secret

To prevent Alice and Bob from mixing up the binder keys, different labels are used for the derivation of the corresponding TLS secrets. For binder keys provisioned outside of TLS, the label `"ext binder"` is used. For resumption keys provisioned as the resumption Master Secret of a previous handshake, the label `"res binder"` is used.

If Alice and Bob choose to perform the TLS handshake based on a PSK, there are multiple possible values that the early secret S_E can take. The actual value of S_E depends on the PSK that Alice selects from those offered by Bob (using their identifiers).

As a result, Bob needs to compute the early secret for *every* PSK he offers to Alice. If Alice selects no PSK from those being offered by Bob, he needs to compute the early secret with a PSK being all zeros.

In the next step, illustrated in *Figure 12.9*, Alice and Bob compute the **Handshake Secret** S_H and the second intermediate secret S_1. The Handshake Secret is derived from the first intermediate secret S_0 and the DHE or ECDHE key share that Alice and Bob exchange during the TLS handshake.

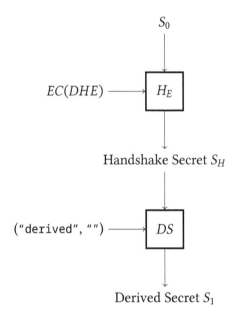

Figure 12.9: Derivation of the TLS handshake secret S_H and the second derived secret S_1

In the fourth step, Alice and Bob derive the `client_handshake_traffic_secret` and `server_handshake_traffic_secret` secrets needed to compute the corresponding handshake traffic keys. This is shown in *Figure 12.10*.

Note how – in addition to using the handshake secret S_H itself – the handshake traffic secrets are derived using not only the `"c hs traffic"` and `"s hs traffic"` labels but also the transcript *trans$_{CHSH}$* of all TLS handshakes starting with ClientHello up until and including the ServerHello message.

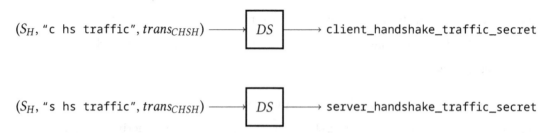

Figure 12.10: Derivation of TLS handshake traffic secrets

Next, as shown in *Figure 12.11*, Alice and Bob derive the *master secret* S_M. This secret will be used for the calculation of the application traffic keys for protecting the bulk application data Alice and Bob want to transmit over the secure TLS channel.

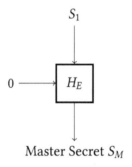

Figure 12.11: Derivation of the TLS master secret

While the early secret, handshake secret, and master secret (as well as the two intermediate derived secrets) can be viewed as raw entropy without any context, traffic secrets and exporter secrets include the TLS handshake context and, as a result, can be used to derive cryptographic keys without any additional context information.

Moreover, multiple invocations of the Derive-Secret function *DS* take the same TLS secret as input but return different outputs because they take different messages as additional input argument.

Finally, the master secret S_M, the corresponding labels and the TLS handshake transcript *trans$_{CHSF}$* are used to derive the first application traffic secrets, the exporter master secret and the resumption master secret (see *Figure 12.12*). Transcript *trans$_{CHSF}$* includes all handshake messages starting from `ClientHello` up until including the Alice's `Finished` message.

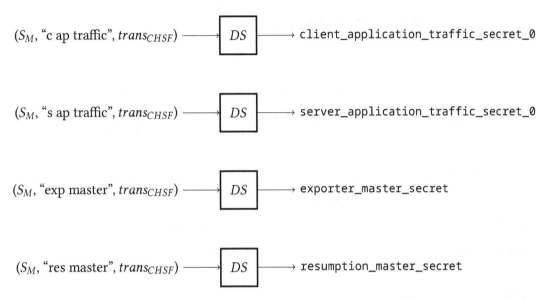

Figure 12.12: Derivation of the TLS application traffic secrets, exporter master secret and resumption master secret

This step concludes the derivation of TLS secrets from the keying material. However, the secrets may be *updated* without having to exchange new key material.

12.4 Updating TLS secrets

At any time after a successful handshake, Alice and Bob can update their application traffic keys using the `KeyUpdate` message. They accomplish this by first deriving new secrets `server_application_traffic_secret_N+1` and `client_application_traffic_secret_N+1` using the HKDF-Expand-Label function H_{EL} as shown in *Figure 12.13*. After that, new application traffic keys are computed using a mechanism we will discuss in the next section.

The TLS 1.3 specification recommends Alice and Bob to delete the n-th server/client application traffic secret and its associated key once the $n + 1$-th secret has been derived and corresponding traffic keys have been computed.

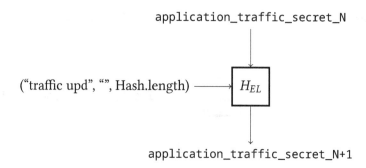

Figure 12.13: Mechanism for updating TLS application traffic secrets

This is another example of a best practice in applied cryptography and security engineering: as soon as cryptographic material is no longer needed, it should be deleted so it cannot fall into Eve's hands. In practice, this means that any device that temporarily stores user's secrets should have an easy-to-invoke function for secure decommissioning.

12.5 TLS keys

TLS uses two types of secret keys. The **Handshake Traffic Keys** are are used for the encryption of the TLS handshake traffic. They are derived from the TLS secrets:

- Alice's key is derived from `server_handshake_traffic_secret`

- Bob's key is derived from `client_handshake_traffic_secret`

The **Application Traffic Keys** are used to encrypt the bulk application data that Bob and Alice transmit during their TLS session. Similar to handshake traffic keys, they are also generated from two different secrets:

- `server_application_traffic_secret` for Alice's key

- `client_application_traffic_secret` for Bob's key

Alice uses her handshake traffic key to encrypt one or more messages to Bob during the TLS handshake: `EncryptedExtensions` and, optionally, `CertificateRequest`, `Certificate`, and `CertificateVerify`.

The `EncryptedExtensions` message contains a list of extensions not necessary for establishing TLS secrets and, in turn, TLS keys. This is an important protocol design decision in TLS 1.3. Previous TLS versions did not have such a mechanism and all data in Alice's reply was transmitted in plaintext. As a result, Eve was able to learn a lot of interesting information about the TLS connection between Alice and Bob. In TLS 1.3, all this information is encrypted.

When Alice authenticates herself to Bob using a certificate, she can optionally request that Bob also prove his identity using a certificate of his own. Alice does this by sending Bob the `CertificateRequest` message.

The `Certificate` message contains Alice's certificate chain which Bob can use to verify Alice's identity. In addition, the `CertificateVerify` message contains an explicit proof that Alice indeed knows the private key corresponding to the certificate that vouches her identity. Finally, Alice also encrypts her Finished message using her handshake traffic key.

Don't worry if some aspects of certificates are unclear to you, such as certificate chains. In a nutshell, certificate chains are sequences of certificates linked together to establish a transitive trust chain from a root certificate to an end-entity certificate. We will cover this topic in detail in *Chapter 10, Digital Certificates and Certificate Authorities.*

Bob uses his handshake traffic key to encrypt the two optional TLS messages, `Certificate` and `CertificateVerify`. Analogous to Alice, Bob uses his handshake traffic key to encrypt his Finished message.

Figure 12.14 shows which TLS messages are encrypted using Alice's and Bob's handshake traffic and application traffic keys. Messages encrypted with Alice's handshake traffic key are shown as $\{ \cdot \}_{k_A}$, and those encrypted with Bob's handshake traffic key as $\{ \cdot \}_{k_B}$. Messages encrypted with Alice's application traffic key are denoted as $[\cdot]_{k_A}$. Messages encrypted with Bob's application traffic key are shown as $[\cdot]_{k_B}$. An asterisk $*$ denotes optional TLS messages.

Figure 12.14: Encrypted messages in a TLS 1.3 session

12.5.1   Exporter values

Exporter values are computed using the Derive-Secret DS and the HKDF-Expand-Label H_{EL} functions as shown in *Figure 12.15*. The input secret can be either early_exporter_master_secret or exporter_master_secret. Bob and Alice use early_exporter_master_secret when they need an exporter for 0-RTT data. For all other cases, the TLS 1.3 standard requires them to use exporter_master_secret.

If the TLS endpoint does not provide a context, a zero-length context_value is used, which yields the same result as an empty context.

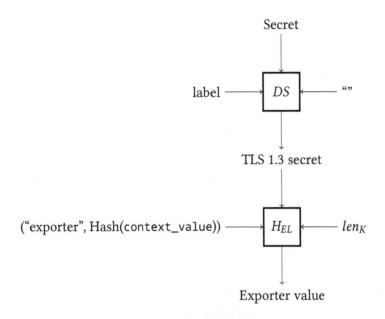

Figure 12.15: Generation of TLS exporter values

12.5.2 Generation of TLS keys

In TLS 1.3, cryptographic keys are generated using the HKDF-Expand-Label function. Alice and Bob derive the keys either from a pre-shared secret key *PSK* they know in advance, or from a DHE- or ECDHE-based secret they establish during the TLS handshake.

The PSK can be established out of band. For example, if Alice is a device provisioning service and Bob is a smart home device from the same manufacturer, the PSK can be distributed in the manufacturing phase in the plant environment, which the company would typically consider secure.

Alternatively, the PSK can be derived from the `resumption_master_secret` secret that Alice and Bob established in one of their previous TLS sessions.

If Alice and Bob use the Diffie-Hellman key exchange protocol, they exchange information about the group they want to use for it: either the multiplicative group in a finite field (DHE) or an elliptic curve (ECDHE). After that, they agree either on finite field Diffie-Hellman parameters (for DHE) or elliptic curve Diffie-Hellman parameters (for ECDHE).

For the moment, we can ignore the details of the underlying cryptography. We will come back to this topic and cover public-key cryptography, Diffie-Hellman key exchange, and elliptic curve cryptography in *Chapter 7, Public-Key Cryptography*, and *Chapter 8, Elliptic Curves*.

Every TLS traffic key actually consists of the key itself and a so-called *initialization vector*. The initialization vector is an input needed when using certain block cipher modes of operation. We will cover initialization vectors and the requirements they have to fulfill in more detail in *Chapter 14, Block Ciphers and Their Modes of Operation*. For the time being, you can simply view the initialization vector as additional (public) input to the encryption function.

TLS traffic keys and their corresponding initialization vectors are generated using the HKDF-Expand-Label function with the following input values:

- One of the derived TLS secrets

- A value indicating the purpose of the key to be generated, for example, a label or context information

- The length of the key to be generated

In the TLS 1.3 specification in RFC 8446, all keys used by Alice to encrypt handshake or application traffic are referred to as `server_write_key`. The corresponding initialization vectors are called `server_write_iv`. By analogy, Bob's traffic keys are called `client_write_key` and the corresponding initialization vectors `client_write_iv`.

What makes each traffic key – and its associated initialization vector – unique is the TLS secret used as input to the HKDF-Expand-Label function. For example, Alice's key for encrypting data during TLS handshake is computed as follows:

```
server_write_key = HKDF-Expand-Label(server_handshake_traffic_secret,
"key", "", key_length)
```

But Alice's application traffic key for encrypting application data right after the TLS handshake is computed as follows:

```
server_write_key =
HKDF-Expand-Label(server_application_traffic_secret_0, "key", "",
key_length)
```

Note how the string input `"key"` is used to indicate that the output of the HKDF-Expand-Label function is a cryptographic key, not the initialization vector. This is a good example of how different keying material can be generated using the same function and the same secret, but different labels.

Table 12.2 shows which TLS secrets and labels are used to generate the different TLS keys. No additional context information is used for generating the keys because the different TLS secrets already carry the relevant context thanks to the labels and transcripts that were used as inputs to function *DS* to derive these TLS secrets.

Type	TLS key	TLS Secret	Label
0	k_B	`client_early_traffic_secret`	"key"
0	iv_B	`client_early_traffic_secret`	"iv"
H	k_A	`server_handshake_traffic_secret`	"key"
H	iv_A	`server_handshake_traffic_secret`	"iv"
H	k_B	`client_handshake_traffic_secret`	"key"
H	iv_B	`client_handshake_traffic_secret`	"iv"
A	k_A	`server_application_traffic_secret_N`	"key"
A	iv_A	`server_application_traffic_secret_N`	"iv"
A	k_B	`client_application_traffic_secret_N`	"key"
A	iv_B	`client_application_traffic_secret_N`	"iv"

Table 12.2: TLS secrets and labels used for the TLS key calculation

TLS 1.3 has three different types of cryptographic keys used in different contexts: encryption of 0-RTT application data, encryption of TLS handshake messages, and application of the bulk application data transmitted in a TLS session.

The types of the keys for these contexts is denoted by 0, H, and A, respectively. Bob's key –
denoted as `client_write_key` in RFC 8446 – is k_B in *Table 12.2*. Bob's initialization vector
is denoted as iv_B. Similarly, Alice's key – specified as `server_write_key` in RFC 8446 – is
denoted by k_A and Alice's initialization vector as iv_A.

12.5.3   Key update

After the TLS handshake, both Alice and Bob can update their traffic keys at any point in
time by sending the `KeyUpdate` message. Alice's new traffic key is generated by deriving
`server_application_traffic_secret_N+1` from `server_application_traffic_secret_N`
as follows:

```
server_application_traffic_secret_N+1 =
HKDF-Expand-Label(server_application_traffic_secret_N, "traffic upd",
"", Hash.length)
```

After that, the new traffic key is computed using the HKDF-Expand-Label function as
described previously. Similarly, Bob's new traffic key is generated by first computing this:

```
client_application_traffic_secret_N+1 =
HKDF-Expand-Label(client_application_traffic_secret_N, "traffic upd",
"", Hash.length)
```

Afterwards, HKDF-Expand-Label is applied to generate the new traffic key.

After having seen how the TLS keys are generated from the TLS secrets, we now take a
detailed look at what exactly the TLS handshake messages for agreeing on a cryptographic
setting and shared keys look like.

12.6   TLS key exchange messages

During the TLS handshake, the Bob and the Alice negotiate the cryptographic settings for
the key establishment and agree upon shared secret keys using **Key Exchange Messages**.

These keys are used to protect the later part of the handshake itself as well as the subsequent application data transmitted between Bob and Alice.

We saw in *Chapter 6, Transport Layer Security at a Glance,* that there are a number of different handshake messages used depending on the chosen key exchange option and the current state of the protocol.

The handshake messages must be sent in the order specified by the TLS protocol. Whenever Alice or Bob receive an out-of-order handshake message, they immediately abort the handshake and signal the error by transmitting the unexpected_alert message.

This illustrates two good practices in cryptographic protocol design. First, the expected order of messages must be unambiguous in any given situation to avoid misinterpretations both on Alice's and on Bob's side. Second, because any deviation from the specified protocol must be treated as a potential attack attempt, the protocol must be stopped immediately, and the other party must be notified about the cause of the failure. The error message not only allows the other party to terminate the protocol but also leaves an audit trace for a potential investigation later on.

Technically speaking, handshake messages are transmitted by passing them to the TLS record layer, where they are encapsulated into one or more TLSPlaintext or TLSCiphertext data structures.

12.6.1 Cryptographic negotiation

Bob, the client, starts cryptographic negotiation by sending the ClientHello message to Alice, the server. This message contains the information about Bob's crytographic capabilities.

The first piece of information in ClientHello is a list of **Authenticated Encryption with Associated Data (AEAD)** algorithms and HKDFs that Bob can compute. We will have more to tell about these specific algorithms in *Chapter 15, Authenticated Encryption,* and *Chapter 11, Hash Functions and Message Authenication Codes,* respectively.

In TLS jargon, such combinations of cryptographic algorithms supported by an endpoint are referred to as *cipher suites*, and ClientHello contains a list of *symmetric cipher suites* defining pairs of AEAD and HKDF algorithms that the client supports.

TLS defines the naming convention for symmetric cipher suites as *TLS_AEAD_HASH = VALUE*, where *TLS* stands for the TLS protocol, *AEAD* denotes the AEAD algorithm for protecting TLS records together with the key size, *HASH* is the hash function used in HKDF, and *VALUE* is a two-byte identifier assigned to that particular cipher suite in the TLS specification. As an example, the symmetric cipher suite TLS_AES_128_GCM_SHA256 refers to the AEAD scheme based on the AES block cipher in **Galois Counter Mode (GCM)** with 128 bits as the key size and SHA-256 as the hash functions. This cipher suite has the associated identifier 0x13,0x01.

The supported_groups and key_share extensions contain the second piece of cryptographic information in the ClientHello message. A TLS extension is simply a data structure composed of the extension type (defined in the TLS standard) and extension data specific to that extension type:

```
struct {
    ExtensionType extension_type;
    opaque extension_data<0..2^16-1>;
} Extension;
```

The supported_groups extension tells Alice (the server) which groups Bob is able to use for the DHE- or ECDHE-related computations. The key_share extension lists the DHE or ECDHE shares for some or all of these groups. We will have more to say about these topics in *Chapter 8, Elliptic Curves*. For now, it is sufficient to know that Alice and Bob need to agree on these parameters to be able to use the Diffie-Hellman key agreement we briefly touched upon in previous chapters.

ClientHello further contains the signature_algorithms extension. It lists digital signature algorithms that Bob (the client) can use. As a result, Alice must use one of these algorithms so that Bob can verify Alice's digital signature.

Moreover, Bob can add `signature_algorithms_cert` to the `ClientHello` message indicating certificate-specific signature algorithms. These are the signature algorithms Bob is able to support for verification of the digital signature of a certificate.

Finally, `ClientHello` might contain the `pre_shared_key` extension listing the identities of all symmetric keys known to Bob, the client, as well as the `psk_key_exchange_modes` extension that tells Alice, the server, which specific key exchange modes can be used with the pre-shared symmetric keys.

This is a good example of how interoperability between different communicating parties can be achieved in a secure manner. Essentially, Bob proposes to Alice a set of options he considers secure and Alice can choose any subset she wants and deems to be secure. Because these cryptographic options are defined in the TLS 1.3 standard, only secure choices are possible (note that in older TLS versions, there are still insecure choices available). If Alice and Bob cannot agree on a common subset, Alice terminates the protocol.

This scheme ensures an important security property. While the endpoints' capability to negotiate is retained – and so the protocol works with a wide range of systems – neither Bob nor Alice can force the protocol to use insecure cryptographic parameters. If this were possible, Eve could impersonate one of the endpoints and break TLS security by supplying weak parameters. In *Chapter 7, Public-Key Encryption*, we will see in detail why this would work.

If Alice chooses to establish shared secret keys for the secure communication channel using DH or ECDH key agreement, she selects the cipher suite, the DH or ECDH group and the key share, and the signature algorithm and the certificate to authenticate herself to Bob. For this to work, however, Alice's choices must match one of the values in Bob's `supported_groups` and `signature_algorithms` extensions. If this is not the case, the TLS protocol specification requires Alice to terminate the handshake and to send Bob a `handshake_failure` or `insufficient_security` message.

Here we see another example of a good practice in (cryptographic) protocol design: the response to a protocol failure and the error handling are well defined. Namely, if the parameter negotiation is unsuccessful, the protocol is terminated. It is also exactly specified which communicating party does what: Alice terminates the handshake and sends an error message to Bob. The error handling itself is explicit and well defined – transmission of a `handshake_failure` or `insufficient_security` message – and so leaves a kind of paper trail that's useful for debugging, auditing, or digital forensics.

If Alice chooses to use a PSK instead, she needs to select one of the key establishment modes listed in Bob's `psk_key_exchange_modes` extension in the `ClientHello` message. If the PSK is used alone, that is, without combining it with DH or ECDH key agreement, it doesn't matter whether Alice supports any of the parameters listed in Bob's `supported_groups` extension.

If Alice selects a DH or ECDH group that does not match Bob's `key_share` extension in the initial `ClientHello` message, Alice has to reply with a `HelloRetryRequest` message. Otherwise, if there is an overlap between the cryptographic parameters chosen by Alice and the cryptographic parameters offered by Bob, Alice indicates her choices in the `ServerHello` message, a reply to `ClientHello`.

If a PSK shall be used, `ServerHello` contains the `pre_shared_key` extension telling Bob which PSK he needs to select. If the DH or ECDH key agreement shall be used, `ServerHello` contains the `key_share` extension with Alice's DH or ECDH key share.

In addition, if Alice authenticates herself to Bob using a digital certificate (more on digital certificates in *Chapter 10, Digital Certificates and Certification Authorities*), Alice will transmit to Bob the messages `Certificate` and `CertificateVerify`.

12.6.2 ClientHello

According to TLS specification, `ClientHello` must be the first message Bob sends to Alice. Bob must also send `ClientHello` if Alice has responded with `HelloRetryRequest` message because of a mismatch in their cryptographic parameters. In the latter case, Bob must respond with the same `ClientHello` message, altering only specific parameter values.

If `HelloRetryRequest` contains a `key_share` extension, Bob must adjust his list of key shares to include a key share from the indicated group. If Bob's initial `ClientHello` message contained the `early_data` extension, it must be removed from subsequent `ClientHello` because the TLS specification forbids sending early data after a `HelloRetryRequest` response.

If Alice's `HelloRetryRequest` response includes a `cookie` extension, Bob must add this extension to his subsequent `ClientHello`. This extension allows Alice to offload state information to Bob, so she can send `HelloRetryRequest` without storing the state.

Finally, if it is present, Bob may update the `pre_shared_key` extension and, optionally, add, remove, or alter the `padding` extension length. The fact that only specific changes are permitted to `ClientHello` illustrates another interesting aspect: the TLS 1.3 specification deliberately reduces the complexity of the protocol and, thus, the complexity of the software or hardware needed to execute the protocol, by limiting the number of valid changes. As we saw in *Chapter 1, Role of Cryptography in the Connected World*, complexity is an enemy of security. So, in practice, this simple constraint helps to prevent implementation bugs that might turn into security vulnerabilities.

Another notable TLS 1.3 design decision is to forbid renegotiation. If Alice successfully completes the cryptographic negotiation with Bob, but later on – at any point in time – receives a `ClientHello` message, Alice terminates their TLS connection and sends Bob the `unexpected_message` message. This is a new feature within TLS 1.3 that was added because of earlier **Renegotiation Attacks**, in which an attacker Mallory makes the victim send a request for a protected resource to a TLS server. This request is stored by the attacker and not forwarded to the server. Instead Mallory sets up a TLS session of her own and requests a different protected resource. To authenticate the request, many TLS servers initiated a session renegotiation by sending a new `ServerHello` message. The attacker can now respond with the stored `ClientHello` message from the stored earlier request.

The basic problem here is that there is no logical connection between requests made within different TLS sessions. In order to avoid these problems, session renegotiation is forbidden in TLS 1.3 even if a TLS session in an earlier version is to be renegotiated to version 1.3. In other words, if Alice has established a TLS connection based on a version of TLS previous to 1.3, and she receives a TLS 1.3 ClientHello in a renegotiation, she must stick to the previous TLS protocol version. The detailed structure of the ClientHello message is shown in *Listing 25*.

The legacy_version constant exists for historical reasons. Previous to TLS 1.3, this message field indicated the highest TLS version number that Bob supports, and it was used to negotiate the TLS version between Bob and Alice.

```
uint16 ProtocolVersion;
opaque Random[32];
uint8 CipherSuite[2]; /* Cryptographic suite selector */

struct {
    ProtocolVersion legacy_version = 0x0303; /* TLS v1.2 */
    Random random;
    opaque legacy_session_id<0..32>;
    CipherSuite cipher_suites<2..2^16-2>;
    opaque legacy_compression_methods<1..2^8-1>;
    Extension extensions<8..2^16-1>;
} ClientHello;
```

Listing 25: ClientHello message structure

In turned out, however, that the implementation of TLS version negotiation was flawed in many TLS servers. As a result, servers would reject a well-formed ClientHello message where the TLS version number was higher than the one supported by the server.

To resolve this *Version Intolerance* issue in TLS 1.3, Bob communicates his preferred TLS versions in the supported_versions extension. The legacy_version field must be set to the constant 0x0303 which stands for TLS version 1.2.

Thus, Alice recognizes the TLS 1.3 ClientHello message based on the value 0x0303 of the legacy_version field and the value 0x0304 present in the supported_versions extension as the highest TLS version supported by Bob.

The random field in the ClientHello message contains a 32-byte random number generated using a cryptographically secure random number generator. We will see in the following chapters what this number is used for.

As the name indicates, legacy_session_id is another legacy field in the ClientHello message. Prior to version 1.3, TLS had a dedicated session resumption feature. In TLS 1.3, this feature was merged with PSKs, in that the secret negotiated in the previous session is treated like a PSK in the resumed session. In the current TLS version, this field is set to 0 unless compatibility mode is used (see RFC 8446 [147], Appendix D, for details).

cipher_suites lists symmetric cryptography settings supported by Bob. In particular, cipher_suites includes the symmetric algorithm for protecting TLS records as well as the hash function to be used in the HKDF algorithm, for example, TLS_AES_256_GCM_SHA384. These settings are listed in Bob's descending preference order.

If cipher_suites lists cipher suites that Alice does not know, cannot compute, or does not want to use, she must ignore these cipher suites and treat others as usual. If Bob wants to perform the TLS handshake using a PSK, he has to indicate at least one cipher suite that defines the hash function to be used with the PSK for deriving further secrets using an HKDF.

The legacy_compression_methods field is also a legacy from previous TLS versions and must be set to 0 in TLS 1.3. Prior to version 1.3, TLS supported compression. The algorithms supported by Bob were listed in legacy_compression_methods. The mandatory value 0 in TLS 1.3 corresponds to no compression, and Alice is required to terminate the TLS handshake – and send Bob an illegal_parameter message – if this field has any value different from zero. However, if a TLS 1.3 server receives a version 1.2 or earlier ClientHello message, it must follow the protocol defined for that specific TLS version.

Using the extensions field, Bob can request extended functionality from Alice. If Bob sends an extension request, Alice typically answers with the corresponding extension response. If Bob requests extended functionality that is not supported by Alice, Bob may terminate the TLS handshake.

In TLS 1.3, the ClientHello message always contains extensions because it includes the mandatory supported_versions extension. If this is not the case, Alice will interpret that ClientHello as a TLS 1.2 message.

Once Bob transmits ClientHello, he must wait for a ServerHello or HelloRetryRequest message from Alice. In addition, if Bob uses early data, he may send this data to Alice while waiting for her next handshake message.

12.6.3   ServerHello

Upon receiving a ClientHello message from Bob, Alice responds with the ServerHello message to continue the TLS handshake – if Alice is able to select a feasible set of cryptographic parameters based on the choices offered by Bob in his ClientHello message. The structure of ServerHello is shown in *Listing 26*.

```
struct {
    ProtocolVersion legacy_version = 0x0303; /* TLS v1.2 */
    Random random;
    opaque legacy_session_id_echo<0..32>;
    CipherSuite cipher_suite;
    uint8 legacy_compression_method = 0;
    Extension extensions<6..2^16-1>;
} ServerHello;
```

Listing 26: ServerHello message structure

The legacy_version field – as you have surely already guessed – is a remnant from previous TLS versions. It was used for version negotiation and contained the TLS version number that Alice selected for that TLS connection.

However, some middleboxes prevent a TLS connection when they encounter a new TLS version number unknown to them in the ServerHello message. A middlebox is a network device that transforms, inspects, filters, and manipulates network traffic beyond mere packet forwarding, for example, a firewall, a network address translator, a load balancer, or a deep packet inspection appliance [182].

To address this downside in TLS 1.3, Alice indicates the TLS version she wants to use in the `supported_versions` extension and sets the `legacy_version` field to 0x0303, the code for TLS 1.2.

The `random` field is a 32-byte random number that must be generated using a cryptographically secure random number generator. This number is generated by Alice and is completely independent from the random number in `ClientHello`.

The TLS 1.3 specification in RFC 8446 requires the use of a cryptographically secure **Pseudorandom Number Generator (PRNG)**. Most modern operating systems provide such a mechanism. As an example, the special `/dev/urandom` file in Linux-based systems provides the interface to the Linux kernel's random number generator and can be used as PRNG (see *Listing 27*). As an alternative, most modern cryptographic libraries provide suitable PRNGs.

```
$ hexdump -C -n 8 /dev/urandom
00000000  41 32 c8 61 53 e8 39 d3   |A2.aS.9.|
$ hexdump -C -n 8 /dev/urandom
00000000  30 db cc 9e 7f 03 43 8a   |0.....C.|
```

Listing 27: Output of Linux /dev/urandom PRNG

Random numbers are used in TLS in public message fields such as the `random` field in `ClientHello` and `ServerHello` messages, and for the generation of the keying material itself. As discussed in *Chapter 3, A Secret to Share*, a cryptographically secure PRNG must be designed in such a way that attacker Eve cannot predict its future output or determine its internal state from previously observed output. Formally, this is captured in the requirement that an attacker cannot efficiently distinguish the output sequence of a PRNG from a truly random sequence of the same length. If a PRNG used in a TLS handshake is insecure and Eve can (partially) predict its output, she can immediately break the security of the TLS connection between Alice and Bob.

The `legacy_session_id_echo` field contains the `legacy_session_id` value from Bob's `ClientHello` message. If Bob receives a `ServerHello` message with a `legacy_session_id_echo` value that does not match the value he sent to Alice in `ClientHello`, Bob immediately terminates the TLS handshake and sends Alice an `illegal_parameter` message.

`legacy_session_id_echo` is also an example of a cryptographic best practice to explicitly verify that what Alice heard is what Bob actually said. When Alice and Bob see different data in a protocol execution, it creates an opportunity for Eve and Mallory to break its security by tricking Alice or Bob to misinterpret the data they see.

The `cipher_suite` field contains the single cipher suite that Alice selected from the list of cipher suites offered by Bob in `cipher_suites` extension in his `ClientHello` message. If Alice selects a cipher suite that was not offered by Bob, Bob terminates the TLS handshake with an `illegal_parameter` message.

The `legacy_compression_method` field consists of a single byte that is always 0 in TLS 1.3.

Finally, the `extensions` field contains a list of – well, you guessed it – extensions. The `ServerHello` message is only allowed to include TLS extensions needed to agree on the cryptographic parameters and the TLS version. Therefore, TLS 1.3 `ServerHello` always contains the `supported_versions` extension and either the `pre_shared_key` or `key_share` extension (or both when a pre-shared symmetric key is used in combination with DH or ECDH key agreement).

The `ServerHello` message in TLS 1.3 also includes a mechanism that allows limited protection against downgrade attacks. In a nutshell, if a TLS 1.3 Alice negotiates a TLS 1.2 or TLS 1.1 connection, it must set the last eight bytes of the `random` field to the values 44 4F 57 4E 47 52 44 01 or 44 4F 57 4E 47 52 44 00, respectively, which means DOWNGRD in ASCII code.

12.6.4   HelloRetryRequest

If Alice receives a `ClientHello` message from Bob with a set of cryptographic parameters that Alice does not support or does not want to use, she responds with a `HelloRetryRequest` message. `HelloRetryRequest` has the same format as the `ServerHello` message, and the `legacy_version`, `legacy_session_id_echo`, `cipher_suite`, `legacy_compression_method` message fields have the same meaning.

Alice's `HelloRetryRequest` contains the `supported_versions` extension to tell Bob which TLS version Alice is using. In addition, it typically includes a minimal set of TLS extensions that tell Bob how – if this is possible for him – to adjust his choice of cryptographic parameters, transmitted in the subsequent `ClientHello`, so they match what Alice supports. With the exception of the optional `cookie` extension, `HelloRetryRequest` may not contain any extensions that Bob did not offer in his initial `ClientHello` message.

Upon receiving `HelloRetryRequest`, Bob uses the `supported_versions`, `cipher_suite`, and legacy-related TLS extensions we previously described to find out which TLS version Alice supports. If the information in these extensions has no effect on Bob's cryptographic parameter choice – that is, if it does not change the `ClientHello` message – Bob terminates the handshake and sends the `illegal_parameter` message to Alice.

Bob also terminates the handshake and sends Alice an `unexpected_message` message if he receives a second `HelloRetryRequest` message in the same TLS connection.

If none of the conditions for terminating the handshake apply, Bob processes all extensions he received from Alice in the `HelloRetryRequest` message and replies with an updated `ClientHello` to match Alice's settings.

If Bob receives a `HelloRetryRequest` message with a cipher suite that he did not offer in `ClientHello`, he terminates the handshake. Moreover, when Bob receives a second `ServerHello` (following `HelloRetryRequest` and the updated `ClientHello` messages), he checks that the cipher suite in `HelloRetryRequest` is identical to that in the second `ServerHello`. If this is not the case, Bob terminates the handshakes and sends Alice an `illegal_parameter` message.

Finally, Alice's TLS version in the `supported_versions` extension in the `HelloRetryRequest` message must be identical to the TLS version in the second `ServerHello` message. Otherwise, Bob terminates the handshake and sends Alice an `illegal_parameter` message.

This finishes our discussion of the TLS key exchange messages. Because of the many possible options, but also because of the need for backward compatibility, this was a rather lengthy and technical section.

12.7 Summary

In this chapter, we took a detailed look at the TLS specification and the various secrets and keys it defines. Specifically, we have seen how different keys used for different contexts are derived from initial secrets – either PSKs or a secret coming from a Diffie-Hellman key exchange.

We have also tried to highlight various best practices in cryptography engineering deployed within TLS: different keys for different purposes, well-defined fallback and alert procedures in case of protocol errors, and the destruction of obsolete keying material.

In the next chapter, we will take a step back and see how the cryptographic primitives we discussed in the previous chapters fit together to form the TLS Handshake protocol.

13

TLS Handshake Protocol Revisited

In previous chapters, you learned about the cryptographic primitives and mechanisms required to understand the inner workings of the TLS 1.3 handshake. Now is a good time to look at the TLS handshake from a bird's-eye view.

In this chapter, we will zoom out of the cryptographic details and revisit how the individual steps combine in the overall scheme of things. More precisely, we will discuss the TLS handshake protocol with the help of state machines for the TLS server and TLS client specified in RFC 8446. Moreover, we will show you how you can use s_client, a TLS client program from the popular OpenSSL toolkit, to conduct your own experiments with TLS.

Upon completion of the chapter, you will have a comprehensive understanding of how the individual protocol steps fit together, both on Alice's and on Bob's side. In terms of skills acquired, you will gain the following:

- A good overview of the entire TLS handshake

- Familiarity with the states of a TLS server and a TLS client, and the messages that trigger state transitions

- Knowledge about OpenSSL, a popular open source TLS toolkit

- An understanding of how to use s_client, part of the OpenSSL toolkit, to experiment with or debug TLS connections

13.1   TLS client state machine

Appendix A of RFC 8446, the IETF specification of TLS 1.3, summarizes valid states and state transitions for TLS 1.3 server and client. The client state machine is shown in *Figure 13.1*. Labels in square brackets indicate actions the client performs only under specific circumstances. Label $k = x$ indicates that the key k is set to value x.

Client Bob starts the TLS handshake by sending the ClientHello message to server Alice. If Bob and Alice have agreed upon a secret key in a previous TLS session, Bob may use this key to encrypt early data.

Bob then transitions into state WAIT_SH, denoted by W_{SH}, where he waits for the ServerHello message from Alice. If Bob's ClientHello contains parameter values that Alice does not support, she replies with a HelloRetryRequest message, thereby making Bob switch back to the initial state and re-send ClientHello with different parameters.

If, on the other hand, Bob receives a ServerHello while he is in the state W_{SH}, he sets the secret key and switches to the state WAIT_EE, denoted by W_EE in *Figure 13.1*, where he waits for EncryptedExtensions from Alice.

Upon receiving EncryptedExtensions, Bob switches to the state WAIT_CERT_CR, denoted as W_{CR}, if he wants Alice to authenticate herself using a digital certificate. While in the state W_{CR}, Bob either receives Alice's certificate and switches to state WAIT_CV, denoted as W_{CV}, or receives a CertificateRequest from Alice asking Bob to authenticate himself using a certificate and switches to the state WAIT_CERT, denoted as W_{CE}.

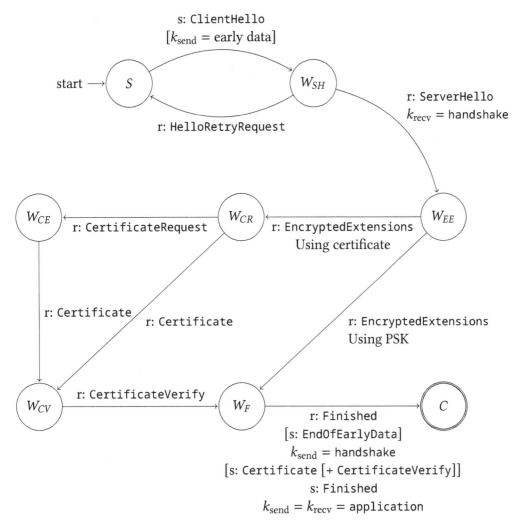

Figure 13.1: State machine and state transitions of a TLS 1.3 client

From W_{CE}, Bob transitions into state W_{CV} upon receiving Alice's certificate. In the next step, upon receiving the CertificateVerify message from Alice, Bob transitions into the WAIT_FINISHED state, denoted as W_F.

Alternatively, while in state W_{EE}, Bob might decide to use a pre-shared secret key and, as a result, let Alice authenticate herself implicitly by using the correct pre-shared key. In this case, Bob switches from W_{EE} to the state W_F.

While in the state W_F, Bob switches to the state CONNECTED, denoted by C, upon receiving the Finished message from Alice. If appropriate, Bob sends EndOfEarlyData as well as his own Certificate and CertificateVerify messages. Finally, Bob sends his Finished message and transitions into state C.

13.2 TLS server state machine

The server state machine is shown in *Figure 13.2*. Like with the client state machine, labels in square brackets indicate actions that the server performs only under specific circumstances.

For server Alice, the TLS handshake is triggered by receiving the ClientHello message from client Bob. Upon receiving this message, Alice transitions to the state RECVD_CH, denoted by R_{CH} in *Figure 13.2*.

If Bob's message contains parameters that Alice does not support, she replies with a HelloRetryRequest and switches into the initial state S.

Otherwise, Alice selects desired parameters from those offered by Bob in his ClientHello and replies with the ServerHello message. In addition, Alice sends EncryptedExtensions, encrypted with the handshake key.

Alice also sends the CertificateRequest message if she wants Bob to authenticate himself using his certificate. Moreover, if Bob has requested Alice to authenticate herself using her certificate, Alice replies with the Certificate and CertificateVerify messages. Alice then sends the Finished message and switches to the state NEGOTIATED, denoted by N.

If 0-RTT mode is desired, Alice uses the early data secret key and switches to the state WAIT_EOED, denoted by W_{EO}, where it receives early data from Bob. Upon receiving Bob's message EndOfEarlyData, Alice transitions to the state WAIT_FLIGHT2, denoted as W_{F2}.

If 0-RTT mode is not desired, Alice simply sets the shared secret key for receiving data to the handshake key and switches to the state W_{F2}.

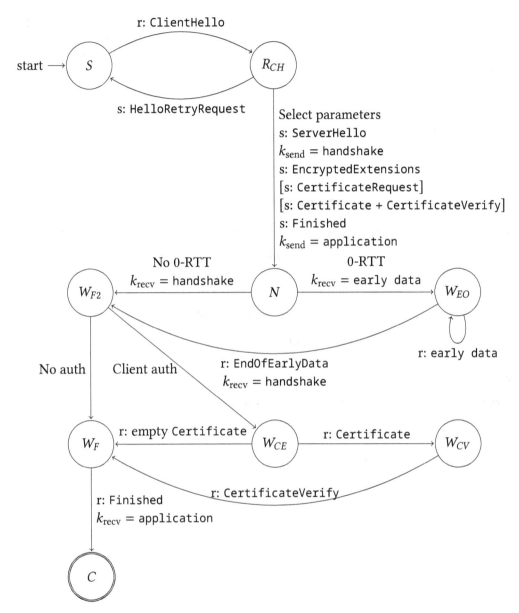

Figure 13.2: State machine and state transitions of a TLS 1.3 server

If Alice does not want Bob to authenticate himself, she switches directly to the state WAIT_FINISHED, denoted by W_F. Otherwise, she transitions into the state WAIT_CERT, denoted by W_{CE}, where she waits for the Certificate message from Bob.

If Alice receives Bob's Certificate while in state W_{CE}, she switches to the state WAIT_CV, denoted by W_{CV}. Alice then waits for the CertificateVerify message from Bob and, upon receiving this message, switches to W_F. Alternatively, if Alice receives an empty Certificate, she transitions directly to W_F.

Finally, while in state W_F, Alice sets the shared secret key to the application key and switches to the state CONNECTED, denoted by C.

13.3   Finished message

Bob's Finished is the final message in the TLS handshake protocol. This message authenticates the handshake as well as the secret shared keys that Alice and Bob agreed upon.

Both Alice and Bob (when he receives Alice's Finished message while in state W_F) verify the correctness of this message's contents and immediately terminate the TLS handshake with decrypt_error if the verification fails.

After Alice and Bob transmitted their Finished messages and successfully verified the received Finished message, they can send and receive application data over the secure channel established using the TLS handshake.

Alternatively, Alice and Bob may transmit data before receiving the peer's Finished message in the following situations:

- Bob sends 0-RTT data.

- Alice sends application data after sending her first *flight*, that is, after her ServerHello message. However, since the TLS handshake is incomplete, she has no assurance of Bob's identity or liveness—that is, the ClientHello message could have been replayed—and Bob does not have these guarantees regarding Alice.

The shared secret key for computing the Finished message is derived from the BaseKey using the HKDF function. More precisely, the key for the Finished message is computed as shown in *Listing 28*.

```
finished_key = HKDF-Expand-Label(BaseKey, "finished", "",
Hash.length)
```

Listing 28: Computation of the key for the Finished *message*

The structure of the Finished message is shown in *Listing 29*. The value of verify_data is computed as:

```
verify_data} = HMAC(finished_key, Transcript-Hash(Handshake Context,
Certificate*, CertificateVerify*))
```

where Certificate and CertificateVerify are only included if they are present.

```
struct {
    opaque verify_data[Hash.length];
} Finished;
```

Listing 29: Structure of the Finished *message*

Any data transmitted after the Finished message is encrypted using the corresponding application traffic shared secret key. This also includes all alert messages sent by Alice in response to Bob's Certificate and CertificateVerify messages.

13.4 Early data

Bob has to send an EndOfEarlyData message upon receiving Alice's Finished message if Alice sent early_data in her EncryptedExtensions message.

If Alice did not send the early_data in the EncryptedExtensions, then Bob does not send the EndOfEarlyData message. EndOfEarlyData indicates that all 0-RTT application_data messages – if any were sent – were successfully transmitted and the following messages are secured using the handshake traffic keys.

13.5 Post-handshake messages

In TLS 1.3, Alice and Bob can send further messages after their main handshake. These post-handshake messages have the handshake content type and are encrypted under the corresponding application traffic key.

13.5.1 The NewSessionTicket message

Any time after receiving Bob's `Finished` message, Alice can send a `NewSessionTicket` message. `NewSessionTicket` creates a unique link between the value of the ticket and the secret pre-shared key that is derived from `resumption_master_secret` (see *Section 12.2, TLS secrets*, in *Chapter 12, Secrets and Keys in TLS 1.3*, for more details).

Bob, in turn, can use this pre-shared key for future handshakes with Alice by including that ticket value in the `pre_shared_key` extension in his `ClientHello` message.

Alice can also send Bob multiple tickets. As an example, she could send a new ticket following the post-handshake authentication so she can encapsulate the additional client authentication state. Moreover, multiple tickets are beneficial for Bob if he wants to open multiple HTTPS connections to Alice in parallel or to speed up connection setup across address families and interfaces using a technique such as *Happy Eyeballs*, as specified in RFC 8305.

Importantly, every ticket can only be resumed with a TLS cipher suite that has the same KDF hash function as the one used during the establishment of the original connection. Moreover, Bob is only allowed to resume if the new SNI value is valid for Alice's certificate that she used to prove her identity to Bob in the original TLS session.

The structure of the `NewSessionTicket` message is shown in *Listing 30*. The element `ticket_lifetime` contains the lifetime of the ticket in seconds, defined from the time the ticket was issued. The maximum value Alice is allowed to use is 604,800 seconds, which is equivalent to seven days. If `ticket_lifetime` is set to zero, the ticket should be discarded immediately.

```
struct {
    uint32 ticket_lifetime;
    uint32 ticket_age_add;
    opaque ticket_nonce<0..255>;
    opaque ticket<1..2^16-1>;
    Extension extensions<0..2^16-2>;
} NewSessionTicket;
```

Listing 30: Structure of the `NewSessionTicket` *message*

Moreover, Bob is not allowed to cache a ticket for longer than seven days regardless of the `ticket_lifetime` value, and he may discard the ticket earlier according to his local policy. Alice, on the other hand, can treat a ticket as valid for a shorter time period than the `ticket_lifetime` value.

The `ticket_age_add` variable stores a random, securely generated value used for obscuring the age of the ticket that Bob includes in his `pre_shared_key` extension. This value is added to Bob's ticket age modulo 2^{32} to obtain an obscured value that is then sent by Bob. Alice generates a fresh `ticket_age_add` value for every ticket she sends.

`ticket_nonce` is a unique value across all tickets that Alice issues in the same TLS connection. `ticket` is the ticket value used as the **pre-shared secret key (PSK)** identity. The ticket itself maybe either a self-encrypted, self-authenticated value or a database lookup key.

Finally, the `extensions` variable contains a set of extension values for that ticket. At the time of this writing, the only extension that the TLS 1.3 standard defines for the `NewSessionTicket` message is `early_data`, which indicates that the ticket can be used to send 0-RTT data. It contains the `max_early_data_size` value, which defines the maximum number of bytes of 0-RTT data that Bob may send using this ticket.

The pre-shared secret key associated with the ticket is computed as follows:

```
HKDF-Expand-Label(resumption_master_secret, "resumption",
ticket_nonce, Hash.length)
```

Recall that since `ticket_nonce` is unique for every `NewSessionTicket` message in a given TLS session, a different pre-shared secret key will be generated for every ticket. Technically, Alice could issue new tickets to indefinitely extend the lifetime of the keying material derived during the initial non-PSK handshake. However, TLS specification recommends limiting the total lifetime of such keying material based on the lifetime of Bob's certificate, the likelihood of certificate revocation, and the time since Bob's `CertificateVerify` signature.

13.5.2   Post-handshake authentication

If Bob sent the `post_handshake_auth` extension, Alice can ask Bob to authenticate himself any time after their handshake by sending Bob a `CertificateRequest` message. In that case, Bob must reply with the corresponding authentication messages:

- If Bob decides to authenticate himself, he replies with `Certificate`, `CertificateVerify`, and `Finished` messages

- If Bob decides to ignore Alice's authentication request, he replies with a `Certificate` message that contains no certificates, followed by a `Finished` message

If Bob receives a `CertificateRequest` message without having sent the `post_handshake_auth` extension, Bob terminates the TLS session and sends Alice an `unexpected_message` alert.

Interestingly, because TLS client authentication might involve the user typing in a secret – for instance, if the TLS client is a web browser and the user has to type in their password – servers must tolerate a delayed response from a TLS client. This also includes scenarios where the server receives an arbitrary number of messages between transmitting the `CertificateRequest` message and receiving the corresponding response from the TLS client.

13.5.3   Key and initialization vector update

Alice and Bob use the `KeyUpdate` message to signal that they are updating the sending cryptographic keys on their respective ends. `KeyUpdate` can be sent by either Alice or Bob after they transmit their `Finished` message.

If, on the other hand, the KeyUpdate message is received before the Finished message, the TLS session must be terminated with an unexpected_message alert.

Following the KeyUpdate message, the transmitting party must encrypt all of their data using the next generation of the derived secret keys. Similarly, the receiving party must update their receiving keys upon receiving the KeyUpdate message.

The format of the KeyUpdate message is shown in *Listing 31*. The value of the request_update field determines whether the receiving party should reply with their own KeyUpdate message. If request_update contains any other value than O or 1, then the receiving party immediately terminates the TLS session and responds with an illegal_parameter alert.

```
enum {
    update_not_requested(0),
    update_requested(1),
    (255)
} KeyUpdateRequest;

struct {
    KeyUpdateRequest request_update;
} KeyUpdate;
```

Listing 31: Structure of the KeyUpdate *message*

If request_update is set to update_requested, the recipient must reply with their own KeyUpdate message, with request_update set to update_not_requested, to avoid an infinite loop.

Moreover, a TLS party might receive an arbitrary number of messages between transmitting a KeyUpdate requesting a key update and receiving the other party's KeyUpdate message. However, because the secret keys for sending and receiving data are derived from independent traffic secrets, using the old receive traffic secret has no effect on the forward secrecy of data transmitted prior to the sending party changing the keys.

13.6   OpenSSL s_client

OpenSSL is an open source project implementing the OpenSSL software, a commercial-grade, feature-rich toolkit for cryptography and TLS [137]. OpenSSL's technical decision making is governed by the **OpenSSL Technical Committee (OTC)** and the software is published under an Apache-style license, making it suitable for both non-commercial and commercial purposes.

At the time of this writing, the latest stable OpenSSL version is the 3.1 series, which the OpenSSL project will support until March 14, 2025. In addition, OpenSSL 3.0 series is available as a **Long-Term Support (LTS)** version, which will be supported until September 7, 2026.

The OpenSSL source code is hosted at `https://github.com/openssl/openssl`. The software includes the following:

- `libssl`, the implementation of TLS protocol versions up to TLS 1.3

- `libcrypto`, a feature-rich cryptography library that is the basis for `libssl`, but can also be used as a standalone library

- The `openssl` command-line tool, which, among other things, can be used for the generation of cryptographic keys and digital certificates, computation of hash functions and message authentication codes, encryption and decryption, and TLS client and server tests

One of the command-line tools, namely, `openssl-s_client`, implements a generic TLS client that connects to remote hosts using the TLS protocol. In practice, this tool is mostly used for diagnostic purposes. In our case, however, `openssl-s_client` is a great way to experiment with TLS: see the protocol at work to increase your understanding.

13.6.1   Installing OpenSSL

Before we can start experimenting with `openssl-s_client`, we first need to install the OpenSSL toolkit. The easiest way to install OpenSSL is to use the source code tarballs available at `https://www.openssl.org/source/`. At the time of this writing, the latest stable OpenSSL tarball is `https://www.openssl.org/source/openssl-3.1.0.tar.gz`.

If you are on a Linux or macOS system, you likely already have OpenSSL installed, although probably in a different version than 3.1.0. You therefore need to be careful to not mess things up on your system. If you are on a Windows system, you would first need an appropriate Linux environment, such as WSL or Cygwin, where you could install OpenSSL.

We recommend to use a Docker container instead. Docker is a popular OS-level virtualization solution where software runs in so-called containers. Docker containers are isolated runtime environments created from Docker images, read-only files containing all source code, libraries, dependencies, tools, and runtime for running an application. Docker images can be created from Dockerfiles that specify what goes into the image. We prepared a repository on GitHub that contains a Dockerfile to build an image with a fully functional OpenSSL 3.1.0 installation. To use it and build the Docker image, execute the following commands:

```
$ gh repo clone duplys/tls_lab
$ cd tls_lab/openssl_docker
$ docker build . -t openssl310
```

You can now start the Docker container by issuing the following command:

```
$ docker container run --rm -it openssl310
```

The `-it` option tells Docker to start the container in interactive mode. The `--rm` option ensures that Docker removes the container after you exit it. Once the container is running, you should see a similar command prompt:

```
root@07c3ba265c69:/opt/openssl#
```

To verify that everything works, you can execute an OpenSSL command in the Docker container prompt. As an example, you can try to access OpenSSL's help pages by issuing the following command:

```
# openssl help
```

Does it work? Congratulations! You have successfully installed OpenSSL on your system.

13.6.2   Using openssl-s_client

Now that we have a working OpenSSL installation, let's look at selected openssl-s_client options for performing basic TLS operations with this tool.

Connecting to a TLS server is done by executing the following command:

```
# openssl s_client -connect servername:443
```

As an example, to connect to the Packt web server using TLS, you need to execute the command:

```
# openssl s_client -connect packtpub.com:443
```

The -connect option takes two arguments: the host name and, optionally, the port to connect to. Packt's website hostname is packtpub.com and the default port a TLS service listens to is 443. This way, we pass packtpub.com:443 as parameters to the -connect option. If no argument is supplied, s_client attempts to connect to the local host on port 4433.

If s_client succeeds in establishing a connection to the TLS server, it displays any data received from the server and transmits all key presses to the server. As an example, we can give an HTTP command such as GET / to retrieve a web page.

When s_client is used in interactive mode – that is, neither the -quiet nor -ign_eof option is given – the tool recognizes the following special commands that must appear at the start of a line:

- The Q command ends the current TLS connection and exits s_client

- The R command renegotiates the TLS session (but this is only relevant for TLS versions 1.2 and below)

- The k command sends a key update message to the TLS server (only available in TLS version 1.3)

- The K command sends a key update message to the TLS server and requests one back (only available in TLS version 1.3)

In addition to the preceding commands, openssl-s_client supports a large set of options that control various aspects of the TLS connection. Detailed information about all options can be found in openssl-s_client's man page at https://www.openssl.org/docs/man 3.1/man1/openssl-s_client.html. The following list describes selected options that we believe to be the most useful when trying to understand and experiment with TLS:

- The -msg option prints all TLS protocol messages, including their hexadecimal representation, in addition to standard information displayed by openssl-s_client.

- The -trace option prints detailed information on the contents of all TLS protocol messages.

- The -msgfile filename option specifies the file where the output of the -msg or -trace options is written to. By default, this information is printed to standard output, that is, to the console.

- The -state option prints the states of the TLS client state machine used by OpenSSL and, hence, by openssl-s_client. The states are printed on separate lines beginning with the string SSL_connect:.

- The -security_debug_verbose option prints security-related debug messages such as checks as to whether specific TLS versions and specific cipher suites are supported. The messages are printed on lines beginning with the string Security callback:.

- The -debug option displays debug information and the hexadecimal representation of the entire TLS network traffic.

- The -tlsextdebug option prints the hex dump, that is, the hexadecimal representation, of all TLS extensions that openssl-s_client received from the TLS server.

- The -status option sends a certificate status request for the TLS server certificate to an OCSP service and prints out the OCSP response.

- The -showcerts option prints the list of certificates transmitted by the TLS server. Note that openssl-s_client does not verify the certificate chain.

- The -sigalgs option instructs openssl-s_client which signature algorithms it must send to the TLS server. Recall that the TLS server selects one of the algorithms in this list based on its preferences or replies with a HelloRetryRequest message if the list contains no algorithm that the server supports. Example strings are given at https://www.openssl.org/docs/man3.1/man3/SSL_CTX_set1_sigalgs.html.

- The -curves curvelist option defines supported curves that openssl-s_client sends to the TLS server. The list of available curves can be obtained with the following command:

```
$ openssl ecparam -list_curves
```

- The -ciphersuites val option defines TLS 1.3 cipher suites that openssl-s_client sends to the TLS server. The list is written using cipher suite names separated by a colon (":"). The names of cipher suites can be obtained using the following command:

```
$ openssl ciphers
```

Some of the results when calling `openssl-s_client` using these options should already be familiar to you, for example, the list of signature algorithms or the list of available curves. Others, such as the names of symmetric cipher algorithms appearing in the list of cipher suites, will be explained in the next part of the book, *Off the Record.*

13.6.3   TLS experiments with `openssl-s_client`

So, what kind of experiments can we do using `openssl-s_client` to better understand how TLS works under the hood? Well, we could start by looking into the protocol messages of an actual TLS session. As an example, we could perform a TLS handshake with the Packt web server:

```
# openssl s_client -connect packtpub.com:443 -msg
```

The output corresponding to the preceding command gives a detailed view of the TLS handshake, including all TLS messages, their length in bytes, and their hex dumps:

```
>>> TLS 1.0, RecordHeader [length 0005]
    16 03 01 01 35
>>> TLS 1.3, Handshake [length 0135], ClientHello
    01 00 01 31 03 03 1c 29 cd 91 3f dc 5e 9e 6b 4f

    -- snip --

<<< TLS 1.2, RecordHeader [length 0005]
    16 03 03 00 7a
<<< TLS 1.3, Handshake [length 007a], ServerHello
    02 00 00 76 03 03 5f f0 44 0e 05 69 25 78 14 cb

    -- snip --

<<< TLS 1.2, RecordHeader [length 0005]
    14 03 03 00 01
<<< TLS 1.2, RecordHeader [length 0005]
    17 03 03 09 f4
```

```
<<< TLS 1.3, InnerContent [length 0001]
    16
<<< TLS 1.3, Handshake [length 000a], EncryptedExtensions
    08 00 00 06 00 04 00 00 00 00
<<< TLS 1.3, Handshake [length 0956], Certificate
    0b 00 09 52 00 00 09 4e 00 05 73 30 82 05 6f 30


    -- snip --

depth=2 C = IE, O = Baltimore, OU = CyberTrust, CN = Baltimore
CyberTrust Root
verify return:1
depth=1 C = US, O = "Cloudflare, Inc.", CN = Cloudflare Inc ECC CA-3
verify return:1
depth=0 C = US, ST = California, L = San Francisco, O = "Cloudflare,
Inc.", CN = packtpub.com
verify return:1
<<< TLS 1.3, \index{OpenSSL client!TLS experiments}Handshake [length
004f], CertificateVerify
    0f 00 00 4b 04 03 00 47 30 45 02 20 7f f9 da ed


    -- snip --
<<< TLS 1.3, Handshake [length 0034], Finished
    14 00 00 30 2a 64 1c 8f e0 f9 f1 ab 2b 3d 7b e8


    -- snip --
>>> TLS 1.2, RecordHeader [length 0005]
    14 03 03 00 01
>>> TLS 1.3, ChangeCipherSpec [length 0001]
    01
>>> TLS 1.2, RecordHeader [length 0005]
    17 03 03 00 45
>>> TLS 1.2, InnerContent [length 0001]
    16
>>> TLS 1.3, Handshake [length 0034], Finished
    14 00 00 30 c1 23 05 61 7b 03 8e c9 d9 b5 1e de


    -- snip --
```

Note that the TLS messages sent by the client are denoted by >>> and the TLS messages sent by the server by <<<. In addition, the command's output includes the certificate presented by the server and the cryptographic settings of the TLS session:

```
Certificate chain
    0 s:C = US, ST = California, L = San Francisco, O = "Cloudflare,
    Inc.", CN = packtpub.com
        i:C = US, O = "Cloudflare, Inc.", CN = Cloudflare Inc ECC CA-3
        a:PKEY: id-ecPublicKey, 256 (bit); sigalg: ecdsa-with-SHA256
        v:NotBefore: Apr  7 00:00:00 2023 GMT; NotAfter: Apr  6
        23:59:59 2024 GMT
    1 s:C = US, O = "Cloudflare, Inc.", CN = Cloudflare Inc ECC CA-3
      i:C = IE, O = Baltimore, OU = CyberTrust, CN = Baltimore
      CyberTrust Root
      a:PKEY: id-ecPublicKey, 256 (bit); sigalg: RSA-SHA256
      v:NotBefore: Jan 27 12:48:08 2020 GMT; NotAfter: Dec 31
      23:59:59 2024 GMT
    ---
Server certificate
-----BEGIN CERTIFICATE-----
MIIFbzCCBRWgAwIBAgIQCjUceIvorTtWOHsotymexDAKBggqhkjOPQQDAjBKMQsw

-- snip --

-----END CERTIFICATE-----
subject=C = US, ST = California, L = San Francisco, O =
"Cloudflare, Inc.",
CN = packtpub.com
issuer=C = US, O = "Cloudflare, Inc.", CN = Cloudflare Inc ECC
CA-3
---
No client certificate CA names sent
Peer signing digest: SHA256
Peer signature type: ECDSA
Server Temp Key: X25519, 253 bits
---
SSL handshake has read 2686 bytes and written 394 bytes
Verification: OK
```

```
- - -
New, TLSv1.3, Cipher is TLS_AES_256_GCM_SHA384
Server public key is 256 bit

-- snip --
```

Next, we might want to know what the ClientHello message sent by openssl-s_client to the Packt web server actually looks like. This can be done using the -trace option:

```
# openssl s_client -connect packtpub.com:443 -trace
```

The corresponding output contains detailed information about ClientHello and the values of its parameters:

```
Sent Record
Header:
  Version = TLS 1.0 (0x301)
  Content Type = Handshake (22)
  Length = 309
    ClientHello, Length=305
      client_version=0x303 (TLS 1.2)
      Random:
        gmt_unix_time=0xF96120B2
        random_bytes (len=28): 2C2985BC3763DE -- snip --
      session_id (len=32): 16BB585F1BAA7C -- snip --
      cipher_suites (len=62)
        {0x13, 0x02} TLS_AES_256_GCM_SHA384
        {0x13, 0x03} TLS_CHACHA20_POLY1305_SHA256
        {0x13, 0x01} TLS_AES_128_GCM_SHA256

        -- snip --

      compression_methods (len=1)
        No Compression (0x00)
      extensions, length = 170
```

```
extension_type=server_name(0), length=17
  0000 - 00 0f 00 00 0c 70 61 63-6b 74 70 75 62 2e 63
  .....packtpub.c
  000f - 6f 6d                                                om
extension_type=ec_point_formats(11), length=4
  uncompressed (0)
  ansiX962_compressed_prime (1)
  ansiX962_compressed_char2 (2)
extension_type=supported_groups(10), length=22
  ecdh_x25519 (29)
  secp256r1 (P-256) (23)
  ecdh_x448 (30)

  -- snip --

extension_type=session_ticket(35), length=0
extension_type=encrypt_then_mac(22), length=0
extension_type=extended_master_secret(23), length=0
extension_type=signature_algorithms(13), length=42
  ecdsa_secp256r1_sha256 (0x0403)
  ecdsa_secp384r1_sha384 (0x0503)
  ecdsa_secp521r1_sha512 (0x0603)

  -- snip --

\index{OpenSSL client!TLS
experiments}extension_type=supported_versions(43), length=5
  TLS 1.3 (772)
  TLS 1.2 (771)
extension_type=psk_key_exchange_modes(45), length=2
  psk_dhe_ke (1)
extension_type=key_share(51), length=38
  NamedGroup: ecdh_x25519 (29)
  key_exchange:  (len=32): F00D50A5796047 -- snip --
```

Now let's take a look at the states of the OpenSSL client state machine as the TLS connection to the Packt web server is being established. We can do this by executing the following command:

```
# openssl s_client -connect packtpub.com:443 -state
```

In the corresponding output, we can see that openssl-s_client starts by sending ClientHello. After that, it transitions through a sequence of states where it receives the ServerHello, EncryptedExtensions, Certificate, CertificateVerify, and Finished messages from the TLS server. As a final step, the client sends its Finished message, thereby completing the TLS handshake:

```
SSL_connect:before SSL initialization
SSL_connect:SSLv3/TLS write client hello
SSL_connect:SSLv3/TLS write client hello
SSL_connect:SSLv3/TLS read server hello
SSL_connect:TLSv1.3 read encrypted extensions

-- snip --

SSL_connect:SSLv3/TLS read server certificate
SSL_connect:TLSv1.3 read server certificate verify
SSL_connect:SSLv3/TLS read finished
SSL_connect:SSLv3/TLS write change cipher spec
SSL_connect:SSLv3/TLS write finished
```

Moreover, we can examine the details of TLS extensions that the Packt web server transmitted using the following command:

```
# openssl s_client -connect packtpub.com:443 -tlsextdebug
```

The corresponding output lists all TLS extensions sent by the server as well as their values in hexadecimal representation:

```
TLS server extension "key share" (id=51), len=36
    0000 - 00 1d 00 20 08 3c 18 21-98 94 30 17 a1 37 00 8f    ...
    .<.!..0..7..
    0010 - c4 07 6f 93 69 46 3a 94-bc 08 f3 82 61 82 ac a7
    ..o.iF:.....a...
    0020 - 73 bb 1e 3f                                         s..?
TLS server extension "supported versions" (id=43), len=2
    0000 - 03 04                                               ..
TLS server extension "server name" (id=0), len=0

-- snip --
```

Finally, let's examine the OCSP response for the digital certificate that the Packt web server has presented to openssl-s_client. We can do this using the following command:

```
# openssl s_client -connect packtpub.com:443 -status
```

The corresponding output shows the OCSP response status, the status of the certificate when the response was generated, and other details:

```
-- snip --

OCSP response:
======================================
OCSP Response Data:
    OCSP Response Status: successful (0x0)
    Response Type: Basic OCSP Response
    Version: 1 (0x0)
    Responder Id: A5CE37EAEBB0750E946788B445FAD9241087961F
    Produced At: Apr 29 20:42:45 2023 GMT
    Responses:
    Certificate ID:
        Hash Algorithm: sha1
```

```
        Issuer Name Hash: 12D78B402C356206FA827F8ED8922411B4ACF504
        Issuer Key Hash: A5CE37EAEBB0750E946788B445FAD9241087961F
        Serial Number: 0A351C788BE8AD3B56387B28B7299EC4
   Cert Status: good
   This Update: Apr 29 20:27:01 2023 GMT
   Next Update: May  6 19:42:01 2023 GMT

   Signature Algorithm: ecdsa-with-SHA256
   Signature Value:
       30:44:02:20:17:4b:4e:d7:99:e4:ec:b3:ea:75:5a:33:bc:7b:
       c7:da:69:30:03:20:99:48:b5:f6:e3:78:a4:dd:ff:78:04:3a:
       02:20:6f:0a:b8:07:b0:40:9e:2c:16:96:6f:de:11:73:1a:fb:
       3d:74:d4:9a:77:61:ae:8e:ac:8d:42:fb:f1:d4:e5:d7
===========================================

-- snip --
```

We encourage you to explore further options of the openssl-s_client tool and experiment with other hosts. You can also adjust the list of signature algorithms or curves that the openssl-s_client supports and observe how the TLS server responds, especially if it does not support any of the algorithms from that list.

13.7   Summary

In this chapter, we looked at the TLS handshake protocol from a bird's-eye view, with the help of TLS client and server state machines. The state machines illustrate how the TLS protocol works on a higher level. In addition, we covered the Finished message and several post-handshake messages in more detail.

We also learned how to use OpenSSL, a popular cryptography and TLS toolkit, and, especially, the s_client OpenSSL tool to experiment with TLS. We discussed how to install and how to use s_client and presented several experiments that you can reproduce and enhance on your own. These experiments allow you to observe TLS at work and take a close look at cryptographic mechanisms and TLS features used in the handshake protocol.

This chapter concludes the second part of the book. In the next part, we will study the TLS record protocol. The record protocol protects application data using shared secret keys established during the TLS handshake. We will start the most fundamental building block of the TLS record protocol: block ciphers, including their modes of operation.

Part 3

Off the Record

The **TLS Record layer** is the part of TLS that actually implements the secure channel between client and server. To do this, cryptographic mechanisms providing *confidentiality, integrity*, and *message authenticity* are needed. As the necessary key material has already been established during the handshake, we may now focus on *symmetric* algorithms, where the client and server use the same key.

Accordingly, in this part, we will cover the basic ideas behind modern block ciphers such as the **Advanced Encryption Standard** (**AES**) and their modes of operation. A rather recent invention is the development of a special mode of operation for block ciphers that can provide confidentiality and message authenticity at the same time. This new concept is called **Authenticated Encryption** and will be covered in depth, since it also used within the record layer of TLS 1.3.

This part contains the following chapters:

- *Chapter 14, Block Ciphers and Their Modes of Operation*

- *Chapter 15, Authenticated Encryption*

- *Chapter 16, The Galois Counter Mode*

- *Chapter 17, TLS Record Protocol Revisited*

- *Chapter 18 TLS Cipher Suites*

14

Block Ciphers and Their Modes of Operation

The TLS Record protocol protects application data sent by Alice and Bob using shared secret keys established during their TLS handshake. We will start our study of the TLS Record protocol with its most fundamental building block: block ciphers. In this chapter, we discuss in detail what block ciphers are, what design principles govern the construction of secure block ciphers, what mathematical objects are used to model block ciphers, and what actual block cipher algorithms used in practice look like.

Block ciphers form an integral part of modern cryptography. However, RFC 8446, the IETF standard specifying TLS 1.3, does not explicitly treat block ciphers. Rather, it points to some related references, including NIST Special Publication 800-38D and IETF's RFC 5116, RFC 6655, and RFC 8439. In contrast, we will cover block ciphers in quite some detail because cryptography of the TLS Record protocol cannot be understood in depth without a solid understanding of block ciphers.

On completion of this chapter, you will have the following:

- A good theoretical understanding of block ciphers, including their mathematical foundations and design principles used to achieve desired security properties

- Familiarity with the most popular block cipher modes of operation, including their working principles, advantages, and disadvantages

- A detailed understanding of how the Advanced Encryption Standard algorithm, the gold standard for block ciphers, works

- Knowledge of how to use OpenSSL to perform encryption using the different modes of operation

But before diving into the details, let's take a step back and take a look at the big picture.

14.1   The big picture

In the last part of the book, we covered in detail the TLS Handshake protocol and the cryptography needed to implement the main security objectives of the TLS Handshake protocol, namely *entity authentication* and *key agreement*. For the latter of these goals, public-key cryptography was needed, for the former, we used both public-key cryptography, especially digital signatures, and symmetric cryptography, especially **message authentication codes (MACs)**.

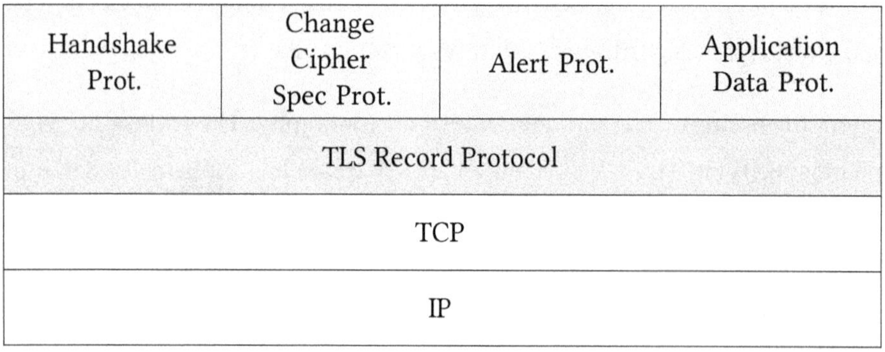

Handshake Prot.	Change Cipher Spec Prot.	Alert Prot.	Application Data Prot.
TLS Record Protocol			
TCP			
IP			

Figure 14.1: TLS subprotocols

But entity authentication and key agreement are only prerequisites of the main goal of TLS, which is *to establish a secure tunnel between client and server, providing **confidentiality, integrity protection, and message authenticity**.* As already briefly discussed in *Chapter 6, Transport Layer Security at a Glance*, it is the task of the TLS Record protocol, located immediately above the transport layer (see *Figure 14.1*), to actually realize this tunnel. In order to do so, it takes a data fragment from a higher layer protocol, for example, HTTP or the TLS Handshake protocol, encrypts and authenticates it (if the necessary key material has already been agreed on), creates a **record header** containing the necessary information for the receiver to process the fragment, and puts the header and the protected data together to form a **record**. Finally, the protected record is transferred to the lower layer protocol.

In earlier TLS versions, the TLS Record protocol first computed a MAC over plaintext, then appended the MAC to the plaintext and finally encrypted the result. But this MAC-then-encrypt order of operation has turned out to be prone to attacks. We will cover some of these attacks in *Chapter 21, Attacks on the TLS Record Protocol*, in *Part 4, Bleeding Hearts and Biting Poodles* of the book. Today, special algorithms called *authenticated ciphers*, providing a more secure combination of encryption and authentication, are used in the TLS Record protocol. These algorithms are discussed in *Chapter 15, Authenticated Encryption*. Authenticated ciphers, in turn, use **block ciphers**, discussed in the present chapter, as their building blocks. Today, block ciphers remain the single most important cryptographic tool for providing confidentiality.

14.2 General principles

A *block cipher* is an encryption function e_K that maps plaintext blocks of fixed size b onto ciphertext blocks of the same size b:

$$e_k : \{0, 1\}^b \to \{0, 1\}^b$$

As indicated by the subscript k, a block cipher is a **symmetric algorithm**, taking a shared key $k \in \mathcal{K}$ as a parameter, where $\mathcal{K}$ is the **keyspace** (see also *Chapter 4, Encryption and*

Decryption). In TLS, the shared key is agreed between client Bob and server Alice during the Handshake protocol, using public-key cryptography. Naturally, a block cipher must be a **bijective** function, or **bijection** for short (see *Section 4.1* in *Chapter 4, Encryption and Decryption*), meaning that there is some inverse function e_k^{-1} that reverses the action of e_k and is used for decryption. Therefore, instead of writing e_k^{-1}, we will often use d_k for the inverse function.

A block cipher processes the plaintext block by block, as opposed to stream ciphers, which process the plaintext bit by bit and which we met already in *Section 4.5.1, Stream ciphers* in *Chapter 4, Encryption and Decryption*. However, note that a block cipher can be turned into a keystream generator for a stream cipher; this is discussed a bit later in the present chapter in *Section 14.4*.

14.2.1 Advantages and disadvantages of block ciphers

Block ciphers achieve high data encryption rate, with hardware implementations being able to encrypt and decrypt at rates of several gigabytes per second. Being symmetric key algorithms, block ciphers have relatively short keys. Moreover, block ciphers can be used as primitives to construct various cryptographic mechanisms, including authenticated encryption with additional data. Finally, block ciphers have a rather extensive history and are generally well-understood cryptographic mechanisms.

On the other hand, as in all symmetric algorithms, the secret key needs to be securely distributed or established in advance (and a good practice in cryptography is to change the key frequently, ideally for each new communication session). Recall that this is also known as the **key distribution problem**. Moreover, the key must remain secret at all communicating parties. If Alice, Bob, and Caroline (a third party in the communication without special features) are using a single key along with a block cipher to secure their communication, it is sufficient for any one of them to lose or leak the secret key, and the security of all three of them will be compromised. On the other hand, if every possible pair of communicating parties has a unique key, then the overall number of keys to be distributed in a secure way becomes very large as it grows quadratically with the number of communicating parties.

In *Chapter 7, Public-Key Cryptography*, we have seen how the key distribution problem can be solved efficiently using asymmetric cryptographic algorithms. Combining these with the speedier symmetric algorithms, especially block ciphers, leads to the hybrid encryption systems we already discussed in *Section 7.11, Hybrid cryptosystems* in *Chapter 7, Public-Key Cryptography*.

14.2.2 Confusion and diffusion

What makes a good block cipher? Claude Shannon was perhaps the first to try and answer this question in a systematic way [162]. He defined two methods *for frustrating a statistical analysis*:

- Assuming that a meaningful plaintext must exhibit some statistical structure, he suggested that the cipher should *dissipate* this structure over the entire ciphertext. This principle is called **diffusion**. Generally, it can be achieved by permuting the symbols in the plaintext block.

- Simply permuting the symbols in a plaintext block will destroy local patterns, but the global plaintext statistics will remain unchanged (for example, permuting the pixels in an image does not change its histogram). In order to obscure the global plaintext statistics, the ciphertext should depend on the plaintext in a very complex way. This principle is called **confusion**. In practice, this principle is realized by a complex substitution of the plaintext symbols.

A good block cipher will contain both components. In order to not give any hints about the plaintext statistics, the substitution and permutation components need to look random, that is, as if having no structure, to the attacker. We will now look at this requirement in detail.

14.2.3   Pseudorandom functions

We start with pseudorandom functions that we briefly touched upon in *Chapter 4, Encryption and Decryption*. Roughly speaking, a pseudorandom function is a deterministic function that appears to be random to any polynomial-time adversary.

Conceptually, a pseudorandom function is a generalization of a pseudorandom generator [97] in that it involves random-looking *functions* instead of random-looking strings. Technically speaking, pseudorandomness is a property of a *distribution* of functions obtained using *keyed functions*. Recall that a keyed function is a two-argument function of the form:

$$f \; : \; \{0,1\}^n \times \{0,1\}^b \rightarrow \{0,1\}^b$$

where the first input is the key k. Typically, the key $k \in \{0,1\}^n$ is chosen and fixed to obtain a single-input function $f_k \; : \; \{0,1\}^b \rightarrow \{0,1\}^b$. Let f_b denote the set of all functions having the same domain and range $\{0,1\}^b$. A keyed function induces a distribution on functions in f_b. The distribution is determined by choosing uniformly a key $k \in \{0,1\}^n$. This selects a specific function f_k from f_b.

The keyed function f is called *pseudorandom* if an efficient adversary cannot distinguish the function f_k from a function f chosen uniformly at random from the set f_b. In other words, no polynomial-time adversary should be able to tell whether it is interacting with f_k or with f. The term *interacting* refers to the fact that the formal definition of a pseudorandom function (see, for instance, [97]) gives the adversary – oftentimes referred to as a probabilistic polynomial-time distinguisher in the cryptographic literature – access to an *oracle* that takes any input x and returns the function value for x. Because both functions f_k and f are deterministic (they are only *chosen* randomly), the oracle returns the same result when it is presented with the same input x. However, if f is a pseudorandom function, no polynomial-time adversary can tell whether the oracle returns $f_k(x)$ or $f(x)$.

Note that pseudorandomness is not a trivial property for a keyed function f because the set f_b, the set of all functions having the same domain and range $\{0,1\}^b$, has $(2^b)^{2^b} = 2^{b \cdot 2^b}$ functions (for each of the 2^b inputs, there are 2^b possible outputs).

On the other hand, because there are 2^n keys, f_k is chosen from a distribution of at most 2^n distinct functions [97]. Yet, the behavior of f_k and a randomly chosen function $f \in f_b$ must appear the same for any polynomial-time adversary.

From the theoretical perspective, cryptographers believe that block ciphers behave like pseudorandom functions. More precisely, they are assumed to behave like a specific type of pseudorandom functions, namely, pseudorandom permutations.

14.2.4 Pseudorandom permutations

Simply put, a permutation is a function that rearranges the order of elements in a set. A random permutation is a permutation that is randomly chosen from all possible permutations for a given set. A pseudorandom permutation looks like a random permutation to any polynomial-time observer, but is actually a deterministic algorithm.

Let $f : \{0, 1\}^n \times \{0, 1\}^b \to \{0, 1\}^b$ again be a length-preserving keyed function that can be efficiently computed; that is, Alice and Bob can compute it in polynomial time. f is a *keyed permutation* if, for every key k, the function f_k is a **bijection**. That is, each element in f_k's domain is mapped to exactly one element in f_k's range, and each element in f_k's range has exactly one preimage in f_k's domain (see *Figure 14.2* and also *Figure 4.3*).

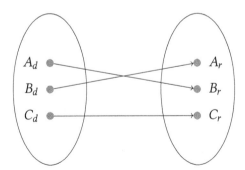

Figure 14.2: Example of a bijective function

Formally, a keyed permutation $f_k(x)$ is considered *efficient* if it can be computed in polynomial time *and* there is a polynomial-time algorithm for computing the inverse

$f_k^{-1}(x)$. The length of $f_k(x)$'s input and output – also referred to as *block size* – is typically identical, but the length of key k can be different from the block size.

The keyed permutation $f_k(x)$ is *pseudorandom* if an efficient adversary, that is, an algorithm running in polynomial time, cannot distinguish f_k from a randomly chosen permutation f. When f_k is used in cryptographic algorithms such as symmetric-key encryption, Alice and Bob need to compute the inverse f_k^{-1} in addition to f_k itself. This could, however, negatively affect security despite f_k being pseudorandom. Consequently, if f_k is used in a cryptographic algorithm, it must be a *strong* pseudorandom permutation. f_k is called a strong pseudorandom permutation if no efficient adversary can distinguish f_k from a permutation chosen at random *even if the adversary has oracle access to f_k^{-1}.*

Basically, pseudorandom permutations are also pseudorandom functions. On the other hand, a pseudorandom function is a pseudorandom permutation if it is a bijection.

Block ciphers, because they must be invertible, are typically modeled as strong pseudorandom permutations. That is, standardized block ciphers are generally assumed to behave like strong pseudorandom permutations. Cryptographers make this assumption so they can formally analyze cryptographic mechanisms that are based on block ciphers.

14.2.5 Substitution-permutation networks and Feistel networks

Modern block ciphers are often constructed as *iterated* functions, where a so-called *round function* $f_k : \{0, 1\}^b \rightarrow \{0, 1\}^b$ is repeatedly applied on the plaintext m, with varying *round keys* $k_1, k_2, \ldots, k_r$. More formally, we can write this process as

$$e_k(m) = f_{k_r}(f_{k_{r-1}}(\ldots f_{k_2}(f_{k_1}(m))))$$

or even

$$e_k(m) = (\circ_{i=1}^r f_{k_i})(m),$$

where $\circ$ stands for the composition of functions. *Figure 14.3* visualizes this process.

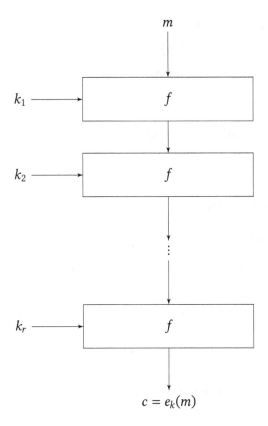

Figure 14.3: Working principle of an iterated block cipher

Here, in each of the r rounds, a different *round key k_i* is derived from k and used as a parameter for the round function. The process of deriving the round keys from k is called *key scheduling.* As the block cipher may be written as the composition of the round functions, each f_{k_i} must be an invertible function. We therefore model the round function in an iterated block cipher as a strong pseudorandom permutation.

Note that in order to build the decryption function d_k, one needs not only to invert the round function but also to apply the round keys in reverse order.

This construction can be efficiently implemented in software because once the round function is implemented, the block cipher is realized by a loop with r iterations.

In order to achieve both confusion and diffusion, the round function should contain a substitution part S (also called an *S-Box*) and a permutation part P (sometimes called a *P-box*). Therefore, this construction principle is also called a *substitution-permutation network*.

The older **Data Encryption Standard (DES)** algorithm, developed in the 1970s by Horst Feistel of IBM, was the dominating block cipher in the 20th century. Its round function f also contains S-boxes and P-boxes, but it is not an iterated block cipher, because the round function does not act on the complete plaintext, but only on its right half R.

More precisely, let L_i and R_i be the left and right halves of the plaintext after i rounds, respectively, then after the next encryption round, the left and right halves are given by

$$L_{i+1} = R_i \text{ and}$$

$$R_{i+1} = L_i \oplus f_{k_i}(R_i),$$

where k_i is the i-th round key. This construction is called a *Feistel network* (see *Figure 14.4*).

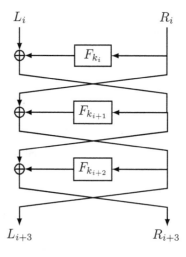

Figure 14.4: Three rounds of a Feistel network

Remarkably, in a Feistel network, the round function does not have to be invertible, because we can solve the equations above for L_i and R_i, provided we know the round key k_i:

$$R_i = L_{i+1} \text{ and}$$

$$L_i = R_{i+1} \oplus f_{k_i}(R_i) = R_{i+1} \oplus f_{k_i}(L_{i+1}).$$

Thus, we can reverse one round of encryption (and therefore decrypt the complete cipher) without having to use the inverse function of the round function. The DES algorithm therefore uses a non-invertible round function: each of its eight S-boxes maps six input bits onto four output bits. We will have to say more on the history of the DES algorithm and its S-boxes shortly.

The DES algorithm has a block length of 64 bits and consists of 16 rounds. Technically, a DES key is 64 bits long, but, allegedly by the intervention of the NSA, this was artificially shortened to 56 bits by making every eighth key bit a **parity bit**. Apart from an exhaustive key search, there have never been any practically relevant cryptographic attacks on the DES, including **differential** [32] and **linear cryptanalysis** [112]. Still, because of the short key length, already in the 1990s one had to resort to the so-called *Triple-DES* or *3DES*, where the DES algorithm is applied three times on the plaintext with three independent 56-bit keys k_1, k_2, k_3. For reasons of backward compatibility, the exact formula is

$$3DES(m) = DES_{k_1}(DES_{k_2}^{-1}(DES_{k_3}(m))).$$

Naturally, this approach does not only triple the key length, but also the computation time. Moreover, the design of the DES algorithm proved to be not efficient enough when encrypting large amounts of data or when being used on platforms with limited resources. Therefore, by the turn of the century, the need for a successor to the DES algorithm became apparent. This successor was called the ***Advanced Encryption Standard*** (**AES**).

14.2.6 Constants in cryptographic algorithms

Specifications of cryptographic algorithms often contain constants. As an example, the SHA-2 family of hash functions specified in the FIPS 180-4 standard must set the initial hash value $H^{(0)}$ before the computation of the SHA algorithm begins. The initial hash value for the SHA-224 function is composed of these eight 32-bit constants:

$$H_0^{(0)} = \texttt{c1059ed8} \qquad\qquad H_4^{(0)} = \texttt{ffc00b31}$$

$$H_1^{(0)} = \texttt{367cd507} \qquad\qquad H_5^{(0)} = \texttt{68581511}$$

$$H_2^{(0)} = \texttt{3070dd17} \qquad\qquad H_6^{(0)} = \texttt{64f98fa7}$$

$$H_3^{(0)} = \texttt{f70e5939} \qquad\qquad H_7^{(0)} = \texttt{befa4fa4}$$

Similarly, the initial hash value for the SHA-256 function consists of the following eight 32-bit constants:

$$H_0^{(0)} = \texttt{6a09e667} \qquad\qquad H_4^{(0)} = \texttt{510e527f}$$

$$H_1^{(0)} = \texttt{bb67ae85} \qquad\qquad H_5^{(0)} = \texttt{9b05688c}$$

$$H_2^{(0)} = \texttt{3c6ef372} \qquad\qquad H_6^{(0)} = \texttt{1f83d9ab}$$

$$H_3^{(0)} = \texttt{a54ff53a} \qquad\qquad H_7^{(0)} = \texttt{5be0cd19}$$

While these constants may seem random at first, they were actually obtained by taking the first 32 bits of the fractional parts of the square roots of the first 8 primes [129]. This might sound counter-intuitive at first, especially if you recall our discussion about the role of entropy in cryptography in *Chapter 3 A Secret to Share.*

However, exactly because these constants were chosen in a deterministic manner, it is extremely unlikely that they were chosen for any specific reason. As a result, we need not be concerned whether they have any implications unknown to us on the security of SHA-224 and SHA-256 functions.

14.2.7 DES S-boxes

On March 17, 1975, the US National Bureau of Standards, the precursor of today's NIST, published the **Data Encryption Standard (DES)**, which quickly became one of the most used cryptographic algorithms worldwide.

As discussed previously, DES is a block cipher based on a Feistel network. At the heart of the DES round function, eight S-boxes ensure the algorithm's security since they are the only non-linear components of the round function [168].

DES was specified in a process that involved a public competition where a cipher submitted by IBM was finally chosen in the second competition round, followed by a public discussion period of about six months. However, the National Bureau of Standards also consulted with the NSA.

After the original algorithm submitted by IBM was sent for review to the NSA, it came back with completely different S-boxes. The modifications were analyzed by the cryptographic community, and there was even an official review conducted on behalf of the US Senate's Select Committee on Intelligence. Despite this, no statistical or mathematical weaknesses were found throughout the 1970s and the 1980s.

This suddenly changed in 1990 after two Israeli cryptographers Eli Biham and Adi Shamir published a novel method for breaking block ciphers called *differential cryptanalysis* [32]. When applying it to DES, cryptographers discovered that DES S-boxes were much more resistant against differential cryptanalysis than randomly chosen S-boxes could ever be.

When Don Coppersmith, one of the IBM cryptographers who designed DES, published original design criteria for DES S-boxes in 1994, the cryptographic community learned that the NSA and IBM knew about differential cryptanalysis as early as 1974. As a result, DES S-boxes were deliberately tweaked to resist differential cryptanalysis but the NSA requested to keep it a secret because the attack was applicable to a wide range of cryptographic algorithms and was considered by the NSA to be a serious risk to national security if it became public.

Fortunately for DES users, the tweak of the DES S-boxes turned out to *increase* the security of the algorithm. However, when unexplained constants are used, there is always the risk of a backdoor. What if Eve is involved in the specification of a cryptographic algorithm – as an example, she could participate in a public competition by submitting her own proposal – and knows a secret attack? She could propose constants that look random at the first sight but are actually carefully chosen to enable that attack.

14.2.8   Nothing-up-my-sleeves numbers

To avoid the risk of backdoors, cryptographers prefer so-called **Nothing-up-My-Sleeves (NUMS)** numbers to be used as constants or initialization values. Simply put, a NUMS number is any number whose origin is easy to explain. That is, it is easy to explain how the number was chosen. Figuratively, the NUMS concept is analogous to a magician demonstrating that they have no objects hidden in their sleeves before performing a magic trick.

As an example, a number composed of the first k digits of π, e or $\sqrt{2}$ would be considered a NUMS number because it is derived from a well-known mathematical constant like π or e, or from a very specific number, such as $\sqrt{2}$, which was probably the first number that ancient Greek mathematicians discovered to be irrational.

How do NUMS numbers make cryptographic algorithms more secure? The idea is that the choice of NUMS numbers is very constrained compared to (seemingly) random numbers. There are infinitely many random numbers. But there are only so many mathematical constants and well-known numbers with very specific mathematical properties, and their digits are given by nature.

As a result, the likelihood of Eve finding a NUMS number that introduces a backdoor or weakens the cryptographic algorithm is extremely low. With random numbers, on the other hand, Eve could simply generate one random number after the other until she finds one that affects the algorithm's security.

Whether this scenario is practical depends on the cryptographic algorithm – are there parameters that are cryptographically weak? – and the computing resources available to Eve. The latter is rather easy to address, especially if Eve is a large organization, let alone a nation state.

14.3 The AES block cipher

In stark contrast to the DES algorithm, whose design criteria were never fully published, the AES was conceived in a very transparent process. After a formal, worldwide *Call for Algorithms* published in 1997 by the NIST, the National Institute of Standards and Technology in the United States, 15 candidate algorithm specifications were submitted, along with reference implementations in C and Java. The goal was to find a block cipher that was *as secure as Triple-DES, but much more efficient.* More specifically, the AES should have a block length of 128 bits and should be able to support variable key lengths of 128, 192, and 256 bits. Further selection criteria, apart from security, were as follows:

- **Versatility:** The selected algorithm should perform uniformly well on all hardware platforms, ranging from chip cards over PCs to **Application-Specific Integrated Circuits(ASICs)** and **Field Programmable Gate Arrays (FPGAs)**.

- **Key agility:** It should be possible to switch to a different key very fast.

- **Simplicity:** The design of the elected algorithm should be as clean and transparent as possible

At the end of the evaluation process, in May 2000, the selected algorithm was announced: it was called *Rijndael* and had been submitted by the Belgian cryptographers Joan Daemen and Vincent Rijmen. All five candidate algorithms that had reached the second stage of the competition were deemed to be very secure. But averaged over all platforms, Rijndael showed the best performance of all candidate ciphers. Moreover, its clean and elegant design was very convincing.

Soon after the NIST had declared Rijndael to be the AES, other standardization organizations followed. Today the AES block cipher is by far the most-used block cipher worldwide.

14.3.1 Overall structure

AES has a fixed block length of 128 bits and, as required by the initial call for algorithms, a flexible key length of 128, 192, or 256 bits. AES is a substitution-permutation network consisting of 10, 12, or 14 rounds, depending on the key length.

The 128 plaintext bits are arranged in a $(4, 4)$ *state matrix A*, where each entry a_{ij} holds a byte of data. These bytes are treated as elements of the finite field $\mathbb{F}_2[X]/P$ with 2^8 elements, where P is the irreducible polynomial

$$P(x) = x^8 + x^4 + x^3 + x + 1$$

(see *Section 7.6, Finite fields* in *Chapter 7, Public-Key Cryptography*). Other than in the DES algorithm, the bytes always retain their structure and are never broken up into smaller parts. This has proven to be advantageous on eight-bit platforms (see [46]).

14.3.2 Round function

The round function f of the AES algorithm has four components (see also *Figure 14.5*):

- **SubBytes**: This is the only non-linear component of the round function. It implements the substitution part in the substitution-permutation network. In software, SubBytes is implemented via a lookup table, but the table entries can be explained mathematically:

  First, each byte b in the state matrix is replaced by its multiplicative inverse in $\mathbb{F}_2[X]/P$. The zero byte 00 is mapped onto itself:

$$b \mapsto g(b) = \begin{cases} b^{-1}, & \text{if } b \neq 00 \\ 00, & \text{otherwise} \end{cases}$$

This map has been shown in [133] to have good resistance against differential and linear cryptanalysis.

However, this simple algebraic expression in itself would lead to a very simple algebraic expression for the complete round function, which could be used to mount other attacks. Therefore the non-linear component g is followed by an affine transformation f. In this transformation, the input byte b is multiplied bitwise by a fixed $(8, 8)$ matrix M, and a constant byte v is added afterward:

$$f(b) = M \times b \oplus v,$$

where

$$M = \begin{pmatrix} 1 & 1 & 1 & 1 & 1 & 0 & 0 & 0 \\ 0 & 1 & 1 & 1 & 1 & 1 & 0 & 0 \\ 0 & 0 & 1 & 1 & 1 & 1 & 1 & 0 \\ 0 & 0 & 0 & 1 & 1 & 1 & 1 & 1 \\ 1 & 0 & 0 & 0 & 1 & 1 & 1 & 1 \\ 1 & 1 & 0 & 0 & 0 & 1 & 1 & 1 \\ 1 & 1 & 1 & 0 & 0 & 0 & 1 & 1 \\ 1 & 1 & 1 & 1 & 0 & 0 & 0 & 1 \end{pmatrix} \text{ and } v = \begin{pmatrix} 0 \\ 1 \\ 1 \\ 0 \\ 0 \\ 0 \\ 1 \\ 1 \end{pmatrix}$$

Summing up, the SubBytes part of the round function is given by

$$\text{SB}(b) = (f \circ g)(b) = f(g(b)),$$

with f and g as defined above.

- **ShiftRows**: The ShiftRows transformation is a simple operation that cyclically shifts the bytes of row i in the state matrix by i places to the left; that is, row 0 is not shifted, row 1 by one place, and so on (see also *Figure 14.5*). As is pointed out in [46], the shifts for the different rows are different in order to achieve optimal diffusion.

- **MixColumns**: Like ShiftRows, this step is part of the permutation component of the round function. MixColumns mixes the entries of each column vector $\vec{v}_j$ of the state matrix by treating the bytes b_{ij} within $\vec{v}_j$ as coefficients of a polynomial p_j of degree ≤ 3:

$$p_j(x) = b_{3j} \cdot x^3 + b_{2j} \cdot x^2 + b_{1j} \cdot x + b_{0j}$$

The mixing is achieved by multiplying each p_j by a fixed polynomial

$$c(x) = 03 \cdot x^3 + 01 \cdot x^2 + 01 \cdot x + 02$$

Like the coefficients of p_j, the coefficients of $c(x)$ are bytes; therefore, they are written as hexadecimal numbers. The multiplication of p_j and c is done modulo $x^4 + 1$, so that the resulting polynomial is of degree ≤ 3 again and its coefficients can be used to populate an output column vector consisting of four bytes again. The coefficients of the polynomial c were carefully chosen to allow for efficient multiplication.

As is shown in [46], p.39, the multiplication by $c(x)$ modulo $x^4 + 1$ can be represented in matrix form by the formula

$$MC(\vec{v}) = \begin{pmatrix} 02 & 03 & 01 & 01 \\ 01 & 02 & 03 & 01 \\ 01 & 01 & 02 & 03 \\ 03 & 01 & 01 & 02 \end{pmatrix} \times \begin{pmatrix} b_0 \\ b_1 \\ b_2 \\ b_3 \end{pmatrix}$$

- **AddRoundKey**: As the last step in each round, a round key k_i, where $1 \leq i \leq r$ is added to the current block. In addition, before the first round, a round key k_0 is added to the plaintext via bitwise XOR.

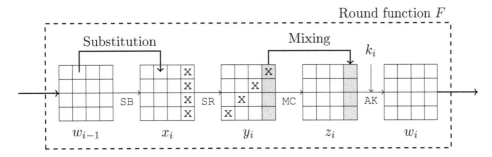

Figure 14.5: Structure of the AES round function. w_{i-1} is the word described by the state before round i. In the last round, the MixColumns step is omitted

14.3.3 Key scheduling

As a round key is added to the 128-bit plaintext block before the first encryption round and at the end of each encryption round, the AES key k needs to be expanded into $r + 1$ different round keys k_i, where each round key has 128 bits and $r \in \{10, 12, 14\}$.

Suppose k has 128 bits. In this case, we are going to do 10 rounds, so we need 11 round keys of 128 bits each. We start by separating k into four 32-bit words W_0, W_1, W_2, W_3. Then the key is expanded by generating more words W_i for $4 \le i \le 43$ by the following algorithm:

- If $i \ge 4$ is **not** a multiple of four, then

$$W_i = W_{i-1} \oplus W_{i-4}$$

- If $i \ge 4$ **is** a multiple of four, then W_{i-1} is first transformed by shifting its four bytes (a, b, c, d) cyclically to the left by one place to get (b, c, d, a). Then SubBytes is applied on each of the bytes and a constant round word c_ℓ is added. The round word is an element of $(\mathbb{F}_2[X]/M)^4$, that is, it consists of four bytes, where each byte is an element of $\mathbb{F}_2[X]/M$, the same finite field as where the elements of the state matrix live. For 128-bit key length, the c_ℓ are defined by

$$\ell = i/4 - 1, c_\ell = (x^\ell, 0, 0, 0)$$

In case you don't want to go through the algebra for yourself, here is a table with the c_ℓ written in hexadecimal form:

ℓ	0	1	2	3	4	5	6	7	8	9
c_ℓ	01	02	04	08	10	20	40	80	1B	36

Table 14.1: Hexadecimal round constants in an AES key schedule

Thus, if $W_{i-1} = (a, b, c, d)$, we get

$$W_i = (\text{SB}(b), \text{SB}(c), \text{SB}(d), \text{SB}(a)) \oplus c_\ell \oplus W_{i-4}$$

Each round key consists of four consecutive words W_i:

$$k_0 = (W_0, W_1, W_2, W_3), k_1 = (W_4, W_5, W_6, W_7), \ldots, k_{11} = (W_{40}, W_{41}, W_{42}, W_{43})$$

For the other key lengths, the expansion algorithm has to be slightly adjusted: a 192-bit key consists of six 32-bit words, and a 256-bit key consists of eight 32-bit words; therefore, for a 192-bit key, the expanding algorithm changes if i is a multiple of six, and for a 256-bit key, it changes if i is a multiple of eight.

Finally, if the key length is 256, there is one more modification of the preceding algorithm: if $i = 4 \mod 8$, then

$$W_i = W_{i-8} \oplus \text{SB}(W_{i-1})$$

We can now formulate the key expansion algorithm in full generality: Suppose k has n bits, where $n \in \{128, 192, 256\}$. Depending on n, we are going to do r rounds, where $r \in \{10, 12, 14\}$, and we are going to expand k into $r + 1$ round keys of 128 bits each.

For this, we first separate k into N 32-bit words $W_0, \ldots, W_{N-1}$, where $N = n/32$. Now we generate more 32-bit words W_i for $N \leq i \leq 4r + 3$ using the following algorithm:

- If $i \geq N$ **is** a multiple of N, let $W_{i-1} = (a, b, c, d)$, where a, b, c, d are bytes. Then

$$W_i = (\text{SB}(b), \text{SB}(c), \text{SB}(d), \text{SB}(a)) \oplus c_\ell \oplus W_{i-N},$$

  where $\ell = i/N - 1$ and c_ℓ as in *Table 14.1*.

- If $N = 8$ and $i = 4 \mod 8$,

$$W_i = W_{i-8} \oplus \text{SB}(W_{i-1})$$

- In all other cases,
$$W_i = W_{i-1} \oplus W_{i-N}$$

Because our space is limited, this concludes our tour of the AES block cipher. There is much more that could be said about AES, especially how some parts of it are motivated by the need to be resistant against certain generic attacks (*linear cryptanalysis* and *differential cryptanalysis*) against block ciphers. If you are interested in these topics, please refer to the book [46] written by the two designers of AES.

We now leave the nuts and bolts of constructing a secure block cipher and turn to the following question: given a secure block cipher, how we should deal with a large number of (possibly identical) plaintext blocks?

14.4 Modes of operation

In the previous sections, we have discussed in detail how a block cipher encrypts a single block of plaintext data. But how should we proceed when faced with a large number of blocks? There are several possible answers to this question, each coming with its own advantages and disadvantages. The different approaches for encrypting a large number of blocks using a certain block cipher are called *modes of operation*.

As of the writing of this book, the following block cipher modes are approved by NIST:

- The modes ECB, CBC, OFB, CFB, CTR, XTS-AES, FF1, and FF3, which can be used to achieve confidentiality

- CMAC mode, which can be used to achieve authentication

- The CCM, GCM, KW, KWP, and TKW modes, which combine confidentiality and message authentication

14.4.1   ECB mode

The **Electronic Code Book (ECB)** mode, shown in *Figure 14.6*, is the most straightforward mode of operation, where the ciphertext is obtained by directly applying the block cipher to the plaintext blocks. More precisely, given a plaintext of l blocks $m_1, \ldots, m_l$, the ciphertext is computed as

$$f_k(m_1), f_k(m_2), \ldots f_k(m_l)$$

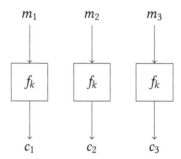

Figure 14.6: Working principle of the ECB mode of operation

From the cryptographic perspective, the ECB mode is insecure regardless of which underlying block cipher is used. This is because ECB is deterministic: any two identical plaintext blocks result in two identical ciphertext blocks. If a block repeats itself in the plaintext, the resulting ciphertext will also contain identical, repeating blocks. Moreover, if a certain plaintext block occurs more often than others, its corresponding cipher block will also occur more often in the ciphertext. More generally, the statistical properties of the plaintext on the block level leak through into the ciphertext, thereby violating Shannon's confusion requirement.

The effect of this leakage can be seen in *Figure 14.7*. The original image of the Linux mascot Tux was drawn by Larry Ewing using the GIMP software; the encrypted image was created by Robert Graham [75]. Since large parts of the original image have a single color, the encrypted image is recognizable as a penguin. Note that this is despite the fact that AES encryption itself cannot be distinguished from a random permutation and, therefore, is considered secure according to the formal definition. As a result, you should never use the ECB mode of operation to directly compute the ciphertext.

 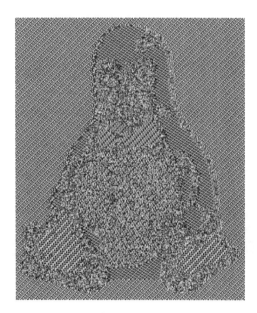

Figure 14.7: On the left, the original image of Tux, the Linux mascot. On the right, the Tux image encrypted using AES in the ECB mode of operation

On a more fundamental level, ECB illustrates an important property of cryptographic constructions: secure cryptographic primitives or building blocks can be combined or used in a way that provides no or very little security. This must be especially taken into account when dealing with large, complex security systems, mechanisms, or protocols.

Let us now do a small experiment by encrypting plaintext using the AES block cipher in the ECB mode of operation. We first need to start the OpenSSL Docker container:

```
$ docker container run --rm -it openssl310
```

In the container, we first create some plaintext and store it in the p.txt file:

```
$ echo -n "cryptographicallcryptographicallcryptographicall" > p.txt
```

With the secret key in place, we can now encrypt the plaintext stored in p.txt using AES in the ECB mode of operation and store the resulting ciphertext in the c.txt file by executing the following:

```
$ openssl enc -aes-128-ecb -in p.txt -out c.txt -K
000102030405060708090a0b0c0d0e0f -nopad
```

To see the encryption result, we have to view the c.txt file in hexadecimal form (because only a subset of values 0-255 represents printable characters). We can use the xxd tool to accomplish this:

```
$ xxd c.txt
00000000: aff4 ad1b b37d 74f6 7087 146e 7aa0 0414  .....}t.p..nz...
00000010: aff4 ad1b b37d 74f6 7087 146e 7aa0 0414  .....}t.p..nz...
00000020: aff4 ad1b b37d 74f6 7087 146e 7aa0 0414  .....}t.p..nz...
```

Every xxd output line shows 16 bytes of c.txt's contents. As you can see, there is a repetition of the block starting with 0xaff4 and ending with 0x0414. This is not a coincidence but the result of our plaintext being composed of a 16-byte string cryptographicall repeated three times. The ECB mode of operation turns this plaintext into a ciphertext consisting of three identical 16-byte blocks.

Filippo Valsorda, a cryptography engineer and open source maintainer, used this ECB property to generate Tux pop art shown in *Figure 14.8*. The different color combinations result from the use of different keys.

Figure 14.8: Filippo Valsorda's Tux pop art using AES encryption in ECB mode with different keys

So, how can we fix this issue? We need to define a mode of operation that maps identical plaintext blocks onto different plaintext blocks.

14.4.2 CBC mode

Cipher Block Chaining (**CBC**), illustrated in *Figure 14.9*, is a mode of operation that chains the ciphertext blocks. CBC encryption is probabilistic, meaning that two identical plaintext blocks will result in two *different* ciphertext blocks:

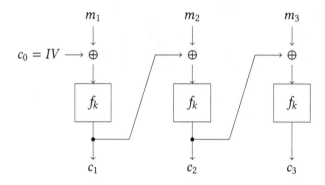

Figure 14.9: Working principle of the CBC mode of operation

The initial ciphertext block c_0 is set to a randomly chosen **initialization vector** (**IV**). The following ciphertext blocks are computed by XORing the plaintext block with the previous ciphertext block and encrypting the result with the underlying block cipher:

$$
\begin{aligned}
c_0 &= IV \\
c_i &= f_k(c_{i-1} \oplus m_i)
\end{aligned}
$$

This construction ensures that identical plaintext blocks will not be mapped onto identical cipher blocks. *Figure 14.10*, created by Robert Graham [75], graphically illustrates this effect. As you can see, the leakage present in ECB encryption is completely eliminated:

Given a ciphertext $c_1, \ldots, c_l$ computed using the CBC mode of operation, the decryption is done by computing

$$
m_i = f_k^{-1}(c_i) \oplus c_{i-1}
$$

Figure 14.10: On the left, the original image of Tux, the Linux mascot. On the right, the Tux image encrypted using AES in the CBC mode of operation

where c_i and m_i denote the corresponding ciphertext and plaintext blocks, and f_k^{-1} denotes the decryption operation performed under key k. To enable decryption, the initialisation vector IV is included in the ciphertext.

Before going on to look at how we can encrypt in CBC mode in OpenSSL, we need to mention two more important properties of the CBC mode:

- A downside of CBC mode is that the encryption (and decryption) cannot be computed in parallel because the encryption of the plaintext block m_i requires the ciphertext block c_{i-1}.

- Because CBC mode uses a random IV, identical plaintexts *never* result in identical ciphertexts. An important consequence of this fact is that CBC encryption mode is **Chosen Plaintext Attack (CPA)**-secure, if we assume the underlying block cipher f to be a pseudorandom permutation. The key idea is to consider an encryption scheme CPA-secure if Eve cannot distinguish between the ciphertexts of two messages of her choice m_0, m_1 even if she has access to an encryption oracle. We will discuss CPA-security in detail later in *Section 15.1.1* in *Chapter 15, Authenticated Encryption*.

To encrypt the plaintext stored in p.txt using AES in the CBC mode of operation, we need an additional 16-byte initialization vector and have to execute the following encryption command:

```
$ openssl enc -aes-128-cbc -in p.txt -out c.txt -K
000102030405060708090a0b0c0d0e0f -iv 000102030405060708090a0b0c0d0e0f0
-nopad$
```

The encryption result is again written to c.txt, and we can use the xxd tool to view the file's contents in hexadecimal form:

```
$ xxd c.txt
00000000: 79a4 8518 4448 04c2 ee96 86df 5ce4 1784  y...DH......\...
00000010: 0973 6960 4b44 62dc 550c abe4 140d bc26  .si`KDb.U......&
00000020: 2f98 c968 da10 f77b 79bc 9100 1f84 6cef  /..h...{y.....l.
```

As you can see, although our plaintext consists of the repeating 16-byte plaintext block cryptographic11, the resulting ciphertext contains no repetitions. In real life, we would, of course, choose a completely random *IV* instead of 0010 ... *f*0. In addition, for every new plaintext (not a plaintext block, though) we would choose a new *IV*.

14.4.3 CBC-MAC

Looking closely at *Figure 14.9* again, we can see that the last cipher block c_3 depends on **all** plaintext blocks m_1, m_2, m_3. Of course this is also true for an arbitrary number of plaintext blocks.

Therefore, one can construct a message authentication code over some plaintext message m called the **CBC-MAC** by encrypting m in CBC mode, using an all-zero block as initialization vector. The CBC-MAC over m is then simply the last resulting cipher block.

While it seems attractive to have a single algorithm that can achieve both confidentiality and authenticity (we will explore this idea further in the next chapter), the CBC-MAC needs to be handled with care.

Assume Eve observes two plaintexts p_1, p_2 along with their corresponding CBC-MACs t_1, t_2. Assume further that the key k_a used to compute the MACs is the same in both cases. Then Eve can construct a third plaintext p_3 having the CBC-MAC t_1 without knowing k_a. Let $p_1 = m_1 \| m_2 \| \dots \| m_N$. Then, Eve sets

$$p_3 = p_2 \| m_1 \oplus t_2 \| m_2 \| \dots \| m_N$$

If the CBC-MAC for p_3 is computed, first p_2 is processed, yielding t_2 as cipher block. So, for the next cipher block, $(m_1 \oplus t_2) \oplus t_2 = m_1$ is encrypted. So, the rest of the computation runs exactly as if p_1 were processed. Therefore, p_1 and p_3 have the same CBC-MAC.

This issue can be avoided by using different keys for different message lengths or by prepending the message length before the actual message.

The CBC-MAC is part of the CCM mode of operation, which we will encounter in *Chapter 15, Authenticated Encryption*.

14.4.4 OFB mode

The **Output Feedback (OFB)** mode, illustrated in *Figure 14.11*, is a mode of operation that uses the underlying block cipher to produce blocks of keying material, which, in turn, is used to encrypt the plaintext messages. Consequently, OFB can be viewed as a stream cipher constructed from an underlying block cipher.

Informally, we can use the output blocks of a secure block cipher as keystream in a stream cipher because of Shannon's *confusion* requirement we discussed at the beginning of this chapter: a cipher block should bear no traces of the statistical structure of the corresponding plaintext block. Consequently, it should have *no statistical structure at all*, which means it should not be distinguishable from a random block:

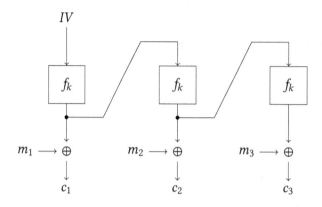

Figure 14.11: Working principle of the OFB mode of operation

To use OFB, the sender must first choose a random initialization vector IV. Using IV and a shared secret k, the encryption is done by computing:

$$y_0 = IV$$
$$y_i = f_k(y_{i-1})$$
$$c_i = m_i \oplus y_i$$

where y_i is the result of encrypting input y_{i-1} with block cipher f under key k. All y_i except y_0 are used as key material that is XORed with the corresponding plaintext block m_i to obtain the ciphertext block c_i.

Similar to CBC, the IV is included in the ciphertext to enable decryption. The decryption is computed as follows:

$$y_0 = IV$$
$$y_i = f_k(y_{i-1})$$
$$m_i = c_i \oplus y_i$$

You can easily see from the above equations that, unlike CBC mode, OFB requires no inverse f^{-1}. In practice, this is especially beneficial in resource-constrained environments such as **Application-Specific Integrated Circuits (ASICs)** or deeply embedded electronics because a *single* function can be used for both encryption and decryption. To use CBC, by contrast, designers must implement two separate functions f and its inverse f^{-1}.

OFB has been shown to be CPA-secure if the underlying f is a pseudorandom function [117]. Moreover, unlike CBC, OFB can be used in a chained manner where the last key material block y_l is used as *IV* for the next plaintext. In contrast, using the last ciphertext block c_l as *IV* for the encryption of the next plaintext renders CBC vulnerable to a chosen plaintext attack. This is because Eve learns c_l and, therefore, *IV*, which will be used to encrypt the next plaintext.

Similar to CBC, OFB encryption and decryption cannot be parallelized. However, the key material y_i can be computed independently from the plaintext to be encrypted or the ciphertext to be decrypted. This, in turn, allows to pre-generate the OFB key stream, making the encryption and decryption itself very fast once the data arrives because it only involves an XOR operation.

If we want to experiment with the OFB mode, we can encrypt our plaintext in p.txt. To use AES in OFB mode, we execute the following command:

```
$ openssl enc -aes-128-ofb -in p.txt -out c.txt -K
000102030405060708090a0b0c0d0e0f -iv 000102030405060708090a0b0c0d0e0f0
-nopad
```

We can once again view the encryption result using the xxd tool. Like with CBC, the ciphertext obtained using OFB contains no repetitions:

```
$ xxd c.txt
00000000: 15a2 1b0d d5bd f731 0f51 ccc6 1cab f886  .......1.Q......
00000010: 59fc a0c8 7faa 1cfc dbfe e2fd 48f1 46d4  Y...........H.F.
00000020: cb7c 6e20 ef2c d2ec 8b84 ac53 51bc 9369  .|n .,.....SQ..i
```

We will now look at an even simpler way to use a block cipher as a key stream generator.

14.4.5 CTR mode

The **Counter (CTR)** mode, illustrated in *Figure 14.12*, is a mode of operation that applies the underlying block cipher f to generate a key stream that is subsequently used for encryption and decryption. Effectively, this makes CTR a stream cipher:

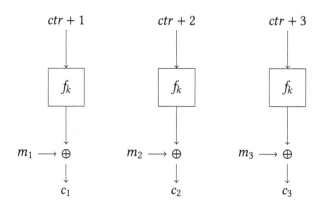

Figure 14.12: Working principle of the CTR mode of operation

To encrypt a plaintext using CTR mode, the sender first chooses a random value for the counter *ctr*. The sender then performs the encryption by generating the key stream and XORing it with the plaintext blocks:

$$
\begin{aligned}
y_i &= f_k(ctr + i) \\
c_i &= m_i \oplus y_i
\end{aligned}
$$

where y_i is the result of encrypting the i-th *ctr* value with block cipher f under key k. The key material y_i is then XORed with the corresponding plaintext block m_i to obtain the ciphertext block c_i.

Decryption using CTR is performed by computing:

$$
\begin{aligned}
y_i &= f_k(ctr + i) \\
m_i &= c_i \oplus y_i
\end{aligned}
$$

From the preceding equations, you can see that CTR, like OFB, requires no inverse function f^{-1}. Moreover, it can be shown that CTR is CPA-secure if f is a pseudorandom function [57].

In contrast to all secure modes of operation discussed so far, both encryption and decryption in CTR mode can be completely parallelized. This is because – as you can easily convince yourself by looking at *Figure 14.12* – the CTR key stream blocks y_i depend only on the counter *ctr* and the shared key k. As a result, y_i can be computed in parallel.

Clearly, since y_i do not depend on the plaintext to be encrypted or ciphertext to be decrypted, the key stream can be pre-generated and cached, similar to OFB. This makes subsequent CTR encryption or decryption very fast.

To encrypt the previously generated plaintext in p.txt using the AES in the CTR mode of operation, we execute the following command:

```
$ openssl enc -aes-128-cbc -in p.txt -out c.txt -K
000102030405060708090a0b0c0d0e0f -iv 00000000000000000000000000000001
-nopad
```

Note that the OpenSSL's option name iv is somewhat misleading in the preceding command since CTR expects a counter value, not an initialization vector. This cryptographic detail was likely ignored to keep the OpenSSL interface as simple as possible.

The resulting ciphertext was written to the c.txt file and we can again view it using the xxd tool:

```
$ xxd c.txt
00000000: 68be 1fec 72f3 b5bc 2f34 1f9e 21dc 0ab4  h...r.../4..!...
00000010: ae5b e4e7 fd3c 33e4 1498 8cb0 e4db 6ff3  .[...<3.......o.
00000020: f4f8 03bb 1e3e 1595 9cf4 d6e6 175b a076  .....>.......[.v
```

Our final mode of operation in this section is particularly well suited for the encryption of entire hard disks.

14.4.6 XTS mode

The **Tweakable Block Cipher with Ciphertext Stealing (XTS)**, shown in *Figure 14.14*, is a mode of operation designed to ensure confidentiality of data stored on block devices, that is, storage devices that use fixed-size data units [58]. XTS is specified in the IEEE standard 1619 [84] and uses the AES block cipher as its underlying cryptographic primitive. For this reason, XTS is oftentimes referred to as XTS-AES.

Conceptually, XTS is a variant of the **XOR-Encrypt-XOR (XEX)** mode of operation proposed in 2004 by the American cryptographer Phillip Rogaway. The XEX mode is illustrated in *Figure 14.13*. It uses a so-called *tweak* t_i that is XORed with the plaintext message m_i before and after it is encrypted using the block cipher f_k.

If t_i is location-specific, XEX is particularly well suited for whole-disk encryption because it can efficiently encrypt consecutive data blocks within a data unit such as a disk sector:

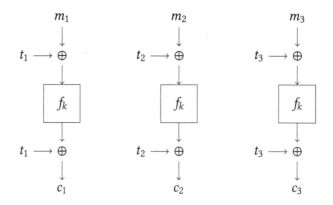

Figure 14.13: Working principle of the XEX mode of operation

XTS mode, shown in *Figure 14.14*, is XEX supplemented with the so-called *ciphertext stealing* , that extends the plaintext so it can be properly processed by a block cipher. More precisely, cipher stealing is an efficient way for using a block cipher to process plaintexts whose size is not an integer multiple of the block size.

Cipher stealing works by processing the last two plaintext blocks in a special way: the second-to-last block's ciphertext is re-used or *stolen* for padding the last plaintext block.

The last block is now padded, which means it has the required length, and can be encrypted in the standard way.

Tweak t is a 128-bit value that encodes the storage location, that is, the block number, of the data being encrypted or decrypted [84]. The symbol α denotes the primitive element in finite field $\mathbb{F}(2^{128})$ whose binary representation is 000...010.

The symbol α^j is the j-th power of the primitive element α, and j is the sequence number of the 128-bit block inside the data unit. The value α^j is multiplied with the 16-byte value obtained by AES encryption (or decryption) operation f_{k_1}.

The symbol $\otimes$ denotes the modular multiplication of two polynomials over the binary Galois field $\mathbb{F}(2)$, taken modulo the polynomial $x^{128} + x^7 + x^2 + x + 1$:

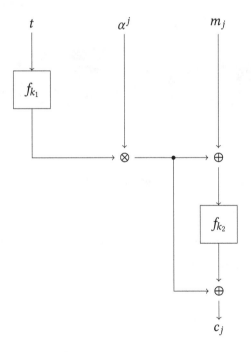

Figure 14.14: Working principle of the XTS mode of operation

The secret key k has a size of 256 or 512 bits and is parsed as a concatenation of two equal-size bitvectors k_1, k_2. In other words, $k = k_1 \| k_2$.

As illustrated in *Figure 14.14*, key k_1 is used for the encryption of the tweak t. The encrypted tweak is multiplied with the term α^j (recall that j is the sequence number of the 128-bit block inside the data unit). The result is XORed with the plaintext m_j and with the encryption result that is computed using key k_2. This way, XTS mode ensures that identical plaintext does not produce identical ciphertext.

To encrypt a plaintext using the AES-XTS mode of operation in our Docker container, we first have to generate a random 16-byte tweak and a random 32-byte secret key:

```
$ openssl rand -hex 16 > t.txt
$ openssl rand -hex 32 > k.txt
```

Then, with tweak and key in place, we perform the encryption of a plaintext stored in the p.txt file and write the result into the c.txt file by calling the following:

```
$ openssl enc -aes-128-xts -in p.txt -out c.txt -K
000102030405060708090a0b0c0d0e0f -iv t.txt -nopad
```

We will now look at how block ciphers are used within TLS.

14.5   Block ciphers in TLS 1.3

In TLS, block ciphers are used for protecting the confidentiality and integrity of data transmitted over the TLS Record layer. More precisely, a block cipher is used for encrypting TLSInnerPlaintext, the plaintext transmitted by Alice and Bob, into encrypted_record in TLSCiphertext structure that is, in turn, transmitted over the wire:

The encryption process is illustrated in *Figure 14.15*. The fragment field in the TLSPlaintext structure contains the actual payload data. The type field in TLSPlaintext contains the subprotocol type, that is, a numeric value encoding the TLS subprotocol type this data has. The enumeration of valid TLS subprotocol types is shown in *Listing 32*.

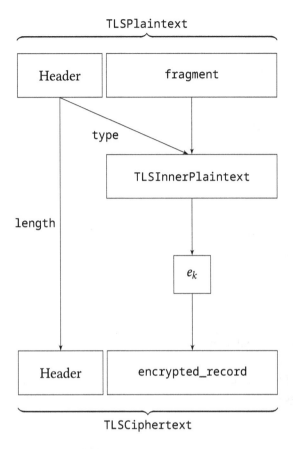

Figure 14.15: Encryption at the TLS Record layer

The subprotocol type and the actual payload are combined into the TLSInnerPlaintext data structure shown in *Listing 32*. This data is then encrypted using a block cipher into the encrypted_record field in TLSCiphertext:

Note that the content type of TLSCiphertext, that is, the opaque_type field, is always set to 23, the numeric code for application_data. This is done in order to hide the actual content type from Eve. The actual type of the TLS record as well as its length – stored in the zeros field of TLSInnerPlaintext – is transmitted within the encrypted field encrypted_record.

```
enum {
    invalid(0),
    change_cipher_spec(20),
    alert(21),
    handshake(22),
    application_data(23),
    (255)
} ContentType;

struct {
    ContentType type;
    ProtocolVersion legacy_record_version;
    uint16 length;
    opaque fragment[TLSPlaintext.length];
} TLSPlaintext;

struct {
    opaque content[TLSPlaintext.length];
    ContentType type;
    uint8 zeros[length_of_padding];
} TLSInnerPlaintext;

struct {
    ContentType opaque_type = application_data; /* 23 */
    ProtocolVersion legacy_record_version = 0x0303; /* TLS v1.2 */
    uint16 length;
    opaque encrypted_record[TLSCiphertext.length];
} TLSCiphertext;
```

Listing 32: TLS 1.3 data structures used in its protocol layer

14.6 Summary

In this chapter, we learned what block ciphers are (encryption functions mapping plaintext blocks of fixed size b onto ciphertext blocks of the same size b), what design principles are used to construct block ciphers (confusion and diffusion), and what theoretical constructions are used to model block ciphers (pseudorandom permutations).

Moreover, we covered iterated block ciphers and substitution-permutation networks, the two major paradigms for designing secure block ciphers. We then studied in detail how AES, the block cipher chosen as a result of a world-wide call for algorithms by the US standardization body NIST, works. Finally, we highlighted the most common modes of operation of block ciphers, including their working principle, advantages, and disadvantages.

In the next chapter, we will take a detailed look at one more mode of operation. It is called **Authenticated Encryption with Additional Data (AEAD)** and plays a crucial role in TLS 1.3. In contrast to the other modes of operation discussed in this chapter, AEAD combines encryption and message authentication in a single algorithm. As a result, in TLS 1.3, AEAD is used to turn plaintexts into encrypted *and* authenticated cipher texts, which are then transmitted over the wire by Alice and Bob.

15

Authenticated Encryption

In the previous chapter, we learned about block ciphers, including the popular AES algorithm, which was standardized by NIST in 2001 and is the workhorse of bulk data encryption on the internet. We also covered the most popular modes of operation of block ciphers.

In this chapter, we will study an advanced concept called **Authenticated Encryption with Additional Data (AEAD)** that is closely linked to modes of operation. AEAD is a fundamental technique used to protect the TLS Record protocol data in TLS 1.3. Unlike the modes of operation discussed in the previous chapter, AEAD combines encryption and message authentication within a *single* cryptographic algorithm. As a result, in TLS 1.3, AEAD ensures both the confidentiality *and* the authenticity of ciphertexts transmitted by Alice and Bob.

Note that earlier versions of TLS use a different scheme to ensure confidentiality and authenticity, namely MAC-then-encrypt (see *Section 15.2.2, MAC-then-encrypt,* in this chapter). However, as will see in this chapter, AEAD has a distinct security advantage over MAC-then-encrypt. In particular, the infamous POODLE attack (see *Section 21.2 in Chapter 21, Attacks on the TLS Record Protocol*) exploits a weakness in an earlier MAC-then-encrypt scheme.

References to AEAD are sprinkled throughout the entire RFC 8446 standard, but most AEAD-related material that we are going to cover in this chapter is found in Chapter 5, *Record Protocol*, of RFC 8446.

Upon completion of the chapter, you will have a good understanding of the theory behind AEAD and be familiar with CCM, a cryptographic algorithm that implements authenticated encryption.

In terms of skills, you learn the following:

- How an AEAD algorithm works in order to combine confidentiality and message authentication in one go

- How the AEAD theory is implemented in the CCM algorithm

- How AEAD is used in TLS 1.3

15.1 Preliminaries

Before diving into the details of authenticated encryption, we must first introduce some security concepts that we will need later on for an in-depth understanding and comparison of different authenticated encryption schemes.

15.1.1 Indistinguishability under a chosen-plaintext attack

Recall that our intuitive understanding of secure encryption is captured in the formal notion of *indistinguishability in the presence of an eavesdropper*. The key idea of indistinguishability is captured in the game – sometimes referred to as an experiment in cryptographic literature – played by Eve and some other party, let's say, Owen:

1. Eve chooses a pair of equal-size messages m_0, m_1.

2. Owen generates a random secret key k and chooses a bit $b \leftarrow \{0, 1\}$ at random.

3. Owen then computes the ciphertext $c = e_k(m_b)$ – referred to as the *challenge ciphertext* – and gives it to Eve. (Note that we use e_k instead of f_k here to denote encryption because the messages m_0, m_1 in this experiment can have a size different from that of a single plaintext block.)

4. Upon receiving c, Eve must guess whether b was 0 or 1. If Eve's guess is correct, we say that Eve succeeds.

A secret key encryption is said to be indistinguishable in the presence of an eavesdropper if Eve succeeds in the above game with a probability P that is at most negligibly greater than $1/2$:

$$P[\text{Eve succeeds}] \leq \frac{1}{2} + negl(n)$$

where $negl(n)$ denotes a function that is negligible in the security parameter n. In *Chapter 4, Encryption and Decryption*, we already learned that a negligible function is a function that decreases faster toward zero with n than the reciprocal of any polynomial. The phrase *security parameter is n* means that the secret key k is an n-bit value $k \leftarrow \{0, 1\}^n$ chosen uniformly at random.

CPA-secure is a stronger notion of security because a chosen-plaintext attack increases Eve's capabilities. If Eve conducts a CPA, she can ask so-called *encryption oracle* Owen for encryption of *multiple* messages that she can choose *adaptively*. Essentially, Eve can freely interact with Owen – by providing him with a plaintext m as input and receiving the resulting ciphertext $c = E_k(m)$ – before having to guess the value of bit b. The modified game now looks like this:

1. Owen generates a random secret key k.

2. Eve can freely interact with Owen, that is, she can ask Owen to compute the ciphertexts for any plaintexts of her choice.

3. Eve chooses a pair of equal-size messages m_0, m_1.

4. Owen chooses a bit $b \leftarrow \{0, 1\}$ at random and computes the challenge ciphertext $c = E_k(m_b)$.

5. Upon receiving c, Eve continues to have oracle access to Owen and must guess whether b was 0 or 1. If Eve's guess is correct, we say that Eve succeeds.

Similar to the previous definition, a secret key encryption is said to be *indistinguishable under a chosen-plaintext attack* (**IND-CPA**) or, equivalently, **CPA-secure**, if Eve succeeds in the above game with a probability P that is at most negligibly greater than $1/2$:

$$P[\text{Eve succeeds}] \leq \frac{1}{2} + negl(n)$$

In other words, an encryption is CPA-secure if Eve cannot distinguish between the encryption of the messages m_0, m_1 even if she has access to an encryption oracle.

Note that Eve could easily succeed if the encryption e_k was deterministic. In that case, all she has to do is to give Owen the messages m_0, m_1 and compare the corresponding ciphertexts c_0, c_1 to the challenge ciphertext. Consequently, to be CPA-secure, the encryption e_k must be *probabilistic* [97]: it must use randomness during the computation of the ciphertext such that no two encryptions of the same plaintext (block) lead to the same ciphertext (block). Clearly, any encryption that is indistinguishable under a CPA is also indistinguishable in the presence of an eavesdropper.

15.1.2   Indistinguishability under a chosen-ciphertext attack

Chosen-Ciphertext Attack (CCA) is a more powerful attack than a chosen-plaintext attack. Recall that in a chosen-plaintext attack Eve is able to encrypt plaintexts of her choice. In a CCA setting, Eve additionally is allowed to *decrypt* ciphertexts of her choice [97]. This ability is formalized by saying that Eve has access to a *decryption oracle*, say, Oscar.

Similar to CPA-security, the formal definition of CCA-security is captured in the following game:

1. Owen or Oscar generates a random secret key k.

2. Eve can ask Owen to compute the ciphertexts for any plaintexts of her choice. Also, she can ask Oscar to compute the plaintexts for any ciphertexts of her choice.

3. Eve then chooses a pair of equal-length messages m_0, m_1.

4. Next, Owen chooses a bit $b \leftarrow \{0, 1\}$ at random and computes the challenge ciphertext $c = e_k(m_b)$.

5. Upon receiving c, Eve continues to have oracle access to Owen and Oscar, but she is not allowed to ask Oscar for the decryption of the challenge ciphertext c.

6. Finally, Eve must guess whether bit b was 0 or 1. If Eve's guess is correct, we say that Eve succeeds.

A secret key encryption is said to have *indistinguishable encryptions under a chosen-ciphertext attack*, also referred to as **IND-CCA** or **CCA-secure**, if Eve succeeds in the above game with a probability p that is at most negligibly greater than $1/2$:

$$P[\text{Eve succeeds}] \leq \frac{1}{2} + negl(n)$$

If, after some extensive interaction with Oscar, Eve finds a way to manipulate ciphertexts and to predict the consequences of these manipulations for the corresponding plaintexts, she can win this game. Therefore, CCA-security implies another very important property of secret key encryption schemes called *non-malleability*.

15.1.3 Non-malleability under a chosen-plaintext attack

The notion of non-malleability is somewhat more involved. We will first try to get an intuitive understanding of why non-malleability is important using a simple example, and then give a formal definition using the game notation equivalent to those for IND-CPA and IND-CCA.

Informally, an encryption scheme is said to be *non-malleable* if, upon observing ciphertext $c = e_k(m)$, Mallory cannot generate a different ciphertext c' that decrypts to a value m' somehow related to m.

A famous example of a malleable cipher is provided by the RSA encryption algorithm. Recall from *Chapter 7, Public-Key Cryptography*, that if Alice has the public key $PK_{Alice} = (e, n)$, a message m is encrypted to

$$c = m^e \mod n.$$

Taking c' to be

$$c' = (a^e \mod n) \cdot c,$$

we see that

$$c' = (a^e \mod n) \cdot (m^e \mod n) = (a \cdot m)^e \mod n,$$

so the corresponding plaintext is $m' = am$.

More generally, in the computational security setting we are currently in, saying that Mallory cannot generate such a c' means that there exists no polynomial time algorithm able to do this. Moreover, requiring m' to be somehow related to m means that there must be a relation $R(m, m')$ between m and m' that can be computed in polynomial time.

To get an intuitive understanding of why the above definition is useful for cryptographic purposes, let's look at a simple example taken from [56]. Assume that Alice, Bob, and a trusted third party Trent are playing a game. The game's objective is for Trent to generate an unbiased bit only with the help of Bob and Alice; that is, Trent himself has no suitable source of entropy he could query.

To achieve the game's objective, the parties use a probabilistic public-key encryption scheme. Recall that probabilistic encryption offers a provable and very strong level of security because it uses randomness in the encryption process. As a result, given a ciphertext, the adversary cannot compute any information about the plaintext.

A classic example of a probabilistic public-key encryption scheme is the Goldwasser-Micali scheme. A simplified definition of the Goldwasser-Micali scheme can be given using the notion of a trapdoor predicate [117].

A *trapdoor predicate* is a Boolean function $B : \{0, 1\}^* \rightarrow \{0, 1\}$ that takes an arbitrary-length bitstring and maps it to either a 0 or a 1. In addition, given a bit v, it is easy to find a random x for which $B(x) = v$. However, computing $B(x)$ for a given x is computationally feasible only if one knows certain trapdoor information.

In other words, if Alice's public key is a trapdoor predicate B, then Bob can encrypt the message bit m_i by randomly selecting a x_i such that $B(x_i) = m_i$ and send x_i to Alice. Because Alice has the trapdoor information, she is able to efficiently compute $B(x_i) = m_i$. Eve, however, can do no better than guessing the value of m_i.

Using the trapdoor predicate notion, the Goldwasser-Micali probabilistic public-key encryption scheme can be defined as follows:

- Encryption: $e(x) = (f(r), x \oplus B(r))$

- Decryption: $d(y, z) = B(f^{-1}(y)) \oplus z$

Here, x is a single-bit plaintext, f is a trapdoor function, B is the trapdoor predicate of f, and r is a random string.

Having defined the public-key encryption scheme, we can now describe the game played by Alice, Bob, and Trent:

1. Trent publishes his public key.

2. Alice and Bob each choose a random bit x_A and x_B, respectively, encrypt it using Trent's public key, and send the ciphertexts c_A and c_B to Trent.

3. Trent decrypts the received messages, XORs the bits x_A and x_B, and announces the result.

Intuitively, because Bob and Alice don't know each other's bit values, we would expect the ciphertexts c_A and c_A to be independent and, therefore, the result of the XOR operation to be unbiased. Surprisingly, however, it turns out to be wrong!

It is easy to show that even given a probabilistic public-key encryption scheme like the one defined above – that is, a scheme offering semantic security against any polynomial time adversary – Mallory can construct a new ciphertext c', which corresponds to the *complement* of Alice's plaintext. To do this, Mallory simply takes Alice's ciphertext

$$c_A = (f(r), x_A \oplus B(r))$$

and modifies it to obtain

$$c' = (f(r), x_A \oplus B(r) \oplus 1)$$

When Trent afterward decrypts the spoofed ciphertext c' instead of Bob's original ciphertext c_B, he obtains:

$$d(y, z') = B(f^{-1}(y)) \oplus z' = B(r) \oplus x_A \oplus B(r) \oplus 1 = x_A \oplus 1$$

instead of the plaintext actually transmitted by Bob:

$$d(y, z) = B(f^{-1}(y)) \oplus z = B(r) \oplus x_A \oplus B(r) = x_A$$

As a result, by replacing Bob's ciphertext c_B with c', Mallory can force Trent's XOR operation to yield a 1 even though she has no idea whether Alice's bit x_A had the value 0 or 1:

$$d(c_A) \oplus d(c') = x_A \oplus (x_A \oplus 1) = 1$$

The example demonstrates that in some cases indistinguishability is not sufficient. In addition, the encryption scheme must be *non-malleable*: if Mallory is given some ciphertext c, it must be computationally infeasible for him to construct a different ciphertext $\tilde{c}$ so that the corresponding plaintexts m and $\tilde{m}$ have some known relationship [117].

In formal terms, the notion of non-malleability can be expressed using the following game with encryption oracle Owen and decryption oracle Oscar:

1. Owen generates a random secret key k.

2. Mallory can ask Owen to compute ciphertexts for an arbitrary number of plaintexts of her choice. In addition, Mallory can ask Oscar to decrypt a set of ciphertexts of her choice, but she can only ask Oscar *once*.

3. Mallory chooses a pair of equal-length messages m_0, m_1.

4. Next – if Mallory has not yet queried the decryption oracle Oscar – Owen chooses a bit $b \leftarrow \{0, 1\}$ at random, computes the challenge ciphertext $c = e_k(m_b)$, adds c to the set of ciphertexts C, and returns c to Mallory.

5. Upon receiving c, Mallory continues to have oracle access to Owen and to Oscar. When Mallory queries Oscar with a set of ciphertexts, Oscar returns the corresponding plaintexts, except for ciphertexts in C. In addition, once Mallory asks Oscar to decrypt a set of ciphertexts, Owen will not compute new challenge ciphertexts.

6. Finally, Mallory must guess whether bit b was 0 or 1. If Mallory's guess is correct, we say that she succeeds.

We say that secret key encryption is *non-malleable under a chosen-ciphertext attack* or, simply, **NM-CPA**, if Mallory succeeds in the above game with a probability p that is at most negligibly greater than $^1/_2$:

$$P[\text{Mallory succeeds}] \leq \frac{1}{2} + negl(n)$$

You might wonder how the above game describes non-malleability without modeling an attacker who alters a ciphertext in some specific way. The reason behind this is that in 2006, the Indian cryptographer Mihir Bellare and the American cryptographer Amit Sahai proved that non-malleability is equivalent to so-called *indistinguishability under a parallel chosen ciphertext attack* where Mallory's queries to the decryption oracle may not depend on the answers to previous queries and must be made all at once [19]. This is exactly the attack that the above game describes.

The next two cryptographic concepts bring us even closer toward our goal of providing confidentiality and authenticity at the same time.

15.1.4   Plaintext integrity

In terms of the integrity of symmetric encryption schemes, the notion of *plaintext integrity* requires an encryption scheme to be designed in such a way that no algorithm running in polynomial time is able to produce a ciphertext that decrypts to a valid message that the sender has never encrypted [18].

In more formal terms, the notion of plaintext integrity is expressed using a game similar to those we previously used for CPA-secure and CCA-secure definitions. The INT-PTX game is as follows:

1. Owen generates a random secret key k.

2. Eve can ask Owen to compute the ciphertext for any plaintext m of her choice. While doing this, Owen adds m to the set of plaintexts $\mathcal{M}$ that Eve asked him to encrypt.

3. Next, Eve must generate the challenge ciphertext c that decrypts to a valid plaintext message m_i and give c to Owen.

4. Owen verifies that c decrypts to a valid message m_i and $m_i \notin \mathcal{M}$. If this is the case, we say that Eve succeeds.

We say that a secret key encryption scheme provides *plaintext integrity*, also referred to as **INT-PTX**, if Eve succeeds in the above game with a probability p that is negligible in the encryption scheme's security parameter n, that is:

$$P[\text{Eve succeeds}] \leq negl(n)$$

In other words, the probability that Eve can generate a ciphertext that decrypts to a valid plaintext message is negligibly small even if Eve has the ability to encrypt any number of chosen plaintexts before she generates the challenge ciphertext c.

As a result, an INT-PTX encryption scheme ensures that Eve won't be able to generate a ciphertext that decrypts to some valid plaintext even if she observed an (arbitrary) large number of encryptions.

15.1.5 Ciphertext integrity

The notion of *ciphertext integrity* requires an encryption scheme to be designed in such a way that no efficient algorithm can compute a valid ciphertext that was not previously produced by the sender, regardless of whether the underlying plaintext is new [18]. Here, *valid* refers to any ciphertext that corresponds to some meaningful plaintext.

The game used to formalize the notion of ciphertext integrity is almost identical to that of plaintext integrity. The only difference is instead of memorizing the plaintext messages he was asked to encrypt, this time Owen memorizes the ciphertexts returned to Eve upon her queries. So, the INT-CTX game is defined as follows:

1. Owen generates a random secret key k.

2. Eve can ask Owen to compute the ciphertext $c' = e_k(m')$ for any plaintext m' of her choice. After each such calculation, before giving c' to Eve, Owen adds c' to the set of ciphertexts C that correspond to the plaintexts Eve asked him to encrypt.

3. Next, Eve must generate the challenge ciphertext c that decrypts to a valid plaintext message m and give c to Owen.

4. Owen verifies that c decrypts to a valid message m and $c \notin C$, in which case we say that Eve succeeds.

Similar to INT-PTX, we say that a secret key encryption scheme provides *ciphertext integrity* (**INT-CTX**) if Eve succeeds in the above game with probability p that is negligible in the security parameter n:

$$P[\text{Eve succeeds}] \leq negl(n)$$

This inequality is just another way of saying that it is practically infeasible for Eve to generate *new* valid ciphertexts even if she has access to an encryption oracle. More precisely, an INT-CTX encryption scheme guarantees that Eve – or, equivalently, any polynomial time algorithm – cannot generate a ciphertext corresponding to a *meaningful* plaintext if neither Bob nor Alice has computed that ciphertext before, even if Eve is allowed to observe an (arbitrary) large number of encryptions for plaintexts of her choice.

We will now take a look at three traditional ways to achieve confidentiality and authenticity and how they fare in terms of the security notions we just introduced.

15.2   Authenticated encryption – generic composition

An **authenticated encryption** (**AE**) scheme is a symmetric-key encryption scheme that provides both confidentiality as well as message integrity and authenticity.

Roughly speaking, sender Alice encrypts her plaintext and, in addition, computes a message authentication code (MAC, see *Chapter 11, Hash Functions and Message Authentication Codes*) over the ciphertext. The MAC serves as a tag to ensure the integrity and authenticity of the ciphertext. Receiver Bob validates the message's integrity and authenticity by recomputing the MAC and checking that it is equal to the MAC attached to Alice's message.

If Bob's verification is successful, he can be sure that the received ciphertext is untampered and was indeed sent by Alice. So, Bob decrypts the ciphertext and processes the obtained plaintext.

The traditional way of implementing AE, called *generic composition*, is a combination of encryption (to achieve confidentiality) and message authentication code (to achieve message integrity and authenticity) [33]. The standard flavors of generic composition are as follows:

- Encrypt-and-MAC

- MAC-then-encrypt

- Encrypt-then-MAC

Intuitively, all three generic composition flavors seem to offer the same level of security. However, as we will soon learn, cryptographers have proven that the security guarantees of these variants can differ depending on what assumptions we make regarding the underlying cryptographic primitives, that is, assumptions regarding the strength of the block cipher and the MAC algorithm used.

15.2.1 Encrypt-and-MAC

The *encrypt-and-MAC* composition encrypts the plaintext and appends the MAC of the plaintext. Using the block cipher encryption e and a message authentication code T, the sender computes:

$$e_{k_e}(m) \parallel T_{k_a}(m)$$

where m is the plaintext message, k_e is the shared secret key for encryption, k_a is the shared secret key for message authentication, and $\parallel$ is a concatenation operation.

The encrypt-and-MAC composition is illustrated in *Figure 15.1*. Sender Alice encrypts plaintext m using the encryption key k_e and, in parallel, computes a message authentication code for m using a second key k_a. Finally, she concatenates the resulting ciphertext $e_{k_e}(m)$ and the MAC $T_{k_a}(m)$ and sends the result to Bob.

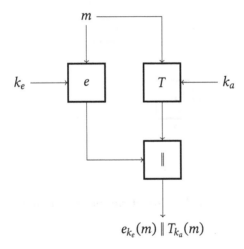

Figure 15.1: Encrypt-and-MAC composition

On the receiver side, Bob first decrypts the ciphertext to obtain plaintext m. He then uses the plaintext to compute the MAC value and compares it to the received MAC value. If the values are equal, Bob is assured that the message was not manipulated and originates from Alice.

15.2.2 MAC-then-encrypt

The *MAC-then-encrypt* composition computes the MAC of the plaintext m, appends the MAC to the plaintext, and encrypts the resulting value:

$$e_{k_e}(m \parallel T_{k_a}(m))$$

The MAC-then-encrypt composition is illustrated in *Figure 15.2*. This time, Alice first computes a MAC for plaintext m using the message authentication key k_a and concatenates the plaintext with the MAC value she has just computed. Alice then encrypts the intermediate value $m \parallel T_{k_a}(m)$ using the encryption key k_e.

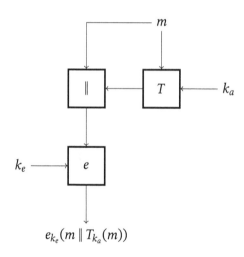

Figure 15.2: MAC-then-encrypt composition

Like with the other two compositions, encrypt-and-MAC and encrypt-then-MAC, the use of two distinct keys $k_e \neq k_a$ is a good practice in cryptographic mechanisms and cryptographic protocols to further increase their security level.

As we have already stressed in earlier chapters, the rationale behind this good practice is that even if Eve or Mallory were to somehow compromise one of the secret shared keys, the other key would remain intact. So, either the encryption or the message authentication would still work. In other words, the compromise of a single key does not lead to a complete compromise of the authenticated encryption mechanism.

Upon receiving Alice's message, Bob decrypts it to obtain plaintext m and its corresponding MAC. Bob then computes the MAC for m using the shared secret key k_a and verifies that the received MAC is equal to the computed MAC. If this is the case, he accepts the message as genuine.

Note that in the MAC-then-encrypt construction, the ciphertext is not protected by the MAC and can be modified by Mallory without being detected. This fact is used in so-called *padding oracle attacks* (see *Chapter 19, Attacks on Cryptography*).

15.2.3 Encrypt-then-MAC

The *encrypt-then-MAC* composition first encrypts the plaintext to obtain the ciphertext $e_{k_e}(m)$, then computes the MAC of the ciphertext, and finally appends the MAC value to the ciphertext:

$$e_{k_e}(m) \parallel T_{k_a}(e_{k_e}(m))$$

The encrypt-then-MAC composition is illustrated in *Figure 15.3*. First, sender Alice encrypts plaintext m using the shared encryption key k_e. She then computes the MAC value for the ciphertext $c = e_{k_e}(m)$ using the message authentication key k_a. Finally, Alice concatenates the ciphertext $e_{k_e}(m)$ with the MAC $T_{k_a}(e_{k_e}(m))$.

After receiving Alice's message, Bob takes the ciphertext $c = e_{k_e}(m)$ and computes the MAC for that ciphertext using key k_a. He then compares the computed MAC with the received MAC. If the values are equal, Bob knows that the message was not manipulated and was sent by Alice. Hence, Bob proceeds by decrypting the ciphertext $e_{k_e}(m)$ using the shared encryption key k_e. If the two MAC values do not agree, however, Bob will refrain from decryption as obviously there has been a transmission error or some other ciphertext manipulation.

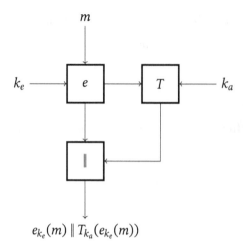

Figure 15.3: Encrypt-then-MAC composition

In the encrypt-then-MAC construction, the ciphertext is protected by the MAC. The encrypt-then-MAC construction therefore avoids the problem of modifiable ciphertext and may be viewed as the most secure way to do generic composition.

15.3   Security of generic composition

In their seminal publication *Authenticated Encryption: Relations among Notions and Analysis of the Generic Composition Paradigm* [18], Bellare and Namprempre analyze the generic compositions encrypt-and-MAC, MAC-then-encrypt, and encrypt-then-MAC, and prove whether these compositions are secure for the notions IND-CPA, IND-CCA, NM-CPA, INT-PTX, and INT-CTX.

The proofs given by Bellare and Namprempre are valid under the assumption that the block cipher used is secure against a chosen-plaintext attack and the MAC algorithm is strongly unforgeable under a chosen-message attack.

Popular cryptographic algorithms we have covered so far – for example, the block cipher AES and the keyed hash function HMAC used for message authentication – are believed to offer such security guarantees. As a result, Bellare and Namprempre emphasize that analyzing the compositions under these assumptions yields a realistic and practically useful result.

Table 15.1 summarizes the security analysis results for the three composite authenticated encryption schemes. Entries marked with ✓ mean that the composition was proven to meet the corresponding security requirement assuming that the block cipher is IND-CPA secure and the message authentication code is strongly unforgeable under a chosen-message attack.

Entries marked with × mean that there exists some IND-CPA secure block cipher and some strongly unforgeable MAC where the composition based on them does not meet the security requirement.

Composition	Confidentiality			Integrity	
	IND-CPA	IND-CCA	NM-CPA	INT-PTX	INT-CTX
Encrypt-and-MAC	×	×	×	✓	×
MAC-then-encrypt	✓	×	×	✓	×
Encrypt-then-MAC	✓	✓	✓	✓	✓

Table 15.1: Security results from [18] for composite authenticated encryption schemes

The results in *Table 15.1* are quite counter-intuitive as they clearly show that the different generic composition variants are *not* equivalent in terms of their security. If we use a block cipher that is IND-CPA-secure and a message authentication code that is strongly unforgeable under a chosen-message attack – a reasonable assumption for standardized cryptographic algorithms – encrypt-then-MAC composition is the most secure.

15.4 Authenticated ciphers

Authenticated ciphers are an alternative to the block cipher and MAC combinations. An authenticated cipher algorithm is functionally equivalent to a cipher and MAC combination, but it is simpler, faster, and oftentimes more secure [11].

In addition to the ciphertext, an authenticated cipher also produces a so-called *authentication tag*. Formally, **Authenticated Encryption (AE)** is defined as:

$$AE_k(P) = (C, T)$$

where K is the secret key, P is the plaintext, C is the ciphertext, and T is the authentication tag.

The inverse operation, **Authenticated Decryption (AD)**, is defined as:

$$AD_k(C, T) = P$$

Analogous to verifying a MAC, if the authentication tag T is invalid, AD_K will return an error to prevent the receiving party from processing the decrypted plaintext since the ciphertext C was manipulated.

Authenticated encryption, among other things, prevents chosen-ciphertext attacks where an adversary creates ciphertexts and asks the legitimate party (an oracle in cryptographic parlance) for the corresponding plaintexts.

15.4.1 Authenticated encryption with associated data

In this section, by *associated data* we mean any data that should be authenticated but not encrypted. There are some scenarios where it is useful to have such data.

For example, say you want to transmit a network packet composed of a header and a payload. You can encrypt the payload to prevent anyone but the legitimate receiver (or a group of legitimate receivers if you use a group key) from accessing it, but you can't encrypt the header as it contains information needed to route the packet to the correct recipient. At the same time, you still want to *authenticate* the header so that the receiving party can verify the packet's authenticity, that is, verify that it actually comes from the expected sender.

In such a situation, you can use an AEAD algorithm. In an AEAD algorithm, cleartext data (the associated data) is attached to a ciphertext along with an authentication tag T. If the cleartext or the ciphertext is corrupted, the authentication tag cannot be validated by the receiver and the ciphertext will not be decrypted.

Formally, we can define the AEAD operation as:

$$AEAD_K(P, A) = (C, A, T)$$

where K is the secret key, P is the plaintext, and A is the associated data. The output of the AEAD operation is a triple consisting of the ciphertext C, the associated data A (which is unencrypted), and an authentication tag T. As required, AEAD leaves A unchanged, while the ciphertext C is the encryption of the plaintext P. The authentication tag T depends on both C and A. Therefore, the receiver can only successfully verify T if both C and A have not been modified.

Conversely, we can define **authenticated decryption with associated data (ADAD)** as:

$$ADAD_K(C, A, T) = (P, A)$$

If we perform AEAD with empty authenticated data A, it becomes a normal authenticated cipher AE. If we instead leave the plaintext P empty, AEAD becomes a MAC.

Because an AEAD cipher provides confidentiality as well as message integrity and authentication, it eliminates the need to implement a separate MAC algorithm like HMAC. Among other things, this allows you to reduce the number of algorithms a TLS endpoint must implement.

15.4.2   Avoiding predictability with nonces

Recall that an encryption scheme is called *probabilistic* if it returns different ciphertexts when the same plaintext is repeatedly encrypted. Otherwise, an attacker could figure out that the same plaintext was encrypted multiple times. To this end, block ciphers and stream ciphers typically use an extra, non-secret but changing parameter called a *nonce*: a number used only once. Authenticated ciphers are no different, as they also want to avoid the visibility of plaintext patterns in the ciphertext. Therefore, when looking at concrete incarnations of AEAD in the next section (and the next chapter), we will see they require an additional parameter N, the nonce.

15.5   Counter with cipher block chaining message authentication code (CCM)

Counter with cipher block chaining message authentication code (CCM) is a block cipher mode of operation that provides authenticated encryption. It was designed by the American computer scientists Russ Housley and Doug L. Whiting, and Dutch cryptographer Niels Ferguson.

CCM is specified in [180] and can be used with 128-bit block ciphers such as AES. As the name suggests, CCM combines two cryptographic primitives:

- CTR mode for achieving confidentiality (see *Section 14.4.5, CTR mode* in *Chapter 14, Block Ciphers and Their Modes of Operation*)

- CBC-MAC construction to ensure message authenticity (see *Section 14.4.3, CBC-MAC* in *Chapter 14, Block Ciphers and Their Modes of Operation*)

In CCM, the two primitives CTR and CBC-MAC are used in the MAC-then-encrypt composition. In the first step, CBC-MAC is applied to compute the MAC value T for the plaintext message m. The MAC and the plaintext are then encrypted using CTR mode.

In contrast to the general case of MAC-then-encrypt composition illustrated in *Figure 15.2*, CCM can be used with the same shared secret key k for both encryption and message authentication without weakening the security guarantees, given that the counter values used in CTR do not collide with the initialization vector used in CBC-MAC. The security of this combination has been proven based on the security of the underlying block cipher [180].

15.5.1 Authenticated encryption with CCM

To apply CCM, sender Alice must provide the following four inputs:

- The shared secret key k_e.

- A nonce n that must be unique within the scope of k_e. (In other words, the set of nonces used with k_e must not contain duplicate values.)

- Plaintext message m.

- Additional authenticated data d. (This data is not encrypted and can be used to authenticate plaintext packet headers or contextual information. If Alice has no data d, she can simply input a zero-length string.)

How to perform authenticated encryption with CCM based on these four inputs is illustrated in *Figure 15.4*.

Alice first applies a formatting function to nonce n, plaintext m, and additional data d to produce a sequence of blocks $B_0, B_1, \dots, B_n$. Alice then computes the authentication tag T using CBC-MAC as shown in *Algorithm 3*, with M being the size of the authentication tag in bytes. This is shown in the lower half of *Figure 15.4*.

Algorithm 3 Computation of MAC value T in CCM using CBC-MAC

Require: Sequence of blocks $B_0, B_1, \dots, B_n$, shared secret key k
Ensure: Message authentication tag T
  $X_1 \leftarrow e_k(B_0)$
  for $i = 1 \dots n$ **do**
    $X_{i+1} \leftarrow e_k(X_i \oplus B_i)$
  end for
  $T \leftarrow$ first M bytes(X_{n+1})
  return T

In the next step, Alice encrypts the plaintext message using CTR mode. Each input A_i to the block cipher is composed of the following:

- A `flags` field, containing information about the message length, the length of the authentication tag, and whether there is additional authenticated data or not

- The nonce n

- The counter value ctr_i

In other words, each 128-bit plaintext block m_i is encrypted to a 128-bit ciphertext block c_i by XORing it with the block cipher output for the value A_i (essentially, the counter value):

$$c_i = m_i \oplus e_k(A_i)$$

Here, e_k is the block cipher's encryption operation under the shared secret key k.

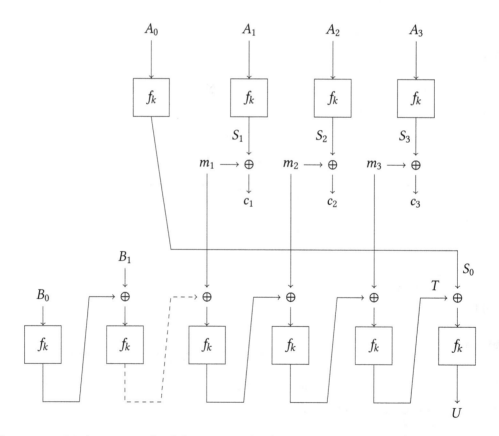

Figure 15.4: Working principle of the CCM mode of operation. The dashed line indicates that a sequence of blocks up to B_n is processed

In the final step, the very first key stream block $S_0 = e_k(A_0)$ is used to encrypt the authentication tag T computed in the first step:

$$U = T \oplus \text{first } M \text{ bytes of } S_0$$

The CCM output consists of the ciphertext c, the concatenation of the ciphertext blocks c_i, and the encryption authentication value U.

15.5.2 Authenticated decryption with CCM

To decrypt and authenticate Alice's message using CCM, Bob must provide the following four inputs:

- The shared secret key k_e

- The nonce n

- Additional authenticated data d

- The encrypted and authenticated message $c \, \| U$

In the first step, Bob computes the key stream $S_i = e_k(A_i)$ and decrypts Alice's message by XORing it with the key stream. As a result, Bob obtains the following:

- The original plaintext message m

- The decrypted MAC value T

In the second step, Bob uses m and the additional authenticated data d to compute the CBC-MAC value T. If the received T and the computed T are equal, Bob accepts Alice's message.

To preserve the security guarantees, the maximum number of block cipher encryption operations in CCM – that is, encryptions in CBC-MAC *and* in CTR – is 2^{61}. In other words, using CCM, Alice can authenticate and encrypt a maximum of roughly 16 million terabytes under the same shared secret k.

Moreover, the nonce n must never be used more than once for a given key k. The reason behind this is that CCM uses CTR mode for encryption and CTR is effectively a stream cipher. Reusing the nonce will therefore lead to repetition of the key stream.

15.6   AEAD in TLS 1.3

In TLS version 1.3 – in contrast to previous TLS versions – all ciphers used to protect the payloads in the TLS Record protocol are AEAD ciphers. As discussed above, an AEAD algorithm takes the following data as input:

- A plaintext to be encrypted and authenticated

- A single shared secret key

- A nonce

- Additional data to be authenticated, but not encrypted

In TLS 1.3, either `client_write_key` or `server_write_key` is the shared secret key. Moreover, one of the two initializations vectors `client_write_iv` (supplied by the client) or `server_write_iv` (supplied by the server) and a sequence number are used for generating the nonce. Finally, the plaintext is stored in the `TLSInnerPlaintext` structure, and the additional data to be authenticated is in the record header:

```
additional_data = TLSCiphertext.opaque_type ||
TLSCiphertext.legacy_record_version || TLSCiphertext.length
```

The output of the AEAD algorithms consists of the ciphertext and authentication tag computed in the authenticated encryption process, as follows:

```
AEADEncrypted = AEAD-Encrypt(write_key, nonce, additional_data,
plaintext)
```

Subsequently, the `encrypted_record` field in the `TLSCiphertext` data structure is set to the `AEADEncrypted` value. When the receiver wants to verify and decrypt the record, it uses the ADAD operation, which takes the following data as input:

- The single shared secret key

- The nonce

- The additional data to be authenticated

- The ciphertext

The plaintext of the encrypted TLS record is then computed as follows:

```
plaintext of encrypted_record = AEAD-Decrypt(peer_write_key, nonce,
additional_data, AEADEncrypted)
```

The ADAD operation produces one of the following outputs. If the decryption failed – for example, because the integrity of the message could not be successfully verified – ADAD returns an error. In that case, the receiving TLS endpoint immediately terminates the TLS connection and sends a `bad_record_mac` message. Otherwise, if the message's authenticity and integrity can be successfully verified, ADAD returns the plaintext.

The TLS 1.3 specification does not allow an AEAD algorithm to produce an expansion larger than 255 bytes. Thus, if a TLS 1.3 endpoint receives a TLS record with `TLSCiphertext.length` larger than $2^{14} + 256$ bytes, it has to end the connection, sending a `record_overflow` alert. The limit is the sum of the maximum `TLSInnerPlaintext` length of $2^{14} + 1$ bytes for `ContentType` and the maximum AEAD expansion of 255 bytes.

15.7 Summary

In this chapter, we covered authenticated encryption and authenticated encryption with additional data. To understand the security implications of different authenticated encryption schemes, we first introduced the security notions IND-CPA, IND-CCA, NM-CPA, INT-PTX, and INT-CTX.

We then studied the encrypt-and-MAC, MAC-then-encrypt, and encrypt-then-MAC variants of generic composition that can be used to construct an authenticated encryption scheme from simpler cryptographic primitives (namely, a block cipher and a message authentication code).

Finally, we had a closer look at the counter with cipher block chaining message authentication code as a concrete example of an AEAD algorithm. Moreover, we looked into how AEAD algorithms are used in TLS 1.3.

In the next chapter, we will take a detailed look at the **Galois/Counter Mode (GCM)**, the mandatory-to-implement AEAD algorithm used in TLS 1.3.

16

The Galois Counter Mode

In the previous chapter, we learned about authenticated encryption and authenticated encryption with additional data. We saw how authenticated encryption can be obtained from simpler cryptographic primitives using generic composition, and we introduced a dedicated counter mode with CBC-MAC (CCM) that provides AEAD.

In TLS 1.3, AEAD is used for protecting all TLS Record protocol payloads. In this chapter, we will study **Galois/Counter Mode (GCM)**, an AEAD algorithm that every TLS 1.3 endpoint must implement. RFC 8446 [147], the specification of TLS 1.3, only references NIST's *Recommendation for Block Cipher Modes of Operation: Galois/Counter Mode (GCM) and GMAC* [57], where GCM is specified. But since GCM is used in the TLS Record protocol, the material we will discuss in this chapter is related to Chapter 5, Record Protocol, of RFC 8446.

Upon completion of the chapter, you will be familiar with GCM's mathematical foundations, architecture, and operation. Moreover, you will have a solid understanding of GCM security guarantees.

These skills will help you to gain an in-depth understanding of how the TLS Record protocol works. In particular, you will learn about the following:

- How the payload data that client Bob and server Alice exchange over their TLS connection is protected both in terms of confidentiality and message integrity and authenticity

- How OpenSSL can be used to measure and compare the performance of individual cryptographic algorithms

16.1 Preliminaries

According to the American security researchers David McGrew and John Viega, "*the Galois/Counter Mode is a block cipher mode of operation that uses universal hashing over a binary Galois field to provide authenticated encryption* [114]."

Before studying the internals of the algorithm, we need to quickly cover two mathematical aspects: the finite field used by GCM and the way multiplication is done in that finite field.

16.1.1 The Galois field $\mathbb{F}_{2^{128}}$

GCM uses multiplication over a finite field. In mathematics, finite fields are also referred to as Galois fields in honor of the 19th-century French mathematician Evariste Galois, hence the name *Galois* counter mode.

We have already encountered finite fields in section 7.6 *Finite Fields* in *Chapter 7, Public-Key Cryptography*. You may go back to that section to refresh your memory, but we are repeating the basic facts here for your convenience.

The field used in GCM has 2^{128} elements, which are represented as polynomials of degree smaller than 128 with coefficients $\in \{0, 1\}$. As there are 128 binary coefficients, we get 2^{128} field elements.

In order to complete the definition of the field, we also need the *field polynomial*

$$P = 1 + \alpha + \alpha^2 + \alpha^7 + \alpha^{128}.$$

In the polynomial representation, the multiplication of two field elements X and Y is performed by multiplying the polynomial representing X with the polynomial representing Y and taking the result modulo P. This means we divide the 256-bit polynomial $X \cdot Y$ by the field polynomial $1 + \alpha + \alpha^2 + \alpha^7 + \alpha^{128}$, and take the 128-bit remainder as the final result. Note that this remainder is a polynomial of degree less than 128 and therefore an element of our field.

To actually compute the multiplication of two finite field elements X and Y, they are treated as bit vectors and processed as shown in algorithm 4, which was given by McGrew and Viega in [114]. The i-th bit of element X is denoted as X_i, where the leftmost bit is X_0 and the rightmost bit is X_{127}. Then,

$$X \cdot Y \mod P = X \cdot (Y_0 + Y_1\alpha + ... Y_{127}\alpha^{127}) \mod P = \sum_{\{i : Y_i=1\}} (X \cdot \alpha^i \mod P)$$

Algorithm 4 implements this formula by repeatedly multiplying X by α modulo P and adding up the results. For this, the multiplication algorithm uses a special field element $R = 11100001 \parallel 0^{120}$. Its polynomial representation is

$$R = 1 + \alpha + \alpha^2 + \alpha^7,$$

so it is equal to the field polynomial without the leading term.

The rightshift function shifts the bits of its argument cyclically by one bit to the right. It is the bitwise equivalent of multiplying X by α. On the other hand, R is chosen so that $\alpha \cdot X \oplus R$ resembles the polynomial $(\alpha \cdot X) \mod P$. If $X_{127} = 0$; however, multiplication by α causes no wrap-around, and $(\alpha \cdot X) \mod P = (\alpha \cdot X)$.

Algorithm 4 Multiplication of Field Elements $\in \mathbb{F}_{2^{128}}$

Require: Elements $X, Y \in \mathbb{F}_{2^{128}}$
Ensure: Multiplication result $Z = X \cdot Y$
  $Z \leftarrow 0$
  $V \leftarrow X$

  for $i = 0 \ \dots \ 127$ **do**
    if $Y_i = 1$ **then**
      $Z \leftarrow Z \oplus V$
    end if
    if $V_{127} = 0$ **then**
      $V \leftarrow \text{rightshift}(V)$
    else
      $V \leftarrow \text{rightshift}(V) \oplus R$
    end if
  end for

  return Z

The addition of two field elements X, Y is simply the addition of two polynomials. Recall the coefficients of polynomials representing the field elements are in $\mathbb{F}_2 = \{0, 1\}$. As a result, addition can be computed as $X \oplus Y$. Moreover, subtraction is identical to addition in $\mathbb{F}_2$.

16.1.2 *GHASH* function

GCM's authentication mechanism is based on a hash function called *GHASH*. The function contains a multiplication by a fixed parameter H within GCM's $\mathbb{F}_{2^{128}}$ field. Effectively, the parameters act like a key and *GHASH* can, therefore, be viewed as a keyed hash function.

Alice and Bob compute the hash key H by encrypting an all-zeros block 0^{128} using their shared secret key k. *GHASH* is then used for compressing the encoding of the additional authenticated data A and the ciphertext C into a single block. Finally, GCM encrypts this block to obtain the authentication tag T.

Notably, while *GHASH* is a keyed hash function, it is *not* a cryptographic hash function. This means, it does not have the security properties of cryptographic hash functions we discussed in *Chapter 11, Hash Functions and Message Authentication Codes.* As a result, it cannot be used for cryptographic purposes outside of the GCM construction.

Like with other GCM functions, the intermediate values of *GHASH* must be kept secret. The function takes the following arguments as input:

- Additional authenticated data A

- Ciphertext blocks C_i

- H, the encryption of 0^{128} (a block of all zeros) obtained under the shared secret key k

GHASH then outputs $GHASH(H, A, C) = X_{m+n+1}$, which is computed as shown in *Algorithm 5.* The term m denotes the rounded up number of 128-bit blocks in A and n denotes the rounded up number of 128-bit blocks in P. In other words, the additional data A consists of $(m-1)128 + v$ bits with $1 \leq v \leq 128$, and plaintext P consists of of $(n-1)128 + u$ bits with $1 \leq u \leq 128$.

Algorithm 5 GCM *GHASH* function.

Require: Encryption H of 0^{128} under key k, additional authenticated data A, ciphertext block C_i

Ensure: X_i

$$
X_i \leftarrow \begin{cases}
0 & \text{for } i = 0 \\
(X_{i-1} \oplus A_i) \cdot H & \text{for } i = 1, \ldots, m-1 \\
(X_{m-1} \oplus (A_m^* \parallel 0^{128-v})) \cdot H & \text{for } i = m \\
(X_{i-1} \oplus C_i) \cdot H & \text{for } i = m+1, \ldots, m+n-1 \\
(X_{m+n-1} \oplus (C_m^* \parallel 0^{128-u})) \cdot H & \text{for } i = m+n \\
(X_{m+n} \oplus (len(A) \parallel len(C))) \cdot H & \text{for } i = m+n+1
\end{cases}
$$

return X_i

16.1.3   The AES-GCM authenticated cipher

GCM is specified in the NIST Special Publication 800-38D [57]. Its great importance for TLS is shown by the fact that it is also a mandatory-to-implement algorithm in TLS 1.3, meaning that every TLS 1.3 endpoint must implement this algorithm. Since [57] requires the use of a NIST-approved 128-bit block cipher, the AES algorithm [127] is the only reasonable choice. As a result, GCM is de facto a mode of operation of the AES algorithm [57].

The **GCM authenticated encryption** operation takes the following four inputs:

- A shared secret key k

- An initialization vector IV (which must be distinct for every GCM invocation under the same key)

- A plaintext message P

- Additional authenticated data A (this data is authenticated, but not encrypted)

Additional data A is used when the information transmitted must be protected in terms of its integrity and authenticity, but must not be encrypted. As an example, the header of a network packet contains information needed for its routing that must be available to intermediate gateways. Thus, while the payload of the packet may be encrypted if confidentiality is desired, the header may not. However, it is desirable to protect the header's integrity and authenticity. There may also be scenarios where is it legally prohibited to encrypt the plaintext message P.

The primary purpose of the initialization vector IV is to act as a nonce. As a result, it must be distinct for every authenticated encryption operation under the same key. As long as distinctiveness can be guaranteed, the IV can be randomly generated. Moreover, the IV is included in the GCM encryption and authentication process so that it is not necessary to add it to the additional authenticated data A.

GCM authenticated encryption is shown in *Algorithm 6*. The output of the operation consists of a ciphertext C and an authentication tag T. The authentication tag applies to the plaintext P and the additional authenticated data A.

Algorithm 6 GCM authenticated encryption operation.

Require: Shared key k, initialization vector IV, plaintext P, additional authenticated data A

Ensure: Ciphertext C, authentication tag T

$H \leftarrow e_k(0^{128})$

if $\text{len}(IV) = 96$ **then**
    $Y_0 \leftarrow IV \parallel 0^{31} \parallel 1$
else
        $Y_0 \leftarrow GHASH(H, \{\}, IV)$
end if

for $i = 1 \ldots n$ **do**
    $Y_i \leftarrow Y_{i-1} + 1$
    if $i < n$ **then**
        $C_i \leftarrow P_i \oplus e_k(Y_i)$
    else
        $C_n \leftarrow P_n \oplus MSB_u(e_k(Y_n))$
    end if
end for

$T \leftarrow MSB_t(GHASH(H, A, C) \oplus e_k(Y_0))$

return C, T

The security strength of the authentication is determined by the desired length of the authentication tag. If plaintext P is empty, GCM acts as a MAC algorithm for the additional authenticated data A. This GCM mode is called **GMAC**.

The **GCM authenticated decryption** operation takes the following five inputs:

- The shared secret key k
- The initialization vector IV
- The ciphertext C
- The additional authenticated data A
- The received authentication tag T

Algorithm 7 shows how GCM authenticated decryption is computed. Recall that the *IV* used in the decryption process must be the same as was used in the encryption process.

The output of the decryption operation is either the plaintext message *P* or a special symbol ⊥ indicating that the integrity and authenticity verification of the received message failed; that is, the received tag and the computed tag did not match. Symbol ⊥ is referred to as FAIL in the GCM standard [57].

Algorithm 7 GCM authenticated decryption operation.

Require: Shared key k, initialization vector IV, ciphertext C, additional authenticated data A, received authentication tag T
Ensure: Plaintext P or symbol ⊥

$H \leftarrow e_k(0^{128})$

if $\text{len}(IV) = 96$ **then**
    $Y_0 \leftarrow IV \parallel 0^{31} \parallel 1$
else
    $Y_0 \leftarrow GHASH(H, \{\}, IV)$
end if

$T' \leftarrow MSB_t(GHASH(H, A, C) \oplus e_k(Y_0))$

for $i = 1 \ldots n$ **do**
    $Y_i \leftarrow Y_{i-1} + 1$

    if $i < n$ **then**
        $C_i \leftarrow P_i \oplus e_k(Y_i)$
    else
        $C_n \leftarrow P_n \oplus MSB_u(e_k(Y_n))$
    end if
end for

if $T = T'$ **then**
    return P
else
    return ⊥
end if

Choosing ⊥ as the output symbol in case of an authentication failure nicely illustrates the concept of *secure defaults*. The decrypting party can rely on GCM to output a symbol that, if the message authentication failed, cannot be confused with valid plaintext. In other words, whenever GCM returns plaintext, the message integrity and authenticity of that message are guaranteed and the decrypting party does not need to perform any additional checks.

Figure 16.1 shows a diagram of the AES-GCM mode applied to one block of associated data A_1 and two blocks of plaintext P_1, P_2. The symbol $\otimes_H$ denotes polynomial multiplication by the hash key H, the authentication key derived from the secret key K. The AES-GCM mode uses a variant of the counter mode (CTR) for encryption.

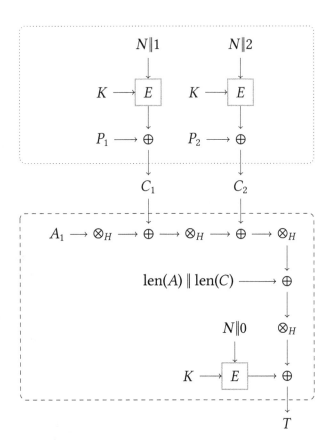

Figure 16.1: Illustration of AES-GCM mode

The operations within the dotted rectangle at the top of *Figure 16.1* are nothing but the **Counter (CTR)** mode of a block cipher. The AES encryption operation denoted by E takes the secret key K and the nonce N concatenated with a counter to produce 128-bit blocks of the key stream that is XOR'ed with the plaintext blocks P_1, P_2, correspondingly. The obtained ciphertext blocks are denoted as C_1, C_2.

The operations within the dashed rectangle at the bottom of *Figure 16.1* correspond to the GHASH function. GHASH takes the associated data A_1 and performs a series of polynomial multiplications $\otimes_H$ and XOR operations $\oplus$ with the hash key H and the ciphertext blocks C_1, C_2. It then takes the result and XORs it with the term $\text{len}(A) \| \text{len}(C)$, which corresponds to the bit length of the associated data A and the bit length of the ciphertext C, respectively.

Finally, the authentication tag T is computed as $T = \text{GHASH}(H, A, C) \oplus E_K(N\|0)$, where E_K is the AES encryption under the secret key K. The hash key H is computed as $H = E_K(0)$, that is, the encryption of the block consisting of a sequence of 0x0 bytes (this step is not shown in *Figure* 16.1).

16.2 GCM security

GCM's biggest security risk is its fragility in case of nonce repetition. NIST's GCM standard [57] requires the following:

The probability that the authenticated encryption function ever will be invoked with the same IV and the same key on two (or more) distinct sets of input data shall be no greater than 2^{-32}.

Moreover, care must be taken that the nonces do not repeat: if the same nonce N is used twice in an AES-GCM computation, an attacker would be able to compute the authentication key H. With the help of H, tags for any ciphertext, associated data, or both can be fabricated.

This is easy to see with a little bit of math. The authentication tag is computed as:

$$T = \text{GHASH}(H, A, C) \oplus E_K(N\|0) \tag{16.1}$$

Now, if we have two tags T_1 and T_2 computed with the same nonce N, we can XOR T_1 and T_2 to obtain the following expression:

$$\text{GHASH}(H, A_1, C_1) \oplus E_K(N\|0) \oplus \text{GHASH}(H, A_2, C_2) \oplus E_K(N\|0) \qquad (16.2)$$

Because $x \oplus x = 0$, the term $E_K(N\|0)$ (the AES encryption of $N\|0$ under the secret key K) will vanish. As a result, the attacker obtains the following expression:

$$\text{GHASH}(H, A_1, C_1) \oplus \text{GHASH}(H, A_2, C_2) \qquad (16.3)$$

Since the values A_1, C_1, A_2, C_2 are known to the attacker and the GHASH function is linear, the attacker can easily determine the hash key H. That, in turn, gives her the ability to forge the authentication tag T for any ciphertext C or associated data A (or both).

In 2016, Böck et al [36] performed an internet-wide scan to investigate issues resulting from nonce reuse within the GCM block cipher mode used in TLS, with particular focus on AES-GCM. In this study, 184 HTTPS servers with repeating nonces were identified. As we have seen previously, this fully breaks the authenticity of the TLS connections. The affected servers included large corporations, financial institutions, and a credit card company. Furthermore, over 70,000 HTTPS servers were discovered that used random nonces. This puts the servers at risk of nonce reuse if a large amount of data is sent over the same connection.

Note in this respect that the NIST GCM standard requires that *the total number of invocations of the authenticated encryption function shall not exceed 2^{32}, including all IV lengths and all instances of the authenticated encryption function with the given key.*

16.3 GCM performance

There is an old saying among cryptographers that the real challenge is not to design a secure algorithm, but one that is secure *and* fast. While this is typically said somewhat jokingly, there is a lot to this saying. Take, for instance, ciphers. It is well known that the *composition of functions* illustrated in *Figure 16.2* can be used to define complicated functions using simpler ones.

Recall that if $f : X \to Y$ and $g : Y \to Z$ are functions, then the composition of g with f, denoted by $g \circ f$, is a function mapping elements of X to elements of Z. Moreover, the composition can be extended to any number of functions $f_1, f_2, \ldots, f_n$ (resulting in the composition $f_n \circ \ldots \circ f_2 \circ f_1$) given that the domain of f_t equals the co-domain of f_{t-1}.

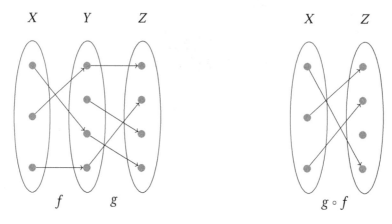

Figure 16.2: Composition $g \circ f$ of functions g and f

In cryptography, ciphers combining a sequence of simpler transformations are called *product ciphers*. So, based on the composition of functions, it is trivial to design a high-security cipher by combining a large number, say in the thousands, of simple substitutions and transpositions.

It is, however, far from trivial to design a cipher that is both secure *and* fast to compute. When David McGrew and John Viega, the authors of GCM, submitted their proposal to NIST, they wrote the following:

There is a compelling need for a mode of operation that can efficiently provide authenticated encryption at speeds of 10 gigabits per second and above in hardware, perform well in software, and is free of intellectual property restrictions. The mode must admit pipelined and parallelized implementations and have minimal computational latency in order to be useful at high data rates. Counter mode has emerged as the best method for high-speed encryption, because it meets those requirements. However, there is no suitable standard message authentication algorithm. This fact leaves us in the situation in which we can encrypt at high speed, but we cannot provide message authentication that can keep up with our cipher.

Let's conduct a small experiment to verify on our own whether GCM's efficiency lives up to the claims of its authors. We can use OpenSSL to compare GCM's performance to that of other authenticated encryption schemes.

Conveniently, OpenSSL implements all authenticated encryption schemes we have discussed so far – CCM and GCM – as well as the ChaCha20-Poly1305 authenticated encryption we will discuss in detail in *Chapter 18, TLS Cipher Suites.*

In addition, OpenSSL implements a mode of operation called **Offset Codebook Mode (OCB)**, which provides authenticated encryption through a combination of a block cipher with a message authentication code in parallel.

To make it simple for you to reproduce the results we're about to show, we will again use the OpenSSL Docker image. It goes without saying that if you want to obtain performance results for a specific system, for example, a specific instruction set architecture, you should run the following commands on the native installation.

To benchmark the performance of cryptographic algorithms, OpenSSL offers a built-in command, `openssl speed`. Using the following command, you can obtain the list of supported algorithms:

```
/opt/openssl# openssl list --cipher-commands
aes-128-cbc    aes-128-ecb    aes-192-cbc    aes-192-ecb
aes-256-cbc    aes-256-ecb    aria-128-cbc   aria-128-cfb
aria-128-cfb1  aria-128-cfb8  aria-128-ctr   aria-128-ecb

-- snip --
```

In order to determine the performance of a specific algorithm, you need to call `openssl speed <algorithm>`. As an example, to test the performance of an AES-128 block cipher in CBC mode, you need to call this:

```
/opt/openssl# openssl speed aes-128-cbc
Doing aes-128-cbc for 3s on 16 size blocks: 149860669 aes-128-cbc's
in 3.00s
Doing aes-128-cbc for 3s on 64 size blocks: 66115959 aes-128-cbc's in
3.00s

-- snip --

The 'numbers' are in 1000s of bytes per second processed.
type              16 bytes       64 bytes      256 bytes   -- snip --
aes-128-cbc  799256.90k   1410473.79k   1447774.12k   -- snip --
```

So, to benchmark GCM against the other authenticated encryption schemes we have seen so far, we can call `openssl speed` with the desired algorithms. For simplicity, we will run the benchmarks on blocks of 8,192 bytes:

```
/opt/openssl# openssl speed -bytes 8192 -evp aes-128-gcm; openssl
speed -bytes 8192 -evp chacha20-poly1305; openssl speed -bytes 8192
-evp aes-128-ccm; openssl speed -bytes 8192 -evp aes-128-ocb

-- snip --

The 'numbers' are in 1000s of bytes per second processed.
type             8192 bytes
AES-128-GCM      5585141.76k

-- snip --

ChaCha20-Poly1305   2215840.43k

-- snip --
```

```
AES-128-CCM      1337092.78k

-- snip --

AES-128-OCB      5607677.95k
```

Table 16.1 summarizes the performance numbers for the four benchmarked authenticated encryption algorithms and the different block sizes that we obtained on our machine. Our comparison is for illustration purposes. If you repeat the experiment, your numbers will be different, but the relative performance of these algorithms should be roughly the same.

Algorithm	Performance (in Kbytes/second)
AES-128-GCM	5,585,141
ChaCha20-Poly1305	2,215,840
AES-128-CCM	1,337,092
AES-128-OCB	5,607,677

Table 16.1: Comparison of the performance of authenticated encryption algorithms using 8,192-byte blocks

While our performance measurement described here is for illustration purposes (see [115] for a scientific treatment on GCM performance), we can still make several observations based on the results in *Table* 16.1:

- GCM is faster than CCM and ChaCha20-Poly1305

- ChaCha20-Poly1305 is faster than CCM

- OCB has a comparable speed to GCM (the reason OCB did not become mainstream is because after its introduction, two U.S. patents have been issued for OCB)

Therefore, we can conclude that TLS 1.3 implements the two fastest authenticated encryption schemes currently available (as we will see in *Chapter 18, TLS Cipher Suites*, GCM is mandatory to implement in TLS 1.3, and ChaCha20-Poly1305 is a so-called *standby cipher* that TLS 1.3 endpoints should support).

16.4 Summary

In this chapter, we studied GCM – the default, mandatory-to-implement authenticated encryption with additional data algorithm used in TLS 1.3. We covered the GCM design and working principles, and we discussed its security.

Moreover, we looked into GCM performance – and why the performance of cryptographic algorithms matters in general – and learned how to benchmark authenticated encryption algorithms covered in this book using OpenSSL.

In the next chapter, we will zoom out of technical and mathematical details and revisit the TLS Record protocol from a higher-level, conceptual perspective. The aim of the next chapter is to understand how the individual cryptographic mechanisms we covered so far fit together to ensure the confidentiality and integrity of data transmitted in TLS records.

17

TLS Record Protocol Revisited

In the previous three chapters, you studied block ciphers and their modes of operation, the AEAD encryption scheme (which aims to provide confidentiality, authenticity, and integrity in a single cryptographic mechanism), and finally the Galois counter mode, a block cipher mode of operation that implements AEAD. It is now time to put these things together.

In this chapter, we will revisit the TLS Record protocol and learn how the preceding cryptographic primitives are combined to protect the payload data transmitted over a TLS connection. In doing this, we will cover Section 5 of the RFC 8446.

We will also get back to OpenSSL's s_client to experimentally investigate the TLS record protocol. This time, however, we will use a debugger to take a look at what happens under the hood in OpenSSL and how the plaintext is turned into an encrypted TLS record.

Upon completing this chapter, you will have a good understanding of how the TLS record protocol works. We will cover the following topics:

- An overview of the record protocol

- Data structures and messages used on the TLS record layer

- How TLS record protection works

- How TLS records are padded and why

- How to debug OpenSSL using the GNU gdb debugger

17.1 TLS Record protocol

The purpose of the TLS Record protocol is to cryptographically protect data in transit using the shared secret keys that Alice and Bob established using the TLS Handshake protocol. More precisely, the Record protocol takes a message that Alice wants to send, partitions the message into one or multiple blocks, protects these records by cryptographic means, and transmits the protected records. When Bob receives this information, the Record protocol ensures that the records are verified regarding their authenticity and integrity, decrypted using the correct key, and reassembled into the original message sent by Alice.

Every TLS record has one of the following four types:

- handshake

- application_data

- alert

- change_cipher_spec

Having types is beneficial because this way multiple higher-level protocols can use the same record layer. If Alice or Bob receive an unexpected record type, they terminate their TLS session and transmit the unexpected_message alert.

The change_cipher_spec is a bit of an exception. If Alice or Bob receive an unencrypted TLS record having change_cipher_spec as type and containing the value 0x01 between the first `ClientHello` and the peer's `Finished` messages, they simply drop this `change_cipher_spec` record. Otherwise, if the value is different from 0x01 or that record is received before the first `ClientHello` or after the peer's `Finished` messages, the receiving party — either Alice or Bob — terminates the TLS connection with the `unexpected_message` alert.

17.2 TLS record layer

The TLS record layer partitions data to be transmitted into `TLSPlaintext` records of up to 2^{14} bytes. The data structure of a TLS 1.3 `TLSPlaintext` record is shown in *Listing 33*.

```
enum {
    invalid(0),
    change_cipher_spec(20),
    alert(21),
    handshake(22),
    application_data(23),
    (255)
} ContentType;

struct {
    ContentType type;
    ProtocolVersion legacy_record_version;
    uint16 length;
    opaque fragment[TLSPlaintext.length];
} TLSPlaintext;
```

Listing 33: Structure of `TLSPlaintext` *records*

The `legacy_record_version` variable denotes the record's TLS version. As of TLS 1.3, `legacy_record_version` is deprecated, and the only requirement in the TLS 1.3 specification is for this field to have the value 0x0303 for all records, except the initial `ClientHello`, which may also have the value 0x0301 for compatibility reasons.

To maximize backward compatibility, the record carrying Bob's first `ClientHello` preferably has version 0x0301, which stands for TLS 1.0. The record carrying Bob's second `ClientHello` or Alice's `ServerHello` has version 0x0303, which stands for TLS 1.2.

The data being sent is stored in the `fragment` variable. TLS treats the `fragment` value as opaque because this data is interpreted and processed by a higher-level protocol specified in the `type` variable of `TLSPlaintext`.

The `length` variable contains the size of the record's `fragment` in bytes. Recall that the maximum size of a TLS 1.3 record is 2^{14} bytes. If Alice or Bob receive a TLS record exceeding this size, they terminate the TLS connection and send a `record_overflow` alert.

The `type` variable contains the high-level protocol that is used to process the fragment contained in the record. Valid protocols are listed in the enumeration `ContentType`. The TLS record layer handles message boundaries based on their `ContentType`:

- `handshake` messages can be put into a single `TLSPlaintext` record or distributed over several records. However, if a handshake message is distributed over several records, no other records are allowed between them. Moreover, handshake messages are not allowed to span key changes. That is, handshake messages that immediately precede a key change must align with the record boundary. Otherwise, the connection is terminated with the `unexpected_message` alert.

- Messages of type `application_data` can be distributed over several `TLSPlaintext` records or combined into a single record. Unlike with `handshake` messages, application data is opaque to TLS and zero-length fragments can be transmitted for `application_data` to protect a TLS session against traffic analysis.

- `alert` messages must be put into a single `TLSPlaintext` record, and multiple alert messages must be distributed over multiple records. That is, a `TLSPlaintext` record of type `alert` contains exactly one message.

So far, we have discussed the structure of the TLS record layer. We now turn to the original purpose of the record layer, namely to protect its payload.

17.3   TLS record payload protection

As illustrated in *Figure 17.1*, before data is transmitted over the wire, the TLS record protection functions – denoted by *E* in *Figure 17.1* – encrypt TLSPlaintext structures into TLSCiphertext structures.

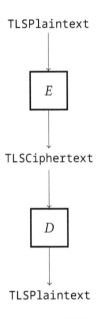

Figure 17.1: Protection of TLS record payload

On the receiver side, TLS record layer functions are used to reverse the process by translating TLSCiphertext structures into TLSPlaintext structures. Every encrypted TLS record is composed of a plaintext header and an encrypted body. The body contains a type and optional padding.

In TLS 1.3, all ciphers used to encrypt TLSPlaintext into TLSCiphertext use the **Authenticated Encryption with Associated Data (AEAD)** mode of operation. Recall that AEAD offers encryption and message authentication in a single cryptographic algorithm that turns plaintext into an authenticated ciphertext. This, in turn, allows the receiving party to verify that the ciphertext was not manipulated while in transit and was indeed sent by the legitimate sender before decrypting the ciphertext.

The structure of the TLS 1.3 `TLSCiphertext` and `TLSInnerPlaintext` record is shown in *Listing 34*. The content field in `TLSInnerPlaintext` is the value of `TLSPlaintext`'s fragment field. That is, content holds the byte encoding of a TLS handshake message, a TLS alert message, or the application data (raw bytes) to be transmitted.

```
struct {
    opaque content[TLSPlaintext.length];
    ContentType type;
    uint8 zeros[length_of_padding];
} TLSInnerPlaintext;

struct {
    ContentType opaque_type = application_data; /* 23 */
    ProtocolVersion legacy_record_version = 0x0303; /* TLS v1.2 */
    uint16 length;
    opaque encrypted_record[TLSCiphertext.length];
} TLSCiphertext;
```

Listing 34: Structure of `TLSCiphertext` *records*

The field type stores the content type of the record. This value is equal to the value of the type field in `TLSPlaintext`. The zeros field contains a sequence of 0s that allows to pad a TLS record.

The opaque_type field of the `TLSCiphertext` structure is always set to application_data. Its constant value of 23 is used to ensure compatibility with middleboxes supporting older TLS versions. The cleartext content of opaque_type is in the field type of `TLSInnerPlaintext`.

Recall from *Chapter 15, Authenticated Encryption*, that an AEAD algorithm *expands* the ciphertext by adding an authentication tag T. The encrypted_record field contains the AEAD-encrypted data from the serialized `TLSInnerPlaintext` structure.

The `length` field holds the size of the `encrypted_record` field of `TLSCiphertext` in bytes. This value is computed as:

$$len(\text{content}) + len(\text{padding}) + 1 + len(\text{expansion added by AEAD algorithm})$$

where $len(\cdot)$ is the size in bytes, and 1 is added for $len(\text{inner content type})$. The maximum `length` value is $2^{14} + 256$ bytes, and the `legacy_record_version` field is always set to the value 0x0303.

Recall that an AEAD algorithm takes as inputs a shared secret key, a nonce, a plaintext, and additional data to be authenticated but not encrypted. The shared secret key is either `client_write_key` or `server_write_key`. The nonce used by the AEAD algorithm is derived from the sequence number and `client_write_iv` or `server_write_iv`. The additional data is the record header; that means it consists of the following data:

```
additional_data = TLSCiphertext.opaque_type ||
TLSCiphertext.legacy_record_version || TLSCiphertext.length
```

The encoded `TLSInnerPlaintext` data structure is the plaintext input of the AEAD algorithm, and the shared secret key used is one of the traffic keys. The output of the AEAD algorithm is computed as follows:

```
AEADEncrypted = AEAD-Encrypt(write_key, nonce, additional_data,
plaintext)
```

Once the AEAD encryption is computed, the `encrypted_record` field of `TLSCiphertext` is set to the `AEADEncrypted` value. To invert the computation – that is, decrypt the ciphertext and verify its integrity and authenticity – the receiver computes the following:

```
plaintext of encrypted_record = AEAD-Decrypt(peer_write_key, nonce,
additional_data, AEADEncrypted)
```

The AEAD decryption and verification routine outputs the plaintext if verification of the message's authenticity and integrity is successful. Otherwise, it outputs an error indicating that something went wrong and, as a result, the receiving party terminates the TLS connection and transmits the `bad_record_mac` alert.

In TLS 1.3, the maximum expansion the AEAD algorithm may output is 255 bytes. If Alice or Bob receive a TLS record with the `length` field of `TLSCiphertext` having a larger value than $2^{14} + 256$ bytes, they terminate the TLS connection and transmit the `record_overflow` alert. This limit is determined by the maximum size of `TLSInnerPlaintext` (2^{14} bytes) plus the size of `ContentType` (1 byte) plus the maximum size of the AEAD expansion (255 bytes).

17.4   Per-record nonce

Alice and Bob keep a 64-bit sequence number for reading and writing TLS records. They increment this number every time they read or write a TLS record.

At the start of a TLS session and whenever the shared secret traffic key is changed, Alice and Bob set this number to zero. The first TLS record transmitted under that key has 0 as its sequence number.

In practice, TLS sequence numbers do not wrap because of their size: in most typical scenarios Alice and Bob exchange much less than 2^{64} records. For the unlikely case where the sequence number must be wrapped, TLS 1.3 specification tells Alice and Bob to either change that secret traffic key or end their TLS connection.

AEAD algorithms specify the range of valid per-record nonce lengths. The record-specific nonce for an AEAD algorithm is constructed like this:

1. The 64-bit sequence number of the TLS record is encoded in the network byte order.

2. In the next step, the encoded number is padded with zeros to the left until it has the length of `iv_length`.

3. Finally, the padded record sequence number is XORed with `client_write_iv` if Bob generates that nonce or with `server_write_iv` if Alice generates that nonce.

Alice and Bob use the resulting value as a per-record nonce. Recall that a nonce – shorthand for *number only used once* – is a (pseudo-) random number used to prevent Mallory from mounting replay attacks where she would record and, later, replay messages originally sent by Alice or Bob. Using nonces, Alice and Bob can add to each of their messages a number that may only be used once, thereby preventing replay attacks.

17.5 Record padding

The TLS 1.3 specification allows Alice and Bob to pad their TLS records by increasing TLSCiphertext's size in order to hide the size of the actual data from Eve.

While this may seem odd at first because the data sent is encrypted, if Eve can determine the size of the encrypted data, she can perform *traffic analysis*. Traffic analysis is one of the oldest attacks on communication and refers to the process of intercepting and examining encrypted messages sent by Alice and Bob in order to deduce information from the size, frequency, or other observable attributes of the encrypted communication. In other words, with traffic analysis Eve can determine communication patterns such as who is talking to whom, how much, how often, and when. Very often, these patterns can be more valuable than the content of the communication itself.

Traffic analysis has its roots in military intelligence. More precisely, it's a technique employed in the branch of signal intelligence used by the military since the beginning of the 20th century. Examples in the military context include the following scenarios:

- If Alice and Bob communicate frequently, the likelihood is high that they are planning something

- If Alice communicates frequently with Bob, and Bob then communicates with Trent, then the command chain Alice → Bob → Trent is very likely

- If Alice and Bob communicate shortly before or after event *A*, and Trent and Claire communicate shortly before or after event *B*, Eve can determine with high likelihood who is involved in which events

Another example where traffic analysis poses a threat is related to privacy. Let's say Alice hosts a website with multiple pages and a specific page P contains a large picture that, when transmitted, must be fragmented into 10 TLS records. Assume that other pages have only text data and, as a result, fit into a single TLS record. Now, if Bob clicks on a link to one of Alice's pages, Eve can easily determine whether Bob is accessing page P based solely on the size of the network traffic transmitted from Alice to Bob.

This example illustrates why traffic analysis can be a very powerful attack: Eve can infer secret information without ever breaking the cryptographic mechanisms used to protect it.

When Alice and Bob generate a TLSCiphertext record, they may pad it with additional bytes up to the maximum length of a record. The padding bytes are simply 0x0 bytes appended to the ContentType field before encryption.

In addition, Alice and Bob can generate application_data type records containing TLSInnerPlaintext with an empty, that is, zero-length, content field. This allows Alice and Bob to generate plausible fake traffic as a countermeasure against traffic analysis. However, TLS 1.3 does not allow Alice and Bob to send handshake or alert type records with an empty content field. If one of them receives such a record, the receiving party terminates the TLS connection and sends an unexpected_message alert.

Padding is automatically verified by the TLS record protocol. When the encrypted_record field of the TLSCiphertext message is decrypted on the receiving end, the record protocol implementation scans this field from its last byte to its first byte until it finds a non-zero byte.

17.6 Limits on key usage

TLS 1.3 specification defines cryptographic limits for the total amount of plaintext that can be securely encrypted using a given set of keys. Assuming that the underlying cryptographic primitives AES or ChaCha20 have no mathematical weaknesses – an assumption made by TLS 1.3 authors – up to $2^{24.5}$ full-size records, that is, about 24 million records, can be securely encrypted using AES-GCM. In the case of ChaCha20/Poly1305, the TLS record sequence number would wrap before the cryptographic limit for this algorithm is reached.

17.7 An experiment with the OpenSSL s_client

We use the OpenSSL s_client again to see the TLS record protocol at work. For this purpose, we use the OpenSSL Docker container from the previous chapter.

17.7.1 Getting started

To start the container, execute the following command:

```
$ docker container run --rm -it openssl310
```

Once the Docker container is up and running, it will give you a command-line prompt similar to the following one, where you can call the s_client tool:

```
root@07c3ba265c69:/opt/openssl#
```

17.7.2 Retrieving a website via TLS

Our goal is to retrieve a web page from the server in order to see what the TLS records look like. To demonstrate this, we will use the website www.cr.yp.to of the American-German mathematician and cryptographer Daniel (Dan) Bernstein, the author of the x25519 elliptic curve.

HTTP uses a GET request method to retrieve a web page. The GET request specifies the path of the page to be retrieved and the HTTP version. The standard HTTP version since the late 1990s is HTTP/1.1 and we will use the root of the web page, denoted by a slash /, as the web page to be retrieved.

Since HTTP is a line-based protocol, the GET request and its parameters go into a single line:

```
GET / HTTP/1.1
```

In addition to the GET method, an HTTP request consists of one or more of so-called *request header fields*. In our case, we need to specify the hostname like this:

```
Host: cr.yp.to
```

The HTTP protocol specifies that the request line GET / HTTP/1.1 must be followed by a carriage return and a new line, and the request header field must be followed by two consecutive carriage returns and line feeds. To address this – because we want to use s_client in interactive mode – we will call the tool with the -crlf option, which translates a line feed from the terminal, that is, the press of the Enter key, into the carriage return + line feed sequence.

So, we start by calling the s_client tool with the -crlf option to deal with carriage return, and -msg and -debug to see detailed information on TLS messages and print the debugging information, including a hex dump of all traffic:

```
root@5026f08a9173:/opt/openssl# openssl s_client -crlf -connect
cr.yp.to:443 -msg -debug
CONNECTED(00000003)
>>> TLS 1.0, RecordHeader [length 0005]
    16 03 01 01 31
>>> TLS 1.3, Handshake [length 0131], ClientHello
    01 00 01 2d 03 03 93 24 7e 4a 6b b9 67 d0 3d dd
    d5 cd cf f6 a6 da 19 a1 75 27 17 ee 26 58 cc 37
    0a 5f a9 04 30 2b 20 92 23 81 9e 72 5f f9 4e 21

    -- snip --
```

After a successful TLS handshake, the `s_client` tool stops and waits for user input:

```
-- snip --

New, TLSv1.2, Cipher is ECDHE-RSA-CHACHA20-POLY1305
Server public key is 2048 bit
Secure Renegotiation IS supported
Compression: NONE
Expansion: NONE
No ALPN negotiated
SSL-Session:
    Protocol  : TLSv1.2
    Cipher    : ECDHE-RSA-CHACHA20-POLY1305
    Session-ID:
    Session-ID-ctx:
    Master-Key: 96260DD02E02C755C804F1EC5DC -- snip --
    PSK identity: None
    PSK identity hint: None
    SRP username: None
    Start Time: 1683835757
    Timeout   : 7200 (sec)
    Verify return code: 0 (ok)
    Extended master secret: yes
---
```

Now we can enter the HTTP `GET` request `GET / HTTP/1.1` and press *Enter*. It will be immediately followed by the debug output:

```
GET / HTTP/1.1
>>> TLS 1.2, RecordHeader [length 0005]
    17 03 03 00 20
write to 0x55ed1055c4b0 [0x55ed10569533] (37 bytes => 37 (0x25))
0000 - 17 03 03 00 20 48 18 81-51 1f 18 1b e8 a0 6a 97   ....
H..Q.....j.
```

```
0010 - be 90 dd 9e a6 b7 e5 8a-e8 c7 e0 80 8d 2f d3 87
............/..
0020 - 69 a1 ef 72 9e                                                     i..r.
```

Next, we need to enter the request header field Host: cr.yp.to. You have to hurry up a bit, though. Otherwise, the server will terminate the TLS session due to a time-out. Also, recall that after entering Host: cr.yp.to, you have to hit *Enter* twice:

```
Host: cr.yp.to
>>> TLS 1.2, RecordHeader [length 0005]
    17 03 03 00 20
write to 0x55ed1055c4b0 [0x55ed10569533] (37 bytes => 37 (0x25))
0000 - 17 03 03 00 20 1a a0 ef-19 30 fd 08 85 03 30 25

>>> TLS 1.2, RecordHeader [length 0005]
    17 03 03 00 12
write to 0x55ed1055c4b0 [0x55ed10569533] (23 bytes => 23 (0x17))
0000 - 17 03 03 00 12 57 0c 8e-ae c1 dd 39 57 a8 d5 38
.....W.....9W..8
0010 - fc 91 9b 32 fb ff 59                              ...2..Y
read from 0x55ed1055c4b0 [0x55ed105653e3] (5 bytes => 5 (0x5))
0000 - 17 03 03 04 10                                    ....
```

After you enter the request header field Host: cr.yp.to and hit *Enter* twice, you will see a large amount of output with the individual TLS protocol messages and, eventually, the HTML payload:

```
<<< TLS 1.2, RecordHeader [length 0005]
    17 03 03 04 10
read from 0x55ed1055c4b0 [0x55ed105653e8] (1040 bytes => 1040
(0x410))
0000 - 2a aa c5 5f 7e d0 4f ac-0d 4d 10 a5 11 91 d8 50
*.._~.O..M.....P
0010 - 69 9a 4e 3a 48 b6 df 2d-cb b3 96 9a fc 91 69 b5
i.N:H..-......i.
```

```
-- snip --

03f0 - 70 d1 0f d4 35 0b e3 fc-fe 5e 6d e6 37 33 e8 54
p...5....^m.73.T
0400 - 6a 69 f4 a5 3c 1a 7d 6d-e5 db d7 be 88 af a3 c1
ji..<.}m........
HTTP/1.1 200 OK
Server: publicfile
Date: Thu, 11 May 2023 20:28:43 GMT
Last-Modified: Wed, 17 Feb 2021 15:13:46 GMT
Content-Type: text/html
Transfer-Encoding: chunked

400
<html>
<head>
<meta http-equiv="content-type" content="text/html; charset=utf-8">
<meta name="viewport" content="width=device-width, initial-scale=1">
<meta name="robots" content="index,follow">
<style type="text/css">

-- snip --
```

Congratulations! You have successfully transmitted HTML data over a secure channel established using the TLS 1.3 protocol. But you might wonder what actually happens to your plaintext input and where those strange byte sequences come from. As an example, the HTTP request GET / HTTP/1.1 was transformed into the following TLS record:

```
GET / HTTP/1.1
>>> TLS 1.2, RecordHeader [length 0005]
    17 03 03 00 20
write to 0x55ed1055c4b0 [0x55ed10569533] (37 bytes => 37 (0x25))
0000 - 17 03 03 00 20 48 18 81-51 1f 18 1b e8 a0 6a 97   ....
H..Q.....j.
```

```
0010 - be 90 dd 9e a6 b7 e5 8a-e8 c7 e0 80 8d 2f d3 87
          .............../..
0020 - 69 a1 ef 72 9e                                                    i..r.
```

The first 5 bytes belong to the TLS record header, which is transmitted in plaintext, that is, the header is *not* encrypted. The first byte is 17 in hexadecimal notation. This is equivalent to 23, the number denoting a TLS record of type application_data. The next two bytes encode the legacy_record_version. Recall that this field has the value 0x0303 for all TLS 1.3 records except the initial ClientHello. The last two bytes of the header store the length of the actual payload, which in our case is 20 in hexadecimal or 32 in decimal. Together with the header, the size of this TLSPlaintext is 37 bytes.

17.7.3   Analyzing the TLS record

What about the 32 payload bytes in the preceding TLS record? How are these bytes computed and where is our original plaintext GET / HTTP/1.1? We can explore these questions by debugging s_client.

The simplest way to do this is using the Dockerfile we supply in the same Git repository you used for experiments with OpenSSL in *Chapter 13, TLS Handshake Protocol Revisited*. With the Git repository that you have previously cloned, execute the following commands:

```
$ cd tls_lab/openssl_debug
$ docker build . -t openssl_debug
$ docker container run --rm -it openssl310_debug
```

You can now start the Docker container by issuing the following command:

```
$ docker container run --rm -it openssl310_debug
```

Once the container is running, you should again see a similar command prompt:

```
root@37cccb0da138:/opt/openssl/openssl-3.1.0/apps#
```

Next, we need to start the GNU debugger gdb and pass it the following options and arguments:

```
root@37cccb0da138:/opt/openssl/openssl-3.1.0/apps# gdb -x
/opt/openssl/openssl-3.1.0/gdbinit --args ./openssl s_client -crlf
-ign_eof -connect cr.yp.to:443 -msg -debug
```

The preceding command tells gdb to use the initialization file gdbinit and start the openssl s_client with the specified options. Once the debugger is running, we set a breakpoint at the s_client_main function, the main function of the OpenSSL s_client, and run the program being debugged using GDB's run command:

```
-- snip --

Reading symbols from ./openssl...
(gdb) b s_client_main
Breakpoint 1 at 0x8bb52: file apps/s_client.c, line 784.
(gdb) run
Starting program: /opt/openssl/openssl-3.1.0/apps/openssl s_client
-crlf
-ign_eof -connect cr.yp.to:443 -msg -debug
warning: Error disabling address space randomization: Operation not
permitted
[Thread debugging using libthread_db enabled]
Using host libthread_db library
"/lib/x86_64-linux-gnu/libthread_db.so.1".

Breakpoint 1, s_client_main (argc=7, argv=0x7ffcea29e990) at
apps/s_client.c:784
784            {
```

Next, we set a breakpoint at the `SSL_write` function and continue – using GDB's c command,
a shorthand for `continue` – the execution of the debugged program until `SSL_write` is
reached. Since we know that the TLS client first writes the TLS handshake protocol
messages, we issue the c command a second time and receive (an empty) `s_client` prompt
waiting for us to enter an HTTP request:

```
(gdb) b SSL_write
Breakpoint 2 at 0x7f95573cfe22: file ssl/ssl_lib.c, line 2131.
(gdb) c
Continuing.
CONNECTED(00000003)


Breakpoint 2, SSL_write (s=0x55992ff9be60, buf=0x55992ff50ad0, num=0)
at
ssl/ssl_lib.c:2131
2131            {
(gdb) c
Continuing.
>>> TLS 1.0, RecordHeader [length 0005]
    16 03 01 01 31
>>> TLS 1.3, Handshake [length 0131], ClientHello
    01 00 01 2d 03 03 bc cc 5a 35 b5 ac c8 21 a9 d1
    30 76 32 20 35 f1 b6 08 3c c7 92 28 8f d3 91 b3

-- snip --

    SRP username: None
    Start Time: 1684177776
    Timeout   : 7200 (sec)
    Verify return code: 20 (unable to get local issuer certificate)
    Extended master secret: yes
---
<empty line for HTTP request>
```

Entering the HTTP request and hitting *Enter* brings us again to the breakpoint at `SSL_write`. The code enters several functions until it reaches the `ssl3_write_bytes` function defined in `ssl/record/rec_layer_s3.c`:

```
GET / HTTP/1.1

Breakpoint 2, SSL_write (s=0x55992ff9be60, buf=0x55992ff50ad0,
num=16) at
ssl/ssl_lib.c:2131
2131            {
(gdb) s
2135                    if (num < 0) {
(gdb) b ssl_write_internal
Breakpoint 3 at 0x7f95573cfaf7: file ssl/ssl_lib.c, line 2027.
(gdb) c
Continuing.

Breakpoint 3, ssl_write_internal (s=0x55992ff9be60,
buf=0x55992ff50ad0,
num=16, written=0x7ffcea29e090) at ssl/ssl_lib.c:2027
2027            {
(gdb) s
2028                    if (s->handshake_func == NULL) {
(gdb) b ssl3_write_bytes
Breakpoint 4 at 0x7f95573f6980: file ssl/record/rec_layer_s3.c, line
346.
(gdb) c
Continuing.

Breakpoint 4, ssl3_write_bytes (s=0x55992ff9be60, type=23,
buf_=0x55992ff50ad0, len=16, written=0x7ffcea29e090) at
ssl/record/rec_layer_s3.c:346
346             {
```

You can see in GDB's output that `ssl3_write_bytes` takes as input a record type set to 23, that is, application data, a buffer `buf_` and a length set to 16.

We can inspect 16 bytes of memory starting at the address of buf_:

```
Breakpoint 4, ssl3_write_bytes (s=0x55992ff9be60, type=23,
buf_=0x55992ff50ad0, len=16, written=0x7ffcea29e090) at
ssl/record/rec_layer_s3.c:346
346          {
(gdb) x/16bx buf_
0x55992ff50ad0:         0x47 0x45 0x54 0x20 0x2f 0x20 0x48 0x54
0x55992ff50ad8:         0x54 0x50 0x2f 0x31 0x2e 0x31 0x0d 0x0a
```

While these bytes values seem odd at first, things become clear when we interpret them using the ASCII codes (in hexadecimal notation): G (0x47) E (0x45) T (0x54) blank (0x20) / (0x2f) blank (0x20) H (0x48) T (0x54) T (0x54) P (0x50) / (0x2f) 1 (0x31) dot (0x2e) 1 (0x31) carriage return (0x0d) new line (0x0a).

Finally, we set a breakpoint at the ssl3_write_bytes function and step through it to see how the plaintext HTTP request is encrypted into a TLSCiphertext record and transmitted to the server:

```
(gdb) b do_ssl3_write
Breakpoint 5 at 0x7f95573f775e: file ssl/record/rec_layer_s3.c, line
664.
(gdb) c
Continuing.

Breakpoint 5, do_ssl3_write (s=0x55992ff9be60, type=23,
buf=0x55992ff50ad0 "GET / HTTP/1.1\r\n", pipelens=0x7ffcea29de90,
numpipes=1,
create_empty_fragment=0, written=0x7ffcea29de00) at
ssl/record/rec_layer_s3.c:664
664          {
(gdb) s

#0  do_ssl3_write (s=0x55992ff9be60, type=23,
```

```
buf=0x55992ff50ad0 "GET / HTTP/1.1\r\n", pipelens=0x7ffcea29de90,
numpipes=1,
create_empty_fragment=0, written=0x7ffcea29de00) at
ssl/record/rec_layer_s3.c:714
714                         || (EVP_MD_CTX_get0_md(s->write_hash) ==
NULL)) {
(gdb) n

-- snip --

989                    if (!BIO_get_ktls_send(s->wbio) &&
!SSL_WRITE_ETM(s) && mac_size != 0) {
(gdb) n
>>> TLS 1.2, RecordHeader [length 0005]
    17 03 03 00 20

-- snip --

(gdb) n
1149              return ssl3_write_pending(s, type, buf, totlen,
written);
(gdb) n
write to 0x55992ff9e270 [0x55992ffa9413] (37 bytes => 37 (0x25))
0000 - 17 03 03 00 20 a1 d4 fa-a0 c3 8b bf e1 23 18 3c   ....
........#.<
0010 - 03 07 95 e0 38 ad 9d b6-57 59 54 00 bb 26 04 bb
....8...WYT..&..
0020 - ac 21 f1 cb 43                                     .!..C
1154         }
```

This concludes our deep dive into the TLS record. We hope you can see how, using OpenSSL's s_client test tool, it is possible to analyze in detail how the TLS record protocol protects its payload.

17.8   Summary

In this chapter, we covered the TLS record layer and learned how cryptographic mechanisms, in particular AEAD algorithms, are used in the TLS record protocol. We described the data structures and messages on the record layer and saw how record payloads are protected. In addition, we discussed per-record nonces and the use of padding for TLS records.

Moreover, we covered how TLS can be further explored – down to nitty-gritty details – by debugging OpenSSL, specifically OpenSSL's s_client test tool. While we did not describe the GNU debugger in detail, the Git repository and instructions for building a Docker image with an OpenSSL 3.1.0 installation suitable for debugging and the GDB commands shown in the examples in this chapter are good starting points for exploring OpenSSL and TLS in more detail.

In the next chapter, we will take a look at TLS 1.3 cipher suites. These are pairs composed of an AEAD algorithm and a hash algorithm to be used with HKDF as a key derivation function. Moreover, we will learn about two additional cryptographic algorithms – ChaCha20 and Poly-1305 – that we haven't covered so far.

18

TLS Cipher Suites

In the previous chapter, we revisited the TLS Record protocol from a higher-level perspective to understand how the individual cryptographic mechanisms – block ciphers, AEAD, and, in particular, the Galois counter mode – fit together to ensure confidentiality and integrity of data transmitted in TLS records.

In this chapter, we will cover TLS 1.3 cipher suites: combinations of ciphers and cryptographic algorithms that any TLS 1.3 endpoint must support and implement. In terms of RFC 8446 material, we will mainly cover the following:

- Subsection 9.1, *Mandatory-to-Implement Cipher Suites*

- Appendix B.4, *Cipher Suites*

In addition, we will introduce two additional cryptographic algorithms – ChaCha20 and Poly-1305 – that can be used in TLS 1.3 and which we have not covered so far.

Upon completion of the chapter, you will have a comprehensive overview of combinations of cryptographic algorithms allowed by the TLS 1.3 standard. More precisely, you will:

- Be familiar with the concept of a standby cipher and, more generally, with the notion and role of cryptographic agility

- Know which cryptographic suites can be used with TLS 1.3

- Understand the inner workings of the ChaCha20 and Poly-1305 algorithms

18.1   Symmetric cipher suites in TLS 1.3

TLS 1.3 specifies a set of so-called *symmetric cipher suites* that Alice and Bob can use to protect the data transmitted via the TLS Record protocol. Each symmetric cipher suite is a pair composed of two cryptographic algorithms:

- An AEAD algorithm used for protecting the confidentiality and integrity of TLS records

- A hash algorithm used within the HKDF function to derive TLS secrets and shared keys

The name of a TLS symmetric cipher suite starts with the string TLS and has the following format:

```
TLS_<AEAD algorithm>_<Hash algorithm>
```

where <AEAD algorithm and <Hash algorithm> are placeholders for specific algorithms. In addition, every cipher suite has a unique 2-byte identification value associated with it.

Table 18.1 shows the symmetric cipher suites that Alice and Bob can use according to the TLS 1.3 standard.

Cipher suite	2-byte identifier
TLS_AES_128_GCM_SHA256	0x13,0x01
TLS_AES_256_GCM_SHA384	0x13,0x02
TLS_CHACHA20_POLY1305_SHA256	0x13,0x03
TLS_AES_128_CCM_SHA256	0x13,0x04
TLS_AES_128_CCM_8_SHA256	0x13,0x05

Table 18.1: Symmetric cipher suites specified in the TLS 1.3 standard.

AEAD algorithms AEAD_AES_128_GCM, AEAD_AES_256_GCM, and AEAD_AES_128_CCM are defined in RFC 5116. The algorithm AEAD_AES_128_CCM_8 is defined in RFC 6655. The hash algorithms are specified in **National Institute of Standards and Technology (NIST)** [129].

18.2 Long-term security

In his famous book *The Cathedral and the Bazaar* [144], the American software developer and open-source advocate Eric Raymond coined the phrase that *"given enough eyeballs, all bugs are shallow"*. Raymond used the phrase – which later became known as the *Linus Law* in honor of Linus Torvalds – to highlight the benefits of the open-source development model, where the peer review conducted by a large developer community is very effective in identifying and fixing software bugs.

As discussed in *Chapter 14, Block Ciphers and Their Modes of Operation*, the AES algorithm was chosen in a worldwide public contest where the entire cryptographic community was able to submit their own proposals and find cryptographic flaws and weaknesses in others. The candidates' algorithms were scrutinized by dozens of world-class cryptographers and leading experts in their respective sub-fields, and this type of contest for selecting cryptographic algorithms to be standardized has become a best practice.

Experts from academia, industry, and national security agencies have carefully investigated any potential weakness that AES might have, yet found nothing practically relevant. Had someone managed to discover a practically-relevant cryptographic flaw in AES after the standard was announced by FIPS, they would have immediately received at least a tenure-track professorship, and certainly a prominent place in the cryptography community's hall of fame. Yet, more than 20 years after AES introduction, no one has found a serious security vulnerability in that block cipher.

Given all these facts, we can say for sure that AES is *the* gold standard! So, a natural question to ask is: why does TLS 1.3 specify a cipher suite with ChaCha20, a second block cipher? The reason, it turns out, is to have a single *standby cipher* that will be ready for adoption as an AES replacement if future advances in cryptanalysis uncover a serious cryptographic weakness in AES.

18.2.1 Advances in cryptanalysis

In June 2013, The Guardian and Washington Post simultaneously published an article about a secret order issued by the United States Foreign Intelligence Surveillance Court ordering Verizon, one of the largest telecommunication providers in the US, to hand over all call records and the metadata of millions Verizon customers to the National Security Agency.

It was the prelude to what eventually became known as the Snowden leaks, a cache of top secret NSA documents revealed by then 29-year-old Edward Snowden, who worked as an intelligence contractor for Booz Allen Hamilton in Hawaii.

One of the documents published by the Washington Post – a summary of a "black budget" for US intelligence gathering activities – contained a statement by James Clapper (at that time, the Director of National Intelligence) that the US National Intelligence Program is *"investing in groundbreaking cryptanalytic capabilities to defeat adversarial cryptography and exploit internet traffic"* [159].

In response to the Snowden leaks, the American cryptographer Bruce Schneier wrote an article for the Wired magazine [159] assessing the alleged groundbreaking cryptographic capabilities. According to Schneier, whatever the NSA's cryptanalytic capabilities were, cryptography would still be the most secure part of an encryption system given that, in practice, social engineering, software bugs, bad passwords, malware, or insecure network configuration are much more likely.

Nevertheless, Schneier speculated that the NSA is very likely to have cryptanalytic techniques that are unknown to the public. The most probable scenario, according to Schneier, is that the NSA achieved some mathematical breakthroughs in the area of public-key cryptography: *"There are a lot of mathematical tricks involved in public-key cryptanalysis, and absolutely no theory that provides any limits on how powerful those tricks can be. [...] It is not unreasonable to assume that the NSA has some techniques in this area that we in the academic world do not"* [159].

While cryptanalytic techniques and theoretical cryptanalytic results are difficult to turn into practical attacks – especially attacks on symmetric key cryptography – Schneier quotes a well-known NSA saying that cryptanalysis only gets better, never worse. He concludes the article by saying it would be *"naive to assume we have discovered all the mathematical breakthroughs in cryptography that can ever be discovered"* [159].

According to the Snowden leaks, the US Department of Defense employed 35,000 people in their cryptologic program, with an annual budget of $11 billion. And this is just one country; numerous nations outside the United States have similar cryptologic programs. As a result, from time to time, we should expect cryptanalytic advances, and occasionally, even groundbreaking results.

A prime example of this is the NSA's role in the improvement of the DES block cipher in the 1970s. Recall that after the original DES algorithm submitted by IBM was sent for review to the NSA, it came back with completely different S-boxes. The modifications were analyzed by the cryptographic community – there was even an official review conducted on behalf of the US Senate's Select Committee on Intelligence – but no statistical or mathematical weaknesses were found throughout the 1970s and the 1980s.

Only in 1990, after Eli Biham and Adi Shamir published differential cryptanalysis, a novel method for breaking block ciphers, did cryptographers discover that DES S-boxes were much more resistant against differential cryptanalysis than randomly chosen S-boxes could ever be.

Finally, when Don Coppersmith, one of the IBM cryptographers who designed DES, published original design criteria for DES S-boxes in 1994, the cryptographic community learned that the NSA and IBM knew about differential cryptanalysis as early as 1974. As a result, DES S-boxes were deliberately tweaked to resist differential cryptanalysis, but the NSA requested to keep it a secret because the attack was applicable to a wide range of cryptographic algorithms and was considered by the NSA to be a serious risk to national security if it became public.

18.2.2   Cryptographic agility

To cope with possible future advances in cryptology, good security systems are built in a way that makes it easy to replace individual cryptographic algorithms with new ones if needed. This design pattern is called *algorithm agility* or *cryptographic agility* (or crypto-agility, for short) and allows maintaining the security of a system, even if a weakness is found in one of its cryptographic primitives.

Bryan Sullivan's talk on cryptographic agility at the BlackHat security conference [169] nicely illustrates how this concept is implemented in practice, in .NET and Java Cryptography architecture frameworks.

Figure 18.1 shows the .NET framework class SHA512CSP implementing the SHA-512 hash function. The SHA512CSP class inherits from the abstract class SHA512, which, in turn, inherits from the abstract class HashAlgorithm.

The HashAlgorithm base class defines a public method called ComputeHash. This method calls an abstract protected method, HashCore, which does the actual hash computation. Hence, the SHA512SCP class that is derived from the HashAlgorithm class must implement its own HashCore method.

In addition, the `HashAlgorithm` class implements a class method called `Create`, which acts as a factory class for classes that derive from `HashAlgorithm`. The method takes the name of the algorithm to be instantiated and creates a new instance of `HashAlgorithm` with the desired hash function. A call to the `ComputeHash` method of the newly created instance performs the actual computation:

```
HashAlgorithm myHash = HashAlgorithm.Create(desiredAlgorithmName);
byte[] result = myHash.ComputeHash(data);
```

The following diagram shows the interdependencies between the various classes related to the base class `HashAlgorithm`:

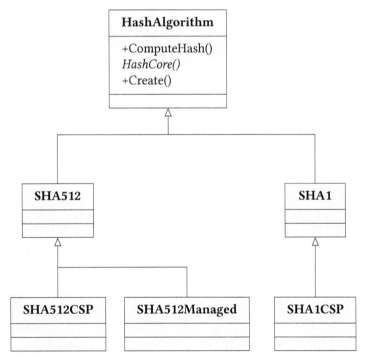

Figure 18.1: Inheritance structure in .NET framework's cryptography part

The software architecture shown in *Figure 18.1* allows developers to write application code *without* hardcoding the hash function to be used.

Instead, the code can load the name of the desired hash algorithm from a database or a configuration file specified by the system administrator. The administrator, in turn, is now able to select the algorithm and the implementation they want to use. For example, they can easily replace the insecure SHA-1 algorithm with the secure SHA-512 algorithm.

18.2.3   Standby ciphers

During the AES contest, 15 submitted algorithms were accepted and their security was analyzed at 3 public workshops and many more peer-reviewed scientific conferences over the course of 4 years.

Even if we assume that other ciphers offer a security level similar to that of AES, every additional cipher that a TLS endpoint must support increases the development, validation, and maintenance cost. So, why have a second encryption algorithm?

The reason for having a second, standby algorithm is *long-term* security. If future advances in cryptanalysis uncover a cryptographic weakness in AES, the second algorithm will be readily available as a drop-in replacement for AES.

The TLS protocol accommodates cryptographic agility by allowing Alice and Bob to negotiate the algorithms they want to use in a particular TLS session. The ability to negotiate algorithms, for one thing, helps to achieve compatibility among heterogeneous devices from different vendors: even if Alice and Bob support different sets of algorithms, they can dynamically select a cipher suite they both support as long as their sets overlap. Simultaneously, the ability to negotiate makes it architecturally easy to include a standby cipher that Alice and Bob can immediately switch to if the mandatory-to-implement cipher becomes cryptographically weak.

In addition – as David McGrew, Anthony Grieco, and Yaron Sheffer outline in [113] – allowing to negotiate algorithms (in other words, providing cryptographic agility) counteracts the proliferation of cryptographic protocols.

Typically, an abundance of cryptographic protocols is worse than an abundance of cryptographic algorithms because it is much easier to replace a cryptographic algorithm than a cryptographic protocol. Why? Because the complexity of a cryptographic algorithm is isolated by a simple interface, while a protocol's complexity is not isolated at all – a protocol must interact with the network stack layers below and above.

The standby cipher must meet the same security and efficiency standards as the mandatory-to-implement cipher. In particular, the standby cipher must undergo an extensive public review process where the cryptographic community has the opportunity to carefully investigate the cipher for any potential security weaknesses. Moreover, the standby cipher must fulfill two additional requirements:

- Its design, that is, its mathematical working principles, must be as independent as possible from that of the mandatory-to-implement cipher. This way, the cryptanalytic advances that weaken the mandatory-to-implement cipher will have the least effect on the standby cipher.

- The mandatory-to-implement cipher is optimized for the existing hardware. The standby cipher must be efficiently computable on the existing hardware as well.

We will now take a look at the standby cipher for the AES.

18.3 ChaCha20

ChaCha20 is a fast block cipher defined in RFC 8439 *ChaCha20 and Poly1305 for IETF Protocols* [131]. The number 20 in the cipher's name refers to a specific ChaCha variant that uses 20 rounds or, equivalently, 80 quarter rounds to compute the ciphertext.

ChaCha20's state is stored in a 4 by 4 matrix consisting of 32-bit unsigned integers. The state representation using a matrix explains why some ChaCha rounds are referred to as *column* rounds while others are referred to as *diagonal* rounds:

```
 0   1   2   3
 4   5   6   7
 8   9  10  11
12  13  14  15
```

18.3.1   ChaCha20 quarter round

The ChaCha20 algorithm's basic operation is the so-called *quarter round*. The quarter round operates on four elements of the ChaCha20 state, hence the name. The four elements are denoted as a, b, c, and d and the quarter round is defined as:

$$a = a + b \quad (\bmod\ 2^{32})$$
$$d = d \oplus a$$
$$d = d \lll 16$$

$$c = c + d \quad (\bmod\ 2^{32})$$
$$b = b \oplus c$$
$$b = b \lll 12$$

$$a = a + b \quad (\bmod\ 2^{32})$$
$$d = d \oplus a$$
$$d = d \lll 8$$

$$c = c + d \quad (\bmod\ 2^{32})$$
$$b = b \oplus c$$
$$b = b \lll 7$$

where $\ll n$ denotes the rotate left by n bits operation, for example:

$$\texttt{0x7998bfda} \ll 7 = \texttt{0xcc5fed3c}$$

The ChaCha20 quarter round is illustrated in *Figure 18.2*. The illustration is based on the code in the *TikZ for Cryptographers* repository maintained by Jean Jérémy [90].

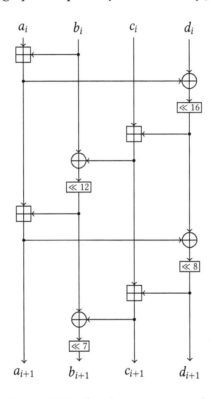

Figure 18.2: ChaCha quarter round

ChaCha20's quarter-round operation is applied to four elements (32-bit unsigned integers) of the cipher's state. So, since the algorithm's state is a 4 by 4 matrix, the full ChaCha20 round requires four quarter rounds.

In RFC 8439, the quarter round is denoted by the function `QUARTERROUND(x, y, z, w)`, which takes the ChaCha20 state's elements at indices x, y, z, and w.

For instance, if the function is called with the argument QUARTERROUND(1, 5, 9, 13), then the quarter round operation is applied to the state's elements marked with an asterisk (and referred to as *column* round):

```
 0   1*   2    3
 4   5*   6    7
 8   9*  10   11
12  13*  14   15
```

18.3.2   The ChaCha20 block function

The ChaCha20 block function takes the following as inputs:

- A 256-bit key

- A 96-bit nonce

- A 32-bit block count parameter

It transforms the cipher's state by executing multiple quarter rounds, and produces a 64-byte pseudorandom output.

Before the round function can be applied, the ChaCha20 state is initialized as follows:

- The first four 4-byte words are set to constants 0x61707865, 0x3320646e, 0x79622d32, and 0x6b206574.

- The next eight 4-byte words are set to 4-byte chunks of the 256-bit ChaCha20 key, by reading the bytes in little-endian order, where the 12th word is a block counter. Because each block has 64 bytes, this 4-byte word is large enough for 256 GB of data.

- The last four 4-byte words are a nonce. The 13th word corresponds to the first 32 bits of the nonce taken as a little-endian integer, and the 16th word corresponds to the last 32 bits of the nonce. The nonce must be repeated for the same key.

With this, the initial value of ChaCha20's state looks like this:

```
cccccccc  cccccccc  cccccccc  cccccccc
kkkkkkkk  kkkkkkkk  kkkkkkkk  kkkkkkkk
kkkkkkkk  kkkkkkkk  kkkkkkkk  kkkkkkkk
bbbbbbbb  nnnnnnnn  nnnnnnnn  nnnnnnnn
```

Here, c stands for the corresponding constant-, k for key-, b for block count-, and n for nonce-bytes.

After the initial state value has been set, ChaCha20 executes 20 rounds (80 quarter rounds) alternating between column and diagonal rounds. The column round is composed of the first 4 quarter rounds, and the diagonal round is composed of the last 4 quarter rounds:

```
QUARTERROUND(0, 4, 8, 12)
QUARTERROUND(1, 5, 9, 13)
QUARTERROUND(2, 6, 10, 14)
QUARTERROUND(3, 7, 11, 15)
QUARTERROUND(0, 5, 10, 15)
QUARTERROUND(1, 6, 11, 12)
QUARTERROUND(2, 7, 8, 13)
QUARTERROUND(3, 4, 9, 14)
```

After the 20 rounds are executed, the output words are added to the original input words (the addition is performed modulo 2^{32}), and the result is serialized by sequencing it in little-endian order.

18.3.3 ChaCha20 encryption algorithm

The ChaCha20 cipher uses the ChaCha20 block function – with the same key and home, and increasing block counter – to generate a key stream block. The key stream blocks are concatenated into a key stream. The cipher subsequently XORs the key stream to the plaintext. *Algorithm 8* shows the complete ChaCha20 encryption process. The notation $p_{i \dots j}$ denotes the i-th to the $(j-1)$-th bytes of variable p.

Alternatively, ChaCha20 XORs the key stream block with a plaintext block before generating the next key stream block. Especially on embedded devices with constrained resources, this mode saves valuable memory. If the plaintext is not a multiple of 512 bits, the superfluous key bits from the last key stream block are discarded.

Algorithm 8 ChaCha20 encryption process.

Require: Arbitrary size plaintext p, 256-bit key k, 96-bit nonce n, and 32-bit initial counter value ctr
Ensure: Encrypted message c

> **for** $j = 0 \ldots \lfloor len(p)/64 \rfloor - 1$ **do**
> $\quad s \leftarrow$ chacha20_block$(k, ctr + j, n)$
> $\quad b \leftarrow p_{64j \ldots (64j+63)}$
> $\quad c \leftarrow c + (b \oplus s)$
> **end for**
>
> **if** $len(p) \mod 64 \neq 0$ **then**
> $\quad j \leftarrow \lfloor len(p)/64 \rfloor$
> $\quad s \leftarrow$ chacha20_block$(k, ctr + j, n)$
> $\quad b \leftarrow p_{64j \ldots len(p)-1}$
> $\quad c \leftarrow c + (b \oplus s)_{0 \ldots len(p) \mod 64}$
> **end if**

> **return** c

To summarize, ChaCha20 takes the following as input:

- A 256-bit key

- A 32-bit initial counter

- A 96-bit nonce

- A plaintext of arbitrary length

It outputs a ciphertext of the same length. ChaCha20's decryption is identical to encryption: the ChaCha20 block function is used to generate the key stream, which is, in turn, XORed with the cipher text to obtain the plaintext.

18.4 Poly1305

Poly1305 is a message authentication code specified in RFC 8439 [131]. It takes a 256-bit one-time key k and an arbitrary length plaintext m, and produces a 128-bit tag used to authenticate message m.

The key k is partitioned into two parts, which RFC 8439 refers to as r and s. The pair (r, s) must be unique and unpredictable for each Poly1305 invocation. The 16-byte part r may be constant, but must undergo the following modification, referred to as *clamping* in RFC 8439:

- The four highest bits of bytes 3, 7, 11, and 15 must be set to 0 (in other words, these bytes must be smaller than 16).

- The two bottom bits of bytes 4, 8, and 12 must be set to 0 (in other words, these bytes must be divisible by 4).

Part s, the other 16-byte part of the secret key k, must be unpredictable. However, r and s can also be (pseudo)randomly generated for each new Poly1305 invocation.

Poly1305 pseudocode is shown in *Algorithm 9*. It takes a 256-bit one-time key and an arbitrary-size message m, and outputs a 128-bit tag t, which is used to verify the integrity and authenticity of message m. First, the key k is divided into r and s, and r is clamped. Next, the constant prime p is set to $2^{130} - 5$ and the accumulator a is set to 0.

In the next step, the plaintext message m is divided into 16-byte blocks. le_bytes_to_num function then reads the block, concatenated with the byte 0x01, as a little-endian number. For example, if the value of a 16-byte block of message m is as follows:

```
43 72 79 70 74 6f 67 72 61 70 68 69 63 20 46 6f
```

then the concatenated result is as follows:

```
6f 46 20 63 69 68 70 61 72 67 6f 74 70 79 72 43 01
```

and the result of assigning n the concatenated value read as the little-endian number is as follows:

```
n = 016f46206369686706172676f7470797243
```

If the message block is 16 bytes long, the above operation is equivalent to adding 2^{128} to the message block. If the block is shorter than 16 bytes, the above operation is equivalent to adding 2^{120}, 2^{112}, 2^{104}, or any other power of 2 down to 2^8 that is evenly divisible by 8. Next, add accumulator a to the number n, and multiply it by r modulo p.

After the loop is finished, add the secret key s to the accumulator a, and return the 128 least significant bits in little-endian order as the tag t.

Algorithm 9 Poly-1305 algorithm.

Require: Arbitrary length message m, 256-bit one-time key k
Ensure: 128-bit tag t
   $r \leftarrow$ le_bytes_to_num($k_{0 \ldots 15}$)
   $r \leftarrow$ clamp(r)
   $s \leftarrow$ le_bytes_to_num($key_{16 \ldots 31}$)
   $a \leftarrow 0$
   $p \leftarrow (1 \ll 130) - 5$

   for $i = 1 \ldots \lceil \text{len}(m)/16 \rceil$ **do**
       $n \leftarrow$ le_bytes_to_num($msg_{16(i-1) \ldots 16i} \parallel 0x01$)
       $a \leftarrow a + n$
       $a \leftarrow (r \cdot a) \mod p$
   end for

   $a \leftarrow a + s$
   return num_to_16_le_bytes(a)

18.4.1   Generating the Poly1305 key using ChaCha20

The Poly1305 key k can be generated pseudorandomly, for example, using the ChaCha20 block function. In this case, Alice and Bob need a dedicated 256-bit session key intended specifically for message authentication.

Generation of the authentication key (r, s) is done by computing the ChaCha20 block function with the following inputs:

- The 256-bit session integrity key that is used as the ChaCha20 key

- The block counter set to 0

- A 96-bit nonce that must be unique for every invocation of the ChaCha20 block function with the same key (therefore, it must *not* be randomly generated)

Computing the ChaCha20 block function produces a 512-bit state. Alice and Bob use the first 256 bits of the state as the one-time key for Poly1305. The first 128 bits are clamped and become part r, and the last 128 bits become part s. *Algorithm 10* shows the Poly1305 key generation process as pseudocode.

Algorithm 10 Poly1305 key generation process

Require: 256-bit key k, 96-bit nonce n
Ensure: Generated key b
   $ctr = 0$
   $b \leftarrow$ chacha20_block(k, ctr, n)
   return $b_{0 \ldots 31}$

ChaCha20 and Poly1305 can be also be used as building blocks within an AEAD construction.

18.5 ChaCha20-Poly1305 AEAD construction

ChaCha20-Poly1305 is a cryptographic algorithm for authenticated encryption with additional data (AEAD, see *Chapter 15, Authenticated Encryption*). Like the two building blocks ChaCha20 and Poly1305, ChaCha20-Poly1305 used in TLS is defined in RFC 8439 [131]. Initially, both building blocks were proposed by the American cryptographer Dan Bernstein [25, 23].

The ChaCha20-Poly1305 AEAD construction is illustrated in *Figure 18.3*. As you can see, the algorithm takes four inputs:

- A 256-bit shared secret key k

- A 96-bit nonce n, which must be different for each ChaCha20-Poly1305 algorithm invocation with the same key

- A plaintext p of arbitrary size

- Arbitrary-sized additional authenticated data d

In the first step, the Poly1305 one-time key k_{ot} is generated using the ChaCha20 block function B as described in *Algorithm 10*.

In the second step, the ChaCha20 encryption process C, discussed previously in this chapter and illustrated in *Algorithm 8* is used to encrypt the plaintext p – using the shared key k and nonce n – with the counter ctr value initially set to 1.

In the last step, the Poly1305 algorithm P is executed using the previously generated one-time key k_{ot} and applied to a message obtained from concatenating the following data:

- Additional authenticated data d (recall this is optional data that is exempt from encryption)

- Padding 0_{p1} of up to 15 zero bytes so that the length of padded d is an integer multiple of 16 (if d's length is an integer multiple of 16, 0_{p1} has the length of 0)

- The ciphertext c

- Padding 0_{p2} of up to 15 zero bytes so that the length of the padded ciphertext c is an integer multiple of 16 (again, if c's length is an integer multiple of 16, 0_{p1} has the length of 0)

- The length of d in bytes $len(d)$

- The length of c in bytes $len(c)$

The output of the Poly1305 algorithm P is a 128-bit tag t that the receiving party will use to verify the integrity and authenticity of the received message, in particular, the received ciphertext c. The overall output of the ChaCha20-Poly1305 AEAD construction is, in turn, the pair (c, t), where c is the enciphered plaintext.

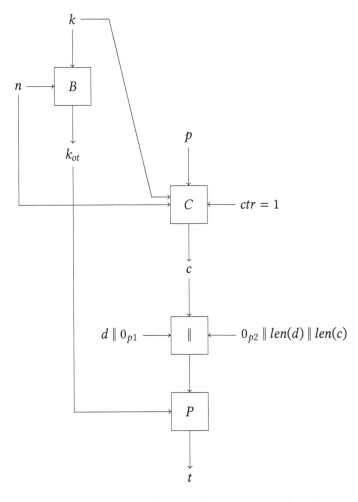

Figure 18.3: The ChaCha20-Poly1305 AEAD algorithm

Decryption using ChaCha20-Poly1305 is almost identical to encryption, except that:

- The ChaCha20 encryption algorithm C is now applied to the ciphertext c, thereby producing the original plaintext p (recall that for ChaCha20, encryption and decryption are identical operations)

- The inputs to the Poly1305 function P are as follows:

  - The padded authenticated data $d \| 0_{p1}$

- The received ciphertext c

- The ciphertext's padding

- The length of c and the length of d: $0_{p2} \parallel len(d) \parallel len(c)$

- Finally, the tag calculated by the receiving party is compared to the received tag, and the message is accepted only if the tags match

Note that one of the benefits of the ChaCha20-Poly1305 AEAD construction is that the *same* key is used for encryption and, effectively, message authentication (because the authentication key is derived from the encryption key using the ChaCha20 block function, as described in the previous section).

18.6 Mandatory-to-implement cipher suites

For compatibility purposes, every TLS endpoint must fulfill a minimum set of requirements. To ensure this, Chapter 9 in RFC 8446 defines three types of compliance requirements:

1. Mandatory-to-implement cipher suites

2. Mandatory-to-implement TLS extensions

3. Protocol invariants that every TLS endpoint and middlebox must follow

If there is no dedicated application profile standard that prescribes different algorithms, TLS 1.3 specification requires a TLS endpoint to implement cipher suites given in *Table 18.2*. Note, however, the difference in the requirement level for the specific cipher suites. The exact meaning of the capital words MUST and SHOULD is defined in IETF RFC 2119, *Key words for use in RFCs to Indicate Requirement Levels*.

The term MUST (or its equivalents, REQUIRED or SHALL) means that the requirement is absolutely mandatory – there is no room for exceptions. In contrast, the term SHOULD (or its equivalent, RECOMMENDED) means that the requirement should be met by default, but there can be situations where the requirement may be ignored for particular reasons. More precisely, to put it in the exact words of RFC 2119, SHOULD means *that there may exist valid reasons in particular circumstances to ignore a particular item, but the full implications must be understood and carefully weighed before choosing a different course. Table 18.2 shows* the requirement levels of the three mandatory-to-implement cipher suites in TLS 1.3.

Cipher suite	Requirement level
TLS_AES_128_GCM_SHA256	MUST
TLS_AES_256_GCM_SHA384	SHOULD
TLS_CHACHA20_POLY1305_SHA256	SHOULD

Table 18.2: Mandatory-to-implement cipher suites in TLS 1.3

Similarly, if no application profile standard is given, TLS 1.3 requires every TLS endpoint to support digital signatures and curves given in *Table 18.3*. The exact meaning of the terms MUST and SHOULD defined in RFC 2119 applies here as well.

Digital signature algorithm or curve	Requirement level
rsa_pkcs1_sha256	MUST
rsa_pss_rsae_sha256	MUST
ecdsa_secp256r1_sha256	MUST
secp256r1	MUST
X25519	SHOULD

Table 18.3: Mandatory-to-implement cipher suites in TLS 1.3

The small number of mandatory-to-implement cipher suites, signature algorithms, and curves greatly reduces the complexity of TLS 1.3 as opposed to earlier versions.

18.7 Summary

In this chapter, we discussed the TLS 1.3 cipher suites, including those that every TLS endpoint must implement. We covered the alternative cipher suite ChaCha20-Poly1305 as well as its building blocks, ChaCha20 block cipher, and Poly1305 message authentication code.

On a more fundamental level, to aid in-depth understanding of TLS cryptography, we discussed how advances in cryptanalysis can affect long-term security, how this risk can be mitigated using cryptographic agility, and how the concept of a standby cipher implements this pattern in TLS 1.3.

This chapter concludes the third part of the book. In the next part, we will change the perspective and look at TLS in general, and TLS 1.3 in particular, from an attacker's point of view. We will first cover attacks on cryptographic schemes and cryptographic protocols from a conceptual, theoretical perspective.

Part 4

Bleeding Hearts and Biting Poodles

In this part, we first give an overview of the attacks on cryptography and then extensively discuss known attacks on previous TLS versions. We show how these attacks work, what TLS security guarantees they undermine, and how the TLS protocol was improved over time to withstand these attacks.

More precisely, we discuss known attacks on the TLS Handshake protocol, on the TLS Record protocol, and on implementations of TLS. After completing this part, you will have a solid understanding of how cryptographic protocols, and in particular, previous TLS versions, are attacked in practice.

This part contains the following chapters:

- *Chapter 19, Attacks on Cryptography*

- *Chapter 20, Attacks on the TLS Handshake Protocol*

- *Chapter 21, Attacks on the TLS Record Protocol*

- *Chapter 22, Attacks on TLS Implementations*

19

Attacks on Cryptography

Winston Churchill, the British statesman and Prime Minister during World War II, famously said: *"Those who fail to learn from history are doomed to repeat it."* This is as valid for cryptography as it is for warfare. In addition, understanding how attacks work – first in general and subsequently on TLS – allows us to build up an in-depth understanding of why TLS is designed the way it is.

In this chapter, we discuss well-known attack types targeting cryptography. We specifically cover attack types relevant to cryptographic protocols such as TLS. The larger part of this chapter deals with attacks on protocols themselves, that is, attacks that are independent of the underlying cryptographic primitives. This is complemented by a brief discussion of attack types targeting cryptographic mechanisms used within a protocol, in particular attacks on encryption schemes and hash functions. We omit attacks on public key cryptography to avoid redundancy since we already discussed the security of Diffie-Hellman key exchange and the security of the RSA cryptosystem in *Chapter 7, Public-Key Cryptography*, and the security of elliptic curves in *Chapter 8, Elliptic Curves*. The security of digital signatures, which are based either on RSA or on elliptic curves, is closely related to the security of these public-key cryptographic primitives and hash functions.

The aim of this chapter is for you to become familiar with the most popular types of attacks on symmetric cryptography and, especially, on cryptographic protocols. This will enable a more in-depth understanding of specific attacks on TLS that we will discuss in the next three chapters.

Recall that the focus of this book is on TLS cryptography. We therefore do not cover popular classes of cyber-attacks such as (distributed) denial of service, traffic analysis, or side-channel attacks, which, instead of cryptography, target the *systems implementing cryptography*. That being said, in *Chapter 22, Attacks on TLS Implementations*, we will look into well-known attacks on TLS implementation, mainly to make you aware of the fact that choosing the right crypto is not enough in practice – you also have to implement, deploy, and operate it in a secure manner.

On completion of the chapter, you will have a good overview of how cryptography – in particular, cryptographic protocols – can be attacked. More precisely, you will know about the following:

- The implications of passive and active as well as local and remote attacks

- The difference between non-interactive and interactive attacks

- The working principle of a number of popular attacks on cryptographic protocols

- Attacks on symmetric encryption schemes and hash functions

19.1   Preliminary remarks

On the most abstract level, a cryptographic protocol such as TLS can be viewed as a cryptographic system, that is, a system that utilizes cryptographic techniques to achieve certain protection goals.

In the present chapter, we will discuss various types of cryptographic attacks. However, we will **not** consider malware-based attacks (see `https://en.wikipedia.org/wiki/`

`Category:Cryptographic_attacks` for a list of various attacks) on end systems where cryptographic algorithms are carried out. The reason for this is that we are mainly interested in the security of cryptographic algorithms, but not in the security of the computing platforms they are running on.

Basically, this means the security of cryptographic systems is evaluated based on the assumption that two important conditions are fulfilled:

- There is some kind of secret – maybe shared, as in symmetric key cryptography, or maybe private, as in Diffie-Hellman key exchange – that is unknown to the adversary.

- The intermediate values of a cryptographic algorithm are not known to the adversary. Take, for example, an iterated block cipher such as AES. If the input and the output for each round and the corresponding sub-operations were known, it would be easy for an attacker to determine the secret key.

A sufficiently powerful malware infecting Alice's computer could essentially read any memory location at any time and thus read any intermediate values. Any subsequent security breaches are not the fault of the cryptographic algorithms used by Alice, however.

Or, to give another example, a malware could see to it that an infected system simply skips (or ignores the result of) a MAC verification step, thereby making it possible for the attacker to send arbitrary code to the victim system and get it executed. Again, this security breach is independent of the underlying MAC algorithm.

19.2 Passive versus active attacks

Arguably, passive and active attacks are the two most fundamental categories describing attacks on cryptography. We already introduced the corresponding attacker models in *Section 2.2* of *Chapter 2, Secure Channel and the CIA Triad*, where we also met two different attackers, Eve (passive) and Mallory (active).

To recap, a passive attack is an attack where the adversary, Eve, is only *eavesdropping* on a communication between the legitimate parties Alice and Bob. In other words, as illustrated in *Figure 19.1*, Eve can only read the (hopefully cryptographically protected) communication messages.

Consequently, a passive attack is only a threat to the confidentiality of information exchanged between Alice and Bob. Importantly, Eve cannot manipulate Alice's or Bob's messages or inject her own messages.

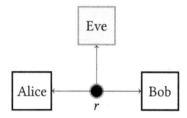

Figure 19.1: In a passive attack, Eve can observe the communication between Alice and Bob

In contrast, in an active attack, the adversary, Mallory, is not only able to read the communication, but may also delete, add, or manipulate messages. In *Figure 19.2*, this ability is indicated by the arrow pointing both ways: to Mallory for her ability to read and from Mallory for her ability to manipulate the communication between Alice and Bob.

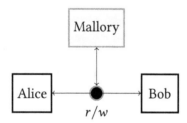

Figure 19.2: In an active attack, Mallory can also manipulate or inject messages

As a result, in addition to compromising confidentiality, an active attack can also compromise the integrity and authenticity of messages sent and received by Alice and Bob. In practice, message integrity and authenticity are often more important than confidentiality because integrity and authenticity are required for safe operation of any cyber-physical system, whereas confidentiality is not. So, active attacks are not only more powerful but are often more dangerous than passive attacks.

19.3 Local versus remote attacks

Geographic constraints imposed on the attacker form the second fundamental attack characteristic in practical cryptography and information security. *Figure 19.3* shows a *local* attack where Mallory needs to be co-located with Bob. What the term *co-located* exactly means depends on the specific attack.

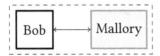

Figure 19.3: Local attack

In some cases, the term *co-located* refers to Mallory residing on the same machine. As an example, imagine an attack where Mallory tries to steal Bob's password from the password file stored on a machine running a Linux operating system that is not connected to the internet. An example might be a machine in a factory. To perform such an attack, Mallory must be logged in on the same system like Bob and therefore must be able to get into the vicinity of that system.

In other cases, a local attack may require Mallory to be connected to the same local network as Bob. If Bob's machines on his computer network trust each other by default and allow every access from within the network, Mallory only needs to get access to that network to extract confidential documents.

What both examples have in common is that Mallory's geographic location is constrained by that of Bob. Of course, a **Local Area Network (LAN)** could span one or more buildings or even an entire campus. Furthermore, the site where the machine storing the password file is located could be in a huge manufacturing facility. Nevertheless, all these locations – however large they might be – are geographically confined.

In some cases, Mallory needs to physically access Bob's hardware. As illustrated in *Figure 19.4*, Mallory gets *inside* Bob's machine or device to be able to directly interact with Bob's hardware.

A prominent example of an attack exploiting physical access is the hacking of embedded devices via JTAG, a standard debug interface on microcontrollers used in such devices. Being designed for debugging and testing, JTAG allows access to and the modification of internal registers and memory, including re-programming and re-configuring the microcontroller. As a result, if Mallory gets access to Bob's JTAG interface, she can easily compromise Bob's system without ever breaking a cryptographic mechanism.

Figure 19.4: Attack requiring physical access

In a remote attack, shown in *Figure 19.5*, Mallory is able to compromise Bob's security from a remote geographical location, typically over the internet. In contrast to a local attack, Mallory has no direct or physical access to Bob's machine. Mallory instead uses poorly protected (or open) network ports or exploits vulnerabilities in the network-facing software or system configuration to gain unauthorized access to Bob's machine.

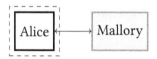

Figure 19.5: Remote attack

On 27 June 2017, a new malware variant — eventually dubbed *NotPetya* by the internet security company Kaspersky who were first to discover the malware — started spreading in Ukraine, France, Germany, Italy, Poland, the United Kingdom, and the United States.

The hackers behind NotPetya initially compromised the software update mechanism of M.E.Doc, a tax software very popular among Ukrainian businesses, by inserting a backdoor. The backdoor remained dormant for at least 6 weeks prior to the attack. Forensic analysis of M.E.Doc's servers revealed that software updates were not applied since 2013, uncovered hacker presence, and a compromised employee's account on the update servers.

The malware subsequently started to quickly spread over networks by exploiting a security vulnerability in Windows operating systems called *EternalBlue*. EternalBlue, a security flaw in the **Server Message Block (SMB)** protocol used for sharing files over Windows networks, was originally discovered by the NSA. It allowed NotPetya to gain access to vulnerable Windows systems without user interaction. By exploiting EternalBlue, the malware was able to spread laterally across computer networks, infecting entire organizations in a very short period of time.

A.P. Moller Maersk A/S, the Copenhagen-based shipping company that transports about 20% of all global shipments, was among the approximately 600 companies hit by NotPetya. Maersk's chief information security officer, Andrew Powell, gave a talk about the incident at Black Hat Europe 2019. According to his account, once a Maersk user was infected in the Odessa office, the malware spread so fast through the Maersk global network that most damage was done within *seven minutes* [139].

Once it infected a system, NotPetya encrypted files and overwrote the system's **Master Boot Record (MBR)**, thereby making the infected system completely unusable. *Figure 19.6* shows the ransom note displayed by the malware on an infected system.

According to Powell, the malware destroyed 49,000 laptops, more than 1,000 applications, all file-sharing systems, the enterprise service bus, VMware vCenter cloud-management servers, and Maersk's DHCP and Active Directory servers at Maersk. Even worse, because NotPetya was designed to also destroy online backups, Maersk's primary and backup Active Directory systems were both irrecoverably damaged [139].

Due to good fortune, Maersk's Lagos office had suffered a power outage while NotPetya was spreading through the company's global network. As a result, Lagos' IT systems, including the backup of Maersk's Active Directory, were not damaged. Subsequently, the Lagos AD node was physically removed and flown to Copenhagen to rebuild the systems from scratch — a process that took over a week.

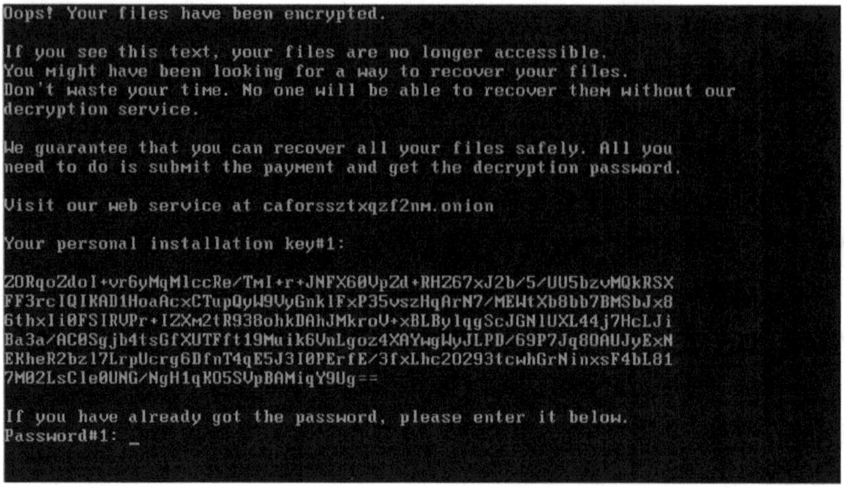

Figure 19.6: Ransom note displayed by NotPetya [156]

Andrew Powell has estimated that NotPetya caused damage, including the cost of recovery efforts, of about $300 million. This is close to the estimates for other large companies, such as the US pharmaceutical giant Merck and the logistics giant FedEx, where, according to the estimates, NotPetya incurred more than $300 million damage in lost business and recovery costs [139].

According to an article published by the Wired online magazine [77], the US White House assessed the total damage inflicted by NotPetya as more than $10 billion. That estimate was confirmed by the former Homeland Security advisor Tom Bassert, who was the most senior cybersecurity official in the US government at the time of the NotPetya attack.

19.3.1   The scalability of local and remote attacks

Why do we care whether an attack is local or remote? The answer is scalability – an attack characteristic closely related to the economic concept of marginal cost. In economics, the marginal cost of goods refers to the additional cost incurred by producing one more unit of those goods. Similarly, the scalability of an attack refers to the additional cost, time, or effort Mallory has to invest to attack one more system or user. If the attack's marginal cost is low, its scalability is high.

Take, for instance, modern cars. One way to attack a vehicle's safety-relevant functionality – albeit not related to information security – is to cut its brake line carrying brake fluid under pressure to activate the brakes. Although somewhat hypothetical, this example is quite illustrative.

In principle, the attack would work. However, it would require Mallory to visit the geographic location of every car she wants to attack. If Mallory were to attack 10,000 vehicles, assuming a 15-minute average attack time per vehicle and 10 hours a day where Mallory can engage gives:

$$10,000/(4 \times 10) = 250 \text{ days}$$

Attacking 100,000 vehicles, therefore, would require 2,500 days or more than 6.5 years, not to mention the financial attack cost. Clearly, such an attack does not scale in practice.

In comparison, assume Mallory knows a zero-day vulnerability that – similar to the famous Jeep hack by Miller and Valasek [120] – can be used to disturb one or more safety-critical **Electronic Control Units** (**ECUs**). If Mallory knows the IP addresses of vulnerable vehicles – an assumption we must make following Kerckhoff's principle from *Chapter 3, A Secret to Share* – she can use an automated script to attack 100,000 cars within a few hours.

Moreover, in contrast to cutting the brake line, Mallory doesn't even need to know how the 0-day vulnerability works; she only needs access to the exploit code. Obviously, such a remote attack is highly scalable and, therefore, a much more serious concern in practice.

19.4 Interactive versus non-interactive attacks

In an *interactive* or *online* attack, Mallory must maintain a connection to and actively interact with her attack target Alice over the *entire* duration of the attack.

Figure 19.7 illustrates the working principle of an interactive attack. To carry out the attack, Mallory sends consecutive requests to Alice and processes Alice's responses until the attack succeeds (or Mallory runs out of computational resources or time).

As an example, assume that Alice runs an SSH server configured to accept a username and a password at the login prompt. In that case, Mallory's attempt to guess that username and password is an interactive attack. The only way Mallory can check whether her guess is correct is by actually entering the guess into Alice's login prompt and, subsequently – maybe with the help of a script, checking whether the login attempt was successful or not. Hence, Mallory must actively interact with Alice for every new guess.

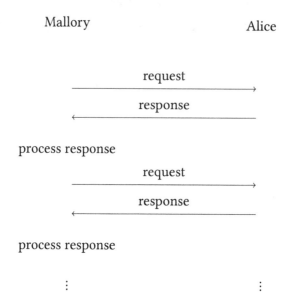

Figure 19.7: Working principle of an interactive attack

In contrast, in a *non-interactive* or *offline* attack, Mallory is able to do the computations offline, without having to interact with Alice. In addition, a non-interactive attack is *verifiable* in the following ways:

- Mallory is able to confirm whether the attack succeeded or not *before* interacting with Alice

- Mallory can recover a long-term secret using offline computation subsequent to an interaction with Alice

Figure 19.8 illustrates the working principle of a non-interactive attack. In this example, Mallory first interacts with Alice and receives Alice's response. Mallory then goes on to process the response offline, without interacting with Alice. After she succeeds (or runs out of computational resources or time), Mallory exploits the results to mount an attack.

A non-interactive attack can be thought of as being composed of two phases. During the initial *online phase*, Mallory acquires the required information. Then, during the *offline phase*, Mallory uses that information to carry out computations to break Alice's security.

As an example, assume that Mallory obtains a copy of the password file from Alice's machine. The password file typically contains hashes rather than plaintext passwords, so Mallory cannot exploit this information directly. However, she can use all the hardware at her disposal to compute hashes for all words from a large dictionary. To perform these computations, Mallory does not need to interact with Alice. Moreover, if Mallory finds a hash value identical to one of those stored in Alice's password file, she knows that the password guess is correct with overwhelming probability. In other words, she can verify that the attack was successful before (again) interacting with Alice.

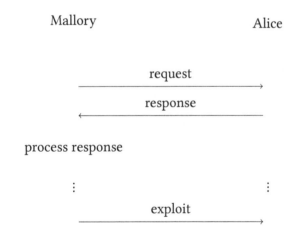

Figure 19.8: Working principle of a non-interactive attack

In general, a non-interactive attack is more dangerous than an interactive attack. Why? Because in an interactive attack, Mallory is constrained by network capabilities such as bandwidth and latency. In the preceding example, every username and password must be transmitted to Alice, and Alice's response must be sent back to Mallory over the network.

So, the network's speed (and how fast Alice processes the login attempt) limits how many combinations Mallory can test in a given time.

More importantly, because Mallory needs to test a large number of username-password pairs, it is easy for Alice to detect the attack. In fact, Alice can easily prevent the attack, for example, by limiting the number of login attempts before locking the account for a predefined period of time.

If Mallory, on the other hand, can mount a non-interactive attack, she can use all the computing power she can afford – checking tens of thousands of username-password combinations per second – without Alice ever being able to notice that.

19.5 Attacks on cryptographic protocols

Recall from *Chapter 2 Secure Channel and the CIA Triad*, that a **cryptographic protocol** is a distributed algorithm defined by a sequence of steps precisely specifying the actions required of two or more entities to achieve a specific cryptographic goal [117].

Attacks on cryptographic protocols typically do not attack the cryptographic primitives they are built of, but the sequence of messages making up the protocol. An attack on a protocol is considered successful if any of the cryptographic goals of the protocol (confidentiality, entity authenticity, or message authenticity) are endangered.

19.5.1 Impersonation attacks

An *impersonation attack* is any deception attempt where Mallory claims to be another entity, say, Bob. What Mallory technically does to trick Alice into believing she is talking to Bob depends on the technical solution used by Alice to verify the identity of her communication peers. Popular examples of such mechanisms, which we also covered in previous chapters, are passwords, secret keys, and digital certificates.

While impersonation attacks are an immediate threat to entity authentication, in many practical scenarios, the ultimate goal of an impersonation attack is to compromise *authorization* and *access control*. While authorization is a security objective that ensures that the policy defining which user is allowed to do what on a given system is adhered to, access control ensures that only authorized users can access the system's resources.

As shown in *Figure 19.9*, if Mallory successfully tricks Alice into believing she is Bob, Alice will grant Mallory Bob's privileges. As a result, Mallory will be able to access all resources that Bob can access and interact with the system in any way that Bob is authorized to do.

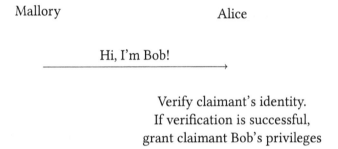

Figure 19.9: Working principle of an impersonation attack

19.5.2 Man-in-the-middle attacks

In a *man-in-the-middle attack*, Mallory secretly places herself between Alice and Bob to either compromise the confidentiality or integrity of their communication. More precisely, Mallory interacts with the communication between Alice and Bob to either read or manipulate their (or insert her own) messages.

Most practical man-in-the-middle attacks work because Alice and Bob believe they are talking directly to each other while, in reality, Mallory sits between them and runs two separate communication sessions, one with Alice and one with Bob. As such, it is an active attack. We do not consider a scenario in which Eve sits between Alice and Bob, merely listening to their communication, to be a man-in-the-middle attack.

We have already encountered an important example of a man-in-the-middle attack in *Figure 7.3*.

Recall from *Chapter 7, Public-Key Cryptography*, that using the Diffie-Hellman protocol, Alice and Bob establish a shared secret k over an insecure communication channel using the following protocol steps:

1. Alice and Bob publicly agree on a cyclic group G and a corresponding generator g.

2. Alice chooses a natural number α, where $1 < \alpha < N$, where N is the order of G. α is *Alice's Private Key SK$_{Alice}$*. She must not disclose this number to any other party.

3. Bob does the same as Alice: he independently chooses a number $1 < \beta < N$ as his private key SK_{Bob}.

4. Alice computes $A = g^\alpha$ in G and sends A to Bob. The number A (together with G and g) can be seen as *Alice's public key*: $PK_{Alice} = (g, G, A)$.

5. Bob computes $B = g^\beta$ in G and sends B to Alice. The number B (together with G and g) can be seen as *Bob's public key*: $PK_{Bob} = (g, G, B)$.

6. Alice computes $K_A = B^\alpha$. Bob computes $K_B = A^\beta$. However, both compute the same value k, because

$$K_A = B^\alpha = (g^\beta)^\alpha = g^{\beta\alpha} = g^{\alpha\beta} = (g^\alpha)^\beta = K_B$$

Alice and Bob can easily compute K_A and K_B, respectively, by computing the powers of group elements. Mallory, on the other hand, would have to solve the discrete logarithm problem for computing K_A or K_B, which is believed to be computationally hard. However, if Alice and Bob do not authenticate each others' public keys, Mallory can place herself in the middle and create two communication channels, as shown in *Figure 19.10*.

In this attack, Mallory intercepts Bob's public key $B = g^\beta$, replaces it with her own public key $M = g^\mu$, and sends M to Alice. Because no message authentication is used, Alice cannot verify that M is not Bob's public key and replies to Mallory (who she erroneously believes to be Bob) with her public key $A = g^\alpha$. In the meantime, Mallory sends Bob her public key M instead of Alice's public key A. Bob also cannot detect that he is actually talking to Mallory and not to Alice.

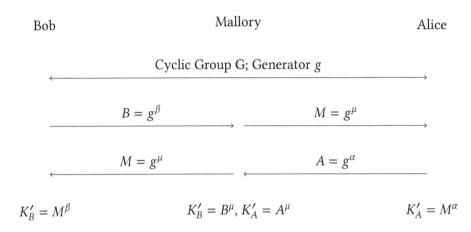

Figure 19.10: Example of a man-in-the-middle attack on unauthenticated Diffie-Hellman key exchange (see also Figure 7.3)

Finally, Alice and Bob compute the shared secret key as $K'_A = M^\alpha$ and $K'_B = M^\beta$ without noticing that they exchanged a key with Mallory rather than with each other. Instead of communicating with each other, Alice and Bob now communicate with Mallory. From this moment on, Mallory can decrypt Bob's messages using K'_B, re-encrypt them using K'_A, and pass them to Alice (and vice versa by re-encrypting Alice's messages using K'_B). Moreover, Mallory can insert any message of her choice by encrypting it using K'_A or K'_B.

A high-profile example of a man-in-the-middle attack is the incident that followed the compromise of Dutch certification authority DigiNotar in 2011. The attack started when one or more hackers breached DigiNotar's web server hosting a vulnerable content management application. The hackers then moved laterally, eventually gaining access to a network segment where all of DigiNotar's root secrets were stored [150].

The root secrets were used to generate the first batch of 128 rogue certificates. This was followed by several more batches, resulting in at least 531 certificates for 53 unique entities. Because the logs of the compromised servers were found to be manipulated and a large number of certificates later discovered in the wild were absent from appropriate databases, it is unknown how many rogue certificates the attackers generated in total.

Because the rogue certificates were generated with embedded OCSP information, the subsequent forensic investigation of DigiNotar's breach was able to track the certificate deployment by examining DigiNotar's OCSP responder logs [150]. The rogue certificates, as it turned out, were used to compromise Iranian Gmail users.

In the days following the breach, an estimated 300,000 IP addresses – the actual man-in-the-middle attack – were presented with fake certificates. Almost all of those IP addresses were located in Iran. The attackers intercepted users attempting to connect to Google's Gmail server and, with the help of a rogue certificate, presented the users with a fake website to collect their Gmail passwords. In total, a staggering 654,313 OCSP requests for the rogue Google certificate were submitted from 298,140 unique IP addresses, 95% of which were within Iran.

19.5.3   Replay attacks

As the name suggests, in a *replay attack*, Mallory reuses or replays information – typically, a message – that she recorded during a previous protocol run. Mallory can replay the message to the same communication party – for instance, sending Alice a message that was originally sent by Alice herself – or to some different communication party – for instance, sending Alice a message that was originally sent by Bob. Despite the original message being authenticated by means of a MAC or a digital signature, the replayed message might still be accepted by Alice as authentic. Replay attacks therefore threaten message authenticity.

The equivalent of a replay attack on persistently stored files is a *restore attack* where Mallory replaces one or more files on Alice's machine with their earlier versions. This might be very dangerous if the files contain configuration data, especially the configuration of network-facing software such as a web server or a firewall. In a restore attack, Mallory can ingest a configuration that is known to be vulnerable – for example, due to a vulnerable software package the web server relies on – and, thus, introduce a weakness she can later on exploit.

The working principle of a replay attack is illustrated in *Figure 19.11*. Alice and Bob use a keyed hash function h_k – effectively, a MAC – to protect the integrity and authenticity of their messages. If no time stamp or nonce (such as a random number or a counter) is used as part of the input for calculating the MAC, Mallory can store the message $D, h(D)$ and, later on, replay it.

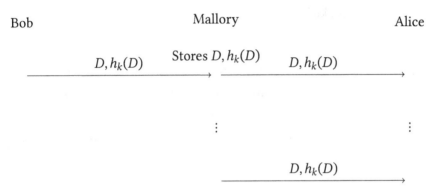

Figure 19.11: Working principle of a replay attack

Now, imagine that Alice is a controller of an automated gate, and the message $D, h(D)$ opens the gate. In our example, it is sufficient for Mallory to capture the message once, when Bob opens the gate. From then on, Mallory can always open the gate by replaying $D, h(D)$. Importantly, this does not require any cryptanalysis and so the attack would work even if the underlying keyed hash function is cryptographically strong.

The reason why a replay attack works in the preceding example is the missing verification of messages' *timeliness* or *freshness*. In other words, because no time stamp, nonce, or other means of contextualization are used, Alice has no way to verify that $D, h(D)$ was not previously sent.

A practical example of a replay attack is so-called *cookie hijacking*. Because HTTP is a stateless protocol, cookies were traditionally the only – and they are still the prevailing – option for persistently storing data on the client.

Persistent cookies are stored on the client's hard drive as long as their expiry date is valid and are frequently used for user identification. A typical example is the case of consecutive visits to a web application.

Web browsers store cookies in known file system locations and in known formats. Thus, if Mallory obtains access to Bob's computer or is able to eavesdrop on the communication between Bob and the web server, she can steal Bob's cookie for some web application, replay a message (URL, cookie), and gain access to that URL as Bob – possibly triggering some action if the web application has a RESTful API.

As an example, assume a web application offers detailed weather information under `https://www.weather.xyz` for payment. Assume further the application uses cookies containing a data item `userID` to identify users. If the application processes HTTP requests to `https://www.weather.xyz` without additionally authenticating the user, Mallory can perform the HTTP requests as Bob if she obtains Bob's cookie.

19.5.4   Interleaving attacks

An *interleaving attack* is a special type of replay attack where Mallory executes multiple protocol sessions in parallel to compromise the protocol's security. Interleaving attacks are hard to spot even for seasoned cryptographers, so we'll use a concrete example to show how such attacks work.

Figure 19.12 shows a cryptographic protocol for establishing a shared secret key. First, Alice sends Bob her name A and a nonce N_A so Bob knows who is trying to communicate with him.

Upon receiving Alice's message, Bob sends a message to the server containing his name B, his nonce N_B, and the pair (A, N_A) encrypted under the secret key k_{BS} shared by Bob and the server. The server, in turn, sends Alice a message containing the following data:

- Bob's nonce N_B

- The triple (B, k_{AB}, N_A) encrypted under secret key k_{AS}, shared by Alice and the server

- The triple (A, k_{AB}, N_B) encrypted under secret key k_{BS}, shared by Bob and the server where k_{AB} is a shared session key that the server generated for Alice and Bob. The first triple (B, k_{AB}, N_A) does the following:

- Tells Alice that the server has indeed been talking to Bob

- Demonstrates that the server's message is fresh (since it contains Alice's nonce N_A)

- Gives Alice the session key k_{AB}

The second triple (A, k_{AB}, N_B) is to be passed to Bob. So, in the final message of the protocol, Alice sends (A, k_{AB}, N_B), encrypted under k_{BS}, and N_B encrypted under k_{AB} to Bob. This message tells Bob that the server has indeed recently talked to Alice (via N_B) and gives him the session key k_{AB}. Moreover, because Alice used the session key k_{AB} to encrypt Bob's nonce N_B, Bob is assured that Alice obtained the session key recently – that is, it guarantees the freshness of this message and that of the session key.

At first glance, the protocol in *Figure 19.12* appears to be secure. It allows Alice and Bob to verify the freshness of the messages they receive and since the session key k_{AB} is generated by the trusted server, there is seemingly no way to compromise security. In reality, however, that protocol is vulnerable to an interleaving attack [170].

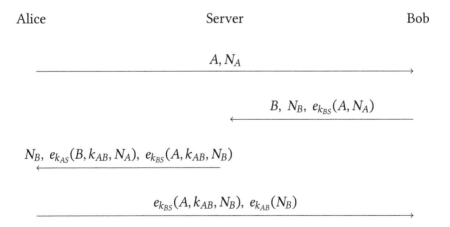

Figure 19.12: Example of a key establishment protocol vulnerable to an interleaving attack

Figure 19.13 illustrates an interleaving attack on the key establishment protocol we just introduced. The attack starts with Mallory either eavesdropping on the initial message from Alice to Bob (alternatively, Mallory could send that message herself). Upon receiving Alice's message, Bob sends a message to the server containing his name B, his nonce N_B, and the pair (A, N_A) encrypted under the secret key k_{BS} shared by Bob and the server. So far, the protocol execution is the same as in the benign case shown in *Figure 19.12*.

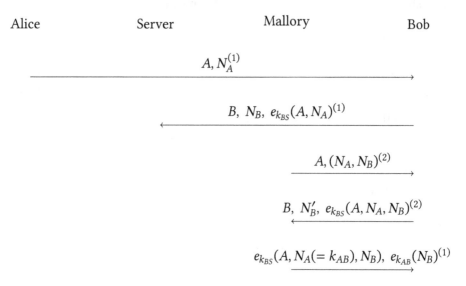

Alice	Server	Mallory	Bob

$$A, N_A^{(1)}$$

$$B,\ N_B,\ e_{k_{BS}}(A, N_A)^{(1)}$$

$$A, (N_A, N_B)^{(2)}$$

$$B,\ N_B',\ e_{k_{BS}}(A, N_A, N_B)^{(2)}$$

$$e_{k_{BS}}(A, N_A(= k_{AB}), N_B),\ e_{k_{AB}}(N_B)^{(1)}$$

Figure 19.13: Interleaving attack on a key establishment protocol

However, after Bob's message to Alice, Mallory initiates a second protocol run pretending to be Alice. She concatenates the nonces from the first protocol run and uses the result (N_A, N_B) as the nonce in the first message of the *second* protocol run. In *Figure 19.13*, messages from the first run are denoted by [(1)] and those from the second protocol by [(2)].

Upon receiving the message $A, (N_A, N_B)^*$ – which Bob believes to come from Alice – Bob responds with a message to the server. In the benign case, this message would be $B,\ N_B,\ e_{k_{BS}}(A, N_A)$. However, because Alice manipulated this message by replacing N_A with (N_A, N_B), Bob responds with $B,\ N_B',\ e_{k_{BS}}(A, N_A, N_B)$. Here, N_B' denotes a nonce Bob chose in the second protocol run that is different from N_B used in the first protocol run.

Mallory intercepts Bob's response B, N'_B, $e_{k_{BS}}(A, N_A, N_B)^{(2)}$ and ends the second protocol run. She then uses the encrypted chunk $e_{k_{BS}}(A, N_A, N_B)$ to construct the last message for the first protocol run:

$$e_{k_{BS}}(A, N_A(= k_{AB}), N_B), \ e_{k_{AB}}(N_B).$$

Because Bob's nonce N_B was previously transmitted in plaintext, the session key k_{AB} is actually N_A and was also transmitted in plaintext, Mallory can compute $e_{k_{AB}}(N_B)$.

As a result, Mallory has successfully impersonated Alice while communicating with Bob and obtained the session key. The attack is an interleaving attack because Mallory uses multiple protocol runs to construct the elements of the last message $e_{k_{BS}}(A, N_A(= k_{AB}), N_B)$, $e_{k_{AB}}(N_B)$. Without the parallel second protocol run, Mallory would not be able to perform the attack.

19.5.5   Reflection attacks

A *reflection attack* is a specific type of an interleaving attack where Mallory sends data she received from Bob in one protocol run back to him in another protocol run. Essentially, Mallory reflects the data back to Bob – hence the name of the attack – in an attempt to trick Bob into providing the answer to his own challenge.

Reflection attacks typically target challenge-response entity authentication protocols. Let's look at a specific example to understand how these attacks work. *Figure 19.14* shows an example challenge-response protocol from [7]. To authenticate Bob, Alice generates a nonce N and sends it to Bob (in clear text). Upon receiving N, Bob encrypts it with the secret key k he shares with Alice and replies with the message $e_k(N)$.

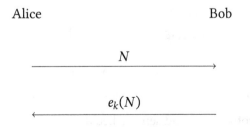

Figure 19.14: Example of a simple challenge-response protocol

Finally, Alice decrypts Bob's message and compares the decrypted nonce with the nonce she sent to Bob. If the two match, Alice knows that the communicating party claiming to be Bob knows the shared secret key k and, therefore, must be Bob.

The protocol can also be initiated by Bob. In that case, Bob generates the nonce and sends it to Alice so she can respond with the encrypted nonce. Bob then verifies Alice's response as a means of verifying her identity.

While the protocol might seem robust at first glance, it is vulnerable to the reflection attack illustrated in *Figure 19.15*:

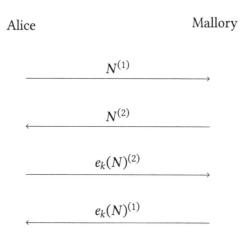

Figure 19.15: Working principle of a reflection attack

Here, Mallory wants to impersonate Bob. After receiving the nonce N from Alice, Mallory creates a second protocol run – messages denoted by $^{(2)}$ – while pretending to be Bob.

However, instead of sending Alice a new nonce, Mallory simply reflects N back to Alice, thereby tricking Alice into providing the response $e_k(N)$ to her own challenge. Mallory then drops the second protocol run and sends Alice the correct response $e_k(N)$ in the first protocol run.

One way to prevent a reflection attack is to include the names of the authenticating parties in the protocol's messages. If Alice's challenge was (A, N) instead of just N, Mallory would not be able to reflect that challenge back to Alice without Alice detecting it. This also explains why it is desirable to have names in protocol messages, authenticate all messages (including the challenge), or use different keys for transmitted and received messages.

We now turn to generic attacks on cryptographic primitives. Mostly, we will discuss the attacks on a conceptual level, as they apply to all encryption or hash algorithms irrespective of their concrete incarnation.

19.6 Attacks on encryption schemes

If Eve attacks an encryption scheme utilizing available ciphertext, she can try to recover either the plaintext of the encrypted messages or the secret key itself used by the encryption scheme.

Recovery of the secret key is typically considered a stronger attack (or, equivalently, a more severe security compromise) than deducing plaintext from the ciphertext. As an example, if Alice and Bob use some standard, pre-defined messages that significantly vary in size – that is, to an extent that is not compensated by padding – Eve can easily guess the plaintext for a given ciphertext even if the encryption scheme is perfectly secret.

On the other hand, to determine the secret key, Eve must find statistical relations between the plaintext and the ciphertext. As far as we know, this is practically impossible for standardized ciphers, let alone for perfectly secret encryption schemes.

19.6.1 Brute-force attack

A *brute-force attack* is simply an exhaustive key search. If Eve attacks a b-bit block cipher that uses an n-bit key and she is given a small number – say, $(n + 4)/b$ – of plaintext-ciphertext pairs encrypted under key k, she can expect to determine k using a brute-force attack after about 2^{k-1} encryption operations *on average*.

How come Eve needs 2^{k-1} encryption operations on average? This is because Eve progresses through the entire key space and, as a result, can expect to find the right key after searching half the key space [117].

19.6.2   Forward search attack

A *forward search attack* can be thought of as a special case of a brute-force attack. If the message space used by Alice and Bob is small or predictable – that is, if the number of plaintext messages that Alice and Bob can possibly send is small or their messages are predictable – Eve can recover the plaintext corresponding to a ciphertext c she observes simply by encrypting all plaintext candidates until she obtains c.

Note that a secure cipher alone does not protect Alice and Bob against this vulnerability. As an example, while AES is considered to be a strong encryption algorithm, the use of AES in ECB mode with a small or predictable message space is nevertheless susceptible to a forward search attack. To protect the confidentiality of their messages, Alice and Bob must instead use probabilistic encryption where two identical plaintexts are never encrypted to the same ciphertext.

19.6.3   Ciphertext-only attack

In a *ciphertext-only attack* (sometimes referred to as a *known ciphertext attack*), Eve tries to deduce either the plaintext or the key used during encryption based solely on the ciphertext she observes. In other words, Eve has no information about the corresponding plaintext. If an encryption scheme is vulnerable to a ciphertext-only attack, it is considered completely insecure.

19.6.4   Known-plaintext attack

In a *known-plaintext attack*, Eve has access to plaintext-ciphertext pairs, that is, to the ciphertext and the corresponding plaintext. Eve's goal is to recover the key used to encrypt the plaintexts.

The known-plaintext attack has its roots in World War II cryptanalysis. British cryptanalysts at Bletchley Park who broke the German Enigma encryption system used a technique based on so-called *cribs*. A crib was a plain language passage believed to occur in an encrypted message.

For example, the daily weather report transmitted by the German military contained the word *Wetter* (German for weather) at the same location in every such message because of style guidelines of military reports. Using cribs, the cryptanalysts were able to test key hypotheses – effectively performing an exhaustive key search – until the correct key for that day was found.

19.6.5 Chosen-plaintext attack

A *chosen-plaintext attack* resembles the known-plaintext attack, but with a fundamental difference that Eve is able to obtain ciphertexts for any plaintexts of her choice. Conceptually, Eve is said to have access to an encryption oracle we introduced in *Chapter 15, Authenticated Encryption*. After querying the encryption oracle, Eve's goal is to recover the secret key.

19.6.6 Padding oracle attacks

Padding oracle attacks exploit the padding validation of encrypted messages – typically in CBC mode decryption – and are a well-known practical example of a chosen-plaintext attack. A typical CBC implementation decrypts all ciphertext blocks, verifies that the padding is correct, removes the padding, and returns the plaintext of the encrypted message. A popular padding is the so-called *PKCS#7* padding defined in RFC 5652 where the value of each added byte is the number of bytes that are added:

```
01
02 02
03 03 03
04 04 04 04
05 05 05 05 05
06 06 06 06 06 06
...
```

Eve exploits the regularity in PKCS#7 padding by crafting specific ciphertexts and submitting them, for instance, to a web server. If that server is vulnerable to padding oracle attacks, it will return an error message indicating invalid padding. This information effectively turns the server into a padding oracle (hence the name of the attack).

But how does the attack work in detail? Recall that the CBC mode of operation works by first setting the initial ciphertext block c_0 to a randomly chosen initialization vector IV. It then computes every subsequent ciphertext block by XORing the plaintext block with the previous ciphertext block and encrypting the result with the underlying block cipher:

$$
\begin{aligned}
c_0 &= IV \\
c_i &= F_k(c_{i-1}) \oplus m_i
\end{aligned}
$$

and the corresponding decryption is computed as:

$$
\begin{aligned}
p_i &= F_k^{-1}(c_i) \oplus c_{i-1} \\
c_0 &= IV
\end{aligned}
$$

where F_k denotes the encryption and F_k^{-1} denotes the decryption of a single plaintext or ciphertext block under key k.

Now, suppose Eve has two ciphertext blocks c_1, c_2 and she wants to recover the corresponding plaintext block p_2. Eve changes the last byte of c_1 to obtain a manipulated ciphertext c_1' and sends (IV, c_1', c_2) to the vulnerable server.

The server, in turn, decrypts the manipulated ciphertext (IV, c_1', c_2) and returns an error message if the padding of the decrypted block p_2' is not valid PKCS#7 padding. If, on the other hand, no error message is returned – that is, if p_2''s padding is valid – Eve learns that the last byte of $F_k^{-1}(c_2) \oplus c_1'$ is 0x01. Because Eve knows c_1' and $F_k^{-1}(c_2) = p_2$, it is trivial for her to calculate the plaintext block p_2 as:

$$
F_k^{-1}(c_2) = p_2 = 0x1 \oplus c_1'
$$

Next, Eve manipulates the last two bytes of c_1 until the server returns no error, that is, until the last two bytes are equal to the valid PKCS#7 padding 0x02 0x02. Recall that Eve already knows the value of c_1's last byte to make $F_k^{-1}(c_2) \oplus c_1'$ equal to `0x01` and so can trivially set c_1's last byte to make that value `0x02`. Eve, therefore, only needs to guess the value of a single byte – namely, the second-last byte of c_1 – which amounts to merely 256 possibilities. She can continue the attack for the remaining bytes of c_2 and, as a result, recover the entire p_2.

The padding oracle attack was originally discovered by the French cryptographer Serge Vaudeney in 2002. SSL, the predecessor of TLS, and the IPSec protocols were vulnerable to this attack.

19.6.7 Adaptive chosen-plaintext attack

In an *adaptive chosen-plaintext attack*, Eve may choose the plaintext depending on the ciphertexts received previously from an encryption oracle. Whereas in a chosen-plaintext attack, Eve has to select the plaintexts *before* the attack begins, in an adaptive chosen-plaintext attack she can choose the plaintext based on the information gathered during the attack.

19.6.8 Chosen-ciphertext attack

In a *chosen-ciphertext attack*, Eve is able to choose ciphertexts for which she then obtains the corresponding plaintexts. In other words, Eve has access to a decryption oracle.

Eve can mount a chosen-ciphertext attack by gaining access to Bob's hardware performing the decryption operation. Obviously, this attack model assumes that Eve cannot directly access the secret key, which is a reasonable assumption given that keys can be stored in a secure memory that cannot be read by the main processor.

Eve's goal is to later on – specifically, without accessing Bob's hardware – deduce the plaintexts for ciphertexts she has not previously seen.

19.6.9 Adaptive chosen-ciphertext attack

If Eve launches an *adaptive chosen-ciphertext attack*, she may choose the ciphertext she wants to submit to the decryption oracle based on a plaintext she received for one or more of the previously submitted ciphertexts.

More formally, an adaptive chosen-ciphertext attack allows Eve to first submit a number of adaptively chosen ciphertexts to be decrypted by a decryption oracle and then attack the encryption scheme based on the results, without querying the oracle with the challenge ciphertext.

19.7 Attacks on hash functions

Recall from *Chapter 11, Hash Functions and Message Authentication Codes*, that a hash function h maps a string of arbitrary length onto a string of fixed length. In this setting, *collisions*, that is, different inputs x_1, x_2 having the same output $h(x_1) = h(x_2)$ have to occur at some point.

In *Chapter 11, Hash Functions and Message Authentication Codes*, we also defined two important properties for a hash function to be considered secure: **Collision Resistance** and the **One-Way Property**. In a nutshell, the first of these properties makes it difficult for Eve to actually find collisions, whereas the second makes it difficult to find *pre-images*, that is to find a matching input string x for a given hash value $h(x)$. All of the attacks in the current section are aimed either at finding collisions or finding pre-images.

19.7.1 Birthday attack

A *birthday attack* exploits the probability of collisions in a hash function – a mathematical property of such functions rooted in probability theory – in order to find two messages that have the same hash value.

Recall from *Chapter 11, Hash Functions and Message Authentication Codes*, that a secure cryptographic hash function must be *second-pre-image resistant*. That means, given message m and hash value $h(m)$, the hash value of m computed using a cryptographically-secure hash function h, it must be computationally hard for Eve to find a second pre-image $\tilde{m}$ such that $h(m) = h(\tilde{m})$.

Clearly, if Eve tries out enough different input messages for the hash function, collisions *must* occur at some point because h maps longer messages onto shorter messages. More precisely, if a given hash value $h(m)$ is n bits long, then Eve can expect to find a second pre-image $\tilde{m}$ after $O(2^n)$ trials. A second pre-image attack is therefore considered successful only if it has a significantly smaller complexity than $O(2^n)$.

A weaker form of attack occurs if Eve manages to find **any** collision, that is, any two messages m_1, m_2 with

$$h(m_1) = h(m_2)$$

without reference to some given hash value. If it is computationally hard for Eve to construct any collisions, the hash function h is called strongly collision resistant.

As before, if Eve tries out enough different messages, collisions will naturally occur at some point, this time after about $2^{n/2}$ trials. This much smaller number (compared to $O(2^n)$) is a consequence of a phenomenon commonly known as the *birthday paradox.*

Consider a room with N people in it. Contrary to intuition, the probability of two people in the room having a birthday on the same day becomes larger than 0.5 as soon as $N > 23$. This is because the number of pairs $P(N)$ that can be formed out of N people grows quadratically with N; more specifically, it is given by:

$$P(N) = \frac{N(N-1)}{2}$$

As a result, as soon as $P(N)$ grows larger than 365, *birthday collisions* will occur with a high probability. This mathematical property can become a concern in a cryptographic setting if the hash function used by Alice allows Eve to find two distinct messages m, m' that have the same hash value. For instance, if Alice has digitally signed m, Eve can append that signature to m' claiming Alice has signed m'.

In a birthday attack, Eve picks messages $m_1, \ldots, m_q$ and computes their hash values $h(m_1), \ldots, h(m_q)$. Eve is said to be successful if she finds a pair of message m_i, m_j that leads to a collision for h. The birthday paradox implies that for a hash function $h : \{0,1\}^* \to \{0,1\}^n$ having 2^n possible hash values, collisions will occur after about $2^{n/2}$ trials.

Consequently, an attack on strong collision resistance is considered successful only if it has a significantly smaller complexity than $O(2^{n/2})$. This also shows that, in general, hash functions with longer hash values can be considered to be more secure than hash functions with shorter hash values.

19.7.2   Dictionary attack

We already learned that a cryptographic hash function is *pre-image resistant*. This is just another way of saying that given a hash value $h(m)$, it is computationally infeasible for Eve to find the pre-image m.

This property is what password security mechanisms in operating systems rely upon. Recall that modern operating systems such as Linux use hash functions to store the hash values of passwords rather than the passwords themselves. The rationale is that even if Eve gets hold of a hashed password, she cannot use it to log in as the victim because the password system requires her to enter the plaintext password. However, because a cryptographic hash function is pre-image resistant, Eve cannot reconstruct the plaintext password from its hash value.

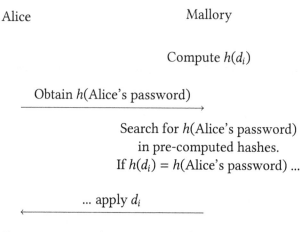

Figure 19.16: Working principle of a dictionary attack

A common way for Eve to defeat pre-image resistance is a *dictionary attack*. In a dictionary attack, Eve systematically computes the hash value for all plaintexts contained in Eve's dictionary, hence the name of the attack. If Eve's goal is to determine the plaintext password given the password's hash value, the dictionary would be typically composed of popular words and their combinations, typical phrases, and a list of common passwords.

Figure 19.16 illustrates the working principle of a dictionary attack. In the initial attack phase (which only needs to be done once), Eve computes the hash values for all dictionary entries d_i using the same hash function h, like Alice.

In the second phase, after obtaining the hash value for Alice's password, Eve searches the pre-computed hashes for the hash value of Alice's password. If Eve finds such a hash value, we say that the dictionary attack succeeded because Eve now knows a plaintext, namely d_i, that yields the desired hash value.

Note that Eve's dictionary entry resulting in Alice's hash value does not necessarily have to be Alice's actual password because any hash function will, at some point, produce collisions. But this doesn't matter in practice since, for example, the password security system only checks if the password entered maps to the hash value stored.

Dictionary attacks were successfully deployed against computer systems – especially against systems that allow weak passwords such as simple words and common phrases found in dictionaries – as early as the late 1980s.

As an example, in early November 1988, the internet – at that time, a collection of networks connecting about 60,000 hosts – was attacked by a virus that broke into **Berkeley Standard Distribution (BSD)** Unix and derivative systems [61]. A group at MIT who discovered and dealt with the virus published their experience and a detailed analysis of the virus in [61].

After entering a vulnerable system, the virus applied a dictionary attack on encrypted passwords stored in /etc/passwd. It used the dictionary attack as the method to verify password guesses in order to avoid being noticed in the system's security logs. The virus first used a built-in dictionary of 432 words and subsequently the local /usr/dict/words file, a 24,474-word spelling dictionary distributed with BSD version 4.3.

An important takeaway from dictionary attacks is that the entropy of the plaintext has a strong effect on the practical security of most cryptographic primitives. If Alice uses only 10 different plaintext messages as input to a hash function or an encryption function, it is very simple for Eve to find their pre-images even if these functions themselves are computationally secure. This, in turn, illustrates the difference between the security of a cryptographic primitive itself and the security of its mode of operation.

19.7.3   Rainbow tables

In 1980, Martin Hellman – the cryptographer who, four years earlier, published the Diffie-Hellman key agreement protocol – proposed a method for achieving a time-memory trade-off in an exhaustive search attack [80]. Hellman's method assumes a chosen plaintext attack with a plaintext p_0, which is encrypted with a secret key k as

$$c = e_k(p_0)$$

and Eve's task is to find k. We first define function f as:

$$f(k) = R(\ e_k(p_0)\ )$$

with R being a simple reduction. The $f(k)$ function generates a key from a key and so can be used to generate key chains.

The reduction used by Hellman in [80] is simply dropping the last 8 bits of the ciphertext because – remember, it's 1980! – Hellman uses DES to illustrate his method. Recall that DES encryption operates on a 64-bit plaintext block and produces a 64-bit ciphertext block using a 56-bit key.

Note that Hellman's method works for any one-way function. So, while the example given in the original paper uses DES encryption, Eve can equally well use the method to break cryptographic hash functions.

During the pre-computation phase, Eve chooses the parameters m and t to trade off time against memory. Eve first draws m *starting points* $S_1, \ldots, S_m$ uniformly at random from the key space. For $1 \le i \le m$, she lets

$$X_{i0} = S_i$$

and computes

$$X_{ij} = f(X_{i,j-1})$$

for $1 \le j \le t$. Recall that the way f is defined, all elements X_{ij} are keys.

The last element in the i-th key chain, referred to as an *endpoint*, is equal to $f^t(S_i)$ and is denoted by E_i as shown in *Figure 19.17*.

$$S_1 = X_{10} \xrightarrow{f} X_{11} \xrightarrow{f} X_{12} \xrightarrow{f} \cdots \xrightarrow{f} X_{1t} = E_1$$

$$S_2 = X_{20} \xrightarrow{f} X_{21} \xrightarrow{f} X_{22} \xrightarrow{f} \cdots \xrightarrow{f} X_{2t} = E_2$$

$$\vdots \qquad\qquad\qquad \vdots$$

$$S_m = X_{m0} \xrightarrow{f} X_{m1} \xrightarrow{f} X_{m2} \xrightarrow{f} \cdots \xrightarrow{f} X_{3t} = E_m$$

Figure 19.17: Pre-computed hash chains

To reduce the memory needed to store the pre-computations, Eve discards all intermediate values X_{ij} and only stores the pairs (S_i, E_i), sorted by E_i.

Now, suppose that Alice chooses a key k' and computes the ciphertext $c_0 = e_{k'}(p_0)$. After intercepting that ciphertext, Eve applies reduction R to compute

$$Y_1 = R(c_0) = f(k')$$

Eve can now check whether Y_1 is an endpoint. If Y_1 is not an endpoint, the key is not in the next-to-last column in *Figure 19.17*. If, on the other hand, $Y_1 = E_i$, then either k' is in the next to last column (that is, $k' = X_{i,t-1}$) or E_i has more than one inverse image. The latter event is referred to as a *false alarm*.

If $Y_1 = E_i$, Eve uses S_i to re-compute $X_{i,1}$, $X_{i,2}$, ... until she can compute $X_{i,t-1}$ and check whether $k' = X_{i,t-1}$ by verifying that decryption $d_{k'=X_{i,t-1}}(c_0)$ yields the chosen plaintext p_0.

If Y_1 is not an endpoint or a false alarm occurred (because E_i has more than one inverse image), Eve computes

$$Y_2 = f(Y_1)$$

and checks whether Y_2 is an endpoint. If Y_2 is not an endpoint, the key k is not in the $t-2$nd column. On the other hand, if $Y_2 = E_i$, Eve checks whether $k = X_{i,t-2}$. Eve continues to compute $Y_3 = f(Y_2)$, ..., $Y_t = f(Y_{t-1})$ to check whether the key is in the $t-3$rd, $t-4$th, and so on – up to 0th – column in *Figure 19.17*.

In other words, to determine k', Eve generates a chain of keys starting with $Y_1 = R(c_0)$ and up to the length t. If Alice computed c_0 using a key that is contained in the table, then Eve will eventually generate the key that matches the last key (the endpoint) in the corresponding chain. As an example, if Alice's key k' is X_{22} in *Figure 19.17*, then calculating $f^{t-2}(X_{22})$ will result in a key equal to the endpoint E_2.

Because the last key is stored with its corresponding first key (the starting point), Eve can recompute the entire key chain, including the key that comes just before $R(c_0)$, that is, the key that Alice used to compute c_0.

However, because the reduction function R in Hellman's method is an arbitrary reduction of the ciphertext space in the key space, it is possible that key chains starting at different keys will collide and merge. Each merge, in turn, reduces the number of keys that are covered by the table. Even worse, the probability that a new chain will merge with an existing one increases with the size of the table.

In 2003, the Swiss cryptographer Philippe Oechslin observed that it is better to generate multiple tables using a different reduction function for each table [134]. While collisions are still possible, the chains do not merge because different tables use different reduction functions.

Based on this observation, Oechslin proposed a new type of chain, which he referred to as *rainbow chains*. Rainbow chains can collide within a single table, but are very unlikely to merge [134] because they use a different reduction function R_i for every element in the key chain. As a result, if there is a collision between two chains, they will only merge if the collision appears at the same position in both chains. Otherwise, the chains will continue with a different reduction function and, thus, will not merge.

To find Alice's key k' in a rainbow table, Eve proceeds in the same way as with Hellman's method, only using different reduction functions. To check whether c_0 is an endpoints, she computes R_{t-1}. If one of the endpoints is equal to R_{t-1}, Eve uses the corresponding starting point to rebuild the key chain, in particular, the next to the last chain element. If none of the endpoints is equal to R_{t-1}, Eve checks whether k' is in the second-last column using R_{t-2}, f_{t-1}, in the third-last column using $R_{t-3}, f_{t-2}, f_{t-1}$, and so on.

But why *rainbow* chains and *rainbow* tables? During his presentation at the Crypto 2003 conference, Oechslin added colors to the original graphic from his paper. The colored graphic is shown in *Figure 19.18* and explains the rainbow association.

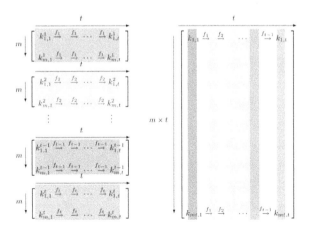

Figure 19.18: Colored graphic in Oechslin's Crypto 2003 talk used to illustrate rainbow tables

19.8 Summary

In this chapter, we discussed common attacks on cryptography. We mostly focused on attacks relevant to cryptographic protocols such as TLS, that is, attacks that are independent of the underlying cryptographic primitives. We then complemented our discussion with attacks on symmetric and asymmetric encryption schemes and hash functions. The security of digital signatures, which are based either on RSA or on elliptic curves, relies on the security of these cryptographic primitives.

In the next chapter, we will cover actual, real-world attacks on the TLS Handshake protocol. The material covered in this chapter will make it easier for you to understand those attacks.

20

Attacks on the TLS Handshake Protocol

The Handshake protocol is the most complex part of TLS because it has several targets to hit at once: it not only needs a key to be established between client and server in a secure (i.e. authenticated) manner, but also the protocol to do this must be negotiated. Finally, the client and server must agree on a set of symmetric algorithms to encrypt and authenticate their subsequent communication. It should come as no surprise that such a complex protocol is prone to many attacks.

Attacks on the Handshake protocol tend to be more severe than attacks on the Record protocol (which we will cover in the next chapter) because they do not attack single messages, but try to find out the key for the entire TLS session or even impersonate one of the communicating parties. On the other hand, all of these attacks require a rather strong attacker model, a *man-in-the-middle* with full control of the communication channel between client and server.

In what follows, we try to give a rather complete overview of the published attacks on the TLS handshake for TLS versions up to and including version 1.2. After reading this chapter, you should have a good understanding of the following:

- How the Handshake protocol of old TLS versions can be attacked on various levels

- How severe these attacks are

- How these attacks have influenced the design of the Handshake of TLS 1.3

20.1   Downgrade attacks

As we have seen in *Chapter 18, TLS Cipher Suites,* the TLS protocol allows Alice and Bob to negotiate cryptographic settings for the TLS connection they want to establish.

The ability to negotiate cryptographic parameters has a twofold benefit. First, it ensures maximum possible compatibility in the heterogeneous landscape of TLS endpoints. As long as Alice and Bob share a single TLS cipher suite, they both support and a single security setting they are willing to accept – for instance, that server Alice authenticates herself using a certificate and client Bob does not need to authenticate himself – they will be able to establish a TLS connection.

Second, it enables cryptographic agility. Without negotiation, all TLS clients on the internet would have to transition to the new cryptographic algorithm at once, or else parts of the TLS ecosystem would stop working. With negotiation, this transition can happen gradually, allowing a grace period during which older TLS endpoints can be updated and without disrupting operations.

The downside of this flexibility is that negotiation enables so-called *downgrade attacks.* Downgrade attacks use negotiation mechanisms to weaken the cryptographic protocol by making Alice and Bob choose weak security parameters or weak cryptographic algorithms.

20.1.1   Taxonomy of downgrade attacks

In [2], Alashwali and Rasmussen introduced a taxonomy for downgrade attacks on TLS. Their taxonomy classifies attacks based on the following attributes:

- The **protocol element** that is targeted (cryptographic algorithm, protocol version, or protocol layer)

- The **type of vulnerability** that enables the attack (implementation vulnerability, design vulnerability, or trust-model vulnerability)

- The **attack method** (modification, deletion, or insertion of protocol messages)

- The **level of damage** that the attack causes (broken or weakened security)

The term *design vulnerability* denotes a flaw in the protocol design, that is, a security flaw in the protocol specification. In contrast to an implementation vulnerability, Eve and Mallory can exploit a design vulnerability even if the protocol's implementation is error free.

The term *trust-model vulnerability* denotes a flaw in the protocol ecosystem's architectural aspect and the trusted parties involved in this architecture. As a result, Eve and Mallory can exploit a trust-model vulnerability even if both the protocol design and the implementation are secure.

20.1.2   Cipher suite downgrade attacks

In a *cipher suite downgrade attack*, Mallory forces Alice and Bob to use weaker cryptographic algorithms than they intend to use.

Figure 20.1 shows a simple example of a downgrade attack on TLS 1.2. The example assumes a certificate-based unilateral server authentication using ephemeral Diffie-Hellman key exchange:

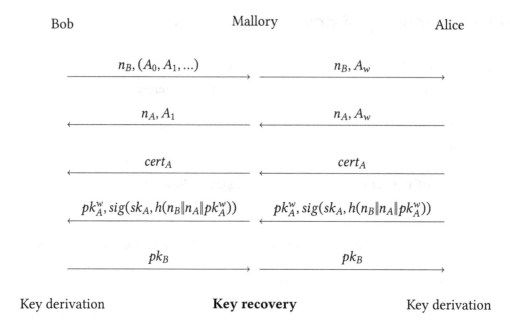

Figure 20.1: *Example of a downgrade attack on simplified TLS 1.2*

The attack works like this:

1. Bob initiates the TLS handshake by sending his nonce n_B and a list of cipher suites $(A_0, A_1, ...)$ within his `ClientHello` message to Alice. We may assume that Bob's list contains only cryptographically strong cipher suites from which Alice can choose. However, Mallory intercepts Bob's message and modifies it to contain only a single weak export-grade cipher suite A_w containing, for example, a 512-bit DHE group for key establishment.

2. As a result, if Alice supports export-grade cipher suites – for instance, to ensure backward compatibility with legacy TLS clients – she will select cipher suite A_w, as this is the only option available to her. She then sends her nonce n_A and the cipher suite A_w to Bob.

3. To prevent being detected, Mallory modifies Alice's message by replacing A_w with A_1. Bob, in turn, receives n_A, A_1 and has no way to detect Mallory's presence.

4. Next, Alice sends her digital certificate $cert_A$ followed by her (weak) public key parameters pk_A^w within her ServerKeyExchange message. She also signs the nonces n_B, n_A and her public key parameters pk_A^w.

5. Because in TLS 1.2 and below, Alice's signature does not cover her cipher suite choice – in our example, the cipher suite A_w, Bob cannot tell whether the selected cipher suite is cryptographically strong or not. As a result, Bob will not recognize the public key parameters sent by Alice as weak.

6. In the next step, Bob sends his own public key parameters pk_B to Alice so they both can compute the PreMasterSecret PMS, the MasterSecret MS, and the shared client and server session keys.

7. Because of the weak public-key parameters that Alice has sent, Mallory is able to recover the private exponents from Alice's public key and compute the PreMasterSecret. In particular, Mallory can fake the final finished messages from Bob and Alice so that the initial manipulation of the cipher suites goes unnoticed.

As a result, Mallory is able to compute all secrets and keys established between Alice and Bob for that particular session and, therefore, completely break the TLS session. The attack does not, however, have any impact on earlier or future TLS sessions between Alice and Bob.

20.1.3 The Downgrade Dance

Originally, the *Downgrade Dance* is a mechanism to negotiate a commonly supported TLS version for client and servers during the TLS handshake. However, up to and including TLS version 1.2, the messages of the negotiation process are not authenticated, so that an active attacker acting as a man-in-the-middle can misuse this mechanism and enforce a lower protocol version upon client Bob and server Alice.

Figure 20.2 shows how the attack works: Mallory simply suppresses all ClientHello messages from Bob and answers them in the name of Alice by a FatalHandshakeError, until Bob sends a `ClientHello` containing a TLS version number that suits Mallory. Mallory now forwards the `ClientHello` from Bob to Alice:

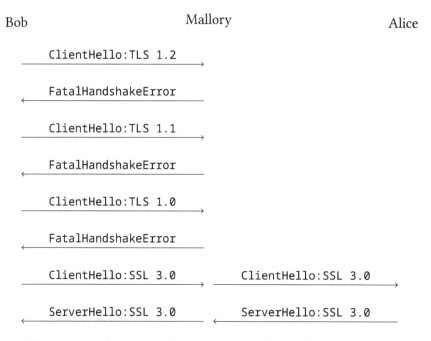

Figure 20.2: The Downgrade Dance. Although Bob and Alice both support TLS version 1.2, they are forced to negotiate SSL version 3.0 by Mallory

Provided Alice accepts the low protocol version proposed by Bob, the handshake continues normally after the Downgrade Dance. Note that Alice and Bob cannot detect the early manipulations by Mallory because the Handshake messages are only protected by the final `finished` message if the Handshake has been successfully completed.

Clearly, simply downgrading the protocol version is not a goal for Mallory in itself. Rather, by downgrading the protocol version, Mallory can take advantage of vulnerabilities and weaker cryptographic algorithms from earlier protocol versions. The SLOTH (see *Section 20.3, SLOTH*, in this chapter) and POODLE (see *Section 21.2, POODLE*, in *Chapter 21, Attacks on the TLS Record Protocol*) attacks are prime examples of this tactic.

Note that with TLS 1.3, the Downgrade Dance will not happen anymore: a TLS 1.3 server Alice that is asked by the client to negotiate a lower protocol version **must** include the seven bytes 44 4F 57 4E 47 52 44 (ASCII code for DOWNGRD) as the last bytes of the `ServerRandom` number in their `ServerHello` message.

These bytes are authenticated (i.e., signed by Alice) and cannot be changed by Mallory. They indicate to the client that the server supports version 1.3 and downgrading is going on. If the negotiated TLS version is lower than the version supported by the client, something is obviously wrong. Moreover, SSL 3.0 must not be negotiated by TLS servers later than version 1.1 (see [16]) because of its many security problems.

In the next sections we will see how these downgrade attack templates can be turned into real-life attacks.

20.2 Logjam

Logjam (see [1]) represents the practical implementation of the attack template shown in *Figure 20.1* with respect to the DHE key-establishment protocol. Here, the server is tricked into selecting a weak export-grade DHE cipher suite such as this:

$$A_w = \text{TLS\_DHE\_RSA\_EXPORT\_WITH\_DES40\_CBC\_SHA}$$

As discussed earlier, the client therefore receives weak key parameters and uses them to generate a shared secret that can be computed by Mallory, despite having negotiated a stronger cipher suite. The underlying weakness, the lack of early authentication of the cipher suite selected by the server, is resolved in TLS 1.3.

20.3 SLOTH

SLOTH [31] uses a weaker form of second-preimage resistance for a hash function h, namely *chosen-prefix collision resistance*. Given two prefixes P_1 and P_2, it should be computationally hard to find a pair of values x_1, x_2 so that

$$h(P_1 \| x_1) = h(P_2 \| x_2)$$

The use of MD5 and SHA-1 is mandated in TLS 1.0 and TLS 1.1 and is still possible in TLS 1.2. However, these older hash functions are not chosen-prefix collision resistant. This weakness can be used by an attacker either to manipulate the initial handshake messages in order to downgrade the negotiated cipher suites or to break client/server authentication. The possibility of these attacks leads to the deprecation of MD5-based signatures in TLS 1.3.

The attacker in this scenario is a man-in-the-middle with sufficient computing resources to generate the chosen-prefix collisions within a short time frame. The attack is based on the fact that, for example, the ClientHello can include extensions that the server does not understand or support and will consequently ignore. Similarly, ServerCertificateRequest can include an optional list of distinguished names of certificate authorities the server trusts. Again, such a list may include arbitrary data the client will ignore if it does not recognize them. These arbitrary parts give an attacker room to generate chosen-prefix collisions.

20.4   Padding oracle attacks on TLS handshake

The term *oracle* originally comes from complexity theory, where it is used to compare the complexity of two computational problems P_1, P_2.

Suppose we can solve P_1 efficiently (i.e., in polynomial time), if there is a polynomial-time algorithm A to solve P_2. In this situation, we say that P_1 *polytime reduces to* P_2, or

$$P_1 \leq_p P_2$$

Informally, we can say that P_2 is at least as hard as P_1 ([117]). Now, the (hypothetical) algorithm A that can efficiently solve P_2 is called an *oracle* for P_2.

As an example, let P_1 be the RSA-problem and P_2 be the integer factorization problem. Recall from *Chapter 7, Public-Key Cryptography*, that the RSA problem means we have to find the plaintext m, given the ciphertext

$$c = m^e \mod n$$

and the public key (e, n), while the integer factorization problems is to find the prime factors of a given integer.

Now it is easy to see that if we had an oracle that provides us with the prime factors of n in polynomial time, we could also solve the RSA problem, namely by computing the secret key d and then using d to decipher c. Thus, we have shown that

$$\text{RSA Problem} \leq_p \text{Integer Factorization}$$

Surprisingly, the seemingly abstract concept of an oracle has important applications in various practical attacks on TLS. In this setting, you may think of an oracle simply as some technical system that is able to provide certain information that would not be available otherwise.

For example, old versions of the TLS Handshake protocol are susceptible to so-called *padding oracle attacks* when Alice and Bob use RSA-based key agreement. If RSA is used, Bob generates a 48-byte `PreMasterSecret` consisting of 2 fixed bytes describing the TLS protocol version and 46 random bytes as illustrated in *Figure 20.3*. Bob then encrypts that `PreMasterSecret` using the public RSA key from Alice's certificate and sends the result to Alice in an encrypted message. Alice, in turn, decrypts Bob's message and uses the `PreMasterSecret` to generate `master_secret`, the secret used for computing TLS key material [5].

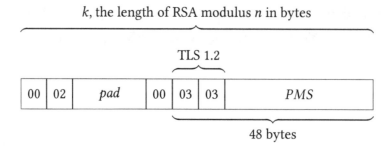

Figure 20.3: PKCS#1 padding used in TLS 1.2

Recall that TLS messages must be correctly padded according to PKCS #1 padding. But what does Alice do if the padding of a TLS message received from Bob is incorrect? In old TLS versions, Alice would, for example, send a *bad TLS padding* message, allowing Mallory to distinguish between correct and incorrect paddings.

These differences give rise to a padding oracle that Mallory can use to launch a *padding oracle attack* that completely compromises the TLS session's security. In particular, Mallory chooses a large number of ciphertexts and determines the `PreMasterSecret` without the knowledge of Alice's private RSA key – based on whether the individual plaintexts corresponding to Mallory's chosen ciphertexts have valid PKCS #1 padding or not. Alternatively, Mallory can use this attack to forge Alice's signature.

The first one to recognize this was the Swiss cryptographer Daniel Bleichenbacher. In 1998, Bleichenbacher published a paper describing chosen ciphertext attacks against protocols based on the RSA encryption standard PKCS#1. Later on, his work became known simply as the *Bleichenbacher attack*.

20.5   Bleichenbacher attack

Long before Bleichenbacher published this work, it was well known that plain RSA is vulnerable to chosen-ciphertext attacks. If Eve wants to decrypt the ciphertext $c \equiv m^d$ (mod n) that Bob encrypted for Alice, she can choose a random integer s and ask Alice to decrypt an apparently innocuous message $c' \equiv s^e c$ (mod n).

If Alice, thinking she is decrypting ciphertexts received from a legitimate party such as Bob, returns Eve the result $m' \equiv (c')^d \pmod{n}$, Eve can easily recover the original message m by computing $m \equiv m' s^{-1} \pmod{n}$. This works because:

$$m' s^{-1} \equiv (c')^d s^{-1} \pmod{n}$$

and for the term $(c')^d s^{-1}$ it holds that:

$$(c')^d s^{-1} \equiv (s^e c)^d s^{-1} \equiv s^{ed} c^d s^{-1} \pmod{n}$$

Moreover, because $ed \pmod{n} \equiv 1$ by the definition of the RSA algorithm, Eve can easily determine m because:

$$s^{ed} c^d s^{-1} \equiv s^1 c^d s^{-1} \equiv c^d \equiv m \pmod{n}$$

In his publication [34], Bleichenbacher showed that Eve can also decrypt any ciphertext c if she has access to an *oracle* that for every ciphertext returns whether the corresponding plaintext has a valid PKCS #1 padding.

20.5.1 The attack

Bleichenbacher's attack is based on the observation that any plaintext m that has a valid PKCS #1 padding is larger than or equal to the k-byte number 00 02 ... 00 and less than the k-byte number 00 03 ... 00.

In other words, if we define number $B = 2^{8(k-2)}$ – which is an $8(k-2)$-bit number with the binary representation 100 ... 00 – then for every m with a valid PKCS #1 padding, it holds that:

$$2B \leq m < 3B$$

As a result, if Eve can trick Alice into decrypting some ciphertext $c' = c s^e = m'^e \pmod{n}$ and learns that the corresponding plaintext $m' = ms$ has a valid PKCS #1 padding, then

Eve knows that:

$$2B \leq m' < 3B$$

and since $m' = ms \pmod{n}$, the preceding inequality can be rewritten as:

$$2B \leq ms \pmod{n} < 3B$$

Next, note that the definition of the modulus operator states that there exists an integer r such that:

$$ms \pmod{n} = ms - rn$$

and we can therefore rewrite the inequality once again as:

$$2B \leq ms - rn < 3B \qquad\qquad (20.1)$$

By subtracting the term ms, we can further simplify the inequality to obtain a representation where only the middle term contains an unknown:

$$2B - ms \leq -rn < 3B - ms$$

As you can easily verify, we can further simplify the inequality by first multiplying it by -1 and then dividing it by n:

$$(ms - 2B)/n \geq r > (ms - 3B)/n$$

That still leaves us with an inequality with two unknown terms r and m. However, we known that m is limited to the interval $2B \leq m < 3B$. Therefore, we can replace ms in the left term with $3B$ and replace ms in the right term with $2B$ to obtain:

$$(3Bs - 2B)/n \geq r > (2Bs - 3B)/n \qquad\qquad (20.2)$$

Eve starts the attack by generating a large number of random integers $s_0, s_1, s_2, ...$ and letting Alice, the padding oracle, decrypt ciphertexts $cs_0, cs_1, cs_2, ...$ For every cs_i whose corresponding plaintext has a valid PKCS #1 padding, Eve computes the interval for r_i using inequality 20.2 and adds r_i to the set R.

In the next step, Eve computes intervals for the plaintext m she wants to obtain by plugging in the values $r_i \in R$ into inequality 20.1

$$2B \leq ms - r_in < 3B$$

which she transforms into:

$$2B + r_in \leq ms < 3B + rn$$

and, finally, into:

$$(2B + r_in)/s \leq m < (3B + rn)/s$$

Eve keeps only those intervals for m that intersect with the interval $2B \leq m < 3B$. By obtaining more and more such intersections, Eve eventually determines an interval spanning only a single value, namely the plaintext m she wants to obtain.

Figure 20.4 illustrates Eve's strategy to determine the unknown plaintext m. Initially, m is confined to the interval $2B \geq m < 3B$. In the second step, Eve determines the intervals for r_0 and keeps only their intersection with the original interval $2B \geq m < 3B$. The intersection is smaller than the original interval.

In every subsequent step, using the corresponding r_i value, Eve determines new intervals for m and their intersection with the interval from the previous step. This way, the interval where m is located gets smaller with every step and eventually contains a single value, namely the unknown plaintext m.

initial *m* interval

Step 1

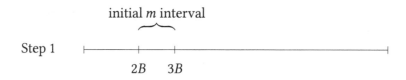

2B   3B

new *m* interval after intersection with intervals for r_0

Step 2

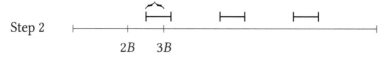

2B   3B

$\vdots$

Figure 20.4: Determining plaintext m as the intersection of intervals

In the two decades after its publication, Bleichenbacher's attack turned into the foundation of all oracle attacks on RSA-based TLS handshakes.

20.5.2   Countermeasures

Daniel Bleichenbacher published his attack at the CRYPTO'98 conference, which took place in August 1998. RFC 2246 *The TLS Protocol Version 1.0* draft version 0.6, released on November 12, 1998, added a note that an attack has been discovered against TLS servers that use RSA with PKCS #1-encoded messages.

In order to prevent Bleichenbacher's attack, the RFC 2246 draft recommends to *"treat incorrectly formatted messages in a manner indistinguishable from correctly formatted RSA blocks. Thus, when it receives an incorrectly formatted RSA block, a server should generate a random 48-byte value and proceed using it as the premaster secret"* [5].

20.6   Improvements of Bleichenbacher's attack

After its publication in 1998, it quickly became clear that Bleichenbacher's attack could be extended on various levels to yield even more practical attacks on TLS.

20.6.1   Bad version oracles

In 2003, Klima, Pokorny, and Rosa published a practical attack on RSA-based TLS sessions that extracts the TLS pre-master secret from a TLS 1.0 handshake [101]. Their attack extends Bleichenbacher's attack by exploiting the TLS version number check over PKCS #1 plaintexts as an oracle.

As shown in *Figure 20.3*, a TLS message with the correct PKCS #1 padding contains two bytes that denote the TLS version. These bytes were originally introduced to thwart so-called *version rollback attacks* where Mallory tries to trick Alice into switching to an older TLS version, preferrably – from Mallory's perspective – with weaker cryptographic algorithms or shorter and, therefore, fewer secure keys.

Klima, Pokorny, and Rosa, however, observed that many then-current TLS implementations returned an error when one of these bytes had a different value than what server Alice expected. Based on this observation, they defined a *bad version oracle*: whenever there is no error message, for some $c = m^e \pmod{n}$ of Eve's choice, she knows that the corresponding plaintext m has a valid PKCS #1 padding.

From here, Eve can apply the original Bleichenbacher attack to invert the RSA encryption. This, in turn, allows Eve to accomplish two different things: she can either extract the pre-master secret from the TLS handshake message or trick Alice into signing a message of Eve's choice.

Klima, Pokorny, and Rosa conducted practical experiments with their attack and determined that at the time of their publication, about two-thirds of several hundred randomly chosen TLS servers were vulnerable to their attack.

20.6.2   Side channel attacks

In 2014, a group of German security researchers discovered four new side channels leading to Bleichenbacher-style oracles and demonstrated Bleichenbacher attacks on **Java Secure Socket Extension (JSSE)** (Java's built-in SSL/TLS implementation) as well as on hardware security appliances that used a specific accelerator chip for TLS [119].

Notably, these latter attacks were the first practical timing attacks against TLS. The timing differences observed by the researchers over a switched network were between 1 and 23 microseconds, allowing them to extract the TLS pre-master secret in a realistic measurement setup.

20.6.3 DROWN

In 2016, a group of academic and industrial researchers from Israel, Germany, and the United States published a new cross-protocol attack called **Decrypting RSA using Obsolete and Weakened eNcryption (DROWN)** that uses a protocol-level Bleichenbacher-style oracle in SSL version 2 to decrypt TLS traffic [12].

To decrypt a 2,048-bit RSA TLS ciphertext using DROWN, Eve must observe 1,000 TLS handshakes, initiate 40,000 SSLv2 connections, and perform 2^{50} offline computations. While 2^{50} sounds like a large number at first, the researchers implemented DROWN and were able to decrypt a TLS 1.2 handshake that uses a 2,048-bit RSA public key in less than 8 hours.

In a second iteration, the researchers improved their attack by exploiting vulnerabilities in the handshake code of the then-current versions of the OpenSSL cryptographic library. The researchers discovered that these vulnerabilities create even more powerful Bleichenbacher oracles that facilitate a significant reduction in the amount of computation required for DROWN. With the improved attack, the TLS ciphertext could be decrypted in 1 minute on a single CPU.

By performing internet-wide scans, the researchers determined that at the time of their publication, 33% of HTTPS servers were vulnerable to the generic DROWN attack and 22% were vulnerable to the improved DROWN attack.

20.6.4 ROBOT

Return Of Bleichenbacher's Oracle Threat (ROBOT) is not the name of an attack, but the acronym of a large-scale campaign performed in 2018 by Böck, Somorovsky, and Young in order to evaluate how widespread Bleichenbacher's RSA vulnerability was on the internet [35]. Their results showed that 20 years after the original publication by Daniel Bleichenbacher, almost one-third of the top 100 domains in the Alexa Top 1 Million list – including well-known tech companies such as Facebook and Paypal – were affected by that vulnerability.

To demonstrate how dangerous Bleichenbacher's attack is in practice, Böck, Somorovsky, and Young signed a message using the private key of `facebook.com`'s HTTPS certificate.

In 2019, a group of researchers around Eyal Ronen and Adi Shamir performed a new evaluation of then-current popular TLS implementations in order to determine whether they exhibit information leakages that lead to Bleichenbacher-style oracles [154].

They discovered that most TLS implementations were vulnerable to attacks that exploit information leakage from various micro-architectural side channels in order to implement a padding oracle. The oracle, in turn, can be used to decrypt or sign a message.

20.7 Insecure renegotiation

In 2009, Marsh Ray and Steve Dispensa, two employees of a company providing a multi-factor authentication solution that was eventually acquired by Microsoft and integrated into Azure, discovered a renegotiation-related vulnerability in then-current TLS versions that allowed Mallory to inject an arbitrary amount of chosen plaintext into the beginning of the application protocol stream [111].

Conceptually, then-current TLS versions were vulnerable to insecure renegotiation because server Alice did not verify whether the source – that is, her communication peer – of the old and the new data in a TLS session was the same.

Using the insecure renegotiation attack, Mallory can inject data that Alice will process as if it came from Bob. For instance, in a web application, Mallory can inject an unauthenticated HTTP request and trick Alice into processing that request in the context of the authenticated user Bob.

Technically, the attack is carried out in three steps [150]:

1. Mallory intercepts Bob's TLS handshake request to Alice and suspends that request.

2. Mallory then opens a TLS connection to Alice and sends her the attack payload P.

3. Finally, Mallory passes Bob's original TLS handshake request to Alice.

Figure 20.5 illustrates how the attack works against a web application secured using TLS [150]:

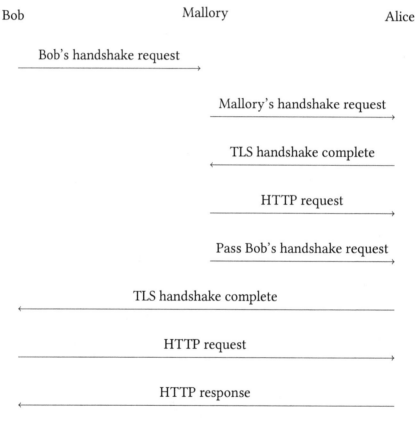

Figure 20.5: Insecure renegotiation

After suspending Bob's TLS handshake, Mallory initiates her own TLS session with Alice and sends an HTTP request for the target page, with a *partial header line* (no newline at the end) that is deliberately left incomplete to neutralize the first line of Bob's subsequent HTTP request:

```
GET /target.jsp HTTP/1.0
X-Ignore:
```

Once Mallory passes Bob's original TLS handshake request to Alice, Alice and Bob establish their TLS session. From Bob's perspective, the TLS session has just started, so he might send an HTTP request like this one:

```
GET /index.jsp HTTP/1.0
Cookie: JSESSIONID=5A644E...257
```

From Alice's perspective, however, Bob's TLS handshake is a renegotiation (because Alice has already established a valid TLS session with Mallory). As a result, Alice will pass Bob's HTTP request to the web application, in the same context as Mallory's request.

The web application does not care whether a renegotiation occurred in the middle of an HTTP request and will stitch the two HTTP requests together, resulting in the following:

```
GET /target.jsp HTTP/1.0
X-Ignore: GET /index.jsp HTTP/1.0
Cookie: JSESSIONID=5A644E...257
```

As a result, Mallory can impersonate Bob – using the authentication cookie that Bob transmits in the header of his HTTP request – while interacting with the web application.

Conceptually, insecure renegotiation vulnerability results from a missing validation that both HTTP requests originate from the same communication entity. Instead, Alice simply interprets both HTTP requests as part of the same data stream.

20.8 Triple Handshake attack

In the Triple Handshake attack [29], an attacker posing as a man-in-the-middle causes two separate TLS connections, namely one from client Bob to attacker Mallory and another from attacker Mallory to server Alice, to share the same `PreMasterSecret` (*PMS*) and the same `sessionID`. In two subsequent handshakes, client authentication is broken by Mallory because application layer data sent by Mallory is accepted as authentic messages coming from Bob by Alice. In this respect, the Triple Handshake attack is similar to insecure renegotiation. In this case, however, the client authentication (via signatures and certificates) within TLS is attacked, while insecure renegotiation targets higher-layer authentication mechanisms such as username/password.

20.8.1 The attack

In the first handshake (shown in *Figure 20.6*), the TLS 1.2 client Bob deliberately connects to a server run by Mallory, not knowing that Mallory is malicious. Having received Bob's `clientHello` message, Mallory turns around and connects, as a client, to server Alice using the same `clientRandom` (*CR*).

Next, Mallory forwards Alice's `serverRandom` (*SR*) and `sessionID` (*SID*) to Bob. Moreover, as we have seen, Mallory can force Bob and Alice to use RSA for key establishment by offering the corresponding cipher suites as the only option. This means Bob sends $E_{PK_{Mallory}}(PMS)$ as his key exchange message to Mallory, where *PMS* is the `PreMasterSecret` chosen by Bob.

Now Mallory can decrypt *PMS*, re-encrypt it, and send it to Alice. Basically, the result of the first handshake are two sessions sharing the same key materials and session parameters (*SID*, *MS*, *CR*, *SR*), but having different server certificates and finished messages. The latter is caused by the fact that Mallory had to manipulate the cipher suites offered by Bob. Note that at this point authentication is not yet broken because Bob is aware he is connected to Mallory, while Alice is connected to some anonymous client.

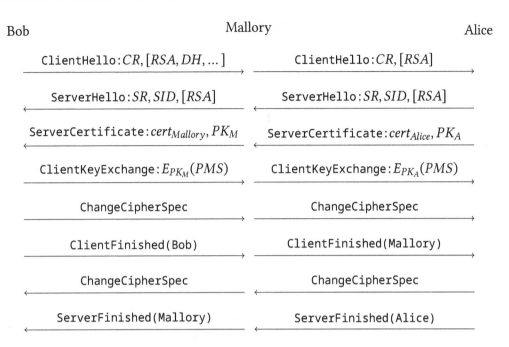

Figure 20.6: The first handshake in the Triple Handshake attack. Afterwards, the two sessions on the left and on the right have the same MasterSecret *and* SessionID

In the second handshake (see *Figure 20.7*), client Bob reconnects to Mallory and asks to *resume* their previous session [29] (see *Section 6.5.3* in *Chapter 6, Transport Layer Security at a Glance*). Mallory, in turn, reconnects to server Alice and asks to resume their previous session as well. Since all the relevant parameters on the two resumed sessions are the same, Mallory can in fact simply forward the abbreviated handshake messages to Bob and Alice unchanged. On completion of the abbreviated handshake, the two connections again have the same keys, but now they also have the same Finished messages. Mallory knows the new connection keys, so he can continue to send encrypted data on either connection towards Bob or Alice, as is shown at the bottom of *Figure 20.7*.

At this point of the attack Bob still (rightly) believes he has established a connection with Mallory, and Alice still believes that she has a connection with some anonymous client, so neither of them has been impersonated yet. This happens in the third and final handshake of the attack.

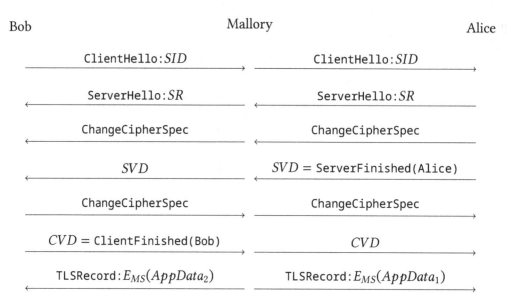

Figure 20.7: The second handshake in the Triple Handshake attack. Both sessions now also have the same Finished *messages. CVD and SVD stand for* Client Verfication Data *and* Server Verfication Data, *respectively*

Before the third handshake, server Alice has to require a session renegotiation, including client authentication, on its connection with Mallory, possibly in response to Mallory's request for some restricted resource. Mallory forwards the renegotiation request to client Bob.

Provided Bob agrees to authenticate with his client certificate at Mallory, both connections engage in a full renegotiation handshake with client authentication. This handshake is transported via the Record Layer of the previous session, that is, the session established in the second handshake.

According to RFC 5746, which defines the TLS Renegotiation Indication Extension ([148]), the Finished messages from the previous handshake must be present within the ClientHello and ServerHello messages of the new session. This is done to create a cryptographic binding between the new and the original session.

However, in the third handshake within the attack scenario described here, Mallory simply forwards all messages from Bob to Alice and back again (see *Figure 20.8*). The handshake completes successfully since the expected Finished values on both connections are the same.

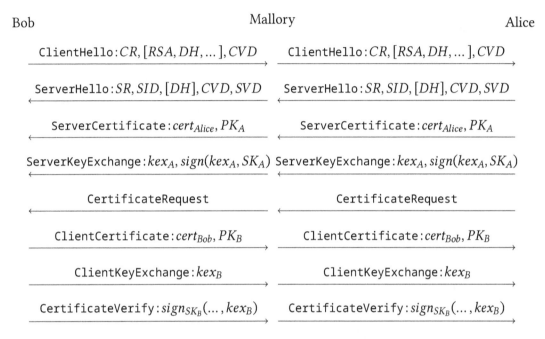

Figure 20.8: The third handshake in the Triple Handshake attack. Mallory stays completely passive and does not know the key agreed between Alice and Bob. Regardless, Alice accepts earlier messages from Mallory after the second handshake, assuming they are coming from Bob

At the end of the third handshake, Mallory no longer knows the connection keys or the master secret; they are known only to Bob and Alice. Consequently, Mallory is not able to read or send messages on these connections any more.

However, because the new session is authenticated and cryptographically bound to the earlier session, Alice will regard the $AppData_1$ sent after the second handshake as authentic data coming from Bob.

20.8.2   Countermeasures in TLS 1.3

While the attack did not have a large impact in practice, it showed that client authentication in TLS 1.2 was insufficiently implemented. In doing so, it had a profound influence on TLS 1.3 protocol design:

- RSA-based key establishment was removed from the available cipher suites in favour of Diffie-Hellman-based protocols. Moreover, the groups used for Diffie-Hellman (multiplicative group of a finite field or elliptic curve point group) must be chosen from a pre-configured list (see *Section 7.10 Public-Key Cryptography in TLS 1.3*, in *Chapter 7, Public-Key Cryptography* and *Section 8.5, Elliptic Curves in TLS 1.3*, in *Chapter 8, Elliptic Curves*).

- As we saw in *Chapter 12, Secrets and Keys in TLS 1.3*, the transcript-hash of all handshake messages prior to the establishment of the PreMasterSecret *PMS* affects the derivation of the MasterSecret (*MS*). This way, the MasterSecret is bound to the connection it was established within.

20.9   Summary

In this chapter, we covered attacks on TLS Handshake protocol. Since Alice and Bob use the handshake to establish the shared MasterSecret for their current TLS session, any successful attack on the handshake completely breaks the security of that TLS session.

While we looked into the attacks' details, there are also some general lessons to be learned from these attacks. Downgrade attacks provide a practical example on how the presence of insecure configuration options and, on a more general level, legacy options kept for backward compatibility, can easily undermine security.

SLOTH illustrates that outdated cryptographic primitives are dangerous not only in theory, but also in practice. Intuitively, one might be tempted to think that theoretical weaknesses are difficult – or even impossible – to exploit in practice. SLOTH shows that a clever attacker is able to get around these difficulties.

Padding oracle attacks such as Bleichenbacher and its numerous improvements show how even solid cryptography can be broken if Mallory learns something about intermediate results of a cryptographic computation. Unfortunately, implementing cryptography in a way that exhibits no discernible variances when processing different inputs is surprisingly hard [92].

Insecure renegotiation is an excellent example of why it is important that both communication parties have the same view of the cryptographic protocol they execute. Insecure renegotiation happens due to the fact that when Mallory passes Bob's TLS handshake request, Bob interprets the situation differently from Alice.

Finally, in the Triple Handshake attack, Mallory manages to break message authentication because an earlier unauthenticated message from Mallory is treated by Alice as if it belongs to some later, authenticated session between Alice and Bob. This shows that all keying material Alice and Bob agree upon in a specific session must be bound to that session.

In the next chapter, we will study attacks on the TLS Record protocol. In contrast to attacks described in this chapter, attacks on TLS records aim to extract data transmitted in the encrypted records.

21

Attacks on the TLS Record Protocol

In the previous chapter, we learned about attacks on the TLS Handshake protocol. Those attacks exploit either protocol-level weaknesses – as in the case of the triple handshake or TLS downgrade attacks – or the existence of padding oracles that allow Mallory to extract the TLS pre-shared key.

In this chapter, we study attacks on the TLS Record protocol. Among other things, you will learn the following:

- How the timing of the messages coming from Alice, the TLS server, can be used to create a padding oracle similar to the one we discussed in the previous chapter (albeit targeting the TLS Record protocol)

- How predictable initialization vectors can be used to attack the CBC mode of operation

- How lossless data compression can undermine the security of an encryption scheme even if the scheme itself is cryptographically secure

Upon completing this chapter, you will have a good overview and good understanding of the attacks targeting the TLS Record protocol. Note, however, that most of these attacks are only applicable to TLS versions older than 1.3. On a more fundamental level, you will learn what common underlying weaknesses these attacks exploit.

In terms of skills, you will develop the ability to spot characteristics such as non-constant algorithm execution time or data compression that can render encryption systems insecure in practice.

21.1 Lucky 13

In 2013, Nadhem AlFardan and Kenneth Paterson, two researchers from the Information Security Group at Royal Holloway, University of London, published a new attack that can recover plaintexts by exploiting timing differences in the decryption process of then-current TLS versions 1.1 and 1.2 [4].

Lucky 13 – we will explain the reason for the attack's unusual name in a moment – targets the TLS Record protocol. More specifically, it exploits an implementation detail stemming from a recommendation in the TLS 1.1 and 1.2 standards.

If, during decryption, Alice encounters a TLS record with malformed padding, she still has to perform MAC verification to prevent trivial timing attacks (we will talk more about timing attacks and, in general, side-channel attacks in *Chapter 22, Attacks on TLS Implementations*). The question is, what data should Alice use for that calculation?

The TLS 1.1 and 1.2 standards recommend checking the MAC as if it had a zero-length padding. They also remark that *"this leaves a small timing channel, since MAC performance depends to some extent on the size of the data fragment, but it is not believed to be large enough to be exploitable, due to the large block size of existing MACs and the small size of the timing signal."*

AlFardan and Paterson discovered that this recommendation indeed introduces a timing signal and that – contrary to the statement in the standards – this timing signal *can* be exploited to compromise TLS security.

21.1.1   The encryption process

The TLS Record protocol of the vulnerable TLS versions uses a **MAC-Encode-Encrypt** (**MEE**) construction. As shown in *Figure 21.1*, sender Bob first computes the MAC tag using the actual payload to be transmitted and certain header bytes as input to the MAC algorithm. All MAC algorithms in TLS 1.1 and 1.2 are HMAC based, with MD5, SHA-1, and SHA-256 being the available hash functions. The header consists of an 8-byte sequence number *SQN*, which Bob increments with each transmitted TLS record, and a 5-byte field *HDR*, which holds a 2-byte version field, a 1-byte type field, and a 2-byte length field.

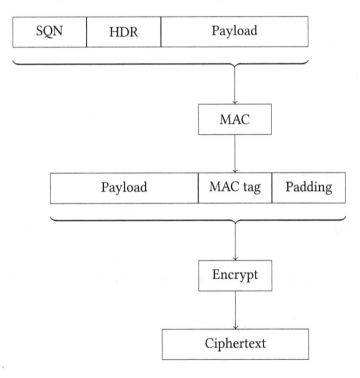

Figure 21.1: TLS 1.1 encryption process. The order of operations is MAC-Encode-Encrypt (MEE)

Next, Bob computes padding bytes to ensure that the byte length of the final data that will be encrypted is an integer multiple of the block cipher's block size. To ensure that receiver Alice can tell the actual data and the padding apart, the padding bytes must follow a specific format.

In TLS 1.1 and 1.2, padding must consist of at least one byte, and the value of padding bytes must be equal to the number of bytes added. So, valid padding sequences are $0x00$ when no bytes were added, $0x01\|0x01$ when 1 padding byte was added, $0x02\|0x02\|0x02$ when 2 padding bytes were added, and so on.

Finally, to encrypt the data using the CBC mode of operation, Bob concatenates the payload, the MAC tag, and the padding into an integer number of plaintext blocks p_j, and computes the ciphertext blocks as:

$$c_j = e_k(p_j \oplus c_{j-1})$$

where c_0 is the initialization vector and the supported block ciphers are DES, 3DES, or AES in the case of TLS 1.1 and 3DES or AES in the case of TLS 1.2.

Later in this chapter, we will see that the MEE construction together with the CBC mode of operation gives rise to several more attacks.

21.1.2 The timing signal

You may be wondering where the timing signal originates from in the encryption process illustrated in *Figure 21.1*. That source, it turns out, is the HMAC algorithm. Recall from *Chapter 11, Hash Functions and Message Authentication Codes*, that the HMAC construction applies the underlying hash function h to the message m twice, in an iterated manner:

$$T = h((k_a \oplus \mathsf{opad})\|h((k_a \oplus \mathsf{ipad})\|m))$$

This, in turn, leads to the following data-dependent timing behavior of the HMAC algorithm when it is implemented in a straightforward manner:

- Messages of up to 55 bytes can be encoded into a single 64-byte block. As a result, such messages require four hash function invocations, two for the inner and two for the outer hash.

- In contrast, messages of 56 to 115 bytes are encoded in two 64-byte blocks and, therefore, require five hash function invocations, three for the inner and two for the outer hash.

This means it is possible by measuring computation times for the HMAC to distinguish between messages that are shorter than 56 bytes and those that are 56 bytes or longer.

21.1.3 The attack

How can Eve exploit the HMAC timing signal to recover a plaintext from an encrypted TLS record? To see this, let c^* be a ciphertext block whose corresponding plaintext p^* Eve wants to recover. Let c' be the ciphertext block preceding the block c^*.

Now, let Δ be a 16-byte block and c_Δ a ciphertext of the form:

$$c_\Delta = c_1 \| c_2 \| c' \oplus \Delta \| c^*$$

where the ciphertext block $c' \oplus \Delta$ is an XOR-masked version of c' – that is, it's the result of Eve XORing the original ciphertext block c' with a 16-byte value Δ of her choice – and c^* is the last ciphertext block.

The corresponding 64-byte plaintext is:

$$p = p_1 \| p_2 \| p_3 \| p_4$$

and – because we are using the CBC mode of operation – the plaintext block p_4 is related to the unknown, targeted plaintext p^* in this specific manner:

$$p_4 = d_k(c^*) \oplus (c' \oplus \Delta) = (d_k(c^*) \oplus c') \oplus \Delta = p^* \oplus \Delta$$

For illustration purposes, assume that SHA-1 is the hash function used in the HMAC algorithm (the attack works also for MD5 and SHA-256). In that case, the MAC tag is 20 bytes long.

As you can see in *Figure 21.1*, after decrypting ciphertext c_Δ into plaintext p, Alice must do the following:

1. Retrieve the payload from p by discarding padding and the received MAC tag.

2. Compute a MAC tag for the message $SQN\|HDR\|\text{Payload}$.

3. Compare the computed MAC tag to the received one.

Because of the length of the $SQN\|HDR$ header – namely, 13 bytes, which also gives the attack its name – there are three possible outcomes when Alice calculates the MAC tag:

- **Outcome 1:** p_4 ends with byte 0x00. In this case, 1 padding byte is removed from p and the next 20 bytes are interpreted as the MAC tag. As a result, the remaining $64 - 21 = 43$ bytes are interpreted as the payload, and Alice computes the MAC for a $13 + 43 = 56$-byte message $SQN\|HDR\|\text{Payload}$.

- **Outcome 2:** p_4 ends with a valid padding pattern of at least 2 bytes. In this case, at least 2 padding bytes are removed from p, and the next 20 bytes are interpreted as the MAC tag. Consequently, at most $64 - 22 = 42$ remaining bytes are interpreted as the payload, and Alice computes the MAC for the message $SQN\|HDR\|\text{Payload}$ of at most 55 bytes.

- **Outcome 3:** p_4 ends with any other byte pattern. In that case, the padding is invalid and – following the TLS 1.1 RFC recommendation – Alice treats plaintext p as if it had *no* padding at all. As a result, the last 20 bytes of p are interpreted as the MAC tag and the remaining $64 - 20 = 44$ bytes are interpreted as the payload. Alice, therefore, computes the MAC for a $13 + 44 = 57$-byte message $SQN\|HDR\|$Payload.

In all three cases, the MAC verification will fail. However, whereas in cases 1 and 3 the hash function will be executed 5 times, it will be only executed 4 times in case 2. So, Eve can distinguish case 2 from cases 1 and 3 by measuring how fast Alice replies with a TLS error message.

When Eve detects case 2, she knows that (given the plaintext has no specific structure) the likeliest padding pattern is $0x01\|0x01$. This is because any longer padding pattern, such as $0x02\|0x02\|0x02$, is about 256 times less likely. Thus, Eve can infer that p_4 ends with $0x01\|0x01$ and, based on the relation $p_4 = p^* \oplus \Delta$, recover the last two bytes of p^*.

Because Eve must correctly guess only the last two bytes of Δ to provoke case 2, she will succeed after 2^{16} trials in the worst case. This is just a little more than 16 thousand trials and is, therefore, feasible in practice.

Once Eve has determined the last two bytes of p^*, she repeats the attack with a new mask Δ', which is a modification of Δ in the third-to-last byte. This is even simpler than the initial hypothesis because now Eve only needs to guess one byte. Hence, Eve needs at most 14×2^8 trials to reveal all remaining 14 bytes of p^*.

AlFardan and Paterson discovered that then-actual versions of popular cryptographic libraries such as OpenSSL, GnuTLS, NSS, PolarSSL, CyaSSL, and Java's BouncyCastle and OpenJDK were vulnerable to the attack. *Figure 21.2* shows the median of Alice's decryption time for the different values of byte 15, where value 0xFE leads to a padding corresponding to case 2.

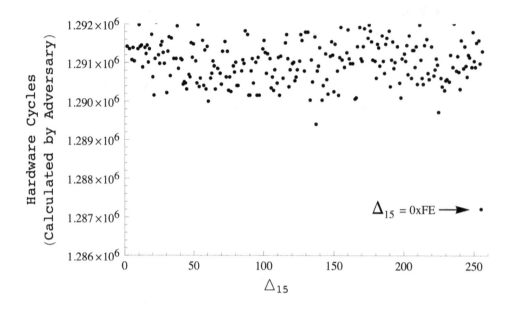

Figure 21.2: TLS median network timings measured by Alfardan and Paterson using the OpenSSL library [4]

As expected, the correct guess leads to a shorter processing time, even when the times are measured over the network.

21.2 POODLE

POODLE stands for **Padding Oracle On Downgraded Legacy Encryption** and was discovered in 2014 by Möller, Duong, and Kotowicz [122]. The name shows that the attack combines two other attacks described in *Chapter 19, Attacks on Cryptography*, and in *Chapter 20, Attacks on the TLS Handshake Protocol*, namely the padding oracle attack and the protocol downgrade attack. By exploiting some characteristics of SSL 3.0, Möller et al. could turn these two into one of the most severe attacks on TLS.

Basically, POODLE is an attack on SSL3.0. Although at the time the attack was published, the underlying weakness was already fixed in TLS 1.2 by introducing authenticated encryption into the TLS Record protocol, the attack remained relevant because of the downgrade dance explained in the previous chapter.

21.2.1 Attacker model

At the heart of the problem lies the MAC-then-encrypt construction deployed by SSL 3.0 described in *Chapter 15, Authenticated Encryption,* and shown in *Figure 21.1*. Because the SSL 3.0 cipher suites use either the (insecure) RC4 stream cipher (see *Section 4.5.2 in Chapter 4, Encryption and Decryption*) or any block cipher in CBC mode (see *Chapter 14, Block Ciphers and Their Modes of Operation*), SSL 3.0 servers will in most cases negotiate a CBC-based cipher suite.

However, it turned out that in connection with the CBC mode of operation, the MAC-then-encrypt construction can be used by an active attacker, Mallory, to deduce parts of the TLS record plaintext. In particular, we are assuming that apart from being able to eavesdrop on and modify messages sent from client Bob to server Alice, Mallory can also see to it that Bob sends encrypted HTTP POST requests to Alice that have been specially crafted by Mallory. For this to happen, Mallory needs to make Bob's browser execute some specific JavaScript code, which might happen after Bob has visited a malicious website controlled by Mallory.

21.2.2 The attack

In the MAC-then-encrypt construction, the MAC is applied to the plaintext only, but does not cover the padding bytes added to the plaintext before encryption. In particular, this holds true for the last padding byte, which in SSL3.0 is always equal to the number N of padded bytes. By making Bob's browser send HTTPS requests of a certain length to Alice, Mallory can make sure that a complete 16-byte block is always padded, which means $N = 15$.

Assume client Bob sends the record

$$c = IV \| C_1 \| C_2 \| \ldots \| C_n$$

to server Alice, where $C_1, C_2, \ldots C_n$ are cipher blocks and IV is the initialization vector for the CBC mode. Mallory now replaces the last cipher block C_n with some interesting block C_i and sends the following modified record instead:

$$\tilde{c} = IV \| C_1 \| C_2 \| \ldots C_{n-1} \| C_i$$

If Alice does not send an error message back, this means $\tilde{c}$ could be successfully decrypted by her. From this, Mallory can deduce that the last plaintext block $\tilde{P}_n$ must have the correct padding number $N = 15$ as its last byte. Now $\tilde{P}_n$ is given by

$$\tilde{P}_n = F_k^{-1}(C_i) \oplus C_{n-1}.$$

Thus, by XORing the last byte of C_{n-1}, Mallory can compute the last byte of $F_k^{-1}(C_i)$. Finally, Mallory can compute the last byte of the interesting plaintext block P_i. This is because in CBC mode,

$$P_i = F_k^{-1}(C_i) \oplus C_{i-1}.$$

However, this will only work in 1 of 256 cases. In all other cases, Alice will strip an incorrect number of padding bytes from the plaintext and the MAC cannot be verified. Mallory must therefore ensure that Bob sends a large number of encrypted HTTP POST requests to Alice, all of which contain a resource path and some string parameter controlled by Mallory. These HTTP requests must also contain interesting data unknown to Mallory, for example, an authentication cookie. Because in SSL 3.0 the IV is the last cipherblock of the previous TLS record, all those POST requests will lead to different records, even if the requests are identical.

Mallory can decrypt other encrypted bytes in C_i by shifting them to the end of C_i. This is done by manipulating the HTTPS requests sent out by Bob using a technique called *bytewise privilege* (see [55]): by increasing the length of the requested resource path, Mallory can push the interesting bytes further toward the end of C_i. Since the overall length of the request must be constant, Mallory at the same time shortens the length of the string parameter in the requests.

21.3   BEAST

Browser Exploit Against SSL/TLS (BEAST) [55] is an attack on the CBC-based encryption of the record layer in SSL 3.0 and TLS 1.0. It is not a padding oracle but uses the predictability of the IV (as mentioned previously, the IV is the last cipher block of the previous TLS record in these versions) instead of attacking one byte of the first cipher block in CBC mode. Using the bytewise privilege technique described earlier, Mallory can move interesting bytes within this cipher block and step-by-step decrypt the complete first cipher block. Still, because the attack is restricted to the first cipher block after the IV, the impact of BEAST was rather limited because the contents of the first plaintext block are usually known. However, BEAST pointed to the fact that there is a serious problem with CBC mode within the TLS record layer.

The attacker model is basically the same as for POODLE, that is, Mallory is a man-in-the-middle who is able to eavesdrop on and manipulate messages sent to the server, along with the ability to make the client send HTTPS requests crafted by him.

21.3.1   The attack

Let's assume Mallory is interested in some unknown plaintext block m_1, which must be the first plaintext block. The CBC mode encrypts m_1 to

$$c_1 = F_k(c_0 \oplus m_1),$$

where F_k is the block cipher and $c_0 = IV$. Mallory observes c_1. Because he also knows c_0, he can craft a new request to be sent by the client with the second plaintext block

$$\tilde{m}_2 = m_0 \oplus c_0 \oplus c_1,$$

where m_0 is some plaintext chosen by Mallory. This gets encrypted to

$$\tilde{c}_2 = F_k(c_1 \oplus \tilde{m}_2) = F_k(m_0 \oplus c_0).$$

Mallory now observes $\tilde{c}_2$ and uses an important fact to distinguish between m_0 and m_1: *if m_0 is equal to m_1, then $\tilde{c}_1 = \tilde{c}_2$.*

This means IND-CPA (see *Section 15.1.1* in *Chapter 15, Authenticated Encryption*) is broken if the CBC mode is used with a predictable IV. The next step for Mallory is to make sure that the unknown plaintext m_1 and m_0 differ only by a single byte b, which is easy because most of the information in the first plaintext block (HTTP method, path, etc.) is known. As there are only 255 possibilities for b, it can be computed by Mallory by crafting at most 255 requests with the same m_1 and different m_0.

21.3.2   Countermeasures

Later versions of TLS, starting with version 1.1, use pseudorandomly generated IVs so that Mallory does not know the IV in advance. Still, because of the downgrade dance, patches were needed for TLS 1.0 and SSL 3.0. These patches make sure that the first plaintext block is always a meaningless dummy block that does not contain any sensitive data, such as authentication cookies.

21.4   Sweet32

SWEET32 [30] is a generic attack against block ciphers with a block size of 64 bits in CBC mode, such as DES or 3DES. However, it has special relevance for TLS because until TLS 1.1, 3DES was mandatory to implement for a TLS library, and TLS 1.2 still contains corresponding cipher suites.

21.4.1 The attack

Recall that in the CBC mode of some block cipher F_k, the i-th plaintext block P_i is encrypted as

$$C_i = F_k(P_i \oplus C_{i-1}).$$

If a large amount of plaintext is encrypted, there might be another plaintext block P_j that generates the same cipher block. Such an occurrence is called a *collision*. In this case, we have

$$C_j = C_i = F_k(P_j \oplus C_{j-1}).$$

This means the input block to F_k must be the same:

$$P_i \oplus C_{i-1} = P_j \oplus C_{j-1},$$

or finally,

$$P_i \oplus P_j = C_{i-1} \oplus C_{j-1}.$$

As the right-hand side is known, the attacker learns $P_i \oplus P_j$. This knowledge can be useful in these cases:

- If some secret information P_i, for example, an authentication cookie, is repeatedly sent by the victim

- If some portion P_j of the plaintext is known

These two conditions are usually fulfilled in HTTP requests. As we have learned in *Chapter 11, Hash Functions and Message Authentication Codes*, collisions for a 64-bit block will occur after encrypting about 2^{32} blocks. However, because not all plaintext blocks carry valuable information, according to [30] a practical attack on cookies requires about 2^{35} blocks, which corresponds to 256 GB of data. In order to generate the required large number of HTTPS requests to some target server, Mallory injects some corresponding JavaScript into the victim's browser and captures the encrypted traffic. In their proof-of-concept attack demo, the authors of [30] were able to recover a two-block cookie from 610 GB of HTTPS traffic, captured over 30.5 hours.

21.4.2   Countermeasures in TLS 1.3

In TLS 1.3, all DES-based cipher suites are deprecated. Moreover, the CBC mode is not used anymore; instead, the **Galois Counter Mode (GCM)** is used for encryption and message authentication (see *Chapter 16, The Galois Counter Mode*).

21.5   Compression-based attacks

Earlier in this chapter, we learned how error messages or timing behavior of Alice's TLS implementation create a side channel providing information about the inner workings of the decryption process. Eve can, in turn, use this information to construct an oracle allowing her to compromise TLS security.

It turns out that lossless compression can also create a similar side channel. In a nutshell, lossless compression allows Eve to extract plaintext from an encrypted communication if she knows or can guess certain characteristics of the plaintext (for example, if she correctly guesses that some string *s* is present in the plaintext).

Between 2012 and 2016, security researchers published four attacks on TLS – CRIME, TIME, BREACH, and HEIST – that exploit the compression side channel. To understand these attacks in depth, let's first look at how some common lossless compression algorithms work.

21.5.1   Lossless compression algorithms

In a *lossless compression algorithm*, the input data is encoded in such a way that its length is decreased. After decoding, however, all of the input data can be reconstructed. The opposite of lossless compression is *lossy compression*, which is common when encoding multimedia data. Here, some of the input data that is deemed unimportant for audiovisual perception are actually thrown away by the algorithm and cannot be reconstructed. In what follows, however, we will only be concerned with lossless compression and therefore frequently omit the attribute *lossless*.

A very common compression algorithm used in internet protocols (and elsewhere) is called **DEFLATE**. It was designed by the American computer scientist Phil Katz for version 2.0 of his archiving tool PKZIP released in 1993. In 1996, the algorithm was also specified in RFC 1951. Technically, DEFLATE combines a so-called Huffman code with the LZ77 data compression algorithm.

Huffman codes are a specific type of optimal codes commonly used in lossless or lossy data compression algorithms, for example, in ZIP and JPEG. The process of finding such codes is called Huffman coding, and it was discovered in 1952 by the American computer science pioneer David Huffman [201].

The output of Huffman coding is a variable-length code generated based on the occurrence frequency of input symbols. Frequently used symbols are encoded using fewer bits than less frequent symbols.

As an example, in the sentence *this is an example of a huffman tree*, the space character occurs seven times, the character "f" occurs three times, and the character "x" occurs once. The Huffman code generated from the character frequencies in that sentence encodes the space character as the 3-bit sequence 111, character "f" as the 4-bit sequence 1101, and character "x" as the 5-bit sequence 10010.

As a result, Huffman codes reduce the overall data size. In the preceding example, encoding the sentence using the Huffman code requires 135 bits as opposed to 288 bits if the 36 characters in the sentence were to be encoded using 8 bits each.

In 1977, the Israeli computer scientist Abraham Lempel and the Israeli electrical engineer Jacob Ziv published a lossless data compression algorithm, **LZ77**. The algorithm works by replacing repeated occurrences of symbol sequences with references to a previous occurrence of that sequence in the input data. Every repeated sequence is replaced by a pair of numbers called the distance-length pair, thereby reducing the size of the data.

As an example, the phrase

```
Google is so googley
```

would be encoded to

```
Google is so g(-13, 5)y.
```

To achieve the compression by identifying recurring symbol sequences, LZ77 must keep track of a pre-configured amount of the most recent data using a data structure called the sliding window. During the encoding process, a sliding window is used to find repeating sequences. During decoding, it is used to interpret the references made occurrences by the encoder. The size of the sliding window – typical values being 2 KB, 4 KB, or 32 KB – determines how many symbols the encoder can use to search for and create references.

21.5.2   The compression side channel

Back in 2002, John Kelsey, a cryptographer working for Certicom at that time, published a paper [98] describing how lossless data compression, when used in cryptosystems, can leak information about the encrypted plaintext.

More precisely, Kelsey showed that under certain circumstances, the size of the ciphertext leaks information about the plaintext when lossless compression is applied to the plaintext. He referred to this information as the *compression side channel.*

The existence of a compression side channel is quite dangerous because it means that Eve can learn certain things about the plaintext from its corresponding ciphertext without ever breaking the encryption algorithm. In addition, Kelsey observed that the compression side channel is fundamentally different from side channels, such as the algorithm's power consumption or execution time (which we will cover in the next chapter), in that it is a property of the algorithm, not the implementation. That is, *any* implementation that uses lossless compression is vulnerable.

As we saw previously, lossless compression works by identifying repeating patterns in the input data and replacing them with references. Thus, if Eve knows the length of encrypted messages that contain s or is able to append s to the messages before they are compressed and encrypted, she can determine the presence of s in a previously unseen encrypted message with non-negligible probability.

Kelsey argued that such *string detection* attacks are feasible in practice and gave the following example for a long string detection with partially chosen plaintext.

Assume that Eve wants to determine whether some long string s appears often in a set of messages $m_0, m_1, \ldots, m_{n-1}$. She can do this using a string detection attack such as this one:

1. First, Eve acquires the compressed and encrypted versions of all m_i. From these messages, she learns their compressed output lengths.

2. In the next step, Eve acquires the compressed and encryption versions of all messages $m_i \| s$.

3. In the third step, Eve determines the length of compressed string s when the corresponding lossless compression algorithm is used.

4. Finally, Eve computes the average $a = (\sum m_i \| s - m_i)/n$. If a is substantially less than the length of compressed s, it is very likely that s is present in many of the messages.

Let's apply this example in the internet setting. To authenticate users, websites use cookies. If the cookie is compressed and encrypted, Mallory cannot simply read it. However, if she can send HTTP requests from Bob's web browser, Mallory can determine the cookie's value using a string detection attack.

Assume that the value of the secret cookie is `abcd1234efgh5678`. Say Mallory correctly guesses part of the secret value and sends the following `GET` request:

```
GET www.alice.com/app.html?some_parameter=abcd
```

In this case, the size of the compressor's output and, in turn, the ciphertext will be smaller because the string abcd occurs multiple times in the HTTP request:

```
GET /app.html?some_parameter=abcd HTTP/1.1
Host: www.alice.com
Cookie: sessionid=abcd1234efgh5678
```

As a result, by making guesses for several bytes and checking the resulting size of the encrypted HTTP request, Mallory will be able to determine the cookie's value.

Importantly, Mallory doesn't have to guess the entire cookie at once (which would be practically infeasible if the cookie is large enough). Instead, she only needs to guess a few bytes at a time, and this can be easily done because a k-byte string can only have 2^{8k} values.

21.5.3 Brief history of compression in TLS

Both TLS version 1.0 released in 1999 [47] and TLS version 1.1 released in 2006 [48] specify compression for TLS records.

One of the parameters Alice and Bob agree upon during a TLS 1.0 or TLS 1.1 handshake is the compression method – the compression algorithm Alice and Bob use to compress data before it is encrypted.

Technically, the compression algorithms translate the `TLSPlaintext` data structure into the `TLSCompressed` data structure shown in *Listing 35*.

Here, `length` is the byte length of the `fragment` variable, and it should not be larger than $2^{14} + 1,024$ bytes. The `fragment` variable, in turn, holds the compressed form of `TLSPlaintext.fragment`:

```
struct {
    ContentType type;        /* same as TLSPlaintext.type */
    ProtocolVersion version;/* same as TLSPlaintext.version */
    uint16 length;
    opaque fragment[TLSCompressed.length];
} TLSCompressed;
```

Listing 35: The `TLSCompressed` *data structure*

In TLS 1.0 and 1.1, Alice and Bob compress all TLS records using the compression algorithm defined in their current session state. There is always an active compression algorithm. At a minimum, all TLS 1.0 and 1.1 implementations must support `CompressionMethod.null`, the identity operation, effectively corresponding to the compression algorithm being deactivated.

Importantly, compression algorithms that are allowed by the TLS 1.0 and 1.1 standards must be lossless – for instance, algorithms such as DEFLATE – and they are not allowed to increase the content length by more than 1,024 bytes.

Due to several attacks that we are going to study next, TLS 1.2 has limited compression, and TLS 1.3 has completely removed compression from the protocol design. Notably, there is even the RFC 8996 [124], which formally deprecates TLS versions 1.0 and 1.1 by moving them to the Historic status.

21.5.4 CRIME

In 2012, security researchers Juliano Rizzo and Thai Duong published a practical attack exploiting the compression side channel [153]. They named their attack **Compression Ratio Info-leak Made Easy** or **CRIME**, for short.

CRIME has even received a dedicated **Common Vulnerabilities and Exposures (CVE)** identifier, namely CVE-2012-4929. CVE is a system that provides information about publicly known security vulnerabilities and exposures to enable vulnerability management automation. Each CVE identifier is unique and contains information about the vulnerability as well as pointers, for example, to security advisories of the affected vendors. One of the best known is the **National Vulnerability Database (NVD)**, operated by the United States government, a well-known public source where CVEs can be looked up.

If Alice and Bob use a vulnerable TLS version up to and including TLS 1.2, Eve can employ CRIME to extract the plaintext from encrypted HTTP headers. She does this by making a series of guesses for a string in the HTTP request – that is, by manipulating that string – and observing the length of the corresponding encrypted traffic. If the value of the string in the HTTP request matches the value of the unknown string in the encrypted HTTP header, lossless compression kicks in and the size of the encrypted traffic is reduced.

Why is this a problem for Alice and Bob? Well, among other things, an HTTP header contains cookies. Cookies are commonly used for user authentication in web applications. As a result, if Eve can extract a cookie transmitted in Bob's HTTP header, she can impersonate Bob to Alice. In web security, this is known as *session hijacking*.

To launch the CIME attack, Eve has to trick Bob into downloading and executing a malicious JavaScript code that Eve can use to craft the HTTP requests with her guess of the secret string in the encrypted HTTP header. In addition, Eve must be capable of assuming the man-in-the-middle role to observe the encrypted network traffic from Bob to Alice and, in particular, the length of the individual network messages.

From the cryptanalytic perspective, CRIME is a combination of a chosen plaintext attack and the information an attacker can obtain through the compression side channel. That, in turn, means IND-CPA (see *Section 15.1.1* in *Chapter 15, Authenticated Encryption*) is broken: Eve can distinguish the ciphertext based on whether it contains the string she has guessed (in the HTTP request) or not.

Exploitation of the compression side channel in CRIME comes as no surprise given that Rizzo and Duang are also the authors of the BEAST attack we previously discussed. To protect against CRIME, data compression was banned in TLS 1.3.

21.5.5 TIME

Less than a year after CRIME was published, security researchers Tal Be'ery and Amichai Shulman presented a new attack they called **Timing Info-leak Made Easy (TIME)** [17]. Conceptually, TIME can be seen as an improvement of the CRIME attack because it eliminates two constraints from the attacker model, and therefore requires a less powerful attacker.

CRIME targets secret values contained in a compressed HTTP request. However, soon after CRIME was published, TLS stopped supporting HTTP request compression, thereby making CRIME less dangerous in practice.

TIME, on the other hand, targets HTTP *responses*. Because a typical HTTP response is much larger than the HTTP request, compressing the responses is a popular technique used by web servers to speed up data transmission. As a result, the compression feature exploited by TIME – and, therefore, TIME's attacker model – has more practical relevance.

CRIME's second constraint relates to network access. To mount the CRIME attack, Eve must have access to the encrypted network traffic. In other words, she not only must trick Bob into executing malicious JavaScript code, but also needs to be in a man-in-the-middle position where she can intercept Bob's encrypted traffic.

TIME, on the other hand, uses *differential timing analysis* to infer the size of the encrypted data. More precisely, Eve guesses the secret value she wants to extract and measures differences in the transmission time of Alice's encrypted HTTP response to Bob. If a sufficiently large part of Eve's guess is correct, the payload of the HTTP response will be smaller and, therefore, the transmission time will be shorter.

The main advantage of exploiting the timing side channel rather than inspecting the encrypted traffic is that the time measurement can be done in the JavaScript code. In other words, Eve does not need man-in-the-middle access to the network traffic transmitted between Alice and Bob. This makes a huge difference. Think about our discussion of local versus remote attacks in chapter 19, *Attacks on Cryptography*. In practice, the requirement to observe Bob's network traffic most likely means that Eve must get access to Bob's wireless local area network. Eve must be *co-located* with Bob while she performs the attack. On the face of it, CRIME looks like a remote attack because it targets network traffic. The need for Eve to access Bob's traffic, however, makes CRIME a *local* attack.

On the other hand, basically any malicious website that Bob visits can have JavaScript code embedded in it that launches the TIME attack, so TIME is a *remote* attack.

But how does Eve manage to measure small timing differences over the internet? It turns out that she can do this using the so-called *congestion window* (see *Figure 21.3*), a feature of the TCP protocol that underlies TLS [150]. To avoid the link between the sender and the receiver becoming overloaded with too much traffic, TCP's congestion window limits the number of bytes that can be transmitted at once.

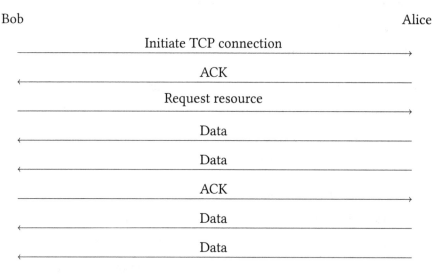

Figure 21.3: Working principle of the TCP congestion window

If the payload to be sent is larger than the congestion window, the sender transmits the first part of the payload that fits into the congestion window, waits for the TCP acknowledgment message from the receiver, and transmits the remaining data. This, in turn, introduces one **Round-Trip Time (RTT)**. *Figure 21.3* shows an example where the congestion window has the size of two TCP segments. After Bob requests a resource, for example, a web page, Alice sends two segments of payload data – the size of the congestion window – and suspends the transmission waiting for Bob to acknowledge he received that data.

By correctly guessing part of the secret value, Eve can make the compressed HTTP response fit exactly into a single congestion window. As a result, a change of one byte in the payload will reduce the response time by one RTT. As an example, an RTT for data transmission between London and New York is approximately 90 ms [150] and therefore can be measured in JavaScript.

However, Eve must be able to inject her guesses into the page (served by Alice) that contains the secret Eve wants to extract. This means that the web application Eve is targeting must mirror some data transmitted in the HTTP request to this application in its HTTP response.

21.5.6 BREACH

In the second half of 2013, security researchers Yoel Gluck, Neal Harris, and Angelo Prado published a modification of CRIME that they called **Browser Reconnaissance and Exfiltration via Adaptive Compression of Hypertext (BREACH)** [72]. Instead of targeting HTTP requests, BREACH uses the CRIME technique to attack HTTP responses.

The authors are motivated by observing that although TLS-level compression was disabled after CRIME's publication, HTTP compression remains popular on the web. Moreover, it is common to include secrets such as **Cross-Site Request Forgery (CSRF)** tokens and user-defined input in the same HTTP response and, therefore, in the same compression context. That, in turn, allowed the authors to apply CRIME to HTTP responses, without relying on TLS compression.

The publication [72] illustrates BREACH using an example attack on **Outlook Web Access (OWA)**. When Bob has established an active OWA session, he transmits the following HTTP request:

```
GET /owa/?ae=Item&t=IPM.Note&a=New&id=canary=<guess>
```

He then receives the following HTTP response:

```
<span id=requestUrl>https://malbot.net:443/owa/forms/
basic/BasicEditMessage.aspx?ae=Item&amp;t=IPM.Note&
amp;a=New&amp;id=canary=<guess></span>
...
<td nowrap id="tdErrLgf"><a
href="logoff.owa?canary=d634cda866f14c73ac135ae858c0d894">Log
Off</a></td>
```

canary is the CSRF token. Importantly, the string canary= is repeated in the HTTP response. As a result, the size of the response is affected by the lossless compression such as DEFLATE used by HTTP. For example, if the first character of <guess> matches the first character of canary, DEFLATE will compress the HTTP response even further. Thus, by observing the size of the encrypted traffic, Eve can determine whether her guess was correct or not. Once the guess is correct, Eve proceeds to guess the next byte in canary.

For the OWA example, the BREACH authors were able to extract the encrypted CSRF tokens about 95% of the time, often in under 30 seconds. That also explains the title of their talk given at BlackHat USA 2013: *SSL, Gone in 30 Seconds*.

BREACH's attack model is equivalent to that of CRIME: Eve must be able to execute JavaScript on Bob's computer and must have access to Bob's network traffic. In addition – like with TIME – the web application needs to reflect user-controlled input and the secret, for instance, the CSRF token of the currently active session, in the HTTP response.

Notably, BREACH is agnostic to the TLS version because it does not require TLS-level compression. Compression of HTTP responses is a common technique at the HTTP level. Consequently, if a web application is vulnerable to BREACH, simply updating the TLS version is not sufficient.

21.5.7 HEIST

In 2016, Mathy Vanhoef and Tom Van Goethem, two security researchers from Belgium, published yet another attack on TLS that exploits the compression side channel. They called their attack **HTTP Encrypted Information can be Stolen through TCP-windows (HEIST)** [175].

HEIST exploits a side channel leaking the exact size of any cross-origin response. Because this side channel is on the TCP level, HEIST allows us to mount CRIME and BREACH attacks purely in the web browser. With HEIST, Eve does not need man-in-the-middle access to Bob's network traffic, and so she can mount CRIME and BREACH attacks *remotely*.

To measure the response times, HEIST uses a JavaScript concept called **Promise**. A Promise is a JavaScript object representing the eventual completion or failure of an asynchronous operation such as an HTTP request to a server. One such example is a GET request to retrieve a web page. A Promise object is always in one of three states:

- **Pending**: The initial state where the Promise is neither fulfilled nor rejected

- **Fulfilled**: A state that the Promise enters upon a successful completion of the asynchronous operation

- **Rejected**: A state that the Promise enters if the asynchronous operation fails

When a Promise is created, JavaScript immediately returns a Promise object. But the Promise itself is either eventually fulfilled or rejected based on the outcome of the fetch() process. Typically, the then() method is used to specify what code shall be executed in case the Promise is fulfilled or rejected.

Vanhoef and Van Goethem observed that the resolution of a Promise happens as soon as the first byte of the corresponding response is received and recognized the security implications of this behavior. Once the client receives the first byte of the response, the JavaScript code is notified by resolving the Promise and can start processing the response while it is still streaming in. If the response is larger than TCP's maximum segment size, it will be split by the server into multiple segments and transmitted according to the congestion window size. After each such transmission, the server waits for a TCP acknowledgment message, ACK, from the client.

Thus, the resolution of a Promise coincides with the receipt of the initial congestion window. Consequently, if Eve can determine when the requested resource – for example, a web page – was completely downloaded, she can determine whether the response fits into a single congestion window. It turns out that Eve can accomplish this using JavaScript's Resource Timing API. This API provides methods that return the time when a request was initiated and when it was completed. *Listing 36* shows how the performance.getEntries() method can be used to obtain the times of a request and determine when the response was completely fetched using the responseEnd attribute:

```javascript
fetch('https://example.com/foo').then(
    function(response) {
        // first byte of `response` received!
        T1 = performance.now();
    }
);


setInterval(function() {
    var entries = performance.getEntries();
    var lastEntry = entries[entries.length - 1];
    if (lastEntry.name == 'https://example.com/foo') {
        T2minT1 = lastEntry.responseEnd - T1;
    }
}, 1)
```

Listing 36: Example JavaScript code for obtaining timing information

Using the example code in *Listing 36*, Eve can send an HTTP `GET` request to fetch `https://example.com/foo`, determine the point in time when the first response byte arrives by executing `T1 = performance.now()`, and determine the point in time when the response was completely received by calling `lastEntry.responseEnd`. Finally, by computing the time difference `T2minT1 = lastEntry.responseEnd - T1`, Eve is able to find out whether the response fits into a single congestion window or not.

Moreover, Vanhoef and Van Goethem demonstrated that the exact size of the response can be calculated based on the timing information when a parameter of the HTTP request is reflected in the corresponding HTTP response.

Thus, to determine the secret value, Eve can simply repeatedly guess the values of the reflected parameter until she finds the largest possible guess for which the HTTP response still fits into the congestion window.

21.6 Summary

In this chapter, we covered attacks on the TLS Record protocol. Although we discussed the technical aspects of all these attacks, there were also some general lessons presented in this chapter.

Lucky 13 is a very educational example of how a seemingly innocuous theoretical weakness that is being ignored can become a critical security vulnerability over time. While Lucky 13 was introduced in 2013, the first practical padding oracle attack on CBC had already been described in 2002 by the French cryptographer Serge Vaudeney [176]. Yet it took over 10 years and the publication of Lucky 13 by AlFardan and Paterson for this type of attack to be taken seriously.

The BEAST attack illustrates that cryptographic notions such as IND-CPA that, on the face of it, are very theoretical, do have their value in practical, real-world security.

The POODLE attack is a good example of security risks posed by insecure legacy systems. In theory, POODLE is an attack on SSL 3.0 and, because at the time of its publication the underlying weakness was already fixed in TLS 1.2, should not have caused any problems.

In practice, POODLE remained a threat to TLS because of the downgrade dance and the typically slow pace of upgrading legacy systems in the field.

Finally, the attacks exploiting the compression side channel demonstrate how the interaction of seemingly unrelated functions – lossless data compression of the plaintext and encryption – can lead to unanticipated, emerging properties such as a timing side channel.

In the next chapter, we will look into attacks that exploit implementation bugs in software stacks that implement TLS.

22

Attacks on TLS Implementations

In the previous chapter, we discussed attacks on the TLS Record protocol. Among other things, we learned how timing side channels can be used to create padding oracles, how predictable initialization vectors can be exploited to attack the CBC mode of operation, and how lossless data compression can compromise the security of an encryption scheme even if the scheme itself is cryptographically secure.

In this chapter, we will take a detailed look at attacks exploiting bugs in TLS software implementations. Among other things, we will cover the following topics:

- Security vulnerabilities resulting from implementing complex specifications

- Security implications of Alice and Bob having a different view of the cryptographic protocol they are executing

- Attacks that exploit so-called *taint-style* vulnerabilities – processing input data without checking that it was not manipulated by Mallory

- Implications of implementation bugs in random number generators

- Security risks when modern, secure protocols are combined with legacy protocols

- Practical implications of implementation-level vulnerabilities

Upon completion of the chapter, the reader will understand why implementation-level security vulnerabilities are easy to introduce into the code base, are hard to spot, and have high impact on security of real-world systems.

22.1 SMACK

In 2015, a group of French security researchers with Benjamin Beurdouche systematically tested the then-popular open source TLS implementations for state-machine-related bugs and uncovered multiple critical security vulnerabilities that have been dormant in these libraries for years [28]. They called these vulnerabilities *State Machine Attacks on TLS* (**SMACK**).

In several previous chapters, for example, in *Chapter 6 Transport Layer Security at a Glance*, *Chapter 8 Elliptic Curves*, *Chapter 12* Secrets and Keys in TLS 1.3, and *Chapter 18 TLS Cipher Suites*, we learned that TLS supports a variety of protocol versions, authentication modes, key exchange alternatives, and protocol extensions.

TLS implementations typically consist of functions for parsing and generating messages, and for performing cryptographic operations. The message sequence – which message to expect or which message to generate as a response – is managed by the TLS peer's state machine, which accepts or transmits the next message based on its state and the negotiated parameters for that TLS session.

The researchers observed that most TLS cipher suites and protocol extensions are defined in their own RFCs. As a result, the composite state machine that a TLS library has to implement is not standardized. This, in turn, requires developers implementing TLS to merge specifications from different RFCs into a single state machine that correctly switches between the protocol modes. This task is, however, error-prone, as illustrated by a simple example from [28] depicted in *Figure 22.1*.

Suppose a developer implements a (fictional) TLS cipher suite where the TLS client sends a *Hello* message and then expects to receive message A and then message B before replying with a *Finished* message.

Now assume that in the next TLS library version, the developer must implement an additional TLS cipher suite where – if this new suite was negotiated at the beginning of the TLS handshake – the TLS client expects to receive message C and then message B.

To reuse the message parsing and generation code for *Hello* and *Finished*, the developer might be tempted to modify the composite state machine so that, after receiving *Hello*, it can receive either A or C, followed by either B or D. While this simple composition implements both TLS cipher suites, it also allows unintended message sequences such as *Hello, A, D, Finished*.

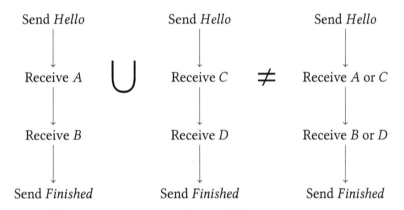

Figure 22.1: Incorrect union of exemplary state machines

Intuitively, you might think that allowing unintended message sequences such as *Hello, A, D, Finished* does not effect security because Alice and Bob will send only valid message sequences and any attempt by Mallory to insert an incorrect message will be detected when Alice and Bob compare their communication transcripts.

This is, however, not the case. If Bob's state machine accepts the sequence *Hello, A, D, Finished*, until he and Alice compare their transcripts, Bob is executing an unknown handshake protocol with no a priori security guarantees. As an example, the code for processing message *D* may be expected to always run after the code processing message *C*. Given *Hello, A, D, Finished*, *D*'s code may unintentionally use an uninitialized data structure that it expected to be filled by *C*'s code. Alternatively, it could leak secrets received in *A* or allow authentication steps to be skipped.

Using a combination of automated testing and manual source code analysis, the researchers conducted a systematic analysis of state machines implemented in then-current versions of open source TLS libraries [28]. While the individual state machines were correct, the researchers identified numerous TLS implementations that contained flaws in their *composite* state machines.

Some of these flaws had no effect on security. Others, however, turned out to be critical vulnerabilities that can be exploited by a remote attacker to undermine TLS security. More specifically, the researchers discovered several ways to impersonate a TLS server to a client running a flawed TLS implementation. One such attack, referred to as SKIP, simply skips the handshake messages. Another attack, which the researchers called FREAK, factors the server's export-grade RSA key.

22.2 FREAK

FREAK stands for *Factoring RSA Export Keys*. The attack was discovered in 2017 ([27]) and can be seen as a variant of the cipher suite downgrade attack shown in *Figure 20.1* with respect to RSA as a key establishment mechanism. It works if server Alice supports weak, export-grade RSA cipher suites. Interestingly, client Bob may even support only strong RSA cipher suites for the attack to work.

More specifically, in the FREAK attack, Mallory modifies the cipher suite list sent by the client to be

$$A_w = \texttt{TLS\_RSA\_EXPORT\_WITH\_DES40\_CBC\_SHA}$$

and forwards it to the server.

If the server accepts this cipher suite and sends a corresponding ServerHello back, Mallory modifies it to a stronger, non-export RSA cipher suite, as follows:

$$A_1 = \text{TLS\_RSA\_WITH\_3DES\_EDE\_CBC\_SHA}$$

The client now ought to use the strong RSA public key contained in the server's certificate for securely transporting PreMasterSecret to the server. However, along with its certificate, the server also sends a ServerKeyExchange message containing an ephemeral export-grade RSA public key with a 512-bit module. Because of a state machine composition bug in OpenSSL, the client silently accepts this message and the server's strong public key is replaced with the weak public key in the ServerKeyExchange message. It is because of this bug that FREAK is classified here as an attack on TLS implementations.

The client then uses the weak ephemeral RSA key to encrypt PreMasterSecret. Today, such a 512-bit RSA modulus can be factorized within hours. While this may still be too long for the ongoing handshake, even ephemeral keys are often reused for days.

22.3 Truncation attacks

The TLS record protocol takes each message from the higher layer application protocol (usually HTTP) and protects it with in a single TLS record. TLS may also *fragment* the message before encrypting it. The TLS security services of integrity and authentication therefore only refer to single messages or their fragments.

In a *truncation attack*, an attacker acting as man-in-the-middle suppresses complete TLS records or fragments, with the result that client and server become de-synchronized with respect to their current state: For example, a client having sent a logout request to the server assumes that they are logged out. If the logout request is suppressed by Mallory (e.g., by injecting an unencrypted TCP FIN packet), however, the server will continue to assume the client is logged in.

In [167], the authors demonstrate the potential of this kind of attack to take control of Microsoft Live accounts. By using simple traffic analysis, they found out that packets carrying logout requests to `account.live.com` tended to be between 474 and 506 bytes long, and simply dropped all packets within this range. If client Bob now leaves his terminal, believing he has successfully logged out, Mallory can take over his account if he has the capability to access Bob's terminal.

In another variant of truncation attacks, in section III of [29], the authors show how cookie-based authentication can be compromised by truncating HTTP headers. When setting an authentication cookie, the server provides the URL of the requested response, the cookie, and a `secure` flag within its `Set-Cookie` header. The `secure` flag makes sure the authentication cookie is sent only via HTTPS. Mallory now triggers a request from the client to a URL that has just the right length so that the first TLS fragment of the server response ends *before* the `secure` flag in the `Set-Cookie` header. Mallory then suppresses the second fragment containing the `secure` flag. As a consequence, the cookie will be sent by the client in plaintext via HTTP.

While these attacks are quite severe, it seems that security in these cases mainly depends on secure application logic. For example, the described attack against authentication cookies was only possible because some browsers accepted incomplete HTTP responses. Moreover, as is pointed out in [167], clients need to be reliably notified about server-side state changes.

22.4 Heartbleed

In 2014, Google's security team member Neel Mehta privately reported an implementation bug to OpenSSL's developer team. The same bug was independently discovered by security engineers working for Codenomicon, a Finnish security company specialized in network security that was eventually acquired by Synopsys. Following its disclosure, Heartbleed was assigned the CVE number CVE-2014-0160.

At the time of Heartbleed's disclosure, more than half a million web servers – about 17% of all web servers using TLS at that time – were believed to be vulnerable to the attack. More importantly, Heartbleed allowed attackers to steal the servers' private keys.

The private key SK_{Alice} of a TLS server is its long-term secret corresponding to the public key in the server's certificate. If Eve manages to compromises Alice's private key, this has grave consequences: Eve can impersonate Alice and decrypt any future communication between server Alice and her clients. If the private key was used to establish a shared secret in a previous TLS session, Eve can decrypt this earlier communication as well.

For this reason, the non-profit digital rights group Electronic Frontier Foundation, technology magazine Ars Technica, and the American cryptographer Bruce Schneier described the Heartbleed bug as *catastrophic*. Joseph Steinberg, the cybersecurity columnist at the American business magazine Forbes, wrote that Heartbleed might be "*the worst vulnerability found (at least in terms of its potential impact) since commercial traffic began to flow on the Internet.*"

22.4.1 TLS Heartbeat extension

The name Heartbleed is a pun on the TLS *Heartbeat extension* proposed in 2012 in RFC 6520. The name alludes to the fact that the Heartbleed attack exploits an implementation bug accidentally introduced with the Heartbeat extension's implementation into OpenSSL version 1.0.1.

The Heartbeat extension specifies a mechanism for testing whether the TLS peer is still active and, as a result, keep the TLS session alive without the need for costly session renegotiation.

The Heartbeat protocol runs on top of the TLS Record protocol and consists of two message types: `HeartbeatRequest` and `HeartbeatResponse`. At any time during an active TLS session, Alice and Bob can receive a `HeartbeatRequest` message and are expected to answer it with a corresponding `HeartbeatResponse` message.

The Heartbeat protocol allows the sender to verify that the TLS peer can be reached and is alive. If no `HeartbeatResponse` message is received after some amount of time, the sender of the `HeartbeatRequest` (whether Alice or Bob) may terminate the TLS session.

Listing 37 shows the data structure of the TLS Heartbeat message specified in RFC 6520. It consists of the message type, an arbitrary payload, and padding:

```
struct {
    HeartbeatMessageType type;
    uint16 payload_length;
    opaque payload[HeartbeatMessage.payload_length];
    opaque padding[padding_length];
} HeartbeatMessage;
```

Listing 37: The `HeartbeatMessage` *data structure*

RFC 6520 specifies that a `HeartbeatMessage` cannot be larger than 2^{14} bytes or `max_fragment_length` when it is negotiated between Alice and Bob according to the specification in RFC 6066.

The `type` variable of the `HeartbeatMessage` data structure can be either `heartbeat_request` or `heartbeat_response`. Unsurprisingly, the `payload_length` variable contains the size of the arbitrary payload; the length of the `payload_length` variable itself is two bytes. If the TLS peer receives a Heartbeat message where `payload_length` is too large, they must silently discard that message. Finally, `padding` contains at least 16 bytes of random content that must be ignored by the receiver.

The receiver of a `HeartbeatRequest` message must reply with a `HeartbeatResponse` message that contains an exact copy of the payload in the received `HeartbeatRequest`. If `HeartbeatResponse` does not contain the expected payload, the receiving TLS peer terminates the TLS session.

22.4.2   The Heartbleed bug

Heartbleed is the result of improper input validation – more precisely, a missing bounds check – in the OpenSSL implementation of the TLS Heartbeat extension. Technically, the bug is a buffer over-read, where an attacker can read more data than what was intended by the designer (see *Figure 22.2*).

Figure 22.2: The Heartbleed Bug (source: xkcd.com/154)

Listing 38 shows an OpenSSL version vulnerable to Heartbleed. The code stores the Heartbeat message type in `unsigned short` hbtype and increments pointer *p by one byte. It then calls the n2s() macro to write the 16-bit length of the Heartbeat payload into the payload variable and to increment *p by two bytes. Finally, p1 is set to point to the payload's contents.

```
/* Read type and payload length first */
hbtype = *p++;
n2s(p, payload);
pl = p;

-- snip --

if (hbtype == TLS1_HB_REQUEST) {
    unsigned char *buffer, *bp;
    int r;
    /* Allocate memory for the response */
    buffer = OPENSSL_malloc(1 + 2 + payload + padding);
    bp = buffer;
    /* Enter response type, length and copy payload */
    *bp++ = TLS1_HB_RESPONSE;
    s2n(payload, bp);
    memcpy(bp, pl, payload);
    bp += payload;
    /* Random padding */
    RAND_pseudo_bytes(bp, padding);
```

Listing 38: The Heartbleed bug

If the received Heartbeat message has the type TLS1_HB_REQUEST, the code proceeds by creating a bp buffer of 1 + 2 + payload + padding bytes. It then sets the message type to TLS1_HB_RESPONSE and increments the bp buffer pointer by one byte. Finally, the code uses the s2n() macro to write the 16-bit payload length to memory, increment bp by two bytes, and copy payload number of bytes from the received payload (which is pointed to by p1) into the reply payload.

Recall that Eve controls the Heartbeat request message and, thus, can manipulate it at will. So, she can set the payload length – stored in the payload variable in the above code – to 64 KB but the payload itself – pointed to by the pl variable – to just one byte.

Because the vulnerable code in *Listing 38* does not check the actual size of the payload in the Heartbeat request, the memcpy() function will read beyond the end of the received payload, thereby reading from the server process's memory. This memory, in turn, holds sensitive information such as passwords, decrypted messages, or Alice's private keys.

In other words, as illustrated in [200], whereas a benign Heartbeat request would ask Alice to *return a four-byte payload*, 0x01020304, a malicious Heartbeat request would ask her to *return a 2^{16}-byte payload*, 0x01020304, causing Alice to return 0x01020304 followed by whatever $2^{16} - 4$ bytes happen to be in her process's active memory.

Even worse, sending a second Heartbeat message will read another 64 KB, thereby allowing Eve to repeat the attack and extract a large amount of Alice's internal memory.

22.4.3 The bugfix

The bugfix for the Heartbleed bug is shown in *Listing 39*. It is a simple bounds check using the actual TLS record length in the s3->rrec data structure.

```
hbtype = *p++;
n2s(p, payload);
if (1 + 2 + payload + 16 > s->s3->rrec.length)
    return 0; /* silently discard per RFC 6520 sec. 4 */
pl = p;
```

Listing 39: The Heartbleed bugfix

The s3->rrec.length variable contains the actual record length, while payload is the payload length provided in the Heartbeat request. If the term 1 + 2 + payload + 16 is larger than s3->rrec.length, Alice knows immediately that this Heartbeat message contains a wrong payload variable and, therefore, is likely manipulated. In that case, the dtls1_process_heartbeat function silently terminates as specified in RFC 6520.

22.5   Insecure encryption activation

Systems that use older plaintext protocols require backward compatibility. In this case, Alice and Bob start the communication without encryption and must explicitly upgrade it to use TLS. As an example, if they use **Simple Mail Transfer Protocol (SMTP)**, published by American computer scientists Jon Postel and Suzanne Sluizer in 1981 (RFC 788), they have to use the STARTTLS command to start a TLS session.

The need to explicitly activate secure communication creates additional attack vectors if application code running on Alice's or Bob's machine contains implementation flaws – not programming bugs, but logical mistakes in the implementation affecting its security [150].

One such flaw is missing STARTTLS enforcement. When a legacy protocol can be used without encryption, Bob's software is responsible for enforcing the desired security level. A common flaw in such software is to request encryption but proceed without it if Alice doesn't offer it. As a result, Mallory can intercept the plaintext messages transmitted between Alice and Bob and simply remove the STARTTLS message to make sure that Alice and Bob continue their communication in plaintext.

Another such flaw is the buffering of insecure plaintext. If Bob's software does not reset the protocol state after the encryption starts, Mallory can manipulate messages she would otherwise have no access to. In particular, she can inject payload into plaintext messages that will be processed *after* the encryption is activated, tricking Alice and Bob into believing they are processing messages secured by TLS while these messages actually contain Mallory's payload.

22.6   Random number generation

In *Chapter 3 A Secret to Share*, we learned that the security of most protocols and mechanisms depends on the generation of random sequences of bits or numbers. These sequences must have a sufficient length and be *random* in a very specific sense: We do not want an attacker to be able to guess part of or the whole sequence.

Why? Recall the example from *Chapter 3 A Secret to Share*: The size of the key space of the AES-256 encryption algorithm is 2^{256}. If the AES-256 key was selected using a truly random source, Eve would have to try on average 2^{255} candidate keys before she found the correct key.

However, if Alice generates the key by first choosing a 32-bit random number and then turning it into a 256-bit key using some complicated but *deterministic* expansion algorithm *E*, then Eve needs to try only 2^{31} possible keys on average (obtained by running every possible 32-bit random number through *E*). To prevent this, Alice and Bob must generate the keys using bits from truly random sources. Cryptographers use the concept of entropy to describe the randomness of a source.

Implementation bugs can undermine TLS security by affecting entropy used in TLS's cryptographic operations. An example of such vulnerability is a bug introduced in Debian, a very popular Linux distribution, in September 2006 and discovered by Debian developer Luciano Bello in 2008.

```
/* Don't add uninitiatilised data.
    MD_Update(&m, buf, j);
*/
    MD_Update(&m, (unsigned char *)&(md_c[0]), sizeof(md_c));
    MD_Final(&m, local_md);
    md_c[1]++;
```

Listing 40: Implementation bug in Debian etch

As shown in *Listing 40*, Debian developers accidentally commented out – effectively, removed – the code line `MD_Update(&m, buf, j);` that was feeding entropy into Debian's pseudo-random number generator [150]. As a result, the input to the pseudo-random number generator had only 16 bits of entropy. All Eve had to do is to try merely 2^{15} possible values on average for any cryptographic operation, for instance, to guess private keys generated by Alice using the vulnerable software:

22.7 BERserk attack

In 2014, Intel's advanced threat research team and the French security researcher Antoine Delignat-Lavaud discovered a critical vulnerability in the then-current version of Mozilla's **Network Security Services (NSS)** cryptographic library [85]. The attack was assigned the CVE number CVE-2014-1569.

The researchers gave the vulnerability the name *BERserk*, which is a pun on the **Basic Encoding Rules (BER)** encoding format. BER is a set of rules specified in International Telecommunications Union's ASN.1 standard for encoding data into binary form.

NSS versions vulnerable to BERserk do not ensure that the BER encoding of an ASN.1 length is correctly formed. This, in turn, allows Mallory to forge RSA signatures using the PKCS#1 v1.5 RSA Signature Forgery attack published earlier by Daniel Bleichenbacher.

According to the PKCS#1 v1.5 standard, a plaintext's hash to be signed must be padded as follows:

```
00 01 FF FF .. FF FF 00 DigestInfo MessageDigest
```

where `DigestInfo` is the ASN.1 encoding of the hash algorithm used to compute the hash of the plaintext message.

In 2006, Bleichenbacher published a signature forgery attack against implementations of RSA signature verification with a low public exponent that do not completely validate PKCS#1 v1.5 padding when decrypting the encoded message from an RSA signature [85].

Suppose the RSA signature verification uses a public key with a small encryption exponent $e = 3$. A vulnerable implementation scans the DER-encoded message for padding bytes `0xFF .. 0xFF` until it finds the separator byte `0x00`. It then continues to validate `DigestInfo` and `MessageDigest` without verifying that there are no extra bytes *after* `MessageDigest`.

As a result, Mallory can insert extra bytes after `MessageDigest`:

```
00 01 FF FF FF FF FF FF FF FF 00 DigestInfo MessageDigest ExtraBytes
```

In a man-in-the-middle scenario, Mallory can make Alice process that modified encoded message. It turns out that `ExtraBytes` allows Mallory to forge RSA signatures – without knowing the RSA private key d – for arbitrary messages when the public exponent is small.

22.8 Cloudbleed

In 2017, Tavis Ormandy, a vulnerability researcher in Google's Project Zero team, reported a security vulnerability in Cloudflare's edge servers [76]. Cloudflare is a large **Content Delivery Network (CDN)** that operates a global network of servers that cache and deliver website content to end users from the server location closest to them.

Because of the vulnerability, the software running on Cloudflare's edge servers – more precisely, an HTML parser – was reading past the end of a buffer and returning contents from the servers' internal memory such as HTTP cookies, authentication tokens, and the bodies of HTTP POST requests.

Cloudflare reported that during the peak time, a period of about five days, 1 in every 3,300,000 HTTP requests to Cloudflare's edge servers potentially resulted in a memory leak [76].

The proof of concept by Tavis Ormandy returned private messages from major dating sites, full messages from a well-known chat service, online password manager data, frames from adult video sites, and hotel bookings. Due to its similarity to Heartbleed, the bug was soon named *Cloudbleed*.

Numerous Cloudflare services need to parse and modify HTML requests and pages, for example, to insert Google Analytics tags, rewrite HTTP links to HTTPS links, exclude parts of a page from bad bots, or modify the HTML code of a web page. To achieve this, the services must parse HTML to identify elements that have to be changed.

To generate HTML parsers, Cloudflare initially used the Ragel state machine compiler tool. Every HTML parser was described in its own `.rl` file. Eventually, though, the company decided that Ragel-based parsers had become too complex to maintain and, therefore, started writing a new parser called `cf-html` to replace Ragel. At the time of the bug discovery, Cloudflare was migrating from the old Ragel to the new `cf-html` parser.

Both `cf-html` and the old Ragel-based parser were implemented as NGINX modules compiled into Cloudflare's NGINX builds. These NGINX filter modules parse buffers (blocks of memory) containing HTML responses, make modifications as necessary, and pass the buffers onto the next filter [76].

Analyses performed after Tavis Ormandy's report showed that the Cloudbleed bug was present in Cloudflare's Ragel parser for many years but did not lead to memory leaks because of the way internal NGINX buffers were used. Unfortunately, introducing `cf-html` changed the buffering in a subtle way that, in turn, enabled the information leakage.

Once Cloudflare realized that the bug was caused by the use of the `cf-html` parser, they quickly disabled its multiple features using the corresponding feature flags they refer to as *global kill switches*. For example, the email obfuscation global kill switch was activated 47 minutes after Cloudflare received information about the security incident.

22.8.1   Details of the the Cloudbleed bug

To build a Ragel-based parser, the Ragel code is automatically transformed into C code. The C code is then compiled into an executable. Unfortunately, the generated C code contained a bug shown in *Listing 41*.

```
/* generated code */
if ( ++p == pe )
    goto _test_eof;
```

Listing 41: Cloudbleed bug

The `if` statement in *Listing 41* is supposed to check whether the end of the buffer, the address pointed to by pe, is reached. However, because the `==` operator is used, that `if` statement evaluates to `false` in *two* cases:

- When `++p` points to an address less than pe, that is, the end of buffer is not reached yet

- When `++p` points to an address larger than pe, that is, when `++p` is beyond the end of the buffer

As a result, if, after being incremented, pointer p does not point exactly to address pe, it will be allowed to jump over the buffer end. Interestingly, the bug in the generated C code is actually the result of a programming error in the Ragel description of the parser. That is, the Ragel code that Cloudflare developers wrote contained an error that led to the bug in the generated code.

A second interesting aspect is that the bug was dormant in Cloudflare's production code for multiple years. However, as long as the old Ragel-based parser was used, the buggy code was never executed. This changed when Cloudflare's engineers added the new `cf-html` parser.

22.9 Timing attacks

In the previous two chapters, we learned about attacks on the TLS Handshake and the TLS Record protocols, which use a padding oracle to compromise TLS security guarantees. In most cases, the padding oracle is a by-product of *data-dependent timing differences* that occur when a TLS implementation processes the received TLS messages.

While these attacks target the TLS Handshake or TLS Record protocol, the underlying reason – namely, the leakage of information about internally processed data – is an implementation issue. In cryptography, attacks that exploit such information are called *side channel attacks*.

More precisely, side channel attacks exploit unintended information leakage caused by the physical properties of the implementation of a cryptographic algorithm. Using the leaked information, Eve can infer intermediate values processed by the cryptographic algorithm and, based on these values, extract the secret values.

22.9.1   Side channel attacks

In side channel attacks, Eve exploits information that the implementation of a cryptographic algorithm leaks through so-called *side channels*. Side channels are observable physical quantities, such as the execution time of a cryptographic algorithm's implementation or the instantaneous power consumption or electromagnetic emanations of a cryptographic circuit, that depend on the intermediate values processed by the implementation of that cryptographic algorithm. *Figure 22.3* gives an overview of side channels known to leak data-dependent information.

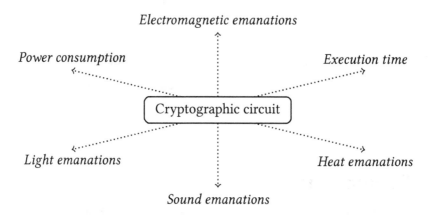

Figure 22.3: Various side channels leaking information about the intermediate values processed by the implementation of a cryptographic algorithm

As an example, *Algorithm 11* shows a naive implementation of the square-and-multiply algorithm. The algorithm is often used to compute the modular exponentiation operation in the RSA public-key-encryption scheme (see also *Chapter 7, Public-Key Cryptography*) because it reduces the number of multiplications required by exploiting binary representation of the exponent. However, unfortunately for Alice and Bob, the naive implementation in *Algorithm 11* has a timing side channel.

The multiplication $b \leftarrow A \cdot b$ (mod n) in the loop iteration i is calculated only if the corresponding bit k_i in the exponent is 1 and is omitted otherwise. As a result, if Eve can precisely measure the execution time of each loop iteration, she can determine the secret bits of the RSA exponent. The data-dependent execution time variation therefore constitutes the so-called *side channel leakage.*

Algorithm 11 The Square–and–multiply algorithm [117].

Require: $a \in \mathbb{Z}_n$, integer $0 < k < n$ whose binary representation is $k = \sum_{i=0}^{t} k_i 2^i$
Ensure: a^k (mod n)
  $b \leftarrow 1$
  if $k = 0$ **then**
    return b
  end if
  $A \leftarrow a$
  if $k_0 = 1$ **then**
    $b \leftarrow a$
  end if
  for i in 1 to t **do**
    $A \leftarrow A^2$ (mod n)
    if $k_i = 1$ **then**
      $b \leftarrow A \cdot b$ (mod n)
    end if
  end for
  return b

In general, a side channel leakage is the measured variation of the observed physical quantity, for example, execution time or instantaneous power consumption, during the execution of a cryptographic algorithm. As an example, *Figure 22.4* shows the instantaneous power consumption of an AES circuit for different Hamming distance values – the number of bits at which two consecutive values differ – for intermediate data processed by AES.

The power consumption in *Figure 22.4* around sample #45 is equivalent to the Hamming distance between the current value of an intermediate register and the result of the SubBytes operation that overwrites the current value.

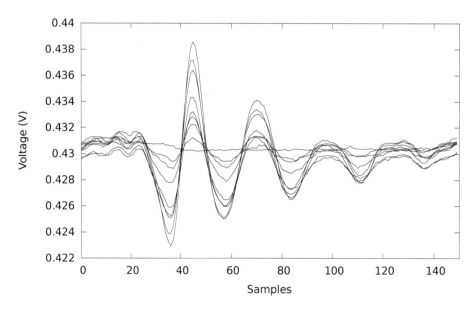

Figure 22.4: Power consumption of an AES hardware implementation when the output of the SubBytes operation is stored in an intermediate register

This is because in CMOS technology, the power consumption of storing a value in a register is proportional to the number of bit flips in that register when the old value is overwritten with the new one.

22.9.2   Raccoon

The Raccoon attack [118] provides an example of a timing attack against the TLS handshake. It allows attackers under certain conditions to get hold of the `PreMasterSecret` established in course of the TLS handshake. However, the authors of [118] themselves say this:

The vulnerability is really hard to exploit and relies on very precise timing measurements and on a specific server configuration to be exploitable.

The attack

Raccoon exploits the fact that according to the specification of TLS 1.2 (and all previous versions), all leading zero bytes in `PreMasterSecret` shall be deleted before the *PMS* is used in further computations. As the resulting *PMS* serves as input into the key derivation function KDF , which is in turn based on hash functions with different timing profiles, precise timing measurements may enable an attacker to find out whether the PMS starts with zero or not.

For example, if Diffie-Hellman is used to establish the PMS, Mallory could eavesdrop the values g^α mod p sent by the client (where α is the client's private key) in a `ClientKeyExchange` message, resend it to the server, and determine via precise time measurements whether the resulting PMS starts with zero or not.

In order to go beyond the leading byte of the PMS, Mallory constructs a series of related values $g^{\mu_i} \cdot g^\alpha$ mod p and sends them to the server. These lead to `PreMasterSecrets`

$$PMS(i) = g^{\mu_i\beta} \cdot g^\beta \quad \text{mod } p,$$

where β is the private key of the server. Note that this will only work if the server either uses static Diffie-Hellman or reuses ephemeral Diffie-Hellman keys for multiple connections.

Based on the server timing behavior, the attacker can find out which values will lead to `PreMasterSecrets`, starting with zero. This enables the attacker to construct a set of equations to compute the original PMS established between the client and the server.

Countermeasures in TLS 1.3

TLS 1.3 does not support static Diffie-Hellman-based key establishment. Apart from key establishment based on **pre-shared keys (PSKs)**, only ephemeral **Diffie-Hellman (DHE)** or **ephemeral elliptic-curve-based Diffie-Hellman (ECDHE)** are available.

Their efficiency and the lack of detection makes side channel attacks a serious threat for any security system. Therefore, special design guidelines and dedicated countermeasures must be implemented to defend cryptographic circuits, in particular block ciphers, against this type of attack.

22.10 Summary

This chapter completes *Part 4 Bleeding Hearts and Biting Poodles*, which was concerned with attacks on previous version of TLS. The attacks we covered in this chapter exploit implementation bugs rather than protocol weaknesses or vulnerabilities in underlying cryptographic mechanisms.

The SMACK and FREAK attacks are practical examples of how easily mistakes happen when you have to implement complex cryptographic protocols and algorithms. Indeed, to put it in the words of Bruce Schneier, *complexity is the enemy of security*. Remember: we had an initial discussion on this topic in the very first chapter of this book.

Truncation attacks show why it is important that both Alice and Bob have the same view of the cryptographic protocol they are executing. If Bob thinks they are both in state x but Alice thinks they are in state y, the security of the whole protocol may be compromised.

The danger of making assumptions about input data – in other words, data that might come from Eve or be manipulated by Mallory – is illustrated by Heartbleed. It is also yet more evidence that programming is inherently hard, and so extra effort must be invested in validating the implementations of cryptographic systems.

Along similar lines, Heartbleed shows that getting the specification right does not guarantee the security of an actual system. Right from the start, RFC 6520 correctly specified that if a TLS peer receives a Heartbeat message where payload_length is too large, they must silently discard that message; however, that specification was not implemented accordingly.

Cloudbleed, once again, illustrates how sneaky bugs can be and that dormant bugs can exist in source code even if the implementation does not show any vulnerable behavior today. It also shows that software companies with professional developers on their payroll are susceptible to implementation-level security vulnerabilities in the same manner as open source projects with voluntary maintainers and contributors.

Moreover, Cloudbleed is a practical example of security problems caused by switching from one technology to another. On the positive side, it shows that having kill switches to immediately turn off a deployed feature is one of the best patterns for building secure systems.

Implementation bugs degrading the quality of random number generation highlight that entropy is fundamental and, at the same time, hard to test. While a collection of statistical tests might have uncovered the Debian bug, simple tests won't work. Testing the remaining cryptographic functions, say, block cipher and hash function implementations, with known-answer-tests will not reveal missing entropy.

Insecure encryption invocation illustrates how the use of legacy protocols in conjunction with modern, secure protocols can undermine the system's security. Raccoon is yet another example of how side channel leakage can be exploited to extract secrets.

Finally, there is a more general insight to be learned from the attacks described in this chapter: while they have nothing to do with cryptography, the financial damage caused by Heartbleed alone very likely exceeds that of all cryptanalytic attacks on TLS taken together.

It thus seems appropriate to close this chapter – and the book – with a quote by Niels Ferguson and Bruce Schneier [65]: *Cryptography is fiendishly difficult. Even seasoned experts design systems that are broken a few years later. [At the same time, cryptography] is one of the easy parts of a security system. [...] Cryptography is the easy part because there are people who know how to do a reasonably good job. [...] The rest of the security system contains problems that we don't know how to solve.*

Bibliography

[1] David Adrian, Karthikeyan Bhargavan, Zakir Durumeric, Pierrick Gaudry, Matthew Green, J Alex Halderman, Nadia Heninger, Drew Springall, Emmanuel Thomé, Luke Valenta, et al. Imperfect Forward Secrecy: How Diffie-Hellman Fails in Practice. In *Proceedings of the 22nd ACM SIGSAC Conference on Computer and Communications Security*, pages 5–17, 2015.

[2] Eman Salem Alashwali and Kasper Rasmussen. What's in a Downgrade? A Taxonomy of Downgrade Attacks in the TLS Protocol and Application Protocols Using TLS. In *Security and Privacy in Communication Networks: 14th International Conference*, pages 468–487. Springer, 2018.

[3] Nadhem AlFardan, Daniel J. Bernstein, Kenneth G. Paterson, Bertram Poettering, and Jacob C. N. Schuldt. On the Security of RC4 in TLS. In *22nd USENIX Security Symposium (USENIX Security 13)*, pages 305–320, Washington, D.C., 2013. USENIX Association.

[4] Nadhem J AlFardan and Kenneth G Paterson. Lucky Thirteen: Breaking the TLS and DTLS Record Protocols. In *IEEE Symposium on Security and Privacy (S&P)*, pages 526–540. IEEE, 2013.

[5] Christopher Allen and Tim Dierks. RFC 2246: The TLS Protocol Version 1.0, 1999.

[6] American National Standards Institute. ANSI X9.62: Public Key Cryptography for the Financial Services Industry: The Elliptic Curve Digital Signature Algorithm (ECDSA). `https://standards.globalspec.com/std/1955141/ANSI%20X9.62`,

2005. [Online; accessed 11-February-2023].

[7] Ross Anderson. *Security Engineering: A Guide to Building Dependable Distributed Systems.* John Wiley & Sons, 2020.

[8] Elena Andreeva, Charles Bouillaguet, Orr Dunkelman, Pierre-Alain Fouque, Jonathan Hoch, John Kelsey, Adi Shamir, and Sébastien Zimmer. New Second-Preimage Attacks on Hash Functions. *Journal of Cryptology*, 29:657–696, 2016.

[9] Manos Antonakakis, Tim April, Michael Bailey, Matt Bernhard, Elie Bursztein, Jaime Cochran, Zakir Durumeric, J Alex Halderman, Luca Invernizzi, Michalis Kallitsis, et al. Understanding the Mirai Botnet. In *26th USENIX security symposium (USENIX Security 17)*, pages 1093–1110, 2017.

[10] Protecting Keys with the Secure Enclave. `https://developer.apple.com/docume ntation/security/certificate_key_and_trust_services/keys/protecting_ke ys_with_the_secure_enclave`, 2022. Online; accessed 21-December-2022.

[11] Jean-Philippe Aumasson. *Serious Cryptography: A Practical Introduction to Modern Encryption.* No Starch Press, 2017.

[12] Nimrod Aviram, Sebastian Schinzel, Juraj Somorovsky, Nadia Heninger, Maik Dankel, Jens Steube, Luke Valenta, David Adrian, J Alex Halderman, Viktor Dukhovni, et al. {DROWN}: Breaking TLS Using {SSLv2}. In *25th USENIX Security Symposium (USENIX Security 16)*, pages 689–706, 2016.

[13] Philip Ball. First Quantum Computer to Pack 100 Qubits Enters Crowded Race. `https://www.nature.com/articles/d41586-021-03476-5`, 2021. [Online; accessed 12-January-2023].

[14] Elaine Barker. SP 800-175B Rev.1: Guideline for Using Cryptographic Standards in the Federal Government: Cryptographic Mechanisms, 2020. Last accessed 15 August 2020.

[15] R. Barnes, K. Bhargavan, B. Lipp, and C. Wood. RFC 9180: Hybrid Public Key Encryption, 2022.

[16] Richard Barnes, Martin Thomson, Alfredo Pironti, and Adam Langley. Deprecating Secure Sockets Layer Version 3.0. Technical report, 2015.

[17] Tal Be'ery and Amichai Shulman. A Perfect CRIME? Only TIME Will Only TIME Will Tell Tell. Technical report, BlackHat Europe, 2013. [Online; accessed 17-September-2023].

[18] Mihir Bellare and Chanathip Namprempre. Authenticated Encryption: Relations Among Notions and Analysis of the Generic Composition Paradigm. *Journal of Cryptology*, 21(4):469–491, 2008.

[19] Mihir Bellare and Amit Sahai. Non-Malleable Encryption: Equivalence Between Two Notions, and an Indistinguishability-based Characterization. *Cryptology ePrint Archive*, 2006.

[20] Tim Berners-Lee. Information Management: A Proposal. Technical report, CERN, 1989.

[21] Tim Berners-Lee and Robert Cailliau. WorldWideWeb: Proposal for a HyperText Project. Technical report, CERN, 1990.

[22] Daniel Bernstein and Tanja Lange. SafeCurves: Choosing Safe Curves for Elliptic-Curve Cryptography. https://safecurves.cr.yp.to/, 2022. [Online; accessed 14-January-2023].

[23] Daniel J Bernstein. The Poly1305-AES message-authentication code. In *Fast Software Encryption: 12th International Workshop, FSE 2005, Paris, France, February 21-23, 2005, Revised Selected Papers 12*, pages 32–49. Springer, 2005.

[24] Daniel J Bernstein. Curve25519: New Diffie-Hellman Speed Records. In *International Workshop on Public Key Cryptography*, pages 207–228. Springer, 2006.

[25] Daniel J Bernstein et al. ChaCha, a Variant of Salsa20. In *Workshop record of SASC*, volume 8, pages 3–5. Citeseer, 2008.

[26] Guido Bertoni, Joan Daemen, Michaël Peeters, and Gilles Van Assche. Keccak. In

Advances in Cryptology–EUROCRYPT 2013, pages 313–314. Springer, 2013.

[27] Benjamin Beurdouche, Karthikeyan Bhargavan, Antoine Delignat-Lavaud, Cédric Fournet, Markulf Kohlweiss, Alfredo Pironti, Pierre-Yves Strub, and Jean Karim Zinzindohoue. A Messy State of the Union: Taming the Composite State Machines of TLS. *Communications of the ACM*, 60(2):99–107, 2017.

[28] SMACK: State Machine AttaCKs. https://mitls.org/pages/attacks/SMACK, 2015. [Online; accessed 24-September-2023].

[29] Karthikeyan Bhargavan, Antoine Delignat Lavaud, Cédric Fournet, Alfredo Pironti, and Pierre Yves Strub. Triple handshakes and cookie cutters: Breaking and fixing authentication over TLS. In *2014 IEEE Symposium on Security and Privacy*, pages 98–113. IEEE, 2014.

[30] Karthikeyan Bhargavan and Gaëtan Leurent. On the Practical (In-)Security of 64-bit Block Ciphers: Collision Attacks on HTTP over TLS and OpenVPN. In *Proceedings of the 2016 ACM SIGSAC Conference on Computer and Communications Security*, pages 456–467, 2016.

[31] Karthikeyan Bhargavan and Gaëtan Leurent. Transcript Collision Attacks: Breaking Authentication in TLS, IKE, and SSH. In *Network and Distributed System Security Symposium–NDSS 2016*, 2016.

[32] Eli Biham and Adi Shamir. Differential Cryptanalysis of DES-like Cryptosystems. *Journal of Cryptology*, 4:3–72, 1991.

[33] J. Black. *Authenticated Encryption*, pages 52–61. Springer US, Boston, MA, 2011.

[34] Daniel Bleichenbacher. Chosen Ciphertext Attacks Against Protocols Based on the RSA Encryption Standard PKCS# 1. In *Advances in Cryptology (CRYPTO)*, pages 1–12. Springer, 1998.

[35] Hanno Böck, Juraj Somorovsky, and Craig Young. Return Of {Bleichenbacher's} Oracle Threat ({{{{{ROBOT}}}}}). In *USENIX Security Symposium*, pages 817–849, 2018.

[36] Hanno Böck, Aaron Zauner, Sean Devlin, Juraj Somorovsky, and Philipp Jovanovic. Nonce-Disrespecting Adversaries: Practical Forgery Attacks on GCM in TLS. Cryptology ePrint Archive, 2016. https://eprint.iacr.org/2016/475.

[37] Andrej Bogdanov and Alon Rosen. Pseudorandom Functions: Three Decades Later. Cryptology ePrint Archive, 2017. https://eprint.iacr.org/2017/652.

[38] Fabrice Boudot, Pierrick Gaudry, Aurore Guillevic, Nadia Heninger, Emmanuel Thomé, and Paul Zimmermann. Comparing the Difficulty of Factorization and Discrete Logarithm: a 240-digit Experiment. In *Annual International Cryptology Conference*, pages 62–91. Springer, 2020.

[39] Matthew Briggs. An Introduction to the General Number Field Sieve. Master's thesis, Virginia Polytechnic Institute and State University, Blacksburg, Virginia, 4 1998.

[40] Britannica, The Editors of Encyclopaedia. World Wide Web. [Online; accessed 01-October-2022].

[41] Bruce Schneier. New NSA Leak Shows MITM Attacks Against Major Internet Services, 2013. [Online; accessed 6-March-2023].

[42] Bundesamt für Sicherheit in der Informationstechnik. Technical Guideline TR-03111: Elliptic Curve Cryptography. https://www.bsi.bund.de/SharedDocs/Downloads /EN/BSI/Publications/TechGuidelines/TR03111/BSI-TR-03111_V-2-0_pdf.p df, 2012. [Online; accessed 21-January-2023].

[43] CA/Browser Forum. Baseline Requirements Documents (SSL/TLS Server Certificates). https://cabforum.org/baseline-requirements-documents, 2023. [Online; accessed 26-November-2023].

[44] CERN. A Short History of the Web. [Online; accessed 01-October-2022].

[45] Cloudflare. LavaRand in Production: The Nitty-Gritty Technical Details, 2022. [Online; accessed 17-August-2022].

[46] Joan Daemen and Vincent Rijmen. *The Design of Rijndael*. Springer, 2002.

[47] Tim Dierks and Christopher Allen. RFC 2246: The TLS Protocol Version 1.0. Technical report, IETF Network Working Group, 1999.

[48] Tim Dierks and Eric Rescorla. RFC 4346: The Transport Layer Security (TLS) Protocol Version 1.1. Technical report, IETF Network Working Group, 2006.

[49] Whitfield Diffie and Martin E Hellman. New Directions in Cryptography. *IEEE Transactions on Information Theory*, 22(6), 1976.

[50] Whitfield Diffie, Paul C Van Oorschot, and Michael J Wiener. Authentication and Authenticated Key Exchanges. *Designs, Codes and Cryptography*, 2(2):107–125, 1992.

[51] Digicert. How to Enable Certificate Transparency, 2023. [Online; accessed 10-March-2023].

[52] John F Dooley. *History of Cryptography and Cryptanalysis: Codes, Ciphers, and their Algorithms.* Springer, 2018.

[53] Benjamin Dowling, Marc Fischlin, Felix Günther, and Douglas Stebila. A Cryptographic Analysis of the TLS 1.3 Handshake Protocol. *Journal of Cryptology*, 34(4):37, 2021.

[54] Peter J. Downey. Multics Security Evaluation: Password and File Encryption Techniques. Technical report, Electronic Systems Div HANSCOM AFB MASS, 1977.

[55] Thai Duong and Juliano Rizzo. Here Come the ⊕ Ninjas. *Unpublished manuscript*, 320, 2011.

[56] Cynthia Dwork. *Non-Malleability*, pages 849–852. Springer US, Boston, MA, 2011.

[57] Morris J Dworkin. Recommendation for Block Cipher Modes of Operation: Galois/Counter Mode (GCM) and GMAC. Technical report, National Institute of Standards and Technology (NIST), 2007.

[58] Morris J Dworkin. SP 800-38e: Recommendation for Block Cipher Modes of Operation: The XTS-AES Mode for Confidentiality on Storage Devices, 2010.

[59] D Eastlake 3rd. RFC 6066: Transport Layer Security (TLS) Extensions: Extension

Definitions, 2011.

[60] Yitayal Kedir Ebrahim. Security Analysis of Website Certificate Validation, 2020.

[61] Mark W Eichin and Jon A Rochlis. With Microscope and Tweezers: An Analysis of the Internet Virus of November 1988. In *IEEE Symposium on Security and Privacy*, volume 7, 1989.

[62] Taher ElGamal. A Public-Key Cryptosystem and a Signature Scheme Based on Discrete Logarithms. *IEEE Transactions on Information Theory*, 31(4):469–472, 1985.

[63] Federal Office for Information Security. BSI TR-02102-1: "Cryptographic Mechanisms: Recommendations and Key Lengths" Version: 2022-1. `https://www.bsi.bund.de/SharedDocs/Downloads/EN/BSI/Publications/TechGuidelines/TG02102/BSI-TR-02102-1.html`, 2022. [Online; accessed 12-August-2022].

[64] Federal Office for Information Security. BSI TR-02102-1: "Cryptographic Mechanisms: Recommendations and Key Lengths" Version: 2023-1. `https://www.bsi.bund.de/SharedDocs/Downloads/EN/BSI/Publications/TechGuidelines/TG02102/BSI-TR-02102-1.pdf?__blob=publicationFile`, 2023. [Online; accessed 21-February-2023].

[65] Niels Ferguson and Bruce Schneier. *Practical Cryptography*, volume 141. Wiley New York, 2003.

[66] Scott Fluhrer, Itsik Mantin, and Adi Shamir. Weaknesses in the Key Scheduling Algorithm of RC4. In *International Workshop on Selected Areas in Cryptography*, pages 1–24. Springer, 2001.

[67] Dan Forsberg, Günther Horn, Wolf-Dietrich Moeller, and Valtteri Niemi. *LTE Security*. John Wiley & Sons, 2012.

[68] John Franks, Phillip Hallam-Baker, Jeffrey Hostetler, Scott Lawrence, Paul Leach, Ari Luotonen, and Lawrence Stewart. HTTP Authentication: Basic and Digest Access Authentication. Technical report, The Internet Society, Network Working Group, 1999.

[69] Steve Fyffe and Tom Abate. Stanford Cryptography Pioneers Whitfield Diffie and Martin Hellman win ACM 2015 A.M. Turing Award. *Standord News Service*, 2016. [Online; accessed 17-December-2023].

[70] Megan Garber. Here Is the First Book Ever Ordered on Amazon, 2012. [Online; accessed 2-October-2022].

[71] Flavio D Garcia, David Oswald, Timo Kasper, and Pierre Pavlidès. Lock It and Still Lose It—on the ({In) Security} of Automotive Remote Keyless Entry Systems. In *25th USENIX security symposium (USENIX Security 16)*, 2016.

[72] Yoel Gluck, Neal Harris, and Angelo Prado. BREACH: Reviving the CRIME Attack. Technical report, BlackHat USA, 2013. [Online; accessed 17-September-2023].

[73] Google Official Blog. A new Approach to China, 2010. [Online; accessed 14-July-2022].

[74] Timothy Gowers, June Barrow-Green, and Imre Leader. *The Princeton Companion to Mathematics*. Princeton University Press, 2010.

[75] Robert Graham. ECB Penguin Demonstration. `https://github.com/robertdavid graham/ecb-penguin`, 2022. [Online; accessed 05-October-2023].

[76] John Graham-Cumming. Incident Report on Memory Leak Caused by Cloudflare Parser Bug. `https://blog.cloudflare.com/incident-report-on-mem ory-leak-caused-by-cloudflare-parser-bug/`, 2017. [Online; accessed 27-September-2023].

[77] Andy Greenberg. The Untold Story of NotPetya, the Most Devastating Cyberattack in History. *Wired Magazine*, 2018. [Online; accessed 11-July-2023].

[78] Andres Guadamuz. Trouble with Prime Numbers: DeCSS, DVD and the Protection of Proprietary Encryption Tools. *Journal of Information, Law & Technology*, 3, 2002.

[79] Mike Hamburg. Ed448-Goldilocks, a New Elliptic Curve. Cryptology ePrint Archive, 2015. [Online; accessed 12-January-2023].

[80] Martin Hellman. A Cryptanalytic Time-Memory Trade-Off. *IEEE Transactions on Information Theory*, 26(4):401–406, 1980.

[81] Cormac Herley, Paul C Van Oorschot, and Andrew S Patrick. Passwords: If We're so Smart, Why are we Still Using Them? In *International Conference on Financial Cryptography and Data Security*, pages 230–237. Springer, 2009.

[82] Jeffrey Hoffstein, Jill Pipher, and Joseph H Silverman. *Introduction to Mathematical Cryptography*, volume 1. Springer, 2008.

[83] Troy Hunt. Have I Been Pwned (HIBP), 2022. [Online; accessed 23-September-2022].

[84] Institute of Electrical and Electronics Engineers (IEEE). IEEE 1619-2018: Standard for Cryptographic Protection of Data on Block-Oriented Storage Devices. `https://ieeexplore.ieee.org/document/8637988`, 2019. [Online; accessed 21-May-2023].

[85] Intel Advanced Threat Research and Antoine Delignat-Lavaud. BERserk Vulnerability: Part 1, 2014.

[86] Internet Research Task Force (IRTF). RFC 7748: Elliptic Curves for Security. `https://www.rfc-editor.org/rfc/rfc7748`, 2016. [Online; accessed 08-January-2023].

[87] Internet Security Research Group. Annual Report, 2021. [Online; accessed 13-July-2022].

[88] Internet Security Research Group (ISRG). Let's Encrypt Stats. `https://letsencrypt.org/stats/`, 2023. [Online; accessed 17-December-2023].

[89] J. C. Jones. Introducing CRLite: All of the Web PKI's Revocations, Compressed, 2023. [Online; accessed 6-March-2023].

[90] Jérémy Jean. TikZ for Cryptographers. `https://www.iacr.org/authors/tikz/`, 2016. [Online; accessed 06-June-2023].

[91] Don Johnson, Alfred Menezes, and Scott Vanstone. The Elliptic Curve Digital Signature Algorithm (ECDSA). `https://www.cs.miami.edu/home/burt/learning/Csc609.142/ecdsa-cert.pdf`, 2001. [Online; accessed 11-February-2023].

[92] Marc Joye and Francis Olivier. *Side-Channel Analysis*. Springer US, 2011.

[93] David Kahn. *The Codebreakers: The Comprehensive History of Secret Communication from Ancient Times to the Internet*. Simon and Schuster, 1996.

[94] B Kaliski, J Jonsson, and A Rusch. RFC 8017: PKCS# 1: RSA Cryptography Specifications Version 2.2, 2016.

[95] Burt Kaliski. *Pseudorandom Function*, pages 995–995. Springer US, Boston, MA, 2011.

[96] Burt Kaliski and A Rusch. RFC 8018: PKCS# 5: Password-Based Cryptography Specification Version 2.1, 2017.

[97] Jonathan Katz and Yehuda Lindell. *Introduction to Modern Cryptography*. CRC press, 2020.

[98] John Kelsey. Compression and Information Leakage of Plaintext. In *Fast Software Encryption (FSE)*, volume 2365 of *Lecture Notes in Computer Science*, pages 263–276. Springer, 2002.

[99] John Kelsey, Bruce Schneier, and Niels Ferguson. Yarrow-160: Notes on the Design and Analysis of the Yarrow Cryptographic Pseudorandom Number Generator. In *Selected Areas in Cryptography: 6th Annual International Workshop*, pages 13–33. Springer, 2001.

[100] Franziskus Kiefer. TL;DR – Hybrid Public Key Encryption. `https://www.franzi skuskiefer.de/p/tldr-hybrid-public-key-encryption/`, 2022. Online; accessed 21-December-2022.

[101] Vlastimil Klíma, Ondrej Pokornỳ, and Tomáš Rosa. Attacking RSA-based Sessions in SSL/TLS. In *International Workshop on Cryptographic Hardware and Embedded Systems (CHES)*, pages 426–440. Springer, 2003.

[102] Neal Koblitz, Alfred J Menezes, Yi-Hong Wu, and Robert J Zuccherato. *Algebraic Aspects of Cryptography*, volume 198. Springer, 1998.

[103] Hugo Krawczyk, Mihir Bellare, and Ran Canetti. RFC2104: HMAC: Keyed-Hashing

for Message Authentication, 1997.

[104] Hugo Krawczyk and Pasi Eronen. RFC 5869: HMAC-based Extract-and-Expand Key Derivation Function (HKDF). Technical report, 2010.

[105] Kaoru Kurosawa. *Hybrid Encryption*, pages 570–572. Springer US, Boston, MA, 2011.

[106] Ralph Langner. Stuxnet: Dissecting a Cyberwarfare Weapon. *IEEE Security & Privacy*, 9(3):49–51, 2011.

[107] Frederic Lardinois. IBM Unveils its 433 Qubit Osprey Quantum Computer. `https://techcrunch.com/2022/11/09/ibm-unveils-its-433-qubit-osprey-quantum-computer/`, 2022. [Online; accessed 12-January-2023].

[108] James Larisch, David Choffnes, Dave Levin, Bruce M. Maggs, Alan Mislove, and Christo Wilson. CRLite: A Scalable System for Pushing All TLS Revocations to All Browsers. In *2017 IEEE Symposium on Security and Privacy (SP)*, pages 539–556, 2017.

[109] Moses Liskov. *Fermat Primality Test*, pages 221–221. Springer US, Boston, MA, 2005.

[110] A Malpani, S Galperin, and C Adams. X. 509 Internet Public-Key Infrastructure Online Certificate Status Protocol – OCSP. Technical report, Internet Engineering Task Force (IETF), 2013.

[111] Marsh Marsh Ray and Steve Dispensa. Renegotiating TLS. `https://ww1.prweb.com/prfiles/2009/11/05/104435/RenegotiatingTLS.pdf`, 2009. [Online; accessed 05-September-2023].

[112] Mitsuru Matsui. Linear Cryptanalysis Method for DES Cipher. In *Workshop on the Theory and Application of of Cryptographic Techniques*, pages 386–397. Springer, 1993.

[113] David McGrew, Anthony Grieco, and Yaron Sheffer. IETF Draft: Selection of Future Cryptographic Standards. `https://www.ietf.org/archive/id/draft-mcgrew-standby-cipher-00.txt`, 2013. [Online; accessed 06-June-2023].

[114] David McGrew and John Viega. The Galois/Counter Mode of Operation (GCM).

Submission to NIST Modes of Operation Process, 2004.

[115] David A. McGrew and John Viega. The Security and Performance of the Galois/Counter Mode of Operation (Full Version). Cryptology ePrint Archive, 2004. `https://eprint.iacr.org/2004/193`.

[116] McMillan, Robert. The World's First Computer Password? It Was Useless Too, 2012. [Online; accessed 20-September-2022].

[117] Alfred J Menezes, Paul C Van Oorschot, and Scott A Vanstone. *Handbook of Applied Cryptography*. CRC press, 1996.

[118] Robert Merget, Marcus Brinkmann, Nimrod Aviram, Juraj Somorovsky, Johannes Mittmann, and Jörg Schwenk. Raccoon Attack: Finding and Exploiting {Most-Significant-Bit-Oracles} in {TLS-DH (E}). In *30th USENIX Security Symposium (USENIX Security 21)*, pages 213–230, 2021.

[119] Christopher Meyer, Juraj Somorovsky, Eugen Weiss, Jörg Schwenk, Sebastian Schinzel, and Erik Tews. Revisiting {SSL/TLS} Implementations: New Bleichenbacher Side Channels and Aattacks. In *USENIX Security Symposium*, pages 733–748, 2014.

[120] Charlie Miller and Chris Valasek. Remote Exploitation of an Unaltered Passenger Vehicle, 2015. [Online; accessed 16-July-2022].

[121] Miva. The History Of E-Commerce: How Did It All Begin?, 2022. [Online; accessed 2-October-2022].

[122] Bodo Möller, Thai Duong, and Krzysztof Kotowicz. This POODLE Bites: Exploiting the SSL 3.0 Fallback. *Security Advisory*, 21:34–58, 2014.

[123] Cristopher Moore and Stephan Mertens. *The Nature of Computation*. OUP Oxford, 2011.

[124] Kathleen Moriarty and Stephen Farrell. RFC 8996: Deprecating TLS 1.0 and TLS 1.1. Technical report, Internet Engineering Task Force (IETF), 2021.

[125] Ware Myers. Can Software for the Strategic Defense Initiative Ever be Error-Free?

Computer, 19(11):61–67, 1986.

[126] National Institute of Standards and Technology. Recommendation for Key Management: Part 1 – General, 2023. [Online; accessed 13-September-2023].

[127] National Institute of Standards and Technology (NIST). Advanced Encryption Standard (AES). *Federal Information Processing Standards (FIPS) Publication 197*, 2001.

[128] National Institute of Standards and Technology (NIST). Digital Signature Standard (DSS). https://csrc.nist.gov/publications/detail/fips/186/4/final, 2013. [Online; accessed 08-January-2023].

[129] National Institute of Standards and Technology (NIST). Secure Hash Standard (SHS). https://nvlpubs.nist.gov/nistpubs/FIPS/NIST.FIPS.180-4.pdf, 2015. [Online; accessed 21-January-2023].

[130] Newswire. New Research: Most People Have 70-80 Passwords. https://www.news wire.com/news/new-research-most-people-have-70-80-passwords-21103705, 2020. [Online; accessed 26-November-2023].

[131] Yoav Nir and Adam Langley. RFC 8439: ChaCha20 and Poly1305 for IETF Protocols. https://www.rfc-editor.org/rfc/rfc8439, 2018. [Online; accessed 08-June-2023].

[132] NIST Computer Security Resource Center. Glossary: Key Transport, 2022. Last accessed 15 August 2020.

[133] Kaisa Nyberg. Differentially Uniform Mappings for Cryptography. In *Advances in Cryptology—EUROCRYPT'93: Workshop on the Theory and Application of Cryptographic Techniques*, pages 55–64. Springer, 1994.

[134] Philippe Oechslin. Making a Faster Cryptanalytic Time-Memory Trade-Off. In *Annual International Cryptology Conference*, pages 617–630. Springer, 2003.

[135] National Institute of Standards and Technology. Federal Information Processing

Standard (FIPS) NIST FIPS 186-5, Digital Signature Standard (DSS), 2023.

[136] B O'Higgins, W Diffie, L Strawczynski, and R De Hoog. Encryption and ISDN-A Natural Fit. In *Proceedings of the 1987 International Switching Symposium*, pages 863–869, 1987.

[137] OpenSSL: Cryptography and SSL/TLS Toolkit. https://www.openssl.org, 2023. [Online; accessed 30-April-2023].

[138] Karmela Padavic-Callaghan. IBM Unveils World's Largest Quantum Computer at 433 Qubits. https://www.newscientist.com/article/2346074-ibm-unveils -worlds-largest-quantum-computer-at-433-qubits/, 2021. [Online; accessed 12-January-2023].

[139] Eric Parizo. Maersk CISO Says NotPeyta Devastated Several Unnamed US firms. *Dark Reading Magazine*, 2019. [Online; accessed 11-July-2023].

[140] Wouter Penard and Tim van Werkhoven. On the Secure Hash Algorithm Family. *Cryptography in Context*, pages 1–18, 2008.

[141] Project Nayuki. Elliptic Curve Point Addition in Projective Coordinates. https://www.nayuki.io/page/elliptic-curve-point-addition-in-projective-coo rdinates. [Online; accessed 18-January 2023].

[142] PurpleSec. Cyber security statistics: The ultimate list of stats data, & trends for 2022, 2022. [Online; accessed 24-September-2022].

[143] Stefan Pütz and Roland Schmitz. Secure Interoperation Between 2G and 3G Mobile Radio Networks. In *1st International Conference on 3G Mobile Communication Technologies*. IET, 2000.

[144] Eric S Raymond. The Cathedral and the Bazaar, 1998.

[145] E Rescorla. RFC 5705: Keying Material Exporters for Transport Layer Security (TLS), 2010.

[146] Eric Rescorla. *SSL and TLS: Designing and Building Secure Systems*. Addison-Wesley

Reading, 2000.

[147] Eric Rescorla et al. RFC 8446: The Transport Layer Security (TLS) Protocol Version 1.3. *Internet Engineering Task Force (IETF)*, 25, 2018.

[148] Eric Rescorla, Marsh Ray, Steve Dispensa, and Nasko Oskov. RFC 5746: Transport Layer Security (TLS) Renegotiation Indication Extension, 2010.

[149] Eric Rescorla, Hannes Tschofenig, and Nagendra Modadugu. The Datagram Transport Layer Security (DTLS) Protocol Version 1.3. *Internet Engineering Task Force*, 2019.

[150] Ivan Ristić. *Bulletproof TLS and PKI: Understanding and Deploying SSL/TLS and PKI to Secure Servers and Web Applications*. Feisty Duck, 2022.

[151] Ronald L Rivest, Adi Shamir, and Leonard Adleman. A method for obtaining digital signatures and public-key cryptosystems. *Communications of the ACM*, 21(2):120–126, 1978.

[152] Rivest, Ron. Website of Ron Rivest, Computer Science and Artificial Intelligence Laboratory (CSAIL), MIT. `http://people.csail.mit.edu/rivest/photos/rsa-photo.jpeg`, 2023. [Online; accessed 17-December-2023].

[153] Juliano Rizzo and Thai Duong. The CRIME attack. `https://docs.google.com/presentation/d/11eBmGiHbYcHR9gL5nDyZChu_-1Ca2GizeuOfaLU2HOU/edit`, 2012. [Online; accessed 15-September-2023].

[154] Eyal Ronen, Robert Gillham, Daniel Genkin, Adi Shamir, David Wong, and Yuval Yarom. The 9 Lives of Bleichenbacher's CAT: New Cache Attacks on TLS Implementations. In *IEEE Symposium on Security and Privacy (S&P)*, pages 435–452. IEEE, 2019.

[155] Scott Rose, Oliver Borchert, Stu Mitchell, and Sean Connelly. Zero Trust Architecture. Technical report, National Institute of Standards and Technology, 2020.

[156] Jay Rosenberg. NotPetya Returns as Bad Rabbit. `https://intezer.com/blog/resea`

`rch/notpetya-returns-bad-rabbit/`, 2017. [Online; accessed 23-December-2023].

[157] Peter Schneider. Tutorial: 5G Mobile Network Security Essentials. In *First ITG Workshop on IT Security (ITSec)*. Tübingen University, 2020.

[158] Bruce Schneier. *Applied Cryptography: Protocols, Algorithms, and Source Code in C.* John Wiley & Sons, 2007. 2nd Edition.

[159] Bruce Schneier. What Exactly Are the NSA's 'Groundbreaking Cryptanalytic Capabilities'? `https://www.wired.com/2013/09/black-budget-what-exactly-are-the-nsas-cryptanalytic-capabilities/`, 2013. [Online; accessed 06-June-2023].

[160] Claus-Peter Schnorr. Efficient Identification and Signatures for Smart Cards. In *Advances in Cryptology—CRYPTO'89*, pages 239–252. Springer, 1990.

[161] C. E. Shannon. Communication Theory of Secrecy Systems. *The Bell System Technical Journal*, 28(4):656–715, 1949.

[162] Claude E Shannon. Communication Theory of Secrecy Systems. *The Bell system technical journal*, 28(4):656–715, 1949.

[163] Peter W Shor. Algorithms for Quantum Computation: Discrete Logarithms and Factoring. In *Proceedings 35th Annual Symposium on Foundations of Computer Science*, pages 124–134. IEEE, 1994.

[164] Peter W Shor. Polynomial-Time Algorithms for Prime Factorization and Discrete Logarithms on a Quantum Computer. *SIAM Review*, 41(2):303–332, 1999.

[165] Dan Shumow and Niels Ferguson. On the Possibility of a Back Door in the NIST SP800-90 Dual EC PRNG. In *Proc. Crypto*, volume 7, 2007.

[166] Joseph H Silverman. *The Arithmetic of Elliptic Curves*, volume 106. Springer, 2009.

[167] Ben Smyth and Alfredo Pironti. Truncating {TLS} Connections to Violate Beliefs in Web Applications. In *7th USENIX Workshop on Offensive Technologies (WOOT 13)*, 2013.

[168] Douglas R Stinson. *Cryptography: Theory and Practice*. Chapman and Hall/CRC, 2005.

[169] Bryan Sullivan. Cryptographic Agility: Defending Against the Sneakers Scenario. `https://infocondb.org/con/black-hat/black-hat-usa-2010/cryptographic-agility-defending-against-the-sneakers-scenario`, 2010. [Online; accessed 09-June-2023].

[170] Paul Syverson. A Taxonomy of Replay Attacks. In *Proceedings The Computer Security Foundations Workshop VII*, pages 187–191. IEEE, 1994.

[171] Dermot Turing. *X, Y & Z: The Real Story of how Enigma was Broken*. The History Press, 2018.

[172] Jan Van Leeuwen. *Handbook of Theoretical Computer Science (vol. A) Algorithms and Complexity*. MIT Press, 1991.

[173] Paul C Van Oorschot. *Computer Security and the Internet: Tools and Jewels from Malware to Bitcoin*. Springer, 2021.

[174] Hans Van Vliet, Hans Van Vliet, and JC Van Vliet. *Software Engineering: Principles and Practice*, volume 13. John Wiley & Sons Hoboken, NJ, 2008.

[175] Mathy Vanhoef and Tom Van Goethem. HEIST: HTTP Encrypted Information Can be Stolen through TCP-windows. Technical report, BlackHat USA, 2016. [Online; accessed 17-September-2023].

[176] Serge Vaudenay. Security Flaws Induced by CBC Padding—Applications to SSL, IPSEC, WTLS. In *International Conference on the Theory and Applications of Cryptographic Techniques*, pages 534–545. Springer, 2002.

[177] Joachim von Zur Gathen. *CryptoSchool*. Springer, 2015.

[178] Samuel S Wagstaff Jr. History of Integer Factorization. `https://www.cs.purdue.edu/homes/ssw/chapter3.pdf`, 2021. [Online; accessed 03-April-2023].

[179] Wayback Machine. Operation Aurora Hit Google, Others by George Kurtz, 2010.

[Online; accessed 14-July-2022].

[180] Doug Whiting, Russ Housley, and Niels Ferguson. Counter with CBC-MAC (CCM). RFC 3610, 2003.

[181] Wikipedia contributors. Lehman's laws of software evolution — Wikipedia, the free encyclopedia, 2021. [Online; accessed 7-July-2022].

[182] Wikipedia contributors. Middlebox — Wikipedia, The Free Encyclopedia, 2021. [Online; accessed 30-October-2022].

[183] Wikipedia contributors. Atmospheric noise — Wikipedia, the free encyclopedia, 2022. [Online; accessed 17-August-2022].

[184] Wikipedia contributors. CERN — Wikipedia, The Free Encyclopedia, 2022. [Online; accessed 1-October-2022].

[185] Wikipedia contributors. Diffie-Hellman Key Exchange — Wikipedia, The Free Encyclopedia, 2022. [Online; accessed 5-July-2022].

[186] Wikipedia contributors. Emergence — Wikipedia, The Free Encyclopedia, 2022. [Online; accessed 11-July-2022].

[187] Wikipedia contributors. Forward Secrecy — Wikipedia, The Free Encyclopedia, 2022.

[188] Wikipedia contributors. Hybrid cryptosystem — Wikipedia, The Free Encyclopedia. `https://en.wikipedia.org/w/index.php?title=Hybrid_cryptosystem&oldid=1` `081587206`, 2022. [Online; accessed 11-December-2022].

[189] Wikipedia contributors. Kerckhoffs's Principle — Wikipedia, The Free Encyclopedia, 2022. [Online; accessed 29-July-2022].

[190] Wikipedia contributors. Market for Zero-Day Exploits — Wikipedia, The Free Encyclopedia, 2022. [Online; accessed 21-July-2022].

[191] Wikipedia contributors. Moore's Law — Wikipedia, The Free Encyclopedia, 2022. [Online; accessed 7-July-2022].

[192] Wikipedia contributors. One-time pad — Wikipedia, the free encyclopedia, 2022. [Online; accessed 28-August-2022].

[193] Wikipedia contributors. Operation Aurora — Wikipedia, The Free Encyclopedia, 2022. [Online; accessed 13-July-2022].

[194] Wikipedia contributors. Quicksort — Wikipedia, the free encyclopedia, 2022. [Online; accessed 29-August-2022].

[195] Wikipedia contributors. Randomized algorithm — Wikipedia, the free encyclopedia, 2022. [Online; accessed 28-August-2022].

[196] Wikipedia contributors. Timeline of E-Commerce — Wikipedia, The Free Encyclopedia. `https://en.wikipedia.org/w/index.php?title=Timeline_of_e-commerce&oldid=1097161867`, 2022. [Online; accessed 8-October-2022].

[197] Wikipedia contributors. Wired Equivalent Privacy — Wikipedia, The Free Encyclopedia, 2022. [Online; accessed 25-July-2022].

[198] Wikipedia contributors. Zero Trust Security Model — Wikipedia, The Free Encyclopedia, 2022. [Online; accessed 13-July-2022].

[199] Wikipedia contributors. DigiNotar — Wikipedia, The Free Encyclopedia, 2023. [Online; accessed 6-March-2023].

[200] Wikipedia contributors. Heartbleed — Wikipedia, The Free Encyclopedia. `https://en.wikipedia.org/w/index.php?title=Heartbleed&oldid=1174551550`, 2023. [Online; accessed 25-September-2023].

[201] Wikipedia contributors. Huffman Coding — Wikipedia, The Free Encyclopedia. `https://en.wikipedia.org/w/index.php?title=Huffman_coding&oldid=1168706432`, 2023. [Online; accessed 12-September-2023].

[202] Maurice Vincent Wilkes. *Time Sharing Computer Systems*. Elsevier Science Inc., 1972.

[203] Tatu Ylonen. SSH – Secure Login Connections over the Internet. In *Proceedings of*

the 6th USENIX Security Symposium, volume 37, pages 40–52, 1996.

[204] Paul Zimmermann. The ECMNET Project. `https://members.loria.fr/PZimmerma nn/records/ecm/intro.html`, 2023. [Online; accessed 14-April-2023].

Index

www.packtpub.com

Subscribe to our online digital library for full access to over 7,000 books and videos, as well as industry leading tools to help you plan your personal development and advance your career. For more information, please visit our website.

Why subscribe?

- Spend less time learning and more time coding with practical eBooks and Videos from over 4,000 industry professionals
- Improve your learning with Skill Plans built especially for you
- Get a free eBook or video every month
- Fully searchable for easy access to vital information
- Copy and paste, print, and bookmark content

Did you know that Packt offers eBook versions of every book published, with PDF and ePub files available? You can upgrade to the eBook version at www.packtpub.com and as a print book customer, you are entitled to a discount on the eBook copy. Get in touch with us at customercare@packtpub.com for more details.

At www.packtpub.com, you can also read a collection of free technical articles, sign up for a range of free

Other Books You Might Enjoy

If you enjoyed this book, you may be interested in these other books by Packt:

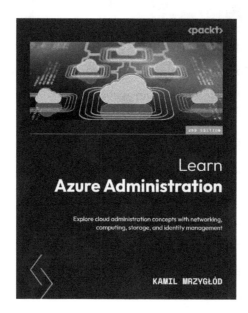

Learn Azure Administration - Second Edition

Kamil Mrzygłód

ISBN: 978-1-83763-611-2

- Discover the workings of Azure Load Balancer, grasp its use cases, and configure load balancer rules
- Gain insights into various solutions for provisioning infrastructure and configuration
- Create and configure workspaces, query data in Log Analytics, and visualize data
- Plan and deploy virtual networks and configure network security groups
- Validate and verify multiple authentication and authorization scenarios

Malware Science

Shane Molinari

ISBN: 978-1-80461-864-6

- Understand the science behind malware data and its management lifecycle
- Explore anomaly detection with signature and heuristics-based methods
- Analyze data to uncover relationships between data points and create a network graph
- Discover methods for reverse engineering and analyzing malware
- Use ML, advanced analytics, and data mining in malware data analysis and detection
- Explore practical insights and the future state of AI's use for malware data science
- Understand how NLP AI employs algorithms to analyze text for malware detection

Packt is searching for authors like you

If you're interested in becoming an author for Packt, please visit `authors.packtpub.com` and apply today. We have worked with thousands of developers and tech professionals, just like you, to help them share their insight with the global tech community. You can make a general application, apply for a specific hot topic that we are recruiting an author for, or submit your own idea.

Share Your Thoughts

Now you've finished *TLS Cryptography In-Depth*, we'd love to hear your thoughts! Scan the QR code below to go straight to the Amazon review page for this book and share your feedback or leave a review on the site that you purchased it from.

https://packt.link/r/1804611956

Your review is important to us and the tech community and will help us make sure we're delivering excellent quality content.

Download a free PDF copy of this book

Thanks for purchasing this book!

Do you like to read on the go but are unable to carry your print books everywhere? Is your eBook purchase not compatible with the device of your choice?

Don't worry, now with every Packt book you get a DRM-free PDF version of that book at no cost.

Read anywhere, any place, on any device. Search, copy, and paste code from your favorite technical books directly into your application.

The perks don't stop there, you can get exclusive access to discounts, newsletters, and great free content in your inbox daily

Follow these simple steps to get the benefits:

1. Scan the QR code or visit the link below

https://packt.link/free-ebook/9781804611951

2. Submit your proof of purchase

3. That's it! We'll send your free PDF and other benefits to your email directly

www.ingramcontent.com/pod-product-compliance
Lightning Source LLC
Chambersburg PA
CBHW060633060326
40690CB00020B/4384